DATE DUE

MY 29 97			
MAY 5			
JY 9 '98			
DE 3 99			
NO 8 00			
NO 27 00			
AP 21 03			
MY 25 06			
2/23/08			
AP 7 08			
NO 5 10			

JANE AUSTEN'S LETTERS

Jane Austen's Letters

Collected and Edited by

DEIRDRE LE FAYE

THIRD EDITION

Oxford   New York

OXFORD UNIVERSITY PRESS

lon Street, Oxford OX2 6DP
ork
Bogota Bombay
own Dar es Salaam
Delhi Florence Hong Kong Istanbul Karachi
Kuala Lumpur Madras Madrid Melbourne
Mexico City Nairobi Paris Singapore
Taipei Tokyo Toronto
and associated companies in
Berlin Ibadan

Oxford is a trade mark of Oxford University Press

First published 1995
Fifth impression 1996

British Library Cataloguing in Publication Data
Data available

Library of Congress Cataloging in Publication Data
Austen, Jane, 1775-1817.
[Correspondence]
Jane Austen's letters—collected and edited by
Deirdre Le Faye.—3rd ed.
_p. cm._
Includes bibliographical references (p.) and indexes.
1. Austen, Jane, 1775-1817—Correspondence.
2. Novelists, English—19th century—Correspondence.
I. Le Faye, Deirdre. II. Title.
_PR4036.A4 1995 823'.7—dc20 94-3650_
ISBN 0-19-811764-7

Printed in Great Britain
on acid-free paper by
Bookcraft (Bath) Ltd.
Midsomer Norton, Avon

ACKNOWLEDGEMENTS

THE present editor would like to express her particular and personal thanks and gratitude to the heirs of R. A. Austen-Leigh, for years of friendship and encouragement; to David Gilson, for advice and for sharing information gained from his study of the Jane Austen letters in the Pierpont Morgan Library; and to the late Mrs Jo Modert, whose book gave the locations of letters as at 1990.

Thanks are also given to the following owners of letters, or copy letters, as at 1993: the great-grandsons of Adm. Sir Francis Austen; the Jane Austen Memorial Trust; Joan Austen-Leigh (Mrs Denis Mason Hurley); the Australian National Library, Canberra; Mr Roger W. Barrett; the Bodleian Library, Oxford; Mr James M. W. Borg; the Trustees of the Boston Public Library, Boston, Mass.; Lord Brabourne; the British Library, London; Cambridge University Library; the Trustees of the Charnwood Trust; the Administrative Trustees of the Chevening Estate; the Cleveland H. Dodge Foundation Inc., New York, and Mrs Cleveland E. Dodge jr.; the Fitzwilliam Museum Library, Cambridge; Mr David Gilson; Mrs Raymond Hartz; the Houghton Library of Harvard University, Cambridge, Mass.; Haverford College, Haverford, Pa.; the Impey and Fowle families; Dr Sidney Ives; King's College Library, Cambridge; Mr Michael M. Kloss; Sir Francis Le Marchant, Bt.; S. Lerner, Redmond, Washington, DC; Mrs Lucy Magruder; Maine Historical Society, Portland, Maine; Massachusetts Historical Society, Boston, Mass.; Mr John Murray; New York Public Library, New York; the Historical Society of Pennsylvania, Philadelphia, Pa.; the Pierpont Morgan Library, New York; Princeton University Library (Robert H. Taylor Collection), Princeton, NJ; Public Record Office, London; President and Fellows of St John the Baptist College, Oxford; Torquay Natural History Society.

There are a few letters still in private hands, with whose owners it has proved impossible to make contact.

The editor's grateful thanks are also due to many other friends and correspondents who have provided information and assistance, in some cases over a period of years: Mrs M. I. Ackworth; Katherine A. Armstrong; the great-grandsons of Adm. Sir Francis Austen; members of the Awdry family; Mr J. F. Barker; Dr Peter Beal, Deputy Director,

Books and Manuscripts, Sotheby's; Mr Lee Biondi; Mrs Stephanie Binnall; Miss Jean K. Bowden, Curator of Jane Austen's House, Chawton; Mr and Mrs Joseph Bown; Miss Mary Burkett; Lord Charteris of Amisfield; Christie Manson & Woods International Inc., New York; Mr G. C. R. Clay, for Cooper family information; Mrs Diana Coldicott; Mr B. V. Cooper, Curator of the Torquay Museum; Dr Edward Copeland; Mrs J. E. Downham; Miss Elizabeth Einberg of the Tate Gallery; Mr Michael Finlay; Mr Tony Gibbs; Miss Hero Granger-Taylor; Sir Michael Heathcote, Bt.; Miss Caroline Humphreys; Revd W. A. W. Jarvis; Miss Helen Lefroy; Mr John Leopold and Mr David Thompson of the Horological Dept. of the British Museum; Revd Ralph Mann; Mrs Sarah Markham, FSA; Miss Honoria D. Marsh; Ms Mary Gaither Marshall; Miss Mollie Martin; Dr Meg Mathies; Mr Bernard Nurse, Librarian of the Society of Antiquaries, London; Mrs Diana Parikian; Mrs Pike; Sir Jonathan Portal, Bt., and Mr Christopher Portal; Ms Sheila Rainey; Mr W. Birch Reynardson; Revd G. A. Robson; Mr William St Clair; Mrs Margaret Sawtell, for the loan of her late husband's MS 'The Kintbury Family' (Fowle history); Nancy, Lady Smiley; Prof. G. H. Treitel, QC; Mrs Trimmer; Mr George Holbert Tucker; Miss Janet Wallace; Mr and Mrs George Ward; the Earl of Wemyss; Commander and Mrs D. P. Willan; Mr and Mrs R. L. Willan; Mrs Margaret Wilson, for information on the dispersal of the Austen archive by the first Lord Brabourne; Mr Jeffrey R. Young; and staff of the following institutions: Andover Reference Library; Beaney Institute, Canterbury; Diocesan Record Office, Canterbury; the British Library, London; Victoria and Albert Museum, London; Centre for Kentish Studies (previously Kent Archives Office), Maidstone; The Huntington Library, San Marino, California; Hampshire Record Office, Winchester.

CONTENTS

CONTENTS

INTRODUCTION TO THE
FIRST EDITION

(1932)

JANE AUSTEN's letters have had some detractors and some apologists. They have received little whole-hearted praise even from the 'idolators' of the novels. It has been assumed that they have little interest except for the few brief rays with which they illumine the history of the novels, and would be hardly readable if their author were not otherwise famous. A familiar complaint is that they have nothing to say about the great events that were shaking Europe—a kind of negative criticism seldom elsewhere applied to family correspondence. A familiar defence is that the letters have been robbed of their general interest by Cassandra Austen's pious destruction of all that she supposed might possibly excite general curiosity. We know from their niece Caroline that 'Her letters to Aunt Cassandra (for they were *sometimes* separated) were, I dare say, open and confidential—My Aunt looked them over and burnt the greater part, (as she told me), 2 or 3 years before her own death—She left, or *gave* some as legacies to the Neices—but of those that *I* have seen, several had portions cut out.'[1]

Doubtless this suppression has cost us much that we should value. But we may suspect that it has not materially affected the impression we should have received from a richer survival. The sisters were, for the greater part of their joint lives, together, and in conditions of the closest intimacy. They were from time to time separated by long visits, and then corresponded regularly. But the purpose of their letters was to exchange information not only between themselves, but between two branches of a large family. There are indications that these letters and others like them were read by, and to, a number of people. Even if this had not been so, it would not have been consonant with the sisters' temperament, or with their way of life, to exchange letters of sentiment or disquisition. It would not have suited Jane Austen's sense of propriety to charge her sister sixpence (or thereabouts) for opinions on religion or politics, on life or letters, which were known already, or would keep. But news would not wait, and news must always give satisfaction.

---

[1] *Family Record* 243 and CMCA's MS.

Only on rare and emergent occasions, I believe, was the ordinary tenor of news interrupted.[2]

I must add, though with reluctance, my impression that Cassandra Austen was not the correspondent who best evoked her sister's powers. The letters to the nieces show more flow of fancy, less attention to the business of news. And the two letters,[3] recovered in recent years, to friends outside the family are notably above the average in variety and vigour.

But I would not seem to be apologetic where I see no need for apology. Are these letters in fact uninteresting? I have not found them so. Even if Jane Austen had no other claim to be remembered, her letters would be memorable. Read with attention, they yield a picture of the life of the upper middle class of that time which is surely without a rival. And they depict not only manners, but also persons. Jane Austen's own family, with its ramifications by marriage, is itself a larger—I had almost said, a more ambitious—subject than any she attempted in her novels. And though the characterization is incidental, and hardly ever deliberate, it is by the same hand as Lady Bertram and Mrs Norris. Round the family is grouped a gallery of lesser persons, all of whom— if they are not merely named—acquire some individuality. It is difficult not to remember even Mr Robert Mascall, though we hardly know more of him than that he 'eats a great deal of butter'. There are in these five hundred pages characters chiefly conspicuous for their amiability: Cassandra herself, and Edward, and the two sailors, and Martha Lloyd, and old Mrs Knight. There are public characters—not many of these— like Mr Crabbe, seen or not seen at a distance, or Mr Lushington, MP, MF, who could talk well about Milton; 'I dare say he is ambitious and insincere'. There are brilliant and versatile characters, notably Henry Austen, who reminds us of Henry Tilney and even of Henry Crawford, but had more of 'genius' than any man in the novels; attractive young people, like Fanny Knight and her 'agreeable, idle brothers', Anna Austen, and Mr Haden; mixed characters, like Mrs James Austen, and Miss Sharp, and 'that puss Cassy', and Mr Moore, rector of Wrotham; and farcical characters, like Mrs Henry Digweed, and Mrs Stent, and Miss Milles of Canterbury, whom the late A. B. Walkley guessed to be the prototype of Miss Bates. Many of these persons have, no doubt, assumed some artificial importance to an editor who has made it his

---

[2] 'I am quite dependent on the communications of our friends, or my own wits', 10-11 Jan. 1809.

[3] 29 Nov. 1812; 22 May 1817.

business to hunt for facts about them. I can urge, on the other side, that ten years' intimacy has raised, not lessened, my regard. I cannot be mistaken in the belief that, in their several degrees, they are alive. How they are brought to life, without quotation and almost without description, may be perceived but can hardly be explained.

The letters are, like most letters, occasional, unstudied, and inconsequent. Their themes are accidental; their bulk, that of a quarto sheet. As a series, though they have connexion, they have no coherence; they straggle over twenty years, and lack a plot. Their details, therefore, unlike the details of *Emma*, are not the ingredients or the embellishments of a rounded composition. If they can be called works of art, they are so only because, as their writer reminds us,[4] 'an artist cannot do anything slovenly'. But as fragments—fragments of observation, of characterization, of criticism—they are in the same class as the material of the novels; and in some respects they have a wider range.

But with all their vividness, are these letters trifling? Can they be plausibly called 'a desert of trivialities punctuated by occasional oases of clever malice'?[5] Life, wrote Johnson, 'is made up of little things'. Trifles are dear to all our hearts, if they are attached to the objects of our affection—whether persons or things. 'The Tables are come . . . They are both covered with green baize & send their best Love.'[6] The writer of these letters was never ashamed to be minute. 'You know how interesting the purchase of a spongecake is to me.'[7] The question, for that posterity whom she did not here address, is not whether she wrote of trifles, but whether she makes the small change of her life important, amusing, and endearing to us her unlicensed readers; or, on the contrary, reveals a cold heart, a meagre intelligence, and a petty spirit. We know that Jane Austen the novelist had a genius for the particular; a zest for the small concerns or belongings of her creatures, which her genius made communicable. The readers of *Mansfield Park* were not told how much Mrs Norris gave William Price at parting. But her family knew that Miss Austen could tell them, if she chose, what the 'something considerable' was. So the secret got out, and still delights each new participant. The eager, affectionate interest which the letters show in matters of domestic concern ('Pray, where did the boys sleep?'[8]) is scarcely less infectious.

[4] 17–18 Nov. 1798.
[5] H. W. Garrod in *Essays by Divers Hands* (R. Society of Literature), VIII, 1928.
[6] 8–9 Nov. 1800; and see 24 Aug. 1805; 5–6 Mar. 1814.
[7] 15–17 June 1808.   [8] 3 Nov. 1813.

But the enchantment which enthusiasts have sometimes found in these letters will not be universally admitted. It will be admitted by those only in whose own experience little things—like nicknames, or family jokes, or the arrangement of the furniture—are inseparable from the deeper joys, and even from the deeper sorrows of life; and by those only who find wisdom and humanity in this correspondence, as well as—or in despite of—its devotion to minutiae. To those who do not find these qualities in them, the letters may appear not merely trivial, but hard and cold. Even their professed admirers have deplored their occasional cynicism. The charge should be met, though I ought to confess that I do not well comprehend it. The letters abound in gentle or playful malice; and sharper strokes are frequent. Mr Robert Mascall is not the only person whose character is blasted in a phrase. Some mercy is shown to foolishness:

Dear Mrs Digweed!—I cannot bear that she sh^d not be foolishly happy after a Ball.[9]

But not very much:

If the Brother sh^d luckily be a little sillier than the Colonel, what a treasure for Eliza.[10]

She was highly rouged, & looked rather quietly & contentedly silly than anything else.[11]

There is none at all for meanness or pretence:

They live in a handsome style and are rich, and she seemed to like to be rich, and we gave her to understand that we were far from being so; she will soon feel therefore that we are not worth her acquaintance.[12]

I would not give much for Mr Rice's chance of living at Deane; he builds his hope, I find, not upon anything that his mother has written, but upon the effect of what he has written himself. He must write a great deal better than those eyes indicate if he can persuade a perverse and narrow-minded woman to oblige those whom she does not love.[13]

This may be thought censorious by those who have no taste for satire. But the unpublished portrait of Mrs Rice deserves the charge of cruelty no more and no less than the published portrait of Mrs Norris; and it has been remarked that Jane Austen does justice to the virtues which

[9] 11–12 Oct. 1813. [10] 1–2 Oct. 1808. [11] 12–13 May 1801.
[12] 7–8 Jan. 1807. [13] 25 Jan. 1801.

Mrs Norris had. Whatever be thought of these asperities, they are not spiteful.

The author of *Pride and Prejudice* was not insensible of the beauty of candour; of the virtue which Elizabeth Bennet, praising her sister, calls 'candour without ostentation or design—to take the good of every body's character, and make it still better, and say nothing of the bad'. She, like her Elizabeth, knew that her own distinctive talent lay in an opposite direction. Neither of them scrupled to use it. But it is unfair to conclude, because Miss Austen can be exquisitely wicked, that she was deficient in the softer emotions: just as it is unfair to deny her all romantic sentiment because there, too, she knew her limitations, and declared she 'could no more write a Romance than an Epic Poem'.[14]

As I lay aside the desultory employment of many years, during which I have indulged a harmless curiosity about the births, marriages, and deaths of unimportant people, the details of travel, and the economy of country houses, I cannot forbear to remind myself of the closing sentences of *The Last Chronicle of Barset*:

To me Barset has been a real country, and its city a real city, and the spires and towers have been before my eyes, and the voices of the people are known to my ears, and the pavements of the city ways are familiar to my footsteps.

That Godmersham and Chawton were and are real places, as Barset and Mansfield were not, makes I think no important difference. The miracle of communication is the same.

R. W. CHAPMAN

1932

[14] 1 Apr. 1816.

PREFACE TO THE THIRD EDITION

MORE than sixty years have now passed since Dr Chapman wrote the preceding introduction to his collection of Jane Austen's letters, and in the course of these decades their interest for posterity has become well proven. Literary critics hunt through them for the most minute details of her opinions, actions, family, and friends, as source-material for biographies and for studies on the composition of the novels; social historians immediately turn to them to find Jane's precise and accurate information on contemporary manners, style, and cost of living; and local historians pick out specific references to the places where she lived or visited in order to cast some reflected glory upon their particular territories. In 1952 Dr Chapman produced a second edition augmented by five letters, but since then still more fragments of letters have appeared in the salerooms, and other family manuscripts have become available to researchers; no apology, therefore, is now necessary for the production of a completely new edition which incorporates the results of the latest scholarship. Some explanation of the changes made in this new volume will, however, be useful to the reader.

Continuing research has enabled dates to be found for several letters which Dr Chapman was obliged to leave undated, and this information, coupled with the insertion in correct chronological order of those five letters which were late entries into his second edition, together with the inclusion of new material discovered post-1952, means that quite a number of the letters have changed places in the text and their numeration has had to be changed accordingly. A concordance with the second edition is therefore given in the List of Letters preceding the main body of the work.

It will also be seen that the numeration of the letters is in some cases followed by (A), (C), (D), or (S). The addition of (A) signifies that the letter itself was not composed by Jane Austen, but was either copied out by her or else was one to which she replied; (C) is one of JA's own letters, but where the original manuscript is now missing and the text is known only from a copy or copies made by some other member of the Austen family in later years; (D) is a draft preserved by JA for her own reference, the fair copy of which may or may not also survive; (S) is a section cut from one of her letters at a later date, the provenance of which may be different from that of the remainder of the manuscript. In the few cases where drafts *and* their fair copies exist, both texts are given in full and the provenance of each is given separately.

In the century since the first publication by Lord Brabourne of the letters that had been in his mother's possession, most of those which he subsequently put on the market have reappeared and are owned by libraries or other institutions. In these cases, where it has been possible to check Brabourne's published version against the actual manuscripts, it can be seen that not only did he or his printer transcribe carelessly and on some occasions omit or alter sentences, but that the division of JA's text into paragraphs was nearly always arbitrary and incorrect. Where such comparisons can be made, the texts in this new edition are of course corrected in all respects; however, there remain fourteen letters which have never been seen since the dispersal of the Brabourne archive, and these can only be reprinted here as from the 1884 publication, but with the difference that the texts are run on from beginning to end without any attempt to create such false paragraphs.

Cassandra Austen's weeding-out and censoring of her sister's letters, as mentioned by their niece Caroline Austen, shows itself more in the complete destruction of letters rather than in the excision of individual sentences; the 'portions cut out' usually only amount to a very few words, and from the context it would seem that the subject concerned was physical ailment. This destruction of letters can usually be noticed when the dates of those surviving are compared. When the sisters were apart, they wrote to each other about every three or four days—another letter begun as soon as the previous one had been posted. There is always a first letter from Jane telling Cassandra of the journey from home to the destination; then a series of letters talking about daily events at the other place; and one or more letters planning the journey home. If Cassandra is the traveller, then the first letter is from Jane hoping she had a good journey; the bulk of the sequence is Jane telling Cassandra how life progresses at home; and the last one or two are Jane's anticipation of her sister's speedy and comfortable return trip. Where a series of letters does not contain this pattern and frequency of correspondence, it means that Cassandra destroyed some of the group in later years, when she was planning to bequeath a token few to her nieces as souvenirs of their aunt Jane. Close consideration shows that the destruction was probably because Jane had either described physical symptoms rather too fully (e.g. during the autumn of 1798, when Cassandra was at Godmersham and Mrs Austen was ill at home in

Steventon being nursed by Jane), or else because she had made some comment about other members of the family which Cassandra did not wish posterity to read. An example of this is in Jane's letter of 11–12 October 1813 (no. **91** of the present edition), where she says: 'As I wrote of my nephews with a little bitterness in my last . . .' and then goes on to praise them for their virtuous behaviour in attending a Holy Communion service the previous day. But 'my last' letter does not survive—it was written some time between 25 September and this one begun on 11 October—and Cassandra evidently did not want the younger generation to come across the 'little bitterness' and be hurt by what Jane herself now felt to be an over-hasty criticism which she already repented. Where such gaps occur within a series of letters, this is drawn to the reader's notice by the insertion of [*Letters missing here*]; and where longer periods of time elapse between groups of letters, when perhaps the sisters were at home together, this is marked by

——————

The layout of this edition is planned to give the maximum degree of ease in reading the actual text, so that the letters follow one after the other with only a brief heading of the necessary names and dates; the printed version reflects as closely as possible Jane Austen's own spelling, capitalization, and punctuation, and page-breaks are also noted. The physical details of the manuscripts—size and type of paper, watermarks, postmarks, endorsements, seals and wafers—are given as endnotes, together with information on their provenance and present ownership so far as can be ascertained, and these endnotes also give explanations of now obscure references to contemporary matters. A select bibliography follows the endnotes and a biographical index and a topographical index follow, providing for those who seek more detailed information on the people and places mentioned by Jane; a general index completes the work.

Although, as Dr Chapman said in 1932, it seems unlikely that any very considerable hoard of Jane Austen's letters will hereafter come to light, nevertheless interesting fragments have continued to appear right up to the present time, and others may yet surface as more family archives find their way into modern County Record Offices. Apart from writing frequently to her brothers and their wives, the Leigh-Perrots, and her various cousins, Jane would have had reason to keep in touch with other old friends and connections in Kent, London, Hampshire, and Berkshire, as well as corresponding occasionally with such people as Miss Irvine of Bath, and the Buller family in Colyton, Devon.

Of those letters which do survive, it is very lucky that the majority fall into clearly defined groups which give examples of a variety of recipients and subjects and Jane's approach to both. The letters to Cassandra are the equivalent of telephone calls between the sisters— hasty and elliptical, keeping each other informed of domestic events and occasionally making comments on the news of the day, both local and national. To her brother Frank, away at sea, Jane writes in a more regular and considered style, giving a bulletin of information about all members of the family, such as someone away for a long period would need to know. No doubt similar letters went to Charles—his surviving pocket-books note the receipt of a number of letters from Jane—though unfortunately he preserved only the very last of them, that written during her final illness. As the elder nephews and nieces grow up, the letters to Fanny Knight are those of an 'agony aunt' in the modern sense— giving advice on affairs of the heart to this motherless teenager. Here again, although Lord Brabourne stated that his mother's diaries showed the receipt of 'upwards of thirty letters' (ii. 118), a closer study makes it clear that Fanny records receiving at least forty-seven letters from Jane between 1803 (when her diaries commence) and 1817. Anna's interest in trying to write a novel leads to the group of letters in which Jane sets out her views as to how a natural and credible story should be composed (these letters of course are now of particular interest to literary critics); there are cheerfully teasing letters to young James-Edward Austen as he grows from good-natured schoolboy into charming young Oxford undergraduate; and little joking notes to the much younger Caroline. Outside the family, there is the crisp business correspondence with Crosby & Co. and John Murray regarding publication, and the careful formality of Jane's responses to Lady Morley and the Revd James Stanier Clarke.

Apart from JA's letters, from time to time there appear in the salerooms fragments of text undeniably in her handwriting, but with religious subject-matter, and so quite unlike the style of her usual correspondence. These fragments may perhaps be referred to as 'Sermon Scraps', since their origin is explained in an undated letter written by the Revd James-Edward Austen-Leigh to his daughter Mary-Augusta, soon after the publication of his *Memoir of Jane Austen* in 1870:

I continue to have letters about the Memoir. *At last*, a very civil one from Sir John Lefevre. One came from the Secretary of a Mechanics Institution *at Guernsey*!! with the cool request that I would give them a copy of the Memoir, together with some letter of Aunt Jane's. I might as well be asked by *any* or *every* Mechanics' Institution between Shetland and the coast of France. I declined, explaining that I had none to give, nor any other means of procuring one but such as are open to the public; but I did send not a letter, but an autograph of my aunt. Mamma has found what I had known of but forgotten, an MS sermon partly written out by Aunt Jane for my father. This I have been able to break up into about twenty sentences. I have pasted each on a larger strip of paper, and have added a certificate that it is in her '*handwriting, not her composition.*' One of these I sent to the Guernsey *gentle*men, or *simple* men, whichever name may best fit them. I had some feeling of gratitude to the Island, on account of the pleasant visit which I paid there, with the Le Marchants more than twenty years ago.

The location of several of these Sermon Scraps has been noted by David Gilson in *The Book Collector*, 36: 2 (Summer 1987), 269–70. They are not, however, published in this present volume, as they are in no way concerned with JA's correspondence.

Dr Chapman was reminded of *The Last Chronicle of Barset*, and the present editor is reminded of Nathaniel Hawthorne's comment on Trollope's novels—that they were 'just as real as if some giant had hewn a great lump out of the earth, and put it under a glass case, with all its inhabitants going about their daily business and not suspecting that they were made a show of'. Jane Austen's letters are not 'just as real'—they *are* real, and as we read them we too can watch the daily business of herself, her family, and friends passing before our eyes, and, if we wish, think away two hundred years to participate unseen in their joys and sorrows.

DEIRDRE LE FAYE

1995

LIST OF LETTERS
(and concordance with RWC numeration)

NO.	RWC	DATE	LETTER
1	1	9–10 Jan. 1796	To Cassandra, from Steventon to Kintbury
2	2	14–15 Jan. 1796	To Cassandra, from Steventon to Kintbury
3	3	23 Aug. 1796	To Cassandra, from London to ?Steventon
4	4	1 Sept. 1796	To Cassandra, from Rowling to Steventon
5	5	5 Sept. 1796	To Cassandra, from Rowling to Steventon
6	6	15–16 Sept. 1796	To Cassandra, from Rowling to Steventon
7	7	18 Sept. 1796	To Cassandra, from Rowling to Steventon
8	8	8 Apr. 1798	To Philadelphia Walter, from Steventon to Seal
9	9	24 Oct. 1798	To Cassandra, from Dartford to Godmersham
10	10	27–8 Oct. 1798	To Cassandra, from Steventon to Godmersham
11	11	17–18 Nov. 1798	To Cassandra, from Steventon to Godmersham
12	12	25 Nov. 1798	To Cassandra, from Steventon to Godmersham
13	13	1–2 Dec. 1798	To Cassandra, from Steventon to Godmersham
14	14	18–19 Dec. 1798	To Cassandra, from Steventon to Godmersham
15	15	24–6 Dec. 1798	To Cassandra, from Steventon to Godmersham
16	16	28 Dec. 1798	To Cassandra, from Steventon to Godmersham

List of Letters

NO.	RWC	DATE	LETTER
39	39	14 Sept. 1804	To Cassandra, from Lyme Regis to Ibthorpe
40	40	21 Jan. 1805	To Francis Austen, from Bath to Portsmouth
41	41	22 Jan. 1805	To Francis Austen, from Bath to Portsmouth
42	42	29 Jan. 1805	To Francis Austen, from Bath to Portsmouth
43	43	8–11 Apr. 1805	To Cassandra, from Bath to Ibthorpe
44	44	21–3 Apr. 1805	To Cassandra, from Bath to Ibthorpe
45	45	24 Aug. 1805	To Cassandra, from Godmersham to Goodnestone
46	46	27 Aug. 1805	To Cassandra, from Goodnestone to Godmersham
47	47	30 Aug. 1805	To Cassandra, from Goodnestone to Godmersham
48(C)	—	?24 July 1806	To Fanny Austen (Knight), from Clifton to Godmersham
49	48	7–8 Jan. 1807	To Cassandra, from Southampton to Godmersham
50	49	8–9 Feb. 1807	To Cassandra, from Southampton to Godmersham
51	50	20–2 Feb. 1807	To Cassandra, from Southampton to Godmersham
52	51	15–17 June 1808	To Cassandra, from Godmersham to Southampton
53	52	20–2 June 1808	To Cassandra, from Godmersham to Southampton
54	53	26 June 1808	To Cassandra, from Godmersham to Southampton
55	54	30 June–1 July 1808	To Cassandra, from Godmersham to Southampton
56	55	1–2 Oct. 1808	To Cassandra, from Southampton to Godmersham
57	56	7–9 Oct. 1808	To Cassandra, from Southampton to Godmersham

NO.	RWC	DATE	LETTER
58	57	13 Oct. 1808	To Cassandra, from Southampton to Godmersham
59	58	15–16 Oct. 1808	To Cassandra, from Southampton to Godmersham
60	59	24–5 Oct. 1808	To Cassandra, from Southampton to Godmersham
61	60	20 Nov. 1808	To Cassandra, from Southampton to Godmersham
62	61	9 Dec. 1808	To Cassandra, from Southampton to Godmersham
63	62	27–8 Dec. 1808	To Cassandra, from Southampton to Godmersham
64	63	10–11 Jan. 1809	To Cassandra, from Southampton to Godmersham
65	64	17–18 Jan. 1809	To Cassandra, from Southampton to Godmersham
66	65	24 Jan. 1809	To Cassandra, from Southampton to Godmersham
67	66	30 Jan. 1809	To Cassandra, from Southampton to Godmersham
68(D)	67	5 Apr. 1809	To R. Crosby & Co, from Southampton to London
68(A)	67a	8 Apr. 1809	To Jane Austen, from London to Southampton
69(D)	—	26 July 1809	To Francis Austen, from Chawton to [China]
69	68	26 July 1809	To Francis Austen, from Chawton to [China]
70	69	18–20 Apr. 1811	To Cassandra, from London to Godmersham
71	70	25 Apr. 1811	To Cassandra, from London to Godmersham
72	71	30 Apr. 1811	To Cassandra, from London to Godmersham
73	72	29 May 1811	To Cassandra, from Chawton to Godmersham

NO.	RWC	DATE	LETTER
74	73	31 May 1811	To Cassandra, from Chawton to Godmersham
75	74	6 June 1811	To Cassandra, from Chawton to Godmersham
76(C)	102	?29–31 Oct. 1812	To Anna Austen, from Chawton to Steventon
77	74.1	29–30 Nov. 1812	To Martha Lloyd, from Chawton to Kintbury
78	75	24 Jan. 1813	To Cassandra, from Chawton to Steventon
79	76	29 Jan. 1813	To Cassandra, from Chawton to Steventon
80	77	4 Feb. 1813	To Cassandra, from Chawton to Steventon
81	78	9 Feb. 1813	To Cassandra, from Chawton to Manydown
82	78.1	16 Feb 1813	To Martha Lloyd, from Chawton to Kintbury
83	—	17 Feb. 1813	To ?Francis Austen, from Chawton to ?Deal
84	79	20 May 1813	To Cassandra, from London to Chawton
85	80	24 May 1813	To Cassandra, from London to Chawton
86	81	3–6 July 1813	To Francis Austen, from Chawton to the Baltic
87	82	15–16 Sept. 1813	To Cassandra, from London to Chawton
88	83	16 Sept. 1813	To Cassandra, from London to Chawton
89	84	23–4 Sept. 1813	To Cassandra, from Godmersham to Chawton
90	85	25 Sept. 1813	To Francis Austen, from Godmersham to the Baltic
91	86	11–12 Oct. 1813	To Cassandra, from Godmersham to Chawton

NO.	RWC	DATE	LETTER
92	87	14–15 Oct. 1813	To Cassandra, from Godmersham to Chawton
93	88	21 Oct. 1813	To Cassandra, from Godmersham to London
94	89	26 Oct. 1813	To Cassandra, from Godmersham to London
95	90	3 Nov. 1813	To Cassandra, from Godmersham to London
96	91	6–7 Nov. 1813	To Cassandra, from Godmersham to London
97	92	2–3 Mar. 1814	To Cassandra, from London to Chawton
98	93	5–8 Mar. 1814	To Cassandra, from London to Chawton
99	94	9 Mar. 1814	To Cassandra, from London to Chawton
100	—	21 Mar. 1814	To ?Francis Austen, from London to ?Spithead
101	96	14 June 1814	To Cassandra, from Chawton to London
102	97	23 June 1814	To Cassandra, from Chawton to London
103	95	?mid-July 1814	To Anna Austen, from Chawton to Steventon
104	98	10–18 Aug. 1814	To Anna Austen, from Chawton to Steventon
105	99	23–4 Aug. 1814	To Cassandra, from London to Chawton
106	99.1	2 Sept. 1814	To Martha Lloyd, from London to Bath
107	100	9–18 Sept. 1814	To Anna Austen, from Chawton to Steventon
108	101	28 Sept. 1814	To Anna Austen, from Chawton to Steventon
109	103	18–20 Nov. 1814	To Fanny Knight, from Chawton to Goodnestone

NO.	RWC	DATE	LETTER
110	104	22 Nov. 1814	To Anna Lefroy, from Chawton to Hendon
111	109	?24 Nov. 1814	To Anna Lefroy, from Chawton to Hendon
112	105	29 Nov. 1814	To Anna Lefroy, from London to Hendon
113	107	30 Nov. 1814	To Anna Lefroy, from London to Hendon
114	106	30 Nov. 1814	To Fanny Knight, from London to Godmersham
115	119	?6 Dec. 1814	To Caroline Austen, from Chawton to Steventon
116	—	?late Dec. 1814	To ?Anna Lefroy, from ?Chawton to ?Hendon
117	—	?early Feb.–July 1815	To Anna Lefroy, from ?Chawton to Hendon
118	108	?late Feb.–early Mar. 1815	To Anna Lefroy, from Chawton to Hendon
119	149	?2 Mar. 1815	To Caroline Austen, from Chawton to Steventon
120	110	29 Sept. 1815	To Anna Lefroy, from Chawton to Wyards
121	111	17–18 Oct. 1815	To Cassandra, from London to Chawton
122(A) (D)	—	?20/21 Oct. 1815	To John Murray, from London to London
123	112	30 Oct. 1815	To Caroline Austen, from London to Chawton
124(D)	114	3 Nov. 1815	To John Murray, from London to London
124	114	3 Nov. 1815	To John Murray, from London to London
125(D)	113	15 Nov. 1815	To James Stanier Clarke, from London to London
125(A)	113*a*	16 Nov. 1815	To Jane Austen, from London to London

NO.	RWC	DATE	LETTER
126	115	23 Nov. 1815	To John Murray, from London to London
127	116	24 Nov. 1815	To Cassandra, from London to Chawton
128	117	26 Nov. 1815	To Cassandra, from London to Chawton
129	118	2 Dec. 1815	To Cassandra, from London to Chawton
130	121	11 Dec. 1815	To John Murray, from London to London
131(C)	122	11 Dec. 1815	To John Murray, from London to London
132(D)	120	11 Dec. 1815	To James Stanier Clarke, from London to London
132(A)	120a	?21 Dec. 1815	To Jane Austen, from London to [London]
133	122.1	14 Dec. 1815	To Charles Thomas Haden, from London to London
134(A)	123a	27 Dec. 1815	To Jane Austen, from Saltram to Chawton
134(D)	123	31 Dec. 1815	To Lady Morley, from Chawton to Saltram
134	—	31 Dec. 1815	To Lady Morley, from Chawton to Saltram
135	124	?Dec. 1815–Jan. 1816	To Anna Lefroy, from Chawton to Wyards
136	148	?early 1816	To Catherine Ann Prowting, from Chawton to Chawton
137	125	13 Mar. 1816	To Caroline Austen, from Chawton to Steventon
138(A)	126a	27 Mar. 1816	To Jane Austen, from Brighton to London
138(D)	126	1 Apr. 1816	To James Stanier Clarke, from Chawton to Brighton
139	127	1 Apr. 1816	To John Murray, from Chawton to London

NO.	RWC	DATE	LETTER
140	128 & 128.1	21 Apr. 1816	To Caroline Austen, from Chawton to Steventon
141(C)	129	23 June 1816	To Anna Lefroy, from Chawton to Wyards
142	130	9 July 1816	To James Edward Austen, from Chawton to Steventon
143	131	15 July 1816	To Caroline Austen, from Chawton to Steventon
144	132	4 Sept. 1816	To Cassandra, from Chawton to Cheltenham
145	133	8–9 Sept. 1816	To Cassandra, from Chawton to Cheltenham
146	134	16–17 Dec. 1816	To James Edward Austen, from Chawton to Steventon
147(C)	135	?Dec. 1816	To Anna Lefroy, from Chawton to Wyards
148	136	8 Jan. 1817	To Cassandra Esten Austen, from Chawton to London
149	137	23 Jan. 1817	To Caroline Austen, from Chawton to Steventon
150(C)	139	24 Jan. 1817	To Alethea Bigg, from Chawton to Streatham
151	140	20–1 Feb. 1817	To Fanny Knight, from Chawton to Godmersham
152	138	26 Feb. 1817	To Caroline Austen, from Chawton to Steventon
153	141	13 Mar. 1817	To Fanny Knight, from Chawton to Godmersham
154	141.1	14 Mar. 1817	To Caroline Austen, from Chawton to Steventon
155	142	23–5 Mar. 1817	To Fanny Knight, from Chawton to Godmersham
156	143	26 Mar. 1817	To Caroline Austen, from Chawton to Steventon
157	144	6 Apr. 1817	To Charles Austen, from Chawton to London

List of Letters

NO.	RWC	DATE	LETTER
158	—	27 Apr. 1817	To Cassandra, from Chawton to Chawton
159	145	22 May 1817	To Anne Sharp, from Chawton to Doncaster
160	146	27 May 1817	To James Edward Austen, from Winchester to Oxford
161(C)	147	?28/29 May 1817	To ?Frances Tilson from Winchester to ?London
CEA/1	—	20 July 1817	To Fanny Knight, from Winchester to Godmersham
CEA/2	—	28 July 1817	To Anne Sharp, from Chawton to [Doncaster]
CEA/3	—	29 July 1817	To Fanny Knight, from Chawton to Godmersham

1. *To Cassandra Austen*

Steventon: Saturday January 9

In the first place I hope you will live twenty-three years longer. Mr Tom Lefroy's birthday was yesterday, so that you are very near of an age.[1] After this necessary preamble I shall proceed to inform you that we had an exceeding good ball last night, and that I was very much disappointed at not seeing Charles Fowle of the party, as I had previously heard of his being invited. In addition to our set at the Harwoods' ball, we had the Grants, St Johns, Lady Rivers, her three daughters and a son, Mr and Miss Heathcote, Mrs Lefevre, two Mr Watkins, Mr J. Portal, Miss Deanes, two Miss Ledgers, and a tall clergyman who came with them, whose name Mary[2] would never have guessed. We were so terrible good as to take James in our carriage, though there were three of us before; but indeed he deserves encouragement for the very great improvement which has lately taken place in his dancing. Miss Heathcote is pretty, but not near so handsome as I expected. Mr H. began with Elizabeth,[3] and afterwards danced with her again; but *they* do not know how *to be particular*. I flatter myself, however, that they will profit by the three successive lessons which I have given them. You scold me so much in the nice long letter which I have this moment received from you, that I am almost afraid to tell you how my Irish friend[4] and I behaved. Imagine to yourself everything most profligate and shocking in the way of dancing and sitting down together. I *can* expose myself, however, only *once more,* because he leaves the country soon after next Friday, on which day we *are* to have a dance at Ashe after all. He is a very gentlemanlike, good-looking, pleasant young man, I assure you. But as to our having ever met, except at the three last balls, I cannot say much; for he is so excessively laughed at about me at Ashe, that he is ashamed of coming to Steventon, and ran away when we called on Mrs Lefroy a few days ago. We left Warren at Dean Gate, in our way home last night, and he is now on his road to town. He left his love, &c., to you, and I will deliver it when we meet. Henry goes to Harden[5] to-day in his way to his Master's degree. We shall feel the loss of these two most agreeable young men exceedingly, and shall have nothing to console us till the arrival of the Coopers on Tuesday. As they will stay here till the Monday following, perhaps Caroline will go to the Ashe ball with me, though I dare say she will not. I danced twice with Warren last night, and once with Mr Charles Watkins, and, to my inexpressible astonishment, I entirely escaped John Lyford. I was forced to fight hard for it, however. We had a very good supper, and the greenhouse was illuminated in a very elegant manner. We had a visit yesterday morning from Mr Benjamin Portal, whose eyes are as handsome as ever. Everybody is extremely anxious for your return, but as you cannot come home by the Ashe ball, I am glad that I have not fed them with false hopes. James danced with Alethea,[6] and cut up the turkey last night with great perseverance. You say nothing of the silk stockings; I flatter myself, therefore, that Charles[7] has not purchased any, as I cannot very well afford to pay for them; all my money is spent in buying white gloves and pink persian.[8] I wish Charles had been at Manydown, because he would have given you some description of my friend, and I think you must be impatient to hear something about him. Henry is still hankering after the Regulars, and as his project of purchasing the adjutancy of the Oxfordshire[9] is now over, he has got a scheme in his head about getting a lieutenancy and adjutancy in the 86th, a new-raised regiment, which he fancies will be ordered to the Cape of Good Hope.[10] I heartily hope that he will, as usual, be disappointed in this scheme. We have trimmed up and given away all the old paper hats of Mamma's manufacture; I hope you will not regret the loss of yours. After I had written the above, we received a visit from Mr Tom Lefroy and his cousin George. The latter is really very well-behaved now;[11] and as for the other, he has but *one* fault, which time will, I trust, entirely remove—it is that his morning coat is a great deal too light. He is a very great admirer of Tom Jones, and therefore wears the same coloured clothes, I imagine, which *he* did when he was wounded.[12] *Sunday.*—By not returning till the 19th, you will exactly contrive to miss seeing the Coopers, which I suppose it is your wish to do. We have heard nothing from Charles[13] for some time. One would suppose they must have sailed by this time, as the wind is so favourable. What a funny name Tom[14] has got for his vessel! But he has no taste in names, as we well know, and I dare say he christened it himself. I am sorry for the Beaches' loss of their little girl, especially as it is the one so much like me. I condole with Miss M. on her losses and with Eliza[15] on her gains, and am ever yours,

J. A.

To Miss Austen,
Rev. Mr Fowle's,
Kintbury,
Newbury.

[*Letter missing here, dated Tuesday 12 or Wednesday 13 January 1796*]

2. *To Cassandra Austen*

Thursday 14–Friday 15 January 1796

Steventon Thursday [January 14]

I have just received yours & Mary's letter & I thank you both, tho' their contents might have been more agreeable. I do not at all expect to see you on tuesday since matters have fallen out so unpleasantly, & if you are not able to return till after that day, it will hardly be possible for us to send for you before Saturday; tho' for my own part I care so little about the Ball that it would be no sacrifice to me to give it up for the sake of seeing you two days earlier. We are extremely sorry for poor Eliza's Illness—I trust however that she has continued to recover since you wrote, & that you will none of you be the worse for your attendance on her. What a good-for-nothing-fellow Charles is to bespeak the stockings—I hope he will be too hot all the rest of his life for it!—I sent you a letter yesterday to Ibthorp, which I suppose you will not receive at Kintbury. It was not very long or very witty, & therefore if you never receive it, it does not much signify. I wrote principally to tell you that the Coopers were arrived and in good health—the little boy is very like Dr Cooper & the little girl is to resemble Jane,[1] they say. Our party to Ashe to-morrow night will consist of Edward Cooper, James (for a Ball is nothing without *him*), Buller, who is now staying with us, & I—I look forward with great impatience to it, as I rather expect to receive an offer from my friend in the course of the evening. I shall refuse him, however, unless he promises to give away his white Coat.

I am very much flattered by your commendation of my last Letter, for I write only for Fame, and without any view to pecuniary Emolument.— Edward[2] is gone to spend the day with his friend, John Lyford, & does not return till to-morrow. Anna[3] is now here; She came up in her chaise to spend the day with her young Cousins; but she does not much take

3

to them or to anything about them, except Caroline's Spinning-wheel. I am very glad to find from Mary that Mr & Mrs Fowle[4] are pleased with you. I hope you will continue to give satisfaction.

How impertinent you are to write to me about Tom,[5] as if I had not opportunities of hearing from him myself. The *last* letter that I received from him was dated on friday the 8th, and he told me that if the wind should be favourable on Sunday, which it proved to be, they were to sail from Falmouth on that Day. By this time therefore they are at Barbadoes I suppose. The Rivers are still at Manydown, and are to be at Ashe tomorrow. I intended to call on the Miss Biggs yesterday had the weather been tolerable. Caroline, Anna & I have just been devouring some cold Souse,[6] & it would be difficult to say which enjoyed it most—

Tell Mary that I make over Mr Heartley & all his Estate to her for her sole use and Benefit in future, & not only him, but all my other Admirers into the bargain wherever she can find them, even the kiss which C. Powlett wanted to give me, as I mean to confine myself in future to Mr Tom Lefroy, for whom I donot care sixpence. Assure her also as a last & indubitable proof of Warren's indifference to me, that he actually drew that Gentleman's picture for me, & delivered it to me without a Sigh.

Friday.—At length the Day is come on which I am to flirt my last with Tom Lefroy, & when you receive this it will be over——My tears flow as I write, at the melancholy idea. Wm. Chute called here yesterday. I wonder what he means by being so civil. There is a report that Tom[7] is going to be married to a Litchfield Lass. John Lyford & his Sister bring Edward home to day, dine with us, & we shall all go together to Ashe. I understand that we are to draw for Partners.—I shall be extremely impatient to hear from you again, that I may know how Eliza is, & when you are to return. With best Love, &c., I am affec:^tely yours

J: Austen

Miss Austen
The Rev. Mr Fowle's,
Kintbury,
Newbury

3. *To Cassandra Austen*

Tuesday 23 August 1796[1]

Cork Street[2] Tuesday morning

My dear Cassandra

Here I am once more in this Scene of Dissipation & vice, and I begin already to find my Morals corrupted.—We reached Staines yesterday I donot [*know omitted*] when, without suffering so much from the Heat as I had hoped to do. We set off again this morning at seven o'clock, & had a very pleasant Drive, as the morning was cloudy & perfectly cool—I came all the way in the Chaise from Hertford Bridge.——

Edward & Frank[3] are both gone out to seek their fortunes; the latter is to return soon & help us seek ours. The former we shall never see again. We are to be at Astley's[4] to night, which I am glad of. Edward has heard from Henry this morning. He has not been at the Races, at all, unless his [*p. 2*] driving Miss Pearson over to Rowling one day can be so called. We shall find him there on Thursday.

I hope you are all alive after our melancholy parting Yesterday, and that you pursued your intended avocation with Success.——

God Bless You—I must leave off, for we are going out. Yrs very affec:tely

J: Austen

Every Body's Love

[*Address missing*]

[*Letter(s) missing here*]

4. *To Cassandra Austen*

Thursday 1 September 1796

Rowling: Thursday September 1

My dearest Cassandra

The letter which I have this moment received from you has diverted me beyond moderation. I could die of laughter at it, as they used to say at school. You are indeed the finest comic writer of the present age. Since I wrote last, we have been very near returning to Steventon so early as next week. Such, for a day or two, was our dear brother Henry's scheme, but at present matters are restored, not to what they were, for my absence seems likely to be lengthened still farther. I am sorry for it, but what can I do? Henry leaves us to-morrow for Yarmouth,[1] as he wishes very much to consult his physician there, on whom he has great reliance. He is better than he was when he first came, though still by no means well. According to his present plan, he will not return here till about the 23rd, and bring with him, if he can, leave of absence for three weeks, as he wants very much to have some shooting at Godmersham,[2] whither Edward and Elizabeth are to remove very early in October. If this scheme holds, I shall hardly be at Steventon before the middle of that month; but if you cannot do without me, I could return, I suppose, with Frank if he ever goes back. He enjoys himself here very much, for he has just learnt to turn, and is so delighted with the employment, that he is at it all day long. I am sorry that you found such a conciseness in the strains of my first letter. I must endeavour to make you amends for it, when we meet, by some elaborate details, which I shall shortly begin composing. I have had my new gown made up, and it really makes a very superb surplice. I am sorry to say that my new coloured gown is very much washed out, though I charged everybody to take great care of it. I hope yours is so too. Our men had but indifferent weather for their visit to Godmersham, for it rained great part of the way there and all the way back. They found Mrs Knight remarkably well and in very good spirits. It is imagined that she will shortly be married again. I have taken little George once in my arms since I have been here, which I thought very kind. I have told Fanny[3] about the bead of her necklace, and she wants very much to know where you found it. To-morrow I shall be just like Camilla[4] in Mr Dubster's summer-house; for my Lionel will have taken away the ladder by which I came here, or at least by which I intended to get away, and here I must stay till his return. My situation, however, is somewhat preferable to hers, for I am very happy here, though I should be glad to get home by the end of the month. I have no idea that Miss Pearson will return with me. What a fine fellow Charles[5] is, to deceive us into writing two letters to him at Cork! I admire his ingenuity extremely, especially as he is so great a gainer by it. Mr and Mrs Cage and Mr and Mrs Bridges dined with us yesterday. Fanny[6] seemed as glad to see me as anybody, and enquired very much after you, whom she supposed to be making your wedding-clothes. She is as handsome as ever, and somewhat fatter. We had a very pleasant day, and some *liqueurs* in the evening. Louisa's figure is very much improved; she is as stout again as she was.[7] Her face, from what I could see of it one evening, appeared not at all altered. She and the gentlemen walked up here on Monday night—she came in the morning with the Cages from Hythe. Lady Hales, with her two youngest daughters, have been to see us. Caroline is not grown at all coarser than she was, nor Harriet at all more delicate. I am glad to hear so good an account of Mr Charde, and only fear that my long absence may occasion his relapse. I practise every day as much as I can—I wish it were more for his sake. I have heard nothing of Mary Robinson[8] since I have been [here]. I expect to be well scolded for daring to doubt, whenever the subject is mentioned. Frank has turned a very nice little butter-churn for Fanny. I do not believe that any of the party were aware of the valuables they had left behind; nor can I hear anything of Anna's gloves. Indeed I have not enquired at all about them hitherto. We are very busy making Edward's shirts, and I am proud to say that I am the neatest worker of the party. They say that there are a prodigious number of birds hereabouts this year, so that perhaps *I* may kill a few. I am glad to hear so good an account of Mr Limprey and J. Lovett. I know nothing of my mother's handkerchief, but I dare say I shall find it soon.

I am very affectionately yours,

Jane

Miss Austen,
Steventon,
Overton,
Hants.

[*Possibly a letter missing here*]

5. *To Cassandra Austen*

Monday 5 September 1796

Rowling Monday 5th Sept^r

My dear Cassandra

I shall be extremely anxious to hear the Event of your Ball, & shall hope to receive so long & minute an account of every particular that I shall be tired of reading it. Let me know how many besides their fourteen Selves & M^r & Mrs Wright, Michael[1] will contrive to place about their Coach, and how many of the Gentlemen, Musicians & Waiters, he will have persuaded to come in their Shooting Jackets. I hope John Lovett's accident will not prevent his attending the Ball, as you will otherwise be obliged to dance with M[r] Tincton the whole Evening. Let me know how[2] J. Harwood deports himself without the Miss Biggs;— and which of the Marys[3] will carry the day with my Brother James. *We* were at a Ball on Saturday I assure you. We dined at Goodnestone & in the Evening danced two Country Dances & the Boulangeries.—I opened the Ball with Edw:[d] Bridges; the other couples,[4] were Lewis Cage & Harriot, Frank and Louisa, Fanny & George. Eliz:[th] played one Country dance, Lady Bridges[5] the other, which She made Henry[6] dance with her; and Miss Finch played the Boulangeries—On reading over the last three or four Lines, I am aware of my having expressed myself in so doubtful a manner that if I did not tell you to the contrary, You might imagine it was Lady Bridges who made Henry dance with her, at the same time that she was playing—which if not impossible must appear a very improbable Event to you.—But it was Eliz: who danced ——.

[*p. 2*] We supped there, & walked home at night under the shade of two Umbrellas.—To-day the Goodnestone Party begins to disperse & spread itself abroad. M[r] & M[rs] Cage & George repair to Hythe. Lady Waltham, Miss Bridges[7] & Miss Mary Finch to Dover, for the health of the two former.—I have never seen Marianne at all.——

On Thursday M[r] & M[rs] Bridges return to Danbury; Miss Harriot Hales accompanies them to London in her way to Dorsetshire. Farmer Clarinbould died this morning, & I fancy Edward means to get some of his Farm if he can cheat Sir Brook enough in the agrement.—We have just got some venison from Godmersham, which the two M[r] Harveys are to devour tomorrow;[8] and on friday or Saturday the Goodnestone people are to finish their Scraps. Henry[9] went away on friday as he purposed *without fayl*[10]—; You will hear from him soon I imagine, as he talked of writing to Steventon shortly. M[r] Richard Harvey is going to be married; but as it is a great secret, & only known to half the Neighbourhood, you must not mention it. The Lady's name is Musgrove.—I am in great Distress.—I cannot determine whether I shall give Richis[11] half a guinea or only five Shillings when I go away. Counsel me, amiable Miss Austen, and tell me which will be the most.— We walked Frank last night to Crixhall ruff,[12] and he appeared much edified. Little Edward was breeched yesterday for good & all, and was whipped, into the Bargain. Pray remember me to Everybody who does not enquire after me. Those who do, remember me without bidding.

[*End of p. 2; second leaf of letter (pp. 3 and 4) missing. Postscript written upside down at top of first page*]

Give my Love to Mary Harrison, & tell her I wish whenever she is attached to a young Man, some *respectable* Dr Marchmont[13] may keep them apart for five Volumes.

[*Address missing*]

[*Letters missing here*]

6. *To Cassandra Austen*

Thursday 15–Friday 16 September 1796

Rowling Thursday 15th Sep:^{tr}—

My dear Cassandra

We have been very gay since I wrote last; dining at Nackington, returning by Moonlight, and everything quite in Stile, not to mention Mr Claringbould's Funeral[1] which we saw go by on Sunday. I beleive I told you[2] in a former Letter that Edward had some idea of taking the name of Claringbould; but that scheme is over, tho' it would be a very eligible as well as a very pleasant plan, would any one advance him Money enough to begin on. We rather expected Mr Milles to have done so on Tuesday; but to our great Surprise, nothing was said on the subject, and unless it is in your power to assist your Brother with five or six Hundred pounds, he must entirely give up the idea. At Nackington we met Lady Sondes' picture over the Mantlepeice in the Dining room, and the pictures of her three Children in an Antiroom, besides Mr Scott, Miss Fletcher, Mr Toke, Mr J. Toke, and the Archdeacon Lynch. Miss Fletcher and I were very thick, but I am the thinnest of the two—She wore her purple Muslin, which is pretty enough, tho' it does not become her complexion. [*p. 2*] There are two Traits in her Character which are pleasing; namely, she admires Camilla, & drinks no cream in her Tea. If you should ever see Lucy,[3] You may tell her, that I scolded Miss Fletcher for her negligence in writing, as she desired me to do, but without being able to bring her to any proper sense of Shame—That Miss Fletcher says in her defence that as every Body whom Lucy knew when she was in Canterbury, has now left it, she has nothing at all to write to her about. By *Everybody*, I suppose Miss Fletcher means that a

9

new set of Officers have arrived there—. But this is a note of my own.—Mrs Milles, Mr John Toke, & in short every body of any Sensibility enquired in tender Strains after You; and I took an opportunity of assuring Mr J. T. that neither he nor his Father need longer keep themselves single for You—. We went in our two Carriages to Nackington; but how we divided, I shall leave you to surmise, merely observing that as Eliz: and I were without either Hat or Bonnet, it would not have been very convenient for us to go in the Chair.—We went by Bifrons, & I contemplated with a melancholy pleasure, the abode of Him, on whom I once fondly [*p. 3*] doated.—We dine to day at Goodnestone, to meet my Aunt Fielding[4] from Margate, and a Mr Clayton, her professed Admirer; at least so I imagine. Lady Bridges has received very good accounts of Marianne, who is already[5] certainly the better for her Bathing.—So—his royal Highness Sir Thomas Williams has at length sailed—; the Papers say "on a Cruize." But I hope they are gone to Cork, or I shall have written in vain. Give my Love to Jane,[6] as she arrived at Steventon Yesterday, I dare say. I sent a message to Mr Digweed from Edward, in a letter to Mary Lloyd, which [she][7] ought to receive to day; but as I know that the Harwoods are not very exact as to their Letters, I may as well repeat it to You—. Mr Digweed is to be informed that Illness has prevented Seward's coming over to look at the intended Repairs at the Farm, but that he will come, as soon as he can. Mr Digweed may also be informed if you think proper, that M^r & Mrs Milles are to dine here tomorrow, and that Mrs Joan Knatchbull is to be asked to meet them.—Mr Richard Harvey's match is put off, till he has got a Better Christian name, of which he has great Hopes. Mr Children's two Sons are both going to be married, John & George—. They are to have one wife between them; a Miss Holwell, who belongs to the Black Hole at Calcutta.——

[*p. 4*] I depend on hearing from James very soon; he promised me an account of the Ball, and by this time he must have collected his Ideas enough, after the fatigue of dancing, to give me one. Edward & Fly[8] went out yesterday very early in a couple of Shooting Jackets, and came home like a couple of Bad Shots, for they killed nothing at all. They are out again to day, & are not yet returned.—Delightful Sport!—They are just come home; Edward with his two Brace, Frank with his Two and a half. What amiable Young Men!

Friday—Your Letter & one from Henry are just come, and the contents of both accord with my Scheme more than I had dared expect—

In one particular[9] I could wish it otherwise, for Henry is very indifferent indeed—. You must not expect us quite so early however as wednesday the 20th—on that day se'night according to our present plan we may be with You. Frank had never any idea of going away before Monday the 26th. I shall write to Miss Pearson immediately & press her returning with us, which Henry thinks very likely, & particularly eligible.

[*End of p. 4; next paragraph written upside down at top of first page*]

Till we know whether She accompanies us or not, we can say nothing in reply to my Father's kind offer—. As to the mode of our travelling to Town, *I* want to go in a Stage Coach, but Frank[10] will not let me. As You are likely to have the Williams' & Lloyds with You next week, You would hardly find room for us then—.

[*Next two paragraphs written upside down between the lines on p. 3*]

If anybody wants anything in Town, they must send their Commissions to Frank, as *I* shall merely pass thro' it.—

The Tallow Chandler is Penlington, at the Crown & Beehive Charles Street, Covent Garden.

[*Final postscript written below the address panel on p. 4*]

Buy Mary Harrison's Gown by all means. You shall have mine for ever so much money, tho' if I am tolerably rich when I get home, I shall like it very much myself.

[J. A.][11]

Miss Austen
Steventon
Overton
Hants.

7. *To Cassandra Austen*

Rowling Sunday 18th Sept:r —

My dear Cassandra,

This morning has been spent in Doubt & Deliberation; in forming plans, and removing Difficulties, for it ushered in the Day with an

Event which I had not intended should take place so soon by a week. Frank has rec:^d his appointment on Board the Captn John Gore, commanded by the Triton,[1] and will therefore be obliged to be in Town on wednesday—& tho' I have every Disposition in the world to accompany him on that day, I cannot go on the Uncertainty of the Pearsons being at Home; as I should not have a place to go to, in case they were from Home.—I wrote to Miss P— on friday, & hoped to receive an answer from her this morning, which would have rendered everything smooth & Easy, and would have enabled us to leave this place tomorrow, as Frank on first receiving his Appointment intended to do. He remains till Wednesday [*p. 2*] merely to accomodate me. I have written to her again today and desired her to answer it by return of post—On Tuesday therefore I shall positively know whether they can receive me on Wednesday—. If they cannot, Edward has been so good as to promise to take me to Greenwich on the Monday following which was the day before fixed on, if that suits them better—. If I have no answer at all on Tuesday, I must suppose Mary[2] is not at Home, & must wait till I do hear; as after having invited her to go to Steventon with me, it will not quite do, to go home and say no more about it.—

My Father will be so good as to fetch home his prodigal Daughter from Town, I hope, unless he wishes me to walk the Hospitals, Enter at the Temple, or mount Guard at St James.[3] It will hardly be in Frank's power to take me home; nay, it certainly will not. I shall write again as soon as I get to [*p. 3*] Greenwich—.

What dreadful Hot weather we have!—It keeps one in a continual state of Inelegance.—If Miss Pearson should return with me, pray be careful not to expect too much Beauty. I will not pretend to say that on a *first veiw*, she quite answered the opinion I had formed of her.—My Mother I am sure will be disappointed, if she does not take great care. From what I remember of her picture, it is no great resemblance. I am very glad that the idea of returning with Frank occurred to me, for as to Henry's coming into Kent again, the time of its taking place is so very uncertain, that I should be waiting for *Deadmen's Shoes*.

I had once determined to go with Frank tomorrow & take my chance &cr; but they dissuaded me from so rash a step—as I really think on consideration it would have been; for if the Pearsons were not at home, I should inevitably fall a Sacrifice to the arts of some fat Woman[4] who would make me drunk with Small Beer——

[*p. 4*] Mary[5] is brought to bed of a Boy; both doing very well. I shall leave you to guess what Mary, I mean.— Adeiu, with best Love to all your agreable Inmates. Donot let the Lloyds go on any account before I return, unless Miss P— is of the party.

How ill I have written. I begin to hate myself.

Y^{rs} ever—J: Austen—

The Triton is a new 32 Frigate,[6] just launched at Deptford.—Frank is much pleased with the prospect of having Capt: Gore under his command.

Miss Austen
Steventon
Overton
Hants

[*Letter(s) missing here, late September 1796*]

———

8. *To Philadelphia Walter*

Sunday 8 April 1798

Steventon Sunday April 8th

My dear Cousin[1]

As Cassandra is at present from home, You must accept from my pen, our sincere Condolance on the melancholy Event which Mrs Humphries[2] Letter announced to my Father this morning.—The loss of so kind & affectionate a Parent,[3] must be a very severe affliction to all his Children, to yourself more especially, as your constant residence with him has given you so much the more constant & intimate Knowledge of his Virtues.—But the very circumstance which at present enhances your loss, must gradually reconcile you to it the better;—the Goodness which made him valuable on Earth, will make him Blessed in Heaven.—This consideration must bring comfort to yourself, to my Aunt, & to all his family & friends; & this comfort must be heightened by the consideration of the little Enjoyment he was able to receive from this World for some time past, [*p. 2*] & of the small degree of pain attending his last hours.—I will not press you to write before you would otherwise feel equal to it, but when you can do it without pain, I hope we shall receive from you as good an account of my Aunt & Yourself, as can be expected in these early days of Sorrow.——

My Father & Mother join me in every kind wish, & I am my dear Cousin,

Yours affec:^{tely}

Jane Austen

[Miss Walter
Seal
Sevenoaks
Kent][4]

────────

9. *To Cassandra Austen*

Wednesday 24 October 1798

'Bull and George', Dartford Wednesday October 24

My dear Cassandra

You have already heard from Daniel,[1] I conclude, in what excellent time we reached and quitted Sittingbourne, and how very well my mother bore her journey thither. I am now able to send you a continuation of the same good account of her. She was very little fatigued on her arrival at this place, has been refreshed by a comfortable dinner, and now seems quite stout. It wanted five minutes of twelve when we left Sittingbourne, from whence we had a famous pair of horses, which took us to Rochester in an hour and a quarter; the postboy seemed determined to show my mother that Kentish drivers were not always tedious, and really drove as fast as *Cax*.[2] Our next stage was not quite so expeditiously performed; the road was heavy and our horses very indifferent. However, we were in such good time, and my mother bore her journey so well, that expedition was of little importance to us; and as it was, we were very little more than two hours and a half coming hither, and it was scarcely past four when we stopped at the inn. My mother took some of her bitters at Ospringe, and some more at Rochester, and she ate some bread several times. We have got apartments up two pair of stairs, as we could not be otherwise accommodated with a sitting-room and bed-chambers on the same floor, which we wished to be. We have one double-bedded and one single-bedded room; in the former my mother and I are to sleep. I shall leave you to guess who is to occupy the other. We sate down to dinner a little after five, and had some beef-steaks and a boiled fowl, but no oyster sauce. I should have

begun my letter soon after our arrival but for a little adventure which
prevented me. After we had been here a quarter of an hour it was
discovered that my writing and dressing boxes had been by accident put
into a chaise which was just packing off as we came in, and were driven
away towards Gravesend in their way to the West Indies. No part of my
property could have been such a prize before, for in my writing-box
was all my worldly wealth, 7*l*., and my dear Harry's deputation.[3] Mr
Nottley immediately despatched a man and horse after the chaise, and
in half an hour's time I had the pleasure of being as rich as ever; they
were got about two or three miles off. My day's journey has been
pleasanter in every respect than I expected. I have been very little
crowded and by no means unhappy. Your watchfulness with regard to
the weather on our accounts was very kind and very effectual. We had
one heavy shower on leaving Sittingbourne, but afterwards the clouds
cleared away, and we had a very bright *chrystal* afternoon. My father is
now reading the 'Midnight Bell',[4] which he has got from the library, and
mother[5] sitting by the fire. Our route to-morrow is not determined. We
have none of us much inclination for London, and if Mr Nottley will
give us leave, I think we shall go to Staines through Croydon and
Kingston, which will be much pleasanter than any other way; but he is
decidedly for Clapham and Battersea. God bless you all!

Yours affectionately,

J. A.

I flatter myself that *itty Dordy*[6] will not forget me at least under a
week. Kiss him for me.

Miss Austen,
Godmersham Park,
Faversham.

[*Letter missing here, dated Thursday 25 October 1798*]

10. *To Cassandra Austen*

Saturday 27–Sunday 28 October 1798

Steventon Saturday Oct: 27th

My dear Cassandra
    Your letter was a most agreable surprize to me to day, & I have taken
a long sheet of paper to shew my Gratitude. We arrived here yesterday

between 4 & 5, but I cannot send you quite so triumphant an account
of our last day's Journey as of the first & second.—Soon after I had
finished my letter from Staines, my Mother began to suffer from the
exercise & fatigue of travelling so far, & she was a good deal indisposed
from that particular kind of evacuation which has generally preceded
her Illnesses—. She had not a very good night at Staines, & felt a heat
in her throat as we travelled yesterday morning, which seemed to fore-
tell more Bile—. She bore her Journey however much better than I had
expected, & at Basingstoke where we stopped more than half an hour,
received much comfort from a Mess of Broth, & the sight of Mr Lyford,
who recommended her to take 12 drops of Laudanum when she went to
Bed, as a Composer, which she accordingly did.—It is by no means
wonderful that her Journey should have produced some Kind of visita-
tion;—I hope a few days will entirely remove it.—James called on us
just as we were going to Tea, & my Mother was well enough to talk
very chearfully to him, before she went to Bed.—Lyford has promised
to call, in the course of a few days, & then they will settle about the
Dandelion Tea;—the receipts for which were shewn him at Basingstoke,
& he approved of them highly; they will only require some slight alteration to be better adapted to my Mother's Constitution. [*p. 2*] James
seems to have taken to his old Trick of coming to Steventon inspite of
Mary's reproaches, for he was here before Breakfast, & is now paying
us a second visit.—Mary is quite well he says, & uncommonly large;[1]—
they were to have dined here to day, but the weather is too bad. I have
had the pleasure of hearing that Martha is with them;—James fetched
her from Ibthrop on Thursday, & she will stay with them till she re-
moves to Kintbury.—We met with no adventures at all in our Journey
yesterday, except that our Trunk had once nearly slipt off, & we were
obliged to stop at Hartley to have our wheels greazed.—While my
Mother & Mr Lyford were together, I went to Mrs Ryders, & bought
what I intended to buy, but not in much perfection.—There were no
narrow Braces for Children, & scarcely any netting silk; but Miss Wood
as usual is going to Town very soon, & will lay in a fresh stock.—I
gave 2^s/3^d a yard for my flannel, & I fancy it is not very good; but it
is so disgraceful & contemptible an article in itself, that its' being comparatively good or bad is of little importance. I bought some Japan Ink[2]
likewise, & next week shall begin my operations on my hat, on which
You know my principal hopes of happiness depend.—I am very grand
indeed;—I had the dignity of dropping out my mother's Laudanum last

night, I carry about the keys of the Wine & Closet; & twice since I began this letter, have had orders to give in the Kitchen: Our dinner was very good yesterday, & the Chicken boiled perfectly tender; therefore I shall not be obliged to dismiss Nanny on that account.—Almost every thing [*p. 3*] was unpacked & put away last night;—Nanny chose to do it,[3] & I was not sorry to be busy.—I have unpacked the Gloves & placed yours in your drawer.—Their colour is light & pretty, & I beleive exactly what we fixed on.—Your letter was chaperoned here by one from M[rs] Cooke, in which she says that *Battleridge*[4] is not to come out before January; & she is so little satisfied with Cawthorn's dilatoriness that she never means to employ him again. M[rs] Hall of Sherbourn was brought to bed yesterday of a dead child, some weeks before she expected, oweing to a fright.—I suppose she happened unawares to look at her husband.—There has been a great deal of rain here for this last fortnight, much more than in Kent; & indeed we found the roads all the way from Staines most disgracefully dirty.—Steventon lane has its full share of it, & I donot know when I shall be able to get to Deane.—I hear that Martha is in better looks & Spirits than she has enjoyed for a long time; & I flatter myself she will now be able to jest openly about M[r] W.[5]—The Spectacles which Molly found[6] are my Mother's, the Scissors my father's.—We are very glad to hear such a good account of your Patients,[7] little & great. My dear itty Dordy's remembrance of me is very pleasing to me; foolishly pleasing, because I know it will be over so soon. My attachment to him will be more durable; I shall think with tenderness & delight on his beautiful & smiling Countenance & interesting Manners, till a few years have turned him into an ungovernable, ungracious fellow.—The Books from Winton are all unpacked & put away;—the Binding has compressed them most conveniently, & there is now very good room in the Bookcase for all that we wish to have there.—I beleive the Servants were very glad to see us, Nanny was I am sure; she confesses that it was very dull, & yet she had her Child with her till last Sunday. I understand that there are some Grapes left, but I beleive not many;—they must be gathered as soon as possible, or this Rain will entirely rot them. [*p. 4*] I am quite angry with myself for not writing closer; why is my alphabet so much more sprawly than Yours? Dame Tilbury's daughter has lain-in—Shall I give her any of your Baby Cloathes?—The Lace Man was here only a few days ago; how unfortunate for both of us that he came so soon!— Dame Bushell washes for us only one week more, as Sukey has got a place.—John Steevens' wife undertakes our Purification; She does not look as if anything she touched would ever be clean, but who knows?— We do not seem likely to have any other maidservant at present, but Dame Staples will supply the place of one.—Mary has hired a young Girl from Ashe, who has never been out to service, to be her Scrub, but James fears her not being strong enough for the place. Earle Harwood has been to Deane lately, as I think Mary wrote us word; & his family then told him that they would receive his wife, if she continued to behave well for another Year.—He was very grateful, as well he might; their behaviour throughout the whole affair has been particularly kind.— Earle & his wife live in the most private manner imaginable at Portsmouth, without keeping a servant of any kind.—What a prodigious innate love of virtue she must have, to marry under such circumstances!—. It is now saturday Even^g but I wrote the cheif of this in the morning.—My Mother has not been down at all today; the Laudanum made her sleep a good deal, & upon the whole I think she is better;— I shall be able to be more positive on this subject I hope tomorrow. My father & I dined by ourselves—How strange!—He & John Bond are now very happy together, for I have just heard the heavy step of the latter along the passage.—James Digweed called today, & I gave him his brother's deputation.[8] Charles Harwood too has just called to ask how we are, in his way from Dummer, whither he has been conveying Miss Garrett, who is going to return to her former residence in Kent.— I *will* leave off, or I shall not have room to add a word tomorrow.— Sunday.—My Mother has had a very good night, & tho' she did not get up to breakfast, feels much better to day.—I have rec:^d my Aunt's letter, & thank you for your Scrap.—I will write to Charles soon.— Pray give [*back to top of first page, upside down*] Fanny & Edward a Kiss from me—& ask George if he has got a new Song for me.—Tis really very kind in my Aunt to ask us to Bath again;[9] a kindness that deserves a better return than to profit by it.——

Yours Ever

J. A.

Miss Austen
Godmersham Park
Faversham
Kent.   Single Sheet

[*Letters missing here*]

11. *To Cassandra Austen*

Saturday 17–Sunday 18 November 1798

Saturday, November 17, [1798][1]

My dear Cassandra

If you paid any attention to the conclusion of my last letter, you will be satisfied, before you receive this, that my mother has had no relapse, and that Miss Debary comes.[2] The former continues to recover, and though she does not gain strength very rapidly, my expectations are humble enough not to outstride her improvements. She was able to sit up nearly eight hours yesterday, and to-day I hope we shall do as much.[3] . . . So much for my patient—now for myself. Mrs Lefroy did come last Wednesday, and the Harwoods came likewise, but very considerately paid their visit before Mrs. Lefroy's arrival, with whom, in spite of interruptions both from my father and James, I was enough alone to hear all that was interesting, which you will easily credit when I tell you that of her nephew[4] she said nothing at all, and of her friend[5] very little. She did not once mention the name of the former to *me*, and I was too proud to make any enquiries; but on my father's afterwards asking where he was, I learnt that he was gone back to London in his way to Ireland, where he is called to the Bar and means to practise. She showed me a letter which she had received from her friend a few weeks ago (in answer to one written by her to recommend a nephew of Mrs Russell to his notice at Cambridge), towards the end of which was a sentence to this effect: 'I am very sorry to hear of Mrs Austen's illness. It would give me particular pleasure to have an opportunity of improving my acquaintance with that family—with a hope of creating to myself a nearer interest. But at present I cannot indulge any expectation of it.' This is rational enough; there is less love and more sense in it than sometimes appeared before, and I am very well satisfied. It will all go on exceedingly well, and decline away in a very reasonable manner. There seems no likelihood of his coming into Hampshire this Christmas, and it is therefore most probable that our indifference will soon be mutual, unless his regard, which appeared to spring from knowing nothing of me at first, is best supported by never seeing me. Mrs Lefroy made no remarks on the letter, nor did she indeed say anything about him as relative to me. Perhaps she thinks she has said too much already. She saw a great deal of the Mapletons while she was in Bath. Christian is still in a very bad state of health, consumptive, and not likely to recover. Mrs Portman is not much admired in Dorsetshire; the good-natured world, as usual, extolled her beauty so highly, that all the neighbourhood have had the pleasure of being disappointed. My mother desires me to tell you that I am a very good housekeeper, which I have no reluctance in doing, because I really think it my peculiar excellence, and for this reason—I always take care to provide such things as please my own appetite, which I consider as the chief merit in housekeeping. I have had some ragout veal, and I mean to have some haricot mutton tomorrow. We are to kill a pig soon. There is to be a ball at Basingstoke next Thursday. Our assemblies have very kindly declined ever since we laid down the carriage,[6] so that dis-convenience and dis-inclination to go have kept pace together. My father's affection for Miss Cuthbert is as lively as ever, and he begs that you will not neglect to send him intelligence of her or her brother, whenever you have any to send. I am likewise to tell you that one of his Leicestershire sheep, sold to the butcher last week, weighed 27 lb. and ¼ per quarter. I went to Deane with my father two days ago to see Mary, who is still plagued with the rheumatism, which she would be very glad to get rid of, and still more glad to get rid of her child, of whom she is heartily tired. Her nurse is come, and has no particular charm either of person or manner; but as all the Hurstbourne world pronounce her to be the best nurse that ever was, Mary expects her attachment to increase. What fine weather this is! Not very becoming perhaps early in the morning, but very pleasant out of doors at noon, and very wholesome—at least everybody fancies so, and imagination is everything. To Edward, however, I really think dry weather of importance. I have not taken to fires yet. I believe I never told you that Mrs Coulthard and Anne, late of Manydown, are both dead, and both died in childbed. We have not regaled Mary with this news. Harry St. John is in Orders, has done duty at Ashe, and performs very well. I am very fond of experimental housekeeping, such as having an ox-cheek now and then; I shall have one next week, and I mean to have some little dumplings put into it, that I may fancy myself at Godmersham. I hope George was pleased with my designs. Perhaps they would have suited him as well had they been less elaborately finished; but an artist cannot do anything slovenly. I suppose baby grows[7] and improves. *Sunday.*—I have just received a note from James to say that Mary was brought to bed last night, at eleven o'clock, of a fine little boy,[8] and that everything is going on very well. My mother had desired to know nothing of it before it should be all over, and we were clever enough to prevent her having any suspicion of it, though Jenny, who had been left here by her mistress, was sent for home. . . . I called yesterday on Betty Londe,? who enquired particularly after you, and said she seemed to miss you very much, because you used to call in upon her very often. This was an oblique reproach at me, which I am sorry to have merited, and from which I will profit. I shall send George another picture when I write next, which I suppose will be soon, on Mary's account. My mother continues well.

Yours,
J. A.

Miss Austen,
Godmersham.

[*?Letter missing here, 20–2 November 1798*]

12. *To Cassandra Austen*

Sunday 25 November 1798

Steventon: Sunday November 25

My dear Sister

I expected to have heard from you this morning, but no letter is come. I shall not take the trouble of announcing to you any more of Mary's children, if, instead of thanking me for the intelligence, you always sit down and write to James. I am sure nobody can desire your letters so much as I do, and I don't think anybody deserves them so well. Having now relieved my heart of a great deal of malevolence, I will proceed to tell you that Mary continues quite well, and my mother tolerably so. I saw the former on Friday, and though I had seen her comparatively hearty the Tuesday before, I was really amazed at the improvement which three days had made in her. She looked well, her spirits were perfectly good, and she spoke much more vigorously than Elizabeth did when we left Godmersham. I had only a glimpse at the child, who was asleep; but Miss Debary told me that his eyes were large, dark, and handsome. *She* looks much as she used to do, is netting herself a gown in worsteds, and wears what Mrs Birch would call a *pot hat*. A short and compendious history of Miss Debary! I suppose you have heard from Henry himself that his affairs are happily settled. We do not know who furnishes the qualification.[1] Mr Mowell[2] would have readily given it, had not all his Oxfordshire property been engaged for a similar purpose to the Colonel.[3] Amusing enough! Our family affairs are rather deranged at present, for Nanny[4] has kept her bed these three or four days, with a pain in her side and fever, and we are forced to have two charwomen, which is not very comfortable. She is considerably better now, but it must still be some time, I suppose, before she is able to do anything. You and Edward will be amused, I think, when you know that Nanny Littlewart[5] dresses my hair. The ball on Thursday was a very small one indeed, hardly so large as an Oxford smack.[6] There were but seven couples, and only twenty-seven people in the room. The Overton Scotchman[7] has been kind enough to rid me of some of my money, in exchange for six shifts and four pair of stockings. The Irish[8] is not so fine as I should like it; but as I gave as much money for it as I intended, I have no reason to complain. It cost me 3s. 6d. per yard. It is rather finer, however, than our last, and not so harsh a cloth. We have got 'Fitz-Albini';[9] my father has bought it against my private wishes, for it does not quite satisfy my feelings that we should purchase the only one of Egerton's works of which his family are ashamed. That these scruples, however, do not at all interfere with my reading it, you will easily believe. We have neither of us yet finished the first volume. My father is disappointed—*I* am not, for I expected nothing better. Never did any book carry more internal evidence of its author. Every sentiment is completely Egerton's. There is very little story, and what there is told in a strange, unconnected way. There are many characters introduced, apparently merely to be delineated. We have not been able to recognise any of them hitherto, except Dr and Mrs Hey and Mr Oxenden, who is not very tenderly treated. You must tell Edward that my father gives 25s. a piece to Seward for his last lot of sheep, and, in return for this news, my father wishes to receive some of Edward's pigs. We have got Boswell's 'Tour to the Hebrides', and are to have his 'Life of Johnson'; and, as some money will yet remain in Burdon's hands,[10] it is to be laid out in the purchase of Cowper's works. This would please Mr Clarke, could he know it. By the bye, I have written to Mrs. Birch among my other writings, and so I hope to have some account of all the people in that part of the world before long. I have written to Mrs E. Leigh too, and Mrs Heathcote has been ill-natured enough to send me a letter of enquiry; so that altogether I am tolerably tired of letter-writing, and, unless I have anything new to tell you of my mother or Mary, I shall not write again for many days; perhaps a little repose may restore my regard for a pen. Ask little Edward whether Bob Brown wears a great coat this cold weather.

[J. A.][11]

Miss Austen,
Godmersham Park.

[*?Letter missing here, 28–9 November 1798*]

13. *To Cassandra Austen*

Saturday 1–Sunday 2 December 1798

Steventon: December 1

My dear Cassandra

I am so good as to write to you again thus speedily, to let you know that I have just heard from Frank. He was at Cadiz, alive and well, on October 19, and had then very lately received a letter from you, written as long ago as when the 'London' was at St Helen's. But his *raly* latest intelligence of us was in one from me of September 1, which I sent soon after we got to Godmersham. He had written a packet full for his dearest friends in England, early in October, to go by the 'Excellent'; but the 'Excellent' was not sailed, nor likely to sail, when he despatched this to me. It comprehended letters for both of us, for Lord Spencer, Mr Daysh, and the East India Directors.[1] Lord St Vincent had left the fleet when he wrote, and was gone to Gibraltar, it was said to superintend the fitting out of a private expedition from thence against some of the enemies' ports; Minorca or Malta were conjectured to be the objects. Frank writes in good spirits, but says that our correspondence cannot be so easily carried on in future as it has been, as the communication between Cadiz and Lisbon is less frequent than formerly. You and my mother,[2] therefore, must not alarm yourselves at the long intervals that may divide his letters. I address this advice to you two as being the most tender-hearted of the family. My mother made her *entrée* into the dressing-room[3] through crowds of admiring spectators yesterday afternoon, and we all drank tea together for the first time these five weeks. She has had a tolerable night, and bids fair for a continuance in the same brilliant course of action to-day.[4] . . . Mr Lyford was here yesterday; he came while we were at dinner, and partook of our elegant entertainment. I was not ashamed at asking him to sit down to table, for we had some pease-soup, a sparerib, and a pudding. He wants my mother to look yellow and to throw out a rash, but she will do neither. I was at Deane yesterday morning. Mary was very well, but does not gain bodily strength very fast. When I saw her so stout on the third and sixth days, I expected to have seen her as well as ever by the end of a fortnight. James went to Ibthorp yesterday to see his mother and child.[5] Letty[6] is with Mary at present, of course exceedingly happy, and in raptures with the child. Mary does not manage matters in such a way as to make me want to lay in myself. She is not tidy enough in her appearance; she has no dressing-gown to sit up in; her curtains are all too thin, and things are not in that comfort and style about her which are necessary to make such a situation an enviable one. Elizabeth was really a pretty object with her nice clean cap put on so tidily and her dress so uniformly white and orderly. We live entirely in the dressing-room now, which I like very much; I always feel so much more elegant in it than in the parlour. No news from Kintbury yet. Eliza[7] sports with our impatience. She was very well last Thursday. Who is Miss Maria Montresor going to marry, and what is to become of Miss Mulcaster? I find great comfort in my stuff gown, but I hope you do not wear yours too often. I have made myself two or three caps to wear of evenings since I came home, and they save me a world of torment as to hair-dressing, which at present gives me no trouble beyond washing and brushing, for my long hair is always plaited up out of sight, and my short hair curls well enough to want no papering. I have had it cut lately by Mr Butler. There is no reason to suppose that Miss Morgan is dead after all. Mr Lyford grati-fied us very much yesterday by his praises of my father's mutton, which they all think the finest that was ever ate. John Bond begins to find himself grow old, which John Bonds ought not to do, and unequal to much hard work; a man is therefore hired to supply his place as to labour, and John himself is to have the care of the sheep. There are not more people engaged than before, I believe; only men instead of boys. I fancy so at least, but you know my stupidity as to such matters. Lizzie Bond is just apprenticed to Miss Small, so we may hope to see her able to spoil gowns in a few years. My father has applied to Mr May for an alehouse for Robert, at his request, and to Mr Deane,[8] of Winchester, likewise. This was my mother's idea, who thought he would be proud to oblige a relation of Edward[9] in return for Edward's accepting his money. He sent a very civil answer indeed, but has no house vacant at present. May expects to have an empty one soon at Farnham, so per-haps Nanny may have the honour of drawing ale for the Bishop.[10] I shall write to Frank to-morrow. Charles Powlett gave a dance on Thursday, to the great disturbance of all his neighbours, of course, who, you know, take a most lively interest in the state of his finances, and live in hopes of his being soon ruined. We are very much disposed to like our new maid; she knows nothing of a dairy, to be sure, which, in our family, is rather against her, but she is to be taught it all. In short, we have felt the inconvenience of being without a maid so long, that we are determined to like her, and she will find it a hard matter to displease us. As yet, she seems to cook very well, is uncommonly stout, and says she can work well at her needle. *Sunday.*—My father is glad to hear so good an account of Edward's pigs, and desires he may be told, as encouragement to his taste for them, that Lord Bolton is particularly curious in *his* pigs, has had pigstyes of a most elegant construction built for them, and visits them every morning as soon as he rises.

Affectionately yours,
J. A.

Miss Austen,
Godmersham Park,
Faversham.

[*Several letters missing here*]

14. *To Cassandra Austen*

Tuesday 18–Wednesday 19 December 1798

Steventon Tuesday Dec:^r 18th

My dear Cassandra
    Your letter came quite as soon as I expected, and so your letters will always do, because I have made it a rule not to expect them till they come, in which I think I consult the ease of us both.—It is a great satisfaction to us to hear that your Business[1] is in a way to be settled, & so settled as to give you as little inconvenience as possible.—You are very welcome to my father's name, & [as][2] to his Services if they are ever required in it.—I shall keep *my* ten pounds too to wrap myself up in next winter.[3]—I took the liberty a few days ago of asking your Black velvet Bonnet to lend me its cawl, which it very readily did, & by which I have been enabled to give a considerable improvement of dignity to my Cap, which was before too *nidgetty* to please me.—I shall wear it

on Thursday, but I hope you will not be offended with me for following your advice as to its ornaments only in part—I still venture to retain the narrow silver round it, put twice round without any bow, & instead of the black military feather shall put in the Coquelicot one, as being smarter;—& besides Coquelicot is to be all the fashion this winter.—After the Ball, I shall probably make it entirely black.—I am sorry that our dear Charles begins to feel the Dignity of Ill-usage.—My father will write to Admiral Gambier.[4]—He must already have received so much satisfaction from his acquaintance with & Patronage of Frank, that he will be delighted I dare say to have another of the family introduced to him.—I think it would be very right in Charles to address Sir Tho[ss] on the occasion; tho' I cannot approve of *your* scheme of writing to him (which you communicated to [*p. 2*] me a few nights ago) to request him to come home & convey You to Steventon.—To do you justice however, You had some doubts of the propriety of such a measure yourself.—I am very much obliged to my dear little George for his messages, for his *Love* at least;—his *Duty* I suppose was only in consequence of some hint of my favourable intentions towards him from his father or Mother.—I am sincerely rejoiced however that I ever was born,[6] since it has been the means of procuring him a dish of Tea.[7]—Give my best Love to him. This morning has been made very gay to us, by visits from our two lively Neighbours M[r] Holder & M[r] John Harwood.—I have received a very civil note from M[rs] Martin requesting my name as a Subscriber to her Library which opens the 14th of January, & my name, or rather Yours is accordingly given. My Mother finds the Money.—Mary subscribes too, which I am glad of, but hardly expected.—As an inducement to subscribe M[rs] Martin tells us that her Collection is not to consist only of Novels, but of every kind of Literature &c &c—She might have spared this pretension to *our* family, who are great Novel-readers & not ashamed of being so;—but it was necessary I suppose to the self-consequence of half her Subscribers.—I hope & imagine that Edward Taylor is to inherit all Sir Edw: Dering's fortune as well as all his own fathers.—I took care to tell M[rs] Lefroy of your calling on her Mother, & she seemed pleased with it.—I enjoyed the hard black Frosts of last week very much, & one day while they lasted walked to Deane by myself.—I do not know that I ever did such a thing in my life before.—Charles Powlett has been very ill, but is getting well again;—his wife is discovered to be everything that the Neighbourhood could wish her, silly & cross as well as extravagant.

Earle Harwood & his friend M[r] Bailey came to Deane yesterday, but are not to stay above a day or two.—Earle has got the ap: [*p. 3*] :pointment to a Prison ship at Portsmouth, which he has been[8] for some time desirous of having; & he & his wife are to live on board for the future.—We dine now at half after Three, & have done dinner I suppose before you begin—We drink tea at half after six.—I am afraid you will despise us.—My father reads Cowper to us in the evening, to which I listen when I can. How do you spend your Evenings?—I guess that Eliz:[th] works, that you read to her, & that Edward goes to sleep.—My Mother continues hearty, her appetite & nights are very good, but her Bowels are still not entirely settled, & she sometimes complains of an Asthma, a Dropsy, Water in her Chest & a Liver Disorder. The third Miss Irish Lefroy is going to be married to a M[r] Courtenay, but whether James or Charles I do not know.—Miss Lyford is gone into Suffolk with her Brother & Miss Lodge—. Everybody is now very busy in making up an income for the two latter. Miss Lodge has only 800£ of her own, & it is not supposed that her Father can give her much, therefore the good offices of the Neighbourhood will be highly acceptable.—John Lyford means to take pupils.—James Digweed has had a very ugly cut—how could it happen?—It happened by a young horse which he had lately purchased, & which he was trying to back into its stable;—the Animal kicked him down with his forefeet, & kicked a great hole in his head;—he scrambled away as soon as he could, but was stunned for a time, & suffered a good deal of pain afterwards.—Yesterday he got up the Horse again, & for fear of something worse, was forced to throw himself off.—*Wednesday.*—I have changed my mind, & changed the trimmings of my Cap this morning; they are now such as you suggested;—I felt as if I should not prosper if I strayed from your directions, & I think it makes me look more like Lady Conyngham[9] now than it did before, which is all that one lives for now.—I beleive I *shall* make my new gown like my robe, but the back of the latter is all in a peice with the tail, & will 7 yards enable me to copy it in that respect? Mary went to Church [*p. 4*] on Sunday, & had the weather been smiling, we should have seen her here before this time.—Perhaps I may stay at Manydown as long as Monday, but not longer.—Martha sends me word that she is too busy to write to me now, & but for your letter,[10] I should have supposed her deep in the study of Medicine preparatory to their removal from Ibthrop.—The letter to Gambier goes to day.—I expect a very stupid Ball, there will be nobody worth dancing with, & nobody worth talking to but Catherine; for I beleive Mrs Lefroy will not be there; Lucy is to go with Mrs Russell.[11]—People get so horridly poor & economical in this part of the World, that I have no patience with them.—Kent is the only place for happiness, Everybody is rich there;—I must do similar justice however to the Windsor neighbourhood.—I have been forced to let James & Miss Debary have two sheets of your Drawing paper, but they sha'nt have any more.—There are not above 3 or 4 left, besides one of a smaller & richer sort.—Perhaps you may want some more if you come thro' Town in your return, or rather buy some more, for your wanting it will not depend on your coming thro' Town I imagine.—I have just heard from Martha, & Frank—his letter was written on the 12th Nov:^r—all well, & nothing particular.

J. A.

Miss Austen
Godmersham Park
Faversham
Kent

15. *To Cassandra Austen*

Monday 24–Wednesday 26 December 1798

Steventon Monday Night Dec:^r 24th

My dear Cassandra,

I have got some pleasant news for you, which I am eager to communicate, & therefore begin my letter sooner, tho' I shall not *send* it sooner than usual.—Admiral Gambier in reply to my father's application writes as follows.—"As it is usual to keep young officers in small vessels, it being most proper on account of their inexperience, & it being also a situation where they are more in the way of learning their Duty, Your Son has been continued in the Scorpion; but I have mentioned to the Board of Admiralty his wish to be in a Frigate, and when a proper opportunity offers & it is judged that he has taken his Turn in a small Ship, I hope he will be removed.—With regard to your Son now in the London, I am glad I can give you the assurance that his promotion is likely to take place very soon, as Lord Spencer has been so good as to say he would include him in an arrangement that he proposes making in a short time relative to some promotions in that quarter."—There!—I may now finish my letter, & go & hang myself, for I am sure I can neither write nor do anything which will not appear insipid to you after this.—*Now* I really think he will soon be made, & only wish we could communicate our fore-knowledge of the Event, to him whom it principally concerns.—My father has written to Daysh to desire that he will inform us if he can, when the Commission is sent.—Your cheif wish is now ready to be accomplished; & could Lord Spencer give happiness to Martha[1] at the same time, what a joyful heart he would make of Yours!—I have sent the same extract of the sweets of Gambier to Charles, who poor fellow! tho' he sinks into nothing but an humble attendant on the Hero of the peice, will I hope be contented with the prospect held out to him.—By what the Admiral [*p. 2*] says it appears as if he had been designedly kept in the Scorpion—. But I will not torment myself[2] with Conjectures & suppositions; Facts shall satisfy me.—Frank had not heard from any of us for ten weeks, when he wrote to me on the 12th of November, in consequence of Lord S[t] Vincents being removed to Gibraltar.—When his Commission is sent however, it will not be so long on its' road as our letters, because all the Government dispatches are forwarded by Land to his Lordship from Lisbon, with great regularity.—I returned from Manydown this morning, & found my Mother certainly in no respect worse than I left her.—She does not like the cold Weather, but that we cannot help.—I spent my time very quietly & very pleasantly with Catherine. Miss Blachford is agreable enough; I do not want People to be very agreable, as it saves me the trouble of liking them a great deal.—I found only Catherine & her when I got to Manydown on Thursday, we dined together & went together to Worting to seek the protection of M[rs] Clarke, with whom were Lady Mildmay, her eldest son, & a M[r] & M[rs] Hoare.—Our Ball was very thin, but by no means unpleasant.—There were 31 People & only[3] 11 Ladies out of the Number, & but five single women in the room.—Of the Gentlemen present You may have some idea from a list of my Partners. M[r] Wood, G. Lefroy, Rice, a M[r] Butcher (belonging to the Temples, a sailor & not of the 11th Light Dragoons) M[r] Temple (not the horrid one of all) M[r] W[m] Orde (Cousin to the Kingsclere Man) M[r] John Harwood & M[r] Calland, who appeared as usual with his hat in his hand, & stood every now & then behind Catherine & me to be talked to & abused for not dancing.—We teized him however[4] into it at last;—I was very glad to see him again after so long a separation, & he was altogether rather the Genius & Flirt of the Evening.—He enquired after You.—There were twenty Dances [*p. 3*] & I danced them all, & without any fatigue.—I was glad to find myself capable of dancing so much & with so much satisfaction as I did;—from my slender enjoyment of the Ashford Balls,[5] (as Assemblies for dancing) I had not thought myself equal to it, but in cold weather & with few couples I fancy I could just as well dance for a week together as for half an hour.—My black Cap was openly admired by M[rs] Lefroy, & secretly I imagine[6] by every body else in the room.—*Tuesday.*—I thank you for your long letter, which I will endeavour to deserve by writing the rest of this as closely as possible.— I am full of Joy at much of your information; that you should have been to a Ball, & have danced at it, & supped with the Prince,[7] & that you should meditate the purchase of a new muslin Gown are delightful circumstances.—*I* am determined to buy a handsome one whenever I can, & I am so tired & ashamed of half my present stock that I even blush at the sight of the wardrobe which contains them.—But I will not be much longer libelled by the possession of my coarse spot, I shall turn it into a petticoat very soon.—I wish you a merry Christmas, but *no* compliments of the Season.—Poor Edward! It is very hard that he who has everything else in the World that he can wish for, should not have good health too.—But I hope with the assistance of Bowel complaints, Faintnesses & Sicknesses, he will soon be restored to that Blessing likewise.—If his nervous complaint proceeded from a suppression of something that ought to be thrown out, which does not seem unlikely,[8] the first of those Disorders may really be a remedy, & I sincerely wish it may, for I know no one more deserving of happiness without alloy than Edward is.—My Mother's spirits are *not* affected by her complication of disorders; on the contrary they are altogether as good as ever; nor are you to suppose that these maladies are often thought of.[9]—She has at times had a tendency towards another which always releives her, & that is, a gouty swelling & sensation about the ancles.—I cannot determine what to do about my new Gown; I wish such things were to be bought ready made.—I have some hopes of meeting Martha at the Christening[10] at Deane next Tuesday, & shall see what she can do for me.—I want to have something suggested which will give me no trouble of thought or direction.—Again I return to my Joy that you danced at Ashford, & that you supped with the Prince.—I can perfectly comprehend M[rs] Cage's distress & perplexity.—She has all those kind of foolish & incomprehensible feelings which would make her fancy herself uncomfortable in such a party.—I love her however inspite of all her Nonsense. Pray give t'other Miss Austen's comp[ts] to Edw: Bridges when you see him again. [*p. 4*] I insist upon your persevering in your design of buying a new Gown; I am sure you must want one, & as you will have 5^{Gs} due in a week's time, I am certain you may afford it very well, & if you think you cannot, I will give you the Body lining.—Of my charities to the poor since I came home, you shall have a faithful account.—I have given a p^r of Worsted Stock^{gs} to Mary Hutchins, Dame Kew, Mary Steevens & Dame Staples; a shift to Hannah Staples, & a shawl to Betty Dawkins; amounting in all to about half a guinea.—But I have no reason to suppose that the Battys *would* accept of anything, because I have not made them the offer.—I am glad to hear such a good account of Harriot Bridges; she goes on now as young Ladies of 17 ought to do; admired & admiring; in a much more rational way than her three elder Sisters, who had so little of that kind of Youth.[11]—I dare say she fancies Major Elrington as agreable as Warren, & if she can think so, it is very well.—I was to have dined at Deane to day, but the weather is so cold that I am not sorry to be kept at home by the appearance of Snow.—We are to have Company to dinner on friday; the three Digweeds & James.—We shall be a nice silent party I suppose.—Seize upon the Scissors as soon as you possibly can on the receipt of this. I only fear your being too late to secure the prize. The Lords of the Admiralty will have enough of our applications at present, for I hear from Charles that he has written to Lord Spencer himself to be removed. I am afraid his serene Highness will be in a passion, & order some of our heads to be cut off.— My Mother wants to know whether Edwd has ever made the Hen House which they planned together.—I am rejoiced to learn from Martha that they certainly continue at Ibthrop, & I have just heard that I am sure of meeting Martha at the Christening.—You deserve a longer letter than this; but it is my unhappy fate seldom to treat people so well as they deserve.—God bless You.— Yours affec:^{tely} Jane Austen.

[*End of p. 4 –postscript written below address panel*]

Wednesday.—The Snow came to nothing yesterday, so I *did* go to Deane, & returned home at 9 o'clock at night in the little carriage—& without being very cold.—Miss Debary dines with us on friday as well as the Gentlemen.

Miss Austen
Godmersham Park
Faversham
Kent

16. *To Cassandra Austen*

My dear Cassandra

Frank is made.—He was yesterday raised to the Rank of Commander, & appointed to the Petterel Sloop, now at Gibraltar.—A Letter from Daysh has just announced this, & as it is confirmed by a very friendly one from Mr Mathew to the same effect transcribing one from Admiral Gambier to the General,[1] We have no reason to suspect the truth of it.—As soon as you have cried a little for Joy, you may go on, & learn farther that the India House[2] have taken *Captn Austen's* Petition into Consideration—this comes from Daysh—& likewise that Lieut. Charles John Austen is removed to the *Tamer* Frigate—this comes from the Admiral.—We cannot find out where the Tamer is, but I hope we shall now[3] see Charles here at all Events. [*p. 2*] This Letter is to be dedicated entirely to Good News.—If you will send my father an account of your Washing & Letter expences &c, he will send You a draft for the amount[4] of it, as well as for your next quarter, & for Edward's Rent.—If you don't buy a muslin Gown now on the strength of this Money, & Frank's promotion, I shall never forgive[5] You.—

Mrs Lefroy has just sent me word that Lady Dortchester means to invite me to her Ball on the 8th of January, which tho' an humble Blessing compared with what the last page records, I do not consider as any Calamity. I cannot write any more now, but I have written enough to make you very happy, & therefore may safely conclude.—

Yours affec:^{ly}
Jane.

Steventon
Friday Decr 28th

Miss Austen
Godmersham Park
Faversham
Kent

[*Letter(s) missing here*]

17. *To Cassandra Austen*

Tuesday 8–Wednesday 9 January 1799

Steventon Tuesday Jan^{ry} 8th—[1799][1]

My dear Cassandra

You must read your letters over *five* times in future before you send them, & then perhaps you may find them as entertaining as I do.—I laughed at several parts of the one which I am now answering.—Charles is not come yet, but he must come this morning, or he shall never know what I will do to him. The Ball at Kempshott is this Evening, & I have got him an invitation, though I have not been so considerate as to get him a *Partner*. But the cases are different between him & Eliza Bailey, for he is not in a dieing way, & may therefore be equal to getting a partner for himself.—I beleive I told You that Monday was to be the Ball Night, for which, & for all other Errors into which I may ever have led You, I now humbly ask your pardon.—Elizabeth is very cruel about my writing Music;—& as a punishment for her, I should insist upon always writing out all hers for her[2] in future, if I were not punishing myself at the same time.—I am tolerably glad to hear that Edward's income is so good a one—as glad as I can at anybody's being rich besides You & me—& I am thoroughly rejoiced to hear of his present to you.—I am not to wear my white sattin cap tonight after all; I am to wear a Mamalouc cap[3] instead, which Charles Fowle sent to Mary, & which she lends me.—It is all the fashion now, worn at the Opera, & by Lady Mildmays at Hackwood Balls—I hate describing such things, & I dare say You will be able to guess what it is like—. I have got over the dreadful epocha of Mantuamaking much better than I expected.— My Gown is made very much like my blue one, which you always told me sat very well, with only these variations;—the sleeves are short, the wrap fuller, the apron comes over it, & a band of the same completes the whole.—

I assure You that I dread the idea of going to Bookham as much as you can do; but I am not without hopes that something may happen to prevent it; Theo' has lost his Election at Baliol, & perhaps they may not be able to see company for some time.[4]—They talk of going to Bath too in the Spring, & perhaps they may be overturned in their way down, & all laid up for the summer.

[*p. 2*] Wednesday.—I have had a cold & weakness in one of my eyes for some days, which makes Writing neither very pleasant nor very profitable, & which will probably prevent my finishing this letter my-self.—My Mother has undertaken to do it for me, & I shall leave the Kempshott Ball for her. You express so little anxiety about my being murdered under Ash Park Copse by Mrs Hulbert's servant, that I have a great mind not to tell you whether I was or not, & shall only say that I did not return home that night or the next, as Martha kindly made room for me in her bed, which was the shut-up one in the new Nurs-ery.—Nurse & the Child slept upon the floor; & there we all were in some confusion & great comfort;—the bed did exceedingly well for us, both to lie awake in⁵ & talk till two o'clock, & to sleep in the rest of the night.—I love Martha better than ever, & I mean to go & see her if I can, when she gets home.—We all dined at the Harwoods on Thurs-day, & the party broke up the next morning.—This complaint in my eye has been a sad bore to me, for I have not been able to read or work in any comfort since friday, but one advantage will be derived from it, for I shall be such a proficient in Music by the time I have got rid of my cold, that I shall be perfectly qualified in *that* Science at least to take Mr Roope's office at Eastwell next summer; & I am sure of Eliz:^th's recom-mendation, be it only on Harriot's account.—Of my Talent in Draw-ing I have given specimens in my letters to You, & I have nothing to do, but to invent a few hard names for the Stars.—Mary grows rather more reasonable about her Child's beauty, & says that she does not think him really handsome; but I suspect her moderation to be some-thing like that of W—W—'s Mama.⁶—Perhaps Mary has told you that they are going to enter more into Dinner parties; the Biggs & Mr Holder dine there tomorrow & I am to meet them; I shall sleep there. Catherine has the honour of giving her name to a set,⁷ which will be composed of two Withers, two Heathcotes, a Blachford, & no Bigg except herself. She congratulated me last night on Frank's promotion as if she really felt the Joy she talked of.—My sweet little George!—I am delighted to hear that he has such an inventive Genius as to face-making—. I ad-mired his yellow wafer very much, & hope he will chuse the wafer for your next letter.—I wore my Green shoes last night, & took my *white fan* with me; I am very glad he never threw it into the River.—Mrs Knights giving up the Godmersham Estate to Edward was no such prodigious act of Generosity⁸ after all it seems, for she has reserved herself an income out of it still;—this ought to be known, that her conduct may not be over-rated.—I rather think Edward shews the most Magnanimity of the two, in accepting her Resignation with such Incumbrances.—The more I write, the better my Eye gets, so [*p. 3*] I shall at least keep on till it is quite well, before I give up my pen to my Mother.—Mrs Bramston's little moveable apartment[9] was tolerably filled last night by herself, Mrs H. Blackstone, her two daughters & me.—I do not like the Miss Blackstones; indeed I was always determined not to like them, so there is the less merit in it.—Mrs Bramston was very civil, kind & noisy.—I spent a very pleasant evening, cheifly among the Manydown party—. There was the same kind of supper as last Year, & the same want of chairs.—There were more Dancers than the Room could conveniently hold, which is enough to constitute a good Ball at any time.—I do not think I was very much in request—. People were rather apt not to ask me till they could not help it;—One's Consequence you know varies so much at times without any particular reason—. There was one Gentleman, an officer of the Cheshire, a very good looking young Man, who I was told wanted very much to be introduced to me;—but as he did not want it quite enough to take much trouble in effecting it, We never could bring it about.—I danced with Mr John Wood again, twice with a Mr South[10] a lad from Winchester who I suppose is as far from being related to the Bishop of that Diocese as it is possible to be, with G. Lefroy & J. Harwood, who I think takes to me rather more than he used to do.—One of my gayest actions was sitting down two Dances in preference to having Lord Bolton's eldest son for my Partner, who danced too ill to be endured.—The Miss Charterises were there, & play'd the parts of the Miss Edens with great spirit.—Charles never came!—Naughty Charles. I suppose he could not get superseded in time—.—Miss Debary has replaced your two sheets of Drawing paper, with two of superior size & quality; so I do not grudge her having them at all now.—Mr Ludlow & Miss Pugh of Andover are lately married, & so is Mrs Skeete of Basingstoke & Mr French, Chemist of Reading.—I do not wonder at your wanting to read *first impressions*[11] again, so seldom as you have gone through it, & that so long ago.—I am much obliged to you for meaning to leave my old petticoat behind You; I have long secretly wished it might be done, but had not courage to make the request. Pray mention the name of Maria Montresor's Lover when you write next, my Mother wants to know it, & I have not courage to look back into your letters to find it out.—I shall not be able to send this till tomorrow, & You will be disappointed on friday; I am very sorry for it, but I cannot help it.—The partnership between Jeffereys Toomer & Legge[12] is dissolved—the two latter are melted away into nothing, & it is to be hoped that Jeffereys will soon break for the sake of a few heroines whose money he may have.—

[*p. 4*] I wish you Joy of your Birthday twenty times over.—I *shall* be able to send this to the post to day, which exalts me to the utmost pinnacle of human felicity, & makes me bask in the sunshine of Prosperity, or gives me any other sensation of pleasure in studied Language which You may prefer.—Do not be angry with me for not filling my Sheet[13]—& beleive me yours affec:ly J. A.

Miss Austen
Godmersham Park
Faversham
Kent

[*Letters missing here*]

18. *To Cassandra Austen*

Monday 21–Wednesday 23 January 1799

Steventon: Monday January 21

My dear Cassandra

I will endeavour to make this letter more worthy your acceptance than my last, which was so shabby a one that I think Mr Marshall could never charge you with the postage.[1] My eyes have been very indifferent since it was written, but are now getting better once more; keeping them so many hours open on Thursday night, as well as the dust of the ball-room, injured them a good deal. I use them as little as I can, but *you* know, and *Elizabeth* knows, and everybody who ever had weak eyes knows, how delightful it is to hurt them by employment, against the advice and entreaty of all one's friends. Charles leaves us to-night. The 'Tamar' is in the Downs, and Mr Daysh advises him to join her there directly, as there is no chance of her going to the westward. Charles does not approve of this at all, and will not be much grieved if he should be too late for her before she sails, as he may then hope to get into a better station. He attempted to go to town last night, and got as far on his road thither as Dean Gate; but both the coaches were full, and we had the pleasure of seeing him back again. He will call on Daysh to-morrow to know whether the 'Tamar' has sailed or not, and if she is still at the Downs he will proceed in one of the night coaches to Deal. I want to go with him, that I may explain the country to him properly between Canterbury and Rowling, but the unpleasantness of returning by myself deters me. I should like to go as far as Ospringe with him very much indeed, that I might surprise you at Godmersham. Martha writes me word that Charles was very much admired at Kintbury, and Mrs Lefroy never saw anyone so much improved in her life, and thinks him handsomer than Henry. He appears to far more advantage here than he did at Godmersham, not surrounded by strangers and neither oppressed by a pain in his face or powder in his hair. James christened Elizabeth Caroline[2] on Saturday morning, and then came home. Mary, Anna, and Edward have left us of course; before the second went I took down her answer to her cousin Fanny. Yesterday came a letter to my mother from Edward Cooper to announce, not the birth of a child, but of a living; for Mrs Leigh has begged his acceptance of the Rectory of Hamstall-Ridware in Staffordshire, vacant by Mr Johnson's death. We collect from his letter that he means to reside there, in which he shows his wisdom. Staffordshire is a good way off; so we shall see nothing more of them till, some fifteen years hence, the Miss Coopers are presented to us, fine, jolly, handsome, ignorant girls. The living is valued at 140*l.* a year, but perhaps it may be improvable. How will they be able to convey the furniture of the dressing-room so far in safety? Our first cousins[3] seem all dropping off very fast. One is incorporated into the family, another dies, and a third goes into Staffordshire. We can learn nothing of the disposal of the other living.[4] I have not the smallest notion of Fulwar's having it. Lord Craven has probably other connections and more intimate ones, in that line, than he now has with the Kintbury family. Our ball on Thursday was a very poor one, only eight couple and but twenty-three people in the room; but it was not the ball's fault, for we were deprived of two or three families by the sudden illness of Mr Wither, who was seized that morning at Winchester with a return of his former alarming complaint. An express was sent off from thence to the family; Catherine and Miss Blachford were dining with Mrs Russell. Poor Catherine's distress must have been very great. She was prevailed on to wait till the Heathcotes could come from Wintney, and then with those two and Harris proceeded directly to Winchester. In such a disorder his danger, I suppose, must always be great; but from this attack he is now rapidly recovering, and will be well enough to return to Manydown, I fancy, in a few days. It was a fine thing for conversation at the ball. But it deprived us not only of the Biggs, but of Mrs Russell too, and of the Boltons and John Harwood, who were dining there likewise, and of Mr Lane, who kept away as related to the family. Poor man!—I mean Mr Wither—his life is so useful, his character so respectable and worthy, that I really believe there was a good deal of sincerity in the general concern expressed on his account. Our ball was chiefly made up of Jervoises and Terrys, the former of whom were apt to be vulgar, the latter to be noisy. I had an odd set of partners: Mr Jenkins, Mr Street, Col Jervoise, James Digweed, J. Lyford, and Mr Briggs, a friend of the latter. I had a very pleasant evening, however, though you will probably find out that there was no particular reason for it; but I do not think it worth while to wait for enjoyment until there is some real opportunity for it. Mary behaved very well, and was not at all fidgetty. For the history of her adventures at the ball I refer you to Anna's letter. When you come home you will have some shirts to make up for Charles. Mrs Davies frightened him into buying a piece of Irish when we were in Basingstoke. Mr Daysh supposes that Captain Austen's commission has reached him by this time. Tuesday.—Your letter has pleased and amused me very much. Your essay on happy fortnights is highly ingenious, and the talobert skin[5] made me laugh a good deal. Whenever I fall into misfortune, how many jokes it ought to furnish to my acquaintance in general, or I shall die dreadfully in their debt for entertainment. It began to occur to me before you mentioned it that I had been somewhat silent as to my mother's health for some time, but I thought you could have no diffi- culty in divining its exact state—you, who have guessed so much stranger things. She is tolerably well—better upon the whole than she was some weeks ago. She would tell you herself that she has a very dreadful cold in her head at present; but I have not much compassion for colds in the head without fever or sore throat. Our own particular little brother[6] got a place in the coach last night, and is now, I suppose, in town. I have no objection at all to your buying our gowns there, as your imagination has pictured to you exactly such a one as is necessary to make me happy. You quite abash me by your progress in notting, for I am still without silk. You must get me some in town or in Canterbury; it should be finer than yours. I thought Edward would not approve of Charles being a crop,[7] and rather wished you to conceal it from him at present, lest it might fall on his spirits and retard his recovery. My father fur- nishes him with a pig from Cheesedown; it is already killed and cut up, but it is not to weigh more than nine stone; the season is too far ad- vanced to get him a larger one. My mother means to pay herself for the salt and the trouble of ordering it to be cured by the sparibs, the souse, and the lard. We have had one dead lamb. I congratulate you on Mr E. Hatton's good fortune. I suppose the marriage will now follow out of hand. Give my compliments to Miss Finch. What time in March may we expect your return in? I begin to be very tired of answering people's questions on that subject, and, independent of *that*, I shall be very glad to see you at home again, and then if we can get Martha and shirk . . . who will be[8] so happy as we? I think of going to Ibthorp in about a fortnight. My eyes are pretty well, I thank you, if you please. Wednesday, 23rd.—I wish my dear Fanny many returns of this day, and that she may on every return enjoy as much pleasure as she is now receiving from her doll's-beds. I have just heard from Charles, who is by this time at Deal. He is to be Second Lieutenant, which pleases him very well. The 'Endymion' is come into the Downs, which pleases him likewise. He expects to be ordered to Sheerness shortly, as the 'Tamar' has never been refitted. My father and mother made the same match for you last night, and are very much pleased with it. *He* is a beauty of my mother's.

Yours affectionately,
Jane[9]

Miss Austen,
Godmersham Park,
Faversham,
Kent

[*Letters missing here*]

19. *To Cassandra Austen*

Friday 17 May 1799

No. 13—Queen's Square—Friday May 17.th

My dearest Cassandra,

Our Journey yesterday went off exceedingly well; nothing occurred to alarm or delay us;—We found the roads in excellent order, had very good horses all the way, & reached Devizes with ease by 4 o'clock.— I suppose John[1] has told you in what manner we were divided when we left Andover, & no alteration was afterwards made. At Devizes we had comfortable rooms, & a good dinner to which we sat down about 5; amongst other things we had Asparagus & a Lobster[2] which made me wish for you, & some cheesecakes on which the children[3] made so delightful a supper as to endear the Town of Devizes to them for a long time. Well, here we are at Bath; we got here about one o'clock, & have been arrived just long enough to go over the house, fix on our rooms, & be very well pleased with the whole of it. Poor Eliz: has had a dismal ride of it from Devizes, for it has rained almost all the way, & our first veiw of Bath has been just as gloomy as it was last November twelvemonth. I have got so many things to say, so many things equally unimportant, that I know not on which to decide at present, & shall therefore go & eat with the Children.—We stopt in Paragon as we came along, but as it was [*p. 2*] too wet & dirty for us to get out, we could only see Frank,[4] who told us that his Master was very indifferent, but had had a better night last night than usual. In Paragon we met M[rs] Foley & M[rs] Dowdeswell with her yellow shawl airing out—& at the bottom of Kingsdown Hill we met a Gentleman in a Buggy, who on a minute examination turned out to be D[r] Hall—& D[r] Hall in such very deep mourning that either his Mother, his Wife, or himself must be dead. These are all of our acquaintance who have yet met our eyes.— I have some hopes of being plagued about my Trunk;—I *had* more a few hours ago, for it was too heavy to go by the Coach which brought Thomas & Rebecca from Devizes, there was reason to suppose that it might be too heavy likewise for any other Coach, & for a long time we could hear of no Waggon to convey it.—At last however, we unluckily discovered that one was just on the point of setting out for this place— but at any rate, the Trunk cannot be here till tomorrow—so far we are safe—& who knows what may not happen to procure a farther delay.—I put Mary's letter into the Post office at Andover with my own hand.—We are exceedingly pleased with the House; the rooms are quite as large as we expected, M[rs] Bromley is a fat woman in mourning, & a little black kitten runs about the Staircase.—Eliz: has the apartment within the Drawing room; she wanted my Mother to have it, but as there [*p. 3*] was no bed in the inner one, & the stairs are so much easier of ascent or my Mother so much stronger than in Paragon as not to regard the double flight, it is settled for us to be above; where we have two very nice sized rooms, with dirty Quilts & everything comfortable. I have the outward & larger apartment, as I ought to have; which is quite as large as our bed room at home, & my Mother's is not materially less.—The Beds are both as large as any at Steventon; & I have a very nice chest of Drawers & a Closet full of shelves—so full indeed that there is nothing else in it, & should therefore be called a Cupboard rather than a Closet I suppose. Tell Mary that there were some Carpenters at work in the Inn at Devizes[5] this morning, but as I could not be sure of their being M[rs] W. Fowle's relations, I did not make myself known to them. I hope it will be a tolerable afternoon; when first we came, all the Umbrellas were up, but now the Pavements are getting very white again.—My Mother does not seem at all the worse for her Journey, nor are any of us I hope, tho' Edw:^d seemed rather fagged last night, & not very brisk this morning, but I trust the bustle of sending for Tea, Coffee & Sugar &c., & going out to taste a cheese himself will do him good.—

There was a very long list of Arrivals here, in the Newspaper yesterday, so that we need not immediately dread absolute Solitude—& there is a public Breakfast in Sydney Gardens every morning, so that we shall not be wholly starved.—Eliz: has just had a very [*p. 4*] good account of the three little Boys—. I hope you are very busy & very comfortable—. I find no difficulty in doing my Eyes.—I like our situation very much—it is far more chearful than Paragon, & the prospect from the Drawingroom window at which I now write, is rather picturesque, as it commands a perspective veiw of the left side of Brock Street, broken by three Lombardy Poplars in the Garden of the last house^6 in Queen's Parade.—

I am rather impatient to know the fate of my best gown, but I suppose it will be some days before Frances can get through the Trunk— In the mean time, I am with many thanks for your trouble in making it, as well as marking my Silk Stockings Y^rs very affec:^ly

Jane

A great deal of Love from everybody.

Miss Austen,
Steventon,
Overton,
Hants

[*Letters missing here*]

20. *To Cassandra Austen*

Sunday 2 June 1799

13, Queen Square—Sunday June 2^d

My dear Cassandra

I am obliged to you for two letters, one from Yourself & the other from Mary, for of the latter I knew nothing till on the receipt of Yours yesterday, when the Pigeon Basket was examined & I received my due.—As I have written to her since the time which ought to have brought me her's, I suppose she will consider herself as I chuse to consider her, still in my debt.—I will lay out all the little Judgement I have in endeavouring to get such stockings for Anna as she will approve;—but I do not know that I shall execute Martha's commission at all, for I am not fond of ordering shoes, & at any rate they shall all have flat heels.—What must I tell you of Edward?—Truth or Falsehood?—I will try the former, & you may chuse for yourself another time.—He was better yesterday than he had been for two or three days before, about as well as while he was at Steventon[1]—He drinks at the Hetling Pump, is to bathe tomorrow, & try Electricity on Tuesday;—he proposed the latter himself to D[r] Fellowes, who made no objection to it, but I fancy we are all unanimous in expecting no advantage from it. At present I have no great notion of our staying here beyond the Month.—I heard from Charles last week;—they were to sail on Wednesday.—My Mother seems remarkably well.—My Uncle overwalked himself at first [*p. 2*] & can now only travel in a Chair, but is otherwise very well.—My Cloak is come home, & here follows the pattern of its' lace.

—If you do not think it wide enough, I can give 3[d] a yard more for yours, & not go beyond the two Guineas, for my Cloak altogether does not cost[2] quite two pounds.—I like it very much, & can now exclaim with delight, like J. Bond at Hay-Harvest, "This is what I have been looking for these three years."—I saw some Gauzes in a shop in Bath Street yesterday at only 4[s] a yard, but they were not so good or so pretty as mine.—Flowers are very much worn, & Fruit is still more the thing.—Eliz: has a bunch of Strawberries, & I have seen Grapes, Cherries, Plumbs & Apricots—There are likewise Almonds & raisins, french plumbs & Tamarinds at the Grocers, but I have never seen any of them in hats.—A plumb or green gage would cost three shillings;—Cherries & Grapes about 5 I beleive—but this is at some of the dearest Shops;[3]—My Aunt has told me of a very cheap one near Walcot Church, to which I shall go in quest of something for You.—I have never seen an old Woman at the Pump room.—Eliz: has given me a hat, & it is not only a pretty hat, but a pretty *stile* of hat too—It is something like Eliza's[4]—only instead of being all straw, half of it is narrow purple ribbon.—I flatter myself however that you can understand very little of it, from this description—. Heaven forbid that I should ever offer such encouragement to Explanations, as to give a clear one on any occasion myself.—But I must write no more of . . . [*six or seven lines cut away at top of p. 3*] . . . it so.—I spent friday evening with the Mapletons, & was obliged to submit to being pleased inspite of my inclination. We took a very charming walk from 6 to 8 up Beacon Hill, & across some fields to the Village of Charlcombe, which is sweetly situated in a little green Valley, as a Village with such a name ought to be.—Marianne is sensible & intelligent, and even Jane considering how fair she is, is not unpleasant. We had a Miss North & a Mr Gould of our party;—the latter walked home with me after Tea;—he is a very Young Man, just entered of Oxford, wears Spectacles, & has heard that Evelina⁵ was written by Dr Johnson.—I am afraid I cannot undertake to carry Martha's Shoes home, for tho' we had plenty of room in our Trunks when we came, We shall have many more things to take back, & I must allow besides for *my* packing.—There is to be a grand gala on tuesday evening in Sydney Gardens;—a Concert, with Illuminations & fireworks;—to the latter Eliz: & I look forward with pleasure, & even the Concert will have more than its' usual charm with me, as the Gardens are large enough for me to get pretty well beyond the reach of its sound.—In the morning Lady Willoughby is to present the Colours to some Corps of Yeomanry or other, in the Crescent—& that such festivities may have a proper commencement, we think of going to . . . [*six or seven lines cut away at top of p. 4*] . . . I am quite pleased with Martha & Mrs Lefroy for wanting the pattern of our Caps, but I am not so well pleased with Your giving it to them—. Some wish, some prevailing Wish is necessary to the animation of everybody's Mind, & in gratifying this, You leave them to form some other which will not probably be half so innocent.—I shall not forget to write to Frank.—Duty & Love &c.

Yours affec:^ly Jane

[*Postscript below address panel*]

My Uncle is quite surprised at my hearing from you so often—but as long as we can keep the frequency of our correspondence from Martha's Uncle,⁶ we will not fear our own.—

Miss Austen
Steventon
Overton
Hants   June 2^d

[*Letters missing here*]

21. *To Cassandra Austen*

Tuesday 11 June 1799

13, Queen Square Tuesday June 11th.

My dear Cassandra

Your letter yesterday made me very happy. I am heartily glad that You have escaped any share in the Impurities of Deane, & not sorry as it turns out that our stay here has been lengthened.—I feel tolerably secure of our getting away next week, tho' it is certainly possible that we may remain till Thursday the 27th—I wonder what we shall do with all our intended visits this summer?—I should like to make a compromise with Adlestrop, Harden & Bookham that Martha's spending the summer at Steventon should be considered as our respective visits to them all.—Edward has been pretty well for this last Week, & as the Waters have never *dis*agreed with him in any respect, We are inclined to hope that he will derive advantage from them in the end;—everybody encourages us in this expectation, for they all say that the effect of the Waters cannot be negative, & many are the instances in which their benefit is felt afterwards more than on the spot.—He is more comfortable here than I thought he would be, & so is Eliz:—tho' they will both I beleive be very glad to get away, the latter especially— Which one can't wonder at *somehow*.—So much for Mrs Piozzi.[1]—I had some thoughts of writing the whole of my letter in her stile, [*p. 2*] but I beleive I shall not.—Though you have given me unlimited powers concerning Your Sprig, I cannot determine what to do about it, & shall therefore in this & in every future letter continue to ask you for further directions.—We have been to the cheap Shop, & very cheap we found it, but there are only flowers made there, no fruit—& as I could get 4 or 5 very pretty sprigs of the former for the same money which would procure only one Orleans plumb, in short could get more for three or four Shillings than I could have means of bringing home, I cannot decide on the fruit till I hear from you again.—Besides, I cannot help thinking that it is more natural to have flowers grow out of the head than fruit.—What do you think on that subject?—I would not let Martha read First Impressions again upon any account, & am very glad that I did not leave it in your power.—She is very cunning, but I see through her design;—she means to publish it from Memory, & one more perusal must enable her to do it.—As for Fitzalbini, when I get home she shall have it, as soon as ever she will own that Mr Elliott is handsomer

44

than M[r] Lance—that fair Men are preferable to Black—for I mean to take every opportunity of rooting out her prejudices.—Benjamin Portal is here. How charming that is!—I do not exactly know why, but the phrase followed so naturally that I could not help putting it down.— My Mother saw him the other day, but without making herself known to him.—I am very glad You liked my Lace, & so are You & so is Martha—& we are all glad together.—I have got your Cloak home, which [*p. 3*] is quite delightful!—as delightful at least as half the circumstances which are called so.—I do not know what is the matter with me to day, but I cannot write quietly; I am always wandering away into some exclamation or other.—Fortunately I have nothing very particular to say.—We walked to Weston one evening last week, & liked it very much.—Liked *what* very much? Weston?—no—*walking* to Weston—I have not expressed myself properly, but I hope you will understand me.—We have not been to any public place lately, nor performed anything out of the common daily routine of N° 13, Queen Square, Bath—. But to day we were to have dashed away at a very extraordinary rate, by dining out, had it not so happened that we do not go.—Edward renewed his acquaintance lately[2] with M[r] Evelyn who lives in the Queen's parade & was invited to a family dinner, which I beleive at first Eliz: was rather sorry at his accepting, but yesterday M[rs] Evelyn called on us & her manners were so pleasing that we liked the idea of going very much.—The Biggs would call her a nice Woman.— But M[r] Evelyn who was indisposed yesterday, is worse to day & we are put off.—It is rather impertinent to suggest any household care to a Housekeeper, but I just venture to say that the Coffee Mill will be wanted every day while Edw: is at Steventon as he always drinks Coffee for Breakfast.—Fanny desires her Love to You, her Love to Grandpapa, her Love to Anna, & her Love to Hannah;—the latter particularly is to be remembered.— Edw:[d] desires his Love to You, to Grandpapa, to Anna, to little Edw:[d], to Aunt James & Uncle James, & he hopes all your Turkies & Ducks & Chicken & Guinea Fowls are very well—& he wishes You very much to send him a printed Letter & so does Fanny—& they both rather think[3] they shall answer it.—EA[4]

[*p. 4*] "On more accounts than one you wished our stay here to be lengthened beyond last Thursday."—There is some Mystery in this. What have you going on in Hampshire besides the *Itch* from which you want to keep us?—D[r] Gardiner was married yesterday to M[rs] Percy & her three daughters.—Now I will give you the history of Mary's veil, in the purchase of which I have so considerably involved you that it is my duty to economise for you in the flowers.—I had no difficulty in getting a muslin veil for half a guinea, & not much more in discovering afterwards that the Muslin was thick, dirty & ragged, & would therefore by no means do for a united Gift.—I changed it consequently as soon as I could, & considering what a state my imprudence had reduced me to, I thought myself lucky in getting a black Lace one for 16 shillings—. I hope the half of that sum will not greatly exceed what You had intended to offer up on the altar of Sister-in-law affection.—Yours affe:

Jane.

[Postscript upside down at top of first page]

They do not seem to trouble You much from Manydown. I have long wanted to quarrel with them, & I beleive I shall take this opportunity.—There is no denying that they are very capricious!—for they like to enjoy their elder Sisters company⁵ when they can.

Miss Austen,
Steventon,
Overton,
Hants
June 11th

[Letter(s) missing here]

22. *To Cassandra Austen*

Wednesday 19 June 1799

13, Queen Square—Wednesday June 19th.

My dear Cassandra

The Children were delighted with your letters, as I fancy they will tell you themselves before this is concluded.—Fanny expressed some surprise at the wetness of the Wafers, but it did not lead to any suspicion of the Truth.—Martha & You were just in time with your commissions, for two o'clock on monday was the last hour of my receiving them;—the office is now closed.—John Lyford's history is a melancholy one.—I feel for his family; & when I know that his Wife was really fond of him, I will feel for her too, but at present I cannot help thinking their loss the greatest.—Edward has not been well these last two days; his appetite has failed him, & he has complained of sick &

uncomfortable feelings, which with other Symptoms make us think of the Gout—perhaps a fit of it might cure him, but I cannot wish it to begin at Bath.—He made an important purchase Yesterday; no less so than a pair of Coach Horses; his friend Mr Evelyn found them out & recommended them, & if the judgement of a Yahoo[1] can ever be depended on, I suppose it may now, for I beleive Mr Evelyn has all his life thought more of Horses than of anything else.—Their Colour is black & their size not large—their price sixty Guineas, of which the Chair Mare was taken as fifteen—but this is of course to be a secret.—Mrs Williams need not pride herself on her knowledge of Dr Mapleton's Success here;—She knows no more than [*p. 2*] everybody else knows in Bath.—There is not a Physician[2] in the place who writes so many Prescriptions as he does—I cannot help wishing that Edward had not been tied down to Dr Fellowes, for had he come disengaged, we should all have recommended Dr Mapleton; my Uncle & Aunt as earnestly as ourselves.—I do not see the Miss Mapletons very often, but just as often as I like; We are always very glad to meet, & I do not wish to wear out our satisfaction.—Last Sunday We all drank tea in Paragon; my Uncle is still in his flannels, but is getting better again.—On Monday, Mr Evelyn was well enough for us to fulfil our engagement with him;—the visit was very quiet & uneventful; pleasant enough.—We met only another Mr Evelyn, his cousin, whose wife came to Tea.— Last night we were in Sidney Gardens again, as there was a repetition of the Gala which went off so ill on the 4th.—We did not go till nine, & then were in very good time for the Fire-works, which were really beautiful, & surpassing my expectation;—the illuminations too were very pretty.—The weather was as favourable, as it was otherwise a fortnight ago.—The Play on Saturday[3] is *I hope* to conclude our Gaieties here, for nothing but a lengthened stay will make it otherwise. We go with Mrs Fellowes.—Edward will not remain at Steventon longer than from Thursday to the following Monday I beleive, as the Rent-day is to be fixed for the *consecutive* friday.—I can recollect nothing more to say at present;—perhaps Breakfast may assist my ideas. [*p. 3*] I was deceived—my breakfast supplied only two ideas, that the rolls were good, & the butter bad;—But the Post has been more friendly to me, it has brought me a letter from Miss Pearson. You may remember that I wrote to her above two months ago about the parcel under my care, & as I had heard nothing from her since, I thought myself obliged to write again two or three days ago, for after all that had passed[4] I was determined that the Correspondence should never cease thro' my means—. This second Letter has produced an apology for her silence, founded on the Illness of several of the family.—The exchange of packets is to take place through the medium of Mr Nutt, probably one of the Sons belonging to Woolwich Academy, who comes to Overton in the beginning of July.—I am tempted to suspect from some parts of her Letter, that she has a matrimonial project in veiw—I shall question her about it when I answer her Letter; but all this you know is *en Mystere* between ourselves.—Edward has seen the Apothecary to whom Dr Millman recommended him, a sensible, intelligent Man, since I began this—& he attributes his present little feverish indisposition to his having ate something unsuited to his Stomach.—I do not understand that Mr Anderton suspects the Gout at all;—The occasional particular glow in the hands & feet, which we considered as a symptom of that Disorder, he only calls the effect of the Water in promoting a better circulation of the blood. I cannot help thinking from your account of Mrs E. H. that Earle's vanity has tempted him to invent the account of her former way of Life, that his triumph in securing her might be greater;—I dare say she was nothing but an innocent Country Girl in fact.—Adeiu—. I shall not write again before Sunday, unless anything particular happens.

Yours Ever Jane.

[*p. 4—letters dictated by the children*]

My dear Cassandra

I thank you for your pretty letter;—My little Brothers were very well when Mama heard from Sackree. I have given all your messages except to my Uncle & Aunt Perrot, & I have not seen them since I had your letter. I am very happy at Bath, but I am afraid Papa is not much better for drinking the Waters.—Mama's best Love.—Is the other chaffinche's nest in the Garden hatched?—Your affec: Neice FAC—P.S.—Yes, I shall be very glad to go home & see brothers.

My dear Aunt Cassandra—I hope you are very well. Grandmama hopes the white Turkey lays, & that you have eat up the black one.—We like Gooseberry Pye & Gooseberry pudding very much.—Is that the same Chaffinches Nest that we saw before we went away? & pray will you send me another printed Letter when You write to Aunt Jane again—If You like it.—EA

[*Postscript by JA, below address panel*]

We shall be with you on Thursday to a very late Dinner—later I suppose than my Father will like for himself—but I give him leave to eat one before. You must give us something very nice, for we are used to live well.

Miss Austen
Steventon
Overton
Hants

June 19th

[?*Letter missing on Sunday 23 June*]

---

23. *To Cassandra Austen*

Saturday 25–Monday 27 October 1800

Steventon Saturday Even:ᵍ Oct:ʳ 25th.

My dear Cassandra

I am not yet able to acknowledge the receipt of any parcel from London, which I suppose will not occasion you much surprise.—I was a little disappointed to day, but not more than is perfectly agreable; & I hope to be disappointed again tomorrow, as only one coach comes down on sundays.—You have had a very pleasant Journey of course, & have found Elizabeth & all the Children very well on your arrival at Godmersham, & I congratulate you on it. Edward is rejoicing this evening I dare say to find himself once more at home, from which he fancies he has been absent a great while.—His son left behind him the very fine chesnuts which had been selected for planting at Godmersham, & the drawing of his own which he had intended to carry to George;— the former will therefore be deposited in the soil of Hampshire instead of Kent; the latter, I have already consigned to another Element. We have been exceedingly busy ever since you went away. In the first place we have had to rejoice two or three times every day at your having such very delightful weather for the whole of your Journey—& in the second place we have been obliged to take advantage of the delightful weather ourselves by going to see almost all our Neighbours.—On Thursday we walked to Deane, Yesterday to Oakley Hall & Oakley, & to day to Deane again.—At Oakley Hall we did a great deal— eat some¹ [*p. 2*] sandwiches all over mustard, admired Mʳ Bramston's

49

Porter & Mrs Bramston's Transparencies, & gained a promise from the latter of two roots of hearts-ease, one all yellow & the other all purple, for you. At Oakley we bought ten pair of worsted stockings, & a shift.— The shift is for Betty Dawkins, as we find she wants it more than a rug.—She is one of the most grateful of all whom Edward's charity has reached, or at least she expresses herself more warmly than the rest, for she sends him a "sight of thanks." This morning we called at the Harwoods, & in their dining-room found Heathcote & Chute for ever[2] —Mrs Wm Heathcote & Mrs Chute—the first of whom took a long ride yesterday morning with Mrs Harwood into Lord Carnarvon's Park & fainted away in the evening, & the second walked down from Oakley Hall attended by Mrs Augusta Bramston. They had meant to come on to Steventon afterwards, but we knew a trick worth two of that.—If I had thought of it in time, I would have said something civil to her about Edward's never having had any serious idea of calling on Mr Chute while he was in Hampshire; but unluckily it did not occur to me.—Mrs Heathcote is gone home to day; Catherine had paid her an early visit at Deane in the morning, & brought a good account of Harris.—James went to Winchester fair yesterday, & bought a new horse; & Mary has got a new maid—two great acquisitions, one comes from Folly Farm, is about five years old, used to draw, & thought very pretty; & the other is neice to Dinah at Kintbury.—James called by my father's desire on Mr Bayle to inquire into the cause of his being so horrid.— [*p. 3*] Mr Bayle did not attempt to deny his being horrid, & made many apologies for it;—he did not plead his having a drunken self, he talked only of a drunken foreman &c, &c, & gave hopes of the Table's being at Steventon on monday se'night next.—We have had no letter since you left us, except one from Mr Serle of Bishop's Stoke to enquire the character of James Elton.—Our whole Neighbourhood is at present very busy greiving over poor Mrs Martin, who has totally failed in her business, & had very lately an execution in her house.—Her own brother & Mr Rider are the principal creditors, & they have seized her effects in order to prevent other people's doing it.—There has been the same affair going on, we are told, at Wilson's, & my hearing nothing of you makes me apprehensive that You, your fellow travellers & all your effects, might be seized by the Bailiffs when you stopt at the Crown & sold altogether for the benefit of the creditors. In talking of Mr Deedes's new house, Mrs Bramston told us one circumstance, which, that we should be ignorant of it before must make Edward's conscience fly into his face; she told us that one of the sitting rooms at Sandling,³ an oval room with a Bow at one end, has the very remarkable & singular feature of a fireplace with a window, the centre window of the Bow, exactly over the mantlepeice.—*Sunday.*—This morning's unpromising aspect makes it absolutely necessary for me to observe once more how peculiarly fortunate you have been in your weather, and then I will drop the subject for ever.—Our Improvements have advanced very well;—the Bank [*p. 4*] along the *Elm Walk* is sloped down for the reception of Thorns & Lilacs; & it is settled that the other side of the path is to continue turf'd & be planted with Beech, Ash, & Larch.—*Monday.* I am glad I had no means of sending this yesterday, as I am now able to thank you for executing my Commissions so well.—I like the Gown very much & my Mother thinks it very ugly.—I like the Stockings also very much & greatly prefer having only two pair of that quality, to three of an inferior sort.—The Combs are very pretty, & I am much obliged to you for your present; but am sorry you should make me so many.—The Pink Shoes are not particularly beautiful, but they fit me very well—the others are faultless.—I am glad that I have still my Cloak to expect. Among my other obligations, I must not omit to number your writing me so long a letter in a time of such hurry. I am amused by your going to Milgate at last—& glad that you have so charming a day for your Journey home.—

[*End of p. 4—next paragraph upside down at top of first page*]

The weather does not know how to be otherwise than fine.—I am surprised that Mʳˢ Marriot should not be taller—Surely You have made a mistake.—Did Mʳ Roland make you look well?—

Yours affec:ˡʸ

JA.

[*Postscript below address panel*]

My father approves his Stockings very highly—& finds no fault with any part of Mʳˢ Hancock's bill except the charge of 3ˢ. 6ᵈ for the Packing box.—

Miss Austen
Godmersham Park
Faversham
Kent

24. *To Cassandra Austen*

Saturday 1 November 1800

Steventon Saturday Nov:ʳ 1ˢᵗ.

My dear Cassandra

You have written I am sure, tho' I have received no letter from you since your leaving London;—the Post, & not yourself must have been unpunctual.—We have at last heard from Frank; a letter from him to You came yesterday, & I mean to send it on as soon as I can get a ditto, (*that* means a frank,) which I hope to do in a day or two.—En attendant, You must rest satisfied with knowing that on the 8ᵗʰ of July the Petterell with the rest of the Egyptian Squadron was off the Isle of Cyprus, whither they went from Jaffa for Provisions &c., & whence they were to sail in a day or two for Alexandria, there to wait the result of the English proposals for the Evacuation of Egypt. The rest of the letter, according to the present fashionable stile of Composition, is cheifly Descriptive; of his Promotion he knows nothing, & of Prizes he is guiltless.—Your letter is come; it came indeed twelve lines ago, but I could not stop to acknowledge it before, & I am glad it did not[1] arrive till I had completed my first sentence, because the sentence had been made ever since yesterday, & I think forms a very good beginning.— Your abuse of our Gowns amuses, but does not discourage me; I shall take mine to be made up next week, & the more I look at it, the better it pleases me.—My Cloak came on tuesday, & tho' I expected a good deal, the beauty of the lace astonished me.—It is too handsome to be worn, almost too handsome to be looked at.—The Glass is all safely arrived also, & gives great satisfaction. [*p. 2*] The wine glasses are much smaller than I expected, but I suppose it is the proper size.—*We* find no fault with your manner of performing any of our commissions, but if you like to think yourself remiss in any of them, pray do.—My Mother was rather vexed that you could not go to Penlington's, but she has since written to him, which does just as well.—Mary is disappointed of course about her Locket, & of course delighted about the Mangle which is safe at Basingstoke.—You will thank Edward for it on their behalf &c. &c., & as you know how much it was wished for, will not feel that you are inventing Gratitude.—Did you think of our Ball on thursday evening, & did you suppose me at it?—You might very safely, for there I was.—On wednesday morning it was settled that Mʳˢ Harwood, Mary & I should go together, & shortly afterwards a very civil note of invitation for me came from Mrs Bramston, who wrote I beleive as soon as she knew of the Ball. I might likewise have gone with Mrs Lefroy, & therefore with three methods of going, I must have been more at the Ball than anybody else.—I dined & slept at Deane.— Charlotte & I did my hair, which I fancy looked very indifferent; nobody abused it however, & I retired delighted with my success.—It was a pleasant Ball, & still more good than pleasant, for there were nearly 60 people, & sometimes we had 17 couple.—The Portsmouths, Dorchesters, Boltons, Portals & Clerks were there, & all the meaner & more usual &c. &c.'s.—There was a scarcity of Men in general, & a still greater scarcity of any that were good for much.—I danced nine dances out of ten, five with Stephen Terry, T. Chute & James Digweed & four with Catherine.—There was commonly [*p. 3*] a couple of ladies standing up together, but not often any so amiable as ourselves.—I heard no news, except that Mr Peters who was not there, is supposed to be particularly attentive to Miss Lyford.—You were enquired after very prettily, & I hope the whole assembly now understands that you are gone into Kent, which the families in general seemed to meet in ignorance of.—Lord Portsmouth surpassed the rest in his attentive recollection of you, enquired more into the length of your absence, & concluded by desiring to be "remembered to you when I wrote next."—Lady Portsmouth had got a different dress on, & Lady Bolton is much improved by a wig.—The three Miss Terries were there, but no Anne;— which was a great disappointment to me; I hope the poor girl had not set her heart on her appearance that Even^g so much as I had.—Mr Terry is ill, in a very low way. I said civil things for Edward to Mr Chute, who amply returned them by declaring that had he known of my brother's being at Steventon he should have made a point of calling on him to thank him for his civility about the Hunt.—I have heard from Charles, & am to send his shirts by half dozens as they are finished;—one sett will go next week.—The Endymion is now waiting only for orders, but may wait for them perhaps a month.—Mr Coulthard was unlucky in very narrowly missing another unexpected Guest at Chawton, for Charles had actually set out & got half the way thither in order to spend one day with Edward, but turned back on discovering the distance to be considerably more than he had fancied, & finding himself & his horse to be very much tired.—I should regret it the more if his friend Shipley had been of the party, for Mr Coulthard might not² have been so well pleased to see only one come at a time.

[*p. 4*] Miss Harwood is still at Bath, & writes word that she never was in better health & never more happy.—Jos: Wakeford[3] died last saturday, & my father buried him on Thursday. A deaf Miss Fonnereau is at Ashe, which has prevented Mrs Lefroy's going to Worting or Basingstoke during the absence of Mr Lefroy.—My Mother is very happy in the prospect of dressing a new Doll which Molly has given Anna. My father's feelings are not so enviable, as it appears that the farm cleared 300£ last year.—James & Mary went to Ibthrop for one night last monday, & found Mrs Lloyd not in very good looks.—Martha has been lately at Kintbury, but is probably at home by this time.—Mary's promised maid has jilted her, & hired herself elsewhere.—The Debaries persist in being afflicted at the death of their Uncle, of whom they now say they saw a great deal in London.—Love to all.—I am glad George remembers me.—Yours very affec:^tely

JA.

[*End of p. 4, next paragraph upside down at top of first page*]

I wore at the Ball your favourite gown, a bit of muslin of the same round my head, border'd with Mrs Cooper's[4] band—& one little Comb.—

[*Postcript below address panel*]

I am very unhappy.—In re-reading your letter I find I might have spared any Intelligence of Charles.—To have written only what you knew before!—You may guess how much I feel.—

Miss Austen
Godmersham Park
Faversham
Kent

[*?Letter missing here*]

25. *To Cassandra Austen*

Saturday 8–Sunday 9 November 1800

Steventon Saturday Even^g—Nov:^r 8.

My dear Cassandra,

Having just finished the first volume of les Veillees du Chateau,[1] I think it a good opportunity for beginning a letter to you while my mind

is stored with Ideas worth transmitting.—I thank you for so speedy a
return to my two last, & particularly thank you for your anecdote of
Charlotte Graham & her cousin Harriot Bailey, which has very much
amused both my Mother & myself. If you can learn anything farther of
that interesting affair I hope you will mention it.—I have two messages; let me get rid of them, & then my paper will be my own.—Mary
fully intended writing to you by Mr Chute's frank, & only happened
intirely to forget it—but will write soon—& my father wishes Edward
to send him a memorandum in your next letter, of the price of the
hops.—The Tables are come, & give general contentment. I had not
expected that they would so perfectly suit the fancy of us all three, or
that we should so well agree in the disposition of them; but nothing
except their own surface can have been smoother;—The two ends put
together form our constant Table for everything, & the centre peice
stands exceedingly well under the glass; holds a great deal most commodiously, without looking awkwardly.—They are both covered with
green baize & send their best Love.—The Pembroke has got its destination by the sideboard, & my mother has great delight in keeping her
Money & papers locked up.—The little Table which used to stand
there, has most conveniently taken itself off into the best bed-room, &
we are now [*p. 2*] in want only of the chiffoniere, which is neither
finished nor come.—So much for that subject; I now come to another,
of a very different nature, as other subjects are very apt to be.—Earle
Harwood has been again giving uneasiness to his family, & Talk to the
Neighbourhood;—in the present instance however he is only unfortunate & not in fault.—About ten days ago, in cocking a pistol in the
guard-room at Marcou, he accidentally shot himself through the Thigh.
Two young Scotch Surgeons in the Island were polite enough to propose taking off the Thigh at once, but to that he would not consent; &
accordingly in his wounded state was put on board a Cutter & conveyed to Haslar Hospital at Gosport; where the bullet was extracted,
& where he now is I hope in a fair way of doing well.—The surgeon
of the Hospital wrote to the family on the occasion, & John Harwood
went down to him immediately, attended by James, whose object in
going was to be the means of bringing back the earliest Intelligence to
M^r & Mrs Harwood, whose anxious sufferings particularly those of the
latter, have of course been dreadful. They went down on tuesday, &
James came back the next day, bringing such favourable accounts as
greatly to lessen the distress of the family at Deane, tho' it will probably
be a long while before Mrs Harwood can be quite at ease.—*One* most

material comfort however they have; the assurance of it's being really an accidental wound, which is not only positively declared by Earle himself, but is likewise testified by the particular direction of the bullet. Such a wound could not have been received in a duel.—At present he is going on very well, but the Surgeon will not declare him to be in no danger.—John Harwood came back last night, & will probably go to him again soon. James had not time at Gosport to take any other steps towards seeing Charles, than the very few which conducted [*p. 3*] him to the door of the assembly room in the Inn, where there happened to be a Ball on the night of their arrival. A likely spot enough for the discovery of a Charles; but I am glad to say that he was not of the party, for it was in general a very ungenteel one, & there was hardly a pretty girl in the room.—I cannot possibly oblige you by not wearing my gown, because I have it made up on purpose to wear it a great deal, & as the discredit will be my own, I feel the less regret.—You must learn to like it yourself & make it up at Godmersham; it may easily be done; it is only protesting it to be very beautiful, & you will soon think it so.—Yesterday was a day of great business with me; Mary drove me all in² the rain to Basingstoke, & still more all in the rain back again, because it rained harder; & soon after our return to Dean a sudden invitation & an own postchaise took us to Ash Park, to dine tete a tete with Mʳ Holder, Mʳ Gauntlett & James Digweed; but our tete a tete was cruelly reduced by the non-attendance of the two latter—. We had a very quiet evening, I beleive Mary found it dull, but I thought it very pleasant. To sit in idleness over a good fire in a well-proportioned room is a luxurious sensation.—Sometimes we talked & sometimes we were quite silent; I said two or three amusing things, & Mʳ Holder made a few infamous puns.—I have had a most affectionate letter from Buller; I was afraid he would oppress me by his felicity³ & his love for his Wife, but this is not the case; he calls her simply Anna without any angelic embellishments, for which I respect & wish him happy—and throughout the whole of his letter indeed he seems more engrossed by his feelings towards our family, than towards her, which You know cannot give any one disgust.—He is very pressing in his invitation to us all to come & see him at Colyton, & my father is very much inclined to go there next Summer.—[*p. 4*] It is a circumstance that may considerably assist the Dawlish scheme.—Buller has desired me to write again, to give him more particulars of us all.—Mʳ Heathcote met with a genteel little accident the other day in hunting; he got off to lead his horse over a hedge or a house or a something, & his horse in his haste trod upon his leg, or rather ancle I beleive, & it is not certain whether the small bone is not broke.—Harris seems still in a poor way, from his bad habit of body; his hand bled again a little the other day, & Dr Littlehales has been with him lately. Martha has accepted Mary's invitation for Ld Portsmouth's Ball.—He has not yet sent out his *own* invitations, but *that* does not signify; Martha comes, & a Ball there must be.—I think it will be too early in her Mother's absence for me to return with her.— Mr Holder told Wm Portal a few days ago that Edward objected to the narrowness of the path which his plantation has left in one part of the Rookery.—Wm Portal has since examined it himself, acknowledges it to be much too narrow, & promises to have it altered. He wishes to avoid the necessity of removing the end of his plantation with it's newly-planted Quick &c, but if a proper footpath cannot be made by poking away the bank on the other side, he will not spare the former.—I have finished this on sunday morning

& am Y^rs Ever JA.

[End of p. 4—two paragraphs upside down at the top of p. 1]

I hope it is true that Edward Taylor is to marry his cousin Charlotte. Those beautiful dark Eyes will then adorn another Generation at least in all their purity.—

Mr Holder's paper tells us that sometime in last August, Capt: Austen & the Petterell were very active in securing a Turkish Ship[4] (driven into a Port in Cyprus by bad weather) from the French.—He was forced to burn her however.—You will see the account in the Sun I dare say.—

[Final paragraph upside down between the lines of p. 1]

Sunday Evening.

We have had a dreadful storm of wind in the forepart of this day, which has done a great deal of mischeif among our trees.—I was sitting alone in the dining room, when an odd kind of crash startled me—in a moment afterwards it was repeated; I then went to the window, which I reached just in time to see the last of our two highly valued Elms descend into the Sweep!!!!! The other, which had fallen I suppose in the first crash, & which was the nearest to the pond, taking a more easterly direction sunk amongst our screen of Chesnuts & firs, knocking down one spruce fir, beating off the head of another, & stripping the two corner chesnuts of several branches, in its fall.—This is not all—. One large Elm out of two on the left hand side, as you enter what I call the Elm walk, was likewise blown down, the Maypole bearing the weathercock was broke in two, & what I regret more than all the rest, is that all the three Elms which grew in Hall's meadow & gave such ornament to it, are gone.—Two were blown down, & the other so much injured that it cannot stand.—I amˢ happy to add however that no greater Evil than the loss of Trees has been the consequence of the Storm in this place, or in our immediate neighbourhood.—We greive therefore in some comfort.—

[*Postscript below address panel*]

You spend your time just as quietly & comfortably as I supposed you would.—We have all seen & admired Fanny's letter to her Aunt.—The Endymion sailed on a cruize last friday.

Miss Austen
Godmersham Park
Faversham
Kent

26. *To Martha Lloyd*

Wednesday 12–Thursday 13 November 1800

Steventon Wednesday Evenᵍ Nov:ʳ 12ᵗʰ.

My dear Martha

I did *not* receive your note yesterday till after Charlotte had left Deane, or I would have sent my answer by her, instead of being the means, as I now must be, of lessening the Elegance of your new Dress for the Hurstbourn Ball by the value of 3ᵈ.—You are very good in wishing to see me at Ibthrop so soon, & I am equally good in wishing to come to you; I beleive our Merit in that respect is much upon a par, our Self-denial mutually strong.—Having paid this tribute of praise to the Virtue of both, I shall have done with Panegyric & proceed to plain matter of fact.—In about a fortnight's time I hope to be with you; I have two reasons for not being able to come before; I wish so to arrange my visit as to spend some days with you after your Mother's return, in the 1ˢᵗ place that I may have the pleasure of seeing her, & in the 2ᵈ, that I may have a better chance of bringing you back with me.—Your promise in my favour was not quite absolute, but if your Will is not perverse, You & Iⁱ will do all in our [*p. 2*] power to overcome your scruples of conscience.—I hope we shall meet next week to talk all this over, till we have tired ourselves with the very idea of my visit, before my visit begins.—Our invitations[2] for the 19th are arrived, & very curiously are they worded.—Mary mentioned to you yesterday poor Earle's unfortunate accident I dare say; he does not seem to be going on very well; the two or three last posts have brought rather less & less favourable accounts of him. This morning's letter states the apprehensions of the Surgeon that the violent catchings of his Patient have done material injury to the bone, which from the first has appeared so nearly broken that any particular irritation or sudden movement might make the fracture certain.—John Harwood is gone to Gosport again to day.—We have two families of friends that are now in a most anxious state; for tho' by a note from Catherine this morning there seems now to be a revival of hope at Manydown,[3] it's continuance may be too reasonably doubted.—M[r] Heathcote however who has broken the small bone of his leg, is so good as to be doing very well. It would be really too much to have three people to care for!—

Mary has heard from Cassandra to day; she is [*p. 3*] now gone with Edward & Elizabeth to the Cages for two or three Nights.—You distress me cruelly by your request about Books; I cannot think of any to bring with me, nor have I any idea of our wanting them. I come to you to be talked to, not to read or hear reading. I can do *that* at home; & indeed I am now laying in a stock of intelligence to pour out on you as *my* share of Conversation.—I am reading Henry's History of England,[4] which I will repeat to you in any manner you may prefer, either in a loose, disultary, unconnected strain, or dividing my recital as the Historian divides it himself, into seven parts, The Civil & Military—Religion—Constitution—Learning & Learned Men—Arts & Sciences —Commerce Coins & Shipping—& Manners;—so that for every evening of the week there will be a different subject; The friday's lot, Commerce, Coin & Shipping, You will find the least entertaining; but the next Eveng:'s portion will make amends.—With such a provision on my part, if you will do your's[5] by repeating the French Grammar, & M[rs] Stent will now & then ejaculate some wonder about the Cocks & Hens, what can we want?—Farewell for a short time—You are to dine here on tuesday to meet James Digweed, whom you must wish to see before he goes into Kent.—We all unite in best Love, & I am

Y[r] very affec[te] JA.—

[*p. 4*] It is reported at Portsmouth that Sir T. Williams is going to be married—It has been reported indeed twenty times before, but Charles is inclined to give some credit to it now, as they hardly ever see him on board, & he looks very much like a Lover.—

Thursday.—The Harwoods have received a much better account of Earle this morning; & Charles, from whom I have just had a letter, has been assured by the Hospital-Surgeon that the Wound is in as favourable a state as can be.

Miss Lloyd
Up-Hurstbourne
Andover

[*Letters missing here*]

27. *To Cassandra Austen*

Thursday 20–Friday 21 November 1800

Steventon Thursday Nov:^{r} 20th.

My dear Cassandra
    Your letter took me quite by surprise this morning; you are very welcome however, & I am very much obliged to you.—I beleive I drank too much wine last night at Hurstbourne; I know not how else to account for the shaking of my hand to day;—You will kindly make allowance therefore for any indistinctness of writing by attributing it to this venial Error.—Naughty Charles did not come on tuesday; but good Charles came yesterday morning. About two o'clock he walked in on a Gosport Hack.—His feeling equal to such a fatigue is a good sign, & his finding no fatigue in it a still better.—We walked down to Deane to dinner, he danced the whole Evening, & to day is no more tired than a gentleman ought to be.—Your desiring to hear from me on Sunday will perhaps bring on you a more particular account of the Ball than you may care for, because one is prone to think much more of such things the morning after they happen, than when time has entirely driven them out of one's recollection.—It was a pleasant Evening, Charles found it remarkably so, but I cannot tell why, unless the absence of Miss Terry—towards whom his conscience reproaches him with now being perfect indifferent—was a releif to him.—There were only twelve dances, of which I danced nine,[1] & was merely prevented from dancing the rest by the want of a partner.—We began at 10, supped at 1, & were at Deane before 5.—There were but 50 people in the room; very few families indeed from our side of the Country, & not many more from the other.—[*p. 2*] My partners were the two St Johns, Hooper Holder—and very prodigious—Mr Mathew, with whom I called the last, & whom I liked the best of my little stock.—There were very few Beauties, &

such as there were, were not very handsome. Miss Iremonger did not look well, & M[rs] Blount was the only one much admired. She appeared exactly as she did in September, with[2] the same broad face, diamond bandeau, white shoes, pink husband, & fat neck.—The two Miss Coxes were there; I traced in one the remains of the vulgar, broad featured girl who danced at Enham eight years ago;—the other is refined into a nice, composed looking girl like Catherine Bigg.—I looked at Sir Thomas Champneys & thought of poor Rosalie;[3] I looked at his daughter & thought her a queer animal with a white neck.—M[rs] Warren, I was constrained to think a very fine young woman, which I much regret. She has got rid of some part of her child, & danced away with great activity, looking by no means very large.—Her husband is ugly enough; uglier even than his cousin John; but he does not look so *very* old.— The Miss Maitlands are both prettyish; very like Anne;[4] with brown skins, large dark eyes, & a good deal of nose.—The General[5] has got the Gout, & M[rs] Maitland the Jaundice.—Miss Debary, Susan & Sally all in black, but without any Statues, made their appearance, & I was as civil to them as their bad breath would allow me. They told me nothing new of Martha.—I mean to go to her on Thursday, unless Charles should determine on coming over again with his friend Shipley for the Basingstoke ball, in which case I shall not go till friday.—I shall write to you again however before I set off, & I shall hope to hear from you in the mean time. If I do not stay for the Ball, I would not on any account do so uncivil a thing [*p. 3*] by the Neighbourhood as to set off at that very time for another place, & shall therefore make a point of not being later than Thursday *morning*.—Mary said that I looked very well last night; I wore my Aunt's gown & handkercheif, & my hair was at least tidy, which was all my ambition.—I will now have done with the Ball; & I will moreover go and dress for dinner.— *Thursday Even[g]* Charles leaves us on saturday, unless Henry should take us in his way to the Island, of which we have some hopes, & then they will probably go together on sunday.—The young lady whom it is suspected that Sir Thomas is to marry, is Miss Emma Wabshaw;—she lives somewhere between Southampton & Winchester, is handsome, accomplished, ami- able, & everything but rich.—He is certainly finishing his house[6] in a great hurry.—Perhaps the report of his being to marry a Miss Fanshawe might originate in his attentions to this very lady; the names are not unlike.—Miss Summers has made my gown very well indeed, & I grow more & more pleased with it.—Charles does not like it, but my father & Mary do; my Mother is very much reconciled to it, & as for James, he gives it the preference over everything of the kind he ever saw; in proof of which I am desired to say that if you like to sell yours, Mary will buy it.—We had a very pleasant day on monday at Ashe; we sat down 14 to dinner in the study, the dining room being not habitable from the Storm's having blown down it's chimney.—Mrs Bramston talked a good deal of nonsense, which Mr Bramston & Mr Clerk seemed almost equally to enjoy.—There was a whist & a casino table, & six outsiders.—Rice & Lucy[7] made love, Mat: Robinson fell asleep, James & Mrs Augusta[8] alternately read Dr Jenner's pamphlet[9] on the cow pox, & I bestowed my company by turns on all. On enquiring of Mrs Clerk, I find that Mrs Heathcote made a great blunder in her news of the Crooks & Morleys; it is young Mr Crooke who is to marry the second Miss Morley—& it is the Miss Morleys instead of the second Miss Crooke, who were the beauties at the Music meeting.—This seems a more likely tale, a better devised Impostor.—The three Digweeds all came on tuesday, & [*p. 4*] we played a pool at Commerce.—James Digweed left Hampshire to day. I think he must be in love with you,[10] from his anxiety to have you go to the Faversham Balls, & likewise from his supposing, that the two Elms fell from their greif at your absence.— Was not it a galant idea?—It never occurred to me before, but I dare say it was so.—Hacker has been here to day, putting in the fruit trees.— A new plan has been suggested concerning the plantation of the new inclosure on the right hand side of the Elm Walk—the doubt is whether it would be better to make a little orchard of it, by planting apples, pears & cherries, or whether it should be larch, Mountain-ash & acacia.— What is your opinion?—I say nothing, & am ready to agree with anybody.—You & George[11] walking to Eggerton!—What a droll party! —Do the Ashford people still come to Godmersham Church every Sunday in a cart?—It is *you* that always disliked Mr N. Toke so much, not *I*.—I do not like his wife, & I do not like Mr Brett, but as for Mr Toke, there are few people whom I like better.—Miss Harwood & her friend have taken a house 15 miles from Bath; she writes very kind letters, but sends no other particulars of the situation—Perhaps it is one of the first houses in Bristol.—Farewell.—Charles sends you his best love—& Edward his worst—[*back to top of p. 1, upside down*] If you think the distinction improper, you may take the worst yourself.—He will write to you when he gets back to his Ship—& in the meantime desires you will consider me as

Y^r affec: Sister

JA.

Charles likes my Gown now.—

[*Upside down between the lines of p. 1*] I rejoice to say that we have just had another letter from our dear Frank—It is to you, very short, written from Larnica in Cyprus & so lately as the 2ᵈ of October.—He came from Alexandria & was to return there in 3 or 4 days, knew nothing of his promotion, & does not write above twenty lines, from a doubt of the letter's ever reaching you & an idea of all letters being open'd at Vienna.—He wrote a few days before to you from Alexandria by the Mercury, sent with dispatches to Lord Keith.—Another letter must be oweing to us besides this—*one* if not *two*—because none of these are to me.—

Henry comes tomorrow, for one night only.—

My Mother has heard from Mʳˢ E. Leigh—. Lady S&S- & her daughter[12] are going to remove to Bath;—Mʳˢ Estwick is married again to a Mʳ Sloane, a young Man under age—without the Knowledge of either family—He bears a good character however.—

[*Postscript below address panel*]

Friday.—I have determined to go on thursday, but of course not before the post comes in.—Charles is in very good looks indeed. I had the comfort of finding out the other evening who all the fat girls with short noses were that disturbed me at the 1ˢᵗ H. Ball. They all prove to be Miss Atkinsons of Enham.

Miss Austen
Godmersham Park
Faversham
Kent

[*Letters missing here*]

28. *To Cassandra Austen*

Sunday 30 November–Monday 1 December 1800

Ibthrop Sunday Nov:ʳ 30ᵗʰ

My dear Cassandra

Shall you expect to hear from me on Wednesday or not?—I think you will, or I should not write, as the three days & half which have passed since my last letter was sent, have not produced many materials towards filling another sheet of paper.—But like Mrs Hastings, "I do not despair—" & you perhaps like the faithful Maria[1] may feel still more certain of the happy Event.—I have been here ever since a quarter after three on thursday last, by the Shrewsbury Clock,[2] which I am fortunately enabled absolutely to ascertain, because Mrs Stent once lived at Shrewsbury, or at least at Tewksbury.—I have the pleasure of thinking myself a very welcome Guest, & the pleasure of spending my time very pleasantly.—Martha looks very well, & wants me to find out that she grows fat; but I cannot carry my complaisance farther than to beleive whatever she asserts on the subject.—Mrs Stent gives us quite as much of her Company as we wish for, & rather more than she used to do; but perhaps not more than is to our advantage in the end, because it is too dirty even for such desperate Walkers as Martha[3] & I to get out of doors, & we are therefore confined to each other's society from morning till night, with very little variety of Books or Gowns. Three of the Miss Debaries called here the morning after [*p. 2*] my arrival, but I have not yet been able to return their civility;—You know it is not an[4] uncommon circumstance in this parish to have the road from Ibthrop to the Parsonage much dirtier & more impracticable for walking than the road from the Parsonage to Ibthrop.—I left my Mother very well when I came away, & left her with strict orders to continue so.—My Journey was safe & not unpleasant;—I spent an hour in Andover, of which Messrs Painter & Redding[5] had the larger part;—twenty minutes however fell to the lot of Mrs Poore & her mother, whom I was glad to see in good looks & spirits.—The latter asked me more questions than I had very well time to answer; the former I beleive is very big; but I am by no means certain;—she is either very big, or not at all big, I forgot to be accurate in my observation at the time, & tho' my thoughts are now more about me on the subject, the power of exercising them to any effect is much diminished.—The two youngest boys only were at home; I mounted the highly-extolled Staircase & went into the elegant Drawing room,[6] which I fancy is now Mrs Harrison's apartment;—and in short did everything that extraordinary Abilities can be supposed to compass in so short a space of time.—

The Endless Debaries are of course very well acquainted with the lady who is to marry Sir Thomas, & all her family. I pardon them however, as their description of her is favourable.—Mrs Wapshire is a widow, with several sons & daughters, a good fortune, & a house in Salisbury; where Miss Wapshire has been for many years a distinguished beauty.—[*p. 3*] She is now seven or eight & twenty, & tho' still hand-some less handsome than she has been.—This promises better, than the bloom of seventeen; & in addition to this, they say that she has always been remarkable for the propriety of her behaviour, distinguishing her far above the general class of Town Misses, & rendering her of course very unpopular among them.—I hope I have now gained the real truth, & that my letters may in future go on without conveying any farther[7] contradictions of what was last asserted about Sir Thomas Williams & Miss Wapshire.—I wish I could be certain that her name were Emma; but her being the Eldest daughter[8] leaves that circumstance doubtful. At Salisbury the match is considered as certain & as near at hand.—Martha desires her best love, & will be happy to welcome any letter from you to this house, whether it be addressed to herself or to me—And in fact, the difference of direction will not be material.—*She* is pleased with my Gown, & particularly bids me say that if you could see me in it for five minutes, she is sure you would be eager to make up your own.—I have been obliged to mention this, but have not failed to blush the whole time of my writing it.—Part of the money & time which I spent at Andover were devoted to the purchase of some figured cambric muslin for a frock for Edward—a circumstance from which I derive two pleas-ing reflections; it has in the first place opened to me a fresh source of self-congratulation on being able to make so munificent a present, & secondly it has been the means of informing me that the very pretty manufacture in question may be bought for 4^s.6^d. p^r y^d—yard & half wide.—Martha has promised to return with me, & our plan is to [have] a nice black frost[9] for walking to Whitchurch, & there throw ourselves into [*p. 4*] a postchaise, one upon the other, our heads hanging out at one door, & our feet at the opposite.—If you have never heard that Miss Dawes has been married these two months, I will mention it in my next.—Pray do not forget to go to the Canterbury Ball. I shall despise you all most insufferably if you do.—By the bye, there will not be any Ball, because Delmar lost so much by the Assemblies last winter that he has protested against opening his rooms[10] this year.—I have charged my Myrmidons to send me an account of the Basingstoke Ball; I have placed my spies at different places that they may collect the more; & by so doing, by sending Miss Bigg to the Townhall itself, & posting my Mother at Steventon I hope to derive from their various observations[11] a good general idea of the whole.—*Monday.*—Martha has this moment received your letter—I hope there is nothing in it requiring an immediate answer as we are at dinner, & she has neither time to read nor I to write. — Y^{rs} Ever

JA.

Miss Austen
Godmersham Park
Faversham
Kent

[*Letters missing here*]

29. *To Cassandra Austen*

Saturday 3–Monday 5 January 1801

Steventon Saturday Jan:^{ry} 3^{d}

My dear Cassandra

As you have by this time received my last letter, it is fit that I should begin another; & I begin with the hope, which is at present uppermost in my mind, that you often wore a white gown in the morning, at the time of all the gay party's being with you. Our visit at Ash Park last Wednesday, went off in a come-cá way; we met Mr Lefroy & Tom Chute, played at cards & came home again. — James & Mary dined here on the following day, & at night Henry set off in the Mail for London. — He was as agreable as ever during his visit, & has not lost anything in Miss Lloyd's estimation. — Yesterday, we were quite alone, only our four selves; — but to day the scene is agreably varied by Mary's driving Martha to Basingstoke, & Martha's afterwards dining at Deane. — My Mother looks forward with as much certainty as you can do, to our keeping two Maids — my father is the only one not in the secret. — We plan having a steady Cook, & a young giddy Housemaid, with a sedate, middle aged Man, who is to undertake the double office of Husband to the former & sweetheart to the latter. — No Children of course to be allowed on either side. — You feel more for John Bond, than John Bond deserves; — I am sorry to lower his Character, but he is not ashamed to own himself, that he has no doubt at all of getting a good place, & that he had even an offer many years ago from a Farmer Paine of taking him into his Service whenever he might quit my father's. — There are three parts of Bath which we have thought of as likely to have Houses in them. — Westgate Buildings, Charles Street, &

some of the short streets leading from Laura Place or Pulteney St:—
Westgate Buildings, tho' quite in the lower part of the Town [*p. 2*] are
not badly situated themselves; the street is broad, & has rather a good
appearance. Charles Street however I think is preferable; The Buildings
are new, & it's nearness to Kingsmead fields would be a pleasant circumstance.—Perhaps you may remember, or perhaps you may forget
that Charles Street leads from the Queen Square Chapel to the two
Green park-Streets.—The Houses in the Streets near Laura Place I
should expect to be above our price.—Gay Street would be too high,
except only the lower house on the left hand side as you ascend; towards *that* my Mother has no disinclination;—it used to be lower rented
than any other house in the row, from some inferiority in the apartments. But above all other's, her wishes are at present fixed on the
corner house in Chapel row, which opens into Prince's Street. Her
knowledge of it however is confined only to the outside, & therefore
she[1] is equally uncertain of it's being really desirable as of its being to
be had.—In the meantime she assures you that she will do everything
in her power to avoid Trim S^t altho' you have not expressed the fearful
presentiment of it, which was rather expected.—We know that Mrs Perrot
will want to get us into Axford Buildings, but we all unite in particular
dislike of that part of the Town, & therefore hope to escape. Upon all
these different situations, You & Edward may confer together, & your
opinion of each will be expected with eagerness.—As to our Pictures,[2]
the Battlepeice, Mr Nibbs, Sir Wm East, & all the old heterogenous,
miscellany, manuscript, Scriptoral peices dispersed over the House are
to be given to James.—Your own Drawings will not cease to be your
own—& the two paintings on Tin will be at your disposal.—My Mother
says that the French agricultural Prints in the best bed-room were given
by Edward to his two Sisters. Do you or he know anything about it?—
She has written to my Aunt & We are all impatient for the answer.—
I do not know how[3] to give up the idea of our both going to Paragon
in May;—*Your* going I consider as indispensably necessary, & I shall
not like being [*p. 3*] left behind; there is no place here or hereabouts
that I shall want to be staying at—& tho' to be sure the keep of two will
be more than of one, I will endeavour to make the difference less by
disordering my Stomach with Bath bunns; & as to the *trouble* of
accomodating us, whether there are one or two, it is much the same.—
According to the first plan, my mother & our two selves are to travel
down together; & my father follow us afterwards—in about a fortnight
or three weeks.—We have promised to spend a couple of days at Ibthrop

in our way.—We must all meet at Bath you know before we set out for the Sea, & everything considered I think the first plan as good as any. My father & mother wisely aware of the difficulty of finding in all Bath such a bed as their own, have resolved on taking it with them;—All the beds indeed that we shall want are to be removed, viz:—besides theirs, our own two, the best for a spare one, & two for servants—and these necessary articles will probably be the only material ones that it [wou]ld answer to send down.—I do not think it will be worth while to remove any of our chests of Drawers.—We shall be able to get some of a much more commo[dious form] made of deal, & painted to look very neat; & I flatter myself that for little comforts of all kinds, our apartment will be one of the most complete things of the sort all over Bath—Bristol included.—We have thought at times of removing the side-board, or a pembroke table, or some other peice of furniture—but upon the whole it has ended in thinking that the trouble & risk of the removal would be more than the advantage of having them at a place, where everything may be purchased. Pray send your opinion.—Martha has as good as promised to come to us again in March.—Her spirits are better than they were.—I have now attained the true art of letter-writing, which we are always told, is to express on paper exactly what one would say to the same person by word of mouth; I have been talking to you almost as fast as I could the whole of this letter.—[*p. 4*] Your Christmas Gaieties are really quite surprising; I think they would satisfy even Miss Walter[4] herself.—I hope the ten shillings won by Miss Foote[5] may make everything easy between her & her cousin Frederick.—So, Lady Bridges in the delicate language of Coulson Wallop is *in for it!*[6]—I am very glad to hear of the Pearsons' good fortune[7]—It is a peice of promotion which I know they looked forward to as very desirable some years ago, on Capt: Lockyer's illness. It brings them[8] a considerable increase of Income, & a better house.—My Mother bargains for having no trouble at all in furnishing our house in Bath—& I have engaged for your willingly undertaking to do it all.—I get more & more reconciled to the idea of our removal. We have lived long enough in this Neighbourhood, the Basingstoke Balls are certainly on the decline, there is something interesting in the bustle of going away, & the prospect of spending future summers by the Sea or in Wales is very delightful.—For a time we shall now possess many of the advantages which I have often[9] thought of with Envy in the wives of Sailors or Soldiers.—It must not be generally known however that I am not sacrificing a great deal in quitting the Country—or I can expect to inspire no tenderness, no interest in those we leave behind.—The threatened Act of Parliament[10] does not seem to give any alarm.—

[*Upside down at top of p. 1*]

My father is doing all in his power to encrease his Income by raising his Tythes &c, & I do not despair of getting very nearly six hundred a year.—In what part of Bath do you mean to place your *Bees?*—We are afraid of the South Parade's being too hot.

[*Postscript below address panel*]

Monday.—Martha desires her best Love, & says a great many kind things about spending some time with you in March—& depending on a large return from us both in the Autumn.—Perhaps I may not write again before Sunday.—

Y[rs] affec:[ly] JA.

Miss Austen
Godmersham Park
Faversham
Kent

30. *To Cassandra Austen*

Thursday 8–Friday 9 January 1801

Steventon Thursday Jan:[ry] 8th—

My dear Cassandra,

The "Perhaps" which concluded my last letter being only a "perhaps", will not occasion your being over-powered with Surprise I dare say, if you *should* receive this before tuesday, which unless circumstances are very perverse will be the case.—I received yours with much general Philanthropy & still more peculiar good will two days ago; & I suppose I need not tell you that it was very long, being written on a foolscap sheet, & very entertaining, being written by You.—M[r] Payne[1] has been dead long enough for Henry to be out of mourning for him before his last visit, tho' we knew nothing of it till about that time. Why he died, or of what complaint, or to what Noblemen he bequeathed his four daughters in marriage we have not heard.—I am glad that the Wildmans' are going to give a Ball, & hope you will not fail to benefit both yourself & me, by laying out a few kisses in the purchase of a frank.—I beleive you are right in proposing to delay the Cambric muslin, & I submit with a kind of voluntary reluctance.—Mr Peter Debary has declined Dean Curacy; he wishes to be settled nearer London. A foolish reason—! as if Deane were not near London in comparison of Exeter or York.—Take the whole World through, & he will find many[2] more places at a greater distance from London than Deane, than he will at a less.—What does he think of Glencoe or Lake Katherine?—I feel rather indignant that any possible objection should be raised against so valuable a peice of preferment, so delightful a situation!—that Deane should not be universally allowed to be as near the Metropolis as any other Country Village.—[*p. 2*] As this is the case however, as Mr Peter Debary has shewn himself a Peter[3] in the blackest sense of the Word, We are obliged to look elsewhere for an heir; & my father has thought it a necessary compliment to James Digweed to offer the Curacy to him, tho' without considering it as either a desirable or an eligible situation for him.—Unless he is in love with Miss Lyford, I think he had better not be settled exactly in this Neighbourhood, & unless he is very much in love with her indeed, he is not likely to think a salary of 50£ equal in value or efficacy to one of 75£.—Were *you* indeed to be considered as one of the fixtures of the house![4]—but you were never actually erected in it either by Mr Egerton Brydges or Mrs Lloyd.—Martha & I dined yesterday at Deane to meet the Powletts & Tom Chute, which we did not fail to do.—Mrs Powlett was at once expensively & nakedly dress'd;—we have had the satisfaction of estimating her Lace & her Muslin; & she said too little to afford us much other amusement.—Mrs John Lyford is so much pleased with the state of widowhood as to be going to put in for being a widow again;—she is to marry a Mr Fendall, a banker in Gloucester, a man of very good fortune, but considerably older than herself & with three little children.—Miss Lyford has never been here yet; she can come only for a day, & is not able to fix the day.—I fancy Mr Holder will have the Farm, & without being obliged to depend on the accomodating spirit of Mr William Portal; he will probably have it for the remainder of my father's lease.—This pleases us all much better than it's falling into the hands of Mr Harwood or Farmer Twitchen.—Mr Holder is to come in a day or two to talk to my father on the subject, & then John Bond's interest will not be forgotten.—I have had a letter to day from Mrs Cooke. Mrs Lawrel is going to be married to a Mr Hinchman,[5] a rich East Indian. I hope Mary will be satisfied with this proof [*p. 3*] of her cousin's Existence & Welfare, & cease to torment herself with the idea of his bones being bleaching in the Sun on Wantage Downs.—Martha's visit is drawing towards it's close, which we all four sincerely regret.—The wedding-day[6] is to be celebrated on the 16th because the 17th falls on saturday—& a day or two before the 16th Mary will drive her sister to Ibthrop to find all the festivity she can in contriving for everybody's comfort, & being thwarted or teized by almost everybody's temper.—Fulwar, Eliza, & Tom Chute are to be of the party;—I know of nobody else.—I was asked, but declined it.—Eliza has seen Lord Craven at Barton, & probably by this time at Kintbury, where he was expected for one day this week.—She found his manners very pleasing indeed.—The little flaw of having a Mistress now living with him at Ashdown Park, seems to be the only unpleasing circumstance about him.—From Ibthrop, Fulwar & Eliza are to return with James & Mary to Deane.—The Rices are *not* to have an house on Weyhill;—for the present he has Lodgings in Andover, & they are in veiw of a dwelling hereafter in Appleshaw, that village of wonderful Elasticity, which stretches itself out for the reception of everybody who does not wish for a house on Speen Hill.—Pray give my love to George, tell him that I am very glad to hear he can skip so well already, & that I hope he will continue to send me word of his improvement in the art.—I think you judge very wisely in putting off your London visit—& I am mistaken if it be not put off for some time.— You speak with such noble resignation of Mrs Jordan & the Opera House that it would be an insult to suppose consolation required—but to prevent your thinking with regret of this rupture of your engagement with Mr Smithson, I must assure you that Henry suspects him to be a great Miser.—

[*p. 4*] *Friday.* No answer from my Aunt.—She has no time for writing I suppose in the hurry of selling furniture, packing Cloathes & preparing for their removal to Scarletts.—You are very kind in planning presents for me to make, & my Mother has shewn me exactly the same attention—but as I do not chuse to have Generosity dictated to me, I shall not resolve on giving my Cabinet to Anna till the first thought of it has been my own. Sidmouth is now talked of as our Summer abode; get all the information therefore about it that you can from Mrs C. Cage. My father's old Ministers are already deserting him to pay their court to his Son; the brown Mare, which as well as the black was to devolve on James at our removal, has not had patience to wait for that, & has settled herself even now at Deane.—The death of Hugh Capet, which like that of Mr Skipsey[7]—tho' undesired was not wholly unexpected, being purposely effected, has made the immediate possession of the Mare very convenient; & everything else I suppose will be seized by degrees in the same manner.—Martha & I work at the books every day.—Yours affec:^ly JA.

Miss Austen
Godmersham Park
Faversham
Kent

31. *To Cassandra Austen*

Wednesday 14–Friday 16 January 1801

Steventon Wednesday Jan^ry–14th.

Poor Miss Austen!—It appears to me that I have rather oppressed you of late by the frequency of my letters. You had hoped not to hear from me again before tuesday, but Sunday shewed you with what a merciless Sister you had to deal.—I cannot recall the past, but you shall not hear from me quite so often in future.—Your letter to Mary was duly received before she left Dean with Martha yesterday morning, & it gives us great pleasure to know that the Chilham Ball was so agreable & that you danced four dances with Mr Kemble.—Desirable however as the latter circumstance was I cannot help wondering at it's taking place;—Why did you dance four dances with so stupid a Man?—why not rather dance two of them with some elegant brother-officer who was struck with your appearance as soon as you entered the room?—Martha left you her best Love; she will write to you herself in a short time; but trusting to my memory rather than her own, she has nevertheless desired me to ask you to purchase for her two bottles of Steele's Lavender Water when you are in Town, provided you should go to the Shop on your own account;—otherwise you may be sure that she would not have you recollect the request.—James dined with us yesterday, wrote to Edward in the Evening, filled three sides of paper, every line inclining too much towards the North-East, & the very first line of all scratched out, and this morning he joins his Lady in the fields of Elysium & Ibthrop.—Last friday was a very busy day with us. [*p. 2*] We were visited by Miss Lyford & Mr Bayle.—The latter began his operations in the house, but had only time to finish the four sitting-rooms; the rest is deferred till the spring is more advanced & the days longer.—He took his paper of appraisement away with him, & therefore we only know the Estimate he has made of one or two articles of furniture, which my father particularly enquired into. I understand however that he was of opinion that the whole would amount to more than two hundred pounds, & it is not imagined that this will comprehend the Brewhouse, & many other &c. &c.—Miss Lyford was very pleasant, & gave my mother such an account of the houses in Westgate Buildings, where Mrs Lyford lodged four years ago, as made her think of a situation there with great pleasure; but your opposition will be without difficulty, decisive, & my father in particular who was very well inclined towards the Row before, has now ceased to think of it entirely.—At present the Environs of Laura-place seem to be his choice. His veiws on the subject are much advanced since I came home; he grows quite ambitious, & actually requires now a comfortable & a creditable looking house.—On Saturday Miss Lyford went to her long home—that is to say, it was a long way off; & soon afterwards a party of fine Ladies issuing from a well-known, commodious green Vehicle, their heads full of Bantam-Cocks & Galinies,^{1} entered the house.—Mrs Heathcote, Mrs Harwood, Mrs James Austen, Miss Bigg, Miss Jane Blachford. Hardly a day passes in which we do not have some visitor or other; yesterday came Mrs Bramstone, who is very sorry that she is to lose us, & afterwards Mr Holder, who was shut up for an hour with my father & James in a most aweful manner.—John Bond est a lui.—Mr Holder was perfectly willing to take him on exactly the same terms with my father, & John seems exceedingly well satisfied.—The comfort of not changing his home is a very material one to him. [*p. 3*] And since such are his unnatural feelings his belonging to Mr Holder is the every thing needful; but otherwise there would have been a situation offering to him which I had thought of with particular satisfaction, viz = under Harry Digweed, who if John had quitted Cheesedown would have been eager to engage him as superintendant at Steventon, would have kept an horse for him to ride about on, would probably have supplied him with a more permanent home, & I think would certainly have been a more desirable Master altogether.—John & Corbett are not to have any concern with each other;—there are to be two Farms & two Bailiffs.—We are of opinion that it would be better in only one.—This morning brought my Aunt's reply, & most thoroughly affectionate is it's tenor. She thinks with the greatest pleasure of our being settled in Bath; it is an event which will attach her to the place more than anything else could do, &c., &c.— She is moreover very urgent with my mother not to delay her visit in Paragon if she should continue unwell, & even recommends her spending the whole winter with them.—At present, & for many days past my mother has been quite stout, & she wishes not to be obliged by any relapse to alter her arrangements.—M^r and Mrs Chamberlayne are in Bath, lodging at the Charitable Repository;—I wish the scene may suggest to Mrs C. the notion of selling her black beaver bonnet for the releif of the poor.—Mrs Welby has been singing Duetts with the Prince of Wales.[2]—My father has got above 500 Volumes to dispose of;—I want James to take them at a venture at half a guinea a volume.—The whole repairs of the parsonage at Deane, Inside & out, Coachbox, Basket & Dickey will not much exceed 100£.—Have you seen that Major Byng,[3] a nephew of Lord Torrington is dead?—That must be Edmund.—

[*p. 4*] *Friday.* I thank you for yours, tho' I should have been more grateful for it, if it had not been charged 8^d. instead of 6^d., which has given me the torment of writing to Mr Lambould on the occasion.—I am rather surprised at the Revival of the London visit—but Mr Doricourt has travelled; he knows best.[4] That James Digweed has refused Dean Curacy I suppose he has told you himself—tho' probably the subject has never been mentioned between you.—Mrs Milles flatters herself falsely; it has never been Mrs Rice's wish to have her son settled near herself—& there is now a hope entertained of her relenting in favour of Deane.—Mrs Lefroy & her son in law were here yesterday; *she* tries not to be sanguine, but *he* was in excellent Spirits.—I rather wish they may have the Curacy. It will be an amusement to Mary to superintend their Household management, & abuse them for expense, especially as Mrs L. means to advise them to put their washing out.—

[*End of p. 4, complimentary close below address panel*]

Yours affec:^ly JA.—

Miss Austen
Godmersham Park
Faversham
Kent

[*Possibly a letter missing here*]

32. *To Cassandra Austen*

Wednesday 21–Thursday 22 January 1801

Steventon Wednesday Jan^ry 21st.

Expect a most agreable Letter; for not being overburdened with subject—(having nothing at all to say)—I shall have no check to my Genius from beginning to end.—Well—& so, Frank's letter has made you very happy, but you are afraid he would not have patience to stay for the Haarlem, which you wish him to have done as being safer than the Merchantman.—Poor fellow! to wait from the middle of November to the end of December, & perhaps even longer! it must be sad work!— especially in a place where the ink is so abominably pale.—What a surprise to him it must have been on the 20th of Oct:r to be visited, collar'd & thrust out of the Petterell by Capt:n Inglis!—He kindly passes over the poignancy of his feelings in quitting his Ship, his Officers & his Men.—What a pity it is that he should not be in England at the time of this promotion, because he certainly would have had an appoint- ment!—so everybody says, & therefore it must be right for me to say it too.—Had he been really here, the certainty of the appointment I dare say would not have been half so great—but as it could not be brought to the proof, his absence will be always a lucky source of regret.—Eliza talks of having read in a Newspaper that all the 1st Lieut:s of the Frigates whose Captains were to be sent into Line-of-Battle ships, were to be promoted to the rank of Commander—. If it be true, Mr Valentine may afford himself a fine Valentine's knot, & Charles may perhaps become 1st of the Endymion—tho' I suppose Capt: Durham is too likely to bring a villain with him under that denomination. [*p. 2*] I dined at Deane yesterday, as I told you I should;—& met the two Mr Holders.—We played at Vingt-un, which as Fulwar was unsuccessful,[1] gave him an opportunity of exposing himself as usual.—Eliza says she is quite well, but she is thinner than when we saw her last, & not in very good looks. I suppose she has not recovered from the effects of her illness in December.—She cuts her hair too short over her forehead, & does not wear her cap far enough upon her head—in spite of these many disadvantages however, I can still admire her beauty.—They all dine here to day. Much good may it do us all. William & Tom are much as usual; Caroline is improved in her person; I think her now really a pretty Child. She is still very shy, & does not talk much. Fulwar goes next month into Gloucestershire, Leicestershire & Warwickshire, & Eliza spends the time of his absence at Ibthrop & Deane; she hopes therefore to see you before it is long. Lord Craven was prevented by Company at home, from paying his visit at Kintbury, but as I told you before, Eliza is greatly pleased with him, & they seem likely to be on the most friendly terms.—Martha returns into this country next tuesday, & then begins her two visits at Deane.—I expect to see Miss Bigg every day, to fix the time for my going to Manydown; I think it will be next week, & I shall give you notice of it if I can, that you may direct to me there.—The Neighbourhood have quite recovered the death of Mrs Rider—so much so, that I think they are rather rejoiced at it now; her Things were so very dear!—& Mrs Rogers is to be all that is desirable. Not even Death itself can fix the friendship of the World.—

[*p. 3*] You are not to give yourself the trouble of going to Penlingtons when you are in Town; my father is to settle the matter when he goes there himself; You are only to take special care of the Bills of his in your hands, & I dare say will not be sorry to be excused the rest of the business.—*Thursday*. Our party yesterday was very quietly pleasant. To day we all attack Ash Park, & tomorrow I dine again at Deane. What an eventful Week!—Eliza left me a message for you which I have great pleasure in delivering; She will write to you & send you your Money next Sunday.—Mary has likewise a message—. She will be much obliged to you if you can bring her the pattern of the Jacket & Trowsers, or whatever it is, that Elizth:'s boys wear when they are first put into breeches—; or if you could bring her an old suit itself she would be very glad, but that I suppose is hardly do-able. I am happy to hear of Mrs Knight's amendment, whatever might be her complaint. I cannot think so ill of her however inspite of your insinuations as to suspect her of having lain-in.—I do not think she would be betrayed beyond an *Accident* at the utmost.—The Wylmots being robbed must be an amusing thing to their acquaintance, & I hope it is as much their pleasure as it seems their avocation to be subjects of general Entertainment.—I have a great mind not to acknowledge the receipt of your letter, which I have just had the pleasure of reading, because I am so ashamed to compare the sprawling lines of this with it!—But if I say all that I have to say, I hope I have no reason to hang myself.—Caroline^2 was only brought to bed on the 7th of this month, so that her recovery does seem pretty rapid.—[*p. 4*] I have heard twice from Edward on the occasion, & his letters have each been exactly what they ought to be—chearful & amusing.—He dares not write otherwise to *me*—but perhaps he might be obliged to purge himself from the guilt of writing Nonsense by filling his shoes with whole pease for a week afterwards.—Mrs G.^{3} has left him 100£—his Wife & son 500£ each. I join with you in wishing for the Environs of Laura place, but do not venture to expect it.— My Mother hankers after the Square^4 dreadfully, & it is but natural to suppose that my Uncle will take *her* part.—It would be very pleasant to be near Sidney Gardens!—we might go into the Labyrinth every day.— You need not endeavour to match my mother's mourning Calico—, she does not mean to make it up any more.—Why did not J. D.⁵ make his proposals to you? I suppose he went to see the Cathedral, that he might know how he should like to be married in it.—Fanny shall have the Boarding-school⁶ as soon as her Papa gives me an opportunity of sending it—& I do not know whether I may not by that time have worked myself up into so generous a fit as to give it to her for ever.—

[*Postscript below address panel*]

We have a Ball on Thursday too—. I expect to go to it from Manydown.—Do not be surprised, or imagine that Frank is come if I write again soon. It will only be to say that I am going to M- & to answer your [ques]tion about my Gown.

[J. A.]⁷

Miss Austen
Godmersham Park
Faversham
Kent

33. *To Cassandra Austen*

Steventon Sunday January 25.

I have nothing to say about Manydown, but I write because you will expect to hear from me, and because if I waited another day or two, I hope your visit to Goodnestone would make my letter too late in its arrival. I dare say I shall be at M. in the course of this week, but as it is not certain you will direct to me at home. I shall want two new coloured gowns for the summer, for my pink one will not do more than clear me from Steventon. I shall not trouble you, however, to get more than one of them, and that is to be a plain brown cambric muslin, for morning wear; the other, which is to be a very pretty yellow and white cloud, I mean to buy in Bath. Buy two brown ones, if you please, and both of a length, but one longer than the other—it is for a tall woman. Seven yards for my mother, seven yards and a half for me; a dark brown, but the kind of brown is left to your own choice, and I had rather they were different, as it will be always something to say, to dispute about which is the prettiest. They must be cambric muslin. How do you like this cold weather? I hope you have all been earnestly praying for it as a salutary relief from the dreadfully mild and unhealthy season preceding it, fancying yourself half putrified from the want of it, and that now you all draw into the fire, complain that you never felt such bitterness of cold before, that you are half starved, quite frozen, and wish the mild weather back again with all your hearts. Your unfortunate sister was betrayed last Thursday into a situation of the utmost cruelty. I arrived at Ashe Park before the Party from Deane, and was shut up in the drawing-room with Mr Holder alone for ten minutes. I had some thoughts of insisting on the housekeeper or Mary Corbett being sent for, and nothing could prevail on me to move two steps from the door, on the lock of which I kept one hand constantly fixed. We met nobody but ourselves, played at *vingt-un* again, and were very cross.[1] On Friday I wound up my four days of dissipation by meeting William Digweed at Deane, and am pretty well, I thank you, after it. While I was there a sudden fall of snow rendered the roads impassable, and made my journey home in the little carriage much more easy and agreeable than my journey down. Fulwar and Eliza left Deane yesterday. You will be glad to hear that Mary is going to keep another maid. I fancy Sally is too much of a servant to find time for everything, and Mary thinks Edward is not so much out of doors as he ought to be; there is therefore to be a girl in the nursery. I would not give much for Mr Rice's chance of living at Deane; he builds his hope, I find, not upon anything that his mother has written, but upon the effect of what he has written himself. He must write a great deal better than those eyes indicate if he can persuade a perverse and narrow-minded woman to oblige those whom she does not love. Your brother Edward makes very honourable mention of you, I assure you, in his letter to James, and seems quite sorry to part with you. It is a great comfort to me to think that my cares have not been thrown away, and that you are respected in the world. Perhaps you may be prevailed on to return with him and Elizabeth into Kent, when they leave us in April, and I rather suspect that your great wish of keeping yourself disengaged has been with that view. Do as you like; I have overcome my desire of your going to Bath with my mother and me. There is nothing which energy will not bring one to. Edward Cooper is so kind as to want us all to come to Hamstall this summer, instead of going to the sea, but we are not so kind as to mean to do it. The summer after, if you please, Mr Cooper, but for the present we greatly prefer the sea to all our relations. I dare say you will spend a very pleasant three weeks in town. I hope you will see everything worthy notice, from the Opera House to Henry's office in Cleveland Court; and I shall expect you to lay in a stock of intelligence that may procure me amusement for a twelvemonth to come. You will have a turkey from Steventon while you are there, and pray note down how many full courses of exquisite dishes M. Halavant[2] converts it into. I cannot write any closer. Neither my affection for you nor for letter-writing can stand out against a Kentish visit. For a three months' absence I can be a very loving relation and a very excellent correspondent, but beyond that I degenerate into negligence and indifference. I wish you a very pleasant ball on Thursday, and myself another, and Mary and Martha a third, but they will not have theirs till Friday, as they have a scheme for the Newbury Assembly. Nanny's husband is decidedly against her quitting service in such times as these, and I believe would be very glad to have her continue with us. In some respects she would be a great comfort, and in some we should wish for a different sort of servant. The washing would be the greatest evil. Nothing is settled, however, at present with her, but I should think it would be as well for all parties if she could suit herself in the meanwhile somewhere nearer her husband and child than Bath. Mrs H. Rice's place would be very likely to do for her. It is not many, as she is herself aware, that she is qualified for. My mother has not been so well for many months as she is now. Adieu. Yours sincerely, JA.

Miss Austen
Godmersham Park
Faversham
Kent

[*Letters missing here*]

34. *To Cassandra Austen*

Manydown Wednesday[1] Feb:ry 11th.

My dear Cassandra

As I have no Mr Smithson to write of *I* can date my letters.—Yours to my Mother has been forwarded to me this morning, with a request that I would take on me the office of acknowledging it. I should not however have thought it necessary to write so soon, but for the arrival of a letter from Charles to myself.—It was written last Saturday from off the Start, & conveyed to Popham Lane by Captn Boyle in his way to Midgham. He came from Lisbon in the Endymion, & I will copy Charles' account of his conjectures about Frank.—"He has not seen my brother lately, nor does he expect to find him arrived, as he met Capt: Inglis at Rhodes going up to take command of the Petterel as he was coming down, but supposes he will arrive in less than a fortnight from this time, in some ship which is expected to reach England about that time with dispatches from Sir Ralph Abercrombie."—The event must shew what sort of a Conjuror Capt: Boyle is.—The Endymion has [*p. 2*] not been plagued with any more prizes.—Charles spent three pleasant days in Lisbon.—They were very well satisfied with their Royal Passenger,[2] whom they found fat, jolly & affable, who talks of Ly Augusta as his wife & seems much attached to her.—When this letter was written, the Endymion was becalmed, but Charles hoped to reach Portsmouth by monday or tuesday; & as he particularly enquires for Henry's direction, you will e'er long I suppose receive further intelligence of him.—He received my letter, communicating our plans, before he left England, was much surprised of course, but is quite reconciled to them, & means to come to Steventon once more while Steventon is ours.—Such I beleive are all the particulars of his Letter, that are worthy of travelling into the Regions of Wit, Elegance, fashion, Elephants & Kangaroons.[3] My visit to Miss Lyford begins tomorrow, & ends on Saturday, when I shall have an opportunity of returning here at no expence as the Carriage must take Cath:[4] to Basingstoke.—She meditates your returning into Hampshire[5] together, & if the Time should accord, it would not be undesirable. She talks of staying only a fortnight, & as that will bring your stay in Berkeley Street to three weeks, I suppose you would not wish to make it longer.—[*p. 3*] Do not let this however retard your coming down, if you had intended a much earlier return.—I suppose whenever you come, Henry would send you in his Carriage a stage or two, where you might be met by John, whose protection you would we imagine think sufficient for the rest of your Journey. He might ride on the Bar, or might even sometimes meet with the accomodation of a sunday-chaise.[6]—James has offered to meet you anywhere, but as that would be to give him trouble without any counterpoise of convenience, as he has no intention of going to London at present on his own account, we suppose that you would rather accept the attentions of John.—We spend our time here as quietly as usual. One long morning visit is what generally occurs, & such a one took place yesterday. We went to Baugherst.—The place is not so pretty as I expected, but perhaps the Season may be against the beauty of Country.

The house seemed to have all the comforts of little Children, dirt & litter. Mr Dyson as usual looked wild, & Mrs Dyson as usual looked big.—Mr Bramston called here the morning before,—et voila tout.— I hope you are as well satisfied with having my coloured Muslin gown as a white one. [*p. 4*] Everybody sends their Love—& I am sincerely Yours,

JA.

Miss Austen
24, Upper Berkeley Street
Portman Square
London.

[*Letters missing here*]

35. To Cassandra Austen

Tuesday 5–Wednesday 6 May 1801

Paragon—Tuesday May 5th

My dear Cassandra

I have the pleasure of writing from my *own* room up two pair of stairs, with everything very comfortable about me. Our Journey here was perfectly free from accident or Event; we changed Horses at the end of every stage, & paid at almost every Turnpike;—we had charming weather, hardly any Dust, & were exceedingly agreable, as we did not speak above once in three miles.—Between Luggershall & Everley we made our grand Meal, and then with admiring astonishment perceived in what a magnificent manner¹ our support had been provided for—;—We could not with the utmost exertion consume above the twentieth part of the beef.—The cucumber will I beleive be a very acceptable present, as my Uncle talks of having enquired the price of one lately, when he was told a shilling.—We had a very neat chaise from Devizes; it looked almost as well as a Gentleman's, at least as a very shabby Gentleman's—; inspite of this advantage however We were above three hours coming from thence to Paragon, & it was half after seven by *Your* Clocks before we entered the house. [*p. 2*] Frank, whose black head was in waiting in the Hall window, received us very kindly;

and his Master & Mistress did not shew less cordiality.—They both look very well, tho' my Aunt has a violent cough. We drank tea as soon as we arrived, & so ends the account of our Journey, which my Mother bore without any fatigue.—How do you do to day?—I hope you improve in sleeping—I think you must, because *I* fall off;—I have been awake ever since 5 & sooner, I fancy I had too much cloathes over my stomach;[2] I thought I *should* by the feel of them before I went to bed, but I had not courage to alter them.—I am warmer here without any fire than I have been lately with an excellent one.—Well—& so the Good news is confirmed, & Martha triumphs.[3]—My Uncle & Aunt seemed quite surprised that you & my father were not coming sooner. —I have given the Soap & the Basket;—& each have been kindly received.—*One* thing only among all our Concerns has not arrived in safety;—when I got into the Chaise at Devizes I discovered that your Drawing Ruler was broke in two;—it is just at the Top where the crosspeice is fastened on.—I beg pardon.—There is to be only one more Ball;—next monday is the day.—The Chamberlaynes are still here; I begin to think better of M^rs C-, and upon recollection beleive she has rather a long chin than otherwise, as she remembers us in Gloucestershire[4] when we were very charming young Women.—[*p. 3*] The first veiw of Bath in fine weather does not answer my expectations; I think I see more distinctly thro' Rain.—The Sun was got behind everything, and the appearance of the place from the top of Kingsdown, was all vapour, shadow, smoke & confusion.—I fancy we are to have a House in Seymour S^t or thereabouts. My Uncle & Aunt both like the situation—. I was glad to hear the former talk of all the Houses in New King S^t as too small;—it was my own idea of them.—I had not been two minutes in the Dining room before he[5] questioned me with all his accustomary[6] eager interest about Frank & Charles, their veiws & intentions.—I did my best to give information.—I am not without hopes of tempting Mrs Lloyd to settle in Bath;—Meat is only 8^d per pound, butter 12^d & cheese 9½^d.[7] You must carefully conceal from her however the exorbitant price of Fish;—a salmon has been sold at 2^s: 9^d p^r pound the whole fish.—The Duchess of York's removal is expected to make that article more reasonable—& till it really appears so, say nothing about salmon.—

Tuesday Night.—When my Uncle went to take his second glass of water, I walked with him, & in our morning's circuit we looked at two Houses in Green Park Buildings, one of which pleased me very well.— We walked all over it except into the Garrets;—the dining-room is of a comfortable size, just as large as you like to fancy it, the 2^d room about 14 ft. square;—The apartment over the Drawing-room pleased me particularly, because it is divided into two, the smaller one a very nice sized Dressing-room, which upon occasion might admit a bed. The aspect is South-East.—The only doubt is about the Dampness of the Offices, of which there were symptoms.—

[*p. 4*] Wednesday.—Mrs Mussell has got my Gown, & I will endeavour to explain what her intentions are.—It is to be a round Gown, with a Jacket, & a Frock front, like Cath: Bigg's to open at the side.— The Jacket is all in one with the body, & comes as far as the pocketholes;—about half a quarter of a yard deep I suppose all the way round, cut off straight at the corners, with a broad hem.—No fullness appears either in the Body or the flap;—the back is quite plain, in this form;—⊓—and the sides equally so.—The front is sloped round to the bosom & drawn in—& there is to be a frill of the same to put on occasionally when all one's handkercheifs are dirty—which frill *must* fall back.—She is to put two breadths & a half in the tail, & no Gores;— Gores not being so much worn as they were;—there is nothing new in the sleeves,—they are to be plain, with a fullness of the same falling down & gathered up underneath, just like some of Marthas—or perhaps a little longer.—Low in the back behind, & a belt of the same.— I can think of nothing more—tho' I am afraid of not being particular enough.—My Mother has ordered a new Bonnet, & so have I;—both white chip, trimmed with white ribbon.—I find my straw bonnet looking very much like other peoples & quite as smart.—Bonnets of Cambric Muslin [*end of p. 4, continued upside down at top of p. 1*] on the plan of Ly Bridges' are a good deal worn, & some of them are very pretty; but I shall defer one of that sort till your arrival.—Bath is getting so very empty that I am not afraid of doing too little.—Black gauze Cloaks are worn as much as anything.—I shall write again in a day or two.— Best Love.

Yrs Ever JA.

[*Postscript below address panel*]

We have had Mrs Lillingstone & the Chamberlaynes to call on us.— My Mother was very much struck with the odd looks of the two latter; *I* have only seen *her*. Mrs Busby drinks tea & plays at Cribbage here tomorrow; & on friday I beleive we go to the Chamberlaynes.—Last night we walked by the Canal.

Miss Austen
Mrs Lloyd's
Up Hurstbourne
Andover

[*Possibly a letter missing here*]

36. *To Cassandra Austen*

Tuesday 12–Wednesday 13 May 1801

Paragon Tuesday May 12th.

My dear Cassandra

My Mother has heard from Mary[1] & I have heard from Frank; we
therefore know something now of our concerns in distant quarters, &
You I hope by some means or other are equally instructed, for I do not
feel inclined to transcribe the letter of either.—You know from Elizabeth I dare say that my father & Frank, deferring their visit to Kippington
on account of Mr M. Austen's absence are to be at Godmersham to day;
& James I dare say has been over to Ibthrop by this time to enquire
particularly after Mrs Lloyd's health, & forestall whatever intelligence
of the Sale I might attempt to give.—sixty one Guineas & a half for the
three Cows gives one some support under the blow of only Eleven
Guineas for the Tables.—Eight for my Pianoforte, is about what I
really expected to get; I am more anxious to know the amount of my
books, especially as they are said to have sold well.—

My Adventures since I wrote last, have not been very numerous; but
such as they are, they are much at your service.—We met not a creature at Mrs Lillingstone's, & yet were not so very stupid [*p. 2*] as I
expected, which I attribute to my wearing my new bonnet & being in
good looks.—On sunday we went to Church twice, & after evening
service walked a little in the Crescent fields, but found it too cold to stay
long. Yesterday morning we looked into a House in Seymour S^t which
there is reason to suppose will soon be empty, and as we are assured
from many quarters that no inconvenience from the river is felt in those
Buildings, we are at liberty to fix in them if we can;—but this house
was not inviting;—the largest room downstairs, was not much more
than fourteen feet square, with a western aspect.—In the evening I
hope you honoured my Toilette & Ball with a thought; I dressed myself

as well as I could, & had all my finery much admired at home. By nine o'clock my Uncle, Aunt & I entered the rooms & linked Miss Winstone on to us.—Before tea, it was rather a dull affair; but then the beforetea did not last long, for there was only one dance, danced by four couple.— Think of four couple, surrounded by about an hundred people, dancing in the upper rooms at Bath!—After tea we *cheered up*; the breaking up of private parties sent some scores more to the Ball, & tho' it was shockingly & inhumanly thin for this place, there were people enough I suppose to have made five or six very pretty Basingstoke assemblies.— I then got Mr Evelyn to talk to, & Miss Twisleton to look at; and I am proud to say that I have a very good [*p. 3*] eye at an Adultress, for tho' repeatedly assured that another in the same party was the *She*, I fixed upon the right one from the first.—A resemblance to Mrs Leigh was my guide. She is not so pretty as I expected; her face has the same defect of baldness as her sister's, & her features not so handsome;—she was highly rouged, & looked rather quietly & contentedly silly than any-thing else.—Mrs Badcock & two young Women were of the same party, except when Mrs Badcock thought herself obliged to leave them, to run round the room after her drunken Husband.—His avoidance, & her pursuit, with the probable intoxication of both, was an amusing scene.— The Evelyns returned our visit on saturday;—we were very happy to meet, & all that;—they are going tomorrow into Gloucestershire, to the Dolphins for ten days.—Our acquaintance Mr Woodward is just married to a Miss Rowe, a young lady rich in money & music.—I thank you for your Sunday's letter, it is very long & very agreable—. I fancy you know many more particulars of our Sale than we do—; we have heard the price of nothing but the Cows, Bacon, Hay, Hops, Tables, & my father's Chest of Drawers & Study Table.—Mary is more minute in her account of their own Gains than in ours—probably being better informed in them.—I will attend to Mrs Lloyd's commission—& to her abhorrence of Musk when I write again.—I have bestowed three calls of enquiry on the Mapletons, & I fancy very beneficial ones to Marianne, as I am always told that she is better. I have not seen any of them.— Her complaint is a billious fever.—I like my dark gown very much indeed, colour, make, & everything.—I mean to have my new white one made up now, in case we should go to the rooms again next monday, which is to be really the last time. [*p. 4*] *Wednesday*. Another stupid party last night; perhaps if larger they might be less intolerable, but here there were only just enough to make one card table, with six people to look over, & talk nonsense to each other. Ly Fust, Mrs Busby & a M^rs

Owen sat down with my Uncle to Whist within five minutes after the three old *Toughs* came in, & there they sat with only the exchange of Adm: Stanhope for my Uncle till their chairs were announced.—I cannot anyhow continue to find people agreable;—I respect Mrs Chamberlayne for doing her hair well, but cannot feel a more tender sentiment.—Miss Langley is like any other short girl with a broad nose & wide mouth, fashionable dress, & exposed bosom.—Adm: Stanhope is a gentlemanlike Man, but then his legs are too short, & his tail too long.—Mrs Stanhope could not come; I fancy she had a private appointment with Mr Chamberlayne, whom I wished to see more than all the rest.—My Uncle has quite got the better of his lameness, or at least his walking with a stick is the only remains of it.—He & I are soon to take the long-plann'd walk to the Cassoon²—& on friday we are all to accompany Mrs Chamberlayne & Miss Langley to Weston. My Mother had a letter yesterday from my father; it seems as if the W. Kent scheme³ were entirely given up.—He talks of spending a [*end of p. 4, continued below address panel*] fortnight at Godmersham & then returning to Town.—

Y^rs Ever JA.

[Postscript upside down at top of p. 1]

Excepting a slight cold, my Mother is very well; she has been quite free from feverish or billious complaints since her arrival here.

Miss Austen
Mrs Lloyd's
Hurstbourn Tarrant
Andover

[Letters missing here]

37. *To Cassandra Austen*

Thursday 21–Friday 22 May 1801

Paragon Thursday May 21st

My dear Cassandra

To make long sentences upon unpleasant subjects is very odious, & I shall therefore get rid of the one now uppermost in my thoughts as soon as possible.—Our veiws on G.P. Buildings seem all at an end; the observation of the damps still remaining in the offices of an house which has been only vacated a week, with reports of discontented families & putrid fevers, has given the coup de grace.—We have now nothing in veiw.—When you arrive, we will at least have the pleasure of examining some of these putrifying Houses again;—they are so very desirable in size & situation, that there is some satisfaction in spending ten minutes within them.—I will now answer the enquiries in your last letter. I cannot learn any other explanation of the coolness between my Aunt & Miss Bond than that the latter felt herself slighted by the former's leaving Bath last summer without calling to see her before she went.— It seems the oddest kind of quarrel in the World; they never visit, but I beleive they speak very civilly if they meet; My Uncle & Miss Bond certainly do. The 4 Boxes of Lozenges at 1^s–1^d–½ per box, amount as I was told to 4^s–6^d, and as the sum was so trifling, I thought it better to pay at once than contest the matter. I have just heard from Frank; my father's plans are now fixed; you will see him at Kintbury on friday, and unless inconvenient to you We are to see you both here on Monday the 1st of June.—Frank has an invitation to Milgate [*p. 2*] which I beleive he means to accept.—Our party at Ly Fust's was made up of the same set of people that you have already heard of; the Winstones, Mrs Chamberlayne, Mrs Busby, Mrs Franklyn & Mrs Maria Somerville; yet I think it was not quite so stupid as the two preceding parties here.—The friendship between Mrs Chamberlayne & me which you predicted has already taken place, for we shake hands whenever we meet. Our grand walk to Weston[1] was again fixed for Yesterday, & was accomplished in a very striking manner; Every one of the party declined it under some pretence or other except our two selves, & we had therefore a tete a tete; but *that* we should equally have had after the first two yards, had half the Inhabitants of Bath set off with us.—It would have amused you to see our progress;—we went up by Sion Hill, & returned across the fields;—in climbing a hill Mrs Chamberlayne is very capital; I could with difficulty keep pace with her—yet would not flinch for the World.— on plain ground I was quite her equal—and so we posted away under a fine hot sun, *She* without any parasol or any shade to her hat, stopping for nothing, & crossing the Church Yard at Weston with as much expedition as if we were afraid of being buried alive.—After seeing what she is equal to, I cannot help feeling a regard for her.—As to Agreableness, she is much like other people.—Yesterday Evening we had a short call from two of the Miss Arnolds, who came from Chippenham on Business; they are very civil, and not too genteel, and upon hearing that we wanted a House recommended one at Chippenham.—This morning we have been[2] visitted again by M^rs & Miss Holder; they wanted us to fix an evening for drinking tea with them, but my Mother's still remaining cold allows her to decline everything of the kind.—As *I* had a [*p. 3*] separate invitation however, I beleive I shall go some afternoon. It is the fashion to think them both very detestable, but they are so civil, & their gowns look so white & so nice (which by the bye my Aunt thinks an absurd pretension in this place) that I cannot utterly abhor them, especially as Miss Holder owns that she has no taste for Music.— After they left us, I went with my Mother to help look at some houses in New King Street, towards which she felt some kind of inclination— but their size has now satisfied her;—they were smaller than I expected to find them. One in particular out of the two, was quite monstrously little;—the best of the sittingrooms not so large as the little parlour at Steventon, and the second room in every floor about capacious enough to admit a very small single bed.—We are to have a tiny party here tonight; I hate tiny parties—they force one into constant exertion.— Miss Edwards & her father, Mrs Busby & her nephew Mr Maitland, & Mrs Lillingstone are to be the whole;—and I am prevented from setting my black cap at Mr Maitland by his having a wife & ten Children.—My Aunt has a very bad cough; do not forget to have heard about *that* when you come, & I think she is deafer than ever. My Mother's cold disordered her for some days, but she seems now very well;—her resolution as to remaining here, begins to give way a little; she will not like being left behind & will be glad to compound Matters with her enraged family.—You will be sorry to hear that Marianne Mapleton's disorder has ended fatally; she was beleived out of danger on Sunday, but a sudden relapse carried her off the next day.—So affectionate a family must suffer severely; & many a girl on early death has been praised into an Angel I beleive, on slighter pretensions to Beauty, Sense [*p. 4*] & Merit than Marianne.—Mr Bent seems *bent* upon being very detestable, for he values the books at only 70£. The whole World is in a conspiracy to enrich one part of our family at the expence of another.—Ten shillings for Dodsley's Poems[3] however please me to the quick, & I do not care how often I sell them for as much. When Mrs Bramston has read them through I will sell them again.—I suppose You can hear nothing of your Magnesia.—

Friday. You have a nice day[4] for your Journey in whatever way it is to be performed,—whether in the Debary's Coach or on your own twenty toes.—When you have made Martha's bonnet you must make her a cloak of the same sort of materials; they are very much worn here, in different forms—many of them just like her black silk spencer, with a trimming round the armholes instead of Sleeves;—some are long before, & some long all round like C. Bigg's.—Our party last night supplied me with no new ideas for my Letter—. Y^rs Ever JA.

[Postscript below address panel]

The Pickfords are in Bath & have called here.—*She* is the most elegant looking Woman I have seen since I left Martha—*He* is as raffish in his appearance as I would wish every Disciple of Godwin⁵ to be.—We drink tea tonight with Mrs Busby.—I scandalized her Nephew cruelly; he has but three Children instead of Ten.—

Best Love to everybody.

Miss Austen
The Rev:^d F. C. Fowle's
Kintbury
Newbury

[Letter of ?23 May missing]

38. *To Cassandra Austen*

Tuesday 26 – Wednesday 27 May 1801

Paragon—Tuesday May 26th

My dear Cassandra

For your letter from Kintbury & for all the compliments on my writing which it contained, I now return you my best thanks.—I am very glad that Martha goes to Chilton; a very essential temporary comfort her presence must afford to Mrs Craven, and I hope she will endeavour to make it a lasting one by exerting those kind offices in favour of the Young Man, from which you were both with-held in the case of the Harrison family¹ by the mistaken tenderness of one part of ours.—The Endymion came into Portsmouth on Sunday, & I have sent Charles a short letter by this day's post.—My adventures since I wrote to you three days ago have been such as the time would easily contain; I walked yesterday morning with Mrs Chamberlayne to Lyncombe & Widcombe, and in the evening I drank tea with the Holders.—Mrs Chamberlayne's pace was not quite so magnificent on this second trial as in the first; it was nothing more than I could keep up with, without effort; & for many, many Yards together on a raised narrow footpath I led the way.—The Walk was very beautiful [*p. 2*] as my companion agreed, whenever I made the observation—And so ends our friendship, for the Chamberlaynes leave Bath in a day or two.—Prepare likewise for the loss of Lady Fust, as you will lose before you find her.—My evening visit was by no means disagreable. Mrs Lillingston came to engage Mrs Holder's conversation, & Miss Holder & I adjourned after tea into the inner Drawingroom to look over Prints & talk pathetically. She is very unreserved & very fond of talking of her deceased brother & Sister, whose memories she cherishes with an Enthusiasm which tho' perhaps a little affected, is not unpleasing.—She has an idea of your being remarkably lively; therefore get ready the proper selection of adverbs, & due scraps of Italian & French.—I must now pause to make some observation on Mrs Heathcote's having got a little Boy;—I wish her well to wear it out—& shall proceed:—Frank writes me word that he *is* to be in London tomorrow; some money Negociation from which he hopes to derive advantage, hastens him from Kent, & will detain him a few days behind my father in Town.—I have seen the Miss Mapletons this morning; Marianne was buried yesterday, and I called without ex-pecting to be let in, to enquire after them all.—[*p. 3*] On the servant's invitation however I sent in my name, & Jane & Christiana who were walking in the Garden came to me immediately, and I sat with them about ten minutes.—They looked pale & dejected, but were more com-posed than I had thought probable.—When I mentioned your coming here on Monday, they said that they should be very glad to see you.— We drink tea to night with Mrs Lysons;—Now this, says my Master[2] will be mighty dull.—On friday we are to have another party, & a sett of new people to you.—The Bradshaws & Greaves's, all belonging to one another, and I hope the Pickfords.—Mrs Evelyn called very civilly on sunday, to tell us that Mr Evelyn had seen Mr Philips the proprietor of N° 12 G. P. B. and that Mr Philips was very willing to raise the kitchen floor;—but all this I fear is fruitless—tho' the water may be kept out of sight,[3] it cannot be sent away, nor the ill effects of its' nearness be excluded.—I have nothing more to say on the subject of Houses;—except that we were mistaken as to the aspect of the one in Seymour Street, which instead of being due West is Northwest.—I assure you inspite of what I might chuse to insinuate in a former letter, that I have seen very little of Mr Evelyn since my coming here; I met him this morning for only the 4th time, & as to my anecdote about Sidney Gardens, I made the [*p. 4*] most of the Story because it came in

to advantage, but in fact he only asked me whether I were to be at Sidney Gardens in the evening or not.—There is now something like an engagement between us & the Phaeton, which to confess my frailty I have a great desire to go out in;—whether it will come to anything must remain with him.—I really beleive he is very harmless; people do not seem afraid of him here, and he gets Groundsel for his birds & all that.—My Aunt will never be easy till she visits them;—she has been repeatedly trying to fancy a necessity for it now on our accounts, but she meets with no encouragement.—She ought to be particularly scrupulous in such matters, & she says so herself—but nevertheless———
—Well—I am come home from Mrs Lysons as yellow as I went;—You cannot like your yellow gown half so well as I do, nor a quarter neither. Mr Rice & Lucy are to be married, one on the 9th & the other on the 10th of July.—Y^rs affec:^ly JA.

[Continued on p. 1, upside down between the lines]

Wednesday.—I am just returned from my Airing in the very bewitching Phaeton & four, for which I was prepared by a note from Mr E. soon after breakfast: We went to the top of Kingsdown—& had a very pleasant drive: One pleasure succeeds another rapidly—On my return I found your letter & a letter from Charles on the table. The contents of yours I suppose I need not repeat to you; to thank you for it will be enough.—I give Charles great credit for remembering my Uncle's direction, & he seems rather surprised at it himself.—He has received 30£ for his share of the privateer & expects 10£ more—but of what avail is it to take prizes if he lays out the produce in presents to his Sisters. He has been buying Gold chains & Topaze Crosses[4] for us;—he must be well scolded.—The Endymion has already received orders for taking Troops to Egypt—which I should not like at all if I did not trust to Charles' being removed from her somehow or other before she sails. He knows nothing of his own destination he says,— but desires me to write directly as the Endymion will probably sail in 3 or 4 days.—He will receive my yesterday's letter to day, and I shall write again by this post to thank & reproach him.—We shall be unbearably fine.—I have made an engagement for you for Thursday the 4th of June; if my Mother & Aunt should not go to the fireworks,[5] which I dare say they will not, I have promised to join Mr Evelyn & Miss Wood—Miss Wood has lived with them you know ever "since my Son died—"

[Postscript below address panel]

I will engage Mrs Mussell as you desire. She made my dark gown very well & may therefore be trusted I hope with Yours—but she does not always succeed with lighter Colours.—My white one I was obliged to alter a good deal.—Unless anything particular occurs, I shall not write again.

Miss Austen
The Rev:^d F. C. Fowle's
Kintbury
Newbury

<hr>

[*Letter missing here*]

39. *To Cassandra Austen*

Friday 14 September 1804
Lyme, Friday Sept. 14.

My dear Cassandra

I take the first sheet of this fine striped paper[1] to thank you for your letter from Weymouth, & express my hopes of your being at Ibthrop before this time. I expect to hear that you reached it yesterday Evening, being able to get as far as Blandford on wednesday.—Your account of Weymouth contains nothing which strikes me so forcibly as there being no Ice in the Town; for every other vexation I was in some measure prepared; & particularly for your disappointment in not seeing the Royal Family[2] go on board on tuesday, having already[3] heard from Mr Crawford that he had seen you in the very act of being too late. But for there being no Ice, what could prepare me!—Weymouth is altogether a shocking place I perceive, without recommendation of any kind, & worthy only of being frequented by the inhabitants of Gloucester.[4]—I am really very glad that we did not go there, & that Henry & Eliza saw nothing in it to make them feel differently.—You found my letter at Andover I hope yesterday, & have now for many hours been satisfied that your kind anxiety on my behalf was as much thrown away as kind anxiety usually is. I continue quite well, in proof of which I have bathed again this morning. It was absolutely necessary that I should have the little fever & indisposition, which I had;[5]—it has been all the fashion this week in Lyme. Miss Anna Cove was confined for a day or two, & her Mother thinks she was saved only by a timely Emetic (prescribed by Dr Robinson) from a serious illness;—and Miss Bonham has been [*p. 2*] under Mr Carpenter's care for several days, with a sort of nervous fever, and tho' she is now well enough to walk abroad, she is still very tall & does not come to the Rooms.—We all of us,[6] attended them, both on Wednesday Evening, & *last Evening*, I suppose I must say, or Martha will think Mr Peter Debary slighted.—My Mother had her pool of Commerce each night & divided the first with Le Chevalier,[7] who was lucky enough to divide the other with somebody else.—I hope he will always win enough to empower him to treat himself with so great an indulgence as cards must be to him. He enquired particularly after you, not being aware of your departure.—We are quite settled in our Lodgings by this time, as you may suppose, & everything goes on in the usual order. The servants behave very well & make no difficulties, tho' nothing certainly can exceed the inconvenience of the Offices, except the general Dirtiness of the House & furniture, & all it's Inhabitants.— Hitherto the weather has been just what we could wish;—the continu- ance of the dry Season is very necessary to our comfort.—I endeavour as far as I can to supply your place, & be useful & keep things in order; I detect dirt in the Water-decanter as fast as I can, and give the Cook physic, which she throws off her Stomach. I forget whether she used to do this, under your administration.—James is the delight of our lives; he is quite an uncle Toby's annuity[8] to us.—My Mother's shoes were never so well blacked before, & our plate never looked so clean.—He waits extremely well, is attentive, handy, quick, & quiet, and in short has a great many more than all the cardinal virtues, (for the cardinal virtues in themselves have been so often possessed that they are no longer worth having)—& amongst the rest, that of wishing to go to Bath, as I understand from Jenny.—He has the laudable thirst I fancy[9] for Travelling, which in poor James Selby[10] was so much reprobated; & part [*p. 3*] of his disappointment in not going with his Master, arose from his wish of seeing London.—My Mother is at this moment read- ing a letter from my Aunt. Yours to Miss Irvine, of which she had had the perusal—(which by the bye, in your place I should not like) has thrown them into a quandary about Charles & his prospects. The case is, that my Mother had previously told my Aunt, without restriction, that a sloop (which my Aunt calls a Frigate) was reserved in the East for Charles; whereas you had replied to Miss Irvine's enquiries on the subject with less explicitness & more caution.—Never mind—let them puzzle on together—As Charles will equally go to the E. Indies, my Uncle cannot be really uneasy, & my Aunt may do what she likes with her frigates.—She talks a great deal of the violent heat of the Weather—

We know nothing of it here.—My Uncle has been suffering a good deal lately; they mean however to go to Scarlets about this time, unless prevented by bad accounts of Cook.—The Coles have got their infamous plate[11] upon our door.—I dare say *that* makes a great part of the massy plate so much talked of.—The Irvines' house is nearly completed—I beleive they are to get into it on tuesday;—My Aunt owns it to have a comfortable appearance, & only "hopes the kitchen may not be damp".—I have not heard from Charles yet, which rather surprises me;—some ingenious addition of his own to the proper direction perhaps prevents my receiving his letter. I have written to Buller;—& I have written to M[r] Pyne, on the subject of the broken Lid;—it was valued by Anning here, we were told, at five shillings, & as that appeared to us beyond the value of all the Furniture in the room[12] together, We have referred ourselves to the Owner. The Ball last night was pleasant, but not full for Thursday. My Father staid very contentedly till half past nine—we went a little after eight—& then walked home with James & a Lanthorn, tho' I beleive the Lanthorn was not lit, as the Moon was up. But this Lanthorn may sometimes be a great convenience to him.—My Mother & I staid about an hour later. Nobody asked me the two first dances—the two next I danced with M[r] Crawford—& had I chosen to stay longer might have danced with M[r] Granville, [*p. 4*] M[rs] Granville's son—whom my dear friend Miss Armstrong offered to introduce to me—or with a new, odd looking Man who had been eyeing me for some time, & at last without any introduction asked me if I meant to dance again.—I think he must be Irish by his ease, & because I imagine him to belong to the Hon[ble] Barnwalls, who are the son & son's wife of an Irish Viscount—bold, queerlooking people, just fit to be Quality at Lyme.—M[rs] Feaver & the Schuylers went away, I do not know where, last tuesday, for some days; & when they return, the Schuylers I understand are to remain here a very little while longer.—I called yesterday morning—(ought it not in strict propriety be termed Yester-Morning?) on Miss Armstrong, & was introduced to her father & Mother. Like other young Ladies she is considerably genteeler then her Parents; M[rs] Armstrong sat darning a p[r] of Stockings the whole of my visit—. But I do not mention this at home, lest a warning should act as an example.—We afterwards walked together for an hour on the Cobb; she is very conversable in a common way; I do not perceive Wit or Genius—but she has Sense & some degree of Taste, & her manners are very engaging. She seems to like people rather too easily—she thought the Downes pleasant &c &c. I have seen nothing of M^r & Mrs Mawhood. My Aunt mentions Mrs Holder's being returned from Cheltenham; so, her summer ends before theirs begins.—Hooper was heard of well at the Madeiras.—Eliza[13] would envy him.—[*end of p. 4, continued upside down at top of p. 1*] I need not say that we are particularly anxious for your next Letter, to know how you find Mrs Lloyd & Martha.—Say Everything kind for us to the latter—The former I fear must be beyond any remembrance of, or from, the Absent.—Y^rs affec:^ly

JA.

[*Postscript below address panel*] I hope Martha thinks you looking better than when she saw you in Bath.—Jenny has fasten'd up my hair to day in the same manner that she used to do up Miss Lloyd's, which makes us both [very] happy.—

[*Continued by crossing on p. 1*]

Friday Eveng.—

The Bathing was so delightful this morning & Molly so pressing with me to enjoy myself that I believe I staid in rather too long, as since the middle of the day I have felt unreasonably tired. I shall be more careful another time, & shall not bathe tomorrow, as I had before intended.—Jenny & James are walked to Charmouth this afternoon;— I am glad to have such an amusement for him—as I am very anxious for his being at once quiet & happy.—He can read, & I must get him some books. Unfortunately he has read the 1st vol. of Robinson Crusoe.[14] We have the Pinckards Newspaper however, which I shall take care to lend him.—

Miss Austen
Mrs Lloyd's
Up. Hurstbourn
Andover

[*?Letters missing here*]

---

40. *To Francis Austen*

Monday 21 January 1805

Green Park B^gs Monday Jan^ry 21st

My dearest Frank

I have melancholy news to relate, & sincerely feel for your feelings under the shock of it.—I wish I could better prepare You for it.—But having said so much, Your mind will already forestall the sort of Event which I have to communicate.—Our dear Father has closed his virtuous & happy life, in a death almost as free from suffering as his Children could have wished. He was taken ill on Saturday morning, exactly in the same way as heretofore, an oppression in the head with fever, violent tremulousness, & the greatest degree of Feebleness. The same remedy of Cupping, which had before been so successful, was immediately applied to—but without such happy effects. [*p. 2*] The attack was more violent, & at first he seemed scarcely at all releived by the Operation.—Towards the Evening however he got better, had a tolerable night, & yesterday morning was so greatly amended as to get up[1] & join us at breakfast as usual, walk about with only the help of a stick, & every symptom was then so favourable that when Bowen saw him at one, he felt sure of his doing perfectly well.—But as the day advanced, all these comfortable appearances gradually changed; the fever grew stronger than ever, & when Bowen saw him at ten at night, he pronounc'd his situation to be most alarming.—At nine this morning he came again—& by his desire a Physician was called;—Dr Gibbs—But it was then absolutely a lost case—. Dr Gibbs said that nothing but a Miracle could save him, and about twenty minutes after Ten he drew his [*p. 3*] last gasp.—Heavy as is the blow, we can already feel that a thousand comforts remain to us to soften it. Next to that of the consciousness of his worth & constant preparation for another World, is the remembrance of his having suffered, comparatively speaking, nothing.—Being quite insensible of his own state, he was spared all the pain of separation, & he went off almost in his Sleep.—My Mother bears the Shock as well as possible; she was quite prepared for it, & feels all the blessing of his being spared a long Illness. My Uncle & Aunt have been with us, & shew us every imaginable kindness. And tomorrow we shall I dare say have the comfort of James's presence, as an Express has been sent to him.—We write also of course to Godmersham & Brompton.[2] Adeiu my dearest Frank. The loss of such a Parent must be felt, or we should be Brutes—. I wish I could have given you better preparation—but it has been impossible.—Yours Ever affec^ly

JA.

Capt. Austen
HMS Leopard
Dungeness
New Romney

41. *To Francis Austen*

Tuesday 22 January 1805

Green Park B^{gs} Tuesday Even^g, Jan^{ry} 22^d.

My dearest Frank

I wrote to you yesterday; but your letter to Cassandra this morning, by which we learn the probability of your being by this time at Portsmouth, obliges me to write to you again, having unfortunately a communication as necessary as painful to make to you.—Your affectionate heart will be greatly wounded, & I wish the shock could have been lessen'd by a better preparation;—but the Event has been sudden, & so must be the information of it. We have lost an Excellent Father.—An Illness of only eight & forty hours carried him off yesterday morning between ten & eleven. He was seized on saturday with a return of the feverish complaint, which he had been subject to for the three last years; evidently a more violent attack from the first, as the applications which had before produced almost immediate releif, seemed for some time to afford him scarcely any.—On Sunday however he [*p. 2*] was much better, so much so as to make Bowen quite easy, & give us every hope of his being well again in a few days.—But these hopes gradually gave way as the day advanced, & when Bowen saw him at ten that night he was greatly alarmed.—A Physician was called in yesterday morning, but he was at that time past all possibility of cure—& Dr Gibbs & Mr Bowen had scarcely left his room before he sunk into a Sleep from which he never woke.—Everything I trust & beleive was done for him that was possible!—It has been very sudden!—within twenty four hours of his death he was walking with only the help of a stick, was even reading!—We had however some hours of preparation, & when we understood[1] his recovery to be hopeless, most fervently did we pray for the speedy release which ensued. To have seen him[2] languishing long, struggling for Hours, would have been dreadful!—& thank God! we were all spared from it. Except the restlessness & confusion of high Fever, he did not suffer—[*p. 3*] & he was mercifully spared from knowing that he was about to quit the Objects so beloved, so fondly cherished as his wife & Children ever were.—His tenderness as a Father, who can do justice to?—My Mother is tolerably well; she bears up with great fortitude, but I fear her health must suffer under such a shock.—An express was sent for James, & he arrived here this morning before eight o'clock.—The Funeral is to be on Saturday, at Walcot Church.—

The Serenity of the Corpse is most delightful!—It preserves the sweet, benevolent smile which always distinguished him.—They kindly press my Mother to remove to Steventon as soon as it is all over, but I do not beleive she will leave Bath at present. We must have this house for three months longer, & here we shall probably stay till the end of that time.—
    We all unite in Love, & I am affec:^{ly} Yours

JA.

Capt. Austen
HMS Leopard
Portsmouth

Jan^{ry} 23^d

42. *To Francis Austen*

Tuesday 29 January 1805

Green Park B^{gs} Tuesday Jan^{ry} 29.

My dearest Frank
    My Mother has found among our dear Father's little personal property, a small astronomical Instrument which she hopes you will accept for his sake. It is I beleive a Compass & Sun-dial, & is in a Black Chagreen Case. Would You have it sent to you now, & with what direction?—There is also a pair of Scissors for you.—We hope these are articles that may be useful to you, but we are sure they will be valuable.—I have not time for more.

Yours very affec^{ly}

JA.

Capt. Austen
HMS Leopard
Portsmouth

[*Letter missing here*]

43. *To Cassandra Austen*

Monday 8–Thursday 11 April 1805

25 Gay St Monday

My dear Cassandra

Here is a day for you! Did Bath or Ibthrop ever see a finer 8th of April?—It is March & April together, the glare of one & the warmth of the other. We do nothing but walk about; as far as your means will admit I hope you profit by such weather[1] too. I dare say You are already the better for change of place. We were out again last night; Miss Irvine invited us, when I met her in the Crescent, to drink tea with them, but I rather declined it, having no idea that my Mother would be disposed for another Evening visit there so soon; but when I gave her the message I found her very well inclined to go;—and accordingly on leaving Chapel we walked to Lansdown.—Richard Chamberlayne & a young Ripley from Mr Morgan's school, were there; & our visit did very well.— This morning we have been to see Miss Chamberlayne look hot on horseback.—Seven years & four months ago we went to the same Ridinghouse to see Miss Lefroy's[2] performance!—What a different set are we now moving in! But seven years I suppose are enough to change every pore of one's skin, & every feeling of one's mind.—We did not walk long in the Crescent yesterday, it was hot & not crouded enough; so we went into the field, & passed close by Stephen Terry & Miss Seymer again.—I have not yet seen her face, but neither her dress nor air have anything of the Dash or Stilishness which the Browns talked of; quite the contrary indeed, her dress is not even smart, & her appearance very quiet. Miss Irvine says she is never speaking a word. Poor Wretch, I am afraid she is *en Penitence.*—Here has been that excellent Mrs Coulthard calling, while my Mother was out & I was beleived to be so; I always respected her as a good-hearted, friendly woman;—And the Brownes have been here; I find their affidavits on the Table.—The Ambuscade reached Gibraltar on the 9th of March & found all well; so say the papers.—We have had no letters from anybody,—but I expect to hear from Edward tomorrow, & from you soon afterwards.—How happy they are at Godmersham now!—I shall be very glad of [*p. 2*] a letter from Ibthrop, that I may know how you all are there, & particularly yourself. This is nice weather for Mrs J. Austen's going to Speen, & I hope she will have a pleasant visit there. I expect a prodigious account of the Christening dinner; perhaps it brought you at last into the company of Miss Dundas again.—

Tuesday. I received your letter last night, & wish it may be soon followed by another to say that all is over; but I cannot help thinking that Nature will struggle again & produce a revival. Poor woman! May her end[3] be peaceful & easy, as the Exit we have witnessed! And I dare say it will. If there is no revival, suffering must be all over; even the consciousness of Existence I suppose was gone when you wrote. The Nonsense I have been writing in this & in my last letter, seems out of place at such a time; but I will not mind it, it will do you no harm, & nobody else will be attacked by it.—I am heartily glad that you can speak so comfortably of your own health & looks, tho' I can scarcely comprehend the latter being really approved. Could travelling fifty miles produce such an immediate change?—You were looking so very poorly here; everybody seem'd sensible of it.—Is there a charm in an hack postchaise?—But if there were, M[rs] Craven's carriage might have undone it all.—I am much obliged to you for the time & trouble you have bestowed on Mary's cap, & am glad it pleases her; but it will prove a useless gift at present I suppose.—Will not she leave Ibthrop on her Mother's death?—As a companion You will be all that Martha can be supposed to want; & in that light, under those circumstances your visit will indeed have been well-timed, & your presence & support have the utmost value.—Miss Irvine spent yesterday Evening with us, & we had a very pleasant walk to Twerton. On our return we heard with much surprise that M[r] Buller had called while we were out. He left his address, & I am just returned from seeing him & his wife in their Lodgings, 7 Bath S[t]. His Errand as you may suppose, is health. It had been often recommended to him to try Bath, but his coming now seems to have been chiefly in consequence of his sister Susan's[4] wish that he would put himself under the care of M[r] Bowen.—Having so very lately heard from Colyton & that account so tolerable, I was very much astonished—but Buller has been worse again since he wrote to me.—His Habit has always been billious, but I am afraid it must be too late for these waters to do him any good; for tho' he is altogether in a more comfortable state as to Spirits & appetite than [*p. 3*] when I saw him last, & seems equal to a good deal of quiet walking, his appearance is exactly[5] that of a confirmed Decline.—The Children are not come, so that poor M[rs] Buller is away from all that can constitute enjoyment with her.[6]—I shall be glad to be of any use to her, but she has that sort of quiet composedness of mind which always seems sufficient to itself.—

What honour I come to!—I was interrupted by the arrival of a Lady to enquire the character of Anne, who is returned from Wales & ready for service.—And I hope I have acquitted myself pretty well; but having a very reasonable Lady to deal with, one who only required a *tolerable* temper, my office was not difficult.—Were I going to send a girl to school I would send her to this person; to be rational in anything is great praise, especially in the ignorant class of school mistresses—& she keeps the School in the upper Crescent.[7]—Since I wrote so far, I have walked with my Mother to St James Square & Paragon; neither family at home. I have also been with the Cookes trying to fix Mary for a walk this afternoon, but as she was on the point of taking a *long* walk with some other Lady, there is little chance of her joining us. I should like to know how far they are going; she invited me to go with them [&] when I excused myself as rather tired & mentioned my coming from S^t Ja[mes] Square, she said "that *is* a long walk indeed." They want us to drink tea with them tonight, but I do not know whether my Mother will have nerves for it.—We are engaged tomorrow Evening. What request we are in!—Mrs Chamberlayne expressed to her neice her wish of being intimate enough with us to ask us to drink tea with her in a quiet way— We have therefore offered ourselves & our quietness thro' the same medium.—Our Tea & sugar will last a great while.—I think we are just the kind of people & party to be treated about among our relations;—we cannot be supposed to be very rich.—The Mr Duncans called yesterday with their Sisters, but were not admitted, which rather hurt me. In the Evening we met Mr John, & I am sorry[8] to say that he has got a very bad cold—they have all had bad colds—& he has but just caught his.—Jenny is very glad to hear of your being better, & so is Robert, with whom I left a message to that effect—as my Uncle has been very much in earnest about your recovery.—I assure you, you were looking very ill indeed, & I do not beleive much of your being looking well already. People think you in a very bad way I suppose, & pay you Compliments to keep up your Spirits.

[*p. 4*] *Thursday.* I was not able to go on yesterday, all my Wit & leisure were bestowed on letters to Charles & Henry. To the former I wrote in consequence of my Mother's having seen in the papers that the Urania was waiting at Portsmouth for the Convoy for Halifax;—this is nice, as it is only three weeks ago that you wrote by the Camilla.—The Wallop race[9] seem very fond of Nova Scotia. I wrote to Henry because I had a letter from him, in which he desired to hear from me very soon. —His to me was most affectionate & kind, as well as entertaining;—

there is no merit to him in *that*, he cannot help being amusing.—He expresses himself as greatly pleased with the Screen, & says that he does not know whether he is "most delighted with the idea or the Execution."—Eliza of course goes halves in all this, and there is also just such a message of warm acknowledgement from her respecting the Broche as you would expect.—He mentions having sent one of Miss Gibson's Letters[10] to Frank, by favour of Gen: Tilson, now waiting at Spithead. Would it be possible for us to do something like it, through Mr Turner's means?—I did not know before, that the Expedition[11] were going to Frank.—One thing more Henry mentions which deserves your hearing; he offers to meet us on the Sea-coast if the plan, of which Edward gave him some hint, takes place. Will not this be making the Execution of such a plan, more desirable & delightful than Ever.— He talks of the rambles we took together last Summer with pleasing affection.—

[Upside down at top of p. 1]

Mary Cooke did walk with us on tuesday, & we drank tea in Alfred S^t. But we could not keep our Engagement with Mrs Chamberlayne last night, my Mother having unluckily caught a cold which seems likely to be rather heavy.—Buller has begun the Waters, so that it will soon appear whether they can do anything for him.—

[Continued below address panel]

Mrs Buller goes with us to our Chapel tomorrow;—which I shall put down as "Attention ye First." I hope she will keep an account too.—My Mother's cold is not so bad to day as I expected. [It is che]ifly in her head, & she has not fever enough to affe[ct] her appetite.—C. Fowle has this moment left us. He has taken N° 20, from Michaelmas.—Y^rs Ever, JA.

Miss Austen
Up. Hurstbourn
Andover

April 11th

[Letters missing here]

44. *To Cassandra Austen*

Sunday 21–Tuesday 23 April 1805

Gay S^t, Sunday Evening, April 21st

My dear Cassandra

I am much obliged to you for writing to me again so soon; your letter yesterday was quite an unexpected pleasure. Poor Mrs Stent! it has been her lot to be always in the way; but we must be merciful, for perhaps in time we may come to be Mrs Stents ourselves, unequal to anything & unwelcome to everybody.—We shall be very glad to see you whenever you can get away, but I have no expectation of your coming before the 10th or 11th of May.—Your account of Martha is very comfortable indeed, & now we shall be in no fear of receiving a worse. This day, if she has gone to Church, must have been a trial of her feelings, but I hope it will be the last of any acuteness.—James may not be a Man of Business, but as a "Man of Letters" he is certainly very useful; he affords you a most convenient communication with the Newbury Post.— You were very right in supposing I wore my crape sleeves to the Concert, I had them put in on the occasion; on my head I wore my crape & flowers, but I do not think it looked particularly well.—My Aunt is in a great hurry to pay me for my Cap, but cannot find in her heart to give me good money. "If I have any intention of going to the Grand Sydney-Garden Breakfast, if there is any party I wish to join, Perrot will take out a ticket for me."—Such an offer I shall of course decline; & all the service she will render me therefore, is to put it out of my power to go at all, whatever may occur to make it desirable.—Yesterday was a busy day with me, or at least with my feet & my stockings; I was walking almost all day long; I went to Sydney Gardens soon after one, & did not return till four, & after dinner I walked to Weston.—My morning engagement was with the Cookes, & our party consisted of George & Mary, a M^r & Miss Bendish who had been with us at the Concert, & the youngest Miss Whitby;—not Julia, we have done with her, she is very ill, but Mary; Mary Whitby's turn is actually¹ come to be grown up & have a fine complexion & wear great square muslin shawls. I have not expressly enumerated myself among the party, but there I was, & my Cousin George was very kind & talked sense to me every now & then in the intervals of his more animated fooleries with Miss Bendish, who is very young & rather handsome, [*p. 2*] and whose gracious manners, ready wit, & solid remarks put me somewhat in mind of my old

acquaintance Lucy Lefroy.—There was a monstrous deal of stupid quiz-
zing, & common-place nonsense talked, but scarcely any Wit;—all that
border'd on it, or on Sense came from my Cousin George, whom altogether I like very well.—Mʳ Bendish seems nothing more than a tall
young Man.—I met Mʳ F. Bonham the other day, & almost his first
salutation was "So Miss Austen your Cousin is come."—My Evening
Engagement & walk was with Miss Armstrong, who had called on me
the day before, & gently upbraided me in her turn with change of
manners to her since she had been in Bath, or at least of late. Unlucky
me! that my notice should be of such consequence & my Manners so
bad!—She was so well-disposed, & so reasonable that I soon forgave
her, & made this engagement with her in proof of it.—She is really an
agreable girl, so I think I may like her, & her great want of a companion
at home, which may well make any tolerable acquaintance important to
her, gives her another claim on my attention.²—I shall endeavour as
much as possible to keep my Intimacies in their proper place, & prevent
their clashing.—I have been this morning with Miss Irvine; it is not in
my power to return her evening-visits at present. I must pay her as I
can.—On tuesday we are to have a party. It came into my wise head
that tho' my Mother did not go out of an evening, there was no reason
against her seeing her friends at home, & that it would be as well to get
over the Chamberlaynes visit now, as to delay it. I accordingly invited
them this morning; Mrs C. fixed on tuesday, & I rather think they will
all come; the possibility of it will deter us from asking Mʳ & Mʳˢ L. P.
to meet them.—I asked Miss Irvine, but she declined it, as not feeling
quite stout, & wishing to keep quiet;—but her Mother is to enliven our
circle.—Bickerton has been at home for the Easter Holidays, & returns
tomorrow; he is a very sweet boy, both in manner & countenance. He
seems to have the attentive, affectionate feelings of Fulwar-William—
who by the bye is actually fourteen—what are we to do?—I have never
seen Bickerton without his immediately enquiring whether I had heard
from you—from "Miss Cassandra," was his expression at first.—As
far as I can learn, the Family are all very much pleased with Bath, &
excessively overcome by the heat, or the Cold, or whatever happens to
be the weather.—They go on with their Masters & Mistresses, & are
now to have a Miss; Amelia is to take lessons of Miss Sharpe.—[*p. 3*]
Among so many friends, it will be well if I do not get into a scrape; &
now here is Miss Blachford come. I should have gone distracted if the
Bullers had staid.—The Cookes leave Bath next week I beleive, & my
Cousin goes earlier.—The papers announce the Marriage of the Rev:

Edward Bather, Rector of some place in Shropshire to a Miss Emma Halifax—a Wretch!—he does not deserve an Emma Halifax's maid Betty.—Mr Hampson is here; this must interest Martha; I met him the other morning in his way (as he said) to Green Park B^{gs}; I trusted to his forgetting our number in Gay S^t when I gave it him, & so I conclude he has, as he [has *omitted*] not yet called.—Mrs Stanhope has let her house from Midsummer, so we shall get rid of them. She is lucky in disposing of it so soon, as there is an astonishing number of Houses at this time vacant in that end of the Town.—Mrs Elliot is to quit hers at Michaelmas.—I wonder whether Mr Hampson's friend Mr Saunders is any relation to the famous Saunders[3] whose letters have been lately published!—I am quite of your opinion as to the folly of concealing any longer our intended Partnership with Martha, & whenever there has of late[4] been an enquiry on the subject I have always been sincere; & I have sent word[5] of it to the Mediterranean in a letter to Frank.—None of *our* nearest connections I think will be unprepared for it; & I do not know how to suppose that Martha's have not foreseen it.—When I tell you that we have been visiting a Countess this morning, you will immediately with great justice, but no truth, guess it to be Lady Roden.[6] No, it is Lady Leven, the mother of Ld Balgonie. On receiving a message from Lord & Lady Leven thro' the Mackays declaring their intention of waiting on us, we thought it right to go to them. I hope we have not done too much, but the friends & admirers of Charles must be attended to.—They seem very reasonable, good sort of people, very civil, & full of his praise.—We were shewn at first into an empty Drawing-room, & presently in came his Lordship, not knowing who we were, to apologise for the servant's mistake, & tell a lie himself, that Lady Leven was not within.—He is a tall, gentlemanlike looking man, with spectacles, & rather deaf;—after sitting with him ten minutes we walked away; but Lady L. coming out of the Dining parlour as we passed the door, we were obliged to attend her back to it, & pay our visit over again.—She is a stout woman, with a very handsome face.— By this means we had the pleasure of hearing Charles's praises twice over;—they think themselves excessively obliged to him, & estimate him so highly as to wish Ld Balgonie when he is quite recovered, to go out to him.—The young man is much better, & is gone for the confirmation of his health, to Penzance.—There is a pretty little Lady Marianne of the party, to be shaken hands with & asked if she remembers Mr Austen.—

[*p. 4*] *Monday.* The Cookes' place seems of a sort to suit Isaac, if he

means to go to service again, & does not object to change of Country.
He will have a good Soil, & a good Mistress, & I suppose will not mind
taking physic now & then. The only doubt which occurs to me is whether
Mr Cooke may not be a disagreable, fidgetty Master, especially in matters concerning the Garden.—Mr Mant has not yet paid my Mother the
remainder of her money, but she has very lately received his apology
for it, with his hope of being able to close the account shortly.—You
told me some time ago that Tom Chute had had a fall from his horse,
but I am waiting to know how it happened before I begin pitying him,
as I cannot help suspecting it was in consequence of his taking orders;
very likely as he was going to do Duty or returning from it.—
Tuesday. I have not much more to add. My Uncle & Aunt drank tea
with us last night, & in spite of my resolution to the contrary, I could
not help putting forward to invite them again this Evening. I thought
it was of the first consequence to avoid anything that might seem a
slight to them. I shall be glad when it is over, & hope to have no
necessity for having so many dear friends at once again.—I shall write
to Charles by the next Packet, unless You tell me in the meantime of
your intending to do it. Beleive me if you chuse,

Y^r affec^te Sister.

Miss Austen
Ibthrop
Up. Hurstbourn
Andover

[*Letters missing here*]

45. *To Cassandra Austen*

Saturday 24 August 1805

Godmersham Park, Saturday Aug^st 24

My dear Cassandra

How do you do? & how is Harriot's cold?—I hope you are at this
time sitting down to answer these questions.—Our visit to Eastwell
was very agreable, I found Ly Gordon's manners as pleasing as they
had been described, & saw nothing to dislike in Sir Janison, excepting
once or twice a sort of sneer at Mrs Anne Finch. He was just getting into

Talk with Eliz[th] as the carriage was ordered, but during the first part of the visit he said[1] very little.—Your going with Harriot was highly approved of by everyone; & only too much applauded as an act of virtue on your part. I said all I could to lessen your merit.—The M[rs] Finches were afraid you would find Goodnestone very dull; I wished when I heard them say so, that they could have heard M[r] E. Bridges's solicitude on the subject & have known all the amusements that were planned to prevent it.—They were very civil to me, as they always are;—Fortune was also very civil to me in placing M[r] E. Hatton by me at dinner.— I have discovered that Ly Eliz:[th] for a woman of her age & situation, has astonishingly little to say for herself, & that Miss Hatton has not much more.—Her eloquence lies in her fingers; they were most fluently harmonious.—George is a fine boy, & well behaved, but Daniel cheifly delighted me; the good humour of his countenance is quite bewitching. After Tea we had a Cribbage Table, & he & I won two rubbers of his brother & M[rs] Mary.—M[r] Brett was the only person there besides our two families. [*p. 2*] It was considerably past eleven before we were at home, & I was so tired as to feel no envy of those who were at Ly Yates' Ball.—My good wishes for it's being a pleasant one, were I hope successful. Yesterday was a very quiet day with us; my noisiest efforts were writing to Frank, & playing at Battledore & Shuttlecock with William; he & I have practised together two mornings, & improve a little; we have frequently kept it up *three* times, & once or twice *six*. The two Edwards went to Canterbury in the chair, & found M[rs] Knight as you found her I suppose the day before, chearful but weak.—Fanny was met walking with Miss Sharp & Miss Milles, the happiest Being in the World; she sent a private message[2] to her Mama implying as much— "Tell Mama that I am quite Palmerstone!"[3]—If little Lizzy used the same Language, she would I dare say send the same message from Goodnestone.—In the evening we took a quiet walk round the Farm, with George & Henry to animate us by their races & merriment.— Little Edw:[d] is by no means better, & his papa & mama have determined to consult D[r] Wilmot. Unless he recovers his strength beyond what is now probable, his brothers will return to School without him, & he will be of the party to Worthing.—If Sea-Bathing should be recommended he will be left there with us, but this is not thought likely to happen.—I have been used very ill this morning, I have received a letter from Frank which I ought to have had when Eliz[th] & Henry had theirs, & which in it's way from Albany to Godmersham has been to Dover & Steventon. It was finished on y[e] 16th, & tells what theirs told before as to his present situation; he is in a great hurry to be married, & I [*p. 3*] have encouraged him in it, in the letter which ought to have been an answer to his.—He must think it very strange that I do not acknowledge the receipt of his, when I speak of those of the same dates to Eliz: & Henry; & to add to my injuries I forgot to number mine on the outside.—I have found your white mittens, they were folded up within my clean nightcap, & send their duty to you.—Eliz: has this moment proposed a scheme, which will be very much for my pleasure, if equally convenient to the other party;⁴ it is that when you return on monday, I should take your place at Goodnestone for a few days.— Harriot cannot be insincere, let her try for it ever so much, & therefore I defy her⁵ to accept this self-invitation of mine, unless it be really what perfectly suits her.—As there is no time for an answer, I shall go in the Carriage on monday, & can return with you, if my going on to Goodnestone is at all inconvenient.—The Knatchbulls come on Wednesday to dinner, & stay only till Friday morng. at the latest.—Frank's letter to me is the only one that You or I have received since Thursday.—Mʳ Hall walked off this morng. to Ospringe, with no inconsiderable Booty. He charged Eliz:ᵗʰ 5ˢ for every time of dressing her hair, & 5ˢ for every lesson to Sace, allowing nothing for the pleasures of his visit here, for meat drink & Lodging, the benefit of Country air, & the charms of Mʳˢ Salkeld's & Mʳˢ Sace's society.—Towards me he was as considerate, as I had hoped for, from my relationship to you, charging me only 2ˢ.6ᵈ for cutting my hair, tho' it was as thoroughly dress'd after being cut for Eastwell, as it had been for the Ashford Assembly.— [*p. 4*] He certainly respects either our Youth or our poverty.—My writing to you to day prevents Eliz:ᵗʰ'ˢ writing to Harriot, for which Evil I implore the latter's pardon.—Give my best Love to her—& kind remembrance to her Brothers.—Yours very affec:ˡʸ

JA.

You are desired to bring back with you Henry's picture⁶ of Rowling for the Mʳˢ Finches.

As I find on looking into my affairs, that instead of being very rich I am likely to be very poor, I cannot afford more than ten shillings for Sackree; but as we are to meet in Canterbury I need not have mentioned this.—It is as well however, to prepare you for the sight of a Sister sunk in poverty, that it may not overcome your Spirits.

[*Continued upside down at top of p. 1*]

We have heard nothing from Henry[7] since he went.—Daniel told us that he went from Ospringe in one of the Coaches.—

[Postscript below address panel]

Eliz[th] hopes you will not be later here on Monday than 5 o'clock, on Lizzy's account.—

Miss Austen
Goodnestone Farm
Wingham

Bye Bag
Aug[st] 24

46. *To Cassandra Austen*

Tuesday 27 August 1805

Goodnestone Farm Tuesday August 27

My dear Cassandra

We had a very pleasant drive from Canterbury, and reached this place about half-past four, which seemed to bid fair for a punctual dinner at five; but scenes of great agitation awaited us, and there was much to be endured and done before we could sit down to table. Harriot found a letter from Louisa Hatton, desiring to know if she and her brothers were to be at the ball at Deal on Friday, and saying that the Eastwell family had some idea of going to it, and were to make use of Rowling if they did; and while I was dressing she came to me with another letter in her hand, in great perplexity. It was from Captain Woodford, containing a message from Lady Forbes, which he had intended to deliver in person, but had been prevented from doing. The offer of a ticket for this grand ball, with an invitation to come to her house at Dover before and after it, was Lady Forbes's message. Harriot was at first very little inclined, or rather totally disinclined, to profit by her ladyship's attention; but at length, after many debates, she was persuaded by me and herself together to accept the ticket. The offer of dressing and sleeping at Dover she determined on Marianne's account to decline, and her plan is to be conveyed by Lady Elizabeth Hatton. I hope their going is by this time certain, and will be soon known to be so. I think Miss H. would not have written such a letter if she had not been all but sure of it, and a little more. I am anxious on the subject, from the fear of being in the way if they do not come to give Harriot a conveyance. I proposed and pressed being sent home on Thursday, to prevent the possibility of being in the wrong place, but Harriot would not hear of it. There is no chance of tickets for the Mr Bridgeses, as no gentlemen but of the garrison are invited. With a civil note to be fabricated to Lady F., and an answer written to Miss H., you will easily believe that we could not begin dinner till six. We were agreeably surprised by Edward Bridges's company to it. He had been, strange to tell, too late for the cricket match, too late at least to play himself, and, not being asked to dine with the players, came home. It is impossible to do justice to the hospitality of his attentions towards me; he made a point of ordering toasted cheese for supper entirely on my account. We had a very agreeable evening, and here I am before breakfast writing to you, having got up between six and seven; Lady Bridges's room must be good for early rising. Mr Sankey was here last night, and found his patient[1] better, but I have heard from a maidservant that she has had but an indifferent night. Tell Elizabeth that I did not give her letter to Harriot till we were in the carriage, when she received it with great delight, and could read it in comfort. As you have been here so lately, I need not particularly describe the house or style of living, in which all seems for use and comfort; nor need I be diffuse on the state of Lady Bridges's bookcase and corner-shelves upstairs. What a treat to my mother to arrange them! Harriot is constrained to give up all hope of seeing Edward here to fetch me, as I soon recollected that Mr and Mrs Charles Knatchbull's being at Godmersham on Thursday must put it out of the question. Had I waited till after breakfast, the chief of all this might have been spared. The Duke of Gloucester's death[2] sets my heart at ease, though it will cause some dozens to ache. Harriot's is not among the number of the last; she is very well pleased to be spared the trouble of preparation. She joins me in best love to you all, and will write to Elizabeth soon. I shall be very glad to hear from you, that we may know how you all are, especially the two Edwards. I have asked Sophie[3] if she has anything to say to Lizzy in acknowledgement of the little bird, and her message is that, with her love, she is very glad Lizzy sent it. She volunteers, moreover, her love to little Marianne, with the promise of bringing her a doll the next time she goes to Godmersham. John[4] is just come from Ramsgate, and brings a good account of the people there. He and his brother, you know, dine at Nackington; we are to dine at four, that we may walk afterwards. As it is now two, and Harriot has letters to write, we shall probably not get out before.

Yours affectionately,

JA.

Three o'clock. Harriot is just come from Marianne, and thinks her upon the whole better. The sickness has not returned, and a headache is at present her chief complaint, which Henry⁵ attributes to the sickness.

Miss Austen
Edward Austen's Esq.
Godmersham Park
Faversham

47. *To Cassandra Austen*

Friday 30 August 1805

Goodnestone Farm Friday August 30

My dear Cassandra

I have determined on staying here till Monday. Not that there is any occasion for it on Marianne's account, as she is now almost as well as usual, but Harriot is so kind in her wishes for my company that I could not resolve on leaving her to-morrow, especially as I had no reason to give for its necessity. It would be inconvenient to me to stay with her longer than the beginning of next week, on account of my clothes, and therefore I trust it will suit Edward to fetch or send for me on Monday, or Tuesday if Monday should be wet. Harriot has this moment desired me to propose his coming hither on Monday, and taking me back the next day. The purport of Elizabeth's letter makes me anxious to hear more of what we are to do and not to do, and I hope you will be able to write me your own plans and opinions to-morrow. The journey to London is a point of the first expediency, and I am glad it is resolved on, though it seems likely to injure our Worthing scheme.¹ I expect that *we* are to be at Sandling, while *they* are in town. It gives us great pleasure to hear of little Edward's being better, and we imagine, from his mama's expressions, that he is expected to be well enough to return to school with his brothers. Marianne was equal to seeing me two days ago; we sat with her for a couple of hours before dinner, and the same yesterday, when she was evidently better, more equal to conversation, and more cheerful than during our first visit. She received me very kindly, and expressed her regret in not having been able to see you. She is, of course, altered since we saw her in October, 1794. Eleven years could not pass away even in health without making some change, but in her case it is wonderful that the change should be so little. I have not seen her to advantage, as I understand she has frequently a nice colour, and her complexion has not yet recovered from the effects of her late illness. Her face is grown longer and thinner, and her features more marked, and the likeness which I remember to have always seen between her and Catherine Bigg is stronger than ever, and so striking is the voice and manner of speaking that I seem to be really hearing Catherine, and once or twice have been on the point of calling Harriot "Alethea". She is very pleasant, cheerful, and interested in everything about her, and at the same time shows a thoughtful, considerate, and decided turn of mind. Edward Bridges dined at home yesterday; the day before he was at St Albans; to-day he goes to Broome, and to-morrow to Mr Hallett's, which latter engagement has had some weight in my resolution of not leaving Harriot till Monday. We have walked to Rowling on each of the two last days after dinner, and very great was my pleasure in going over the house and grounds. We have also found time to visit all the principal walks of this place, except the walk round the top of the park, which we shall accomplish probably to-day. Next week seems likely to be an unpleasant one to this family on the matter of game. The evil intentions of the Guards[2] are certain, and the gentlemen of the neighbourhood seem unwilling to come forward in any decided or early support of their rights. Edward Bridges has been trying to arouse their spirits, but without success. Mr Hammond, under the influence of daughters and an expected ball, declares he will do nothing. Harriot hopes my brother will not mortify her by resisting all her plans and refusing all her invitations; she has never yet been successful with him in any, but she trusts he will now make her all the amends in his power by coming on Monday. She thanks Elizabeth for her letter, and you may be sure is not less solicitous than myself for her going to town. Pray say everything kind for us to Miss Sharpe, who could not regret the shortness of our meeting in Canterbury more than we did. I hope she returned to Godmersham as much pleased with Mrs Knight's beauty and Miss Milles's judicious remarks as those ladies respectively were with hers. You must send me word that you have heard from Miss Irvine. I had almost forgot to thank you of your letter. I am glad you recommended 'Gisborne',[3] for having begun, I am pleased with it, and I had quite determined not to read it. I suppose everybody will be black for the D. of G. Must we buy lace, or will ribbon do? We shall not be at Worthing so soon as we have been used to talk of, shall we? This will be no evil to us, and we are sure of my mother and Martha being happy together. Do not forget to write to Charles. As I am to return so soon, we shall not send the pincushions.

Yours affectionately, JA

You continue, I suppose, taking hartshorn, and I hope with good effect.

Miss Austen
Edward Austen's Esq.
Godmersham Park
Faversham

48(C). *To Fanny Austen (Knight)*

?*Thursday 24 July 1806*

Lines written by Jane Austen for the amusement of a Niece (afterwards Lady Knatchbull) on the arrival of Captn. & Mrs Austen at Godmersham Park soon after their marriage July 1806.[1]

See they come, post haste from Thanet,
　　Lovely couple, side by side;
They've left behind them Richard Kennet
　　With the Parents of the Bride!

Canterbury they have passed through;
　　Next succeeded Stamford-bridge;
Chilham village they came fast through;
　　Now they've mounted yonder ridge.

Down the hill they're swift proceeding
　　Now they skirt the Park around;
Lo! The Cattle sweetly feeding
　　Scamper, startled at the sound!

Run, my Brothers, to the Pier gate!
　　Throw it open, very wide!
Let it not be said that we're late
　　In welcoming my Uncle's Bride!

To the house the chaise advances;
Now it stops—They're here, they're here!
How d'ye do, my Uncle Francis?
How does do your Lady dear?

———

[*Letter(s) missing here*]

49. *To Cassandra Austen*

Wednesday 7–Thursday 8 January 1807

Southampton Wednesday January 7

My dear Cassandra

You were mistaken in supposing I should expect your letter on Sunday; I had no idea of hearing from you before Tuesday, and my pleasure yesterday was therefore unhurt by any previous disappointment. I thank you for writing so much; you must really have sent me the value of two letters in one. We are extremely glad to hear that Elizabeth is so much better, and hope you will be sensible of still further amendment in her when you return from Canterbury. Of your visit there I must now speak 'incessantly'; it surprises, but pleases me more, and I consider it as a very just and honourable distinction of you, and not less to the credit of Mrs Knight. I have no doubt of your spending your time with her most pleasantly in quiet and rational conversation, and am so far from thinking her expectations of you will be deceived, that my only fear is of your being so agreeable, so much to her taste, as to make her wish to keep you with her for ever. If that should be the case, we must remove to Canterbury, which I should not like so well as Southampton. When you receive this, our guests[1] will be all gone or going; and I shall be left to the comfortable disposal of my time, to ease of mind from the torments of rice puddings and apple dumplings, and probably to regret that I did not take more pains to please them all. Mrs J. Austen has asked me to return with her to Steventon; I need not give my answer; and she has invited my mother to spend there the time of Mrs F. A's confinement, which she seems half inclined to do. A few days ago I had a letter from Miss Irvine, and as I was in her debt, you will guess it to be a remonstrance, not a very severe one, however; the first page is in her usual retrospective, jealous, inconsistent style, but the remainder is chatty and harmless. She supposes my silence may have proceeded from resentment of her not having written to inquire particularly after my hooping cough, &c. She is a funny one. I have answered her letter, and have endeavoured to give something like the truth with as little incivility as I could, by placing my silence to the want of subject in the very quiet way in which we live. Phebe has repented, and stays. I have also written to Charles, and I answered Miss Buller's letter by return of post, as I intended to tell you in my last. Two or three things I recollected when it was too late, that I might have told you; one is, that the Welbys have lost their eldest son by a putrid fever at Eton, and another that Tom Chute is going to settle in Norfolk. You have scarcely ever mentioned Lizzy since your being at Godmersham. I hope it is not because she is altered for the worse. I cannot yet satisfy Fanny as to Mrs Foote's baby's name,[2] and I must not encourage her to expect a good one, as Captain Foote is a professed adversary to all but the plainest; he likes only Mary, Elizabeth, Anne, &c. Our best chance is of 'Caroline', which in compliment to a sister seems the only exception. He dined with us on Friday, and I fear will not soon venture again, for the strength of our dinner was a boiled leg of mutton, underdone even for James; and Captain Foote has a particular dislike to underdone mutton; but he was so good-humoured and pleasant that I did not much mind his being starved. He gives us all the most cordial invitation to his house in the country, saying just what the Williams[3] ought to say to make us welcome. Of them we have seen nothing since you left us, and we hear that they are just gone to Bath again, to be out of the way of further alterations at Brooklands. Mrs F. A. has had a very agreeable letter from Mrs Dickson, who was delighted with the purse, and desires her not to provide herself with a christening dress, which is exactly what her young correspondent wanted; and she means to defer making any of the caps as long as she can, in hope of having Mrs D's present in time to be serviceable as a pattern. She desires me to tell you that the gowns were cut out before your letter arrived, but that they are long enough for Caroline. The *Beds*, as I believe they are called, have fallen to Frank's share to continue, and of course are cut out to admiration. 'Alphonsine' did not do. We were disgusted in twenty pages, as, independent of a bad translation, it has indelicacies which disgrace a pen hitherto so pure;

and we changed it for the 'Female Quixotte',[4] which now makes our evening amusement; to me a very high one, as I find the work quite equal to what I remembered it. Mrs F. A., to whom it is new, enjoys it as one could wish; the other Mary, I believe, has little pleasure from that or any other book. My mother does not seem at all more disappointed than ourselves at the termination of the family treaty;[5] she thinks less of *that* just now than of the comfortable state of her own finances, which she finds on closing her year's accounts beyond her expectation, as she begins the new year with a balance of 30*l.* in her favour; and when she has written her answer to my aunt, which you know always hangs a little upon her mind, she will be above the world entirely. You will have a great deal of unreserved discourse with Mrs K., I dare say, upon this subject, as well as upon many other of our family matters. Abuse everybody but me.

Thursday. We expected James yesterday, but he did not come; if he comes at all now, his visit will be a very short one, as he must return to-morrow, that Ajax and the chair may be sent to Winchester on Saturday. Caroline's new pelisse depended upon her mother's being able or not to come so far in the chair; how the guinea that will be saved by the same means of return is to be spent I know not. Mrs J. A. does not talk much of poverty now, though she has no hope of my brother's being able to buy another horse *next* summer. Their scheme against Warwickshire continues, but I doubt the family's being at Stoneleigh so early as James says he must go, which is May. My mother is afraid I have not been explicit enough on the subject of her wealth; she began 1806 with 68*l.*, she begins 1807 with 99*l.*, and this after 32*l.* purchase of stock. Frank too has been settling his accounts and making calculations, and each party feels quite equal to our present expenses; but much increase of house-rent would not do for either. Frank limits himself, I believe, to four hundred a year. You will be surprised to hear that Jenny is not yet come back; we have heard nothing of her since her reaching Itchingswell, and can only suppose that she must be detained by illness in somebody or other, and that she has been each day expecting to be able to come on the morrow. I am glad I did not know beforehand that she was to be absent during the whole or almost the whole of our friends being with us, for though the inconvenience has not been nothing, I should have feared still more. Our dinners have certainly suffered not a little by having only Molly's head and Molly's hands to conduct them; she fries better than she did, but not like Jenny. We did *not* take our walk on Friday, it was too dirty, nor have we yet done it; we may perhaps do something like it to-day, as after seeing Frank skate, which he hopes to do in the meadows by the beach,[6] we are to treat ourselves with a passage over the ferry. It is one of the pleasantest frosts I ever knew, so very quiet. I hope it will last some time longer for Frank's sake, who is quite anxious to get some skating; he tried yesterday, but it would not do. Our acquaintance increase too fast. He was recognised lately by Admiral Bertie, and a few days since arrived the Admiral and his daughter Catherine to wait upon us. There was nothing to like or dislike in either. To the Berties are to be added the Lances, with whose cards we have been endowed, and whose visit Frank and I returned yesterday. They live about a mile and three-quarters from S. to the right of the new road to Portsmouth, and I believe their house[7] is one of those which are to be seen almost anywhere among the woods on the other side of the Itchen. It is a handsome building, stands high, and in a very beautiful situation. We found only Mrs Lance at home, and whether she boasts any offspring besides a grand pianoforte did not appear. She was civil and chatty enough, and offered to introduce us to some acquaintance in Southampton, which we gratefully declined. I suppose they must be acting by the orders of Mr Lance of Netherton in this civility, as there seems no other reason for their coming near us. They will not come often, I dare say. They live in a handsome style and are rich, and she seemed to like to be rich, and we gave her to understand that we were far from being so; she will soon feel therefore that we are not worth her acquaintance. You must have heard from Martha by this time. We have had no accounts of Kintbury since her letter to me. Mrs F. A. has had one fainting fit[8] lately; it came on as usual after eating a hearty dinner, but did not last long. I can recollect nothing more to say. When my letter is gone, I suppose I shall.

Yours affectionately, JA

I have just asked Caroline if I should send her love to her godmama, to which she answered 'Yes'.

Miss Austen
Godmersham Park
Faversham
Kent

[*Letters missing here*]

50. *To Cassandra Austen*

Sunday 8–Monday 9 February 1807

Southampton Feb. 8th

My dearest Cassandra

My expectation of having nothing to say to you after the conclusion of my last, seems nearer Truth than I thought it would be, for I feel to have but little. I need not therefore be above acknowledging the receipt of yours this morn^g; or of replying to every part of it which is capable of an answer; & you may accordingly prepare for my ringing the Changes of the Glads & Sorrys for the rest of the page.—Unluckily however I see nothing to be glad of, unless I make it a matter of Joy that Mrs Wylmot has another son & that Ld Lucan has taken a Mistress, both of which Events are of course joyful to the Actors;—but to be sorry I find many occasions, the first is that your return is to be delayed, & whether I ever get beyond the first is doubtful. It is no use to lament.—I never heard that even Queen Mary's Lamentation[1] did her any good, & I could not therefore expect benefit from mine.—We are all sorry, & now that subject is exhausted. I heard from Martha yesterday; she spends this week with the Harwoods, goes afterwards with James & Mary for a few days to see Peter Debary & two of his sisters at Eversley—the Living of which he has gained on the death of Sir R. Cope—& means to be here on ye 24th, which will be Tuesday fortnight. I shall be truely glad if she can keep to her day, but dare not depend on it;—& am so apprehensive of farther detention that if nothing else occurs to create it, I cannot help thinking she will marry Peter Debary.—It vexed me that I could not get any fish for Kintbury while their family was large; but so it was, & till last Tuesday I could procure none. I then sent them four pair of small Soals, & should be glad to be certain of their arriving in good time, but I have heard nothing about them since, & had rather hear nothing than Evil.—They cost six shillings, & as they travelled in a Basket which came from Kintbury a few days before with Poultry &c, I insist upon treating you with the Booking *whatever it may be*, You are only Eighteen pence in my debt.—Mrs E. Leigh did not make the slightest allusion to my Uncle's Business, [*p. 2*] as I remember telling you at the time, but you shall hear it as often as you like. My Mother wrote to her a week ago.—Martha's rug is just finished, & looks well, tho' not quite so well as I had hoped. I see no fault in the Border, but the Middle is dingy.—My Mother desires me to say that she will knit one for you, as soon as you return to chuse the colours & pattern. I am sorry I have affronted you on the subject of M[r] Moore, but I do not mean ever to like him; & as to pitying a young woman merely because she cannot live in two places at the same time, & at once enjoy the comforts of being married & single, I shall not attempt it, even for Harriot.[2]—You see I have a spirit, as well as yourself.—Frank & Mary cannot at all approve of your not being at home in time to help them in their finishing purchases, & desire me to say that, if you are not,[3] they shall be as spiteful as possible & chuse everything in the stile most likely to vex you, Knives that will not cut, glasses that will not hold, a sofa without a seat, & a Bookcase without shelves.—Our Garden[4] is putting in order, by a Man who bears a remarkably good Character, has a very fine complexion & asks something less than the first. The Shrubs which border the gravel walk he says are only sweetbriar & roses, & the latter of an indifferent sort;—we mean to get a few of a better kind therefore, & at my own particular desire he procures us some Syringas. I could not do without a Syringa, for the sake of Cowper's Line.[5]—We talk also of a Laburnam.—The Border under the Terrace Wall, is clearing away to receive Currants & Gooseberry Bushes, & a spot is found very proper for Raspberries.—The alterations & improvements within doors too advance very properly, & the Offices will be made very convenient indeed.—Our Dressing-Table is constructing on the spot, out of a large Kitchen Table belonging to the House, for doing which we have the permission of M[r] Husket Lord Lansdown's Painter,—domestic Painter I sh[d] call him, for he lives in the Castle—Domestic Chaplains have given way to this more necessary office, & I suppose whenever the Walls want no touching up, he is employed about my Lady's face.—The morning was so wet that I was afraid we should not be able to see our little Visitor, but Frank who alone could go to Church called for her after Service, & she is now talking away at my side & examining the Treasures of my Writing-desk drawer;—very happy I beleive;—not at all shy of course.—Her name is Catherine & her Sister's Caroline.[6]—She is something like her Brother, & as short for her age, but not so well-looking.[7]—What is become of all the Shyness in the World?—[*p. 3*] Moral as well as Natural Diseases disappear in the progress of time, & new ones take their place.—Shyness & the Sweating Sickness have given way to Confidence & Paralytic complaints.—I am sorry to hear of M[rs] Whitfield's encreasing Illness, & of poor Marianne Bridges's having suffered so much;—these are some of my sorrows, & that M[rs] Deedes is to have another Child I suppose I may lament.—The death of Mrs W. K.[8] we had seen;—I had no idea that anybody liked her, & therefore felt nothing for any Survivor, but I am now feeling away on her Husband's account, and think he had better marry Miss Sharpe.— I have this instant made my present, & have the pleasure of seeing it smiled over with genuine satisfaction. I am sure I may on this occasion call Kitty Foote, as Hastings did H. Egerton,[9] my "very valuable Friend."—*Even^g*.—Our little visitor has just left us, & left us highly pleased with her;—she is a nice, natural, openhearted, affectionate girl, with all the ready civility which one sees in the best Children of the present day;—so unlike anything that I was myself at her age, that I am often all astonishment & shame.—Half her time here was spent at Spillikins; which I consider as a very valuable part of our Household furniture, & as not the least important Benefaction[10] from the family of Knight to that of Austen.—But I must tell you a story. Mary has for some time had notice from Mrs Dickson of the intended arrival of a certain Miss Fowler in this place;—Miss F. is an intimate friend of Mrs D. & a good deal known as such to Mary.—On Thursday last she called here while we were out;—Mary found on our return her card with only her name on it, & she had left word that she w^d call again.— The particularity of this made us talk, & among other conjectures Frank said in joke "I dare say she is staying with the Pearsons."—The connection of the names struck Mary, & she immediately recollected Miss Fowler's having been very intimate with persons so called;—and upon putting everything together we have scarcely a doubt of her being actually staying with the only Family in the place whom we cannot visit.— What a Contretems!—in the Language of France; What an unluckiness! in that of M^{de} Duval[11]—The Black Gentleman has certainly employed one of his menial imps to bring about this complete tho' trifling mischeif.—Miss F. has never called again, but we are in daily expectation of it.—Miss P. has of course given her a proper understanding of the Business;[12]—it is evident that Miss F. did not expect or wish to have the visit returned, & Frank is quite as much on his guard for his wife, as we c^d desire for her sake, or our own.—[*p. 4*] We shall rejoice in being so near Winchester when Edward[13] belongs to it, & can never have our spare bed filled more to our satisfaction than by him. Does he leave Eltham at Easter?—We are reading Clarentine,[14] & are surprised to find how foolish it is. I remember liking it much less on a 2^d reading than at the 1st & it does not bear a 3^d at all. It is full of unnatural conduct & forced difficulties, without striking merit of any kind.— Miss Harrison is going into Devonshire to attend Mrs Dusautoy as usual.—Miss Jackson is married to young Mr Gunthorpe, & is to be very unhappy. He swears, drinks, is cross, jealous, selfish & Brutal;—the match makes *her* family miserable, & has occasioned *his* being disinherited.—The Browns are added to our list of acquaintance; He commands the Sea Fencibles here under Sir Tho.^15 & was introduced at his own desire by the latter when we saw him last week.—As yet the Gentlemen only^16 have visited, as Mrs B. is ill, but she is a nice looking woman & wears one of the prettiest Straw Bonnets in the place.— *Monday.* The Garret-beds are made, & ours will be finished to day. I had hoped it w^d be finished on Saturday, but neither Mrs Hall nor Jenny were able to give help enough for that; & I have as yet done very little & Mary^17 nothing at all. This week we shall do more, & I sh^d like to have all the 5 Beds completed by the end of it.—There will then be the Window [*continued below address panel*] -Curtains, sofa-cover, & a carpet to be altered. I should not be surprised if we were to be visited by James again this week; he gave us reason to expect him soon; & if they go to Eversley he cannot come next week.—[*back to p. 1, crossed*] I am sorry & angry that his Visits should not give one more pleasure; the company of so good & so clever a Man ought to be gratifying in itself;—but his Chat seems all forced, his Opinions on many points too much copied from his Wife's, & his time here is spent I think in walking about the House & banging the Doors, or ringing the Bell for a glass of Water.—

There, I flatter myself I have constructed you a Smartish Letter, considering my want of Materials. But like my dear Dr Johnson^18 I beleive I have dealt more in Notions than Facts.—

I hope your Cough is gone & that you are otherwise well.—And remain with Love, Y^rs affec^tely JA.

Miss Austen
Godmersham Park
Faversham
Kent

[*Letters missing here*]

51. *To Cassandra Austen*

Friday 20–Sunday 22 February 1807

Southampton Friday Feby 20th.

My dear Cassandra

We have at last heard something of Mr Austen's Will. It is beleived at Tunbridge that he has left everything after the death of his widow to Mr M^y Austen's[1] 3^d son John; & as the said John was the only one of the Family who attended the Funeral, it seems likely to be true.—Such ill-gotten Wealth can never prosper!—I really have very little to say *this* week, & do not feel as if I should spread that little into the shew of much. I am inclined for short sentences.—Mary[2] will be obliged to you to take notice how often Eliz^th nurses her Baby[3] in the course of the 24 hours, how often it is fed & with what;—you need not trouble yourself to *write* the result of your observations, your return will be early enough for the communication of them.—You are recommended to bring away some flower-seeds from Godmersham, particularly Mignionette seed.—My Mother has heard this morn^g from Paragon.— My Aunt talks much of the violent colds prevailing in Bath, from which my Uncle has suffered ever since their return, & she has herself a cough much worse than any she ever had before, subject as she has always been to bad ones.—She writes in good humour & chearful spirits how- ever. The negociation between them & Adlestrop[4] so happily over in- deed, what can have power to vex her materially?—Elliston, she tells us has just succeeded to a considerable fortune on the death of an Uncle. I would not have it enough to take *him* from the Stage; *she* should quit her business, & live with him in London.—We could not pay our visit on Monday, the weather altered just too soon; & we have since had a touch of almost everything in the weather way;—two of the severest frosts since the winter began, preceded by rain, hail & snow.—Now we are smiling again.

[*p. 2*] *Saturday.* I have received your letter, but I suppose you do not expect me to be gratified by it's contents. I confess myself much dis- appointed by this repeated delay of your return, for tho' I had pretty well given up all idea of your being with us before our removal, I felt sure that March would not pass quite away without bringing you. Be- fore April comes, of course something else will occur to detain you. But as *you* are happy, all this is Selfishness, of which here is enough for one page.—Pray tell Lizzy that if I had imagined her Teeth to be really out

I should have said before what I say now, that it was a very unlucky fall indeed, that I am afraid it must have given her a great deal of pain, & that I dare say her Mouth looks very comical.—I am obliged to Fanny for the list of Mrs Coleman's Children, whose names I had not however quite forgot; the new one I am sure will be Caroline.⁵—I have got Mr Bowen's Recipe for you, it came in my Aunt's letter.—You must have had more snow at G^m than we had here;—on Wednesday morn^g there was a thin covering of it over the fields & roofs of the Houses, but I do not think there was any left the next day. Everybody used to Southampton says that Snow never lies more than 24 hours near it, & from what we have observed ourselves, it is very true.—Frank's going into Kent depends of course upon his being unemployed, but as the 1st Lord⁶ after promising Ld Moira that Capt. A. should have the first good Frigate that was vacant, has since given away two or three fine ones, he has no particular reason to expect an appointment now.—*He* however has scarcely spoken about the Kentish Journey; I have my information cheifly from her, & she considers her own going thither as more certain if he sh^d be at sea, than if not.—Frank has got a very bad Cough, for an Austen;—but⁷ it does not disable him from making very nice fringe for the Drawingroom-Curtains.—Mrs Day has now got the Carpet in hand, & Monday I hope will be the last day of her employment here. A fortnight afterwards she is to be called again from the shades of her red-check'd bed in an alley near the end of the High Street [*p. 3*] to clean the new House & air the Bedding.—We hear that we are envied our House by many people, & that the Garden is the best in the Town.— There will be green baize enough for Martha's room & ours;—not to cover them but to lie over the part where it is most wanted, under the Dressing Table. Mary is to have a peice of Carpetting for the same purpose; my Mother says *she* does not want any; & it may certainly be better done without in her room than in Martha's & ours, from the difference of their aspect.—I recommend Mrs Grant's Letters,⁸ as a present to the latter;—what they are about, nor how many volumes they form I do not know, having never heard of them but from Miss Irvine, who speaks of them⁹ as a new & much admired work, & as one which has pleased her highly.—I have enquired for the book¹⁰ here, but find it quite unknown. I beleive *I* put five breadths of Linen also into my flounce; I know I found it wanted more than I had expected, & that I sh^d have been distressed if I had not bought more than I beleived myself to need, for the sake of the even Measure, on which we think so differently.—A light morn^g gown will be a very necessary purchase for you,

& I wish you a pretty one. I shall buy such things whenever I am tempted, but as yet there is nothing of the sort to be seen.—We are reading Barretti's other book, & find him dreadfully abusive of poor Mr Sharpe.[11] I can no longer take his part against you, as I did nine years ago.—*Sunday*—This post has brought me Martha's own assurance of her coming on tuesday even^g which nothing is now to prevent except William[12] should send her word that there is no *remedy*[13] on that day.— Her letter was put into the post at Basingstoke on their return from Eversley, where she says they have spent their time very pleasantly; she does not own herself in any danger of being tempted back again however, & as she signs by her maiden name we are at least to suppose her not married yet.—They must have had a cold visit, but as she found it agreable I suppose there was no want of Blankets, & we may trust to her Sister's[14] taking care that her love of many should be known.—She sends me no particulars, having time only to write the needful.—

[*p. 4*] I wish You a pleasant party tomorrow & not more than you like of Miss Hatton's neck.—Lady B.[15] must have been a shameless woman if she named H. Hales as within her Husband's reach. It is a peice of impertinence indeed in a Woman to pretend to fix on anyone, as if she supposed it c^d be only ask & have.—A Widower with 3 children has no right to look higher than his daughter's Governess.—I am forced to be abusive for want of subject,[16] having really nothing to say.—When Martha comes she will supply me with matter; I shall have to tell you how she likes the House & what she thinks of Mary.—You must be very cold today at G^m—We are cold here. I expect a severe March, a wet April, & a sharp May.—And with this prophecy I must conclude.—

My Love to everybody—Y^rs affec^tely J. Austen

Miss Austen
Godmersham Park
Faversham
Kent

[*Letters missing here*]

52. *To Cassandra Austen*

Wednesday 15–Friday 17 June 1808

Godmersham Wednesday June 15

My dear Cassandra

Where shall I begin? Which of all my important nothings shall I tell you first? At half after seven yesterday morning Henry saw us into our own carriage, and we drove away from the Bath Hotel; which, by the bye, had been found most uncomfortable quarters—very dirty, very noisy, and very ill-provided. James began his journey by the coach at five.[1] Our first eight miles were hot; Deptford Hill brought to my mind our hot journey into Kent fourteen years ago; but after Blackheath we suffered nothing, and as the day advanced it grew quite cool. At Dartford, which we reached within the two hours and three-quarters, we went to the Bull, the same inn at which we breakfasted in that said journey, and on the present occasion had about the same bad butter. At half-past ten we were again off, and, travelling on without any adventure reached Sittingbourne by three. Daniel was watching for us at the door of the George, and I was acknowledged very kindly by Mr and Mrs Marshall, to the latter of whom I devoted my conversation, while Mary went out to buy some gloves. A few minutes, of course, did for Sittingbourne; and so off we drove, drove, drove, and by six o'clock were at Godmersham. Our two brothers[2] were walking before the house as we approached, as natural as life. Fanny and Lizzy met us in the Hall with a great deal of pleasant joy; we went for a few minutes into the breakfast parlour, and then proceeded to our rooms. Mary has the Hall chamber. I am in the Yellow room—very literally—for I am writing in it at this moment. It seems odd to me to have such a great place all to myself, and to be at Godmersham without you is also odd. You are wished for, I assure you: Fanny, who came to me as soon as she had seen her Aunt James to her room, and stayed while I dressed, was as energetic as usual in her longings for you. She is grown both in height and size since last year,[3] but not immoderately, looks very well, and seems as to conduct and manner just what she was and what one could wish her to continue. Elizabeth, who was dressing when we arrived, came to me for a minute attended by Marianne, Charles, and Louisa, and, you will not doubt, gave me a very affectionate welcome. That I had received such from Edward also I need not mention; but I do, you see, because it is a pleasure. I never saw him look in better health, and

Fanny says he is perfectly well. I cannot praise Elizabeth's looks, but they are probably affected by a cold. Her little namesake has gained in beauty in the last three years, though not all that Marianne has lost. Charles is not quite so lovely as he was. Louisa is much as I expected, and Cassandra I find handsomer than I expected, though at present disguised by such a violent breaking-out that she does not come down after dinner. She has charming eyes and a nice open countenance, and seems likely to be very lovable. Her size is magnificent. I was agreeably surprised to find Louisa Bridges still here. She looks remarkably well (legacies are very wholesome diet), and is just what she always was. John[4] is at Sandling. You may fancy our dinner party therefore; Fanny, of course, belonging to it, and little Edward,[5] for that day. He was almost too happy, his happiness at least made him too talkative. It has struck ten; I must go to breakfast. Since breakfast I have had a *tete-a-tete* with Edward in his room; he wanted to know James's plans and mine, and from what his own now are I think it already nearly certain that I shall return when they do, though not with them. Edward will be going about the same time to Alton, where he has business with Mr. Trimmer, and where he means his son should join him; and I shall probably be his companion to that place, and get on afterwards somehow or other. I should have preferred a rather longer stay here certainly, but there is no prospect of any later conveyance for me, as he does not mean to accompany Edward[6] on his return to Winchester, from a very natural unwillingness to leave Elizabeth at that time.[7] I shall at any rate be glad not to be obliged to be an incumbrance on those who have brought me here, for, as James has no horse, I must feel in their carriage that I am taking his place. We were rather crowded yesterday, though it does not become me to say so, as I and my boa were of the party, and it is not to be supposed but that a child of three[8] years of age was fidgety. I need scarcely beg you to keep all this to yourself, lest it should get round by Anna's means. She is very kindly inquired after by her friends here, who all regret her not coming with her father and mother. I left Henry, I hope, free from his tiresome complaint, in other respects well, and thinking with great pleasure of Cheltenham and Stoneleigh. The brewery scheme is quite at an end: at a meeting of the subscribers last week it was by general, and I believe very hearty, consent dissolved. The country is very beautiful. I saw as much as ever to admire in my yesterday's journey. *Thursday.* I am glad to find that Anna was pleased with going to Southampton, and hope with all my heart that the visit may be satisfactory to everybody. Tell her that she will hear in a few days from her mamma, who would have written to her now but for this letter. Yesterday passed quite *a la* Godmersham: the gentlemen rode about Edward's farm, and returned in time to saunter along Bentigh with us; and after dinner we visited the Temple Plantations, which, to be sure, is a Chevalier Bayard of a plantation. James and Mary are much struck with the beauty of the place. To-day the spirit of the thing is kept up by the two brothers being gone to Canterbury in the chair. I cannot discover, even through Fanny, that her mother is fatigued by her attendance on the children. I have, of course, tendered my services, and when Louisa[9] is gone, who sometimes hears the little girls read, will try to be accepted in her stead. She will not be here many days longer. The Moores are partly expected to dine here to-morrow or Saturday. I feel rather languid and solitary—perhaps because I have a cold; but three years ago we were more animated with you and Harriot and Miss Sharpe. We shall improve, I dare say, as we go on. I have not yet told you how the new carriage is liked—very well, very much indeed, except the lining, which does look rather shabby. I hear a very bad account of Mrs Whitefield; a very good one of Mrs Knight, who goes to Broadstairs next month. Miss Sharpe is going with Miss Bailey to Tenby. The Widow Kennet succeeds to the post of laundress. Would you believe it my trunk is come already; and, what completes the wondrous happiness, nothing is damaged. I unpacked it all before I went to bed last night, and when I went down to breakfast this morning presented the rug, which was received most gratefully, and met with universal admiration. My frock is also given, and kindly accepted. *Friday.* I have received your letter, and I think it gives me nothing to be sorry for but Mary's[10] cold, which I hope is by this time better. Her approbation of her child's hat makes me very happy. Mrs J. A. bought one at Gayleard's for Caroline, of the same shape, but brown and with a feather. I hope Huxham[11] is a comfort to you; I am glad you are taking it. I shall probably have an opportunity of giving Harriot your message to-morrow; she does not come here, they have not a day to spare, but Louisa and I are to go to her in the morning. I send your thanks to Eliza by this post in a letter to Henry. Lady Catherine is Lord Portmore's daughter. I have read Mr Jefferson's case to Edward, and he desires to have his name set down for a guinea and his wife's for another; but does not wish for more than one copy of the work.[12] Your account of Anna gives me pleasure. Tell her, with my love, that I like her for liking the quay. Mrs J. A. seems rather surprised at the Maitlands drinking tea with you, but that does not prevent my approving it. I hope you had not a disagreeable evening with Miss Austen and her niece. You know how interesting the purchase of a sponge-cake is to me. I am now just returned from Eggerton; Louisa and I walked together and found Miss Maria[13] at home. Her sister we met on our way back. *She* had been to pay her compliments to Mrs. Inman, whose chaise was seen to cross the park while we were at dinner yesterday. I told Sackree that you desired to be remembered to her, which pleased her; and she sends her duty, and wishes you to know that she has been into the great world. She went on to town after taking William to Eltham, and, as well as myself, saw the ladies go to Court on the 4th. She had the advantage indeed of me in being in the Palace.[14] Louisa[15] is not so handsome as I expected, but she is not quite well. Edward and Caroline seem very happy here; he has nice playfellows in Lizzy and Charles. They and their attendant have the boys' attic. Anna will not be surprised that the cutting off her hair is very much regretted by several of the party in this house; I am tolerably reconciled to it by considering that two or three years may restore it again. You are very important with your Captain Bulmore and Hotel Master, and I trust, if your trouble over-balances your dignity on the occasion, it will be amply repaid by Mrs Craven's approbation, and a pleasant scheme to see her. Mrs Cooke has written to my brother James to invite him and his wife to Bookham in their way back, which, as I learn through Edward's means, they are not disinclined to accept, but that my being with them would render it impracticable, the nature of the road affording no conveyance to James. I shall therefore make them easy on that head as soon as I can. I have a great deal of love to give from everybody.

Yours most affectionately, Jane

My mother will be glad to be assured that the size of the rug does perfectly well. It is not to be used till winter.

Miss Austen
Castle Square
Southampton

53. *To Cassandra Austen*

Monday 20–Wednesday 22 June 1808

Godmersham, Monday June 20th.

My dear Cassandra

I will first talk of my visit to Canterbury, as Mrs J. A.'s letter to Anna cannot have given you every particular of it, which you are likely to wish for.—I had a most affectionate welcome from Harriot & was happy to see her looking almost as well as ever. She walked with me to call on Mrs Brydges, when Eliz^th & Louisa went to Mrs Milles';—Mrs B. was dressing & c^d not see us, & we proceeded to the White Friars, where Mrs K. was alone in her Drawing room, as gentle & kind & friendly as usual.—She enquired after every body, especially my Mother & yourself.—We were with her a quarter of an hour before Eliz. & Louisa, hot from Mrs Baskerville's Shop, walked in;—they were soon followed by the Carriage, & another five minutes brought Mr Moore himself, just returned from his morn^g ride. Well!—& what do I think of Mr Moore?—I will not pretend in one meeting to *dislike* him, whatever Mary may say; but I can honestly assure her that I saw nothing in him to admire.—His manners, as you have always said, are gentlemanlike—but by no means winning. He made one formal enquiry after you.—I saw their little girl, & very small & very pretty she is; her features are as delicate as Mary Jane's,[1] with nice dark eyes, & if she had Mary Jane's fine colour, she w^d be quite complete.—Harriot's fondness for her seems just what is amiable & natural, & not foolish.—I saw Caroline[2] also, & thought her very plain.—Edward's plan for Hampshire does not vary. He only improves it with the kind intention of taking me on to Southampton, & spending one whole day with you; & if it is found practicable, Edward Junr[3] will be added to our party for that one day also, which is to be Sunday ye 10th of July.—I hope you may have beds for them. We are to begin our Journey on ye 8th & reach you late on ye 9th.—This morning brought me a letter from Mrs Knight, containing the usual Fee, & all the usual Kindness. She asks me to spend a day or two with her this week, to meet Mrs C. Knatchbull, who with her Husband comes to the W. Friars to day—& I beleive I shall go.—I have consulted Edwd—& think it will be arranged for Mrs J. A.'s going with me one morn^g, my staying the night, & Edward's driving me home the next Even^g.—Her very agreable present[4] will make my circumstances quite easy. I shall reserve half for my Pelisse.—[*p. 2*] I hope, by this early return I am sure of seeing Catherine & Alethea;— & I propose that either with or without them, you & I & Martha shall have a snug fortnight while my Mother is at Steventon.—We go on very well here, Mary finds the Children less troublesome than she expected, & independant of *them*, there is certainly not much to try the patience or hurt the Spirits at Godmersham.—I initiated her yesterday into the mysteries of Inman-ism.[5]—The poor old Lady is as thin & chearful as ever, & very thankful for a new acquaintance.—I had called on her before with Eliz. & Louisa.—I find John Bridges grown very old & black, but his manners are not altered; he is very pleasing, & talks of Hampshire with great admiration.—Pray let Anna have the pleasure of knowing that she is remembered with kindness both by Mrs Cooke & Miss Sharpe. Her manners must be very much worsted by your description of them, but I hope they will improve by this visit.— Mrs Knight finishes her letter with "Give my best love to Cassandra when you write to her."—I shall like spending a day at the White Friars very much.—We breakfasted in the Library this morn^g for the first time, & most of the party have been complaining all day of the heat; but Louisa & I feel alike as to weather, & are cool & comfortable.—Wednesday—The Moores came yesterday in their Curricle between one & two o'clock, & immediately after the noonshine[6] which succeeded their arrival, a party set off for Buckwell to see the Pond dragged;—Mr Moore, James, Edward & James-Edward on horseback, John Bridges driving Mary in his gig.—The rest of us remained quietly & comfortably at home.—We had a very pleasant Dinner, at the lower end of the Table at least; the merriment was cheifly between Edwd Louisa, Harriot & myself.—Mr Moore did not talk so much as I expected, & I understand from Fanny, that I did not see him at all as he is in general;—our being strangers made him so much more silent & quiet. Had I had no reason for observing what he said & did, I sh^d scarcely have thought about him.—His manners to her want Tenderness—& he was a little violent at last about the impossibility of her going to Eastwell.—I cannot see any unhappiness in her[7] however; & as to Kind-heartedness &c. [*p. 3*] she is quite unaltered.—Mary was disappointed in *her* beauty, & thought *him* very disagreable; James admires *her*, & finds *him* conversible & pleasant. I sent my answer by them to Mrs Knight, my double acceptance of her note & her invitation, which I wrote without much effort; for I was rich—& the Rich are always respectable, whatever be their stile of writing:—I am to meet Harriot at dinner tomorrow;—it is one of the Audit days, & Mr M. dines with the Dean,[8] who is just come to Canterbury.—On Tuesday there is to be a family meeting at Mrs C. Milles's. —Lady Bridges & Louisa from Goodnestone, the Moores, & a party from this House, Elizth John Bridges & myself. It will give me pleasure to see Lady B.—she is now quite well.—Louisa goes home on friday, & John with her; but he returns the next day. These are our engagements; make the most of them.—Mr Waller is dead, I see;—I cannot greive about it, nor perhaps can his Widow very much.—Edward began cutting S^{t}foin on saturday & I hope is likely to have favourable weather;—the crop is good.—There has been a cold & sorethroat prevailing very much in this House lately, the Children have almost all been ill with it, & we were afraid Lizzy was going to be very ill one day; she had specks & a great deal of fever.—It went off[9] however, & they are all pretty well now.—I want to hear of your gathering Strawberries, we have had them three times here.—I suppose you have been obliged to have in some white wine, & must visit the Store Closet a little oftener than when you were quite by yourselves.—One begins really to expect the S[t] Albans now, & I wish she may come before Henry goes to Cheltenham, it will be so much more convenient to him. He will be very glad if Frank can come to him in London, as his own Time is likely to be very precious, but does not depend on it.—I shall not forget Charles next week.—So much did I write before breakfast— & now to my agreable surprise I have to acknowledge another Letter from you.—I had not the least notion of hearing before tomorrow, & heard of Russell's being about to pass the Windows without any anxiety. You are very amiable & very clever to write such long Letters; every page of yours has more lines than this, & every line more words than the average of mine. I am quite ashamed—but you have certainly more little events than we have. M[r] Lyford supplies you with a great deal of interesting Matter (Matter Intellectual, not physical)—but I have nothing to say of M[r] Scudamore. [*p. 4*] And now, that is such a sad stupid attempt at Wit, about Matter, that nobody can smile at it, & I am quite out of heart. I am sick of myself, & my bad pens.—I have no other complaint however, my languor is entirely removed.—Ought I[10] to be very much pleased with Marmion?[11]—as yet I am not.—James reads it aloud in the Even[g]—the short Even[g]—beginning at about 10, & broken by supper.—Happy M[rs] Harrison & Miss Austen!—You seem to be always calling on them.—I am glad your various civilities have turned out so well; & most heartily wish you Success & pleasure in your present engagement.—I shall think of you tonight as at Netley, & tomorrow too, that I may be quite sure of being right—& therefore I guess you will not go to Netley at all.—This is a sad story about M[rs] Powlett.[12] I should not have suspected her of such a thing.—She staid the Sacrament I remember, the last time that you & I did.—A hint of it, with Initials, was in yesterday's Courier; & M[r] Moore guessed it to be L[d] Sackville, beleiving there was no other Viscount S. in the peerage, & so it proved—L[d] Viscount Seymour not being there.—Yes, I enjoy my apartment very much, & always spend two or three hours in it after breakfast.—The change from Brompton Quarters to these is material as to Space.—I catch myself going on to the Hall Chamber now & then.—Little Caroline looks very plain among her Cousins, & tho' she is not so headstrong or humoursome as they are, I do not think her at all [*continued below address panel*] more engaging.—Her brother is to go with us to Canterbury tomorrow, & Fanny completes the party. I fancy Mrs K. feels less interest in that branch of the family than any ot[her. I] dare say she will do her *duty* however, by the Boy.—His Uncle Edward talks nonsense to him [*back to p. 1, crossed*] delightfully—more than he can always understand. The two Morrises are come to dine & spend the day with him. Mary wishes my Mother to buy whatever she thinks necessary for Anna's Shifts;—& hopes to see her at Steventon soon after ye 9th of July, if that time is as convenient to my Mother as any other.—I have hardly done justice to what she means on the subject, as her intention is that my Mother sh^d come at whatever time She likes best.—They will be at home on ye 9th.—

I always come in for a morning visit from Crondale, & M^r & Mrs Filmer have just given me my due. He & I talked away gaily of Southampton, the Harrisons Wallers &c.—Fanny sends her best Love to You all, & will write to Anna very soon.—Yours very affec^{ly}

Jane.

[*Postscript on p. 2, crossed*]

I want some news from Paragon.—

I am almost sorry that Rose Hill Cottage sh^d be so near suiting us, as it does not quite.

Miss Austen
Castle Square
Southampton

54. *To Cassandra Austen*

Sunday 26 June 1808

Godmersham, Sunday June 26th

My dear Cassandra

I am very much obliged to you for writing to me on Thursday, & very glad that I owe the pleasure of hearing from you again so soon, to such an agreable cause; but you will not be surprised, nor perhaps so angry as I sh^d be, to find that Frank's History had reached me before, in a letter from Henry.—We are all very happy to hear of his health &

safety;—he wants nothing but a good Prize to be a perfect Character.—
This scheme to the Island is an admirable thing for his wife; she will not
feel the delay of his return, in such variety.—How very kind of M^{rs}
Craven to ask her!—I think I quite understand the whole Island arrangements, & shall be very ready to perform my part in them. I hope
my Mother will go—& I trust it is certain that there will be Martha's
bed for Edward when he brings me home. What can you do with
Anna?—for her bed will probably be wanted for young Edward.[1]—His
Father writes to Dr Goddard to day to ask leave, & we have the Pupil's
authority for thinking it will be granted.—I have been so kindly pressed
to stay longer here, in consequence of an offer of Henry's to take me
back some time in September, that not being able to detail all my ob-
jections to such a plan, I have felt myself obliged to give Edwd & Elizth
one private reason for my wishing to be at home in July.—They feel
the strength of it, & say no more;—& one can rely on their secrecy.—
After this, I hope we shall not be disappointed of our Friends' visit;[2]—
my honour, as well as my affection will be concerned in it.—Elizth has
a very sweet scheme of our accompanying Edward[3] into Kent next
Christmas. A Legacy might make it very feasible;—a Legacy is our
sovereign good.—In the mean while, let me remember that I have now
some money to spare, & that I wish to have my name put down as a
subscriber to Mr Jefferson's works. My last Letter was closed before it
occurred to me how possible, how right, & how gratifying such a
measure w^d be.—Your account [*p. 2*] of your Visitors good Journey,
Voyage, & satisfaction in everything gave me the greatest pleasure.
They have nice weather for their introduction to the Island, & I hope
with such a disposition to be pleased, their general Enjoyment is as
certain as it will be just.—Anna's being interested in the Embarkation
shows a Taste that one values.—Mary Jane's delight in the Water is
quite ridiculous. Elizabeth supposes Mrs Hall will account for it, by the
Child's knowledge of her Father's being at sea.—Mrs J. A. hopes as I
said in my last, to see my Mother soon after her return home, & will
meet her at Winchester on any day, she will appoint.—And now I
beleive I have made all the needful replys & communications; & may
disport myself as I can on my Canterbury visit.—It was a very agreable
visit. There was everything to make it so; Kindness, conversation, &
variety, without care or cost.—Mr Knatchbull from Provender was at
the W. Friars when we arrived, & staid dinner, which with Harriot—
who came as you may suppose in a great hurry, ten minutes after the
time—made our number 6.—Mr K. went away early;—Mr Moore

succeeded him, & we sat quietly working & talking till 10; when he ordered his wife away, & we adjourned to the Dressing room to eat our Tart & Jelly.—Mr M. was not un-agreable, tho' nothing seemed to go right with him. He is a sensible Man, & tells a story well.—Mrs C. Knatchbull & I breakfasted tete a tete the next day, for her Husband was gone to Mr Toke's, & Mrs Knight had a sad headache which kept her in bed. She had had too much company the day before;—after my coming, which was not till past two, she had Mrs M. of Nackington,[4] a M^rs & Miss Gregory, & Charles Graham;[5] & she told me it had been so all the morning.—Very soon after breakfast on friday Mrs C. K.—who is just what we have always seen her—went with me to Mrs Brydges' & Mrs Moore's,[6] paid some other visits while I remained with the latter, & we finished with Mrs C. Milles, who luckily was not at home, & whose new House is a very convenient short cut from the Oaks to the W. Friars.—We found Mrs Knight up & better—but early as it was— only 12 o'clock—we had scarcely taken off our Bonnets before company came, Ly Knatchbull & her Mother; & after them succeeded Mrs White, Mrs Hughes & her two Children, Mr Moore, Harriot & Louisa, & John Bridges, with such short intervals between any, as to [*p. 3*] make it a matter of wonder to me, that Mrs K. & I should ever have been ten minutes alone, or have had any leisure[7] for comfortable Talk.— Yet we had time to say a little of Everything.—Edward came to dinner, & at 8 o'clock he & I got into the Chair, & the pleasures of my visit concluded with a delightful drive home.—M^rs & Miss Brydges seemed very glad to see me.—The poor old Lady looks much as she did three years ago, & was very particular[8] in her enquiries after my Mother;— And from her, & from the Knatchbulls, I have all manner of kind Compliments to give you both. As Fanny writes to Anna by this post, I had intended to keep my Letter for another day, but recollecting that I must keep it two,[9] I have resolved rather to finish & send it now. The two letters will not interfere I dare say; on the contrary, they may throw light on each other.—Mary begins to fancy, because she has received no message on the subject, that Anna does not mean to answer her Letter; but it must be for the pleasure of fancying it.—I think Eliz^th better & looking better than when we came.—Yesterday I introduced James to Mrs Inman;—in the evening John Bridges returned from Goodnestone—& this morn^g before we had left the Breakfast Table we had a visit from Mr Whitfield, whose object I imagine[10] was principally to thank my Eldest Brother for his assistance. Poor Man!—he has now a little intermission of his excessive solicitude on his wife's account, as

she is rather better.—James does Duty at Godmersham today.—The
Knatchbulls had intended coming here next week, but the Rentday
makes it impossible for them to be received, & I do not think there will
be any spare time afterwards. They return into Somersetshire by way
of Sussex & Hants, & are to be at Fareham—& perhaps may be in
Southampton, on which possibility I said all that I thought right—& if
they are in the place, Mrs K. has promised to call in Castle Square;—
it will [be *omitted*] about the end of July.—She seems to have a prospect however of being in that Country again in the Spring for a longer
period, & will spend a day with us if she is.—You & I need not tell
each other how glad we shall be to receive attention from, or pay it to
anyone connected with Mrs Knight.—I cannot help regretting that
now, when I feel enough her equal to relish her society, I see so little
of the latter.—The Milles' of Nackington dine here on friday & perhaps the Hattons.—It is a compliment as much due to me, as a call from
the Filmers.—When you write to the Island, Mary will be glad to have
Mrs Craven [*p. 4*] informed with her Love that she is now sure it will
not be in her power to visit Mrs Craven during her stay there, but that
if Mrs Craven can take Steventon in her way back, it will be giving my
brother & herself great pleasure.—She also congratulates her namesake[11] on hearing from her Husband.—That said namesake is rising in
the World;—she was thought excessively improved in her late visit.—
Mrs Knight thought her so, last year.—Henry sends us the welcome
information of his having had no face-ache since I left them.—You are
very kind in mentioning old Mrs Williams so often. Poor Creature!—
I cannot help hoping that each Letter may tell of her sufferings being
over.—If she wants sugar, I sh^d like to supply her with it.—The Moores
went yesterday to Goodnestone, but return tomorrow. After Tuesday
we shall see them no more—tho' Harriot is very earnest with Edwd to
make Wrotham in his Journey, but we shall be in too great a hurry to
get nearer to it than Wrotham Gate.—He wishes to reach Guilford on
friday night—that we may have a couple of hours to spare for Alton.—
I shall be sorry to pass the door at Seale[12] without calling, but it must
be so;—& I shall be nearer to Bookham than I c^d wish, in going from
Dorking to Guilford—but till I have a travelling purse of my own, I
must submit to such things.—[*continued below address panel*] The Moores
leave Canterbury on friday—& go for a day or two to Sandling.—I
really hope Harriot is altogether very happy—but she cannot feel quite
so much at her ease with her Husband, as the Wives she has been used
to.—[*upside down at top of p. 1*] Good-bye. I hope You have been long

recovered from your worry on Thursday morn^g—& that you do not much mind not going to the Newbury Races.—I am withstanding those of Canterbury. Let that strengthen you.—

Y^{rs} very sincerely
Jane

Miss Austen
Castle Square
Southampton

55. *To Cassandra Austen*

Thursday 30 June–Friday 1 July 1808
Godmersham, Thursday June 30th

My dear Cassandra

I give you all Joy of Frank's return, which happens in the true Sailor way, just after our being told not to expect him for some weeks.—The Wind has been very much against him, but I suppose he must be in our Neighbourhood by this time. Fanny is in hourly expectation of him here.—Mary's visit in the Island is probably shortened by this Event. Make our kind Love & Congratulations to her.—What cold, disagreable weather, ever since Sunday!—I dare say you have Fires every day. My kerseymere Spencer is quite the comfort of our Even^g walks.—Mary thanks Anna for her Letter, & wishes her to buy enough of her new coloured frock to make a shirt handkf.—I am glad to hear of her Aunt Maitland's kind present.—We want you to send us Anna's height, that we may know whether she is as tall as Fanny;—and pray can you tell me of any little thing that w^d be probably acceptable to Mrs F. A.—I wish to bring her something;—has she a silver knife—or w^d you recommend a Broche? I shall not spend more than half a guinea about it.—Our Tuesday's Engagement went off very pleasantly; we called first on Mrs Knight, & found her very well; & at dinner had only the Milles' of Nackington in addition to Goodnestone & Godmersham & Mrs Moore.—Lady Bridges looked very well, & w^d have been very agreable I am sure, had there been time enough for her to talk to me, but as it was, she c^d only be kind & amiable, give me good-humoured smiles & make friendly enquiries.—Her son Edward was also looking very well, & with manners as un-altered as hers. In the Even^g came Mr Moore, Mr Toke, D^r & Mrs Walsby & others;—one Card Table was formed, the rest of us sat & talked, & at half after nine we came away.—Yesterday my two Brothers went to Canterbury, and J. Bridges left us for London in his way to Cambridge, where he is to take his Master's Degree.—Edward & Caroline & their Mama have all had the God-mersham Cold; the former with sorethroat & fever which his Looks are still suffering from.—*He* is very happy here however, [*p. 2*] but I beleive the little girl will be glad to go home;[1] —her Cousins are too much for her.—We are to have Edward, I find, at Southampton while his Mother is in Berkshire for the Races—& are very likely to have his Father too. If circumstances are favourable, that will be a good time for our scheme to Beaulieu.—Lady E. Hatton called here a few mornings ago, her Daughter Eliz[th] with her, who says as little as ever, but holds up her head & smiles & is to be at the Races.—Annamaria was there with M[rs] Hope, but we are to see her here tomorrow.—So much was written before breakfast; it is now half past twelve, & having heard Lizzy read, I am moved down into the Library for the sake of a fire which agreably surprised us when we assembled at Ten, & here in warm & happy solitude proceed to acknowledge this day's Letter. We give you credit for your spirited voyage, & are very glad it was accom-plished so pleasantly, & that Anna enjoyed it so much.—I hope you are not the worse for the fatigue—but to embark at 4 you must have got up at 3, & most likely had no sleep at all.—Mary's not chusing to be at home, occasions a general small surprise.—As to Martha, she had not the least chance in the World of hearing from me again, & I wonder at her impudence in proposing it.—I assure you[2] I am as tired of writ-ing long letters as you can be. What a pity that one should still be so fond of receiving them!—Fanny Austen's Match[3] is quite news, & I am sorry she has behaved so ill. There is some comfort to *us* in her miscon-duct, that we have not a congratulatory Letter to write.—James & Edward are gone to Sandling to day;—a nice scheme for James, as it will shew him a new & fine Country. Edward certainly excels in doing the Honours to his visitors, & providing for their amusement.—They come back this Even[g]—Elizabeth talks of going with her three girls to Wrotham while her husband is in Hampshire;—she is improved in looks since we first came, & excepting a cold, does not seem at all unwell. She is considered indeed as more than usually active for her situation & size.—I have tried to give James pleasure by telling him of his Daughter's Taste, but if he felt, he did not express it.—*I* rejoice in it very sin-cerely.—Henry talks, or rather writes of going to the Downes, if the S[t] Albans continues there—but I hope it will be settled otherwise.—I had everybody's congratulations on her arrival, at Canterbury; — it is pleas-ant to be among people who know one's connections & care about

them; & it amuses me to hear John Bridges talk of "Frank."—[*p. 3*] I
have thought a little of writing to the Downs, but I shall not; it is so
very certain that he w^d be somewhere else when my Letter got there.—
Mr Tho. Leigh is again in Town—or was very lately. Henry met with
him last sunday in St James's Church.—He owned being come up
unexpectedly on Business—which we of course think can be only *one*
business—& he came post from Adlestrop in one day, which—if it c^d
be doubted before—convinces Henry that he will live for ever.—M^rs
Knight is kindly anxious for our Good, & thinks Mr L. P. *must* be
desirous for his *Family's* sake to have everything settled.—Indeed, I do
not know where we are to get our Legacy—but we will keep a sharp
look-out.—Lady B. was all in prosperous Black the other day.—A
Letter from Jenny Smallbone[4] to her Daughter brings intelligence[5] which
is to be forwarded to my Mother, the calving of a Cow at Steventon.—
I am also to give her Mama's Love to Anna, & say that as her Papa[6]
talks of writing her a Letter of comfort she will *not* write, because she
knows it w^d certainly prevent his doing so.—When are calculations
ever right?—I could have sworn that Mary must have heard of the S^t
Albans return, & w^d have been wild to come home, or to be doing
something.—Nobody ever feels or acts, suffers or enjoys, as one expects!—I do not at all regard Martha's disappointment in the Island; she
will like it the better in the end.—I cannot help thinking & re-thinking
of your going to the Island so heroically. It puts me in mind of M^rs
Hastings' voyage down the Ganges,[7] & if we had but a room to retire
into to eat our fruit, we w^d have a picture of it hung there.—Friday July
1st—The weather is mended, which I attribute to my writing about it—
& I am in hopes, as you make no complaint, tho' on the Water & at 4
in the morn^g—that it has not been so cold with you.—It will be two
years tomorrow since we left Bath for Clifton, with what happy feelings
of Escape!—This post has brought me a few lines from the amiable
Frank, but he gives us no hope of seeing him here.—We are not unlikely to have a peep at Henry who, unless the St Albans moves quickly,
will be going to the Downs, & who will not be able to be in Kent
without giving a day or two to Godmersham.—James has heard this
morn^g from Mrs Cooke, in reply to his offer of taking Bookham in his
way home, which is kindly accepted; & Edwd has had a less agreable
answer from Dr Goddard, who actually refuses the petition. [*p. 4*] Being once fool enough to make a rule of never letting a Boy go away an
hour before the Breaking up Hour, he is now fool enough to keep it.[8]—
We are all disappointed.—His Letter brings a double disappointment,

for he has no room for George this summer.—My Brothers returned last night at 10, having spent a very agreable day in the usual routine. They found Mrs D.^9 at home, & Mr D. returned from Business abroad, to dinner. James admires the place very much, & thinks the two Eldest girls handsome—but Mary's beauty has the preference.—The number of Children struck him a good deal, for not only are their own Eleven all at home, but the three little Bridgeses^10 are also with them.—James means to go once more to Cant^y to see his friend Dr Marlowe, who is coming about this time;—*I* shall hardly have another opportunity of going there. In another week I shall be at home—& then, my having been at Godmersham will seem like a Dream, as my visit at Brompton seems already. The Orange Wine will want our Care soon.—But in the meantime for Elegance & Ease & Luxury—; the Hattons' & Milles' dine here today—& I shall eat Ice & drink French wine, & be above Vulgar Economy.^11 [*continued below address panel*] Luckily the pleasures of Friendship, of unreserved Conversation, of similarity of Taste & Opinions, will make good amends for Orange Wine.—

Little Edwd is quite w[ell] again.—

Y^rs affec^ly with Lo[ve] from all, JA.

Miss Austen
Castle Square
Southampton

---

56. *To Cassandra Austen*

Saturday 1–Sunday 2 October 1808

Castle Square, Saturday Octr 1.

My dear Cassandra

Your letter this morning was quite unexpected, & it is well that it brings such good news to counterbalance the disappointment to me of losing my first sentence, which I had arranged full of proper hopes about your Journey, intending to commit them to paper to day, & not looking for certainty till tomorrow.—We are extremely glad to hear of the birth of the Child,^1 & trust everything will proceed as well as it begins;—his Mama has our best wishes, & he our second best for health & comfort—tho' I suppose unless *he* has our best too, we do nothing for *her*.—We are glad it was all over before your arrival;—& I am most happy to find who the Godmother is to be.—My Mother was some time guessing the names.—Henry's present to you gives me great pleasure, & I shall watch the weather for him at this time with redoubled interest.—We have had 4 brace of Birds lately, in equal Lots from Shalden & Neatham.[2]—Our party at M[rs] Duer's produced the novelties of two old M[rs] Pollens & M[rs] Heywood, with whom my Mother made a Quadrille Table; & of M[rs] Maitland & Caroline, & M[r] Booth without his sisters at Commerce.—I have got a Husband for each of the Miss Maitlands;—Col[n] Powlett & his Brother have taken Argyle's inner House, & the consequence is so natural that I have no ingenuity in planning it. If the Brother sh[d] luckily be a little sillier than the Colonel, what a treasure for Eliza.[3]—M[r] Lyford called on tuesday to say that he was disappointed of his son & daughter's coming, & must go home himself the following morn[g];—& as I was determined that he sh[d] not lose every pleasure I consulted him on my complaint. He recommended cotton moistened with oil of sweet almonds, & it has done me good.— I hope therefore to have nothing more to do with Eliza's[4] receipt than to feel obliged to her for giving it[5] as I very sincerely do.—

[*p. 2*] M[rs] Tilson's remembrance gratifies me, & I will use her patterns if I can; but poor Woman! how can she be honestly breeding again?[6]—I have just finished a Handkf. for M[rs] James Austen, which I expect her Husband to give me an opportunity of sending to her ere long. Some fine day in October will certainly bring him to us in the Garden, between three & four o'clock.—*She* hears that Miss Bigg is to be married in a fortnight. I wish it may be so.—About an hour & half after your toils on Wednesday ended, ours began;—at seven o'clock, M[rs] Harrison, her two daughters & two Visitors, with M[r] Debary & his eldest sister walked in; & our Labour was not a great deal shorter than poor Elizabeth's, for it was past eleven before we were delivered.—A second pool of Commerce, & all the longer by the addition of the two girls, who during the first had one corner of the Table & Spillikins to themselves, was the ruin of us; —it completed the prosperity of M[r] Debary however, for he won them both.—M[r] Harrison came in late, & sat by the fire—for which I envied him, as we had our usual luck of having a very cold Even[g]. It rained when our company came, but was dry again before they left us.—The Miss Ballards are said to be remarkably well-informed; their manners are unaffected & pleasing, but they do not talk quite freely enough to be agreable—nor can I discover any right they had by Taste or Feeling to go their late Tour.—Miss Austen & her nephew are returned—but M[r] Choles is still absent;— "still absent" say you, "I did not know that he was gone anywhere"—

Saturday 1–Sunday 2 October 1808

Neither did I know that Lady Bridges was at Godmersham at all, till I was told of her being *still* there, which I take therefore to be the most approved method of announcing arrivals & departures.—Mᵣ Choles is gone to drive a Cow to Brentford, & his place is supplied to us by a Man who lives in the same sort of way by odd jobs, & among other capabilities has that of working in a garden, which my Mother will not forget, if we ever have another garden here.—In general however she thinks much more of Alton, & really expects to move there.—Mʳˢ Lyell's 130 Guineas rent have made a great impression. [*p. 3*] To the purchase of furniture, whether here or there, she is quite reconciled, & talks of the *Trouble* as the only evil.—I depended upon Henry's liking the Alton plan, & expect to hear of something perfectly *unexceptionable*⁷ there, through him.—Our Yarmouth Division⁸ seem to have got nice Lodgings;—& with fish almost for nothing, & plenty of Engagements & plenty of each other, must be very happy.—My Mother has undertaken to cure six Hams for Frank;—at first it was a distress, but now it is a pleasure.—She desires me to say that she does not doubt your making out the Star pattern very well, as you have the Breakfast room-rug to look at.—We have got the 2ᵈ vol. of Espriella's Letters,⁹ & I read it aloud by candlelight. The Man describes well, but is horribly anti-english. He deserves to be the foreigner he assumes. Mᵣ Debary went away yesterday, & I being gone with some partridges to Sᵗ Maries lost his parting visit.—I have heard today from Miss Sharpe, & find that she returns with Miss B.¹⁰ to Hinckley, & will continue there at least till about Christmas, when she thinks they may both travel southward.—Miss B. however is probably to make¹¹ only a temporary absence from Mᵣ Chessyre, & I shᵈ not wonder if Miss Sharpe were to continue with her;—unless anything more eligible offer, she certainly *will*. She describes Miss B. as very anxious that she should do so.—Sunday—I had not expected to hear from you again so soon, & am much obliged to you for writing as you did; but now as you must have a great deal of the business upon your hands, do not trouble yourself with me for the present;—I shall consider silence as good news, & not expect another Letter from you till friday or Saturday.¹²—You must have had a great deal more rain than has fallen here;—Cold enough it has been but not wet, except for a few hours on Wednesday Evenᵍ, & I could have found nothing more plastic than dust to stick in;—now indeed we are likely to have a wet day—& tho' Sunday, my Mother begins it without any ailment.—Your plants were taken in one very [*p. 4*] cold blustering day & placed in the Dining room, & there was a frost the very same night.—

141

If we have warm weather again they are to be put out of doors, if not my Mother will have them conveyed to their Winter quarters.—I gather some Currants every now & then, when I want either fruit or employment.—Pray tell my little Goddaughter[13] that I am delighted to hear of her saying her lesson so well.—You have used me ill, you have been writing to Martha without telling me of it, & a letter which I sent her on wednesday to give her information of you, must have been good for nothing. I do not know how to think that something will not still happen to prevent her returning by ye 10th—And if it does, I shall not much regard it on my own account, for I am now got into such a way of being alone that I do not wish even for her.—The Marquis[14] has put off being cured for another year;—after waiting some weeks in vain for the return of the Vessel he had agreed for, he is gone into Cornwall to order a Vessel built for himself by a famous Man in that Country, in which he means to go abroad a twelvemonth hence.—

[Upside down at top of p. 1]

We had two Pheasants last night from Neatham. Tomorrow Eveng is to be given to the Maitlands;—we are just asked, to meet Mrs Heywood & Mrs Duer.

[Below address panel]

Everybody who comes to Southampton finds it either their duty or pleasure to call upon us; Yesterday we were visited by the eldest Miss Cotterel, just arrived from Waltham. Adeiu—With Love to all, Yrs affecly JA.

Miss Austen
Edward Austen's Esqr
Godmersham Park
Faversham
Kent

57. *To Cassandra Austen*

Friday 7–Sunday 9 October 1808

Castle Square, Friday Oct. 7.—

My dear Cassandra

Your letter on Tuesday gave us great pleasure, & we congratulate you all upon Elizabeth's hitherto happy recovery;—tomorrow or Sunday

I hope to hear of its' advancing in the same stile.—We are also very glad to know that you are so well yourself, & pray you to continue so.—I was rather surprised on Monday by the arrival of a Letter for you from your Winchester Correspondent,[1] who seemed perfectly unsuspicious of your being likely to be at Godmersham;—I took complete possession of the Letter by reading, paying for, & answering it;—and he will have the Biscuits to day,—a very proper day[2] for the purpose, tho' I did not think of it at the time.—I wish my Brother joy of completing his 30th year[3]—& hope the day will be remembered better than it was six years ago.—The Masons are now repairing the Chimney, which they found in such a state as to make it wonderful that it sh[d] have stood so long, & next to impossible that another violent wind should not blow it down. We may therefore thank *you* perhaps for saving us from being thumped with old bricks.—You are also to be thank'd by Eliza's[4] desire for your present to her of dyed sattin, which is made into a bonnet, & I fancy surprises her by its' good appearance.—My Mother is preparing mourning for M[rs] E. K.[5]—she has picked her old silk pelisse to peices, & means to have it dyed black[6] for a gown—a very interesting scheme, tho' just now a little injured by finding that it must be placed in M[r] Wren's hands, for M[r] Chambers is gone.—As for M[r] Floor, he is at present rather low in our estimation; how is your blue gown?—Mine is all to peices.—I think there must have been something wrong in the dye, for in places it divided with a Touch.—There was four shillings thrown away;—to be added [*p. 2*] to my subjects of never failing regret.—We found ourselves tricked into a thorough party at M[rs] Maitlands, a quadrille & a Commerce Table, & Music in the other room. There were two pools at Commerce, but I would not play more than one, for the Stake was three shillings, & I cannot afford to lose that, twice in an even[g]—The Miss Ms. were as civil & as silly as usual.—You know of course that Martha comes today; yesterday brought us notice of it, & the Spruce Beer is brewed in consequence.—On wednesday I had a letter from Yarmouth to desire me to send Mary's flannels & furs &c—& as there was a packing case at hand, I could do it without any trouble.—On Tuesday Even[g] Southampton was in a good deal of alarm for about an hour; a fire broke out soon after nine at Webbes, the Pastrycook, & burnt for some time with great fury. I cannot learn exactly how it originated, at the time it was said to be their Bakehouse, but now I hear it was in the back of their Dwelling house, & that one room was consumed.—The Flames were considerable, they seemed about as near to us as those at Lyme,[7] & to reach higher. One could not but feel uncomfortable, & I began to think of what I should do, if it came to the worst;—happily however the night was perfectly still, the Engines were immediately in use, & before ten the fire was nearly extinguished—tho' it was twelve before everything was considered safe, & a Guard was kept the whole night. Our friends the Duers were alarmed,[8] but not out of their good Sense or Benevolence.—I am afraid the Webbes have lost a great deal—more perhaps from ignorance or plunder than the Fire;—they had a large stock of valuable China, & in order to save it, it was taken from the House, & thrown down anywhere.—The adjoining House, a Toyshop, was almost equally injured—& Hibbs, whose House comes next, was so scared from his senses that he was giving away all his goods, valuable Laces &c, to anybody who w[d] take them.—The Croud in the High S[t] I understand was immense; M[rs] Harrison, who was drinking tea with a Lady at Millar's, could not leave it twelve o'clock.—Such are the prominent features of our fire. Thank God! they were not worse.—[*p. 3*] Saturday.—Thank you for your Letter, which found me at the Breakfast-Table, with my *two* companions.[9]—I am greatly pleased with your account of Fanny; I found her in the summer just what you describe, almost another Sister, & could not have supposed that a neice would ever have been so much to me. She is quite after one's own heart; give her my best Love,[10] & tell her that I always think of her with pleasure.—I am much obliged to you for enquiring about my ear, & am happy to say that M[r] Lyford's prescription has entirely cured me. I feel it a great blessing to hear again.— Your gown shall be unpicked, but I do not remember its' being settled so before.—Martha was here by half past six, attended by Lyddy;— they had some rain at last, but a very good Journey on the whole; & if Looks & Words may be trusted Martha is very happy to be returned. We receive her with Castle Square-Weather, it has blown a gale from the N. W. ever since she came—& we feel ourselves in luck that the Chimney was mended yesterday.—She brings several good things for the Larder, which is now very rich; we had a pheasant & hare the other day from the M[r] Grays of Alton. Is this to entice us to Alton, or to keep us away?—Henry had probably some share in the two last baskets from that Neighbourhood, but we have not seen so much of his handwriting even as a direction to either. Martha was an hour & half in Winchester, walking about with the three boys[11] & at the Pastrycook's.—She thought Edward grown, & speaks with the same admiration as before of his

Manners;—she saw in George a little likeness to his Uncle Henry.—I am glad you are to see Harriot,[12] give my Love to her.—I wish you may be able to accept Lady Bridges's invitation, tho' *I* could not her son Edward's;[13]—she is a nice Woman, & honours me by her remembrance.—Do you recollect whether the Manydown family send about their Wedding Cake?—Mrs Dundas has set her heart upon having a peice from her friend Catherine,[14] & Martha who knows what importance she attaches to the sort of thing, is anxious for the sake of both, that there sh^d not be a disappointment.—Our weather I fancy has been just like yours, we have had *some* very delightful days, our 5th & 6th were what the 5th & 6th of October should always be, but we have always wanted a fire *within* doors, at least except for just the middle of the day.—Martha does not find the Key, which you left in my charge for her, suit the Keyhole—& wants to know whether you think you can have mistaken it.[15]—It should open the interior of her High Drawers— but she is in no hurry about it. [*p. 4*] Sunday—It is cold enough now for us to prefer dining upstairs to dining below without a fire, & being only three we manage it very well, & today with two more we shall do just *as* well, I dare say; Miss Foote[16] & Miss Wethered are coming. My Mother is much pleased with Elizabeth's admiration of the rug—& pray tell Elizabeth that the new mourning gown is to be made double *only* in the body & sleeves.—Martha thanks you for your message, & desires you may be told with her best Love that your wishes are answered & that she is full of peace & comfort here.—I do not think however that *here* she will remain a great while, she does not herself expect that Mrs Dundas will be able to do with her long.[17] She *wishes* to stay with us till Christmas if possible.—Lyddy goes home tomorrow; she seems well, but does not mean to go to service at present.—The Wallops are returned.—Mr John Harrison has paid his visit of duty & is gone.—We have got a new Physician, a Dr Percival, the son of a famous Dr Percival of Manchester,[18] who wrote Moral Tales for Edward to give to me.—When you write again to Catherine thank her on my part for her very kind & welcome mark of friendship. I shall value such a Broche very much.—Goodbye my dearest Cassandra [*continued below address panel*] Y^{rs} very affec^{ly} JA.

Have you written to Mrs E. Leigh?—Martha will be glad to find Anne in work at present, & I am as glad to have her so found.—

We must turn our black pelisses into new, for Velvet is to be very much worn this winter.—

Miss Austen
Edward Austen's Esq'
Godmersham Park
Faversham
Kent

58. *To Cassandra Austen*

Thursday 13 October 1808

Castle Square, Oct' 13.

My dearest Cassandra

I have received your Letter, & with most melancholy anxiety was it
expected, for the sad news¹ reached us last night, but without any particulars; it came² in a short letter to Martha from her sister, begun at
Steventon, & finished in Winchester.—We have felt, we do feel for you
all—as you will not need to be told—for you, for Fanny, for Henry,³
for Lady Bridges, & for dearest Edward, whose loss & whose sufferings seem to make those of every other person nothing.—God be
praised! that you can say what you do of him—that he has a religious
Mind to bear him up, & a Disposition that will gradually lead him to
comfort.—My dear, dear Fanny!—I am so thankful that she has you
with her!—You will be everything to her, you will give her all the
Consolation that human aid can give.—May the Almighty sustain you
all—& keep you my dearest Cassandra well—but for the present I dare
say you are equal to everything.—[*p. 2*] You will know that the poor
Boys⁴ are at Steventon, perhaps it is best for them, as they will have
more means of exercise & amusement there⁵ than they cᵈ have with us,
but I own myself disappointed by the arrangement;—I should have
loved to have them with me at such a time. I shall write to Edward by
this post.—We shall of course hear from you again very soon, & as
often as you can write.—We will write as you desire, & I shall add
Bookham. Hamstall I suppose you write to yourselves, as you do not
mention it.—What a comfort that Mʳˢ Deedes is saved from present
misery & alarm—but it will fall heavy upon poor Harriot—& as for
Lady B.—but that her fortitude does seem truely great, I should fear
the effect of such a Blow & so unlooked for. I long to hear more of you
all.—Of Henry's anguish, I think with greif & solicitude; but he will
exert himself to be of use & comfort. [*p. 3*] With what true simpathy
our feelings are shared by Martha, you need not be told;—she is the

146

friend & Sister under every circumstance.—We need not enter into a Panegyric on the Departed—but it is sweet to think of her great worth—of her solid principles, her true devotion, her excellence in every relation of Life. It is also consolatory to reflect on the shortness of the sufferings which led her from this World to a better.—Farewell for the present, my dearest Sister. Tell Edward that we feel for him & pray for him.—

Y^{rs} affec^{tely}
J. Austen

I will write to Catherine.[6]
Perhaps you can give me some directions about Mourning.

Miss Austen
Edward Austen's Esqr
Godmersham Park
Faversham
Kent

59. *To Cassandra Austen*

Saturday 15–Sunday 16 October 1808

Castle Square, Saturday night, Octr 15.

My dear Cassandra
    Your accounts make us as comfortable as we can expect to be at such a time. Edward's loss is terrible, & must be felt as such, & these are too early days indeed to think of Moderation in greif, either in him or his afflicted daughter—but soon we may hope that our dear Fanny's sense of Duty to that beloved Father will rouse her to exertion. For his sake, & as the most acceptable proof of Love to the spirit of her departed Mother, she will try to be tranquil & resigned.—Does she feel You to be a comfort to her, or is she too much overpowered for anything but Solitude?—Your account of Lizzy is very interesting. Poor Child! One must hope the impression *will* be strong, & yet one's heart aches for a dejected Mind of eight years old.—I suppose you see the Corpse,[1]—how does it appear?—We are anxious to be assured that Edwd will not attend the funeral; but when it comes to the point, I think he must feel it impossible.—Your parcel shall set off on Monday, & I hope the Shoes will fit; Martha & I both tried them on.—I shall send you such of your Mourning as I think most likely to be useful, reserving for myself your Stockings & half the velvet—in which selfish arrangement I know I am

doing what you wish.—*I* am to be in Bombazeen & Crape, according to what we are told is universal *here*; & which agrees [*p. 2*] with Martha's previous observation. My Mourning however will not impoverish me, for by having my velvet Pelisse fresh lined & made up, I am sure I shall have no occasion *this winter* for anything new of that sort.—I take my Cloak for the Lining—& shall send yours on the chance of its' doing something of the same for you—tho' I beleive your Pelisse is in better repair than mine.— *One* Miss Baker makes my gown, & the other my Bonnet, which is to be silk covered with Crape.—I have written to Edwd Cooper, & hope he will not send one of his Letters of cruel comfort to my poor Brother;—& yesterday I wrote to Alethea Bigg, in reply to a Letter from her. She tells us in confidence, that Cath: is to be married on Tuesday se'night.—Mr Hill is expected at Manydown in the course of the ensueing week.—We are desired by Mrs Harrison & Miss Austen to say everything proper for them to Yourself & Edward on this sad occasion—especially that nothing but a wish of not giving additional trouble where so much is inevitable, prevents their writing themselves to express their Concern.—They seem truely to feel concern.—I am glad you can say what you do of Mrs Knight, & of Goodnestone in general;—it is a great releif to me to know that the Shock did not make any of them ill.—But what a task was Yours, to announce it!—*Now* I hope you are not overpowered with Letter-writing, as Henry & John[2] can ease you of many of your Correspondents.—Was Mr Scudamore in the House at the time, was any application attempted, & is the seizure at all accounted for?—Sunday.—As Edward's letter to his son is not come here, we know that you must have been informed as early as friday of [*p. 3*] the Boys being at Steventon, which I am glad of.— Upon your Letter to Dr Goddard's being forwarded to them, Mary wrote to ask whether my Mother wished to have her Grandsons sent to her. We decided on their remaining where they were, which I hope my Brother will approve of. I am sure he will do us the justice of beleiving that in such a decision we sacrificed inclination to what we thought best.—I shall write by the Coach tomorrow to Mrs J. A. & to Edward about their mourning, tho' this day's post will probably bring directions to them on that subject from Yourselves.—I shall certainly make use of the opportunity of addressing our Nephew on the most serious of all concerns, as I naturally did in my Letter to him before. The poor Boys are perhaps more comfortable at Steventon than they could be here, but you will understand *my feelings* with respect to it.—Tomorrow will be a dreadful day for you all!—Mr Whitfield's will be a severe duty!—Glad shall I be to hear that it is over.—That you are for ever in our Thoughts, you will not doubt.—I see your mournful party in my mind's eye under every varying circumstance of the day;—& in the Even^g especially, figure to myself its' sad gloom—the efforts to talk—the frequent summons to melancholy orders & cares—& poor Edward restless in Misery going from one room to the other—& perhaps not seldom upstairs to see all that remains of his Elizabeth.—Dearest Fanny must now look upon herself as his prime source of comfort, his dearest friend; as the Being who is gradually to supply to him, to the extent that is possible, what he has lost.—This consideration will elevate & cheer her.—Adeiu.—You cannot write too often, as I said before.—We are heartily rejoiced [*p. 4*] that the poor Baby gives you no particular anxiety.—Kiss dear Lizzy for us.—Tell Fanny that I shall write in a day or two to Miss Sharpe.—

Yours most truely
J. Austen

My Mother is not ill.

Tell Henry that a Hamper of Apples is gone to him from Kintbury, & that Mr Fowle^3 intended writing on friday (supposing him in London) to beg that the Charts &c may be consigned to the care of the Palmers.^{4}—Mrs Fowle has also written to Miss Palmer to beg she will send for them.—

Miss Austen
Edward Austen's Esqr
Godmersham Park
Faversham
Kent

[*Letter(s) missing here*]

60. *To Cassandra Austen*

Monday 24–Tuesday 25 October 1808

Castle Square Monday October 24

My dear Cassandra

Edward and George came to us soon after seven on Saturday, very well, but very cold, having by choice travelled on the outside, and with no great coat but what Mr Wise,^{1} the coachman, good-naturedly spared them of his, as they sat by his side. They were so much chilled when they arrived, that I was afraid they must have taken cold; but it does not seem at all the case; I never saw them looking better. *They behave extremely*[2] well in every respect, showing quite as much feeling as one wishes to see, and on every occasion speaking of their father with the liveliest affection. His letter was read over by each of them yesterday, and with many tears; George sobbed aloud, Edward's tears do not flow so easily; but as far as I can judge they are both very properly impressed by what has happened. Miss Lloyd, who is a more impartial judge than I can be, is exceedingly pleased with them. George is almost a new acquaintance to me, and I find him in a different way as *engaging as Edward*. We do not want amusement; bilbocatch,[3] at which George is indefatigable, spillikins, paper ships, riddles, conundrums, and cards, with watching the flow and ebb of the river, and now and then a stroll out, keep us well employed; and we mean to avail ourselves of our kind papa's consideration, by not returning to Winchester till quite the evening of Wednesday. Mrs J. A. had not time to get them more than one suit of clothes; their others are making here, and though I do not believe Southampton is famous for tailoring, I hope it will prove itself better than Basingstoke. Edward has an old black coat, which will save *his* having a second new one; but I find that black pantaloons are considered by them as necessary, and of course one would not have them made uncomfortable by the want of what is usual on such occasions. Fanny's letter was received with great pleasure yesterday, and her brother sends his thanks and will answer it soon. We all saw what she wrote, and were very much pleased with it. Tomorrow I hope to hear from you, and tomorrow we must think of poor Catherine.[4] Today Lady Bridges is the heroine of our thoughts, and glad shall we be when we can fancy the meeting over. There will then be nothing so very bad for Edward to undergo. The St Albans, I find, sailed on the very day of my letters reaching Yarmouth, so that we must not expect an answer at present; we scarcely feel, however, to be in suspense, or only enough to keep our plans to ourselves.[5] We have been obliged to explain them to our young visitors, in consequence of Fanny's letter, but we have not yet mentioned them to Steventon. We are all quite familiarised to the idea ourselves; my mother only wants Mrs Seward to go out at Midsummer. What sort of a kitchen garden is there? Mrs J. A. expresses her fear of our settling in Kent, and, till this proposal was made, we began to look forward to it here; my mother was actually talking of a house at Wye. It will be best, however, as it is. Anne has just given her mistress warning; she is going to be married; I wish she would stay her year. On the subject of matrimony, I must notice a wedding in the Salisbury paper, which has amused me very much, Dr Phillot to Lady Frances St Lawrence. *She* wanted to have a husband I suppose, once in her life, and *he* a Lady Frances. I hope your sorrowing party were at church yesterday, and have no longer *that* to dread. Martha was kept at home *by a cold, but I went with my two nephews, and I saw Edward was much affected by the sermon, which, indeed, I could have supposed purposely addressed* to the afflicted, if the text had not naturally come in the course of Dr Mant's observations on the Litany: 'All that are in danger, necessity, or tribulation,' was the subject of it. The weather did not allow us afterwards to get farther than the quay, where George was very happy as long as we could stay, flying about from one side to the other, and skipping on board a collier immediately. In the evening we had the Psalms and Lessons, and a sermon at home, to which they were very attentive; but you will not expect to hear that they did not return to conundrums the moment it *was over*. Their aunt[6] has written pleasantly of them, which was more than I hoped. While I write now, George is most industriously making and naming paper ships, at which he afterwards shoots with horse-chestnuts, brought from Steventon on purpose; and Edward equally intent over the 'Lake of Killarney,'[7] twisting himself about in one of our great chairs. *Tuesday*. Your close-written letter makes me quite ashamed of my wide lines; you have sent me a great deal of matter, most of it very welcome. As to your lengthened stay, it is no more than I expected, and what must be, but you cannot suppose I like it. All that you say of Edward is truly comfortable; I began to fear that when the bustle of the first week was over, his spirits might for a time be more depressed; and perhaps one must still expect something of the kind. If *you* escape a bilious attack, I shall wonder almost as much as rejoice. I am glad you mentioned where Catherine goes today; it is a good plan, but sensible people may generally be trusted to form such. The day began cheerfully, but it is not likely to continue what it should, for them or for us. *We had a little water party* yesterday; I and my two nephews went from the Itchen Ferry up to Northam, where we landed, looked into the 74,[8] and walked home, and it was so much enjoyed that I had intended to take them to Netley today; the tide is just right for our going immediately after noonshine, but I am afraid there will be rain; if we cannot get so far, however, we may perhaps go round from the ferry to the quay. I had not proposed doing more than cross the Itchen yesterday, but it proved so pleasant, and so much to the satisfaction of all, that when we reached the middle of the stream we agreed to be rowed up the river; both the boys rowed great part of the way, and their questions and remarks, as well as their enjoyment, were very amusing; George's enquiries were endless, and his eagerness in everything reminds me often *of his Uncle Henry*. Our evening was equally agreeable in its way; I introduced *speculation*, and it was so much approved that we hardly knew how to leave off. Your idea of an early dinner tomorrow is exactly what we propose, for, after writing the first part of this letter, it came into my head that at this time of year we have not summer evenings. We shall watch the light today, that we may not give them a dark drive tomorrow. They send their best love to papa and everybody, with George's thanks for the letter brought by this post. Martha begs my brother may be assured of her interest in everything relating to him and his family, and of her sincerely partaking our pleasure in the receipt of every good account from Godmersham. Of Chawton I think I can have nothing more to say, but that everything you say about it in the letter now before me will, I am sure, as soon as I am able to read it to her, make my mother consider the plan with more and more pleasure. We had formed the same views on H. Digweed's farm. A very kind and feeling letter is arrived today from Kintbury. Mrs Fowle's sympathy and solicitude on such an occasion you will be able to do justice to, and to express it as she wishes to my brother. Concerning *you*, she says: 'Cassandra will, I know, excuse my writing to her; it is not to save myself but *her* that I omit so doing. Give my best, my kindest love to her, and tell her I feel for her as I know she would for me on the same occasion, and that I most sincerely hope her health will not suffer.' We have just had two hampers of apples from Kintbury, and the floor of our little garret is almost covered. Love to all.

Yours very affectionately,

JA.

Miss Austen
Edward Austen Esq
Godmersham Park
Faversham
Kent

[*Letters missing here*]

61. *To Cassandra Austen*

Sunday 20 November 1808

Castle Square, Sunday Novr 21 [*sic*]

Your letter my dear Cassandra, obliges me to write immediately, that you may have the earliest notice of Frank's intending if possible to go to Godmersham exactly at the time now fixed for your visit to Goodnestone. He resolved almost directly on the receipt of your former Letter, to try for an extension of his Leave of absence that he might be able to go down to you for two days, but charged me not to give you any notice of it, on account of the uncertainty of success;—Now however, I must give it, & now perhaps he may be giving it himself—for I am just in the hateful predicament of being obliged to write what I know will somehow or other be of no use.—He meant to ask for five days more, & if they were granted, to go down by Thursday-night's Mail & spend friday & saturday with you;—& he considered his chance of succeeding, by no means bad.—I hope it will take place as he planned, & that your arrangements with Goodnestone may admit of suitable alteration.—Your news of Edw: Bridges was *quite* news, for I have had no letter from Wrotham.—I wish him happy with all my heart, & hope his choice may turn out according to his own expectations, & beyond those of his Family—And I dare say it will. Marriage is a great Improver—& in a similar situation Harriet[1] may be as amiable as Eleanor.—As to Money, that will come You may be sure, because they cannot do without it.—When you see him again, pray give him our Congratulations & best wishes.—This Match will certainly set John & Lucy[2] going.—There are six Bedchambers at Chawton; Henry wrote to my Mother the other day, & luckily mentioned the number—which is just what [*p. 2*] we wanted to be assured of. He speaks also of Garrets for Storeplaces, one of which she immediately planned fitting up for Edward's Manservant[3]—& now perhaps it must be for our own—for she is already quite reconciled to our keeping one. The difficulty of doing without one, had been thought of before.—His name shall be Robert,[4] if you please.—Before I can tell you of it, you will have heard that Miss Sawbridge is married. It took place I beleive on Thursday, Mrs Fowle has for some time been in the secret, but the Neighbourhood in general were quite unsuspicious. Mr Maxwell *was* Tutor to the young Gregorys—consequently they must be one of the happiest Couple in the World, & either of them worthy of Envy—for *she* must be excessively in love, & *he* mounts from nothing,[5] to a comfortable Home.—Martha has heard him very highly spoken of.—They continue for the present at Speen Hill.—I have a Southampton Match to return for your Kentish one, Capt. G. Heathcote & Miss A. Lyell; I have it from Alethea—& like it, because I had made it before. Yes, the Stoneleigh Business is concluded, but it was not till yesterday that my Mother was regularly informed of it, tho' the news had reached us on Monday Even^g by way of Steventon. My Aunt says as little as may be on the subject by way of information, & nothing at all by way of satisfaction. She reflects on Mr T. Leigh's dilatoriness, & looks about with great diligence & success for Inconvenience & Evil—among which she ingeniously places the danger of her new Housemaids catching cold on the outside of the Coach, when she goes down to Bath—for a carriage makes her sick.— John Binns has been offered their place, but declines it—as she supposes, because he will not wear a Livery.—Whatever be the cause, I like the effect.—In spite of all my Mother's long & intimate knowledge of the Writer, she was not up to the expectation of such a Letter as this; the discontentedness of it shocked & surprised her—but *I* see nothing in it out of Nature—tho' a sad nature. [*p. 3*] She does not forget to wish for Chambers,[6] you may be sure.—No particulars are given, not a word of arrears mentioned—tho' in her letter to James they were in a *general way* spoken of.[7] The amount of them is a matter of conjecture, & to my Mother a most interesting one; she cannot fix any time for their beginning, with any satisfaction to herself, but Mrs Leigh's death—& Henry's two Thousand pounds neither agrees with that period nor any other.— I did not like to own, our previous information of what was intended last July—& have therefore only said that if we could see Henry we might hear many particulars, as I had understood that some confidential conversation had passed between him & Mr T. L. at Stoneleigh. We have been as quiet as usual since Frank & Mary left us;—Mr Criswick called on Martha that very morn^g in his way home again from Portsmouth, & we have had no visitor since.—We called on the Miss Lyells one day, & heard a good account of Mr Heathcote's canvass, the success of which of course exceeds his expectation.—Alethea in her Letter hopes for *my interest*, which I conclude means Edward's—& I take this opportunity therefore of requesting that he will bring in Mr Heathcote.— Mr Lance told us yesterday that Mr H. had behaved very handsomely & waited on Mr Thistlethwaite to say that if *he* (Mr T.) would stand, *he* (Mr H.) would not oppose him; but Mr T. declined it, acknowledging himself still smarting under the payment of late Electioneering Costs.—

The M[rs] Hulberts, we learn from Kintbury, come to Steventon this week, & bring Mary Jane Fowle with them, in her way to M[rs] Nunes;— she returns at Christmas with her Brother.— *Our* Brother[8] we may perhaps see in the course of a few days—& we mean to take the opportunity of his help, to go one night to the play. Martha ought to see the inside of the Theatre once while she lives in Southampton, & I think she will hardly wish to take a second veiw.—The Furniture of Bellevue is to be sold tomorrow, & we shall take it in our usual walk if the Weather be favourable. How could you have a wet day on Thursday?—with us it was a Prince of days, the most [*p. 4*] delightful we have had for weeks, soft, bright, with a brisk wind from the South west;—everybody was out & talking of spring—& Martha & I did not know how to turn back.—On friday Even[g] we had some very blowing weather—from 6 to 9, I think we never heard it worse, even here.— And one night we had so much rain that it forced its' way again into the Storecloset—& tho' the Evil was comparatively slight, & the Mischeif nothing, I had some employment the next day in drying parcels &c. I have now moved still more out of the way.—

Martha sends her best Love, & thanks you for admitting her to the knowledge of the pros & cons about Harriet Foote—she has an interest in all such matters.—I am also to say that she wants to see you.—Mary Jane[9] missed her papa & mama a good deal at first, but now does very well without them.—I am glad to hear of little John's being better;— & hope your accounts of M[rs] Knight will also improve. Adeiu. Remember me affec[tely] to everybody, & beleive me

Ever Yours JA.

Miss Austen
Edw: Austen's Esq[r]
Godmersham Park
Faversham
Kent

[*Letters missing here*]

62. *To Cassandra Austen*

Friday 9 December 1808

Castle Square, Friday Dec[r] 9.—

Many thanks my dear Cassandra, to you & M[r] Deedes, for your joint & agreable composition, which took me by surprise this morning. He has certainly great merit as a Writer, he does ample justice to his subject, & without being diffuse, is clear & correct;—& tho' I do not mean to compare his Epistolary powers with yours, or to give him the same portion of my Gratitude, he certainly has a very pleasing way of winding up a whole, & speeding Truth into the World.—"But all this, as my dear Mrs Piozzi[1] says, is flight & fancy & nonsense—for my Master has his great Casks to mind, & I have my little Children"—It is *you* however in this instance, that have the little Children—& *I* that have the great cask—, for we are brewing Spruce Beer again;—but my meaning really is, that I am extremely foolish in writing all this unnecessary stuff, when I have so many matters[2] to write about, that my paper will hardly hold it all. Little Matters they are to be sure, but highly important.—In the first place, Miss Curling is actually at Portsmouth—which I was always in hopes would not happen.—I wish her no worse however than a long & happy abode there. *Here*, she w^d probably be dull, & I am sure she w^d be troublesome.—The Bracelets[3] are in my possession, & everything I could wish them to be. They came with Martha's pelisse, which likewise gives great satisfaction.—Soon after I had closed my last letter to you, we were visited by Mrs Dickens & her Sisterinlaw Mrs Bertie, the wife of a lately made Admiral;—Mrs F. A. I beleive was their first object—but they put up with us very kindly, & M^rs D- finding in Miss Lloyd a friend of Mrs Dundas had another motive for the acquaintance. She seems a really agreable Woman—that is, her manners are gentle & she knows a great many of our Connections in West Kent.[4]—Mrs Bertie lives in the Polygon, & was out when we returned her visit—which are *her* two virtues.—

[*p. 2*] A larger circle of acquaintance & an increase of amusement is quite in character with our approaching removal.—Yes—I mean to go to as many Balls as possible, that I may have[5] a good bargain. Every body is very much concerned at our going away, & every body is acquainted with Chawton & speaks of it as a remarkably pretty village, & every body knows the House we describe—but nobody fixes on the right.—I am very much obliged to Mrs Knight for such a proof of the interest she takes in me—& she may depend upon it, that I *will* marry Mr Papillon, whatever may be his reluctance or my own.—I owe her much more than such a trifling sacrifice.—Our Ball[6] was rather more amusing than I expected, Martha liked it very much, & I did not gape till the last quarter of an hour.—It was past nine before we were sent for, & not twelve when we returned.—The room was tolerably full, & there were perhaps thirty couple of Dancers;—the melancholy part was to see so many dozen young Women standing by without partners, & each of them with two ugly naked shoulders!—It was the same room in which we danced 15 years ago!— I thought it all over—& inspite of the shame of being so much older, felt with thankfulness that I was quite as happy now as then.—We paid an additional shilling for our Tea, which we took as we chose in an adjoining, & very comfortable room.—There were only 4 dances, & it went to my heart that the Miss Lances (one of them too named Emma!) should have partners only for two.—You will not expect to hear that *I* was asked to dance—but I was—by the Gentleman whom we met *that Sunday*[7] with Capt[n] D'auvergne. We have always kept up a Bowing acquaintance since, & being pleased with his black eyes, I spoke to him at the Ball, which brought on me this civility; but I do not know his name,—& he seems so little at home in the English Language[8] that I beleive his black eyes may be the best of him.—Capt. D'auvergne has got a Ship.—Martha & I made use of the very favourable state of yesterday for walking, to pay our duty at Chiswell—we found M[rs] Lance at home & alone, & sat out three other Ladies who soon came in.—We went by the Ferry, & returned by the Bridge, & were scarcely at all fatigued.—Edward must have enjoyed [*p. 3*] the last two days;—You, I presume had a *cool* drive to Canterbury. Kitty Foote came on Wednesday, & her Even[g] visit began early enough for the last part, the apple pye of our dinner, for we never dine now till five.—Yesterday I, or rather You had a letter from Nanny Hilliard, the object of which is that she w[d] be very much obliged to us if we w[d] get Hannah a place.—I am sorry that I cannot assist her;—if you can, let me know, as I shall not answer the letter immediately. M[r] Sloper is married again, not much to Nanny's, or anybody's satisfaction;—the Lady was Governess to Sir Robert's[9] natural Children, & seems to have nothing to recommend her.—I do not find however that Nanny is likely to lose her place in consequence.—She says not a word of what service she wishes for Hannah, nor what Hannah can do—but a Nursery I suppose, or something of that kind, must be the Thing.—Having now cleared away my smaller articles of news, I come to a communication of some weight—no less than that my Uncle & Aunt are going to allow James £100. a year. We hear of it through Steventon;—Mary sent us the other day an extract from my Aunt's letter on the subject—in which the Donation is made with the greatest kindness, & intended as a Compensation for his loss in the Conscientious refusal of Hampstead Living[10]—£100. a year being all that he had at the time called its' worth—as I find it was always intended at Steventon to

divide the real Income with Kintbury.—Nothing can be more affectionate than my Aunt's Language in making the present, & likewise in
expressing her hope of their being much more together in future, than
to her great regret, they have of late years been.—My Expectations for
my Mother do not rise with this Event. We will allow a little more time
however, before we fly out.—If not prevented by Parish Business, James
comes to us on Monday. The Mrs Hulberts & Miss Murden are their
Guests at present, & likely to continue such till Christmas.—Anna comes
home on ye 19th.—The Hundred a year begins next Ladyday.—I am
glad you are to have Henry with you again; with him & the Boys, you
cannot but have a chearful, & at times even a merry Christmas.—
Martha is so . . . [*two lines cut away at the bottom of p. 3*]

[*p. 4*] We want to be settled at Chawton in time for Henry to come
to us for some Shooting, in October at least;—but a little earlier, &
Edward may visit us after taking his boys back to Winchester;—suppose we name the 4th of Sept^r—will not that do?—I have but one thing
more to tell you. Mrs Hill[11] called on my Mother yesterday while we
were gone to Chiswell—& in the course of the visit asked her whether
she knew anything of a Clergyman's family of the name of *Alford* who
had resided in our part of Hampshire.—Mrs Hill had been applied to,
as likely to give some information of them, on account of their probable
vicinity to Dr Hill's Living—by a Lady, or for a Lady, who had known
M^rs & the two Miss Alfords in Bath, whither they had removed it seems
from Hampshire—& who now wishes to convey to the Miss Alfords
some work, or trimming, which she has been doing for them—but the
Mother & Daughters have left Bath, & the Lady cannot learn where
they are gone to.—While my Mother gave us the account, the probability of its being ourselves, occurred to us, and it had previously struck
herself[12] . . . [*two lines cut away at the bottom of p. 4—text continues
below address panel*] . . . likely—& even indispensably to be *us*, is that
she mentioned Mr Hammond as now having the Living or Curacy,
which the Father had had.—I cannot think who our kind Lady can
be—but I dare say we shall not like the work.—

[*Upside down at top of p. 1*]

Distribute the affec^te Love of a Heart not so tired as the right hand
belonging to it.—Yours Ever Sincerely

JA.

Miss Austen
Edw: Austen's Esqr
Godmersham Park
Faversham
Kent.

[*Letters missing here*]

63. *To Cassandra Austen*

Tuesday 27–Wednesday 28 December 1808

Castle Square, Tuesday Dec: 27.

My dear Cassandra

I can now write at leisure & make the most of my subjects, which is lucky, as they are not numerous this week. Our house was cleared by half-past Eleven on saturday, & we had the satisfaction of hearing yesterday, that the party[1] reached home in safety, soon after 5. I was very glad of your letter this morning, for my Mother taking medicine, Eliza[2] keeping her bed with a cold, & Choles not coming, made us rather dull & dependant on the post. You tell me much that gives me pleasure, but I think not much to answer.—I wish I *could* help you in your Needlework, I have two hands & a new Thimble that lead a very easy life. Lady Sondes' match surprises, but does not offend me;—had her first marriage been of affection, or had there been a grown-up single daughter, I should not have forgiven her—but I consider everybody as having a right to marry *once* in their Lives for Love, if they can—& provided she will now leave off having bad head-aches & being pathetic, I can allow her, I can *wish* her to be happy.—Do not imagine that your picture of your Tete a tete with Sir B-[3] makes any change in our expectations here; he could not be really reading, tho' he held the newspaper in his hand; he was making up his mind to the deed, & the manner of it—I think you will have a letter from him soon.—I heard from Portsmouth yesterday, & as I am to send them more cloathes, they cannot be expecting a very early return to us. Mary's face is pretty well, but she must have suffered a great deal with it—an abscess was formed & open'd. Our Even^g party on Thursday, produced nothing more remarkable than Miss Murden's coming too, tho' she had declined it absolutely in the morn^g, & sitting very ungracious & very silent with us from 7 o'clock, till half after 11—for so late was it, oweing to the Chairmen, before we got rid of them. The last hour, spent in yawning & shivering in a wide circle round [*p. 2*] the fire, was dull enough—but the Tray had admirable success. The Widgeon, & the preserved Ginger were as delicious, as one could wish. But as to our Black Butter,[4] do not decoy anybody to Southampton by such a lure, for it is all gone. The first pot was opened when Frank & Mary were here, & proved not at all what it ought to be;—it was neither solid, nor entirely sweet—& on seeing it, Eliza remembered that Miss Austen had said she did not think it had been boiled enough.—It was made you know when we were absent.— Such being the event of the first pot, I w[d] not save the second, & we therefore ate it in unpretending privacy; & tho' not what it ought to be, part of it was very good.—James means to keep three Horses on this increase of income, at present he has but one; Mary wishes the other two to be fit to carry Women—& in the purchase of one, Edward will probably be called upon to fulfil his promise to his Godson.[5] We have now pretty well ascertained James's Income to be Eleven Hundred Pounds, curate paid, which makes us very happy—the ascertainment as well as the Income.—Mary does not talk of the Garden, it may well be a disagreable subject to her—but her Husband is persuaded that nothing is wanting to make the first new one Good, but trenching, which is to be done by his own servants & John Bond by degrees—not at the expense which trenching the other, amounted to.—I was happy to hear, cheifly for Anna's sake, that a Ball at Manydown was once more in agitation; it is called a Child's Ball, & given by M[rs] Heathcote to W[m]— such was its' beginning at least—but it will probably[6] swell into something more. Edward was invited, during his stay at Manydown, & it is to take place between this & twelfth-day.—M[rs] Hulbert has taken Anna a pair of white shoes on the occasion.—I forgot in my last to tell you, that we hear by way of Kintbury & the Palmers, that they were all well at Bermuda[7] in the beginning of Nov[r].—

Wednesday. Yesterday must have been a day of sad remembrance[8] at G[m]. I am glad it is over.—We spent friday Even[g] with our friends at the Boarding House, & our curiosity was gratified by the sight of their fellow-inmates, M[rs] Drew & Miss Hook, M[r] Wynne & M[r] Fitzhugh, the latter is brother to M[rs] Lance, & very much the Gentleman. He has lived in that House more than twenty years, & poor Man, [*p. 3*] is so totally deaf, that they say he c[d] not hear a Cannon, were it fired close to him; having no cannon at hand to make the experiment, I took it for granted, & talked to him a little with my fingers, which was funny enough.—I recommended him to read Corinna.[9]—Miss Hook is a well-behaved, genteelish Woman; M[rs] Drew wellbehaved without being at all genteel. M[r] Wynne seems a chatty, & rather familiar young Man.—Miss Murden was quite a different creature this last Even[g] from what she had been before, oweing to her having with Martha's help found a situation in the morn[g] which bids very fair for comfort. When she leaves Steventon, she comes to board & lodge with M[rs] Hookey, the Chemist—for there is no M[r] Hookey—. I cannot say that I am in any hurry for the conclusion of her present visit, but I was truely glad to see her comfortable in Mind & spirits;—at her age perhaps one may be as friendless oneself, & in similar circumstances quite as captious.—My Mother has been lately adding to her possessions in plate—a whole Tablespoon & a whole dessert-spoon, & six whole Teaspoons, which makes our sideboard border on the Magnificent. They were mostly the produce of old, or useless silver[10]—I have turned the 11s in the List into 12s, & the Card looks all the better;—A silver Tea-Ladle is also added, which will at least answer the purpose of making us sometimes think of John Warren.—I have laid Lady Sondes' case before Martha—who does not make the least objection to it, & is particularly pleased with the name of Montresor. I do not agree with her there, but I like his rank very much—& always affix the ideas of strong sense, & highly elegant Manners, to a General. I must write to Charles next week. You may guess in what extravagant terms of praise Earle Harwood speaks of him. He is looked up to by everybody in all America.—I shall not tell[11] you anything more of W[m] Digweed's China, as your Silence on the subject makes you unworthy of it. M[rs] H. Digweed looks forward with great satisfaction to our being her neighbours—I w[d] have her enjoy the idea to the utmost, as I suspect there will not [be *omitted*] much in the reality.—With equal pleasure *we* anticipate an intimacy with [*p. 4*] her Husband's Bailiff & his wife, who live close by us, & are said to be remarkably good sort of people.—Yes, yes, we *will* have a Pianoforte, as good a one as can be got for 30 Guineas—& I will practise country dances, that we may have some amusement for our nephews & neices, when we have the pleasure of their company. Martha sends her Love to Henry & tells him that he will soon have a Bill of Miss Chaplin's, about £14—to pay on her account; but the Bill shall not be sent in, till his return to Town.—I hope he comes to you in good health, & in spirits as good as a first return to Godmersham can allow. With his nephews, he will force himself to be chearful, till he really is so.—Send me some intelligence of Eliza,[12] it is a long while since I have heard of her.—We have had Snow on the Ground here almost a week, it is now going, but Southampton must boast no longer.—We all send our Love to Edward Jun[r] & his Brothers—& I hope Speculation is generally liked.

[*Continued below address panel*]

Fare you well.—Y[rs] affec[ly]—J. Austen

My Mother has not been out of doors this week, but she keeps pretty [well]—We have rec[d] through Bookham, an indifferent account of your God Mother.[13]—

Miss Austen
Edward Austen's Esq[r]
Godmersham Park
Faversham
Kent

[*Letters missing here*]

64. *To Cassandra Austen*

Tuesday 10–Wednesday 11 January 1809

Castle Square, Tuesday Jan[y] 10.

I am not surprised my dear Cassandra, that you did not find my last Letter very full of Matter, & I wish this may not have the same deficiency;—but we are doing nothing ourselves to write about, & I am therefore quite dependant upon the Communications of our friends, or my own Wit.—This post brought me two interesting Letters, Yours, & one from Bookham, in answer to an enquiry of mine about your good Godmother, of whom we had lately received a very alarming account from Paragon. Miss Arnold was the Informant there, & she spoke of M[rs] E. L.s having been very dangerously ill, & attended by a Physician from Oxford.—Your Letter to Adlestrop may perhaps bring you information from the spot, but in case it should not, I must tell you that she is better, tho' D[r] Bourne cannot yet call her out of danger;—such was the case, last Wednesday—& M[rs] Cooke's having had no later account is a favourable sign.—I am to hear again from the latter *next* week, but not *this*, if everything goes on well.—Her disorder is an Inflammation on the Lungs, arising from a severe Chill, taken in Church last Sunday three weeks;—her Mind, all pious Composure, as may be supposed.—

George Cooke was there when her Illness began, his Brother has now taken his place.—Her age & feebleness considered, one's fears cannot but preponderate—tho' her amendment has already surpassed the expectation of the Physician, at the beginning.—I am sorry to add that *Becky* is laid up with a complaint of the same kind.—

[*p. 2*] I am very glad to have the time of your return at all fixed, we all rejoice in it, & it will not be later than I had expected. I dare not hope that Mary & Miss Curling may be detained at Portsmouth so long, or half so long—but it would be worth twopence to have it so.—The St Albans perhaps may soon be off to help bring home what may remain by this time of our poor Army,[1] whose state seems dreadfully critical.—The Regency[2] seems to have been heard of only here, my most political Correspondants make no mention of it. Unlucky, that I should have wasted so much reflection on the subject!—I can now answer your question to my Mother more at large, & likewise more at small—with equal perspicuity & minuteness, for the very day of our leaving Southampton is fixed—& if the knowledge is of no *use* to Edward, I am sure it will give him pleasure. Easter Monday, April 3^d is the day; we are to sleep that night at Alton, & be with our friends at Bookham the next, if they are then at home;—there we remain till the following Monday, & on Tuesday April 11th, hope to be at Godmersham.[3] If the Cookes are absent, we shall finish our Journey on ye 5th—These plans depend of course upon the weather, but I hope there will be no settled Cold to delay us materially.—To make you amends for being at Bookham, it is in contemplation to spend a few days at Barton Lodge in our way *out* of Kent.—The hint of such a visit is most affectionately welcomed by Mrs Birch, in one of her odd, pleasant Letters lately, in which she speaks of *us* with the usual distinguished kindness; declaring that she shall not be at all satisfied unless a very *handsome* present[4] is made us immediately, from one Quarter. Fanny's not coming with you, is no more than we expected, & as we have not the hope of a Bed for her, & shall see her so soon afterwards at G^m we cannot wish it otherwise.—[*p. 3*] William will be quite recovered I trust by the time you receive this.—What a comfort his Cross-stitch must have been! Pray tell him that I should like to see his Work very much.—I hope our answers this morn^g have given satisfaction; we had great pleasure in Uncle Deedes' packet—& pray let Marianne know, in private, that I think she is quite right to work a rug for Uncle John's Coffee urn, & that I am sure it must give great pleasure to herself now, & to him when he receives it.—The preference of Brag over Speculation does not greatly surprise me I beleive, because I feel the same myself; but it mortifies me deeply, because Speculation was under my patronage;—& after all, what is there so delightful in a pair-royal of Braggers? it is but three nines, or three Knaves, or a mixture of them.—When one comes to reason upon it, it cannot stand its' ground against Speculation—of which I hope Edward is now convinced. Give my Love to him, if he is.—The Letter from Paragon, before mentioned, was much like those which had preceded it, as to the felicity of its Writer.—They found their House so dirty & so damp, that they were obliged to be a week at an Inn.—John Binns had behaved most unhandsomely & engaged himself elsewhere.—They *have* a Man however, on the same footing, which my Aunt does not like, & she finds both him & the new Maidservant very, very inferior to Robert & Martha.—Whether they mean to have any other Domestics does not appear, nor whether they are to have a Carriage while they are in Bath.— The Holders are as usual, tho' I beleive it is not very usual for them to be happy, which they now are at a great rate, in Hooper's Marriage. The Irvines are not mentioned.—The American Lady[5] improved as we went on—but still the same faults in part recurred.—We are now in Margiana,[6] & like it very well indeed.[7]—We are just going to set off for Northumberland to be shut up in Widdrington Tower, where there must be two or three sets of Victims already immured [*p. 4*] under a very fine Villain.—Wednesday.—Your report of Eliza's health gives me great pleasure—& the progress of the Bank is a constant source of satisfaction. With such increasing profits, tell Henry, that I hope he will not work poor High-diddle so hard as he used to do.—Has your News-paper given a sad story of a M[rs] Middleton, wife of a Farmer in York-shire, her sister & servant being almost frozen to death in the late weather—her little Child quite so?—I hope this sister is not[8] our friend Miss Woodd—& I rather think her Brotherinlaw had moved into Lincolnshire, but their name & station accord too well. M[rs] M. & the Maid are said to be tolerably recovered, but the Sister is likely to lose the use of her Limbs.—Charles's rug will be finished today, & sent tomorrow to Frank, to be consigned by him to M[r] Turner's care—& I am going to send Marmion out with it;—very generous[9] in me, I think.—As we have no letter from Adlestrop, we may suppose the good Woman was alive on Monday, but I cannot help expecting bad news from thence or Bookham, in a few days.—Do you continue quite well?—

[*Continued below address panel*]

Have you nothing to say of your little Namesake?[10]—We join in Love & many happy returns.[11]—

Y^{rs} affec^{ly}
J Austen

[*Postscript upside down at top of p. 1*]

The Manydown Ball was a smaller thing than I expected, but it seems to have made Anna very happy. At *her* age it would not have done for *me*.—

Miss Austen
Edward Austen's Esqr
Godmersham Park
Faversham
Kent

65. *To Cassandra Austen*

Tuesday 17–Wednesday 18 January 1809

Castle Square, Tuesday Jany 17.—

My dear Cassandra

I am happy to say that we had no second Letter from Bookham last week. Yours has brought its usual measure of satisfaction & amusement, & I beg your acceptance of all the Thanks due on the occasion.—Your offer of Cravats is very kind, & happens to be particularly adapted to my wants—but it was an odd thing to occur to you.— Yes—we have got another fall of snow, & are very dreadful; everything seems to turn to snow this winter.—I hope you have had no more illness among you, & that William will be soon as well as ever. His working a footstool for Chawton is a most agreable surprise to me, & I am sure his Grandmama will value it very much as a proof of his affection & Industry—but we shall never have the heart to put our feet upon it.—I beleive I must work a muslin cover in sattin stitch, to keep it from the dirt.—I long to know what his colours are—I guess greens & purples.—Edwd & Henry have started a difficulty respecting our Journey, which I must own with some confusion, had never been thought of by us; but if the former expected by it, to prevent our travelling into Kent entirely he will be disappointed, for we have already determined to go the Croydon road, on leaving Bookham, & sleep at Dartford.— Will not that do?—There certainly does seem no convenient restingplace on the other road.—Anna went to Clanville last friday, & I have hopes of her new Aunt's[1] being really worth her knowing.—Perhaps you may never have heard that James & Mary paid a morn[g] visit there in form some weeks ago, & Mary tho' by no means disposed to like her, was very much pleased with her indeed. *Her* praise to be sure, proves [*p. 2*] nothing more than M[rs] M.'s being civil & attentive to them, but her being so is in favour of her having good sense.—Mary writes of Anna as improved in person, but gives her no other commendation.—I am afraid her absence now may deprive her of one pleasure, for that silly M[r] Hammond is actually to give his Ball—on friday.—We had some reason to expect a visit from Earle Harwood & James this week, but they do not come.—Miss Murden arrived last night at M[rs] Hookey's, as a message & a basket announced to us.—You will therefore return to an enlarged & of course improved society here, especially as the Miss Williamses are come back.—We were agreably surprised the other day by a visit from your Beauty & mine, each in a new Cloth Mantle & Bonnet, & I daresay you will value yourself much on the modest propriety of Miss W.'s taste, hers being purple, & Miss Grace's scarlet. I can easily suppose that your six weeks here will be fully occupied, were it only in lengthening the waist of your gowns. I have pretty well arranged my spring & summer plans of that kind, & mean to wear out my spotted Muslin before I go.—You will exclaim at this—but mine really has signs of feebleness, which with a little care may come to something.—Martha & D[r] Mant are as bad as ever; he runs after her in the street to apologise for having spoken to a Gentleman while *she* was near him the day before.—Poor M[rs] Mant can stand it no longer; she is retired to one of her married Daughters.—We hear through Kintbury that M[rs] Esten was unluckily to lie in at the same time with M[rs] C. A.[2]— When William returns to Winchester Mary Jane[3] is to go to M[rs] Nunes for a month, & then to Steventon for a fortnight, & it seems likely that she & her Aunt Martha may travel into Berkshire together.—We shall not have a Month of Martha after your return—& that Month will be a very interrupted & broken one;—but we shall enjoy ourselves the more, when we *can* get a quiet half hour together.—To set against your new Novel, of which nobody ever heard before & perhaps never may again, We have got *Ida of Athens* by Miss [*p. 3*] Owenson;[4] which must be very clever, because it was written as the Authoress says, in three months.—We have only read the Preface yet; but her Irish Girl does not make me expect much.—If the warmth of her Language could affect the Body, it might be worth reading in this weather.—Adeiu—

I must leave off to stir the fire & call on Miss Murden. *Even^g*. I have done them both, the first very often.—We found our friend as comfortable, as she can ever allow herself to be in cold weather;—there is a very neat parlour behind the Shop for her to sit in, not very light indeed, being a la Southampton, the middle of Three deep—but very lively, from the frequent sound of the pestle & mortar.—We afterwards called on the Miss Williamses, who lodge at Dusautoys; Miss Mary only was at home, & she is in very indifferent health.—Dr Hacket came in while we were there, & said that he never remembered such a severe winter as this, in Southampton before. It is bad, but *we* do not suffer as we did last year, because the wind has been more N.E.-than N.W.—For a day or two last week, my Mother was very poorly with a return of *one* of her old complaints—but it did not last long, & seems to have left nothing bad behind it.—She began to talk of a serious Illness, her two last having been preceded by the same symptoms;—but thank Heaven! she is now quite as well as one can expect her to be in Weather, which deprives her of Exercise.—Miss M. conveys to us a third volume of sermons from Hamstall,⁵ just published; & which we are to like better than the two others;—they are professedly *practical*, & for the use of Country Congregations.—I have just received some verses in an unknown hand, & am desired to forward them to my nephew Edw^d6 at Godmersham.—

"Alas! poor Brag, thou boastful Game! What now avails thine empty name?—

Where now thy more distinguish'd fame?—My day is o'er, & Thine the same.—

For thou like me art thrown aside, At Godmersham, this Christmas Tide;

And now across the Table wide, Each Game save Brag or Spec: is tried."—

"Such is the mild Ejaculation, Of tender hearted Speculation."—

Wednesday.—I expected to have a Letter from somebody today, but I have not. Twice every day, I think of a Letter from Portsmouth.—Miss Murden has been sitting with us this morn^g—as yet she seems very well pleased with her situation. The worst part of her being in Southampton will be the necessity of our walking with her now & then, for she talks so loud that one is quite ashamed, but our Dining hours are luckily very different, which we shall take all reasonable advantage of.—Mrs H^y D. has been brought to bed some time. I suppose *we* must stand to the next. [*p. 4*] The Queen's Birthday⁷ moves the Assembly to this night, instead of last—& as it is always fully attended, Martha and I expect an amusing shew.—We were in hopes of being independant of other companions by having the attendance of Mr Austen & Capt. Harwood, but as they fail us, we are obliged to look out for other help, & have fixed on the Wallops as least likely to be troublesome.—I have called on them this morn^g & found them very willing;—& I am sorry that you must wait a whole week for the particulars of the Even^g.—I propose being asked to dance by our acquaintance Mr Smith, now *Captn* Smith, who has lately re-appeared in Southampton—but I shall decline it.—He saw Charles last August.—What an alarming Bride Mrs Col^n Tilson must have been! Such a parade is one of the most immodest peices of Modesty that one can imagine. To *attract* notice could have been her only wish.—It augurs ill for his family—it announces not *great* sense, & therefore ensures boundless Influence.—I hope Fanny's visit is now taking place.—You have said scarcely anything of her lately, but I trust you are as good friends as ever.—

[*Continued upside down at top of p. 1*]

Martha sends her Love, & hopes to have the pleasure of seeing you when you return to Southampton. You are to understand this message, as being merely for the sake of a Message, to oblige me.—Y^rs affec:^tely—J. Austen.

Henry never sent his Love to me in your last—but I send him Mine.—

Miss Austen
Edwd Austen's Esqr
Godmersham Park
Faversham
Kent

66. *To Cassandra Austen*

Tuesday 24 January 1809

Castle Square, Tuesday Jany 24.

My dear Cassandra

I will give you the indulgence of a letter on Thursday this week, instead of Friday, but I do not require you to write again before Sunday, provided I may beleive you & your finger going on quite well.—Take care of your precious self, do not work too hard, remember that Aunt Cassandras are quite as scarce as Miss Beverleys.[1]—I had the happiness yesterday of a letter from Charles, but I shall say as little about it as possible, because I know *that* excruciating Henry will have had a Letter likewise, to make all my intelligence valueless.—It was written at Bermuda on ye 7 & 10. of Dec^r;—all well, and Fanny still only in expectation of being otherwise. He had taken a small prize[2] in his late cruize; a French schooner laden with Sugar, but Bad weather parted them, & she had not yet been heard of;—his cruize ended Decr 1st—My September Letter was the latest he had received.—This day three weeks you are to be in London, & I wish you better weather—not but that you may have worse, for we have now nothing but ceaseless snow or rain & insufferable dirt to complain of—no tempestuous winds, nor severity of cold. Since I wrote last, we have had something of each, but it is not genteel to rip up old greivances.—You used me scandalously by not mentioning Ed. Cooper's Sermons;—I tell you everything, & it is unknown the Mysteries you conceal from me.—And to add to the rest you persevere in giving[3] a final e to Invalid—thereby putting it out of one's power to suppose Mrs E. Leigh even for a moment, [*p. 2*] a veteran Soldier.—She, good Woman, is I hope destined for some further placid enjoyment of her own Excellence in this World, for her recovery advances exceedingly well.—I had this pleasant news in a letter from Bookham last Thursday, but as the letter was from Mary[4] instead of her Mother, you will guess her account was not equally good from home.— Mrs Cooke had been confined to her bed some days by Illness, but was then better, & Mary wrote in confidence of her continuing to mend. I have desired to hear again soon.—You rejoice me by what you say of Fanny—I hope she will not turn[5] good-for-nothing this ever so long;— We thought of & talked of her yesterday with sincere affection, & wished her a long enjoyment of all the happiness to which she seems born.—While she gives happiness to those about her, she is pretty sure of her own share.—I am gratified by her having pleasure in what I write—but I wish the knowledge of my being exposed to her discerning Criticism, may not hurt my stile, by inducing too great a solicitude. I begin already to weigh my words & sentences more than I did, & am looking about for a sentiment, an illustration or a metaphor in every corner of the room. Could my Ideas flow as fast as the rain in the Storecloset, it would be charming.—We have been in two or three dreadful states within the last week, from the melting of the snow &c.— & the contest between us & the Closet has now ended in our defeat; I have been obliged to move almost everything out of it, & leave it to splash itself as it likes.—You have by no means raised my curiosity after Caleb;[6]—My disinclination for it before was affected, but now it is real; I do not like the Evangelicals.—Of course I shall be delighted when I read it, like other people, but till I do, I dislike it.—I am sorry my verses did not bring any return from Edward, I was in hopes they might—but I suppose he does not rate them high enough.—It [*p. 3*] might be partiality, but they seemed to me purely classical—just like Homer & Virgil, Ovid & Propria que Maribus.[7]—I had a nice, brotherly letter from Frank the other day, which after an interval of nearly three weeks, was very welcome.—No orders were come on friday, & none were come yesterday, or we sh[d] have heard today.—I had supposed Miss C.[8] would share her Cousin's room here, but a message in this Letter proves the Contrary;—I will make the Garret as comfortable as I can, but the possibilities of that apartment are not great.—My Mother has been talking to Eliza about our future home—and *she*, making no difficulty at all of the Sweetheart, is perfectly disposed to continue with us, but till she has written home for *Mother's* approbation, cannot quite decide.—*Mother*[9] does not like to have her so far off;—at Chawton she will be nine or ten miles nearer, which I hope will have its due influence—As for Sally, she means to play John Binns with us, in her anxiety to belong to our Household again. Hitherto, she appears a very good Servant.—You depend upon finding all your plants dead, I hope.—They look very ill I understand.—Your silence on the subject of our Ball, makes me suppose your Curiosity too great for words. We were very well entertained, & could have staid longer but for the arrival of my List shoes to convey me home, & I did not like to keep them waiting in the Cold. The room was tolerably full, & the Ball opened by Miss Glyn;—the Miss Lances had partners, Capt. D'auvergne's friend appeared in regimentals, Caroline Maitland had an Officer to flirt with, & M[r] John Harrison was deputed by Capt. Smith, being himself absent, to ask me to dance.—Everything went well you see, especially after we had tucked M[rs] Lance's neckhandkerf. in behind, & fastened it with a pin.—[*p. 4*] We had a very full & agreable account of M[r] Hammond's Ball, from Anna last night; the same fluent pen has sent similar information I know into Kent.—She seems to have been as happy as one could wish her—& the complacency of her Mama[10] in doing the Honours of the Even[g] must have made *her* pleasure almost as great.—The Grandeur of the Meeting was beyond my hopes.—I should like to have seen Anna's looks & performance—but that sad cropt head must have injured the former.—

Martha pleases herself with beleiving that if *I* had kept her counsel, you w^d never have heard of Dr M.'s^11 late behaviour, as if the very slight manner in which I mentioned it could have been all on which you found your Judgement.—I do not endeavour to undeceive her, because I wish her happy at all events, & know [*continued below address panel*] how highly she prizes happiness of any kind. She is moreover so full of kindness for us both, & sends you in particular so many good wishes about [your] finger, that I am willing to overlook a venial fault; & as Dr M. is a Clergymen [*continued upside down at top of p. 1*] their attachment, however immoral, has a decorous air.—Adeiu, sweet You.—This is greivous news from Spain.—It is well that Dr Moore was spared the knowledge of such a Son's death.^12—Y^rs affec:^ly J. Austen

Anna's hand gets better & better, it begins to be too good for any consequence.—

[*More postscripts crossed on p. 1*]

We send best Love to dear little Lizzy & Marianne in particular.

The Portsmouth paper^13 gave a melancholy history of a poor Mad Woman, escaped from Confinement, who said her Husband & Daughter of the Name of Payne lived at Ashford in Kent. Do You own them?

Miss Austen
Edwd Austen Esqr
Godmersham Park
Faversham
Kent.

67. *To Cassandra Austen*

Monday 30 January 1809

Castle Square, Monday Jany 30.

My dear Cassandra

I was not much surprised yesterday by the agreable surprise of your letter, & extremely glad to receive the assurance of your finger being well again. Here is such a wet Day as never was seen!—I wish the poor little girls had better weather for their Journey;^1 they must amuse themselves with watching the raindrops down the Windows. Sackree I suppose feels quite brokenhearted.—I cannot have done with the weather without observing how delightfully mild it is; I am sure Fanny must enjoy it with us.—Yesterday was a very blowing day; we got to Church however, which we had not been able to do for two Sundays before.—

I am not at all ashamed about the name of the Novel, having been guilty of no insult towards your handwriting; the Dipthong I always saw, but knowing how fond you were of adding a vowel wherever you could, I attributed it to that alone—& the knowledge of the truth does the book no service;—the only merit it could have, was in the name of Caleb, which has an honest, unpretending sound; but in Coelebs,[2] there is pedantry & affectation.—Is it written only to Classical Scholars?—I shall now try to say only what is necessary, I am weary of meandering—so expect a vast deal of small matter concisely told, in the next two pages.—M[rs] Cooke has been very dangerously ill, but is now I hope safe.—I had a letter last week from George, Mary being too busy to write, & at that time[3] the Disorder was called of the Typhus kind, & their alarm considerable—[*p. 2*] but yesterday brought me a much better account from Mary; the origin of the complaint being now ascertained to be Billious, & the strong medicines requisite, promising to be effectual.—M[rs] E. L.[4] is so much recovered as to get into the Dressing-room every day.—A letter from Hamstall gives us the history of Sir Tho. Williams' return;—the Admiral, whoever he might be, took a fancy the Neptune, & having only a worn-out 74 to offer in lieu of it, Sir Tho. declined such a command, & is come home Passenger. Lucky Man! to have so fair an opportunity of escape.—I hope his Wife allows herself to be happy on the occasion, & does not give all her thoughts to being nervous.—A great event happens this week at Hamstall, in young Edward's removal to school; he is going to Rugby & is very happy in the idea of it.—I wish his happiness may last, but it will be a great change, to become a raw school boy from being a pompous Sermon-Writer, & a domineering Brother.—It will do him good I dare say.—Caroline[5] has had a great escape from being burnt to death lately;—as her Husband gives the account, we must beleive it true.—Miss Murden is gone—called away by the critical state of M[rs] Pottinger, who has had another severe stroke, & is without Sense or Speech. Miss Murden wishes to return to Southampton if circumstances suit, but it must be very doubtful.—We have been obliged to turn away Cholles, he grew so very drunken & negligent, & we have a Man in his place called Thomas.—Martha desires me to communicate something concerning herself [*p. 3*] which she knows will give you pleasure, as affording her very particular satisfaction; it is, that she is to be in Town this spring with M[rs] Dundas.—I need not dilate on the subject—you understand enough of the whys & wherefores to enter into her feelings, & to be conscious that of all possible arrangements, it is the one most acceptable to her.—She goes to Barton on leaving us—& the Family remove to Town in April.—What you tell me of Miss Sharpe is quite new, & surprises me a little;—I feel however as you do. She is born, poor thing! to struggle with Evil—& her continuing with Miss B.[6] is I hope a proof that Matters are not always so very bad between them, as her Letters sometimes represent.—Jenny's marriage I had heard of, & supposed you would do so too[7] from Steventon, as I knew you were corresponding with Mary at the time. I hope she will not sully the respectable name she now bears.—Your plan for Miss Curling is uncommonly considerate & friendly, & such as she must surely jump at. Edward's going round by Steventon, as I understand he promises to do, can be no reasonable objection, M[rs] J. Austen's hospitality is just of the kind to enjoy such a visitor.—We were very glad to know Aunt Fatty[8] was in the Country when we read of the Fire.—Pray give my best Comp[ts] to the M[rs] Finches, if they are at G[m]—I am sorry to find that Sir J. Moore[9] has a Mother living, but tho' a very Heroick son, he might not be a very necessary one to her happiness.—Deacon Morrell may be more to M[rs] Morrell.—I wish Sir John had united something of the Christian with the Hero in his death.—Thank Heaven! we have had no one to care for particularly among the Troops—no [*p. 4*] one in fact nearer to us than Sir John himself.—Col. Maitland is safe & well; his Mother & sisters were of course anxious about him, but there is no entering much into the solicitudes of that family.—My Mother is well, & gets out when she can with the same enjoyment, & apparently the same strength as hitherto.—She hopes you will not omit begging M[rs] Seward to get the Garden cropped for us—supposing she leaves the House too early, to make the Garden any object to herself.—We are very desirous of receiving *your* account of the House—for your observations will have a motive which can leave nothing to conjecture & suffer nothing from want of Memory.—For one's own dear Self, one ascertains & remembers everything.—Lady Sondes is an impudent Woman to come back into[10] her old Neighbourhood again; I suppose she pretends never to have married before—& wonders how her Father & Mother came to have her christen'd Lady Sondes.—

[*Continued below address panel*]

The storecloset I hope will never do so again—for much of the Evil is proved to have proceeded from the Gutter being choked up, & we have had it cleared.—We had reason to rejoice in the Child's[11] absence at the time of the Thaw, [*continued upside down at top of p. 1*] for the

Nursery was not habitable.—We hear of similar disasters from almost everybody.—No news from Portsmouth. We are very patient.—Mrs Charles Fowle desires to be kindly remembered to you. She is warmly interested in my Brother & his Family.—

Y^{rs} very affec:^{ly} J. Austen.

Miss Austen
Edwd Austen's Esqr
Godmersham Park
Faversham
Kent

[*Letters missing here*]

68(D). *To Crosby & Co.*

Wednesday 5 April 1809

Gentlemen

In the Spring of the year 1803 a MS. Novel in 2 vol. entitled Susan was sold to you by a Gentleman of the name of Seymour,[1] & the purchase money £10. rec^d at the same time. Six years have since passed, & this work of which I avow myself the Authoress, has never to the best of my knowledge, appeared in print, tho' an early publication was stipulated for at the time of Sale. I can only account for such an extraordinary circumstance by supposing the MS by some carelessness to have been lost; & if that was the case, am willing to supply You with another Copy if you are disposed to avail yourselves of it, & will engage for no farther delay when it comes into your hands.—It will not be in my power from particular circumstances[2] to command this Copy before the Month of August, but then, if you accept my proposal, you may depend on receiving it. Be so good as to send me a Line in answer, as soon as possible, as my stay in this place will not exceed a few days. Should no notice be taken of this Address, I shall feel myself at liberty to secure the publication of my work, by applying elsewhere. I am Gentlemen &c &c

MAD.—

Direct to Mrs Ashton Dennis
Post office, Southampton
[Messrs. Crosbie [*sic*] & Co.,
Stationers' Hall Court
London]

April 5. 1809.

68(A). *From Richard Crosby*

Saturday 8 April 1809

Madam

We have to acknowledge the receipt of your letter of the 5th inst. It is true that at the time mentioned we purchased of Mr Seymour a MS. novel entitled *Susan* and paid him for it the sum of 10£ for which we have his stamped receipt as a full consideration, but there was not any time stipulated for its publication, neither are we bound to publish it, Should you or anyone else [*sic*] we shall take proceedings to stop the sale. The MS. shall be yours for the same as we paid for it.

For R. Crosby & Co
I am yours etc.
Richard Crosby

London
Ap 8 1809
Mrs Ashton Dennis
Post Office
Southampton.

69(D). *To Francis Austen*

Wednesday 26 July 1809

Copy of a letter to Frank, July 26, 1809.

My dearest Frank, I wish you Joy
Of Mary's safety with a boy,[1]
Whose birth has given little pain,
Compared with that of Mary Jane.—
May he a growing Blessing prove,
And well deserve his Parents Love!
Endow'd with Art's & Nature's Good,
Thy name possessing with thy Blood;
In him, in all his ways, may we

Another Francis William see!—
Thy infant days may he inherit,
Thy warmth, nay insolence of spirit;-
We would not with one fault dispense
To weaken the resemblance.
May he revive thy Nursery sin,
Peeping as daringly within,
(His curley Locks but just descried)
With, "Bet, my be not come to bide."
Fearless of danger, braving pain,
And threaten'd very oft in vain,
Still may one Terror daunt his soul
One needful engine of controul
Be found in this sublime array,
A neigbouring [*sic*] Donkey's aweful Bray!—
So may his equal faults as Child
Produce Maturity as mild,
His saucy words & fiery ways
In early Childhood's pettish days
[*p. 2*] In Manhood shew his Father's mind,
Like him considerate & kind;
All Gentleness to those around,
And eager only not to wound.
Then like his Father too, he must,
To his own former struggles just,
Feel his Deserts with honest Glow,
And all his Self-improvement know.—
A native fault may thus give birth
To the best blessing, conscious worth.—

As for ourselves, we're very well,
As unaffected prose will tell.
Cassandra's pen will give our state
The many comforts that await
Our Chawton home[2]—how much we find
Already in it to our mind,
And how convinced that when complete,
It will all other Houses beat,
That ever have been made or mended,
With rooms concise or rooms distended.

You'll find us very snug next year;
Perhaps with Charles & Fanny near—
For now it often does delight us
To fancy them just over-right us.³

J. A.

69. *To Francis Austen*

Wednesday 26 July 1809

Chawton, July 26.—1809.—

My dearest Frank, I wish you joy
Of Mary's safety with a Boy,
Whose birth has given little pain
Compared with that of Mary Jane.—
May he a growing Blessing prove,
And well deserve his Parents' Love!—
Endow'd with Art's & Nature's Good,
Thy name possessing with thy Blood,
In him, in all his ways, may we
Another Francis William see!—
Thy infant days may he inherit,
Thy warmth, nay insolence of spirit;-
We would not with one fault dispense
To weaken the resemblance.
May he revive thy Nursery sin,
Peeping as daringly within,
His curley Locks but just descried,
With "Bet, my be not come to bide."—

Fearless of danger, braving pain,
And threaten'd very oft in vain,
Still may one Terror daunt his Soul,
One needful engine of Controul
[*p. 2*] Be found in this sublime array,
A neighbouring Donkey's aweful Bray.
So may his equal faults as Child,
Produce Maturity as mild!
His saucy words & fiery ways
In early Childhood's pettish days,

177

In Manhood, shew his Father's mind
Like him, considerate & kind;
All Gentleness to those around,
And eager only not to wound.

Then like his Father too, he must,
To his own former struggles just,
Feels [*sic*] his Deserts with honest Glow,
And all his self-improvement know.—
A native fault may thus give birth
To the best blessing, conscious Worth.—

As for ourselves we're very well;
As unaffected prose will tell.—
Cassandra's pen will paint our state,
The many comforts that await
Our Chawton home, how much we find
Already in it, to our mind;
[*p. 3*] And how convinced, that when complete
It will all other Houses beat
That ever have been made or mended,
With rooms concise, or rooms distended.
You'll find us very snug next year,
Perhaps with Charles & Fanny near,
For now it often does delight us
To fancy them just over-right us.—

                                        J. A.—

Captⁿ Austen RN.
26th July

[*Letters missing here*]

70. *To Cassandra Austen*

Thursday 18–Saturday 20 April 1811

Sloane St Thursday April 18.

My dear Cassandra

I have so many little matters to tell you of, that I cannot wait any longer before I begin to put them down.—I spent tuesday in Bentinck S^t; the Cookes called here & took me back; & it was quite a Cooke day, for the Miss Rolles paid a visit while I was there, & Sam Arnold dropt in to tea. The badness of the weather disconcerted an excellent plan of mine, that of calling on Miss Beckford again, but from the middle of the day it rained incessantly. Mary & I, after disposing of her Father & Mother, went to the Liverpool Museum,[1] & the British Gallery,[2] & I had some amusement at each, tho' my preference for Men & Women, always inclines me to attend more to the company than the sight.—Mrs Cooke regrets very much that she did not see you when you called, it was oweing [to some][3] blunder among the servants, for she did not know of our visit till we were gone.—She seems tolerably well; but the nervous part of her Complaint I fear increases, & makes her more & more unwilling to part with Mary.—I have proposed to the latter that she should go to Chawton with me, on the supposition of my travelling the Guildford road—& *she* I do beleive, would be glad to do it, but perhaps it may be impossible; unless a Brother can be at home at that time, it certainly must.—George comes to them to day. I did not see Theo' till late on Tuesday; he was gone to Ilford, but he came back in time to shew his usual, nothing-meaning, harmless, heartless Civility.— Henry, who had been confined the whole day to the Bank, took me in his way home; & after [*p. 2*] putting Life & Wit into the party for a quarter of an hour, put himself & his Sister into a Hackney coach.— I bless my stars that I have done with tuesday!—But alas!—Wednesday was likewise a day of great doings, for Manon[4] & I took our walk to Grafton House,[5] & I have a good deal to say on that subject. I am sorry to tell you that I am getting very extravagant & spending all my Money; & what is worse for *you*, I have been spending yours too; for in a Linendraper's shop to which I went for check'd Muslin, & for which I was obliged to give seven shillings a yard, I was tempted by a pretty coloured muslin, & bought 10 y^{ds} of it, on the chance of your liking it;—but at the same time if it sh^d not suit you, you must not think yourself at all obliged to take it; it is only 3/6 p^r y^d, & I sh^d not in the least mind keeping the whole.—In texture, it is just what we prefer, but its' resemblance to green cruels[6] I must own is not great, for the pattern is a small red spot.—?[I took the opportunity of buying some (*?two words lost here*) for you],[7] & now I beleive I have done all my commissions, except Wedgwood. I liked my walk very much; it was shorter than I had expected, & the weather was delightful. We set off immediately after breakfast & must have reached Grafton House by ½ past 11—, but when we entered the Shop, the whole Counter was thronged, & we waited *full* half an hour before we c^d be attended to. When we were served however, I was very well satisfied with my purchases, my Bugle Trimming at 2/4^{d8} & 3 p^r silk Stock^{gs} for a little less than 12./S. a p^r—In my way back, who sh^d I meet but Mr Moore,[9] just come from Beckenham. I beleive he w^d have passed me, if I had not made him stop—but we were delighted to meet. I soon found however that he had nothing new to tell me, & then I let him go.—Miss Burton has made me a very pretty little [*p. 3*] Bonnet—& now nothing can satisfy me but I must have a straw hat, of the riding hat shape, like Mrs Tilson's; & a young woman in this Neighbourhood is actually making me one. I am really very shocking; but it will not be dear at a Guinea.—Our Pelisses are 17/S. each—she charges only 8/ for the making, but the Buttons seem expensive;—*are* expensive, I might have said—for the fact is plain enough.—We drank tea again yesterday with the Tilsons, & met the Smiths.—I find all these little parties very pleasant. I like Mr S. Miss Beaty[10] is goodhumour itself, & does not seem much besides. We spend tomorrow even^g with them, & are to meet the Col^n & Mrs *Cantelo* Smith, you have been used to hear of; & if she is in good humour, are likely to have excellent singing.—To night I might have been at the Play, Henry had kindly planned our going together to the Lyceum, but I have a cold which I sh^d not like to make worse before Saturday;—so, I stay within, all this day.—Eliza is walking out by herself. She has plenty of business on her hands just now—for the day of the Party is settled, & drawing near;—above 80 people are invited for next tuesday Even^g & there is to be some very good Music, 5 professionals, 3 of them Glee-singers, besides Amateurs.—Fanny will listen to this. One of the Hirelings, is a Capital on the Harp, from which I expect great pleasure.—The foundation of the party was a dinner to Henry Egerton & Henry Walter[11]—but the latter leaves Town the day before. I am sorry—as I wished *her* prejudice to be done away—but sh^d have been more sorry if there had been no invitation.—I am a wretch, to be so occupied with all these Things, as to seem to have no Thoughts

to give to people & circumstances which really supply a far more lasting interest—the Society in which You are—but I do think of you all
I assure you, & want to know all about everybody, & especially about
your visit to the W. Friars;[12] "mais le moyen"[13] not to be occupied by
one's own concerns?—Saturday.—Frank is superseded in the Caledonia.
Henry brought us this news yesterday from M[r] Daysh—& he heard at
the same time that Charles may [*p. 4*] be in England in the course of
a month.—Sir Edw[d] Pellew succeeds Lord Gambier in his command, &
some Captain of his, succeeds Frank; & I beleive the order is already
gone out. Henry means to enquire farther to day;—he wrote to Mary[14]
on the occasion.—This is something to think of.—Henry is convinced
that he will have the offer of something else, but does not think it will
be at all incumbent on him to accept it; & then follows, what will he do?
& where will he live?—I hope to hear from you today. How are you,
as to Health, strength, Looks, stomach &c?—I had a very comfortable
account from Chawton yesterday.—If the Weather permits, Eliza & I
walk into London this morn[g]—*She* is in want of chimney lights for
Tuesday;—& *I*, of an ounce of darning cotton.—She has resolved not
to venture to the Play tonight. The D'Entraigues & Comte Julien cannot come to the Party—which was at first a greif, but she has since
supplied herself so well with Performers that it is of no consequence;—
their not coming has produced our going to them tomorrow Even[g]—
which I like the idea of. It will be amusing to see the ways of a French
circle. I wrote to M[rs] Hill[15] a few days ago, & have received a most kind
& satisfactory answer; my time, the first week in May, exactly suits her;
& therefore I consider my Goings as tolerably fixed. I shall leave Sloane
S[t] on the 1st or 2[d] & be ready for James on ye 9th;—& if his plan alters,
I can take care of myself.—I have explained my veiws here, & everything is smooth & pleasant; & Eliza [*continued below address panel*] talks
kindly of conveying me to Streatham.—We met the Tilsons yesterday
Even[g]—but the singing Smiths sent an excuse—which put our M[rs] Smith
out of hum[our]—[*continued upside down at top of p. 1*]

We are come back, after a good dose of Walking & Coaching, & I
have the pleasure of your letter.—I wish I had James's verses,[16] but
they were left at Chawton. When I return thither, if M[rs] K.[17] will give
me leave, I will send them to her.—Our first object to day was Henrietta
S[t] to consult with Henry, in consequence of a very unlucky change of
the Play for this very night—Hamlet instead of King John—& we are
to go on Monday to Macbeth, instead, but it is a disappointment to us
both.

Love to all. Yours affec:^ly Jane.

Miss Austen
Edwd Austen's Esqre
Godmersham Park
Faversham
Kent

71. *To Cassandra Austen*

Thursday 25 April 1811

Sloane St Thursday April 25.

My dearest Cassandra

I can return the compliment by thanking you for the unexpected pleasure of *your* Letter yesterday, & as I like unexpected pleasure, it made me very happy; And indeed, You need not apologise for your Letter in any respect, for it is all very fine, but not *too* fine I hope to be written again, or something like it. I think Edward will not suffer much longer from heat; by the look of Things this morn^g I suspect the weather is rising into the balsamic Northeast. It has been hot here, as you may suppose, since it was so hot with you, but I have not suffered from it at all, nor felt it in such a degree as to make me imagine it would be anything in the Country. Everybody has talked of the heat, but I set it all down to London.—I give you joy of our new nephew,[1] & hope if he ever comes to be hanged, it will not be till we are too old to care about it.—It is a great comfort to have it so safely & speedily over. The Miss Curlings must be hard-worked in writing so many Letters, but the novelty of it may recommend it to *them*;—Mine was from Miss Eliza, & she says that my Brother[2] may arrive today.—No indeed, I am never too busy to think of S&S.[3] I can no more forget it, than a mother can forget her sucking child; & I am much obliged to you for your enquiries. I have had two sheets to correct, but the last only brings us to W.s first appearance.[4] Mrs K.[5] regrets in the most flattering manner that she must wait *till* May, but I have scarcely a hope of its being out in June.— Henry does not neglect it; he *has* hurried the Printer, & says he will see him again today.—It will not stand still during his absence, [*p. 2*] it will be sent to Eliza.—The *Incomes* remain as they were, but I will get them altered if I can.—I am very much gratified by Mrs K.s interest in it; & whatever may be the event of it as to my credit with her, sincerely wish her curiosity could be satisfied sooner than is now probable. I think she will like my Elinor, but cannot build on any thing else. Our party went off extremely well. There were many solicitudes, alarms & vexations beforehand of course, but at last everything was quite right. The rooms were dressed up with flowers &c, & looked very pretty.—A glass for the Mantlepeice was lent, by the Man who is making their own.—Mr Egerton & Mr Walter came at ½ past 5, & the festivities began with a p^r of very fine Soals. Yes, Mr Walter—for he postponed his leaving London on purpose—which did not give much pleasure at the time, any more than the circumstance from which it rose, his calling on Sunday & being asked by Henry to take the family dinner on that day, which he did—but it is all smooth'd over now;—& she likes him very well.—At ½ past 7 arrived the Musicians in two Hackney coaches, & by 8 the lordly Company^6 began to appear. Among the earliest were George & Mary Cooke, & I spent the greatest part of the even^g very pleasantly with them.—The Draw^g room being soon hotter than we liked, we placed ourselves in the connecting Passage,^7 which was comparatively cool, & gave us all the advantage of the Music at a pleasant distance, as well as that of the first veiw of every new comer.—I was quite surrounded by acquaintance, especially Gentlemen; & what with Mr Hampson, Mr Seymour, Mr W. Knatchbull, Mr Guillemarde, Mr Cure, a Capt Simpson, brother to *the* Capt Simpson, besides Mr Walter & Mr Egerton, in addition to the Cookes & Miss Beckford & Miss Middleton, I had quite as much upon my hands as I could do.—Poor Miss B. has been suffering again from her old complaint, & looks thinner than ever. She certainly goes to Cheltenham the beginning of June. We were all delight & cordiality of course. Miss M. seems very happy, but has not beauty enough to figure in London.—Including everybody we were 66—which was considerably more than Eliza had expected, & quite enough to fill [*p. 3*] the Back Draw^g room, & leave a few to be scattered about in the other, & in the passage.—The Music^8 was extremely good. It opened (tell Fanny) with "Prike pe Parp^9 pin praise pof Prapela"—& of the other Glees I remember, "In peace Love tunes," "Rosabelle," "The red cross Knight," & "Poor Insect." Between the Songs were Lessons on the Harp, or Harp & Piano Forte together—& the Harp Player was Wiepart, whose name seems famous, tho' new to me.—There was one female singer, a short Miss Davis all in blue, bringing up for the Public Line, whose voice was said to be very fine indeed; & all the Performers gave great satisfaction by doing what they were paid for, & giving themselves no airs.—No Amateur could be persuaded to do anything.—The House was not clear till after 12.—If you wish to hear more of it, you must put your questions, but I seem rather to have exhausted than spared the subject.—This said Capt. Simpson told us, on the authority of some other Captn just arrived from Halifax, that Charles was bringing the Cleopatra home, & that she was probably by this time in the Channel—but as Capt. S. was certainly in liquor, we must not quite depend on it.—It must give one a sort of expectation however, & will prevent my writing to him any more.—I would rather he sh^d not reach England till I am at home, & the Steventon party gone. My Mother & Martha both write with great satisfaction of Anna's behaviour. She is quite an Anna with variations—but she cannot have reached her last, for that is always the most flourishing & shewey— she is at about her 3^d or 4th which are generally simple & pretty.—Your Lilacs are in leaf, *ours* are in bloom.—The Horse chesnuts are quite out, & the Elms almost.—I had a pleasant walk in Kensington G^s on Sunday with Henry, Mr Smith & Mr Tilson—everything was fresh & beautiful.—We *did* go to the play after all on Saturday, we went to the Lyceum, & saw the Hypocrite,^{10} an old play taken from Moliere's *Tartuffe*, & were well entertained. Dowton & Mathews were the good actors. Mrs Edwin was the Heroine—& her performance is just what it used to be.—I have no chance of seeing Mrs Siddons.^{11}—She *did* act on Monday, but as Henry was told by the Boxkeeper that he did not think she would, the places, & all thought of it, were given up. I should particularly have liked seeing her in Constance, & could swear at her with little effort for disappointing me.—Henry has been to the Water-colour Exhibition, which open'd on Monday, & is to meet us there again some morn^g—If Eliza cannot go—(& she has a cold at present) Miss Beaty will be invited to be my companion.—Henry leaves Town [*p. 4*] on Sunday afternoon—but he means to write soon himself to Edward—& will tell his own plans.—The Tea is this moment setting out.—Do not have your col^d muslin unless you really want it, because I am afraid I c^d not send it to the Coach without giving trouble here.— Eliza caught her cold on Sunday in our way to the D'Entraigues;—the Horses actually gibbed on this side of Hyde Park Gate—a load of fresh gravel made it a formidable Hill to them, & they refused the collar;— I beleive there was a sore shoulder to irritate.—Eliza was frightened, & we got out—& were detained in the Even^g air several minutes.—The cold is in her chest—but she takes care of herself, & I hope it may not last long.—This engagement prevented Mr Walter's staying late—he had his coffee & went away.—Eliza enjoyed her even^g very much & means to cultivate the acquaintance—& I see nothing to dislike in^{12}

them, but their taking quantities of snuff.—Monsieur the old Count, is a very fine looking man, with quiet manners, good enough for an Englishman—& I beleive is a Man of great Information & Taste. He has some fine Paintings, which delighted Henry as much as the Son's music gratified Eliza—& among them, a Miniature of Philip 5. of Spain, Louis 14.s Grandson, which exactly suited *my* capacity.—Count Julien's performance is very wonderful. We met only Mrs Latouche & Miss East— & we are just now engaged to spend next Sunday Even^g at Mrs L.s—& to meet the D'Entraigues;—but M. le Comte must do without Henry. If he w^d but speak english, *I* would take to him.—[*continued below address panel*] Have you ever mentioned the leaving off Tea to Mrs K.?—Eliza has just spoken of it again.—The Benefit *she* has found from it in sleeping, has been very great.—[*continued upside down at top of p. 1*] I shall write soon to Catherine to fix my day, which will be Thursday.—We have no engagements but for Sunday. Eliza's cold makes quiet adviseable.—Her party is mentioned in this morning's paper.[13] I am sorry to hear of poor Fanny's state.—From *that* quarter I suppose is to be the alloy of her happiness.—I *will* have no more to say.—

Y^{rs} affec^{ly} J. A.

Give my Love particularly to my God-daughter.[14]

Miss Austen
Edwd Austen's Esqre
Godmersham Park
Faversham

[*Letter missing here, ?28–9 April*]

72. To Cassandra Austen

Tuesday 30 April 1811

Sloane St Tuesday.

My dear Cassandra

I had sent off my Letter yesterday before Yours came, which I was sorry for; but as Eliza has been so good as to get me a frank, your questions shall be answered without much further expense to you.— The best direction to Henry at Oxford will be, *The Blue Boar, Cornmarket.*—I do *not* mean to provide another trimming for my Pelisse, for I am determined to spend no more money, so I shall wear it as it is, longer than I ought, & then—I do not know.—My head dress was a Bugle band like the border to my gown, & a flower of Mrs Tilson's.— I depended upon hearing something of the Even^g from Mr W. K.^1 & am very well satisfied with his notice of me. "A pleasing looking young woman";—that must do;—one cannot pretend to anything better now— thankful to have it continued a few years longer!—It gives me sincere pleasure to hear of Mrs Knight's having had a tolerable night at last— but upon this occasion I wish she had another name, for the two *Nights* jingle very much.—We have tried to get Self-controul,^2 but in vain.— I *should* like to know what her Estimate is—[*p. 2*] but am always half afraid of finding a clever novel *too clever*—& of finding my own story & my own people all forestalled. Eliza has just rec^d a few lines from Henry to assure her of the good conduct of his Mare. He slept at Uxbridge on Sunday, & wrote from Wheatfield.—We were not claimed by Hans place yesterday, but are to dine there today.—Mr Tilson called in the even^g—but otherwise we were quite alone all day, & after having been out a good deal, the change was very pleasant.—I like your opinion of Miss Allen^3 much better than I expected, & have now hopes of her staying a whole twelvemonth.—By this time I suppose she is hard at it, governing away—poor creature! I pity her, tho' they *are* my neices. Oh! yes, I remember Miss Emma Plumbtree's *Local* consequence perfectly.—"I am in a Dilemma, for want of an Emma,"

"Escaped from the Lips, Of Henry Gipps."^4—

But really, I was never much more put to it, than in contriving an answer to Fanny's former message. What is there to be said on the subject?—Pery pell^5—or pare pey? or po.—or at the most, Pi pope pey pike pit.—I congratulate Edward on the Weald of Kent Canal-Bill being put off till another Session, as I have just had the pleasure of reading. There is always something to be hoped from Delay.—

"Between Session & Session"
"The first Prepossession"
"May rouse up the Nation"
"And the Villainous Bill"
"May be forced to lie Still"
"Against Wicked Men's will."

[*p. 3*] There is poetry for Edward & his Daughter. I am afraid I shall not have any for you.—I forgot to tell you in my last, that our cousin Miss Payne called in on Saturday & was persuaded to stay dinner.— She told us a great deal about her friend Lady Cath. Brecknell, who is most happily married—& Mr Brecknell is very religious, & has got black Whiskers.—I am glad to think that Edwd has a tolerable day for his drive to Goodnestone, & *very* glad to hear of his kind promise of bringing you to Town. I hope everything will arrange itself favourably. The 16th is now to be Mrs Dundas's day.^6—I mean, if I can, to wait for your return, before I have my new Gown made up—from a notion of their making up to more advantage together—& as I find the Muslin is not so wide as it *used to be*, some contrivance may be necessary.—I expect the Skirt to require one half breadth cut in gores, besides two whole Breadths.—

Eliza has not yet quite resolved on inviting Anna^7—but I think she will.—Yours very affec^ly

Jane.

[*No address*]

[*Letters missing here*]

73. *To Cassandra Austen*

Chawton Wednesday May 29.

It was a mistake of mine, my dear Cassandra, to talk of a 10th child at Hamstall; I had forgot there were but 8 already.—Your enquiry after my Uncle & Aunt were most happily timed, for the very same post brought an account of them. They are again at Gloucester House,^1 enjoying fresh air, which they seem to have felt the want of in Bath, & are tolerably well—but not more than tolerable. My Aunt does not enter into particulars, but she does not write in spirits, & we imagine that she has never entirely got the better of her disorder in the Winter.—Mrs Welby takes her out airing in her Barouche, which gives her a headache—a comfortable proof I suppose of the uselessness of the new Carriage when they have got it.—You certainly must have heard, before I can tell you, that Col. Orde has married our cousin, Marg^t Beckford, the March^ss of Douglas's sister. The Papers say^2 that her Father disinherits her, but I think too well of an Orde, to suppose that she has not a handsome Independance of her own.—The Chicken are all alive, & fit for the Table—but we save them for something grand.—Some of the Flower seeds are coming up very well—but your Mignionette makes a wretched appearance.—Miss Benn has been equally unlucky as to hers; She had seed from 4 different people, & none of it comes up. Our young Piony at the foot of the Fir tree has just blown & looks very handsome; & the whole of the Shrubbery Border [*p. 2*] will soon be very gay with Pinks & Sweet Williams, in addition to the Columbines already in bloom. The Syringas too are coming out.—We are likely to have a great crop of Orleans plumbs—but not many greengages—on the standard scarcely any—three or four dozen perhaps against the wall. I beleive I told you differently when I first came home, but I can now judge better than I could then.—I have had a medley & satisfactory Letter this morn^g from the Husband & Wife at Cowes;[3]—& in consequence of what is related of their plans, we have been talking over the possibility of inviting them here, in their way from Steventon—which is what one should wish to do, & is I daresay what they expect; but supposing Martha to be at home, it does not seem a very easy thing to accomodate so large a party.—My Mother offers to give up her room to Frank & Mary—but there will then be only the Best, for two Maids & three Children.—They go to Steventon about ye 22^d—& I *guess* (for it is quite a guess) will stay there from a fortnight to three weeks.—I must not venture to press Miss Sharpe's coming at present;—we may hardly be at liberty before August.—Poor John Bridges! we are very sorry for his situation, & for the distress of the Family.[4] Lady B. is in *one way* severely tried!—And our own dear Brother suffers a great deal I dare say on the occasion.—I have not much to say of ourselves. Anna is nursing a cold caught in the Arbour at Faringdon, that she may be able to keep her engagement to Maria M.[5] this evening, when I suppose she will make it worse.—[*p. 3*] She did not return from Faringdon till Sunday, when H^t B.[6] walked home with her, & drank tea here.—She was with the Prowtings almost all Monday;—she went to learn to make feather Trimmings of Miss Anne, & they kept her to dinner—which was rather lucky, as we were called upon to meet M^{rs} & Miss Terry the same even^g at the Digweeds—& tho' Anna was of course invited to, I think it always safest to keep her away from the family,[7] lest she sh^d be doing too little or too much. Mrs Terry, Mary & Robert, with my Aunt Harding & her Daughter came from Dummer for a day & a night—all very agreable & very much delighted with the new House, & with Chawton in general.—We sat upstairs—& had Thunder & Lightning as usual. I never knew such a Spring for Thunder storms as it has been!—Thank God!—we have had[8] no bad ones here.—I thought

myself in luck to have my uncomfortable feelings shared by the Mistress
of the House, as that procured Blinds & Candles.—It had been excessively hot the whole day.—Mrs Harding is a goodlooking woman, but
not much like Mrs Toke,⁹ inasmuch as she is very brown & has scarcely
any teeth;—she seems to have some of Mrs Toke's civility, but does not
profess being so silly.—Miss H. is an elegant, pleasing, pretty looking
girl, about 19 I suppose, or 19 & ½, or 19 & ¼, with flowers in her head,
& Music at her fingers ends.—She plays very well indeed. I have seldom heard anybody with more pleasure.—They were at Godington 4
or 5 years ago; my cousin Flora Long was there last year. *My* name is
Diana.¹⁰ How does Fanny like it?—What a change in the weather!—
We have a Fire again now.—

[*p. 4*] Harriet Benn sleeps at the G^t House tonight & spends tomorrow with us; & the plan is that we should all walk with her to drink tea
at Faringdon, for her Mother is now recovered, but the state of the
weather is not very promising at present.—Miss Benn has been returned to her Cottage¹¹ since the beginning of last week, & has now just
got another girl;—she comes from Alton.—For many days Miss B. had
nobody with her but her neice Eliz^th—who was delighted to be her
visitor & her maid. They both dined here on Saturday while Anna was
at Faringdon; & last night, an accidental meeting & a sudden impulse
produced Miss Benn & Maria Middleton at our Tea Table.—If you
have not heard, it is very fit you should, that Mr Harrison has had the
Living of Fareham given him by the Bishop, & is going to reside there;
—And now it is said that Mr Peach (beautiful Wiseacre) wants to have
the Curacy of Overton; & if he *does* leave Wootton, James Digweed
wishes to go there.—Fare you well.—Yours affec^ly

J. Austen

[*Postscript below address panel*]

The Chimneys at the G^t House are done. Mr Prowting has opened
a Gravel pit,¹² very conveniently for my Mother, just at the mouth of
the approach to his House—but it looks a little as if he meant to catch
all his company. Tolerable Gravel.—

Miss Austen
Godmersham Park
Faversham
Kent

74. *To Cassandra Austen*

Friday 31 May 1811

Chawton Friday May 31st.—

My dear Cassandra

I have a magnificent project.—The Cookes have put off their visit to us; they are not well enough to leave home at present, & we have no chance of seeing them till I do not know when—probably never, in this house. This circumstance has made me think the present time would be favourable for Miss Sharp's coming to us; it seems a more disengaged period with us, than we are likely to have later in the Summer; if Frank & Mary do come, it can hardly be before the middle of July, which will be allowing a reasonable length of visit for Miss Sharpe supposing she begins it when you return; & if You & Martha do not dislike the plan, & she can avail herself of it, the opportunity of her being conveyed hither will be excellent.—I shall write to Martha by this post, & if neither You nor she make any objection to my proposal, I shall make the invitation directly—& as there is no time to lose, you must write by return of post if you have any reason for not wishing it done.—It was her intention I beleive to go first to Mrs Lloyd¹—but such a means of getting here may influence her otherwise.—We have had a Thunder storm again this morn^g. Your Letter came to comfort me for it.—I have taken your hint, slight as it was, & have [*p. 2*] written to Mrs Knight, & most sincerely do I hope it will not be in vain. I cannot endure the idea of her giving away her own wheel, & have told her no more than the truth, in saying that I could never use it with comfort;—I had a great mind to add that if she persisted in giving it, I would spin nothing with it but a Rope to hang myself—but I was afraid of making it appear a less serious matter of feeling than it really is.—I am glad you are so well yourself, & wish everybody else were equally so.—I will not say that your Mulberry trees are dead, but I am afraid they are not alive. We shall have pease soon—I mean to have them with a couple of Ducks from Wood Barn & Maria Middleton towards the end of next week.— From Monday to Wednesday Anna is to be engaged at Faringdon, in order that she may come in for the Gaieties of Tuesday² (ye 4th), on Selbourne Common, where there are to be Volunteers & Felicities of all kinds. Harriot B.³ is invited to spend the day with the John Whites, & her Father & Mother have very kindly undertaken to get Anna invited also.—Harriot & Eliz. dined here yesterday, & we walked back with them to Tea;—not my Mother—she has a cold which affects her in the usual way, & was not equal to the walk.—She is better this morn^g & I hope will soon physick away the worst part of it.—It has not confined her; she has got out every day that the weather has allowed her.—Poor Anna is also suffering from *her* cold which is worse today, but as she has no sore throat I hope it may spend itself by Tuesday. She had a delightful Even^g with the Miss Middletons—Syllabub, Tea, Coffee, Singing, Dancing, a Hot Supper, eleven o'clock, everything that can be imagined agreable.—She desires her best Love to Fanny, & will answer her letter before she leaves Chawton, & engages to send her a [*p. 3*] particular account of the Selbourn day. We cannot agree as to which is the eldest of the two Miss Plumbtrees;—send us word.—Have you remembered to collect peices for the Patchwork?—We are now at a stand still. I got up here to look for the old Map, & can now tell you that it shall be sent tomorrow;—it was among the great parcel in the Dining room.—As to my debt of *3^s*.6 to Edward, I must trouble you to pay it, when you settle with him for your Boots.—

We began our China Tea three days ago, & *I* find it very good—my companions know nothing of the matter.—As to Fanny, & her 12 lb. in a twelvemonth, she may talk till she is as black in the face as her own Tea, but I cannot beleive her;—more likely 12 lb. to a quarter.—I have a message to you from Mrs Cooke;—the substance of it is that she hopes you will take Bookham in your way home, & stay there as long as you can, & that when you must leave them, they will convey you to Guildford.—You may be sure that it is very kindly worded—& that there is no want of attendant Comp^ts to my Brother & his family.—I am very sorry for Mary;[4]—but I have some comfort in there being two Curates[5] now lodging in Bookham, besides their own Mr Warneford from Dorking, so that I think she must fall in love with one or the other.—

How horrible it is to have so many people killed![6]—And what a blessing that one cares for none of them!—I return to my Letter writing from calling on Miss Harriot Webb, who is short & not quite straight, & cannot pronounce an R any better than her Sisters—but she has dark hair, a complexion to suit, & I think has the pleasantest countenance & manner of the three—the most natural.—She appears very well pleased with her new Home—& they are all reading with delight Mrs H. More's recent publication[7]—

[*p. 4*] You cannot imagine—it is not in Human Nature to imagine what a nice walk we have round the Orchard.—The row of Beech look very well indeed, & so does the young Quickset hedge[8] in the Garden.—I hear today that an Apricot has been detected on one of the Trees.—

My Mother is perfectly convinced *now* that she shall not be overpower'd by her Cleft Wood—& I beleive would rather have more than less.—

Strange to tell, Mr Prowting was *not* at Miss Lee's wedding—but his Daughters had some cake, & Anna had her share of it.—I continue to like our old Cook quite as well as ever—& but that I am afraid to write in her praise, I could say that she seems just the Servant for us.—Her Cookery is at least tolerable;—her pastry is the only deficiency.—God bless you.—& I hope June will find you well & bring us together.— Y^rs Ever

Jane.

[Postscript below address panel]

I hope you understand that I do not expect you to write on Sunday, if you like my plan.—I shall consider Silence as Consent.

Miss Austen
Edwd Austen's Esqre
Godmersham Park
Faversham

75. *To Cassandra Austen*

Thursday 6 June 1811

Chawton Thursday June 6.

By this time my dearest Cassandra, you know Martha's plans. I was rather disappointed I confess to find that she could not leave Town till after ye 24th, as I had hoped to see you here the week before. The delay however is not great, & everything seems generally arranging itself for your return very comfortably. I found Henry perfectly pre-disposed to bring you to London if agreable to yourself; he has not fixed his day for *going* into Kent, but he must be back again before ye 20th.—You may therefore think with something like certainty of the close of your Godmersham visit, & will have I suppose about a week for Sloane S^t. He travels in his Gig—& should the weather be tolerable, I think you must have a delightful Journey.—I have given up all idea of Miss Sharpe's travelling with You & Martha, for tho' you are both all compliance with my scheme, yet as *you* knock off a week from the end of her visit, & *Martha* rather more from the beginning, the thing is out of the question.—I have written to her to say that after the middle of July we shall be happy to receive her—& I have added a welcome if she could make her way hither *directly*;[1] but I do not expect that she will.— I have also sent our invitation to Cowes.[2]—We are very sorry for the disappointment you have all had in Lady B.'s[3] illness;—but a division of the proposed party is with you by this time, & I hope may have brought you a better account of the rest.—Give my Love & Thanks [*p. 2*] to Harriot;[4]—who has written me charming things of your looks, & diverted me very much by poor M[rs] C. Milles's continued perplexity. —I had a few lines from Henry on Tuesday to prepare us for himself & his friend, & by the time that I had made the sumptuous provision of a neck of Mutton on the occasion, they drove into the Court—but lest you should not immediately recollect in how many hours a neck of Mutton may be certainly procured, I add that they came a little after twelve—both tall, & well, & in their different degrees, agreable.—It was a visit of only 24 hours—but very pleasant while it lasted.—M[r] Tilson took a sketch of the Great House before dinner;—& after dinner we all three walked to Chawton Park, meaning to go into it, but it was too dirty, & we were obliged to keep on the outside. M[r] Tilson admired the Trees very much, but greived that they should not be turned into money.—My Mother's cold is better, & I beleive she only wants dry weather to be very well. It was a great distress to her that Anna sh[d] be absent, during her Uncle's visit—a distress which I could not share.— She does not return from Faringdon till this even[g],—& I doubt not, has had plenty of the miscellaneous, unsettled sort of happiness which seems to suit her best.—We hear from Miss Benn, who was on the Common[s] with the Prowtings, that she was very much admired by the Gentlemen in general.—

I like your new Bonnets exceedingly, yours is a shape which always looks well, & I think Fanny's particularly becoming to her.—[*p. 3*] On Monday I had the pleasure of receiving, unpacking & approving our Wedgwood ware. It all came very safely, & upon the whole is a good match, tho' I think they might have allowed us rather larger leaves, especially in such a Year of fine foliage as this. One is apt to suppose that the Woods about Birmingham must be blighted.—There was no Bill with the Goods—but that shall not screen them from being paid. I mean to ask Martha to settle the account. It will be quite in her way, for she is just now sending my Mother a Breakfast set, from the same place. I hope it will come by the Waggon tomorrow; it is certainly what we want, & I long to know what it is like; & as I am sure Martha has great pleasure in making the present, I will not have any regret.[6] We have considerable dealings with the Waggons at present; a Hamper of Port & Brandy from Southampton, is now in the Kitchen.—Your answer about the Miss Plumtrees, proves you as fine a Daniel as ever Portia was;—for *I* maintained Emma to be the eldest.—We began Pease on Sunday, but our gatherings are very small—not at all like the Gathering in the Lady of the Lake.[7]—Yesterday I had the agreable surprise of finding several scarlet strawberries quite ripe;—had *You* been at home, this would have been a pleasure lost. There are more Gooseberries & fewer Currants than I thought at first.—We must buy currants for our Wine.—

The Digweeds are gone down to see the Stephen Terrys at Southampton, & catch the Kings birthday at Portsmouth. Miss Papillon called on us yesterday, looking handsomer than ever.—Maria Middleton & Miss Benn dine here tomorrow.—[*p. 4*] We are not to enclose any more Letters to Abingdon S^t[8] as perhaps Martha has told you.—

I had just left off writing & put on my Things for walking to Alton, when Anna & her friend Harriot called in their way thither, so we went together. Their business was to provide mourning, against the King's death;[9] & my Mother has had a Bombasin bought for her.—I am not sorry to be back again, for the young Ladies had a great deal to do—& without much method in doing it.—Anna does not come home till tomorrow morn^g—She has written I find to Fanny—but there does not seem[10] to be a great deal to relate of Tuesday. I had hoped there might be Dancing.—Mrs Budd died on Sunday Even^g. I saw her two days before her death, & thought it must happen soon. She suffered much from weakness & restlessness almost to the last. Poor little Harriot seems truely greived. You have never mentioned Harry;[11]—how is he?—

With Love to You all, Y^rs affec^ly

J. A.

Miss Austen
Edw. Austen's Esqre
Godmersham Park
Faversham

[*Letters missing here*]

76(C). *To Anna Austen*

?Between Thursday 29–Saturday 31 October 1812[1]

Miss Jane Austen begs her best thanks may be conveyed to M[rs] Hunter of Norwich for the Threadpaper which she has been so kind as to send her by M[r] Austen, & which will be always very valuable on account of the spirited sketches (made it is supposed by Nicholson or Glover)[2] of the most interesting spots, Tarefield Hall, the Mill, & above all the Tomb of Howard's wife, [*p. 2*] of the faithful representation of which Miss Jane Austen is undoubtedly a good judge having spent so many summers at Tarefield Abbey[3] the delighted guest of the worthy M[rs] Wilson. [It is impossible for any likeness to be more complete.][4] Miss Jane Austen's tears have flowed over each sweet sketch in such a way as would do M[rs] Hunter's heart good to see; if M[rs] Hunter could understand all Miss Jane Austen's interest in the subject she would certainly have the kindness to publish at least 4 vols more about the Flint family,[5] & especially would give many fresh particulars on that part of it which M[rs] H. has hitherto handled too briefly; viz, the history of Mary Flint's marriage with Howard.

Miss Jane Austen cannot close this small epitome of the miniature abridgment of her thanks & admiration [*p. 3*] without expressing her sincere hope that M[rs] Hunter is provided at Norwich with a more safe conveyance to London than Alton can now boast, as the Car of Falkenstein[6] which was the pride of that Town was overturned within the last 10 days.

Miss Austen
Steventon

---

77. *To Martha Lloyd*

Sunday 29–Monday 30 November 1812

Chawton Sunday Nov[r] 29th.

My dear Martha[1]

I shall take care not to count the lines of your *last* Letter; you have obliged me to eat humble-pie indeed; I am really obliged to you however, & though it is in general much pleasanter to reproach than to be grateful, I do not mind it now.—We shall be glad to hear, whenever you can write, & can well imagine that time for writing must be wanting in such an arduous, busy, useful office as you fill at present. You are made for doing good, & have quite as great a turn for it I think as for physicking little Children. The mental Physick which you have been lately applying bears a stamp beyond all common Charity, & I hope a Blessing will continue to attend it.—I am glad you are well & trust you are sure of being so, while you are employed in such a way;—I must hope however that your health may eer long stand the trial of a more common-place course of days, & that you will be able to leave Barton when Mrs D. D. arrives there.—There was no ready-made Cloak at Alton that would do, but Coleby has undertaken to supply one in a few days; it is to be Grey Woollen & cost ten shillings. I hope you like the *sim*[2] of it.—Sally[3] knows your kind intentions & has received your message, & in return for it all, she & I have between us made out [*p. 2*] that she sends her Duty & thanks you for your goodness & means to be a good girl if I please.—I have forgot to enquire as to her wanting anything particularly, but there is no *apparent* deficiency, she looks very neat & tidy. The Calico for her Mother shall be bought soon.—We have been quite alone, except Miss Benn, since 12 o'clock on wednesday, when Edward & his Harem[4] drove from the door; & we have since heard of their safe arrival & happiness at Winchester.—Lizzy was much obliged to you for your message, but *she* had the little room. Her Father having his choice & being used to a very large Bedchamber at home, would of course prefer the ample space of Yours.—The visit was a very pleasant one I really beleive on each side; they were certainly very sorry to go away, but a little of that sorrow must be attributed to a disinclination for what was before them. They have had favourable weather however, & I hope Steventon may have been better than they expected.—We have reason to suppose the change of name[5] has taken place, as we have to forward a Letter to Edward Knight Esqre from the Lawyer who has the management of the business. I must learn to make a better K.—Our next visitor is likely to be William[6] from Eltham in his way to Winchester, as Dr Gabell chuses he should come then before the Holidays, though it can be only for a week. [*p. 3*] If Mrs Barker has any farther curiosity about the Miss Webbs let her know that we are going to invite them for Tuesday even^g—also Capt. & Mrs Clement & Miss Benn, & that Mrs Digweed is already secured.—"But why not Mr Digweed?"—Mrs Barker will immediately say—To that you may answer that Mr D. is going on tuesday to Steventon to shoot rabbits.— The 4 lines on Miss W.[7] which I sent you were all my own, but James afterwards suggested what I thought a great improvement & as it stands in the Steventon Edition. P. & P. is sold. — Egerton gives £110 for it. — I would rather have had £150, but we could not both be pleased, & I am not at all surprised that he should not chuse to hazard so much. — Its' being sold will I hope be a great saving of Trouble to Henry, & therefore must be welcome to me. — The Money is to be paid at the end of the twelvemonth. — You have sometimes expressed a wish of making Miss Benn some present; — Cassandra & I think that something of the Shawl kind to wear over her Shoulders within doors in very cold weather might be useful, but it must not be very handsome or she would not use it. Her long Fur tippet is almost worn out. — If you do not return in time to send the Turkey yourself, we must trouble you for Mr Morton's direction again, as we should be quite as much at a loss as ever. It becomes now a sort of vanity in us not to know Mr Morton's direction with any certainty. — We are just beginning to be engaged in another Christmas Duty, & next to eating Turkies, a very pleasant one, laying out Edward's money for the Poor; & the Sum that passes [*p. 4*] through our hands this year is considerable, as Mrs Knight left £20 to the Parish. — Your nephew William's state seems very alarming. Mary Jane,[8] from whom I heard the other day, writes of him as very uneasy; I hope his Father & Mother are so too. — When you see Miss Murden, give her our Love & Good wishes, & say that we are very sorry to hear of her so often as an Invalid. Poor Mrs Stent I hope will not be much longer a distress to anybody. — All of you that are well enough to look, are now passing your Judgements I suppose on Mrs John Butler; & "is she pretty? or is she not?" is the knotty question. Happy Woman! to stand the gaze of a neighbourhood as the Bride of such a pink-faced, simple young Man! —

Monday. A wettish day, bad for Steventon. — Mary Deedes I think must be liked there, she is so perfectly unaffected & sweet tempered, & tho' as ready to be pleased as Fanny Cage, deals less in superlatives & rapture. — Pray give our best comp^ts to Mrs Dundas & [*continued below address panel*] tell her that we hope soon to hear of her complete recovery. — Yours affec:^ly

J. Austen

Miss Lloyd[9]

78. *To Cassandra Austen*

Sunday 24 January 1813

Chawton Sunday even^g Jany 24.

My dear Cassandra

This is exactly the weather we could wish for, if you are but well enough to enjoy it. I shall be glad to hear that you are not confined to the house by an increase of Cold. Mr Digweed has used us basely. Handsome is as Handsome does; he is therefore a very ill-looking Man. I hope you have sent off a Letter to me by this day's post, unless you are tempted to wait till tomorrow by one of Mr Chute's franks.—We have had no letter since you went away, & no visitor, except Miss Benn who dined with us on friday; but we have received the half of an excellent Stilton cheese—we presume, from Henry.—My Mother is very well & finds great amusement in the glove-knitting; when this pair is finished, she means to knit another, & at present wants no other work.— We quite run over with Books. *She* has got Sir John Carr's Travels in Spain[1] from Miss B. & *I* am reading a Society-Octavo,[2] an Essay on the Military Police & Institutions of the British Empire, by Capt. Pasley[3] of the Engineers, a book which I protested against at first, but which upon trial I find delightfully written & highly entertaining. I am as much in love with the Author as I ever was with Clarkson or Buchanan,[4] or even the two Mr Smiths of the city.[5] The first soldier I ever sighed for; but he does write with extraordinary force & spirit. Yesterday moreover brought us Mrs Grant's Letters, with Mr White's Comp^ts.—But I have disposed of them, Comp^ts & all, for the first fortnight to Miss Papillon—& among so many readers or retainers of Books as we have in Chawton, I dare say there will [*p. 2*] be no difficulty in getting rid of them for another fortnight if necessary.—I learn from Sir J. Carr that there is no Government House at Gibraltar.—I must alter it to the Commissioner's.[6]—Our party on Wednesday was not unagreable, tho' as usual we wanted a better Master of the House, one less anxious & fidgetty, & more conversible. In consequence of a civil note that morn^g from Mrs Clement, I went with her & her Husband in their Tax-cart;[7]— civility on both sides; *I* would rather have walked, & no doubt, *they* must have wished I had.—I ran home with my own dear Thomas[8] at night in great Luxury. Thomas was very useful. We were Eleven altogether, as you will find on computation, adding Miss Benn & two strange

Gentlemen, a Mr Twyford, curate of G^t Worldham who is living in Alton, & his friend Mr Wilkes.—I do not know that Mr T. is anything, except very dark-complexioned, but Mr W. was a useful addition, being an easy, talking, pleasantish young Man;—a *very* young Man, hardly 20 perhaps. He is of St Johns, Cambridge, & spoke very highly of H. Walter as a Schollar;—he said he was considered as the best Classick in the University.—How such a report would have interested my Father!—I could see nothing very promising between Mr P. & Miss P. T.[9]—She placed herself on one side of him at first, but Miss Benn obliged her to move up higher;—& she had an empty plate, & even asked him to give her some Mutton without being attended to for some time.—There might be Design in this, to be sure, on his side;—he might think an empty Stomach the most favourable for Love.—Upon Mrs Digweed's mentioning that she had sent the Rejected Addresses to Mr Hinton, I began talking to her a little about them & expressed my hope of their having amused her. Her answer was, "Oh! dear, [*p. 3*] yes, very much;—very droll indeed;—the opening of the House!—& the striking up of the Fiddles!"—What she meant,[10] poor Woman, who shall say?—I sought no farther.—The Papillons have now got the Book & like it very much; their neice Eleanor has recommended it most warmly to them.—*She* looks like a rejected Addresser. As soon as a Whist party was formed & a round Table threatened, I made my Mother an excuse, & came away; leaving just as many for *their* round Table,[11] as there were at Mrs Grants.—I wish they might be as agreable a set.— It was past 10 when I got home, so I was not ashamed of my dutiful Delicacy.—The Coulthards were talked of you may be sure; no end of *them*; Miss Terry had heard they were going to rent Mr Bramston's house at Oakley, & Mrs Clement that they were going to live at Streatham.—Mrs Digweed & I agreed that the House at Oakley could not possibly be large enough for them, & now we find they have really taken it.—Mr Gauntlett is thought very agreable, & there are *no* Children at all.—The Miss Sibleys want to establish a Book Society in their side of the Country, like ours. What can be a stronger proof of that superiority in ours over the Steventon & Manydown Society, which I have always foreseen & felt?—No emulation of the kind was ever inspired by *their* proceedings; no such wish of the Miss Sibleys was ever heard, in the course of the many years of that Society's existence;— And what are their Biglands & their Barrows, their Macartneys & Mackenzies,[12] to Capt. Pasley's Essay on the Military Police of the British Empire, & the rejected Addresses? I have walked once to Alton, & yesterday Miss Papillon & I walked together to call on the Garnets. She invited herself very pleasantly to be my companion, when I went to propose to her the indulgence of accomodating us about the Letters from the Mountains. *I* had a very agreable walk; if *she* had not, more shame for her, for I was quite as entertaining as she was. Dame G. is pretty well, & we found her surrounded by her well-behaved, healthy, large-eyed Children.[13]—I took her an old Shift & promised her a set of our Linen; & my Companion left some of her Bank Stock[14] with her. [*p. 4*] Tuesday has done its duty, & I have had the pleasure of reading a very comfortable Letter. It contains so much, that I feel obliged to write down the whole of this page & perhaps something in a Cover.[15]— When my parcel is finished I shall walk with it to Alton. I beleive Miss Benn will go with me. She spent yesterday evening with us.—As I know Mary is interested in her not being neglected by her neighbours, pray tell her that Miss B. dined last wednesday at M[r] Papillons—on Thursday with Capt. & M[rs] Clement—friday here—saturday with M[rs] Digweed—& Sunday with the Papillons again.—I had fancied that Martha w[d] be at Barton from last Saturday, but am best pleased to be mistaken. I hope she is now quite well.—Tell her that I hunt away the rogues[16] every night from under her bed; they feel the difference of her being gone.—Miss Benn wore her new shawl last night, sat in it the whole even[g] & seemed to enjoy it very much.—"A very sloppy lane" last friday!—What an odd sort of country you must be in! I cannot at all understand it! It was just greasy here on friday, in consequence of the little snow that had fallen in the night.—Perhaps it *was* cold on Wednesday, yes, I beleive it certainly was—but nothing terrible.—Upon the whole, the Weather for Winter-weather is delightful, the walking excellent.—I cannot imagine what sort of a place Steventon can be!— My Mother sends her Love to Mary, with Thanks for her kind intentions & enquiries as to the Pork, & will prefer receiving her Share from the two *last* Pigs.—She has great pleasure in sending her a pair of Garters, & is very glad that she had them ready knit.—Her Letter to Anna is to be forwarded, if any opportunity offers; otherwise it may wait for her return.—M[rs] Leigh's[17] Letter came this morn[g]—We are glad to hear anything so tolerable of Scarlets.—Poor Charles & his frigate. But there could be no chance of his having one, while it was thought such a certainty.—I can hardly beleive Brother Michael's news;[18] We have no such idea in Chawton at least.—M[rs] Bramstone is the sort of Woman I detest.—M[r] Cottrell is worth ten of her. It is better to be given the Lie direct, than to excite no interest. . . . [*end of p. 4, last leaf of letter missing.*]

[Miss Austen
Steventon]

79. *To Cassandra Austen*

Chawton Friday Jany 29.

I hope you received my little parcel by J. Bond on Wednesday even^g, my dear Cassandra, & that you will be ready to hear from me again on Sunday, for I feel that I must write to you to day. Your parcel is safely arrived & everything shall be delivered as it ought. Thank you for your note. As you had not heard from me at that time it was very good in you to write, but I shall not be so much your debtor soon.—I want to tell you that I have got my own darling Child¹ from London;—on Wednesday I received one Copy, sent down by Falknor, with three lines from Henry to say that he had given another to Charles & sent a 3^d by the Coach to Godmersham; just the two Sets which I was least eager for the disposal of. I wrote to him immediately to beg for my two other Sets, unless he would take the trouble of forwarding them at once to Steventon & Portsmouth—not having an idea of his leaving Town before to day;—by your account however he was gone before my Letter was written. The only evil is the delay, nothing more can be done till his return. Tell James & Mary so, with my Love.—For *your* sake I am as well pleased that it sh^d be so, as it might be unpleasant to you to be in the Neighbourhood at the first burst of the business.—The Advertisement is in our paper to day² for the first time;—*18ˢ*—He shall ask £1-1- for my two next, & £1-8- for my stupidest of all.³—I shall write to Frank, that he may not think himself neglected. Miss Benn dined with us on the very day of the Books coming, & in the even^g we set fairly at it & read half the 1st vol. to her—prefacing that having intelligence from Henry that such a work w^d soon appear we had desired him to send it whenever it came out—& I beleive it passed with her unsuspected.—She was [*p. 2*] amused, poor soul! *that* she c^d not help you know, with two such people⁴ to lead the way; but she really does seem to admire Elizabeth. I must confess that *I* think her as delightful a creature as ever appeared in print, & how I shall be able to tolerate those who do not like *her* at least, I do not know.—There are a few

Typical errors—& a "said he" or a "said she" would sometimes make the Dialogue more immediately clear—but "I do not write⁵ for such dull Elves"

"As have not a great deal of Ingenuity themselves."—The 2ᵈ vol.⁶ is shorter than I cᵈ wish—but the difference is not so much in reality as in look, there being a larger proportion of Narrative in that part. I have lopt & cropt so successfully however that I imagine it must be rather shorter than S. & S. altogether.—Now I will try to write of something else;—it shall be a complete change of subject—Ordination.⁷ I am glad to find your enquiries have ended so well.—If you cᵈ discover whether Northamptonshire is a Country of Hedgerows,⁸ I shᵈ be glad again.— We admire your Charades⁹ excessively, but as yet have guessed only the 1ˢᵗ. The others seem very difficult. There is so much beauty in the Versification however, that the finding them out is but a secondary pleasure.—I grant you that *this is* a cold day, & am sorry to think how cold you will be through the process of your visit at Manydown. I hope you will wear your China Crape. Poor wretch! I can see you shivering away, with your miserable feeling feet.—What a vile Character Mʳ Digweed turns out, quite beyond anything & everything;¹⁰—instead of going to Steventon they are to have a Dinnerparty next tuesday!—I am sorry to say that I could not eat a Mincepie at Mʳ Papillon's; I was rather head-achey that day, & cᵈ not venture on anything sweet except Jelly; but *that* was excellent.—There were no stewed pears, but Miss Benn had some almonds & raisins.—By the bye, she desired to be kindly remembered to you when I wrote last, & I forgot it.—Betsy¹¹ sends her Duty to you & hopes you are well, & her Love to Miss Caroline & hopes she has got rid of her Cough. It was such a pleasure to her to think her Oranges were so well timed, that I dare say she was rather glad to hear of the Cough. . . . *[end of p. 2; second leaf of letter missing; postscript upside down at top of p. 1]*

Since I wrote this Letter we have been visited by Mʳˢ Digweed, her Sister & Miss Benn. I gave Mʳˢ D. her little parcel, which she opened here & seemed much pleased with—& she desired me¹² to make her best Thanks &c. to Miss Lloyd for it.— Martha may guess how full of wonder & gratitude she was.

[Miss Austen
Steventon]

80. *To Cassandra Austen*

Thursday 4 February 1813

Chawton Thursday Feb: 4.

My dear Cassandra

Your letter was truely welcome & I am much obliged to you all for your praise; it came at a right time, for I had had some fits of disgust;[1]—our 2^d evening's reading to Miss Benn had not pleased me so well, but I beleive something must be attributed to my Mother's too rapid way of getting on—& tho' she perfectly understands the Characters herself, she cannot speak as they ought.—Upon the whole however I am quite vain enough & well satisfied enough.—The work is rather too light & bright & sparkling;—it wants shade;—it wants to be stretched out here & there with a long Chapter—of sense if it could be had, if not of solemn specious nonsense—about something unconnected with the story; an Essay on Writing, a critique on Walter Scott, or the history of Buonaparte—or anything that would form a contrast & bring the reader with increased delight to the playfulness & Epigrammatism of the general stile.—I doubt your quite agreeing with me here—I know your starched Notions.—The caution observed at Steventon with regard to the possession of the Book is an agreable surprise to me, & I heartily wish it may be the means of saving you from everything unpleasant;—but you must be prepared for the Neighbourhood being perhaps already informed of there being such a Work in the World, & in the Chawton World! Dummer will do *that* you know.—It was spoken of here one morn^g when Mrs D.[2] called with Miss Benn.—The greatest blunder in the Printing that I have met with is in Page 220—Vol. 3. where two speeches are made into one.—There might as well have been no suppers at Longbourn, but I suppose it was the remains of Mrs Bennet's old Meryton habits.—I am sorry for your disappointment about Manydown, & fear this week must be a heavy one. As far as one may venture to judge at a distance of 20 miles [*p. 2*] you must miss Martha. For *her* sake I was glad to hear of her going, as I suppose she must have been growing anxious, & wanting to be again in scenes of agitation & exertion.—She had a lovely day for her journey. I walked to Alton, & dirt excepted, found it delightful,—it seemed like an old Feby come back again.—Before I set out we were visited by Mrs Edwards, & while I was gone Miss Beckford & Maria, & Miss Woolls & Harriet B. called, all of whom my Mother was glad to see & I very glad to escape.—John M.[3] is sailed, & now Miss B. thinks his Father will really try for a house, & has hopes herself of avoiding Southampton;—this is, as it was repeated to me;—And I can tell the Miss Williamses that Miss Beckford has no intention of inviting them to Chawton.—Well done You—I thought of you at Manydown in the Draw[g] room & in your China Crape;—therefore, you were in the Breakfast parlour in your Brown Bombasin; if I thought of you *so*, you would have been in the Kitchen in your Morning stuff.—I feel that I have never mentioned the Harwoods[4] in my Letters to you, which is shocking enough—but we are sincerely glad to hear all the good of them you send us. There is no chance I suppose, no *danger* of poor M[rs] H.s being persuaded to come to Chawton at present.—I hope John H. will not have more debts brought in, than he likes.—I am pleased with M. T.'s[5] being to dine at Steventon;—it may enable you to be yet more decided with Fanny & help to settle her faith.—Thomas was married on Saturday, the Wedding[6] was kept at Neatham, & that is all I know about it.—Browning is quite a new Broom & at present has no fault. He had lost some of his knowledge of waiting, & is I think rather slow; but he is not noisy & not at all above being taught.—The Back gate is regularly locked.—I did not forget Henry's fee to Thomas.—I had a letter from Henry yesterday, written on Sunday from Oxford; mine had been forwarded to him; Edward's information[7] therefore was correct.[8]—He says that copies were sent to S. & P.[9] at the same time with the others.—He has some thoughts of going to Adlestrop.— ... [*end of p. 2, remainder of letter missing.*]

[Miss Austen
Steventon]

81. *To Cassandra Austen*

Tuesday 9 February 1813

Chawton Tuesday Feb: 9.

This will be a quick return for yours, my dear Cassandra; I doubt its' having much else to recommend it, but there is no saying, it may turn out to be a very long, delightful Letter. What a day was Yesterday! How many impatient, grumbling spirits must have been confined!—We felt for you—I could think of nothing to amuse you but packing up your cloathes. My Mother was quite in distress about Edward & Anna, & will not be quite comfortable till she knows how their Journeys were

settled.—In a few hours You will be transported to Manydown—&
then for Candour & Comfort & Coffee & Cribbage.—Perhaps it will
be your last visit there.[1]—While I think of it, give my Love to Alethea
(Alethea first, mind, she is Mistress) & M[rs] Heathcote—& kind remembrance to Miss Charlotte Williams. Only think of your having at last
the honour of seeing that wonder of wonders her elder Sister!—We are
very sorry for what you tell us of Deane. If M[rs] Heathcote[2] does not
marry & comfort him now, I shall think she is a Maria & has no heart.—
Really, either she or Alethea *must* marry him, or where he is [*sic*] to
look for Happiness?—I am exceedingly pleased that you can say what
you do, after having gone thro' the whole work—& Fanny's praise is
very gratifying;—my hopes were tolerably strong of *her*, but nothing
like a certainty. Her liking Darcy & Eliz[th] is enough. She might hate all
the others, if she would. [*p. 2*] I have her opinion under her own hand
this morning, but your Transcript of it which I read first, was not & is
not the less acceptable.—To *me*, it is of course all praise—but the more
exact truth which she sends *you* is good enough.—We are to see the
Boys[3] for a few hours this day se'night—& I am to order a Chaise for
them—which I propose 5 o'clock for, & having a 3 o'clock dinner.—
I am sorry to find that Sackree was worse again when Fanny wrote; she
had been seized the night before with a violent shivering & Fever, &
was still so ill as to alarm Fanny, who was writing from her room.—
Miss Clewes seems the very Governess they have been looking for
these ten years;—longer coming than J. Bond's last Shock of Corn.—
If she will but only keep Good & Amiable & Perfect!—Clewes & [*sic*]
is better than Clowes.—And is not it a name for Edward to pun on?—
is not a Clew a Nail?—Yes, I beleive I *shall* tell Anna[4]—& if you see
her, & donot dislike the commission, you may tell her for me. You
know that I meant to do it as handsomely as I could. But she will
probably not return in time.—Browning goes on extremely well; as far
as he has been able to do anything out of doors, my Mother is exceedingly pleased.—The Dogs seem just as happy with him as with
Thomas;—Cook & Betsey I imagine a great deal happier.—Poor Cook
is likely to be tried by a wet Season now; but she has[5] not begun lament-
ing much yet.—Old Philmore I beleive is well again. [*p. 3*] My Cold
has been an Off & on Cold almost ever since you went away, but never
very bad; I increase it by walking out & cure it by staying within. On
Saturday I went to Alton, & the high wind made it worse—but by
keeping house ever since, it is almost gone.—I have had Letters from
my Aunt & from Charles within these few days.—My Uncle is quite

confined to his Chair, by a broken Chilblain on one foot & a violent swelling in the other, which my Aunt does not know what to call;—there does not seem pain enough for Gout.—But you had all this history at Steventon perhaps.—She talks of being another fortnight at Scarlets; she is really anxious I can beleive to get to Bath, as they have an apprehension of their House in Pulteney S^{t6} having been broken into.—Charles, his wife, & Eldest & Youngest reached the Namur in health & safety last Sunday se'night; Middle is left in Keppel S^t—Lady W.[7] has taken to her old tricks of ill health again & is sent for a couple of Months among her friends. Perhaps she may make *them* sick.—I have been applied to for information as to the Oath taken in former times of Bell Book & Candle—but have none to give. Perhaps you may be able to learn something of its Origin & Meaning at Manydown.—Ladies who read those enormous great stupid thick Quarto Volumes, which one always sees in the Breakfast parlour there, must be acquainted with everything in the World.—I detest a Quarto.—Capt. Pasley's Book is too good for their Society. They will not understand a Man who condenses his Thoughts into an Octavo. [*p. 4*] I do not mean however to put Mrs H. out of conceit with her Society; if she is satisfied—well;—if she thinks others satisfied—still better;—I say nothing of the complaints which reach me from all quarters.—Kill poor Mrs Sclater if you like it, while you are at Manydown.—Miss Benn dined here on friday, I have not seen her since;—there is still work for one evening more.[8]—I know nothing of the Prowtings. The Clements are at home & are reduced to read. They have got Miss Edgeworth.[9]—I have disposed of Mrs Grant for the 2^d fortnight to Mrs Digweed;—it can make no difference to *her*, which of the 26 fortnights in the Year, the 3 vol^s lay in her House.—It is raining furiously—& tho' only a storm, I shall probably send my Letter to Alton instead of going myself.—I had no thought of your writing by Mr Gray; On Sunday or Tuesday I suppose I shall hear.—

Cook does not think the Mead in a State to be stopped down.

[*Continued upside down at top of p. 1*]

I do not know what Alethea's notions of Letter writing & Note writing may be, but *I* consider her as still in my Debt—[*continued below address panel*]

If Mrs Freeman is anywhere above ground give my best Comp^{ts} to her.

Y^{rs} very affec^{ly}

J. Austen

Tuesday 16 February 1813

Miss Austen
Manydown
By favour of
    Mr Gray.

82. *To Martha Lloyd*

Tuesday 16 February 1813

Chawton Tuesday Feb: 16.

My dear Martha

Your long Letter was valued as it ought, & as I think it fully entitled to a second from me, I am going to answer it now in an handsome manner before Cassandra's return; after which event, as I shall have the benefit of all your Letters to her, I claim nothing more.—I have great pleasure in what you communicate of Anna, & sincerely rejoice in Miss Murden's amendment; & only wish there were more stability in the Character of their two constitutions.—I will not say anything of the weather we have lately had, for if you were not aware of its' being terrible, it would be cruel to put it in your head. My Mother slept through a good deal of Sunday, but still it was impossible not to be disordered by such a sky, & even yesterday she was but poorly. She is pretty well again today, & I am in hopes may not be much longer a Prisoner.—We are going to be all alive from this forenoon to tomorrow afternoon;—it will be over when you receive this, & you may think of me as one not sorry that it is so.—George, Henry & William will soon be here & are to stay the night—and tomorrow the 2 Deedes' & Henry Bridges will be added to our party;—we shall then [*p. 2*] have an early dinner & dispatch them all to Winchester. We have no late account from Sloane S^t & therefore conclude that everything is going on in one regular progress, without any striking change.—Henry was to be in Town again last Tuesday.—I have a Letter from Frank; they are all at Deal again, established once more in fresh Lodgings. I think they must soon have lodged in every house in the Town.—We read of the Pyramus being returned into Port, with interest—& fear Mrs D. D.² will be regretting that she came away so soon.—There is no being up to the tricks of the Sea.—Your friend has her little Boys about her³ I imagine. I hope their Sister enjoyed the Ball at Lady Keith—tho' I do not know that I do much hope it, for it might be quite as well to have her shy & uncomfortable in such a croud of Strangers.—

207

I am obliged to you for your enquiries about Northamptonshire,[4] but do not wish you[5] to renew them, as I am sure of getting the intelligence I want from Henry, to whom I can apply at some convenient moment "sans peur et sans reproche".—I suppose all the World is sitting in Judgement upon the Princess of Wales's Letter.[6] Poor Woman, I shall support her as long as I can, because she *is* a Woman, & because I hate her Husband—but I can hardly [*p. 3*] forgive her for calling herself "attached & affectionate" to a Man whom she must detest—& the intimacy said to subsist between her & Lady Oxford is bad.—I do not know what to do about it;—but if I must give up the Princess, I am resolved at least always to think that she would have been respectable, if the Prince had behaved only tolerably by her at first.—

Old Philmore is got pretty well, well enough to warn Miss Benn out of her House. His son is to come into it.—Poor Creature!—You may imagine how full of cares she must be, & how anxious all Chawton will feel to get her decently settled somewhere.—She will have 3 months before her—& if anything else can be met with, she will be glad enough to be driven from her present wretched abode;—it has been terrible for her during the late storms of wind & rain.—Cassandra has been rather out of luck at Manydown—but that is a House, in which one is tolerably independent of weather.—The Prowtings perhaps come down on Thursday or Saturday, but the accounts of *him* do not improve.—Now I think I may in *Quantity* have deserved your Letter. My ideas of Justice in Epistolary Matters are you know very strict.—With Love from my Mother, I remain Y^{rs} very affec^{ly}

J. Austen

[*p. 4*] Poor John Harwood!—One is really obliged to engage in Pity again on his account—& where there is a lack of money, one is on pretty sure grounds.—So after all, Charles, that thick-headed Charles is the best off of the Family. I rather grudge him his 2,500£.—My Mother is very decided in *selling* Deane—And if it is *not* sold, I think it will be clear that the Proprietor can have no plan of marrying.

Miss Lloyd

83. To ?Francis Austen

Wednesday 17 February 1813

[*Text of letter not preserved*]   . . . . . .

Yours very affec:^{ly}
J. Austen

Chawton Wednesday
    Feb. 17.

―――――

84. To Cassandra Austen

Thursday 20 May 1813

Sloane S^t—Thursday May 20.

My dear Cassandra

Before I say anything else, I claim a paper full of Halfpence on the Drawingroom Mantlepeice; I put them there myself & forgot to bring them with me.—I cannot say that I have yet been in any distress for Money, but I chuse to have my due as well as the Devil.—How lucky we were in our weather yesterday!—This wet morning makes one more sensible of it. We had no rain of any consequence; the head of the Curricle was put half-up three or four times, but our share of the Showers was very trifling, though they seemed to be heavy all round us, when we were on the Hog's-back;¹ & I fancied it might then be raining so hard at Chawton as to make you feel for us much more than we deserved.—Three hours & a q^r took us to Guildford, where we staid barely two hours, & had only just time enough for all we had to do there, that is, eating a long comfortable Breakfast, watching the Carriages, paying Mr Herington & taking a little stroll afterwards. From some veiws which that stroll gave us, I think most highly of the situation of Guildford. We wanted all our Brothers & Sisters to be standing with us in the Bowling Green & looking towards Horsham.—I told Mr Herington of the Currants; he seemed equally surprised & shocked, & means to talk to the Man who put them up. I wish you may find the Currants any better for it.—[*p. 2*] He does not expect Sugars to fall.— I was very lucky in my gloves, got them at the first shop I went to, though I went into it rather because it was near than because it looked at all like a glove shop, & gave only four Shillings for them;—upon

209

hearing which, every body at Chawton will be hoping & predicting that they cannot be good for anything, & their worth certainly remains to be proved, but I think they look very well.—We left Guildford at 20 minutes before 12—(I hope somebody cares for these minutiae) & were at Esher in about 2 hours more.—I was very much pleased with the Country in general—;—between Guildford & Ripley I thought it particularly pretty, also about Painshill & every where else; & from a Mr Spicer's Grounds at Esher which we walked into before our dinner, the veiws were beautiful. I cannot say what we did *not* see, but I should think there could not be a Wood or a Meadow or a Palace or a remarkable spot in England that was not spread out before us, on one side or the other.—Claremont is going to be sold, a Mr Ellis has it now;—it is a House that seems never to have prospered.—At 3, we were dining upon veal cutlets & cold ham, all very good—; & after dinner we walked forward, to be overtaken at the Coachman's time, & before he *did* overtake us we were very near Kingston.—I fancy it was about ½ past 6 when we reached this house, a 12 hours Business, & the Horses did not appear more than reasonably tired. I was very tired too, & very glad to get to bed early, but am quite well to-day. [*p. 3*] Upon the whole it was an excellent Journey & very thoroughly enjoyed by me;—the weather was delightful the greatest part of the day, Henry found it too warm & talked of its' being close sometimes, but to my capacity it was perfection.—I never saw the Country from the Hogsback so advantageously.—We ate 3 of the Buns in the course of that stage, the remaining 3 made an elegant entertainment for M^r & Mrs Tilson who drank tea with us.—Now, little Cass & her attendant are travelling down to Chawton;—I wish the day were brighter for them. If Cassy should have intended to take any sketches while the others dine, she will hardly be able.—How will you distinguish the two Betsies?²—Mrs Perigord arrived a ½ past 3—& is pretty well, & her Mother, for *her*, seems quite well. She sat with me while I breakfasted this morn^g—talking of Henrietta Street, servants & Linen, & is too busy in preparing for the future, to be out of spirits.—If I can, I shall call by & bye on Mrs Hoblyn & Charlotte Craven; Mrs Tilson is going out, which prevents my calling on *her*, but I beleive we are to drink tea with her.—Henry talks of our going to the Water-coloured Exhibition³ tomorrow, & of my calling for him in Henrietta S^t—; if I do, I shall take the opportunity of getting my Mother's gown—; so, by 3 o'clock in the afternoon she may consider herself the owner of 7 y^ds of B^k Sarsenet as completely as I hope Martha finds herself of a 16th of the £20,000.⁴—

I am very snug with the front Drawingroom all to myself & would not say "Thank you" for any companion but You. The quietness of it does me good.—Henry & I are disposed to wonder that the Guildford road should not be oftener preferred to the Bagshot, [*p. 4*] it is not longer, has much more beauty & not more hills.—If I were Charles, I should chuse it; & having him in our thoughts we made enquiries at Esher as to their posting distances.—From Guildford to Esher 14 miles, from Esher to Hyde Park corner 15—which makes it exactly the same as from Bagshot to H. P. corner, changing at Bedfont, 49 miles altogether, each way.—

I have contrived to pay my two visits, though the weather made me a great while about it, & left me only a few minutes to sit with C. C..—She looks very well & her hair is done up with an elegance to do credit to any Education. Her manners are as unaffected & pleasing as ever.—She had heard from her Mother today.—Mrs Craven spends another fortnight at Chilton.—I saw nobody but Charlotte, which pleased me best.—I was shewn up stairs into a Draw^g room, where she came to me, & the appearance of the room, so totally un-school-like, amused me very much. It was full of all [*continued below address panel*] the modern Elegancies—& if it had not been for some naked Cupids over the Mantlepeice, which must be a fine study for Girls, one should never have Smelt Instruction.

Mrs Perigord desires her Duty to all the Ladies.—Y^rs very affec^ly J. A.—

Miss Austen
Chawton
Alton
Hants

85. *To Cassandra Austen*

Monday 24 May 1813

Sloane St Monday May 24.

My dearest Cassandra

I am very much obliged to you for writing to me. You must have hated it after a worrying morning.—Your Letter came just in time to save my going to Remnants, & fit me for Christian's, where I bought Fanny's dimity. I went the day before (Friday) to Laytons[1] as I proposed, & got my Mother's gown, 7 y^ds at 6/6. I then walked into

No. 10,[2] which is all dirt & confusion, but in a very promising way, & after being present at the opening of a new account to my great amusement, Henry & I went to the Exhibition in Spring Gardens.[3] It is not thought a good collection, but I was very well pleased—particularly (pray tell Fanny) with a small portrait of Mrs Bingley,[4] excessively like her. I went in hopes of seeing one of her Sister, but there was no Mrs Darcy;—perhaps however, I may find her in the Great Exhibition[5] which we shall go to, if we have time;—I have no chance of her in the collection of Sir Joshua Reynolds's[6] Paintings which is now shewing in Pall Mall, & which we are also to visit.—Mrs Bingley's is exactly herself, size, shaped face, features & sweetness; there never was a greater likeness. She is dressed in a white gown, with green ornaments, which convinces me of what I had always supposed, that green was a favourite colour with her. I dare say Mrs D. will be in Yellow.—Friday was our worst day as to weather, we were out in a very long & very heavy storm of hail, & there had been others before, but I heard no Thunder.—Saturday was a good deal better, dry & cold.—I gave 2/6 for the Dimity; I do not boast of any Bargains, but think both the Sarsenet & Dimity good of their sort.—

[*p. 2*] I have bought your Locket, but was obliged to give 18^s for it—which must be rather more than you intended; it is neat & plain, set in gold. [*Four or five words cut out*]—We were to have gone to the Somerset house Exhibition on Saturday, but when I reached Henrietta Street Mr Hampson was wanted there, & Mr Tilson & I were obliged to drive about Town after him, & by the time we had done, it was too late for anything but Home.—We never found him after all.—I have been interrupted by Mrs Tilson.—Poor Woman! She is in danger of not being able to attend Lady Drummond Smiths Party tonight. Miss Burdett was to have taken her, & now Miss Burdett has a cough & will not go.— My cousin Caro*line*[7] is her sole dependance.—The events of Yesterday were, our going to Belgrave Chapel in the morn^g, our being prevented by the rain from going to even^g Service at St James, Mr Hampson's calling, Messrs Barlow & Phillips dining here; & M^r & Mrs Tilson's coming in the even^g a l'ordinaire.—*She* drank tea with us both Thursday & Saturday, *he* dined out each day, & on friday we were with them; & they wish us to go to them tomorrow even^g to meet Miss Burdett; but I do not know how it will end. Henry talks of a drive to Hampstead,[8] which may interfere with it.—I should like to see Miss Burdett very well, but that I am rather frightened by hearing that she wishes to be introduced to *me*. If I *am* a wild Beast,[9] I cannot help it. It is not my own fault.—There is no change in our plan of leaving London, but we shall not be with you before Tuesday. Henry thinks Monday would appear too early a day. There is no danger of our being induced to stay longer.

[*p. 3*] I have not quite determined how I shall manage about my Cloathes, perhaps there may be only my Trunk to send by the Coach, or there may be a Bandbox with it.—I have taken your gentle hint & written to Mrs Hill.—The Hoblyns want us to dine with them, but we have refused. When Henry returns he will be dining out a great deal I dare say; as he will then be alone, it will be more desirable;—he will be more welcome at every Table, & every Invitation more welcome to him. He will not want either of us again till he is settled in Henrietta S^t. This is my present persuasion.—And he will not be settled there, really settled, till late in the Autumn—"he will not be come to bide",[10] till after September.—There is a Gentleman in treaty for this house. Gentleman himself is in the Country, but Gentleman's friend came to see it the other day & seemed pleased on the whole.—Gentleman would rather prefer an increased rent to parting with five hundred G^s at once; & if that is the only difficulty, it will not be minded: Henry is indifferent as to the which.—Get us the best weather you can for wednesday, Thursday & Friday. We are to go[11] to Windsor in our way to Henley, which will be a great delight. We shall be leaving Sloane S^t about 12—, two or three hours after Charles's party have begun their Journey.—You will miss them, but the comfort of getting back into your own room will be great!—& then, the Tea & Sugar!—

I fear Miss Clewes is not better, or you w^d have mentioned it.—I shall not write again unless I have any unexpected communication or opportunity to tempt me.—I enclose Mr Heringtons Bill & receipt.

[*p. 4*] I am very much obliged to Fanny for her Letter;—it made me laugh heartily; but I cannot pretend to answer it. Even had I more time, I should not feel at all sure[12] of the sort of Letter that Miss D. would write.[13] I hope Miss Benn is got quite well again & will have a comfortable Dinner with you today.—*Monday even^g*—We have been both to the Exhibition & Sir J. Reynolds',—and I am disappointed, for there was nothing like Mrs D. at either.—I can only imagine that Mr D. prizes any Picture of her too much to like it should be exposed to the public eye.—I can imagine he w^d have that sort [*of omitted*] feeling—that mixture of Love, Pride & Delicacy.—Setting aside this disappointment, I had great amusement among the Pictures; & the Driving about, the Carriage been open, [*sic*] was very pleasant.—I liked my solitary elegance very much, & was ready to laugh all the time, at my being where

I was.—I could not but feel that I had naturally small right to be parading about London in a Barouche.—Henry desires Edward may know that he has just bought 3 dozen of Claret for him (Cheap) & ordered it to be sent down to Chawton.—I should not wonder if we got no farther than Reading on Thursday even^g—& so, reach Steventon only to a reasonable Dinner hour the next day;—but whatever I may write or you may imagine, we [*continued below address panel*] know it will be something different.—I shall be quiet tomorrow morn^g; all my business is done, & I shall only call again upon Mrs Hoblyn &c.—Love to your much [?redu]ced Party.—Y^rs affec^ly,

J. Austen

Miss Austen
Chawton
By favour of
Messrs Gray & Vincent

---

86. *To Francis Austen*

Saturday 3–Tuesday 6 July 1813

Chawton July 3^d 1813

My dearest Frank

Behold me going to write you as handsome a Letter as I can. Wish me good luck.—We have had the pleasure of hearing of you lately through Mary, who sent us some of the particulars of Yours of June 18th (I think) written off Rugen, & we enter into the delight of your having so good a Pilot.—Why are you like Queen Eliz^th?—Because you know how to chuse wise Ministers.—Does not this prove You as great a Captain as she was a Queen?—This may serve as a riddle for you to put forth among your Officers, by way of increasing your proper consequence.— It must be real enjoyment to you, since you are obliged to leave England, to be where you are, seeing something of a new Country, & one that has been so distinguished as Sweden.—You must have great pleasure in it.—I hope you may have gone to Carlscroon.—Your Profession has its' douceurs to recompense for some of its' Privations;—to an enquiring & observing Mind like yours, such douceurs must be considerable.—Gustavus-Vasa, & Charles 12th, & Christiana, & Linneus'— do their Ghosts rise up before You?—I have a great respect for former

Sweden. So zealous as it was for Protestanism! [*sic*]—And I have always fancied it more like England than many Countries;—& according to the Map, many of the names have a strong resemblance[2] to the English. July begins unpleasantly with us, cold & showery, but it is often a baddish month. We had some fine dry weather preceding it, which was very acceptable to the Holders of Hay & the Masters of Meadows—In general it must have been a good Haymaking Season. Edward has got in all his, in excellent order; I speak only of Chawton; [*p. 2*] but here he has had better luck[3] than Mr Middleton ever had in the 5 years that he was Tenant. Good encouragement for him to come again; & I really hope he will do so another Year.—The pleasure to us of having them here is so great, that if we were not the best Creatures in the World we should not deserve it.—We go on in the most comfortable way, very frequently dining together, & always meeting in some part of every day.—Edward is very well & enjoys himself as thoroughly as any Hampshire born Austen can desire. Chawton is not thrown away upon him.—He talks of making a new Garden;[4] the present is a bad one & ill situated, near Mr Papillon's;—he means to have the new,[5] at the top of the Lawn behind his own house.—We like to have him proving & strengthening his attachment to the place by making it better.—He will soon have all his Children about him, Edward, George & Charles are collected already, & another week brings Henry & William.—It is the custom at Winchester for Georges to come away a fortnight before the Holidays, when they are not to return any more; for fear they should overstudy themselves just at last, I suppose.—Really it is a peice of dishonourable accomodation[6] to the Master.—We are in hopes of another visit from our own true, lawful Henry very soon, he is to be *our* Guest this time.—He is quite well I am happy to say, & does not leave it to *my* pen I am sure to communicate to you the joyful news of his being Deputy Receiver[7] no longer.—It is a promotion which he thoroughly enjoys;—as well he may;—the work of his own mind.—He sends you all his own plans of course.—The scheme for Scotland we think an excellent one both for himself & his nephew.[8]—Upon the whole his Spirits are very much recovered.—If I may so express myself, his Mind is not a Mind for affliction. He is too Busy, too active, too sanguine.—Sincerely as he was attached to poor Eliza moreover, & excellently as he behaved to her, he was always so used to be away from her at times, that her Loss is not felt as that of many a beloved Wife might be, especially when all the circumstances of her long [*p. 3*] & dreadful Illness are taken into the account.—He very long knew that she must die, & it was indeed a release at last.—Our mourning for her is not over, or we should now be putting it on again for Mr Thos Leigh— the respectable, worthy, clever, agreable Mr Tho. Leigh, who has just closed a good life at the age of 79, & must have died the possessor of one of the finest Estates in England & of more worthless Nephews & Neices[9] than any other private Man in the united Kingdoms.—We are very anxious to know who will have the Living of Adlestrop, & where his excellent Sister will find a home for the remainder of her days. As yet she bears his Loss with fortitude, but she has always seemed so wrapt up in him, that I fear she must feel it very dreadfully when the fever of Business is over.—There is another female sufferer on the occasion to be pitied. Poor Mrs L. P.[10]—who would now have been Mistress of Stonleigh [*sic*] had there been none of that vile compromise,[11] which in good truth has never been allowed to be of much use to them.—It will be a hard trial.—Charles's little girls were with us about a month, & had so endeared themselves that we were quite sorry to have them go. We have the pleasure however of hearing that they are thought very much improved at home—Harriet in health, Cassy in manners.—The latter *ought* to be a very nice Child—Nature has done enough for her—but Method has been wanting;—we thought her very much improved ourselves, but to have Papa & Mama think her so too, was very essential to our contentment.—She will really be a very pleasing Child, if they will only exert themselves a little.—Harriet is a truely sweet-tempered little Darling.—They are now all at Southend together.—Why do I mention *that*?—As if Charles did not write himself.—I hate to be spending my time so needlessly, encroaching too upon the rights of others.—I wonder whether you happened to see Mr Blackall's marriage[12] in the Papers last Jan^{ry}. *We* did. He was married at Clifton to a Miss Lewis, whose Father had been late of Antigua. I should very much like to know what sort of a Woman she is. He was a peice of Perfection, noisy Perfection himself which I always recollect with regard.—We had noticed a few months before his succeeding to a College Living, the very Living which we remembered his talking of & wishing for; an exceeding good one, Great Cadbury in Somersetshire.—I would wish Miss Lewis to be of a silent turn & rather ignorant, but naturally intelligent & wishing to learn;—fond of cold veal pies, green tea in the afternoon, & a green window blind at night.

[*p. 4*] July 6.—

Now my dearest Frank I will finish my Letter. I have kept it open on the chance of what a Tuesday's post might furnish in addition, & it furnishes the likelihood of our keeping our neighbours at the G^t House some weeks longer than we had expected.—Mr Scudamore, to whom my Brother referred, is very decided as to G^m not being fit to be inhabited at present;—he talks even of two months more being necessary to sweeten it,[13] but if we have warm weather I dare say less will do.— My Brother will probably go down & sniff at it himself & receive his Rents.—The Rent-day has been postponed already.—*We* shall be gainers by their stay, but the young people in general are disappointed, & therefore we c^d wish it otherwise.—

Our Cousins Colonel Thos Austen & Margaretta are going Aid-de-camps to Ireland & Lord Whitworth goes in their Train as Lord Lieutenant;—good appointments for each.—God bless you.—I hope you continue beautiful & brush your hair, but not all off.[14]—We join in an infinity of Love.—Y^rs very affec^ly

Jane Austen

[Postscript upside down at top of p. 1]

You will be glad to hear that every Copy of S.&S. is sold & that it has brought me £140—besides the Copyright, if that sh^d ever be of any value.—I have now therefore written myself into £250.—which only makes me long for more.—I have something in hand—which I hope on the credit of P. & P. will sell well, tho' not half so entertaining.[15] And by the bye—shall you object to my mentioning the Elephant in it, & two or three other of your old Ships?[16]—I *have* done it, but it shall not stay, to make you angry.—They are only just mentioned.

Captn Austen
HMS Elephant
Baltic.

---

87. *To Cassandra Austen*

Wednesday 15–Thursday 16 September 1813

Henrietta St Wednesday—½ past 8—

Here I am, my dearest Cassandra, seated in the Breakfast, Dining, sitting room, beginning with all my might. Fanny will join me as soon as she is dressed & begin her Letter. We had a very good journey— Weather & roads excellent—the three first stages for 1^s-6^d- & our only misadventure the being delayed about a q^r of an hour at Kingston for Horses, & being obliged to put up with a p^r belonging to a Hackney Coach & their Coachman, which left no room on the Barouche Box for Lizzy, who was to have gone her last stage there as she did the first;— consequently we were all 4 within, which was a little crowd;—We arrived at a q^r past 4—& were kindly welcomed by the Coachman, & then by his Master, and then by W^m,[1] & then by Mrs Perigord, who all met us before we reached the foot of the Stairs. M^{de} Bigeon was below dressing us a most comfortable dinner of Soup, Fish, Bouillee, Partridges & an apple Tart, which we sat down to soon after 5, after cleaning & dressing ourselves & feeling that we were most commodiously disposed of.—The little adjoining Dressing-room to our apartment makes Fanny & myself very well off indeed, & as we have poor Eliza's bed our space is ample every way.—Sace arrived safely about ½ past 6. At 7 we set off in a Coach for the Lyceum—were at home again in about 4 hours & ½—had Soup & wine & water, & then went to our Holes. Edward finds his quarters[2] very snug & quiet.—I must get a softer pen.—This is harder. I am in agonies.—I have not yet seen Mr Crabbe.[3]—Martha's Letter is gone to the Post.—

I am going to write nothing but short Sentences. There shall be two full stops in every Line. Layton and Shear's *is* Bedford House. We mean to get there before breakfast if it's possible. For we feel more & more how much we have to do. And how little time. This house looks very nice. It seems like Sloane S^t moved here. I believe Henry is just rid of Sloane S^t—Fanny does not come, but I have Edward seated by me beginning a Letter, which looks natural.

Henry has been suffering from the pain in the face which he has been subject to before. He caught cold at Matlock, & since his return has been paying a little for past pleasure.—It is nearly removed now—but he looks thin in the face—either from the pain, or the fatigues of his Tour, which must have been great.

Lady Robert[4] is delighted with P. & P- and really *was* so as I understand before she knew who wrote it—for, of course, she knows now.— He told her with as much satisfaction as if it were my wish. He did not tell *me* this, but he told Fanny. And Mr Hastings—I am quite delighted with what such a Man writes about it.—Henry sent him the Books after his return from Daylesford—but you will hear the Letter too.

Let me be rational & return to my two full stops.

I talked to Henry at the Play last night. We were in a private Box— Mr Spencer's—Which made it much more pleasant. The Box is directly on the Stage. One is infinitely less fatigued than in the common way.— But Henry's plans are not what one could wish. He does not mean to be at Chawton till ye 29.—He must be in town again by Octr 5.—His plan is to get a couple of days of Pheasant Shooting and then return directly; his wish was to bring you back with him. I have told him your scruples.—He wishes you to suit yourself as to time. And if you cannot come till later, will send for you at any time, as far as Bagshot.—He presumed you w^d not find difficulty in getting so far. I c^d not say you would. He proposed your going with him into Oxfordshire. It was his own thought at first. I could not but catch at it for you.

We have talked of it again this morning (for now we have breakfasted), and I am convinced that if you can make it suit in other respects you need not scruple on his account. If you cannot come back with him on ye 3^d or 4th, therefore, I do hope you will contrive to go to Adlestrop. —By not beginning your absence till about the middle of this month I think you may manage it very well. But you will think all this over. One c^d wish he had intended to come to you earlier, but it cannot be helped.

I said nothing to him of Mrs H. & Miss B–[5] that he might not suppose Difficulties. Shall not you put *them* into our own Room? This seems to me the best plan—& the Maid will be most conveniently near.

Oh, dear me, when I shall ever have done? We *did* go to Layton & Shear's before Breakfast. Very pretty English poplins at 4.3—Irish D^o at 6.0—*more* pretty certainly—beautiful.—

Fanny & the two little girls are gone to take Places for tonight at Covent Garden; Clandestine Marriage & *Midas*.[6] The latter will be a fine show for L. & M.—They revelled last night in Don Juan,[7] whom we left in Hell at ½ past 11.—We had Scaramouch & a Ghost—and were delighted;—I speak of *them*; *my* delight was very tranquil, & the rest of us were sober-minded. Don Juan was the last of 3 musical things; —Five hours at Brighton,[8] in 3 acts—of which one was over before we arrived, none the worse—& The Beehive,[9] rather less flat & trumpery.

I have this moment received £5 from kind, beautiful Edward. Fanny has a similar Gift. I shall save what I can of it for your better leisure in this place. *My* Letter was from Miss Sharpe.—Nothing particular. A letter from Fanny Cage this morning.

4 o'clock.—We are just come back from doing Mrs Tickars, Miss Hare, and Mr Spence. Mr Hall is here; & while Fanny is under his hands, I will try to write a little more.

Miss Hare had some pretty caps, and is to make me one like one of them, only *white* sattin instead of blue. It will be white sattin and lace, and a little white flower perking out of the left ear, like Harriot Byron's feather.[10] I have allowed her to go as far as £1–16. My Gown is to be trimmed everywhere with white ribbon plaited on, somehow or other. She says it will look well. I am not sanguine. They trim with white very much.

I learnt from Mrs Tickars's young Lady, to my high amusement, that the stays now are not made to force the Bosom up at all;—*that* was a very unbecoming, unnatural fashion. I was really glad to hear that they are not to be so much off the shoulders as they were.

Going to Mr Spence's was a sad Business & cost us many tears, unluckily we were obliged to go a 2^d time before he could do more than just look:—we went 1st at ½ past 12 and afterwards at 3. Papa with us each time—&, alas! we are to go again to-morrow. Lizzy is not finished yet. There have been no Teeth taken out however, nor will be I believe, but he finds *hers* in a very bad state, & seems to think particularly ill of their Durableness.—They have been all cleaned, *hers* filed, and are to be filed again. There is a very sad hole between two of her front Teeth.

This not seeing much of Henry. I have just seen him however for 3 minutes, & have read him the Extract from Mrs F. A's Letter—& he says he will write to Mrs Fra. A.[11] about it, & he has no doubt of being attended to as he knows they feel themselves obliged to him.—Perhaps you may see him on Saturday next. He has just started such an idea. But it will be only for a couple of days.

Thursday morning ½ past 7.—Up & dressed and downstairs in order to finish my Letter in time for the Parcel. At 8 I have an appointment with M^{de} B.[12] who wants to show me something downstairs. At 9 we are to set off for Grafton House & get that over before breakfast. Edward is so kind as to walk there with us. We are to be at Mr Spence's again at 11 & from that time shall be driving about I suppose till 4 o'clock at least.—We are if possible to call on Mrs Tilson.

Mr Hall was very punctual yesterday & curled me out at a great rate. I thought it looked hideous, and longed for a snug cap instead, but my companions silenced me by their admiration. I had only a bit of velvet round my head. I did not catch cold however. The weather is all in my favour. I have had no pain in my face since I left you.

We had very good places in the Box next the Stage box—front and 2^d row, the three old ones behind of course.—I was particularly disappointed at seeing nothing of Mr Crabbe. I felt sure of him when I saw

that the boxes were fitted up with Crimson velvet.[13] The new M[r] Terry
was L[d] Ogleby, & Henry thinks he may do; but there was no acting
more than moderate; & I was as much amused by the remembrances
connected with Midas[14] as with any part of it. The girls were very much
delighted, but still prefer Don Juan—& I must say that I have seen
nobody on the stage who has been a more interesting Character than
that compound of Cruelty & Lust.

It was not possible for me to get the Worsteds yesterday. I heard
Edward last night pressing Henry to come to G[m] & I think Henry
engaged to go there after his November collection.[15] Nothing has been
done[16] as to S&S. The Books came to hand too late for him to have time
for it, before he went. M[r] Hastings never *hinted* at Eliza in the smallest
degree.—Henry knew nothing of M[r] Trimmer's death. I tell you these
things, that you may not have to ask them over again.

There is a new Clerk sent down to Alton,[17] a M[r] Edmund Williams,
a young Man whom Henry thinks most highly of—and he turns out to
be a son of the luckless Williamses of Grosvenor Place.

I long to have you hear M[r] H's[18] opinion of P&P. His admiring my
Elizabeth so much is particularly welcome to me.

Instead of saving my superfluous wealth for you to spend, I am going
to treat myself with spending it myself. I hope at least that I shall find
some poplin at Layton & Shears that will tempt me to buy it. If I do,
it shall be sent to Chawton, as half will be for you; for I depend upon
your being so kind as to accept it, being the main point. It will be a
great pleasure to me. Don't say a word. I only wish you could choose
too. I shall send 20 yards.

Now for Bath. Poor F. Cage[19] has suffered a good deal from her
accident. The noise of the White Hart was terrible to her.—They will
keep her quiet, I dare say. *She* is not so much delighted with the place
as the rest of the Party; probably, as she says herself, from having been
less well, but she thinks she sh[d] like it better in the season. The Streets
are very empty now, & the shops not so gay as she expected. They
are at No. 1 Henrietta Street, the corner of Laura Place; and have no
acquaintance at present but the Bramstons.

Lady B. drinks at the Cross Bath, her son at the Hot, and Louisa is
going to Bathe. D[r] Parry seems to be half starving M[r] Bridges;[20] for he
is restricted to much such a Diet as James's Bread, Water and Meat, &
is never to eat so much of that as he wishes;—& he is to walk a great
deal, walk till he drops, I believe, Gout or no Gout. It really is to that
purpose; I have not exaggerated.

Charming weather for you & us, and the Travellers, & everybody. You will take your walk this afternoon & ... [*end of letter missing*]

Miss Austen
Chawton
By favour of Mr Gray[21]

88. *To Cassandra Austen*

Thursday 16 September 1813

Henrietta Street—Thursday—after dinner

Thank you my dearest Cassandra for the nice long Letter I sent off this morning.—I hope you have had it by this time & that it has found you all well,[1] & my Mother no more in need of Leeches.[2]—Whether this will be delivered to you by Henry on Saturday even^g or by the Postman on Sunday morn^g I know not, as he has lately recollected something of an engagement for Saturday which perhaps may delay his visit.[3]—He seems determined to come to you soon however.—I hope you will receive the Gown tomorrow & may be able with tolerable honesty to say that you like the Colour;—it was bought at Grafton House, where, by going very early, we got immediate attendance & went on very comfortably.—I only forgot the one particular thing which I had always resolved to buy there—a white silk Handkf—& was therefore obliged to give six shillings for one at Crook & Besford's—which reminds me to say that the Worsteads ought also to be at Chawton tomorrow & that I shall be very happy to hear they are approved. I had not much time for deliberation. We are now all four of us young Ladies sitting round the Circular Table in the inner room writing our Letters, while the two Brothers are having a comfortable coze in the room adjoining.—It is to be a quiet evening, much to the satisfaction of 4 of the 6.—My Eyes are quite tired of Dust & Lamps.—The Letter you forwarded from Edwd Junr has been duly received. He has been shooting most prosperously at home, & dining at Chilham Castle & with Mr Scudamore. [*p. 2*] My Cap is come home & I like it very much, Fanny has one also; hers is white Sarsenet & Lace, of a different shape from mine, more fit for morning, Carriage wear—which is what it is intended for—& is in shape exceedingly like our own Sattin & Lace of last winter—shaped round the face exactly like it, with pipes & more fullness, & a round crown inserted behind. *My* Cap has a peak in front. Large, full Bows of very narrow ribbon (old twopenny) are the thing.

One over the right temple perhaps, & another at the left ear.—Henry is not quite well.—His Stomach is rather deranged. You must keep him in Rhubarb & give him plenty of Port & Water.—He caught his cold farther back than I told you—before he got to Matlock—somewhere in his Journey from the North—but the ill effects of *that* I hope are nearly gone.—We returned from Grafton House only just in time for breakfast & had scarcely finished breakfast when the Carriage came to the door. From 11 to ½ past 3 we were hard at it;—we *did* contrive to get to Hans Place for 10 minutes. Mrs T.^4 was as affectionate & pleasing as ever; & from her appearance I suspect her to be in the family way. Poor Woman!—Fanny prophecies the Child's coming within 3 or 4 days.^5 After our return, Mr Tilson walked up from the Compting House^6 & called upon us; & these have been all our Visitings.—I have rejoiced more than once that I bought my Writing paper in the Country; we have not had a q^r of an hour to spare.—I enclose the Eighteen pence due to my Mother.—The Rose colour was 6/S, & the other 4/S p^r y^d— There was but 2 y^d & a q^r of the dark slate in the Shop, but the Man promised to match it & send it off correctly.

[*p. 3*] Fanny bought her Irish^7 at Newton's in Leicester Sq^re & I took the opportunity of thinking about your Irish & seeing one peice of the Yard wide at 4/S—& it seemed to me very good—good enough for your purpose.^8—It might at least be worth your while to go there, if you have no other engagements.—Fanny is very much pleased with the Stockings^9 she has bought of Remmington—Silk at 12S.—Cotton at 4.3.—She thinks them great bargains, but I have not seen them yet— as my hair was dressing when the Man & the Stockgs came.—The poor Girls & their Teeth!—I have not mentioned them yet, but we were a whole hour at Spence's, & Lizzy's were filed & lamented over again & poor Marianne had two taken out after all, the two just beyond the Eye teeth, to make room for those in front.—When her doom was fixed, Fanny Lizzy & I walked into the next room, where we heard each of the two sharp hasty Screams.—Fanny's teeth were cleaned too—& pretty as they are, Spence found something to do to them, putting in gold & talking gravely—& making a considerable point of seeing her again before winter;—he had before urged the expediency of L. & M.s being brought to Town in the course of a couple of Months to be farther examined, & continued to the last to press for their all coming to him.— My B^r would not absolutely promise.—The little girls teeth I can suppose in a critical state, but I think he must be a Lover of Teeth & Money & Mischeif to parade about Fannys.—I would not have had him look at mine for a shilling a tooth & double it.—It was a disagreable hour. We then went[10] to Wedgwoods where my B[r] & Fanny chose a Dinner Set.—I beleive the pattern is a small Lozenge in purple, between Lines of narrow Gold;—& it is to have the Crest.

[*p. 4*] We must have been 3 q[rs] of an hour at Grafton House, Edward sitting by all the time with wonderful patience. There Fanny bought the Net for Anna's gown, & a beautiful Square veil for herself.—The Edging . there is very cheap, I was tempted by some, & I bought some very nice plaiting Lace at 3.4.—

Fanny desires me to tell Martha with her kind Love that Birchall assured her there was no 2[d] set of Hook's Lessons[11] for Beginners—& that by my advice, she has therefore chosen her a set by another Composer. I thought she w[d] rather have something than not.—It costs six shillings.—With Love to You all, including Triggs,[12] I remain

Y[rs] very affec[ly] J Austen

Miss Austen
Chawton
By favour of [*left blank*]

[*Letter(s) missing here*]

89. *To Cassandra Austen*

Thursday 23–Friday 24 September 1813

Godmersham Park—Thursday Sept: 23[d]—

My dearest Cassandra

Thank you five hundred & forty times for the exquisite peice of Workmanship which was brought into the room this morng. while we were at breakfast—with some very inferior works of art in the same way, & which I read with high glee—much delighted with everything it told whether good or bad.—It is so rich in striking intelligence that I hardly know what to reply to first. I beleive Finery must have it. I am extremely glad that you like the Poplin, I thought it would have my *Mother's* approbation, but was not so confident of *yours*. Remember that it is a present. Do not refuse me. I am very rich.—M[rs] Clement is very welcome to her little Boy[1] & to my Congratulations into the bargain, if ever you think of giving them. I hope she will do well.—Her sister in Lucina,[2] M[rs] H. Gipps does too well we think;—Mary P.[3] wrote on

Sunday that she had been three days on the Sofa. Sackree does not approve it.—How can Mrs J. Austen be so provokingly ill-judging?—I should have expected better from her professed if not her real regard for my Mother. Now my Mother will be unwell again. Every fault in Ben's[4] blood does harm to hers, & every dinner-invitation[5] he refuses will give her an Indigestion.—Well, there is some comfort in the Mrs Hulberts not coming to you—& I am happy to hear of the Honey.—I was thinking of it the other day.—Let me know when you begin the new Tea—& the new white wine.—My present Elegancies have not yet made me indifferent to such Matters. I am still a Cat if I see a Mouse.—I am glad you like our caps—but Fanny is out of conceit with hers already; she finds that she has been buying a new cap without having a new pattern, which is true enough.—She is rather out of luck, to like neither her gown nor her Cap—but I do not much mind it, because besides that I like them both myself, I consider it as a thing of course at her time of Life—[*p. 2*] one of the sweet taxes of Youth to chuse in a hurry & make bad bargains.—I wrote to Charles yesterday, & Fanny has had a letter from him to day, principally to make enquiries about the time of their visit here, to which mine was an answer beforehand; so he will probably write again soon to fix his week.—I am best pleased that Cassy does not go to you.—Now, what have we been doing since I wrote last? The M^r Ks[6] came a little before dinner on Monday, & Edwd went to the Church with the two Seniors[7]—but there is no Inscription yet drawn up. They are very goodnatured you know & civil & all that—but are not particularly superfine; however, they ate their dinner & drank their Tea & went away, leaving their lovely Wadham in our arms—& I wish you had seen Fanny & me running backwards & forwards with his Breeches from the little chintz to the White room before we went to bed, in the greatest of frights lest he should come upon us before we had done it all.—There had been a mistake in the Housemaids Preparations & *they* were gone to bed.—He seems a very harmless sort of young Man—nothing to like or dislike in him;—goes out shooting or hunting with the two others[8] all the morng.—& plays at whist & makes queer faces in the eveng.—On Tuesday the Carriage was taken to the Painters;—at one time Fanny & I were to have gone in it, cheifly to call on M^rs C- Milles & *Moy*—but we found that they were going for a few days to Sandling & w^d not be at home;—therefore my Brother & Fanny went to Eastwell in the chair instead. While they were gone the Nackington Milles' called & left their cards.—Nobody at home at Eastwell.—We hear a great deal of

Geo. H.'s wretchedness. I suppose he has quick feelings—but I dare say they will not kill him.—He is so much out of spirits however that his friend John Plumptre is gone over to comfort him, at Mr Hatton's desire; he called here this morng. in his way. A handsome young Man certainly, with quiet, gentlemanlike manners.—I set him down as sensible rather than Brilliant.—There is nobody Brilliant nowadays.—He talks of staying a week at Eastwell & then comes to Chilham Cas: for a day or two, & my B^r invited him to come here afterwards, which he seemed very agreable to.—"'T'is Night⁹ & the Landscape is lovely no more", but to make amends for that, our visit to the Tyldens is over. My Brother, [*p. 3*] Fanny, Edwd & I went; Geo: staid at home with W. K.—There was nothing entertaining, or out of the common way. We met only Tyldens & double Tyldens.¹⁰ A Whist Table for the Gentlemen, a grown-up musical young Lady to play Backgammon with Fanny, & engravings of the Colleges at Cambridge¹¹ for me. In the morng. we returned Mrs Sherer's visit.—I like *Mr S.* very much.—Well, I have not half done yet; I am not come up with myself.—My B^r drove Fanny to Nackington & Cant^y yesterday, & while they were gone the Faggs paid their duty.—Mary Oxenden is staying at Cant^y with the Blairs, & Fanny's object was to see her.—The Deedes' want us to come to Sandling for a few days, or at least a day & night;—at present Edwd does not seem well affected—he w^d rather not be asked to go anywhere—but I rather expect he will be persuaded to go for the one day & night. I read him the cheif of your Letter, he was interested & pleased as he ought, & will be happy to hear from you himself.—Your finding so much comfort from his Cows gave him evident pleasure.—I wonder Henry did not go down on Saturday;—he does not in general fall *within* a doubtful Intention.—My face is very much as it was before I came away— for the first two or three days it was rather worse—I caught a small cold in my way down & had some pain every even^g—not to last long, but rather severer than it had been lately. This has worn off however & I have scarcely felt any thing for the last two days.—Sackree is pretty well again, only weak;—much obliged to you for your message &c;— it was very true that she bless'd herself the whole time that the pain was not in her Stomach.—I read all the scraps I could of your Letter to her. She seemed to like it—& says she shall always like to hear anything of Chawton now—& I am to make you Miss Clewes's assurance to the same effect, with Thanks & best respects &c.—The girls are much disturbed at Mary Stacey's not admitting Dame L:¹²—Miss C. & I are sorry but not angry;—we acknowledge Mary Stacey's right & can suppose her to have reason.—Oh!—the Church must have looked very forlorn. We all thought of the empty Pew.[13]—How Bentigh[14] is grown!—& the Cant^y-Hills-Plantation!—And the Improvements *within* are very great.—I admire the Chintz room very much.—We live in the Library except at Meals & have a fire every Even^g—The weather is set about changing;—we shall have a settled wet season soon. I must go to bed.

[*p. 4*] Friday. I am sorry to find that one of the nightcaps here belongs to you—sorry, because it must be in constant wear.—Great Doings again today—Fanny, Lizzy & Mar: are going to Goodnestone for the Fair, which is tomorrow, & stay till Monday, & the Gentlemen are all to dine at Evington. Edwd has been repenting ever since he promised to go & was hoping last night for a wet day—but the morn^g is fair.—I shall dine with Miss Clewes & I dare say find her very agreable.—The invitation to the Fair was general; Edwd positively declined his share of that, & I was very glad to do the same.—It is likely to be a baddish Fair—not much upon[15] the Stall, & neither Mary O. nor Mary P.[16]—It is hoped that the Portfolio may be in Cant^y this morn^g. Sackree's sister found it at Croydon & took it to Town with her, but unluckily did not send it down till she had directions. Fanny C's.[17] screens can be done nothing with, but there are parts of workbags in the parcel, very important in their way.—Three of the Deedes girls are to be at Goodnestone.—We shall not be much settled till this visit is over—settled as to employment I mean;—Fanny & I are to go on with Modern Europe[18] together, but hitherto have advanced only 25 Pages, something or other has always happened to delay or curtail the reading hour.—I ought to have told you before of a purchase of Edward's in Town, he desired you might hear of it, a *Thing* for measuring Timber with,[19] so that you need not have the trouble of finding him in Tapes any longer.—He treated himself with this seven shilling purchase, & bought a new Watch & new Gun for George.—The new gun shoots very well.

[*Continued below address panel*]

Apples are scarce in this Country; £1–5–a sack.—Miss Hinton should take Hannah Knight.—Mrs Driver[20] has not yet appeared.—J. Littleworth & the Grey Poney reached Bath safely.—

[*Continued on p. 1, upside down between the lines*]

A Letter from Mrs Cooke, they have been at Brighton a fortnight, stay at least another & Mary is already much better.—Poor Dr Isham is obliged to admire P. & P.—& to send me word that he is sure he shall not like M^de Darblay's new Novel[21] half so well.—Mrs C. invented it all of course. He desires his comp^ts to you & my Mother.—Of the Adlestrop-Living business Mrs C. says "It can be now no secret, as the Papers for the necessary Dispensations are going up to the Archbishop's Secretary.—However be it known that we all wish to have it understood that George takes this Trust *entirely* to oblige Mr Leigh & never will be a shilling benefited by it. Had my consent been necessary, beleive me I sh^d have withheld it, for I do think it on the part of the Patron a very shabby peice of business.—All these & other *Scrapings* from dear Mrs E. L. are to accumulate no doubt to help Mr Twisleton[22] to a secure admission again into England."—I would wish you therefore to make it known to my Mother as if *this* were the first time of Mrs Cooke's mentioning it to me.—

I told Mrs C. of my Mother's late oppression in *her head.*—She says on that subject—"Dear Mrs Austen's is I beleive an attack frequent at her age & mine. Last year I had for some time the Sensation of a Peck Loaf resting on my head, & they talked of cupping me, but I came off with a dose or two of calomel & have never heard of it since."—

The three Miss Knights & Mrs Sayce are just off;—the weather has got worse since the early morn^g;—whether Miss Clewes & I are to be Tete a Tete, or to have 4 gentlemen to admire us is uncertain.

I am now alone in the Library, Mistress of all I survey[23]—at least I may say so & repeat the whole poem if I like it, without offence to anybody.—

Martha will have wet Races & catch a bad cold;—in other respects I hope she will have much pleasure at them—& that she is free from Earache *now.* I am glad she likes my cap so well.—

I assure you my old one looked so smart yesterday that I was asked two or three times before I set off, whether it was not my new one.—I have this moment seen Mrs Driver driven up to the Kitchen Door. I cannot close with a grander circumstance or greater wit.—

Yours affec:^ly J. A.

[*Postscripts crossed on p. 2*]

I am going to write to Steventon so you need not send any news of me there.

Louisa's best Love & a Hundred Thousand Million Kisses.

Miss Austen
Chawton
Alton
Hants

90. *To Francis Austen*

Saturday 25 September 1813

Godmersham Park—Sept: 25. 1813.

My dearest Frank

The 11th of this month brought me your letter & I assure you I thought it very well worth its 2^s/3^d.—I am very much obliged to you for filling me so long a sheet a [*sic*] paper, you are a good one to traffic with in that way, You pay most liberally;—my Letter was a scratch of a note compared with yours—& then you write so even, so clear both in style & Penmanship, so much to the point & give so much real intelligence that it is enough to kill one.—I am sorry Sweden is so poor & my riddle so bad.—The idea of a fashionable Bathing place in Mecklenburg!—How can people pretend to be fashionable or to bathe out of England!—Rostock Market makes one's mouth water, our cheapest Butcher's meat is double the price of theirs;—nothing under 9^d all this Summer, & I beleive upon recollection nothing under 10^d.—Bread has sunk & is likely to sink more, which we hope may make Meat sink too. But I have no occasion to think of the price of Bread or of Meat where I am now;—let me shake off vulgar cares & conform to the happy Indifference of East Kent wealth.—I wonder whether You & the King of Sweden know that I *was* to come to G^m with my B^r. Yes, I suppose you have rec^d due notice of it by some means or other. I have not been here these 4 years, so I am sure the event deserves to be talked of before & behind as well as in the middle.—We left Chawton on ye 14th,—spent two entire days in Town & arrived here on ye 17th.—My B^r, Fanny, Lizzy, Marianne & I composed this division of the Family, & filled his Carriage, inside & out.—Two post-chaises under the escort of George conveyed eight more across the Country, the Chair brought two, two others came on horseback & the rest by the Coach—& so by one means or another we all are removed.—It puts me in mind of the account of St Paul's Shipwreck,[1] where all are said by different means to reach the Shore in safety. [*p. 2*] I left my Mother, Cassandra & Martha well, & have had good accounts of them since. At present they are quite alone, but they are going to be visited by Mrs Heathcote & Miss Bigg— & to have a few days of Henry's company likewise.—I expect to be here about two months. Edward is to be in Hampshire again in November & will take me back.—I shall be sorry to be in Kent so long without seeing Mary, but am afraid it must be so. She has very kindly invited me to Deal, but is aware of the great improbability of my being able to get there.—It would be a great pleasure to me to see Mary Jane again too, as well as her Brothers, new & old.—Charles & his family I do hope to see; they are coming here for a week in October.—We were accomodated in Henrietta S^t—Henry was so good as to find room for his 3 neices & myself in his House. Edward slept at an Hotel in the next Street.—N° 10 is made very comfortable with Cleaning, & Painting & the Sloane S^t furniture. The front room upstairs is an excellent Dining & common sitting parlour—& the smaller one behind will sufficiently answer his purpose as a Draw^g room.—He has no intention of giving large parties of any kind.—His plans are all for the comfort of his Friends & himself.—M^{de} Bigeon & her Daughter have a Lodging in his neighbourhood & come to him as often as he likes or as they like. M^{de} B. always markets for him as she used to do; & upon our being in the House, was constantly there to do the work.—She is wonderfully re-covered from the severity of her Asthmatic complaint.—Of our three even^{gs} in Town one was spent at the Lyceum & another at Covent Garden;—the Clandestine Marriage was the most respectable of the performances, the rest were Sing-song & trumpery, but did very well for Lizzy & Marianne, who were indeed delighted;—but *I* wanted better acting.—There was no Actor worthy naming.—I beleive the Theatres are thought at a low ebb at present.—Henry has probably sent you his own account of his visit in Scotland. I wish he had had more time & could have gone farther north, & deviated to the Lakes in his way back, but what he was able to do seems to have afforded him great Enjoyment & he met with Scenes of higher Beauty in Roxburghshire than I had supposed the South of Scotland possessed.—Our nephew's gratifica-tion [*p. 3*] was less keen than our Brother's.—Edward is no Enthusiast in the beauties of Nature. His Enthusiasm is for the Sports of the field only.—He is a very promising & pleasing young Man however upon the whole, behaves with great propriety to his Father & great kindness to his Brothers & Sisters—& we must forgive his thinking more of Growse & Partridges than Lakes & Mountains. He & George are out every morn^g either shooting or with the Harriers. They are both good Shots.—Just at present I am Mistress & Miss & altogether here, Fanny being gone to Goodnestone for a day or two, to attend the famous Fair, which makes its yearly distribution of gold paper & coloured persian through all the Family connections.—In this House there is a constant succession of small events, somebody is always going or coming; this morn^g we had Edwd Bridges unexpectedly to breakfast with us, in his

way from Ramsgate where is his wife, to Lenham where is his Church—
& tomorrow he dines & sleeps here on his return.—They have been all
the summer at Ramsgate, for *her* health, she is a poor Honey—the sort
of woman who gives me the idea of being determined never to be
well—& who likes her spasms & nervousness & the consequence they
give her, better than anything else.—This is an illnatured sentiment to
send all over the Baltic!—The Mr Knatchbulls, dear Mrs Knights Brothers dined here the other day. They came from the Friars, which is still
on their hands.—The Elder made many enquiries after you.—Mr Sherer
is quite a new Mr Sherer to me; I heard him for the first time last
Sunday, & he gave us an excellent Sermon—a little too eager sometimes in his delivery, but that is to *me* a better extreme than the want of
animation, especially when it evidently comes from the heart as in him.
The Clerk[2] is as much like you as ever, I am always glad to see him on
that account.—But the Sherers are going away. He has a bad Curate at
Westwell, whom he can eject only by residing there himself. He goes
nominally for three years, & a Mr Paget is to have the Curacy of G^m—
a married Man, with a very musical wife, which I hope may make her
a desirable acquaintance to Fanny.—I thank you very warmly for your
kind consent to my application[3] & the kind hint which followed it.—
I was previously aware of what I sh^d be laying myself open to—but the
truth is that the Secret has spread so far as to be scarcely the Shadow
of a secret now—& that I beleive whenever the 3^d appears, I shall not
even attempt to tell Lies about it.—I shall rather try to make all the
Money than all the Mystery I can of it.[4]—People shall pay for their
Knowledge if I can make them.—Henry heard P. & P. warmly [*p. 4*]
praised in Scotland, by Lady Robt Kerr & another Lady;—& what does
he do in the warmth of his Brotherly vanity & Love, but immediately
tell them who wrote it!—A Thing once set going in that way—one
knows how it spreads!—and he, dear Creature, has set it going so much
more than once. I know it is all done from affection & partiality—but
at the same time, let me here again express to you & Mary my sense of
the *superior* kindness which you have shewn on the occasion, in doing
what I wished.—I am trying to harden myself.—After all, what a trifle
it is in all its Bearings, to the really important points of one's existence
even in this World!—

I take it for granted that Mary has told you of Anna's engagement to
Ben Lefroy. It came upon us without much preparation;—at the same
time, there was *that* about her which kept us in a constant preparation
for something.—We are anxious to have it go on well, there being quite

as much in his favour as the Chances are likely to give her in any Matrimonial connection. I beleive he is sensible, certainly very religious, well connected & with some Independance.—There is an unfortunate dissimularity of Taste between them in one respect which gives us some apprehensions, he hates company & she is very fond of it;—This, with some queerness of Temper on his side & much unsteadiness on hers, is untoward.

[Continued below address panel]

I hope Edward's family-visit to Chawton will be yearly, he certainly means it now, but we must not expect it to exceed *two* months in future.—I do not think however, that *he* found *five* too long this Summer.—He was very happy there.—The new Paint improves this House much, & we find no evil from the smell.

[Continued upside down at top of p. 1]

Poor Mr Trimmer is lately dead, a sad loss to his Family, & occasioning some anxiety to our Brother;—for the present he continues his Affairs in the Son's hands;⁵ a matter of great consequence to *them*—I hope he will have no reason to remove his Business.—I remain

Your very affec^te Sister

J. Austen

[Postscript crossing p. 2]

There is to be a 2^d Edition of S.&S. Egerton advises it.

Captain Austen
HMS Elephant
Baltic.

[Letters missing here]

91. *To Cassandra Austen*

Monday 11–Tuesday 12 October 1813

Godmersham Park Monday Octr. 11th.

You will have Edward's Letter tomorrow. He tells me that he did not send you any news to interfere with mine, but I do not think there is much for anybody to send at present. We had our dinner party on Wed^y with the addition of M^rs & Miss Milles who were under a promise of dining here in their return from Eastwell whenever they paid their visit of duty there, & it happened to be paid on that day.—Both Mother & Daughter are much as I have always found them.—I like the Mother, 1st because she reminds me of Mrs Birch & 2dly because she is chearful & grateful for what she is at the age of 90 & upwards.—The day was pleasant enough. I sat by Mr Chisholme & we talked away at a great rate about nothing worth hearing.—It was a mistake as to the day of the Sherers going being fixed; *they* are ready but are waiting for Mr Paget's answer.—I enquired of Mrs Milles after Jemima Brydges & was quite greived to hear that she was obliged to leave Cant^y some months ago on account of her debts & is nobody knows where.—What an unprosperous Family!—On saturday soon after breakfast Mr J. P.^1 left us for Norton Court.—I like him very much.—He gives me the idea of a very amiable young Man, only too diffident to be so agreable as he might be.—He was out the cheif of each morn^g with the other two— shooting & getting wet through.—Tomorrow we are to know whether he & a hundred young Ladies will come here for the Ball.—I do not much expect any.—The Deedes' cannot meet us, they have Engage-ments at home. I will finish the Deedes' by saying that they are not likely to come here till quite late in my stay—the very last week per-haps^2—& I do not expect to see the Moores at all.—They are not solicited till after Edward's return from Hampshire. Monday, Nov:^r 15th is the day now fixed for our setting out.—Poor Basingstoke Races!— there seem to have been two particularly wretched days on purpose for them;—& Weyhill week^3 does not begin much happier.—We were quite surprised by a Letter from Anna at Tollard Royal^4 last Satur-day—but perfectly approve her going & only regret they should all go so far, to stay so few days. We had Thunder & Lighten^g here on Thurs-day morn^g between 5 & 7—no very bad Thunder, but a great deal of Light^g—It has given the commencement of [*p. 2*] a Season of wind & rain; & perhaps for the next 6 weeks we shall not have two dry days together.—Lizzy is very much obliged to you for your Letter & will answer it soon, but has so many things to do that it may be four or five days before she can. This is quite her own message, spoken in rather a desponding tone.—Your Letter gave pleasure to all of us, we had all the reading of it of course, I *three times*—as I undertook to the great releif of Lizzy, to read it to Sackree, & afterwards to Louisa.—Sackree does not at all approve of Mary Doe & her nuts—on the score of propriety rather than health.—She saw some signs of going after her in

George & Henry, & thinks if you could give the girl a check, by rather reproving her for taking anything seriously about nuts which they said to her, it might be of use.—This, of course, is between our three discreet selves—a scene of triennial bliss.[5]—Mrs Britton called here on Saturday. I never saw her before. She is a large, ungenteel Woman, with self-satisfied & would-be elegant manners.—We are certain of some visitors tomorrow; Edward Bridges comes for two nights in his way from Lenham to Ramsgate & brings a friend—name unknown—but supposed to be a Mr Harpur, a neighbouring Clergyman; & Mr R. Mascall is to shoot with the young Men, which it is to be supposed will end in his staying dinner.—On Thursday, Mr Lushington MP. for Canterbury & Manager of the Lodge Hounds, dines here & stays the night.—He is cheifly Young Edward's acquaintance.—If I can, I will get a frank from him & write to you all the sooner. I suppose the Ashford Ball will furnish something.—As I wrote of my nephews with a little bitterness in my last,[6] I think it particularly incumbent on me to do them justice now, & I have great pleasure in saying that they were both at the Sacrament yesterday. After having much praised or much blamed anybody, one is generally sensible of something just the reverse soon afterwards. Now, these two Boys who are out with the Foxhounds will come home & disgust me again[7] by some habit of Luxury or some proof of sporting Mania—unless I keep it off by this prediction.—They amuse themselves very comfortably in the Even^g—by netting; they are each about a rabbit net, & sit as deedily to it, side by side, as any two Uncle Franks could do.—I am looking over Self Control[8] again, & my opinion is confirmed of its' being an excellently-meant, elegantly-written Work, without anything of Nature or Probability in it. I declare I do not know whether Laura's passage down the American River, is not the most natural, possible, every-day thing she ever does.—

[*p. 3*] *Tuesday.*—Dear me! What is to become of me! Such a long Letter![9]—Two & forty Lines in the 2^d Page.—Like Harriot Byron[10] I ask, what am I to do with my Gratitude?—I can do nothing but thank you & go on.—A few of your enquiries I think, are replied to en avance. The name of F. Cage's Draw^g Master is O'Neil.—We are exceedingly amused with your Shalden news—& your self reproach on the subject of Mrs Stockwell, made me laugh heartily. I rather wondered that Johncock,[11] the only person in the room, could help laughing too.—I had not heard before of her having the Measles. M^rs H- & Alethea's[12] staying till friday was quite new to me; a good plan however—I c^d not have settled it better myself, & am glad they found so much in the house to approve—and I hope they will ask Martha to visit them.—I admire the Sagacity & Taste of Charlotte Williams. Those large dark eyes always judge well.—I will compliment her, by naming a Heroine[13] after her.—Edward has had all the particulars of the Building &c read to him twice over & seems very well satisfied;—a narrow door to the Pantry is the only subject of solicitude—it is certainly just the door which should not be narrow, on account of the Trays—but if a case of necessity, it must be borne.—I *knew* there was Sugar in the Tin, but had no idea of there being enough to last through your Company. All the better.—You ought not to think this new Loaf better than the other, because *that* was the first of 5 which al[l came] together. Something of fancy perhaps, & something of Imagination.—Dear Mrs Digweed!—I cannot bear that she sh^d not be foolishly happy after a Ball.—I hope Miss Yates & her companions[14] were all well the day after their arrival.—I am thoroughly rejoiced that Miss Benn has placed herself in Lodgings—tho' I hope they may not be long necessary.—No Letter from Charles yet.—Southey's Life of Nelson;[15]—I am tired of Lives of Nelson, being that I never read any. I will read this however, if Frank is mentioned in it.—Here am I in Kent, with one Brother in the same County & another Brother's Wife,[16] & see nothing of them—which seems unnatural—It will not last so for ever I trust.—I sh^d like to have Mrs F. A. & her Children here for a week—but not a syllable of that nature is ever breathed.—I wish her last visit had not been so long a one.—I wonder whether Mrs Tilson has ever lain-in.[17] Mention it, if it ever comes to your knowledge, & we shall hear of it by the same post from Henry. Mr Rob. Mascall breakfasted here; he eats a great deal of Butter.—I dined upon Goose[18] yesterday—which I hope will secure a good Sale of my 2^d Edition.—Have you any Tomatas?—Fanny & I regale on them every day.—Disastrous Letters from the Plumptres & Oxendens.—Refusals everywhere—a Blank partout—& it is not quite certain whether [*p. 4*] we go or not;—something may depend upon the disposition of Uncle Edward[19] when he comes—& upon what we hear at Chilham Castle this morn^g—for we are going to pay visits. We are going to each house at Chilham & to Mystole. I shall like seeing the Faggs.—I shall like it all, except that we are to set out so early that I have not time to write as I could wish.—Edwd Bridges's friend is a Mr Hawker I find, not Harpur. I would not have you sleep in such an Error for the World. My Brother desires his best Love & Thanks for all your Information. He hopes the roots of the old Beach [*sic*] have been dug away enough to allow a proper covering of Mould & Turf.—He is sorry for the necessity of build^g the new Coin—but hopes they will contrive that the Doorway should be of the usual width;—if it must be contracted on one side, by widening it on the other.—The appearance need not signify.—And he desires me to say that Your being at Chawton when he is, will be quite necessary. You cannot think it more indispensable than he does. He is very much obliged to you for your attention to everything.—Have you any idea of returning with him to Henrietta S^t & finishing your visit then?—Tell me your sweet little innocent Ideas.— [*continued below address panel*] Everything of Love & Kindness—proper & improper, must now suffice.—

Y^rs very affec^ly
J. Austen

[*Addition at the top of p. 1, in Fanny's hand*]

My Dearest At: Cass:—I have just asked At: Jane to let me write a little in her letter but she does not like it[20] so I won't.—good bye.

Miss Austen
Chawton
Alton
Hants

92. *To Cassandra Austen*

Thursday 14–Friday 15 October 1813

Godmersham Park Thursday Oct. 14.

My dearest Cassandra

Now I will prepare for Mr Lushington, & as it will be wisest also to prepare for his not coming or my not getting a frank I shall write very close from the first & even leave room for the seal[1] in the proper place.— When I have followed up my last with this, I shall feel somewhat less unworthy of you than the state of our Correspondence now requires. I left off in a great hurry to prepare for our morn^g visits—of course was ready a good deal the first, & need not have hurried so much—Fanny wore her new gown & cap.—I was surprised to find Mystole so pretty. The Ladies were at home; I was in luck, & saw Lady Fagg & all her five Daughters, with an old Mrs Hamilton from Cant^y & M^rs & Miss Chapman from Margate into the Bargain.—I never saw so plain a family, five sisters so very plain!—They are as plain as the Foresters or the Franfraddops[2] or the Seagraves or the Rivers' excluding Sophy.—Miss

Sally Fagg has a pretty figure, & that comprises all the good Looks of the family.—It was stupidish; Fanny did her part very well, but there was a lack of Talk altogether, & the three friends in the House only sat by & looked at us.—However Miss Chapman's name is Laura & she had a double flounce to her gown.—You really must get some flounces. Are not some of your large stock of white morn^g gowns just in a happy state for a flounce, too short?—Nobody at home at either House[3] in Chilham.—Edward Bridges & his friend did not forget to arrive. The friend is a Mr Wigram, one of the three & twenty Children of a great rich mercantile Sir Robert Wigram, an old acquaintance of the Footes, but very recently known to Edwd B.—The history of his coming here, is that intending to go from Ramsgate to Brighton, Edw: B. persuaded him to take Lenham in his way, which gave him the convenience of Mr W.'s gig & the comfort of not being alone there; but probably thinking a few days of G^m would be the cheapest & pleasantest way of entertaining his friend & himself, offered a visit here, & here they stay till tomorrow. Mr W. is about 5 or 6 & 20, not ill-looking & not agreable.— He is certainly no addition.—A sort of cool, gentlemanlike manner, but very silent.—They say his name is Henry. A proof how unequally the gifts of Fortune are bestowed.—I have seen many a John & Thomas much more agreable.—[*p. 2*] We have got rid of Mr R. Mascall however;—I did not like *him* either. He talks too much & is conceited— besides having a vulgarly shaped mouth. He slept here on Tuesday; so that yesterday Fanny & I sat down to breakfast with six gentlemen to admire us.—We did not go to the Ball.—It was left to her to decide, & at last she determined against it. She knew that it would be a sacrifice on the part of her Father & Brothers if they went—& I hope it will prove that *she* has not sacrificed much.—It is not likely that there sh^d have been anybody there, whom she w^d care for.—*I* was very glad to be spared the trouble of dressing & going & being weary before it was half over, so my gown & my cap are still unworn.—It will appear at last perhaps that I might have done without either.—I produced my Brown Bombasin yesterday & it was very much admired indeed—& I like it better than ever:—You have given many particulars of the state of Chawton House, but still we want more.—Edward wants to be expressly told that all the Round Tower &c. is entirely down, & the door from the Best room stopt up;—he does not know enough of the appearance of things in that quarter.—He heard from Bath yesterday. Lady B.[4] continues very well & Dr Parry's opinion is that while the Water agrees with her she ought to remain there, which throws their coming

away at a greater Uncertainty than we had supposed.—It will end perhaps in a fit of the Gout which may prevent her coming away.—Louisa
thinks her Mother's being so well may be quite as much oweing to her
being so much out of doors, as to the Water.—Lady B. is going to try
the Hot pump, the Cross Bath being about to be painted.—Louisa is
particularly well herself, & thinks the Water has been of use to her.—
She mentioned our enquiries &c. to M^r & Mrs Alex: Evelyn, & had their
best Comp^ts & Thanks to give in return.—Dr Parry does not expect M^r
E. to last much longer.—Only think of Mrs Holder's being dead!—
Poor woman, she has done the only thing in the World she could possibly do, to make one cease to abuse her.—Now, if you please, Hooper^s
must have it in his power to do more by his Uncle.—Lucky for the little
girl!—An Anne Ekins can hardly be so unfit for the care of a Child as
a Mrs Holder. A letter from Wrotham yesterday, offering an early visit
here;—& M^r & Mrs Moore & one Child are to come on Monday for 10
days.—I hope Charles & Fanny may not fix the same time—but if they
come at all in October they *must*. What is the use of hoping?—The two
parties of Children is the cheif Evil. [*p. 3*] To be sure, here we are, the
very thing has happened, or rather worse, a Letter from Charles this
very morn^g which gives us reason to suppose they may come here to
day. It depends upon the weather, & the weather now is very fine.—No
difficulties are made however & indeed there will be no want of room,
but I wish there were no Wigrams & Lushingtons in the way to fill up
the Table & make us such a motley set.—I cannot spare Mr Lushington
either because of his frank, but Mr Wigram does no good to anybody.—
I cannot imagine how a Man can have the impudence to come into a
Family party for three days, where he is quite a stranger, unless he
knows himself to be agreable on undoubted authority.—He & Edw. B.
are going to ride to Eastwell—& as the Boys are hunting & my B^r is
gone to Cant^y Fanny & I have a quiet morn^g before us.—Edward has
driven off poor Mrs Salkeld.—It was thought a good opportunity of
doing something towards clearing the House.—By her own desire
Mrs Fanny is to be put^6 in the room next the Nursery, her Baby in a
little bed by her;—& as Cassy is to have the Closet within & Betsey
William's little Hole they will be all very snug together.—I shall be
most happy to see dear Charles, & he will be as happy as he can with
a cross Child or some such care pressing on him at the time.—I should
be very happy in the idea of seeing little Cassy again too, did not I fear
she w^d disappoint me by some immediate disagreableness.—We had the
good old original Brett & Toke calling here yesterday, separately.—M^r

Toke I am always very fond of. He enquired after you & my Mother, which adds Esteem to Passion.—The Charles Cages are staying at Godington.—I *knew* they must be staying somewhere soon.—Ed: Hussey is warned out of Pett, & talks of fixing at Ramsgate.—Bad Taste!—He is very fond of the Sea however;—some Taste in that—& some Judgement too in fixing on Ramsgate, as being by the Sea.—The Comfort of the Billiard Table here is very great.—It draws all the Gentlemen to it whenever they are within, especially after dinner, so that my B^r Fanny & I have the Library to ourselves in delightful quiet.— There is no truth in the report of G. Hatton being to marry Miss Wemyss. He desires it may be contradicted.—Have you done anything about our Present to Miss Benn?—I suppose she must have a bed at my Mothers whenever she dines there.—How will they manage as to inviting her when you are gone?—& if they invite how they will contrive to enter- tain her?—Let me know as many of your parting arrangements as you can, as to Wine &c.—I wonder whether the Ink bottle has been filled.— Does Butcher's meat keep up at the same price? & is not Bread lower than 2/6.—Mary's blue gown!—My Mother must be in agonies.—I have a great mind to have *my* blue gown dyed some time or other—I proposed it once to you & you made some objection, I forget what.— It is the fashion of flounces that gives it particular Expediency.—M^rs & Miss Wildman have just been here. Miss is very plain. I wish Lady B. may be returned before we leave G^m that Fanny may spend[7] the time of her Father's absence, at Goodnestone, which is what she would prefer.—*Friday.*—They came last night at about 7. We had given them up, but I still expected them to come. Dessert was nearly over;—a better time for arriving than an hour & ½ earlier. They were late be- cause they did not set out [*p. 4*] earlier & did not allow time enough.— Charles did not *aim* at more than reaching Sittingbourn by 3, which c^d not have brought them here by dinner time.—They had a very rough passage, he w^d not have ventured if he had known how bad it w^d be.— However here they are safe & well, just like their own nice selves, Fanny looking as neat & white this morn^g as possible, & dear Charles all affectionate, placid, quiet, chearful good humour. They are both looking very well, but poor little Cassy is grown extremely thin & looks poorly.—I hope a week's Country air & exercise may do her good. I am sorry to say it can be but a week.—The Baby does not appear so large in proportion as she was, nor quite so pretty, but I have seen very little of her.—Cassy was too tired & bewildered just at first to seem to know anybody—We met them in the Hall, the Women &

Girl part of us—but before we reached the Library she kissed me very affectionately—& has since seemed to recollect me in the same way. It was quite an even^g of confusion as you may suppose—at first we were all walking about from one part of the House to the other—then came a fresh dinner in the Breakfast room for Charles & his wife, which Fanny & I attended—then we moved into the Library, were joined by the Dining room people, were introduced & so forth.—& then we had Tea & Coffee which was not over till past 10.—Billiards again drew all the odd ones away, & Edwd Charles, the two Fannys & I sat snugly talking. I shall be glad to have our numbers a little reduced, & by the time You receive this we shall be only a family, tho' a large family party. Mr Lushington goes tomorrow.—Now I must speak of *him*—& I like him very much. I am sure he is clever & a Man of Taste. He got a vol. of Milton last night & spoke of it with Warmth.—He is quite an M.P.—very smiling, with an exceeding good address, & readiness of Language.—I am rather in love with him.—I dare say he is ambitious & Insincere.—He puts me in mind of Mr Dundas—. He has a wide smiling mouth & very good teeth, & something the same complexion & nose.—He is a much shorter Man, with Martha's Leave. Does Martha never hear from Mrs Craven?—Is Mrs Craven never at home?—We breakfasted in the Dining room today & are now all pretty well dispersed & quiet.—Charles & George are gone out shooting together, to Winnigates & Seaton Wood—I asked on purpose to tell Henry. Mr Lushington & Edwd are gone some other way.—I wish Charles may kill something—but this high wind is against their Sport.—[*p. 5*] Lady Williams is living at the Rose at Sittingbourn, they called upon her Yesterday; she cannot live at Sheerness & as soon as she gets to Sittingbourn is quite well.—In return for all your Matches, I announce that her Brother William is going to marry a Miss Austen of a Wiltshire Family,[8] who say they are related to us.—I talk to Cassy about Chawton; she remembers much but does not volunteer on the subject.—Poor little Love—I wish she were not so very Palmery—but it seems stronger than ever.—I never knew a Wife's family-features have such undue influence.—Papa & Mama have not yet made up their mind as to parting with her or not—the cheif, indeed the only difficulty with Mama is a very reasonable one, the Child's being very unwilling to leave them. When it was mentioned to her, she did not like the idea of it at all.— At the same time, she has been suffering so much lately from Sea sickness, that her Mama cannot bear to have her much on board[9] this winter.—Charles is less inclined to part with her.—I do not know how it will end, or what is to determine it. He desires his best Love to you & has not written because he has not been able to decide.—They are both very sensible of your Kindness on the occasion.—I have made Charles furnish me with something to say about Young Kendall.—He is going on very well. When he first joined the Namur, my B^r did not find him forward enough to be what they call put in the Office, & therefore placed him under the Schoolmaster, but he is very much improved, & goes into the Office now every afternoon—still attending School in the morn^g. This Cold weather comes very fortunately for Edward's nerves with such a House full, it suits him exactly, he is all alive & chearful. Poor James, on the contrary, must be running his Toes into the fire. I find that Mary Jane Fowle was very near returning with her B^{rio} & paying them a visit on board—I forget exactly what hindered her—I beleive their Cheltenham Scheme—I am glad something did.—They are to go to Cheltenham on Monday se 'night. I don't vouch for their going you know, it only comes from one of the Family.—Now I think I have written you a good sized Letter & may deserve whatever I can get in reply.—Infinities of Love. I must distinguish that of Fanny Sen:^r—who particularly desires to be remembered to you all.—Yours very affec^{ly} J. Austen

[*Address written by Mr Lushington*]

Faversham fifteenth October 1813
Miss Austen
Chawton
Alton
Hants

Free
R. Lushington

[*Letter of 19 October 1813 missing*]

93. *To Cassandra Austen*

Thursday 21 October 1813

Godmersham Park Oct. 18

My dear Aunt Cassandra
    I am very much obliged to you for your long letter and for the nice account of Chawton. We are all very glad to hear that the Adams are

gone, and hope Dame Libscombe will be more happy now with her deaffy child, as she calls it, but I am afraid there is not much chance of her remaining long sole mistress of her house. I am sorry you had not any better news to send us of our hare, poor little thing! I thought it would not live long in that *Pondy House*; I don't wonder that Mary Doe is very sorry it is dead, because we promised her that if it was alive when we came back to Chawton, we would reward her for her trouble. Papa is much obliged to you for ordering the scrubby firs to be cut down; I think he was rather frightened at first about the great oak. Fanny quite believed it, for she exclaimed 'Dear me, what a pity, how could they be so stupid!' I hope by this time they have put up some hurdles for the sheep, or turned out the cart-horses from the lawn. Pray tell grandmama that we have begun getting seeds for her; I hope we shall be able to get her a nice collection, but I am afraid this wet weather is very much against them. How glad I am to hear she has had such good success with her chickens, but I wish there had been more bantams amongst them. I am very sorry to hear of poor Lizzie's fate. I must now tell you something about our poor people. I believe you know old Mary Croucher, she gets *maderer* and *maderer* every day. Aunt Jane has been to see her, but it was on one of her rational days. Poor Will Amos hopes your skewers are doing well; he has left his house in the poor Row, and lives in a barn at Builting. We asked him why he went away, and he said the fleas were so starved when he came back from Chawton that they all flew upon him and *eenermost* eat him up. How unlucky it is that the weather is so wet! Poor uncle Charles has come home half drowned every day. I don't think little Fanny is quite so pretty as she was; one reason is because she wears short petticoats, I believe. I hope Cook is better; she was very unwell the day we went away. Papa has given me half-a-dozen new pencils, which are very good ones indeed; I draw every other day. I hope you go and whip Lucy Chalcraft every night. Miss Clewes begs me to give her very best respects to you; she is very much obliged to you for your kind enquiries after her. Pray give my duty to grandmamma and love to Miss Floyd.[1] I remain, my dear Aunt Cassandra, your very affectionate niece,

Elizth. Knight

Thursday. I think Lizzy's letter will entertain you. Thank you for yours just received. To-morrow shall be fine if possible. You will be at Guildford before our party set off. They only go to Key Street,[2] as Mr Street the Purser lives there, and they have promised to dine and sleep with him. Cassy's looks are much mended. She agrees pretty well with her cousins, but is not quite happy among them; they are too many and too boisterous for her. I have given her your message, but she said nothing, and did not look as if the idea of going to Chawton again was a pleasant one. They have Edward's carriage to Ospringe. I think I have just done a good deed—extracted Charles from his wife and children upstairs, and made him get ready to go out shooting, and not keep Mr Moore waiting any longer. Mr and Mrs Sherer and Joseph dined here yesterday very prettily. Edw. and Geo. were absent—gone for a night to Eastling. The two Fannies went to Canty. in the morning, and took Lou. and Cass. to try on new stays. Harriot[3] and I had a comfortable walk together. She desires her best love to you and kind remembrance to Henry. Fanny's best love also. I fancy there is to be another party to Canty. to-morrow—Mr and Mrs Moore and me. Edward thanks Henry for his letter. We are most happy to hear he is so much better. I depend upon you for letting me know what he wishes as to my staying with him or not; you will be able to find out, I dare say. I had intended to beg you would bring one of my nightcaps with you, in case of my staying, but forgot it when I wrote on Tuesday. Edward is much concerned about his pond; he cannot now doubt the fact of its running out, which he was resolved to do as long as possible. I suppose my mother will like to have me write to her. I shall try at least. No; I have never seen the death of Mrs Crabbe.[4] I have only just been making out from one of his prefaces[5] that he probably was married. It is almost ridiculous. Poor woman! I will comfort *him*[6] as well as I can, but I do not undertake to be good to her children. She had better not leave any. Edw. and Geo. set off this day week for Oxford. Our party will then be very small, as the Moores will be going about the same time. To enliven us, Fanny proposes spending a few days soon afterwards at Fredville. It will really be a good opportunity, as her father will have a companion. We shall all three go to Wrotham, but Edwd. and I stay only a night perhaps. Love to Mr Tilson.

Yours very affectionately, J. A.

Miss Austen
10 Henrietta St,
Covent Garden
London

94. *To Cassandra Austen*

Tuesday 26 October 1813

Godmersham Park Tuesday Oct: 26.

My dearest Cassandra

You will have had such late accounts from this place as (I hope) to prevent your expecting a Letter from me immediately, as I really do not think I have wherewithal to fabricate one to day. I suspect this will be brought to you by our nephews, tell me if it is.—It is a great pleasure to me to think of you with Henry, I am sure your time must pass most comfortably & I trust you are seeing improvement in him every day.— I shall be most happy to hear from you again. Your Saturday's Letter however was quite as long & as particular as I could expect.—I am not at all in a humour for writing; I must write on till I am.—I congratulate Mr Tilson & hope everything is going on well. Fanny & I depend upon knowing what the Child's name is to be, as soon as you can tell us. I guess Caroline.[1]—Our Gentlemen are all gone to their Sittingbourn Meeting, East & West Kent in one Barouche together—rather—West Kent driving East Kent.—I beleive that is not the usual way of the County. We breakfasted before 9 & do not dine till ½ past 6 on the occasion, so I hope we three shall have a long Morning enough.—Mr Deedes & Sir Brook—I do not care for Sir Brook's being a Baronet I will put Mr Deedes first because I like him a great deal the best—they arrived together yesterday—for the Bridges' are staying at Sandling— just before dinner;—both Gentlemen much as they used to be, only growing a little older. They leave us tomorrow.—You were clear of Guildford by half an hour & were winding along the pleasant road to Ripley when the Charleses set off on friday.—I hope we shall have a visit [*p. 2*] from them at Chawton in the Spring, or early part of the Summer. They seem well inclined.—Cassy had recovered her Looks almost entirely & I find they do not consider the Namur as disagreeing with her in general—only when the weather is so rough as to make her sick.—Our Canterbury scheme took place as proposed & very pleasant it was, Harriot & I & little George[2] within, my Brother on the Box with the Master Coachman.—I was most happy to find my B^r included in the party, it was a great improvement, & he & Harriot & I walked about together very happily while Mr Moore took his little boy with him to Taylors & Haircutters.—*Our* cheif Business was to call on Mrs Milles, & we had[3] indeed so little else to do that we were obliged to

saunter about anywhere & go backwards & forwards as much as possible to make out the Time & keep ourselves from having two hours to
sit with the good Lady. A most extraordinary circumstance in a Canterbury Morn^g!—*Old Toke* came in while we were paying our visit. I
thought of Louisa.—Miss Milles was queer as usual & provided us with
plenty to laugh at. She undertook in *three words* to give us the history
of Mrs Scudamore's reconciliation, & then talked on about it for half an
hour, using such odd expressions & so foolishly minute that I could
hardly keep my countenance.—The death of Wyndham Knatchbull's
son⁴ will rather supersede the Scudamores. I told her that he was to be
buried at Hatch.—She had heard, with military Honours at Portsmouth.—We may guess how that point will be discussed, evening after
evening.—Oweing to a difference of Clocks, the Coachman did not
bring the Carriage so soon as he ought by half an hour;—anything like
a breach of punctuality was a great offence—& Mr Moore was very
angry—which I was rather glad of—I wanted to see him angry—&
though he spoke to his Servant⁵ in a very loud voice & with a good deal
of heat I was happy to perceive that he did not scold Harriot at all.
[*p. 3*] Indeed there is nothing to object to in his manners to her, & I do
beleive that he makes her—or she makes herself—very happy.—They
do not spoil their Boy.⁶—It seems now quite settled that we go to
Wrotham on Saturday ye 13th, spend Sunday there, & proceed to London on Monday, as before intended.—I like the plan, I shall be glad to
see Wrotham.—Harriot is quite as pleasant as ever; we are very comfortable together, & talk over our Nephews & Neices occasionally as
may be supposed, & with much Unanimity—& I really like M^r M.
better than I expected—see less in him to dislike.—

I begin to perceive that you will have this Letter tomorrow. It is
throwing a Letter away to send it by a visitor, there is never convenient
time for reading it—& Visitor can tell most things as well.—I *had*
thought with delight of saving you the postage—but Money is Dirt.—
If *you* do not regret the loss of Oxfordshire & Gloucestershire *I* will
not—tho' I certainly had wished for your going very much. "Whatever
is, is best."—There has been one infallible Pope⁷ in the World.—George
Hatton called yesterday—& I saw him—saw him for 10 minutes—sat
in the same room with him—heard him talk—saw him Bow—& was
not in raptures.⁸—I discerned nothing extraordinary.—I should speak
of him as a Gentlemanlike young Man—eh! bien tout est dit. We are
expecting the Ladies of the Family this morn^g.—

How do you like your flounce?—We have seen only *plain* flounces.—

I hope you have not cut off the train of your Bombasin. I cannot reconcile myself to giving them up as Morning gowns—they are so very sweet by Candle light.—I would rather sacrifice my Blue one for that purpose;—in short, I do not know, & I do not care.—Thursday or Friday are now mentioned from Bath as the day of setting off. The Oxford scheme is given up.—They will go directly to Harefield—Fanny does not go to Fredville, not yet at least. She has had a Letter of excuse from Mary Plumptre to day. The death of Mr Ripley, their uncle by Marriage & M^r P's very old [*p. 4*] friend, prevents their receiving her.— Poor Blind Mrs Ripley must be felt for, if there is any feeling to be had for Love or Money. We have had another of Edward Bridges' Sunday visits.—I think the pleasantest part of his married Life, must be the Dinners & Breakfasts & Luncheons & Billiards that he gets in this way at G^m. Poor Wretch! He is quite the Dregs of the Family as to Luck.—

I long to know whether you are buying Stockings or what you are doing. Remember me most kindly to M^de B. & Mrs Perigord.—You will get acquainted with my friend Mr Philips & hear him talk from Books— & be sure to have something odd happen to you, see somebody that you do not expect, meet with some surprise or other, find some old friend sitting with Henry when you come into the room.—Do something clever in that way.—Edwd & I settled that you went to St Paul's Covent Garden, on Sunday.—Mrs Hill will come & see you—or else she wont come & see you, & will write instead.—I have had a late account from Steventon, & a baddish one, as far as Ben is concerned.— He has declined a [*continued below address panel*] Curacy (apparently highly eligible) which he might have secured against his taking orders—& upon its' being made rather a serious question, says he has not made up his mind as to taking orders so early—& that if her Father makes a point of it, he must give Anna up rather than do what he does not approve.[9]—He must be maddish. They are going on again, at present [*continued upside down at top of p. 1*] as before—but it cannot last.— Mary says that Anna is very unwilling to go to Chawton & will get home again as soon as she can.[10]—Good bye. Accept this indifferent Letter & think it Long & Good.—Miss Clewes is better for some prescription of Mr Scudamores & indeed seems tolerably stout now.—I find time in the midst of Port & Madeira to think of the 14 Bottles of Mead very often.—Yours very affec^ly, J. A.

[*Crossed on p. 1*]

Lady Elizabeth[11] her second Daughter & the two Mrs Finches have just left us.—The two Latter friendly & talking & pleasant as usual.

[*p. 4, upside down*]

Harriot & Fanny's best Love.—

Miss Austen
10, Henrietta Street
Covent Garden
London

[*?Letter missing here*]

95. *To Cassandra Austen*

Wednesday 3 November 1813

Godmersham Park Wednesday Nov:^er 3^d.

My dearest Cassandra

I will keep this celebrated Birthday[1] by writing to you, & as my pen seems inclined to write large I will put my Lines very close together.— I had but just time to enjoy your Letter yesterday before Edward & I set off in the Chair for Cant^y—& I allowed him to hear the cheif of it as we went along. We rejoice sincerely in Henry's gaining ground as he does, & hope there will be weather for him to get out every day this week, as the likeliest way of making him equal to what he plans for the next.—If he is tolerably well, the going into Oxfordshire will make him better, by making him happier.—Can it be, that I have not given you the minutiae of Edward's plans?—See here they are—To go to Wrotham on Saturday ye 13th, spend Sunday there, & be in Town on Monday to dinner, & if agreable to Henry, spend one whole day with him—which day is likely to be Tuesday, & so go down to Chawton on Wednesday.—But now, I cannot be quite easy without staying a little while with Henry, unless he wishes it otherwise;—his illness & the dull time of year together make me feel that it would be horrible of me not to offer to remain with him—& therefore, unless you know[2] of any objection, I wish you would tell him with my best Love that I shall be most happy to spend 10 days or a fortnight in Henrietta S^t—if he will accept me. I do not offer more than a fortnight because I shall then have been some time from home, but it will be a great pleasure to be with him, as it always is.—I have the less regret & scruple on your account, because I shall see you for a day & a half, & because You will have Edward for at least a week.—My scheme is to take Bookham in my way home for a few days & my hope that [*p. 2*] Henry will be so good as to send me some part of the way thither. I have a most kind repetition of Mrs Cooke's two or three dozen Invitations, with the offer of meeting me anywhere in one of her airings.—Fanny's cold is much better. By dosing & keeping her room on Sunday, she got rid of the worst of it, but I am rather afraid of what this day may do for her; she is gone to Cant^y with Miss Clewes, Liz. & Ma. and it is but roughish weather for any one in a tender state.—Miss Clewes has been going to Cant^y ever since her return, & it is now just accomplishing. Edward & I had a delightful morn^g for our Drive *there*, I enjoyed it thoroughly, but the Day turned off before we were ready, & we came home in some rain & the apprehension of a great deal. It has not done us any harm however.—He went to inspect the Gaol, as a visiting Magistrate, & took me with him.—I was gratified—& went through all the feelings which People must go through I think in visiting such a Building.—We paid no other visits—only walked about snugly together & shopp'd.—I bought a Concert Ticket & a sprig of flowers for my old age.—To vary the subject from Gay to Grave with inimitable address I shall now tell you something of the Bath party—& still a Bath party they are, for a fit of the Gout came on last week.—The accounts of Lady B. are as good as can be under such a circumstance, Dr P.-3 says it appears a good sort of Gout, & her spirits are better than usual, but as to her coming away, it is of course all uncertainty.—I have very little doubt of Edward's going down to Bath, if they have not left it when he is in Hampshire; if he does, he will go on from Steventon, & then return direct to London, without coming back to Chawton.—This detention does not suit his feelings.—It may be rather a good thing however that Dr P. should see Lady B. with the Gout on her. Harriot was quite wishing for it.—The day seems to improve. I wish my pen would too.—Sweet Mr Ogle. I dare say he sees all the Panoramas4 for nothing, has free-admittance everywhere; he is so delightful!—Now, you need not see anybody else.—I am glad to hear of our being likely to have a peep at Charles & Fanny at Christmas, but do not force poor Cass. to stay if she hates it.—You have done very right as to Mrs F. A.—Your tidings of S & S. give [*p. 3*] me pleasure. I have never seen it advertised.—Harriot, in a Letter to Fanny today, enquires whether they sell Cloths for Pelisses at Bedford House—& if they do, will be very much obliged to you to desire them to send her down Patterns, with the Width & Prices—they may go from Charing Cross almost any day in the week—but if it is a *ready money* house[5] it will not do, for the Bru of feu the Archbishop[6] says she cannot pay for it immediately.—Fanny & I suspect they do not deal in the Article.—The Sherers I beleive are now really going to go, Joseph has had a Bed here the two last nights, & I do not know whether this is not the day of moving. Mrs Sherer called yesterday to take leave. The weather looks worse again.—We dine at Chilham-Castle tomorrow, & I expect to find some amusement; but more from the Concert the next day, as I am sure of seeing several that I want to see. We are to meet a party from Goodnestone, Lady B.[7] Miss Hawley & Lucy Foote—& I am to meet Mrs Harrison,[8] & we are to talk about Ben & Anna. "My dear Mrs Harrison, I shall say, I am afraid the young Man has some of your Family Madness—& though there often appears to be something of Madness in Anna too, I think she inherits more of it from her Mother's family than from ours—" That is what I shall say—& I think she will find it difficult to answer me.—I took up your Letter again to refresh me, being somewhat tired; & was struck with the prettiness of the hand; it is really a very pretty hand now & then—so small & so neat!—I wish I could get as much into a sheet of paper.—Another time I will take two days to make a Letter in; it is fatigueing to write a whole long one at once. I hope to hear from you again on Sunday & again on friday, the day before we move.—On Monday I suppose you will be going to Streatham, to see quiet Mr Hill & eat very bad Baker's bread.—A fall in Bread by the bye. I hope my Mother's Bill next week will shew it. I have had a very comfortable Letter from her, one of her foolscap sheets quite full of little home news.—Anna was there the first of the two Days—. An Anna sent away & an Anna fetched are different things.—This will be an excellent time for Ben to pay his visit—now that we, the formidables, are absent. I did not mean to eat, but Mr Johncock has brought in the Tray, so I must.—I am all alone. Edward is gone into his Woods.—At this present time I have five Tables, Eight & twenty Chairs & two fires[9] all to myself.—Miss Clewes is to be invited to go to the Concert with us, there will be my Brother's place & ticket for her, as he cannot go. He & the other connections of the Cages are to meet at Milgate [*p. 4*] that very day, to consult about a proposed alteration of the Maidstone road, in which the Cages are very much interested. Sir Brook comes here in the morn^g, & they are to be joined by Mr Deedes at Ashford.—The loss of the Concert will be no great evil to the Squire.—We shall be a party of three Ladies therefore—& to meet three Ladies.—What a convenient Carriage Henry's is, to his friends in general!—Who has it next?—I am glad William's[10] going is voluntary, & on no worse grounds. An inclination for the Country is a venial fault.—He has more of Cowper than of Johnson in him, fonder of Tame Hares & Blank verse than of the full tide of human Existence at Charing Cross.[11]—Oh! I have more of such sweet flattery from Miss Sharp!—She is an excellent kind friend. I am read & admired in Ireland too.—There is a Mrs Fletcher, the wife of a Judge, an old Lady & very good & very clever, who is all curiosity to know about me—what I am like & so forth—. I am not known to her by *name* however. This comes through Mrs Carrick, not through Mrs Gore—You are quite out there.—I do not despair of having my picture in the Exhibition at last—all white & red, with my Head on one Side;[12]— or perhaps I may marry young Mr D'arblay.[13]—I suppose in the mean-time I shall owe dear Henry a great [*continued below address panel*] deal of Money for Printing &c.[14]—I hope Mrs Fletcher will indulge herself with S & S.—If I *am* to stay in H.St & if you should be writing home soon I wish you wd be so good as to give a hint of it—for I am not likely to write there again these 10 days, having written yes[terday].

[*Continued on p. 1, upside down between the lines*]

Fanny has set her heart upon its' being a Mr Brett who is going to marry a Miss Dora Best of this Country. I dare say Henry has no objection. Pray, where did the Boys sleep?—

The Deedes' come here on Monday to stay till friday—so that we shall end with a flourish the last Canto.—They bring Isabella & one of the Grown ups—& will come in for a Canty Ball on Thursday.—I shall be glad to see them.—Mrs Deedes & I must talk rationally together I suppose.

Edward does not write to Henry, because of my writing so often. God bless you. I shall be so glad to see you again, & I wish you many happy returns of this Day.—Poor Lord Howard! How he does cry about it![15]—Yrs very truly,

J. A.

Miss Austen
10, Henrietta Street
Covent Garden
London

96. To Cassandra Austen

Saturday 6–Sunday 7 November 1813

Saturday Novr 6.—Godmersham Park

My dearest Cassandra

Having half an hour before breakfast—(very snug, in my own room, lovely morn^g, excellent fire, fancy me) I will give you some account of the last two days. And yet, what is there to be told?—I shall get foolishly minute unless I cut the matter short.—We met only the Brittons at Chilham Castle, besides a M^r & Mrs Osborne & a Miss Lee staying in the House, & were only 14 altogether. My B^r & Fanny thought it the pleasantest party they had ever known there & I was very well entertained by bits & scraps.—I had long wanted to see Dr Britton, & his wife amuses me very much with her affected refinement & elegance.—Miss Lee I found very conversible; she admires Crabbe as she ought.—She is at an age of reason, ten years older than myself at least. She was at the famous Ball[1] at Chilham Castle, so of course you remember her.—By the bye, as I must leave off being young, I find many Douceurs in being a sort of Chaperon for I am put on the Sofa[2] near the Fire & can drink as much wine as I like. We had Music in the Even^g, Fanny & Miss Wildman played, & Mr James Wildman sat close by & listened, or pretended to listen.—Yesterday was a day of dissipation all through, first came Sir Brook to dissipate us before breakfast—then there was a call from Mr Sherer, then a regular morn^g visit from Lady Honeywood in her way home from Eastwell—then Sir Brook & Edward set off—then we dined (5 in number) at ½ past 4—then we had coffee, & at 6 Miss Clewes, Fanny & I draved away. We had a beautiful night for our frisks.—We were earlier than we need have been, but after a time Lady B. & her two companions appeared, we had kept places for them & there we sat, all six in a row, under a side wall, I between Lucy Foote & Miss Clewes.—Lady B. was much what I expected, I could not determine whether she was rather handsome or very plain.—I liked her, for being in a hurry to have the Concert over & get away, & for getting away at last with a great deal of decision & promtness [sic], not waiting to compliment & dawdle & fuss about seeing *dear Fanny*,[3] who was half the even^g in another part of the room with her friends the Plumptres. I am growing too minute, so I will go to Breakfast. [*p. 2*] When the Concert was over, Mrs Harrison & I found each other out & had a a [sic] very comfortable little complimentary friendly Chat. She is a sweet

Woman, still quite a sweet Woman in herself, & so like her Sister!—I could almost have thought I was speaking to Mrs Lefroy.—She introduced me to her Daughter, whom I think pretty, but most dutifully inferior to La Mere Beauté.[4] The Faggs & the Hammonds were there, Wm Hammond the only young Man of renown. *Miss* looked very handsome, but I prefer her little, smiling, flirting Sister Julia.—I was just introduced at last to Mary Plumptre, but should hardly know her again. She was delighted with *me* however, good Enthusiastic Soul!—And Lady B. found me handsomer than she expected, so you see I am not so very bad as you might think for.—It was 12 before we reached home. We were all dog-tired, but pretty well today, Miss Clewes says she has not caught cold, & Fanny's does not seem worse. I was so tired that I began to wonder how I should get through the Ball next Thursday, but there will be so much more variety then in walking about, & probably so much less heat that perhaps I may not feel it more. My China Crape is still kept for the Ball. Enough of the Concert.—I had a Letter from Mary[5] Yesterday. They travelled down to Cheltenham last Monday very safely & are certainly to be there a month.—Bath is still Bath. The H. Bridges' must quit them early next week, & Louisa seems not quite to despair of their all moving together, but to those who see at a distance there appears no chance of it.—Dr Parry does not want to keep Lady B. at Bath when she can once move. That is lucky.—You will see poor Mr Evelyn's death. Since I wrote last, my 2^d Edit.[6] has stared me in the face.—Mary tells me that Eliza[7] means to buy it. I wish she may. It can hardly depend upon any more Fyfield Estates.[8]—I cannot help hoping that *many* will feel themselves obliged to buy it. I shall not mind imagining it a disagreable Duty to them, so as they do it. Mary heard before she left home, that it was very much admired at Cheltenham, & that it was given to Miss Hamilton.[9] It is pleasant to have such a respectable Writer named. I cannot tire *you* I am sure on this subject, or I would apologise.—What weather! & what news![10]— We have enough to do to admire them both. I hope You derive your full share of enjoyment from each.

[*p. 3*] I have extended my Lights & increased my acquaintance a good deal within these two days. Lady Honeywood, you know;—I did not sit near enough to be a perfect Judge, but I thought her extremely pretty & her manners have all the recommendations of Ease & goodhumour & unaffectedness;—& going about with 4 Horses, & nicely dressed herself—she is altogether a perfect sort of Woman.—Oh! & I saw Mr Gipps last night—the useful Mr Gipps, whose attentions came in as acceptably to us in handing us to the Carriage, for want of a better Man, as they did to Emma Plumptre.—I thought him rather a good looking little Man.—I long for your Letter tomorrow, particularly that I may know my fate as to London. My first wish is that Henry sh^d really chuse what he likes best; I shall certainly not be sorry if he does not want me.—Morning church tomorrow.—I shall come back with impatient feelings. The Sherers are gone, but the Pagets are not come, we shall therefore have Mr S. again. Mr Paget acts like an unsteady Man. Dr Mant however gives him a very good Character; what is wrong is to be imputed to the Lady.—I dare say the House likes Female Government.— I have a nice long Black & red letter[11] from Charles, but not communicating much that I did not know. There is some chance of a good Ball next week, as far as Females go. Lady Bridges may perhaps be there with some Knatchbulls—Mrs Harrison perhaps with Miss Oxenden & the Miss Papillons—& if Mrs Harrison, then Lady Fagg will come. The shades of Evening are descending & I resume my interesting Narrative. Sir Brook & my Brother came back about 4, & Sir Brook almost immediately set forward again for Goodnestone.—We are to have Edwd B. tomorrow, to pay us another Sunday's visit—the last, for more reasons than one; they all come home on the same day that we go.—The Deedes' do not come till Tuesday. Sophia is to be the Comer. She is a disputable Beauty that I want much to see. Lady Eliz. Hatton & Annamaria called here this morn^g;—Yes, they called,—but I do not think I can say anything more about them. They came & they sat & they went. Sunday.—Dearest Henry! What a turn he has for being ill! & what a thing Bile is!—This attack has probably been brought on in part by his previous confinement & anxiety;—but however it came, I hope it is going fast, & that you will be able to send a very good account of him on Tuesday.—As I hear on Wednesday, of course I shall not expect to hear again on friday. Perhaps a Letter to Wrotham would not have an ill effect. We are to be off on Saturday before the Post comes in, as Edward takes his own Horses all the way. He talks of 9 o'clock. We shall bait at Lenham. [*p. 4*] Excellent sweetness of you to send me such a nice long Letter;—it made its appearance, with one from my Mother, soon after I & my impatient feelings walked in.—How glad I am that I did what I did!—I was only afraid that *you* might think the offer superfluous, but you have set my heart at ease.—Tell Henry that I *will* stay with him, let it be ever so disagreable to him. Oh! dear me!—I have not time or paper for half that I want to say.—There have been two Letters from Oxford, one from George yesterday. They got there very safely, Edwd two hours behind the Coach, having lost his way in leaving London. George writes chearfully & quietly—hopes to have Utterson's rooms soon, went to Lecture on wednesday, states some of his expences, & concludes with saying, "I am afraid I shall be poor."— I am glad he thinks about it so soon.—I beleive there is no private Tutor yet chosen, but my Brother is to hear from Edwd on the subject shortly.—You, & Mrs H.^{12} & Catherine & Alethea going about together in Henry's carriage, seeing sights!—I am not used to the idea of it yet. All that you are to see of Streatham, seen already!—Your Streatham & my Bookham may go hang.—The prospect of being taken down to Chawton by Henry, perfects the plan to me.—I was in hopes of your seeing some illuminations, & you *have* seen them. "I thought you would came, & you *did* came."^{13} I am sorry *he* is not to *came* from the Baltic sooner.—Poor Mary!—My Brother has a Letter from Louisa today, of an unwelcome nature;—they are to spend the winter at Bath!—It was just decided on.—Dr Parry wished it,—not from thinking the Water necessary to Lady B.—but that he might be better able to judge how far his Treatment of her, which is totally different from anything she had been used to—is right; & I [*continued below address panel*] suppose he will not mind having a few more of her Ladyship's guineas.—His system is a Lowering one. He took twelve ounces of Blood from her when the Gout appeared, & forbids Wine &c.—Hitherto, the plan agrees with her.—*She* is very well satisfied to stay, but it is a sore disappointment to Louisa & Fanny.—

[*Continued upside down at the top of p. 1*]

The H. Bridges leave them on Tuesday, & they mean to move into a smaller House. You may guess how Edward feels.—There can be no doubt of his going to Bath now;—I should not wonder if he brought Fanny Cage back with him.—You shall hear from me once more, some day or other.

Yours very affec:^{ly}

J. A.

We do not like Mr Hampson's scheme.^{14}

Miss Austen
10, Henrietta Street
Covent Garden
London

[*Letter missing here*]

97. *To Cassandra Austen*

Wednesday 2–Thursday 3 March 1814

Henrietta St Wednesday March 2^d

My dear Cassandra

You were wrong in thinking of us at Guildford last night, we were at Cobham. On reaching G. we found that John[1] & the Horses were gone on. We therefore did no more there than we had done at Farnham, sit in the Carriage while fresh Horses were put in, & proceeded directly to Cobham, which we reached by 7, & about 8 were sitting down to a very nice roast fowl &c.—We had altogether a very good Journey, & everything at Cobham was comfortable.—I could not pay Mr Herington!—That was the only alas! of the Business. I shall therefore return his Bill & my Mother's £2.—that you may try your Luck.—We did not begin reading[2] till Bentley Green. Henry's approbation hitherto is even equal to my wishes; he says it is very different from the other two, but does not appear[3] to think it at all inferior. He has only married Mrs R. I am afraid he has gone through the most entertaining part.— He took to Lady B. & Mrs N. most kindly, & gives great praise to the drawing of the Characters. He understands them all, likes Fanny & I think foresees how it will all be.—I finished the Heroine[4] last night & was very much amused by it. I wonder James did not like it better. It diverted me exceedingly.—We went to bed at 10. I was very tired, but slept to a miracle & am lovely today; & at present Henry seems to have no complaint. We left Cobham at ½ past 8, stopt to bait & breakfast at Kingston & were in this House considerably before 2—quite in the stile of Mr Knight. [*p. 2*] Nice smiling Mr Barlowe met us at the door, & in reply to enquiries after News, said that Peace was generally expected.—I have taken possession of my Bedroom, unpacked my Bandbox, sent Miss P.'s[5] two Letters to the twopenny post, been visited by M^{de} B.,—& am now writing by myself at the new Table in the front room. It is snowing.—We had some Snowstorms yesterday, & a smart frost at night, which gave us a hard road from Cobham to Kingston; but as it was then getting dirty & heavy, Henry had a pair of Leaders put on from the latter place to the bottom of Sloane S^t.—His own Horses therefore cannot have had hard work.—I watched for *Veils* as we drove through the Streets, & had the pleasure of seeing several upon vulgar heads.—And now, how do you all do? You in particular after the worry of yesterday & the day before. I hope Martha had a pleasant visit again,

255

& that You & my Mother could eat your Beefpudding. Depend upon my thinking of the Chimney Sweeper as soon as I wake tomorrow.— Places are secured at Drury Lane for Saturday, but so great is the rage for seeing Keen[6] that only a 3^d & 4th row could be got. As it is in a front box however, I hope we shall do pretty well.—Shylock.—A good play for Fanny. She cannot be much affected I think.—Mrs Perigord has just been here. I have paid her a Shilling for the Willow.[7] She tells me that we owe her Master for the Silk-dyeing.—My poor old Muslin has never been dyed yet; it has been promised to be done several times.—What wicked People Dyers are. They begin with dipping their own Souls in scarlet sin.—Tell my Mother that my £6.15. was duly received, but placed to *my* account instead of hers, & I have just signed a something which makes it over to her. [*p. 3*] It is Even^g. We have drank tea & I have torn through the 3^d vol. of the Heroine, & do not think it falls off.—It is a delightful burlesque, particularly on the Radcliffe style.— Henry is going on with Mansfield Park; he admires H. Crawford—I mean properly—as a clever, pleasant Man.—I tell you all the Good I can, as I know how much you will enjoy it.—

John Warren & his wife are invited to dine here, to name their own day in the next fortnight.—I do not expect them to come.—Wyndham Knatchbull is to be asked for Sunday, & if he is cruel enough to consent, somebody must be contrived to meet him.—We hear that Mr Keen is more admired than ever. The two vacant places of our two rows, are likely to be filled by Mr Tilson & his Brother Genl Chownes.— I shall be ready to laugh at the sight of Frederick[8] again.—It seems settled that I have the carriage on friday to pay visits, I have therefore little doubt of being able to get to Miss Hares. I am to call upon Miss Spencer: Funny me!—

There are no good Places to be got in Drury Lane for the next fortnight, but Henry means to secure some for Saturday fortnight when You are reckoned upon.—

I wonder what worse thing than Sarah Mitchell You are forced upon by this time!—Give my Love to little Cassandra,[9] I hope she found my Bed comfortable last night & has not filled it with fleas.—I have seen nobody in London yet with such a long chin as Dr Syntax,[10] nor [*p. 4*] Anybody quite so large as Gogmagoglicus.[11]—Yours affec^{ly}

J. Austen

Thursday
My Trunk did not come last night, I suppose it will this morn^g; if not I must borrow Stockings & buy Shoes & Gloves for my visit. I was

foolish not to provide better against such a Possibility. I have great hope however that writing about it in this way, will bring the Trunk presently.—

Miss Austen
Chawton
P^r favor of
E. W. Gray Esqre

98. *To Cassandra Austen*

Saturday 5–Tuesday 8 March 1814

Henrietta St Saturday March 5.

My dear Cassandra

Do not be angry with me for beginning another Letter to you. I have read the Corsair,[1] mended my petticoat, & have nothing else to do.— Getting out is impossible. It is a nasty day for everybody. Edward's spirits will be wanting Sunshine, & here is nothing but Thickness & Sleet; and tho' these two rooms are delightfully warm I fancy it is very cold abroad.—Young Wyndham[2] accepts the Invitation. He is such a nice, gentlemanlike, unaffected sort of young Man, that I think he may do for Fanny;—has a sensible, quiet look which one likes.—Our fate with Mrs L. & Miss E.[3] is fixed for this day senight.—A civil note is come from Miss H. Moore,[4] to apologise for not returning my visit today & ask us to join a small party this Even^g—Thank ye, but we shall be better engaged.—I was speaking to M^de B. this morn^g about a boil'd Loaf, when it appeared that her Master has no raspberry Jam; *She* has some, which of course she is determined he shall have; but cannot you bring him a pot when you come?—

Sunday.—I find a little time before breakfast for writing.—It was considerably past 4 when they arrived yesterday; the roads were so very bad!—as it was, they had 4 Horses from Cranford Bridge. Fanny was miserably cold at first, but they both seem well.—No possibility of Edwd's writing. His opinion however inclines *against* a second prosecution;[5] he thinks it w^d be a vindictive measure. He might think differently perhaps on the spot.—But things must take their chance.—

We were quite satisfied with Kean. I cannot imagine better acting, but the part was too short, & excepting him & Miss Smith, & *she* did not quite answer my expectation, the parts were ill filled & the Play heavy. [*p. 2*] We were too much tired to stay for the whole of Illusion[6] (Nourjahad) which has 3 acts;—there is a great deal of finery &

dancing in it, but I think little merit. Elliston was Nourjahad, but it is
a solemn sort of part, not at all calculated for his powers. There was
nothing of the *best Elliston* about him. I might not have known him, but
for his voice.—A grand thought has struck me as to our Gowns. This
6 weeks mourning[7] makes so great a difference that I shall not go to
Miss Hare, till you can come & help chuse yourself; unless you particularly wish the contrary.—It may be hardly worthwhile perhaps to have
the Gowns so expensively made up; we may buy a cap or a *veil* instead;—but we can talk more of this together.—Henry is just come
down, he seems well, his cold does not increase. I expected to have
found Edward seated at a table writing to Louisa, but I was first.—
Fanny I left fast asleep.—She was doing about last night, when *I* went
to sleep, a little after one.—I am most happy to find there were but *five*
shirts.—She thanks you for your note, & reproaches herself for not
having written to you, but I assure her there was no occasion.—The
accounts are not capital of Lady B.—Upon the whole I beleive Fanny
liked Bath very well. They were only out three Evengs;—to one Play
& each of the Rooms;—Walked about a good deal, & saw a good deal
of the Harrisons & Wildmans.—All the Bridgeses are likely to come
away together, & Louisa will probably turn off at Dartford to go to
Harriot.—Edward is quite [*about five words cut out*].—Now we are come
from Church, & all going to write.—Almost everybody was in mourning last night, but my brown gown did very well. Gen:l Chowne was
introduced to me; he has not much remains of Frederick.—This young
Wyndham does not come after all; a very long & very civil note of
excuse is arrived. It makes one moralize upon the ups & downs of this
Life. [*p. 3*] I have determined to trim my lilac sarsenet with black sattin
ribbon just as my China Crape is, 6d width at bottom, 3d or 4d at top.—
Ribbon trimmings are all the fashion at Bath, & I dare say the fashions
of the two places are alike enough in that point, to content *me*.—With
this addition it will be a very useful gown, happy to go anywhere.—
Henry has this moment said that he likes my M. P. better & better;—
he is in the 3d vol.—I beleive *now* he has changed his mind as to fore-
seeing the end;—he said yesterday at least, that he defied anybody to
say whether H. C. would be reformed, or would forget Fanny in a
fortnight.—I shall like to see Kean again excessively, & to see him with
You too;—it appeared to me as if there were no fault in him anywhere;
& in his scene with Tubal there was exquisite acting. Edward has had
a correspondence with Mr Wickham on the Baigent business, & has
been shewing me some Letters enclosed by Mr W. from a friend of his,

a Lawyer, whom he had consulted about it, & whose opinion is *for* the prosecution for assault, supposing the Boy is acquitted on the first, which he rather expects.—Excellent Letters; & I am sure he must be an excellent Man. They are such thinking, clear, considerate Letters as Frank might have written. I long to know Who he is, but the name is always torn off. He was consulted only as a friend.—When Edwd gave me *his* opinion against the 2^d prosecution, he had not read this Letter, which was waiting for him here.—Mr W. is to be on the Grand Jury. This business must hasten an Intimacy between his family & my Brother's.— Fanny cannot answer your question about button holes till she gets home.—I have never told you, but soon after Henry & I began our Journey, he said, talking of Yours, that he sh^d desire you to come post at his expence, & added something of the Carriage meeting you at Kingston. He has said nothing about it since.—Now I have just read Mr Wickham's Letter, by which it appears that the Letters of his friend were sent to my Brother quite confidentially—therefore do'nt tell. By his expression, this friend must be one of the Judges. [*p. 4*] A cold day, but bright & clean.—I am afraid your planting can hardly have be- gun.—I am sorry to hear that there has been a rise in tea. I do not mean to pay Twining till later in the day, when we may order a fresh sup- ply.—I long to know something of the Mead—& how you are off for a Cook.—*Monday.* Here's a day!—The Ground covered with snow! What is to become of us?—We were to have walked out early to near Shops, & had the Carriage for the more distant.—Mr Richard Snow[8] is dreadfully fond of us. I dare say he has stretched himself out at Chawton too.—Fanny & I went into the Park yesterday & drove about & were very much entertained;—and our Dinner & Even^g went off very well.— Messrs J. Plumptre & J. Wildman called while we were out; & we had a glimpse of them both & of G. Hatton too in the Park. *I* could not produce a single acquaintance.—By a little convenient Listening, I now know that Henry wishes to go to G^m for a few days before Easter, & has indeed promised to do it.—This being the case, there can be no time for your remaining in London after your return from Adlestrop.— You must not put off your coming therefore;—and it occurs to me that instead of my coming here again from Streatham, it will be better for you to join me there.—It is a great comfort to have got at the truth.— Henry finds he cannot set off for Oxfordshire before the Wednes^y which will be ye 23^d; but we shall not have too many days together here previously.—I shall write to Catherine[9] very soon. Well, we have been out, as far as Coventry S^t—; Edwd escorted us there & back to

Newtons, where he left us, & I brought Fanny safe home. It was snowing the whole time. We have given up all idea of the Carriage. Edward & Fanny stay another day, & both seem very well pleased to do so.— Our visit to the Spencers is of course put off.—Edwd heard from Louisa this morn^g. Her Mother does not get better, & Dr Parry talks of her beginning the Waters again; this [*p. 5*] will be keeping them longer in Bath, & of course is not palateable. You cannot think how much my Ermine Tippet is admired both by Father & Daughter. It was a noble Gift.—Perhaps you have not heard that[10] Edward has a good chance of escaping his Lawsuit.[11] His opponent "knocks under." The terms of Agreement are not quite settled.—We are to see "the Devil to pay"[12] to night. I expect to be very much amused.—Excepting Miss Stephens, I dare say Artaxerxes[13] will be very tiresome.—A great many pretty Caps in the Windows of Cranbourn Alley!—I hope when you come, we shall both be tempted.—I have been ruining myself in black sattin ribbon with a proper perl edge; & now I am trying to draw it up into kind of Roses, instead of putting it in plain double plaits.—Tuesday. My dearest Cassandra in ever so many hurries I acknowledge the receipt of your Letter last night, just before we set off for Covent Garden.—I have no Mourning come, but it does not signify. This very moment has Rich^d[14] put it on the Table.—I have torn it open & read your note. Thank you, thank you, thank you.—

Edwd is amazed at the 64 Trees. He desires his Love & gives you notice of the arrival of a Study Table for himself. It ought to be at Chawton this week. He begs you to be so good as to have it enquired for,[15] & fetched by the Cart; but wishes it not to be unpacked till he is on the spot himself. It may be put in the Hall.—Well, Mr Hampson dined here & all that. I was very tired of Artaxerxes, highly amused with the Farce, & in an inferior way with the Pantomime that followed. Mr J. Plumptre joined in the latter part of the Even^g—walked home with us, ate some soup, & is very earnest for our going to [*p. 6*] Cov. Gar. again to night to see Miss Stephens in the Farmers Wife.[16] He is to try for a Box. I do not particularly wish him to succeed. I have had enough for the present.—Henry dines to day with Mr Spencer.—

Yours very affec^ly
J. Austen

Miss Austen
Chawton
By favour of
Mr Gray

99. *To Cassandra Austen*

Wednesday 9 March 1814

Henrietta St Wednesday March 9.

Well, we went to the Play again last night, & as we were out great part of the morning too, shopping & seeing the Indian Jugglers,¹ I am very glad to be quiet now till dressing time. We are to dine at the Tilsons & tomorrow at Mr Spencers.—We had not done breakfast yesterday when Mr J. Plumptre appeared to say that he had secured a Box. Henry asked him to dine here, which I fancy he was very happy to do; & so, at 5 o'clock we four sat down to table together, while the Master of the House was preparing for going out himself.—The Farmer's Wife is a Musical thing in 3 Acts, & as Edward was steady in not staying for anything more, we were at home before 10—Fanny & Mr J. P. are delighted with Miss S, & her merit in singing is I dare say very great; that she gave *me* no pleasure is no reflection upon her, nor I hope upon myself, being what Nature made me on that article. All that I am sensible of in Miss S. is, a pleasing person & no skill in acting.—We had Mathews, Liston & Emery;² of course some amusement.—Our friends were off before ½ past 8 this morn^g, & had the prospect of a heavy cold Journey before them.—I think they both liked their visit very much, I am sure Fanny did.—Henry sees decided attachment³ between her & his new acquaintance.—[*p. 2*] I have a cold too as well as my Mother & Martha. Let it be a generous emulation between us which can get rid of it first.—I wear my gauze gown today, long sleeves & all; I shall see how they succeed, but as yet I have no reason to suppose long sleeves are allowable.—I have lowered the bosom especially at the corners, & plaited black sattin ribbon round the top. Such will be my Costume of Vine leaves & paste. Prepare for a Play the very first evening, I rather think Covent Garden, to see Young in Richard.⁴—I have answered for your little companion's⁵ being conveyed to Keppel S^t immediately.—I have never yet been able to get there myself, but hope I shall soon. What cruel weather this is! And here is Lord Portsmouth married too to Miss Hanson!⁶—Henry has finished Mansfield Park, & his approbation has not lessened. He found the last half of the last volume *extremely interesting*. I suppose my Mother recollects that she gave me no Money for paying Brecknell & Twining; & *my* funds will not supply enough.—

We are home in such good time that I can finish my Letter to night,⁷ which will be better than getting up to do it tomorrow, especially as on account of my Cold, which has been very heavy in my head this Even^g —I rather think of lying in bed later than usual. I would not but be well enough to go to Hertford S^t on any account.—We met only Genl Chowne today, [*p. 3*] who has not much to say for himself.—I was ready to laugh at the remembrance of Frederick, & such a different Frederick as we chose to fancy him to the real Christopher!—Mrs Tilson had long sleeves too, & she assured me that they are worn in the evening by many. I was glad to hear this.—She dines here I beleive next tuesday.—

On friday we are to be snug, with only Mr Barlowe & an evening of Business.—I am so pleased that the Mead is brewed!—Love to all. If Cassandra has filled my Bed with fleas, I am sure they must bite herself.—

I have written to Mrs Hill & care for nobody.

Yours affec^ly
J. Austen

Miss Austen
Chawton
By favor of
Mr Gray.—

100. *To ?Francis Austen*

Monday 21 March 1814

Henrietta St Monday March 21.

[*Main text of p. 1 missing*]

[*top of p. 2*] . . . and only just time enough for what is to be done. And all this, with very few acquaintance in Town & going to no Parties & living very quietly!—What do People do that . . .

[*Remainder of letter missing; postscript upside down at top of p. 1*]

Perhaps before the end of April, *Mansfield Park* by the author of S & S.—P. & P. may be in the World.—Keep the *name* to yourself. I sh^d not like to have it known beforehand. God bless you.—Cassandra's best Love. Yours affec:^ly

J. Austen

101. *To Cassandra Austen*

Tuesday 14 June 1814

Chawton Tuesday June 13. [*sic*]

My dearest Cassandra

Fanny takes my Mother to Alton this morn^g which gives me an op-portunity of sending you a few lines, without any other trouble[1] than that of writing them. This is a delightful day in the Country, & I hope not much too hot for Town.—Well, you had a good Journey I trust & all that;—& not rain enough to spoil your Bonnet.—It appeared so likely to be a wet even^g that I went up to the G^t House between 3 & 4, & dawdled away an hour[2] very comfortably, tho' Edwd was not very brisk. The air was clearer in the Even^g & he was better.—We all five walked together into the Kitchen Garden & along the Gosport Road, & they drank tea with us.—You will be glad to hear that G. Turner has another *situation*—something in the Cow Line near Rumsey, & he wishes to move immediately, which is not likely to be inconvenient to anybody. The new Nursery Man at Alton comes this morn^g, to value the Crops in the Garden.—

The only Letter to day is from Mrs Cooke to me. They do not leave home till July & want me to come to them according to my promise.— And after considering everything, I have resolved on going. My com-panions promote it.—I will not go however till after Edward is gone, that he may feel he has a somebody to give Memorandums to, to the last;—I must give up all help from his Carriage of course.—And at any rate it must be such an Excess of Expense that I have quite made up my mind to it, & do not mean to care. [*p. 2*] I have been thinking of Triggs & the Chair you may be sure, but I know it will end in Posting. They will meet me at Guilford.—In addition to their standing claims on me, they admire Mansfield Park exceedingly. Mr Cooke says "it is the most sensible Novel he ever read"—and the manner in which I treat the Clergy, delights them very much.—Altogether I must go—& I want you to join me there when your visit in Henrietta S^t is over. Put this, into your capacious Head.—

Take care of yourself, & do not be trampled to death in running after the Emperor.[3] The report in Alton yesterday was that they w^d certainly travel this road either to, or from Portsmouth.—I long to know what this Bow of the Prince's will produce.—

I saw Mrs Andrews yesterday. Mrs Browning had seen her before. She is very glad to send an Elizabeth.—

Miss Benn continues the same.—Mr Curtis however saw her yesterday & said her hand was going on as well as possible.—Accept our best Love.—

Yours very affec:^ly
J. Austen

Miss Austen
10, Henrietta Street
By favour of
Mr Gray—

[*? Letters missing here*]

102. *To Cassandra Austen*

Thursday 23 June 1814

Thursday June 23.

Dearest Cassandra

I received your pretty Letter while the Children were drinking tea[1] with us, as Mr Louch was so obliging as to walk over with it. Your good account of every body made us very happy.—I heard yesterday from Frank; when he began his Letter he hoped to be here on Monday, but before it was ended he had been told that the Naval Review w^d not take place till Friday, which w^d probably occasion him some delay, as he cannot get some necessary business of his own attended to, while Portsmouth is in such a bustle. I hope Fanny has seen the Emperor, & then I may fairly wish them all away.—I go tomorrow, & hope for some delays & adventures.—My Mother's Wood is brought in—but by some mistake, no Bavins.[2] She must therefore buy some.—

Henry at Whites![3]—Oh! what a Henry.—I do not know what to wish as to Miss B,[4] so I will hold my tongue & my wishes.

Sackree & the Children set off yesterday & have not been returned back upon us. They were all very well the Evening before.—We had handsome [*p. 2*] presents from the G^t House yesterday, a Ham & the 4 Leeches.—Sackree has left some shirts of her Master's at the School,

which finished or unfinished she begs to have sent by Henry & W^m.—
Mr Hinton is expected home soon, which is a good thing for the Shirts.—
We have called upon Miss Dusautoy & Miss Papillon & been very
pretty.—Miss D. has a great idea of being Fanny Price, she & her
youngest sister together, who is named Fanny.—Miss Benn has drunk
tea with the Prowtings, & I beleive comes to us this even^g. She has still
a swelling⁵ about the fore-finger, & a little discharge, & does not seem
to be on the point of a perfect cure; but her Spirits are good—& she
will be most happy I beleive to accept any Invitation.—The Clements
are gone to Petersfield, to look.—

Only think of the Marquis of Granby⁶ being dead. I hope, if it please
Heaven there should be another Son, they will have better Sponsors &
less Parade.

I certainly do not *wish* that Henry should think again of getting me
to Town. I would rather return straight from Bookham; but if he really
does propose it, I cannot say No, to what will be so kindly intended. It
could be but for a few days however, as my [*p. 3*] Mother would be
quite disappointed by my exceeding the fortnight which I now talk of
as the outside;—at least we could not both remain longer away comfortably.—The middle of July is Martha's time, as far as she has any
time. She has left it to Mrs Craven to fix the day.—I wish she could get
her Money paid, for I fear her going at all, depends upon that.—Instead
of Bath, the Deans Dundases have taken a House at Clifton,—Richmond Terrace—& she is as glad of the change as even You & I should
be—or almost.—She will now be able to go on from Berks & visit
them, without any fears from Heat.—This Post has brought me a Letter
from Miss Sharpe. Poor thing! she has been suffering indeed! but is now
in a comparative state of comfort. She is at Sir W. P.'s, in Yorkshire,⁷
with the Children, & there is no appearance of her quitting them.—Of
course, we lose the pleasure of seeing her here. She writes highly of Sir
W^m—I do so want him to marry her!—There is a Dow: Lady P. pre-
siding there, to make it all right.—The *Man* is the same; but she does
not mention what he is by Profession or Trade.—She does not think
Lady P. was privy to his Scheme on her; but on being in his power,
yielded.—Oh! Sir W^m—Sir W^m—how [*p. 4*] I will love you, if you
will love Miss Sharp!—Mrs Driver &c are off by Collier; but so near
being too late that she had not time to call & leave the Keys herself.—
I have them however;—I suppose, one is the Key of the Linen Press—
but I do not [know *omitted*] what to guess the other.—

The Coach was stopt at the Blacksmith's, & they came running down, with Triggs, & Browning, & Trunks & Bird cages. Quite amusing! My Mother desires her Love & hopes to hear from you.

Yours very affec:^{ly}

J. Austen

[*Postscript upside down at top of p. 1*]

Frank & Mary are to have Mary Goodchild to help as *Under*,[8] till they can get a Cook. *She* is delighted to go.—

[*Second postscript below address panel*]

Best Love at Streatham.

Miss Austen
Henrietta S^t
By favour of
Mr Gray.

[*?Letters missing here*]

---

103. *To Anna Austen*

?mid-July 1814[1]

[*First leaf, pp. 1 and 2, missing*]

    [*p. 3*] . . . I am pretty well in health and work a good deal in the Garden, but for these last 3 or 4 weeks have had weakness in my Eyes; it was well for you it did not come sooner, for I could not now make petticoats, Pockets & dressing Gowns for any *Bride expectant*—I can not wear my spectacles, and therefore can do hardly any work but knitting *white* yarn and platting *white* willow. I write & read without spectacles, and therefore do but little of either—We have a good appearance of Flowers in the Shrubbery and borders, & what is still better, a very good crop of small Fruit, even your Goosberry [*sic*] Tree does better than heretofore, when the Gooseberries are ripe I shall sit upon my Bench, eat them & think of you, tho I can do that without the assistance of ripe gooseberries; indeed, my dear Anna, there is noboddy [*sic*] I think of oftener, very few I love better,—My Eyes are tired so I must quit you—Farewell.

Y^r affect. G: M:

C. Austen

[*p. 4*]

My dear Anna—I am very much obliged to you for sending your MS.[2] It has entertained me extremely, all of us indeed; I read it aloud to your G. M.—& A^t C.—and we were all very much pleased.—The Spirit does not droop at all. Sir Tho:—Lady Helena, & St Julian are very well done—& Cecilia continues to be interesting inspite of her being so amiable.—It was very fit that you should advance her age. I like the beginning of D. Forester very much—a great deal better than if he had been very Good or very Bad.—A few verbal corrections were all that I felt tempted to make—the principal of them is a speech of St Julians to Lady Helena—which you will see I have presumed to alter.—As Lady H. is Cecilia's superior, it w^d not be correct to talk of *her* being introduced; Cecilia must be the person introduced—And I do not like a Lover's speaking in the 3^d person;—it is too much like the formal part of Lord Orville,[3] & I think is not natural. If *you* think differently however, you need not mind me.—I am impatient for more—& only wait for a safe conveyance to return this Book.—Yours affec^{ly}, J. A.

Miss Austen
Steventon

104. *To Anna Austen*

Wednesday 10–Thursday 18 August 1814

Chawton Wednesday Aug: 10.

My dear Anna

I am quite ashamed to find that I have never answered some questions of yours in a former note.—I kept the note on purpose to refer to it at a proper time, & then forgot it.—I like the name "Which is the Heroine?" very well, & I dare say shall grow to like it very much in time—but "Enthusiasm"[1] was something so very superior that every common Title must appear to disadvantage.—I am not sensible of any Blunders about Dawlish. The Library was particularly pitiful & wretched 12 years ago, & not likely to have anybody's publication.—There is no such Title as Desborough[2]—either among the Dukes, Marquisses, Earls,

Viscounts or Barons.—These were your enquiries.—I will now thank
you for your Envelope, received this morning.—I hope Mr W. D. will
come.—I can readily imagine Mrs H. D.^{3} may be very like a profligate
Young Lord—I dare say the likeness will be "beyond every thing"—
Your Aunt Cass:—is as well pleased with St Julian as ever. I am delighted with the idea of seeing Progillian again.

Wednesday 17.—We have just finished the 1st of the 3 Books I had
the pleasure of receiving yesterday; *I* read it aloud—& we are all very
much amused, & like the work quite as well as ever.—I depend upon
getting [*p. 2*] through another book before dinner, but there is really a
great deal of respectable reading in your 48 Pages. I was an hour about
it.—I have no doubt that *6* will make a very good sized volume.—You
must be quite pleased to have accomplished so much.—I like Lord P.-
& his Brother very much;—I am only afraid that Lord P.-'s good nature will make most people like him better than he deserves.—The
whole Portman Family^4 are very good—& Lady Anne, who was your
great dread, you have succeeded particularly well with.—Bell Griffin is
just what she should be.— My Corrections have not been more important than before;—here & there, we have thought the sense might be
expressed in fewer words—and I have scratched out Sir Tho: from
walking with the other Men to the Stables &c the very day after his
breaking his arm—for though I find your Papa *did* walk out immediately after *his* arm was set, I think it can be so little usual as to *appear*
unnatural in a book—& it does not seem to be material that Sir Tho:
should go with them.—Lyme will not do. Lyme is towards 40 miles
distance from Dawlish & would not be talked of there.—I have put
Starcross indeed.—If you prefer *Exeter*, that must be always safe.—I
have also scratched out the Introduction between Lord P. & his Brother,
& Mr Griffin. [*p. 3*] A Country Surgeon (dont tell Mr C. Lyford) would
not be introduced to Men of their rank.—And when Mr Portman is first
brought in, he w^d not be introduced as *the Honble—That* distinction is
never mentioned at such times;—at least I beleive not.—Now, we have
finished the 2^d book—or rather the 5th—I *do* think you had better omit
Lady Helena's postscript;—to those who are acquainted with P. & P it
will seem an Imitation.—And your Aunt C. & I both recommend your
making a little alteration in the last scene between Devereux F. & Lady
Clanmurray & her Daughter. We think they press him too much—
more than sensible Women or well-bred Women would do. *Lady C.* at
least, should have discretion enough to be sooner satisfied with his
determination of not going with them.—I am very much pleased with

Egerton as yet.—I did not expect to like him, but I do; & Susan is a very nice little animated Creature—but St Julian is the delight of one's Life. He is quite interesting.—The whole of his Break-off with Lady H. is very well done.—

Yes—Russel Square is a very proper distance from Berkeley S^t—We are reading the last book.—They must be *two* days going from Dawlish to Bath; They are nearly 100 miles apart.[5]

Thursday. We finished it last night, after our return from drinking tea at the G^t House.—The last Chapter does not please us quite so well, we do not thoroughly like the *Play*; perhaps from having had too much of Plays in that way lately.—And we think you had better not leave England. Let the Portmans go to Ireland, but as you know nothing of the Manners there, you had better not go with them. You will be in danger of giving false representations. Stick [*p. 4*] to Bath & the Foresters. There you will be quite at home.—Your Aunt C. does not like desultory novels, & is rather fearful yours will be too much so, that there will be too frequent a change from one set of people[6] to another, & that circumstances will be sometimes introduced of apparent consequence, which will lead to nothing.—It will not be so great an objection to *me*, if it does. I allow much more Latitude than She does—& think Nature & Spirit cover many sins of a wandering story—and People in general do not care so much about it—for your comfort. I should like to have had more of Devereux. I do not feel enough acquainted with him.— You were afraid of meddling with him I dare say.—I like your sketch of Lord Clanmurray, and your picture of the two poor young girls enjoyments is very good.—I have not yet noticed St Julian's serious conversation with Cecilia, but I liked it exceedingly;—what he says about the madness of otherwise sensible Women, on the subject of their Daughters coming out, is worth its' weight in gold.—I do not see that the language sinks. Pray go on.

Yours very affec:^ly J. Austen

[Postscript below address panel]

Twice you have put Dorsetshire for Devonshire. I have altered it.— Mr Griffin must have lived in Devonshire; Dawlish is half way down the County.—

[Second postscript upside down at top of p. 1]

These bits of Irish belong to you.—They have been in my work bag ever since You were here, & I think they may as well go to their right owner.

Miss Austen.

---

105. *To Cassandra Austen*

Tuesday 23—Wednesday 24 August 1814[1]

23 Hans Place, Tuesday Morn[g]

My dear Cassandra

I had a very good Journey, not crouded, two of the three taken up at Bentley being Children, the others of a reasonable size; & they were all very quiet & civil.—We were late in London, from being a great Load & from changing Coaches at Farnham, it was nearly 4 I beleive when we reached Sloane S[t]; Henry himself met me, & as soon as my Trunk & Basket could be routed out from all the other Trunks & Baskets in the World, we were on our way to Hans Place in the Luxury of a nice large cool dirty Hackney Coach. There were 4 in the Kitchen part of Yalden—& I was told 15 at top, among them Percy Benn; we met in the same room at Egham, but poor Percy was not in his usual Spirits. He would be more chatty I dare say in his way *from* Woolwich.[2] We took up a young Gibson at Holybourn; & in short everybody either *did* come up by Yalden yesterday, or wanted to come up. It put me in mind of my own Coach[3] between Edinburgh & Sterling.—Henry is very well, & has given me an account of the Canterbury Races, which seem to have been as pleasant as one could wish. Everything went well. Fanny had good Partners, M[r] J. P.[4] was her 2[d] on Thursday, but he did not dance with her any more.—This will content you for the present. I must just add however that there were no Lady Charlottes,[5] they were gone off to Kirby—& that Mary Oxenden, instead of dieing, is going to marry W[m] Hammond.—

No James & Edward yet.—Our evening yesterday was perfectly quiet; we only talked a little to M[r] Tilson across the intermediate Gardens; *she* was gone out airing with Miss Burdett.—It is a delightful Place[6]—more than answers my expectation. [*p. 2*] Having got rid of my unreasonable ideas, I find more space & comfort in the rooms than I had supposed, & the Garden is quite a Love. I am in the front Attic, which is the Bedchamber to be preferred. Henry wants you to see it all, & asked whether you w^d return with him from Hampshire; I encouraged him to think you would. He breakfasts here, early, & then rides to Henrietta S^t—If it continues fine, John is to drive me there by & bye, & we shall take an Airing together; & I do not mean to take any other exercise, for I feel a little tired after my long Jumble.—I live in his room downstairs, it is particularly pleasant, from opening upon the garden. I go & refresh myself every now & then, and then come back to Solitary Coolness.—There is *one* maid servant only, a very creditable, cleanlooking young Woman. Richard remains for the present.—

Wednesday Morn^g—My Brother & Edwd arrived last night.—They c^d not get Places the day before. Their business is about Teeth & Wigs, & they are going after breakfast to Scarman's & Tavistock S^t—and they are to return, to go with me afterwards in the Barouche. I hope to do some of my errands today. I got the Willow yesterday, as Henry was not quite ready when I reached Hen^a S^t—I saw Mr Hampson there for a moment. He dines here tomorrow & proposed bringing his son; so I must submit to seeing George Hampson, though I had hoped to go through Life without it.—It was one of my vanities, like your not reading *Patronage*.[7]—After leaving H. S^t—we drove to Mrs Latouches, *they* are always at home—& they are to dine here on friday.—We could do no more, as it began to rain.—We dine at ½ past 4 today, that our Visitors may go to the Play, and [*p. 3*] Henry & I are to spend the even^g with the Tilsons, to meet Miss Burdett, who leaves Town tomorrow.—Mrs T. called on me yesterday.—Is not this all that can have happened, or been arranged?—Not quite.—Henry wants me to see more of his Hanwell favourite,[8] & has written to invite her to spend a day or two here with me. His scheme is to fetch her on Saturday. I am more & more convinced that he will marry again soon, & like the idea of *her* better than of anybody else at hand.

Now, I have breakfasted & have the room to myself again.—It is likely to be a fine day.—How do you all do?—Henry talks of being at Chawton *about* the 1st of Sept^r—He has once mentioned a scheme, which I should rather like—calling on the Birches & the Crutchleys in our way. It may never come to anything, but I must provide for the possibility, by troubling you [to] send up my Silk Pelisse by Collier on Saturday.—I feel it would be necessary on such an occasion;—and be so good as to put up a clean Dressing gown which will come from the Wash on friday.—You need not direct it to be left anywhere. It may take its' chance.—We are to call for Henry between 3 & 4—& I must finish this & carry it with me, as he is not always there in the morn⁸⁹ before the Parcel is made up.¹⁰—And before I set off, I must return Mrs Tilson's visit.—I hear nothing of the Hoblyns & abstain from all enquiry.—

I hope Mary Jane & Frank's Gardens go on well.—Give my Love to them all—Nunna Hat's Love to George.¹¹—A great many People wanted to mo up in the Poach as well as me.—The wheat looked very well all the way, & James says the same of *his* road.—The same good account of Mrs C.'s¹² health continues, & her circumstances mend. She gets farther & farther from Poverty. What a comfort! [*p. 4*] Good bye to You.—Yours very truely & affec^ly

Jane.

All well at Steventon. I hear nothing particular of Ben, except that Edward¹³ is to get him some pencils.—

Miss Austen
Chawton
By favour of
Mr Gray

[*Letters missing here*]

106. *To Martha Lloyd*

Friday 2 September 1814

23 Hans Place Friday Sepr 2^d

My dear Martha

The prospect of a long quiet morning determines me to write to you; I have been often thinking of it before, but without being quite able to do it—and You are too busy, too happy & too *rich* I hope, to care much for Letters.—It gave me very great pleasure to hear that your Money was paid, it must have been a circumstance to increase every enjoyment you can have had with your friends—and altogether I think you must be spending your time most comfortably. The weather can hardly have incommoded you by its' heat.—We have had many evenings here so cold, that I was sure there must be fires in the Country.—How many alterations you must perceive in Bath! & how many People & Things gone by, must be recurring to you!—I hope you will see Clifton. Henry takes me home tomorrow; I rather expect at least to be at Chawton before night, tho' it may not be till early on Sunday, as we shall lengthen the Journey by going round by Sunning Hill;—his favourite Mrs Crutchley lives there, & he wants to introduce me to her.—We offered a visit in our way, to the Birches, but they cannot receive us, which is a disappointment.—He comes back again on Wednesday, [*p. 2*] & perhaps brings James with him; so it was settled, when James was here;—he wants to see Scarman again, as his Gums last week were not in a proper state for Scarman's operations. I cannot tell how much of all this may be known to you already.—I shall have spent my 12 days here very pleasantly, but with not much to tell of them; two or three *very* little Dinner-parties at home, some delightful Drives in the Curricle, & quiet Tea-drinkings with the Tilsons, has been the sum of my doings. I have seen no old acquaintance I think, but Mr Hampson. Henry met with Sir Brook & Lady Bridges by chance, & they were to have dined with us yesterday, had they remained in Town. I am amused by the present style of female dress;—the coloured petticoats with braces over the white Spencers & enormous Bonnets upon the full stretch, are quite entertaining. It seems to me a more marked *change* than one has lately seen.—Long sleeves appear universal, even as *Dress*, the Waists short, and as far as I have been able to judge, the Bosom covered.—I was at a little party last night at Mrs Latouche's, where dress is a good deal attended to, & these are my observations from it.—Petticoats short, & generally, tho' not always, flounced.—The broad-straps belonging to the Gown or Boddice, which cross the front of the Waist, over white, have a very pretty effect I think.—I have seen West's famous Painting, & prefer it to anything of the kind I ever saw before. I do not know that it *is* reckoned superior to his "Healing in the Temple", [*p. 3*] but it has gratified *me* much more,[1] & indeed is the first representation of our Saviour which ever at all contented me. "His Rejection by the Elders", is the subject.—I want to have You & Cassandra see it.—I am extremely pleased[2] with this new House of Henry's, it is everything that could be wished for him, & I have only to hope he will continue to like it as well as he does now, and not be looking out for anything better.—He is in very comfortable health;—he has not been so well, he says, for a twelvemonth.—*His* veiw, & the veiw of those he mixes with, of Politics, is not chearful—with regard to an American war[3] I mean;—they consider it as certain, & as what is to ruin us. The [?Americans] cannot be conquered, & we shall only be teaching them the skill in War which they may now want. We are to make them good Sailors & Soldiers, & [?gain] nothing ourselves.—If we *are* to be ruined, it cannot be helped—but I place my hope of better things on a claim to the protection of Heaven, as a Religious Nation, a Nation inspite of much Evil improving in Religion, which I cannot beleive the Americans to possess.—However this may be, Mr Barlowe is to dine with us today, & I am in some hope[4] of getting Egerton's account[5] before I go away—so we will enjoy ourselves as long as we can. My Aunt does not seem pleased with Capt. & Mrs D. D. for taking a House in Bath, I was afraid she would not like it, but I ho[pe ?they] do.—When I get home, I shall hear [*about five words missing*] . . . [?*shall be very happy to*] find myself at [*nearly all the next line missing*] . . . Miss Benn [*nearly all the bottom line missing*] . . . to hear [*p. 4*] Mrs Digweed's goodhumoured communications. The language of London is flat; it wants her phrase.—Dear me!—I wonder whether you have seen Miss Irvine!—At this time of year, she is more likely to be out of Bath than in.

One of our afternoon drives was to Streatham, where I had the pleasure of seeing Mrs Hill as well & comfortable as usual;—but there is a melancholy disproportion[6] between the Papa & the little Children.—She told me that the Awdrys have taken that sweet S^t Bo[niface that we] passed by [*three or four words missing*] & Ventnor; [*approximately two lines missing, with the conclusion*].

[*Postscript below address panel*]

Pray give my best [com]pts to your Friends. I have not forgotten their parti[cular] claim to my Gratitude as an Author.[7]—We have j[ust hea]rd that Mrs C. Austen is safe in her bed with a Girl.[8] It happened on board a fortnig[ht] before it was expected.

Miss Lloyd
Captn Deans Dundas' RN
Pulteney Street
Bath

107. *To Anna Austen*

Friday 9–Sunday 18 September 1814

Chawton Sept: 9.

My dear Anna

We have been very much amused by your 3 books, but I have a good many criticisms to make—more than you will like. We are not satisfied with Mrs F.'s settling herself as Tenant & near Neighbour to such a Man as Sir T. H. without having some other inducement to go there; she ought to have some friend living thereabouts to tempt her. A woman, going with two girls just growing up, into a Neighbourhood where she knows nobody but one Man, of not very good character, is an awkwardness which so prudent a woman as M^rs F would not be likely[1] to fall into. Remember, she is very prudent;—you must not let her act inconsistently.—Give her a friend, & let that friend be invited to meet her at the Priory, & we shall have no objection to her dining there as she does; but otherwise, a woman in her situation would hardly go there, before she had been visited by other Families.—I like the scene itself, the Miss Lesleys, Lady Anne, & the Music, very much.—Lesley *is* a noble name.—Sir T. H. You always do very well; I have only taken the liberty of expunging one phrase of his, which would not be allowable. "Bless my Heart"—It is too familiar & inelegant. Your G. M. is more disturbed at Mrs F.'s not returning the Egertons visit sooner, than anything else. They ought to have called at the Parsonage before Sunday.—

You describe a sweet place, but your descriptions are often more minute than will be liked. You give too many particulars of right hand & left.—

[*p. 2*] Mrs F. is not careful enough of Susan's health;—Susan ought not to be walking out so soon after Heavy rains, taking long walks in the dirt. An anxious Mother would not suffer it.—I like your Susan very much indeed, she is a sweet Creature, her playfulness of fancy is very delightful. I like her as she is *now* exceedingly, but I am not so well satisfied with her behaviour to George R. At first she seemed all over attachment & feeling, & afterwards to have none at all; she is so extremely composed at the Ball, & so well-satisfied apparently with Mr Morgan. She seems to have changed her Character.—You are now collecting your People delightfully, getting them exactly into such a spot as is the delight of my life;—3 or 4 Families in a Country Village is the very thing to work on—& I hope you will write a great deal more, & make full use of them while they are so very favourably arranged. You are but *now* coming to the heart & beauty of your book; till the heroine grows up, the fun must be imperfect—but I expect a great deal of entertainment from the next 3 or 4 books, & I hope you will not resent these remarks by sending me no more.—We like the Egertons very well, we see no Blue Pantaloons, or Cocks & Hens;— there is nothing to *enchant* one certainly in Mr L. L.—but we make no objection to him, & his inclination to like Susan is pleasing.—The

Sister is a good contrast—but the name of Rachael is as much as I can bear.—They are [*p. 3*] not so much like the Papillons as I expected. Your last Chapter is very entertaining—the conversation on Genius &c. Mr St J.- & Susan both talk in character & very well.—In some former parts, Cecilia is perhaps a little too solemn & good, but upon the whole, her disposition is very well opposed to Susan's—her want of Imagination is very natural.[2]—I wish you could make Mrs F. talk more, but she must be difficult to manage & make entertaining, because there is so much good common sence & propriety about her that nothing can be very *broad*. Her Economy & her Ambition must not be staring.—The Papers left by Mrs Fisher is very good.—Of course, one guesses something.—I hope when you have written a great deal more you will be equal to scratching out some of the past.—The scene with Mrs Mellish, I should condemn; it is prosy & nothing to the purpose—& indeed, the more you can find in your heart to curtail between Dawlish & Newton Priors, the better I think it will be.—One does not care for girls till they are grown up.—Your Aunt C. quite enters into the exquisiteness of that name. Newton Priors[3] is really a Nonpareil.—Milton w^d have given his eyes to have thought of it.—Is not the Cottage taken from Tollard Royal?—

Sunday 18th—I am very glad dear Anna, that I wrote as I did before this sad Event[4] occurred. I have now only to add that your G. Mama does not seem the worse now for the Shock.—I shall be very happy to receive more of your work, if more is ready; & you write so fast, that I have great hopes Mr D.[5] will come freighted back with such a Cargo as not all his Hops or his Sheep could equal the value of.

[*p. 4*] Your Grandmama desires me to say that she will have finished your Shoes tomorrow & thinks they will look very well;—and that she depends upon seeing you, as you promise, before you quit the Country, & hopes you will give her more than a day.—Y^rs affec:^ly

J. Austen

Miss Austen

108. *To Anna Austen*

Chawton Wednesday Sept: 28.

My dear Anna

I hope you do not depend on having your book back again immediately. I keep it that your G:Mama may hear it—for it has not been possible yet to have any public reading. I have read it to your Aunt Cassandra however—in our own room at night, while we undressed— and with a great deal of pleasure. We like the first chapter extremely— with only a little doubt whether Ly Helena is not almost *too* foolish. The matrimonial Dialogue is very good certainly.—I like Susan as well as ever—& begin now not to care at all about Cecilia—she may stay at Easton Court as long as she likes.—Henry Mellish I am afraid will be too much in the common Novel style—a handsome, amiable, unexceptionable Young Man (such as do not much abound in real Life) desperately in Love, & all in vain. But I have no business to judge him so early.—Jane Egerton is a very natural, comprehendable Girl—& the whole of her acquaintance with Susan, & Susan's Letter to Cecilia, very pleasing & quite in character.—But *Miss* Egerton does not entirely satisfy us. She is too formal & solemn, we think, in her advice to her Brother not to fall in love; & it is hardly like a sensible Woman; it is putting it into his head.—We should like a few hints from her better.—[*p. 2*] We feel really obliged to you for introducing a Lady Kenrick, it will remove the greatest fault in the work, & I give you credit for considerable forbearance as an Author in adopting so much of our opinion.—I expect high fun about Mrs Fisher & Sir Thomas.—You have been perfectly right in telling Ben of your work, & I am very glad to hear how much he likes it. *His* encouragement & approbation must be quite "beyond everything."—I do not at all wonder at his not expecting to like anybody so well as Cecilia *at first*, but shall be surprised if he does not become a Susan-ite in time.—Devereux Forester's being ruined by his Vanity is extremely good; but I wish you would not let him plunge into a "vortex of Dissipation". I do not object to the Thing, but I cannot bear the expression;—it is such thorough novel slang— and so old, that I dare say Adam met with it in the first novel he opened.—Indeed I did very much like to know Ben's opinion.—I hope he will continue to be pleased with it, I think he must—but I cannot flatter him with there being much Incident. We have no great right to wonder at his not valueing the name of Progillian. *That* is a source of delight which he hardly ever can be quite competent to.—Walter Scott has no business to write novels, especially good ones.—It is not fair.— [*p. 3*] He has Fame & Profit enough as a Poet, and should not be taking the bread out of other people's mouths.—I do not like him, & do not mean to like Waverley[1] if I can help it—but fear I must.—I am quite determined however not to be pleased[2] with Mrs West's Alicia de Lacy,[3] should I ever meet with it, which I hope I may not.—I think I *can* be stout against any thing written by Mrs West.—I have made up my mind to like no Novels really, but Miss Edgeworth's, Yours & my own.—

What can you do with Egerton to increase the interest for him? I wish you c^d contrive something, some family occurrence to draw out his good qualities more—some distress among Brothers or Sisters to releive by the sale of his Curacy—something to [take] him mysteriously away, & then heard of at York or Edinburgh—in an old great Coat.[4]—I would not seriously recommend anything Improbable, but if you c^d invent something spirited for him, it w^d have a good effect.—He might lend all his Money to Captn Morris—but then he w^d be a great fool if he did. Cannot the Morrises quarrel, & he reconcile them?—Excuse the liberty I take in these suggestions.—

Your Aunt Frank's Housemaid has just given her warning, but whether she is worth your having, or w^d take your place I know not.—She was Mrs Webb's maid before she went to the G^t House. She leaves your Aunt, because she cannot agree with her fellow servants. She is in love with the Man—& her head seems rather turned; he returns her affection, but she fancies every body else is wanting to get him too, & envying her. [*p. 4*] Her previous service must have fitted her for such a place as yours,[5] & she is very active & cleanly.—She is own Sister to the favourite Beatrice. The Webbs are really gone. When I saw the Waggons at the door, & thought of all the trouble they must have in moving, I began to reproach myself for not having liked them better—but since the Waggons have disappeared, my Conscience has been closed again—& I am excessively glad they are gone.—

I am very fond of Sherlock's Sermons,[6] prefer them to almost any.

Your affec^te Aunt

J. Austen

If you wish me to speak to the Maid, let me know.—

Miss Austen
Steventon

—————————

109. *To Fanny Knight*

Friday 18–Sunday 20 November 1814

Chawton Nov: 18.—Friday

I feel quite as doubtful as you could be my dearest Fanny as to *when* my Letter may be finished, for I can command very little quiet time at present, but yet I must begin, for I know you will be glad to hear as soon as possible, & I really am impatient myself to be writing something on so very interesting a subject, though I have no hope of writing anything to the purpose.—I shall do very little more I dare say than say over again, what you have said before.—I was certainly a good deal surprised *at first*—as I had no suspicion of any change in your feelings, and I have no scruple in saying that you cannot be in Love. My dear Fanny, I am ready to laugh at the idea—and yet it is no laughing matter to have had you so mistaken as to your own feelings—And with all my heart I wish I had cautioned you on that point when first you spoke to me;—but tho' I did not think you then so *much* in love as you thought yourself, I did consider you as being attached in a degree—quite sufficiently for happiness, as I had no doubt it would increase with opportunity.—And from the time of our being in London together, I thought you really very much in love.—But you certainly are not at all—there is no concealing it.—What strange creatures we are!—It seems as if your being secure of him (as you say yourself) had made you Indifferent.—There was a little disgust I suspect, at the Races—& I do not wonder at it. His expressions then would not do for one who had rather more Acuteness, Penetration & Taste, than Love, which was your case. And yet, after all, I *am* surprised that the change in your feelings should be so great.—He is, just what he ever was, only more evidently & uniformly devoted to *you*. [*p. 2*] This is all the difference.—How shall we account for it?—My dearest Fanny, I am writing what will not be of the smallest use to you. I am feeling differently every moment, & shall not be able to suggest a single thing that can assist your Mind.— I could lament in one sentence & laugh in the next, but as to Opinion or Counsel I am sure none will [be *omitted*] extracted worth having from this Letter.—I read yours through the very even^g I received it— getting away by myself—I could not bear to leave off, when I had once begun.—I was full of curiosity & concern. Luckily Your Aunt C. dined at the other house, therefore I had not to manoeuvre away from *her*;— & as to anybody else, I do not care.—Poor dear Mr J. P!^1—Oh! dear Fanny, Your mistake has been one that thousands of women fall into. He was the *first* young Man who attached himself to you. That was the charm, & most powerful it is.—Among the multitudes however that make the same mistake with Yourself, there can be few indeed who have so little reason to regret it;—*his* Character & *his* attachment leave you nothing to be ashamed of.—Upon the whole, what is to be done? You certainly *have* encouraged him to such a point as to make^2 him feel

almost secure of you—you have no inclination for any other person—
His situation in life, family, friends, & above all his Character—his
uncommonly amiable mind, strict principles, just notions, good habits—*all* that *you* know so well how to value, *All* that really is of the first
importance—everything of this nature pleads his cause most strongly.—
You have no doubt of his having superior Abilities—he has proved it
at the University—he is I dare say such a Scholar as your agreable, idle
Brothers would ill bear a comparison with.—Oh! my dear Fanny, the
more I write about him, the warmer my feelings become, the more
strongly I feel the sterling worth of such a young Man & the desirable-
ness of your growing in love with him again. I recommend this most
thoroughly.—There *are* such beings in the World perhaps, one in a
Thousand, as the Creature You & I should think perfection, [*p. 3*]
where Grace & Spirit are united to Worth, where the Manners are equal
to the Heart & Understanding, but such a person may not come in your
way, or if he does, he may not be the eldest son of a Man of Fortune,
the Brother of your particular friend, & belonging to your own
County.—Think of all this Fanny. Mʳ J. P.- has advantages which do
not often meet in one person.³ His only fault indeed seems Modesty. If
he were less modest, he would be more agreable, speak louder & look
Impudenter;—and is not it a fine Character, of which Modesty is the
only defect?—I have no doubt that he will get more lively & more like
yourselves as he is more with you;—he will catch your ways if he
belongs to you. And as to there being any objection from his *Goodness*,
from the danger of his becoming even Evangelical, I cannot admit *that*.
I am by no means convinced that we ought not all to be Evangelicals,
& am at least persuaded that they who are so from Reason & Feeling,
must be happiest & safest.—Do not be frightened from the connection
by your Brothers having most wit. Wisdom is better than Wit, & in the
long run will certainly have the laugh on her side; & don't be frightened by the idea of his acting more strictly up to the precepts of the
New Testament than others.—And now, my dear Fanny, having written so much on one side of the question, I shall turn round & entreat
you not to commit yourself farther, & not to think of accepting him
unless you really do like him. Anything is to be preferred or endured
rather than marrying without Affection; and if his deficiencies of Manner &c &c strike you more than all his good qualities, if you continue
to think strongly of them, give him up at once.—Things are now in
such a state, that you must resolve upon one or the other, either to allow
him to go on as he has done, or whenever you are together behave with

a coldness which may convince him that he has been deceiving himself.—I have no doubt of his suffering a good deal for a time, a great deal, when he feels that he must give you up;—but it is no creed of mine, as you must be well aware, that such sort of Disappointments kill anybody.—Your sending the Music was an admirable device, it made everything easy, & I do not know how I could have accounted for the parcel⁴ otherwise; for tho' your dear Papa most conscientiously hunted about till he found me alone in the Din^g-parlour, Your Aunt C. had seen that he *had* a parcel to deliver.—As it was however, I do not think anything was suspected.—We have heard nothing fresh from Anna. I trust she is very comfortable in her new home. Her Letters have been very sensible & satisfactory, with no *parade* of happiness, which I liked them the better for.—I have often known young married Women write in a way I did not like, in that respect.

[*p. 4*] You will be glad to hear that the first Edit: of M.P. is all sold.— Your Uncle Henry is rather wanting me to come to Town, to settle about a 2^d Edit:—but as I could not very conveniently leave home now, I have written him my Will & pleasure, & unless he still urges it, shall not go.—I am very greedy & want to make the most of it;—but as you are much above caring about money, I shall not plague you with any particulars.—The pleasures of Vanity are more within your comprehension, & you will enter into mine, at receiving the *praise* which every now & then comes to me, through some channel or other.—

Saturday.—Mr Palmer spent yesterday with us, & is gone off with Cassy this morn^g. We have been expecting Miss Lloyd the last two days, & feel sure of her to day.—Mr Knight & Mr Edw: Knight are to dine with us.—And on Monday they are to dine with us again, accompanied by their respectable Host & Hostess.⁵—*Sunday*. Your Papa had given me messages to you, but they are unnecessary, as he writes by this post to Aunt Louisa.⁶ We had a pleasant party yesterday, at least *we* found it so.—It is delightful to see him so chearful & confident.—Aunt Cass: & I dine at the G^t House to day. We shall be a snug half dozen.— [*continued below address panel*] Miss Lloyd came, as we expected, yesterday, & desires her Love.—She is very happy to hear of your learning the Harp.—I do not mean to send you what I owe Miss Hare, because I think you would rather not be paid beforehand.—Yours very affec^ly

J. Austen

[*Postscript upside down at top of p. 1*]

Your trying to excite your own feelings by a visit to his room amused me excessively.—The dirty Shaving Rag was exquisite!—Such a circumstance ought to be in print. Much too good to be lost.—

Remember me particularly to Fanny C.[7]—I thought you w^d like to hear from me, while you were with her.

Miss Knight
Goodnestone Farm
Wingham
Kent

110. *To Anna Lefroy*

Tuesday 22 November 1814

My dear Anna

I met Harriet Benn yesterday, she gave her congratulations & desired they might be forwarded to You, and there they are.—Your Father returned to dinner, Mr Wm Digweed who had business with your Uncle, rode with him.—The cheif news from their country is the death of old Mrs Dormer.—Your Cousin Edward goes to Winchester today to see his Brother & Cousins,[1] & returns tomorrow. Mrs Clement walks about in a new Black velvet Pelisse lined with Yellow, & a white Bobbin-net-veil, & looks remarkably well in them.—I think I understand the Country about Hendon from your description. It must be very pretty in Summer.—Should you [?guess] that you were within a dozen miles of the We[n² from] the atmosphere?—I shall break my hea[rt] if yo[u do]not go to Hadley.—

Make everybody at Hendon admire Mansfield Park.—

Your affec: Aunt
J. A.

Tuesday Nov: 22.

To
Mrs B. Lefroy
Hendon

111. *To Anna Lefroy*

?Thursday 24 November 1814[1]

[recto] . . . Mrs Creed's opinion[2] is gone down on my list; but fortunately I may excuse myself from entering M^r [*cut out*] as my paper only

relates to Mansfield Park. I will redeem my credit with him, by writing a close Imitation of "Self-control" as soon as I can;—I will improve upon it;—my Heroine shall not merely be wafted down an American river in a boat by herself, she shall cross the Atlantic in the same way, & never stop till she reaches Gravesent.—

[*verso*] . . . that depends on us to secure it, but you mu[st be] aware that in another person's house one cannot command one's own time or activities, & though your Uncle Henry is so kind as to give us the use of a Carriage while we are with him, it may not be possible for us to turn that Carriage towards Hendon without a[c]tually mounting the Box ourselves;—Your Uncle arrived yesterday by the Gosport—(and only think of the Gosport not being here till ½ past 4!—I [*most of next line missing*] . . .) and takes . . .

[*No address*]

112. *To Anna Lefroy*

I am very much obliged to you, my dear Anna, & should be very happy to come & see you again if I could, but I have not a day disengaged. We are expecting your Uncle Charles tomorrow; and I am to go the next day to Hanwell to fetch some Miss Moores who are to stay here till Saturday; then comes Sunday & Elizth Gibson, and on Monday Your Uncle Henry takes us both to Chawton. It is therefore really impossible, but I am very much obliged to You & to Mr B. Lefroy for wishing it. We should find plenty to say, no doubt, & I should like to hear Charlotte Dewar's Letter; however, though I do not hear it, I am glad she has written to you. I like first Cousins to be first Cousins, & interested about each other. They are but one remove from B^r & S^r—

[*p. 2*] We all came away very much pleased with our visit I assure You. We talked of you for about a mile & a half with great satisfaction, & I have been just sending a very good account of you to Miss Beckford, with a description of your Dress for Susan & Maria^1—Your Uncle & Edw^{d2} left us this morning. The hopes of the Former in his Cause, do not lessen.—We were all at the Play last night, to see Miss O'neal in Isabella.^{3} I do not think she was quite equal to my expectation. I fancy I want something more than can be. Acting seldom satisfies me. I took two Pocket handkerchiefs, but had very little occasion for either. She is an elegant creature however & hugs Mr Younge delightfully.—

[*p. 3*] I am going this morning to see the little girls in Keppel Street. Cassy was excessively interested about your marrying, when she heard of it, which was not till she was to drink your health on the wedding day. She asked a thousand questions, in her usual way—What he said to you? & what you said to him?—And we were very much amused one day by Mary Jane's asking "what Month her *Cousin Benjamin* was born in?"—

If your Uncle⁴ were at home he would send his best Love, but I will not impose any base, fictitious remembrance on You.—Mine I can honestly give, & remain Yʳ affec: Aunt

J. Austen

23, Hans Place
Tuesday Nov: 29.

Mʳˢ B. Lefroy
Hendon

113. *To Anna Lefroy*

Wednesday 30 November 1814

Hans Place, Wednesday¹

My dear Anna

I have been very far from finding your Book an Evil I assure you; I read it immediately—& with great pleasure. I think you are going on very well. The description of Dʳ Griffin & Lady Helena's unhappiness is very good, just what was likely to be.—I am curious to know what the end of *them* will be: The name of Newton-Priors is really invaluable!—I never met with anything superior to it.—It is delightful. —One could live upon the name of Newton-Priors for a twelve-month.—Indeed, I *do* think you get on very fast. I wish other people of my acquaintance could compose as rapidly.—I am pleased with the Dog scene, & with the whole of George & Susan's Love; but am more particularly struck with your *serious* conversations &c.—They are [*p. 2*] very good throughout.—Sᵗ Julian's History was quite a surprise to me; You had not very long known it yourself I suspect—but I have no objection to make to the circumstance—it is very well told—& his having been in love with the Aunt, gives Cecilia an additional Interest with him. I like the Idea;—a very proper compliment to an Aunt!—I rather imagine indeed that Neices are seldom chosen but in compliment to some Aunt or other.² I dare say Ben was in love with me once, & wᵈ never have thought of *You* if he had not supposed me dead of a Scarlet fever.—Yes, I was in a mistake as to the number of Books. I thought I had read 3 before the 3 at Chawton; but fewer than 6 will not do.—I want to see dear Bell Griffin again.—Had not you better give some hint of St Julian's early³ [*p. 3*] [history in the beginning of your story?].

[*No address*]

114. *To Fanny Knight*

Wednesday 30 November 1814

23 Hans Place, Wednesday Nov: 30.

I am very much obliged to you my dear Fanny for your letter, & I hope you will write again soon that I may know You to be all safe & happy at home.—Our visit to Hendon will interest you I am sure, but I need not enter into the particulars of it, as your Papa will be able to answer *almost* every question. I certainly could describe her bed-room, & her Drawers & her Closet better than he can, but I do not feel that I can stop to do it.—I was rather sorry to hear that she *is* to have an Instrument; it seems throwing money away. They will wish the 24 Gs. in the shape of Sheets & Towels six months hence;—and as to her playing, it never can be anything.—Her purple Pelisse rather surprised me.—I thought we had known all Paraphernalia of that sort. I do not mean to blame her, it looked very well & I dare say she wanted it. I suspect nothing worse than its' being got in secret, & not owned to anybody.—She is capable of that you know.—I received a very kind note from her yesterday, to ask me to come again & stay a night with them; I cannot do it, but I was pleased to find that she had the *power* of doing so right a thing. My going was to give them *both* Pleasure¹ very properly.—I just saw Mr Hayter at the Play, & think his face would please me on acquaintance. I was sorry he did not dine here.—It seemed rather odd to me to be in the Theatre, with nobody to *watch* for. I was quite composed myself, at leisure for all the agitation Isabella could raise. [*p. 2*] Now my dearest Fanny, I will begin a subject which comes in very naturally.—You frighten me out of my Wits by your reference. Your affection gives me the highest pleasure, but indeed you must not let anything depend on my opinion. Your own feelings & none but your own, should determine such an important point.—So far however as answering your question, I have no scruple.—I am perfectly convinced that your present feelings, supposing you were to marry *now*, would be sufficient for his happiness;—but when I think how very, very far it is from a *Now*, & take everything that *may be*, into consideration, I dare not say, "determine to accept him." The risk is too great for *you*, unless your own Sentiments prompt it.—You will think me perverse perhaps; in my last letter I was urging everything in his favour, & now I am inclining the other way; but I cannot help it; I am at present more impressed with the possible Evil that may arise to *You* from engaging yourself to him—in word or mind—than with anything else.—When I consider how few young Men you have yet seen much of—how capable you are (yes, I do still think you *very* capable)[2] of being really in love—and how full of temptation the next 6 or 7 years of your Life will probably be—(it is the very period of Life for the *strongest* attachments to be formed)—I cannot wish you with your present very cool feelings to devote yourself in honour to him. It is very true that you never may attach another Man, his equal altogether, but if that other Man has the power of attaching you *more*, he will be in your eyes the most perfect.—I shall be glad if you *can* revive past feelings, & from your unbiassed self resolve to go on as you have done, but this I do not expect, and without it [*p. 3*] I cannot wish you to be fettered. I should not be afraid of your *marrying* him;—with all his Worth, you would soon love him enough for the happiness of both; but I should dread the continuance of this sort of tacit engagement, with such an uncertainty as there is, of *when* it may be completed.—Years may pass, before he is Independant.—You like him well enough to marry, but not well enough to wait.—The unpleasantness of appearing fickle is certainly great—but if you think you want Punishment for past Illusions, there it is—and nothing can be compared to the misery of being bound *without* Love, bound to one, & preferring another. *That* is a Punishment which you do *not* deserve.—I know you did not meet— or rather will not meet to day—as he called here yesterday—& I am glad of it.—It does not seem very likely at least that he sh^d be in time for a Dinner visit 60 m[iles] off. We did not see him, only found his card when we came home at 4.—Your Uncle H. merely observed that he was a day after the Fair.—He asked your Brother on Monday, (when Mr Hayter was talked of) why he did not invite *him* too?—saying, "I know he is in Town, for I met him the other day in Bond S^t—" Edward answered that he did not know where he was to be found.—"Don't you know his Chambers?—" "No."—I shall be most glad to hear from you again my dearest Fanny, but it must not be later than Saturday, as we shall be off on Monday long before the Letters are delivered—and write *something* that may do to be read or told. I am to take the Miss Moores back on Saturday, & when I return I shall hope[3] to find your pleasant, little, flowing Scrawl on the Table.—It will be a releif to me after playing at Ma'ams—for tho' I like Miss H. M. as much as one can at my time of Life after a day's acquaintance, it is uphill work to be talking to those whom one knows so little.—Only *one* comes back with me tomorrow, probably Miss Eliza, & I rather dread it. We shall not have two Ideas in common. She is young, pretty, chattering, & thinking cheifly (I presume) of Dress, Company, & Admiration.—[*p. 4*] Mr Sanford is to join us at dinner, which will be a comfort, and in the even^g while your Uncle & Miss Eliza play chess, he shall tell me comical things & I will laugh at them, which will be a pleasure to both.—I called in Keppel Street & saw them all, including dear Uncle Charles, who is to come & dine with us quietly to day.—Little Harriot sat in my lap—& seemed as gentle & affectionate as ever, & as pretty, except not being quite well. Fanny is a fine stout girl, talking incessantly, with an interesting degree of Lisp and Indistinctness—and very likely may be the handsomest in time.—That puss Cassy, did not shew more pleasure in seeing me than her Sisters, but I expected no better;—she does not shine in the tender feelings. She will never be a Miss O'neal;—more in the Mrs Siddons line.—

Thank you—but it is not settled yet whether I *do* hazard a 2^d Edition.[4] We are to see Egerton today, when it will probably be determined.—People are more ready to borrow & praise, than to buy—which I cannot wonder at;—but tho' I like praise as well as anybody,[5] I like what Edward calls *Pewter* too.—I hope he continues careful of his Eyes & finds the good effect of it. [*continued below address panel*] I cannot suppose we differ in our ideas of the Christian Religion. You have given an excellent description of it. We only affix a different meaning to the Word *Evangelical*.—Yours most affec^ly

J. Austen

Miss Gibson is very glad to go with us.

Miss Knight
Godmersham Park
Faversham
Kent

115. *To Caroline Austen*

?Tuesday 6 December 1814

My dear Caroline

I wish I could finish Stories as fast as you can.—I am much obliged to you for the sight of Olivia, & think you have done for her very well; but the good for nothing Father, who was the real author of all her Faults & Sufferings, should not escape unpunished.—I hope *he* hung himself, or took the sur-name of *Bone* [*p. 2*] or underwent some direful penance or other.—

Yours affec^{ly}
J. Austen

Dec: 6.[1]

[*No address*]

---

116. *To ?Anna Lefroy*

?late December 1814

[*recto*] . . . Thank you for the history of your morning in Town, You know I enjoy particulars, & I was particularly amused with your picture of Grafton House;—it is just so.—How much I should like finding you there one day, seated on your high stool, with 15 rolls of persian before you, & a little black woman just answering your questions in as few words as possible!— . . .

[*verso*] . . . for your very kind invitation, but we are [?afraid it is] quite out of our power to accept it. We are going to [?Hans Place] only for a fortnight, which will not allow of any other visit being taken out of it, and therefore you must not impute it to want of inclination, but of ability.—We shall be much [?disappointed] if we do not see you somehow or other, & shall . . . [*nearly all the next line missing*] . . . st be . . .

[*No address, date or direction*]

117. *To Anna Lefroy*

?between February–July 1815

[*top of p. 3*] . . . from the first, being *born* older, is a very good thing.—
I wish you perseverance & success with all my heart—and have great
confidence of your producing at last, by dint of writing . . . [*nearly all
the next line missing*] . . . work.—Shall . . .

[*top of p. 4*] . . . If You & his Uncles are good friends to little Charles
Lefroy, he will be a great deal the better for his visit;—we thought him
a very fine boy, but terribly in want of Discipline.—I hope he gets a
wholesome thump, or two, whenever it is necessary. [*nearly all the next
line missing*] . . . [?] with us when we . . .

[*No address, date or direction*]

118. *To Anna Lefroy*

?late February–early March 1815

[*middle of p. 3*] . . . We have got "Rosanne"¹ in our Society, and find
it much as you describe it; very good and clever, but tedious. M^rs
Hawkins' great excellence is on serious subjects. There are some very
delightful conversations and reflections on religion: but on lighter top-
ics I think she falls into many absurdities; and, as to love, her heroine
has very comical feelings. There are a thousand improbabilities in the
story. Do you remember the two Miss Ormesdens, introduced just at
last? Very flat and unnatural.—Mlle Cossart is rather my passion.—
Miss Gibson returned to the G^t House last friday, & is pretty well, but
not entirely so. Captn Clement has very kindly offered to drive her out,
& she would like it very much, but no day has yet been quite good
enough, or else she has not been otherwise equal to it.—She sends you
her Love . . . [*nearly all the next line missing*] . . . kind wishes.

[*p. 4*] . . . [I cannot flourish in this east wind]² which is quite against
my skin & conscience.—We shall see nothing of Streatham while we
are in Town;—Mrs Hill is to lye-in of a Daughter³ early in March.—
Mrs Blackstone is to be with her. Mrs Heathcote & Miss Bigg are just
leaving her: the latter writes me word that Miss Blachford *is* married,⁴
but I have never seen it in the Papers. And one may as well be single
if the Wedding is not to be in print.—[*rest of last line with complimentary
close and signature cut away*].

[*Address missing*]

119. *To Caroline Austen*

?Thursday 2 March 1815

... we four sweet Brothers & Sisters dine today at the G^t House. Is not that quite natural?—Grandmama & Miss Lloyd will be by themselves, I do not exactly know what they will have for dinner, very likely some pork ?[—Do you know that ...]

[*No address, date or direction*]

---

120. *To Anna Lefroy*

Friday 29 September 1815

Chawton, Friday Septr 29.

My dear Anna

We told Mr B. Lefroy that if the weather did not prevent us, we should certainly come & see you tomorrow, & bring Cassy, trusting to your being so good as to give her a dinner about one o'clock, that we might be able to be with you the earlier & stay the longer—but on giving Cassy her choice of the Fair or Wyards,[1] it must be confessed that she has preferred[2] the former, which we trust will not greatly affront you;—if it does, you may hope that some little Anna hereafter may revenge the insult by a similar preference of an Alton fair to her Cousin Cassy.—In the meanwhile, we have determined to put off our visit to you till Monday, which we hope will be not less convenient to You.—I wish the weather may not resolve upon other put-offs. I *must* come to you before Wednesday if it be possible, for on that day I am going to London for a week or two with your Uncle Henry, who is expected here on Sunday. If Monday therefore should appear too dirty for walking, & Mr B. L. would be so kind as to come & fetch me to spend some part of the morn^g with you, I should be much obliged to him. Cassy might [*p. 2*] be of the Party, & your Aunt Cassandra will take another opportunity.—

Your G.Mama sends her Love & Thanks for your note. She was very happy to hear the contents of your Packing Case.—She will send the

290

Strawberry roots by Sally Benham, as early next week as the weather may allow her to take them up.—

Yours very affec:^{ly}
My dear Anna
J. Austen

[*No address*]

_____

[*Letters missing here*]

121. *To Cassandra Austen*

Tuesday 17–Wednesday 18 October 1815

Hans Place, Tuesday Oct: 17.

My dear Cassandra

Thank you for your two Letters. I am very glad the new Cook begins so well. Good apple pies are a considerable part of our domestic happiness.—Mr Murray's Letter is come; he is a Rogue[1] of course, but a civil one. He offers £450- but wants to have the Copyright of MP. & S&S included. It will end in my publishing for myself I dare say.—He sends more praise however than I expected. It is an amusing Letter. You shall see it.—Henry came home on Sunday & we dined the same day with the Herrieses—a large family party—clever & accomplished.—I had a pleasant visit the day before. Mr Jackson is fond of eating & does not much like M^r or Miss P.[2]—What weather we have!—What shall we do about it?—The 17th of Oct^r & summer still! Henry is not quite well—a bilious attack with fever—he came back early from H.S^t yesterday & went to bed—the comical consequence[3] of which was that Mr Seymour & I dined together tète a tète.—He is calomeling & therefore in a way to be better & I hope may be well tomorrow. The Creeds of Hendon dine here today, which is rather unlucky—for he will hardly be able to shew himself—& they are all Strangers to me. He has asked Mr Tilson to come & take his place. I doubt our being a very agreable pair.—We are engaged tomorrow to Cleveland Row.[4]—[*p. 2*] I was there yesterday morning.—There seems no idea now of Mr Gordon's going to Chawton—nor of any of the family coming here at present.

Many of them are sick.—Wednesday.—Henry's illness[5] is more serious than I expected. He has been in bed since three o'clock on Monday. It is a fever—something bilious, but cheifly Inflammatory. I am not alarmed—but I have determined to send this Letter today by the post, that you may know how things are going on. There is no chance of his being able to leave Town on Saturday. I asked M[r] Haydon that question today.—M[r] H. is the apothecary from the corner of Sloane S[t]—successor to M[r] Smith, a young Man said to be clever, & he is certainly[6] very attentive & appears hitherto to have understood the complaint. There is a little pain in the Chest, but it is not considered of any consequence. M[r] H. calls it a general Inflammation.—He took twenty ounces of Blood from Henry last night—& nearly as much more this morn[g]—& expects to have to bleed him again tomorrow, but he assures me that he found him *quite* as much better today as he expected. Henry is an excellent Patient,[7] lies quietly in bed & is ready to swallow anything. He lives upon Medicine, Tea & Barley water.—He has had a great deal of fever, but not much pain of any sort—& sleeps pretty well.—*His* going to Chawton will probably end in nothing, as his Oxfordshire Business is so near;—as for myself, You may be sure I shall return as soon as I can. Tuesday is in my brain, but you will feel the Uncertainty of it.—I want to get rid of some of my Things, & therefore shall send down a parcel by Collier on Saturday. Let it be paid for on my own account.—[*p. 3*] It will be mostly dirty Cloathes[8]—but I shall add Martha's Lambswool, your Muslin Handks.—(India at 3/6) your Pens, 3[s]—& some articles for Mary, if I receive them in time from M[rs] Hore.— Cleveland Row of course is given up. M[r] Tilson took a note there this morn[g]. Till yesterday afternoon I was hoping that the Medicine he had taken, with a good night's rest would set him quite to rights. I fancied it only Bile—but they say, the disorder must have originated in a Cold. You must fancy Henry in the back room upstairs—& I am generally there also, working or writing.—I wrote to Edw[d] yesterday, to put off our Nephews till friday. I have a strong idea of their Uncle's being well enough to like seeing them [by] that time.—I shall write to you next by my parcel—two days hence—unless there is anything particular to be communicated before, always excepted.—The post has this moment brought me a letter from Edward. He is likely to come here on Tuesday next, for a day or two's necessary business in his Cause.[9]—

M[rs] Hore wishes to observe to Frank & Mary that she doubts their finding it answer to have Chests of Drawers bought in London, when the expense of carriage is considered. The two Miss Gibsons called here on Sunday, & brought a Letter from Mary, which shall also be put into the parcel. Miss G. looked particularly well.—I have not been able to return their call.—I want to get to Keppel S^t again if I can, but it must be doubtful.—The Creeds are agreable People themselves, but I fear must have had a very dull visit.—[*p. 4*] I long to know how Martha's plans go on. If you have not written before, write by Sunday's post to Hans Place.—I shall be more than ready for news of you by that time.— A change of weather at last!—Wind & Rain.—Mrs Tilson has just called. Poor Woman, she is quite a wretch, always ill.—God bless you.—

Y^{rs} affec:^{ly} J. A.

Uncle Henry was very much amused with Cassy's message, but if she were here now with the red shawl she w^d make him laugh more than w^d do him good.—

Miss Austen
Chawton
Alton

[*Letters missing here*]

122(A)(D). *From Henry Austen*

?Friday 20/Saturday 21 October 1815

A Letter to Mr Murray which Henry dictated a few days after his Illness began, & just before the severe Relapse which threw him into such Danger.—

Dear Sir

Severe Illness has confined me to my Bed ever since I received Yours of ye 15th—I cannot yet hold a pen, & employ an Amuensis [*sic*].—The Politeness & Perspicuity of your Letter equally claim my earliest Exertion.—Your official opinion of the Merits of *Emma*, is very valuable & satisfactory.—Though I venture to differ occasionally from your Critique, yet I assure you the Quantum of your commendation rather exceeds than falls short of the Author's expectation & my own.—The Terms you offer are so very inferior to what we had expected, that I am apprehensive of having made some great Error in my Arithmetical Calculation.—On the subject of the expence & profit of publishing, you must be much better informed than I am;—but Documents in my possession appear to prove that the Sum offered by you for the Copyright of Sense & Sensibility, Mansfield Park & Emma, is not equal to

293

the Money which my Sister has actually cleared by one very moderate Edition of Mansfield Park—(You Yourself expressed astonishment that so small an Edit:¹ of such a work should have been sent into the World) & a still smaller one of Sense & Sensibility.— ...

[*No address*]

123. *To Caroline Austen*

Monday 30 October 1815

Hans Place, Monday nig[ht]
Oct: 30.

My dear Caroline

I have not yet felt quite equal to taking up your Manuscript, but think I shall soon, & I hope my detaining it so long will be no inconvenience.—It gives us great pleasure that you should be at Chawton.¹ I am sure Cassy must be delighted to have you.—You will practise your Music of course, & I trust to you for taking care of my Instrument & not letting it be ill used in any respect.—Do not allow anything to be put on it, but what is very light.—I hope you will try to make out some other tune besides the Hermit.²—Tell your Grandmama that I have written to Mʳˢ Cooke to congratulate her, & that I have heard from Scarlets today; they were [*p. 2*] much shocked by the preparatory Letter which I felt obliged to send last wednesday, but had been made comfortable in comparison, by the receipt of my friday's Letter. Your Papa wrote again by this Post, so that I hope they are now easy.—I am sorry you got wet in your ride; Now that you are become an Aunt,³ you are a person of some consequence & must excite great Interest whatever You do. I have always maintained the importance of Aunts as much as possible, & I am sure of your doing the same now.—Beleive me my dear Sister-Aunt,

Yours affecˡʸ
J. Austen

[*No address*]

124(D). *To John Murray*

Friday 3 November 1815

Sir

My Brother's severe Illness has prevented his replying to Yours of Oct: 15, on the subject of the MS of *Emma*, now in your hands—And as he is, though recovering, still in a state which we are fearful of harrassing by any Business, & I am at the same time desirous of coming to some decision on the affair in question, I must beg the favour of you to call on me here any day that may suit you best, & at any hour in the Even^g or any in the Morn^gr except from 11 to one.—A short conversation may perhaps do more than much Writing.—

My Brother begs his Compts & best Thanks for your polite attention in supplying him with a copy of Waterloo.²

I am Sir

Y^r HumServ^t
Jane Austen

[*No address*]

124. *To John Murray*

Friday 3 November 1815

23, Hans Place, Friday Nov: 3^d

Sir

My Brother's severe Illness has prevented his replying to Yours of Oct: 15, on the subject of the MS of *Emma* now in your hands—and as he is, though recovering, still in a state which we are fearful of harrassing by Business & I am at the same time desirous of coming to some decision on the affair in question, I must request the favour of you to call on me here, on any day after the present that may suit you best, at any hour in the Evening, or any in the Morning except from Eleven to One.—A short conversation may perhaps do more than much Writing.

My Brother begs his Compt^s & best Thanks for your polite attention in supplying him with a Copy of Waterloo.

I am Sir
Your Ob. Hum: Servt
Jane Austen

[*No address*]

125(D). *To James Stanier Clarke*

Wednesday 15 November 1815

Copy of my Letter to M[r] Clarke, Nov: 15.—1815

Sir

I must take the liberty of asking You a question—Among the many flattering attentions which I rec[d] from you at Carlton House, on Monday last, was the Information of my being at liberty to dedicate any future Work to HRH the P. R. without the necessity of any Solicitation on my part. Such at least, I beleived to be your words; but as I am very anxious to be quite certain of what was intended, I intreat you to have the goodness to inform me how such a Permission is to be understood, & whether it is incumbent on me to shew my sense of the Honour, by inscribing the Work now in the Press, to H. R. H.—I sh[d] be equally concerned to appear either presumptuous or Ungrateful.—

I am &c—

[*No address*]

125(A). *From James Stanier Clarke*

Thursday 16 November 1815

Carlton House Nov[r]: 16th: 1815.

Dear Madam

It is certainly not *incumbent* on you to dedicate your work now in the Press to His Royal Highness: but if you wish to do the Regent that honour either now or at any future period, I am happy to send you that permission which need not require any more trouble or solicitation on your Part.

Your late Works, Madam, and in particular Mansfield Park reflect the highest honour on your Genius & your Principles; in every new work your mind seems to increase its energy and powers of discrimination. The Regent has read & admired all your publications.

Accept my sincere thanks for the pleasure your Volumes have given me: in the perusal of them I felt a great inclination to write & say so. And I also dear Madam wished to be allowed to ask you, to delineate in some future Work the Habits of Life and Character and enthusiasm of a Clergyman—who should pass his time between the metropolis & the Country—who should be something like Beatties Minstrel[1]

Silent when glad, affectionate tho' shy
And now his look was most demurely sad
& now he laughed aloud yet none knew why—

Neither Goldsmith—nor La Fontaine in his Tableau de Famille[2]—have in my mind quite delineated an English Clergyman, at least of the present day—Fond of, & entirely engaged in Literature—no man's Enemy but his own. Pray dear Madam think of these things.

Believe me at all times
With sincerity & respect
Your faithful & obliged Servant
J. S. Clarke
Librarian.

P.S.

I am going for about three weeks to Mr Henry Streatfeilds, Chiddingstone Sevenoaks—but hope on my return to have the honour of seeing you again.

Miss Austen
Nº 23
Hans Place
Sloane Street

126. *To John Murray*

Thursday 23 November 1815

Sir

My Brother's note last Monday has been so fruitless, that I am afraid there can be little chance of my writing to any good effect; but yet I am so very much disappointed & vexed by the delays of the Printers[1] that I cannot help begging to know whether there is no hope of their being quickened.—Instead of the Work being ready by the end of the present month, it will hardly, at the rate we now proceed, be finished by the end of the next, and as I expect to leave London early in Dec[r], it is of consequence that no more time should be lost.—Is it likely that the Printers will be influenced to greater Dispatch & Punctuality by knowing that the Work is to be dedicated, by Permission, to the Prince Regent?—If you can make that circumstance operate, I shall be very glad.—My Brother returns *Waterloo*, [*p. 2*] with many thanks for the Loan of it.—We have heard much of Scott's account of Paris;[2]—if it be not incompatible with other arrangements, would you favour us with it—supposing you have any set already opened?—You may depend upon its' being in careful hands.

I remain, Sir,
Y^r ob. HumServ^t
J. Austen

23 Hans Place
Thursday Nov: 23.

Mr Murray

127. *To Cassandra Austen*

Friday 24 November 1815

Hans Place, Friday Nov: 24.

My dearest Cassandra

I have the pleasure of sending you a much better account of *my affairs*, which I know will be a great delight to you. I wrote to Mr Murray yesterday myself, & Henry wrote at the same time to Roworth. Before the notes were out of the House I received three sheets, & an apology from R. We sent the notes however, & I had a most civil one in reply from Mr M. He is so very polite indeed, that it is quite over-coming.—The Printers have been waiting for Paper—the blame is thrown upon the Stationer—but he gives his word that I shall have no farther cause for dissatisfaction.—He has lent us *Miss Williams*[1] & *Scott*, & says that any book of his will always be at *my* service.—In short, I am soothed & complimented into tolerable comfort.—

We had a visit yesterday from Edwd Knight; & Mr Mascall joined him here;—and this morn^g has brought Mr Mascall's Compt^s & two Pheasants.—We have some hope of Edward's coming to dinner today; he will, if he can I beleive.—He is looking extremely well.—Tomor-row Mr Haden is to dine with us.—There's Happiness!—We really grow so fond of Mr Haden that I do not know what to expect.—He, & Mr Tilson & Mr Philips made [*p. 2*] up our circle of Wits last night; Fanny played, & he sat & listened & suggested improvements, till Richard came in to tell him that "the Doctor was waiting for him at Captn Blake's"—and then he was off with a speed that you can ima-gine. He never does appear in the least above his Profession, or out of humour with it, or I should think poor Captn Blake, whoever he is, in a very bad way.—

I must have misunderstood Henry, when I told you that *you* were to hear from him today. He read me what he wrote to Edward;—part of it must have amused him I am sure;—one part alas! cannot be very amusing to anybody.— I wonder that with such Business to worry him, he can be getting better, but he certainly does gain strength, & if you & Edwd were to see him now I feel sure that you w^d think him improved since Monday. He was out yesterday, it was a fine sunshiney day *here*—(in the Country perhaps you might have Clouds & fogs—Dare I say so?—I shall not deceive *you*, if I do, as to my estimation of the Climate of London)—& he ventured, first on the Balcony, & then as far as the Greenhouse. He caught no cold, & therefore has done more today with great delight, & self-persuasion of Improvement; he has been to see Mrs Tilson & the Malings.—By the bye, you may talk to Mr T. of his wife's being better, I saw her yesterday & was sensible of her having gained ground in the last two days.—

[*p. 3*] *Evening.*—We have had no Edward.—Our circle is formed; only Mr Tilson & Mr Haden.—We are not so happy as we were. A message came this afternoon from Mrs Latouche & Miss East, offering themselves to drink tea with us tomorrow—& as it was accepted, here is an end of our extreme felicity in our Dinner-Guest.—I am heartily sorry they are coming! It will be an Even^g spoilt to Fanny & me.— Another little Disappointment.—Mr H. advises Henry's *not* venturing with us in the Carriage tomorrow;—if it were Spring, he says, it w^d be a different thing. One would rather this had not been. He seems to think his going out today rather imprudent, though acknowledging at the same time that he is better than he was in the Morn^g.—Fanny has had a Letter full of Commissions from Goodnestone; we shall be busy about them & her own matters I dare say from 12 till 4.—Nothing I trust will keep us from Keppel Street.—This day has brought a most friendly Letter from Mr Fowle, with a brace of Pheasants. I did not know before that Henry had written to him a few days ago, to ask for them. We shall live upon Pheasants;^{2} no bad Life!—I send you five one pound notes, for fear you should be distressed for little Money.—Lizzy's work is charmingly done. Shall you put it to your Chintz?—A *Sheet* come in this moment. 1st & 3^d vol. are now at 144.—2^d at 48.—I am sure you will like Particulars.—We are not to have the trouble of returning the Sheets to Mr Murray any longer, the Printer's boys bring & carry.

[*p. 4*] I hope Mary continues to get well fast—& I send my Love to little Herbert.^{3}—You will tell me more of Martha's plans of course when you write again.—Remember me most kindly to everybody, & Miss Benn besides.—Yours very affec^{ly}, J. Austen.

I have been listening to dreadful Insanity.—It is Mr Haden's firm beleif that a person *not* musical is fit for every sort of Wickedness.[4]— I ventured to assert a little on the other side, but wished the cause in abler hands.—

[*Continued upside down at top of p. 1*]

Supposing the weather sh^d be very bad on Sunday Even^g I shall not like to send Richard out you know—& in that case, my Dirty Linen must wait a day.

Miss Austen
Chawton

128. *To Cassandra Austen*

Sunday 26 November 1815

Hans Place, Sunday Nov: 26.

My Dearest
The Parcel arrived safely, & I am much obliged to you for your trouble.—It cost 2^s.10—but as there is a certain saving of 2^s.4½ on the other side, I am sure it is well worth doing.—I send 4 p^r of Silk Stock^{gs}— but I do not want them washed at present. In the 3 neckhandfs. I include the one sent down before.—These things perhaps Edwd may be able to bring, but even if he is not, I am extremely pleased with his returning to you from Steventon. It is much better—far preferable.—I *did* mention the P.R- in my note to Mr Murray, it brought me a fine compliment in return; whether it has done any other good[1] I do not know, but Henry thought it worth trying.—The Printers continue to supply me very well, I am advanced in vol. 3. to my *arra*-root, upon which peculiar style of spelling, there is a modest *qu:^{ry}?* in the Margin.—I will not forget Anna's arrow-root.—I hope you have told Martha of my first resolution of letting nobody know that I *might* dedicate &c—for fear of being obliged to do it—& that she is thoroughly convinced of my being influenced now by nothing but the most mercenary motives.—I have paid nine shillings on her account to Miss Palmer; there was no more oweing.—Well—we were very busy all yesterday; from ½ past 11 to 4 in the Streets, working almost entirely for other people, driving from Place to Place after a parcel for Sandling which we could never find, & encountering the miseries of Grafton House [*p. 2*] to get a purple frock for Eleanor Bridges.—We got to Keppel S^t however, which

was all I cared for—& though we could stay only a q^r of an hour, Fanny's calling gave great pleasure & her Sensibility still greater, for she was very much affected at the sight of the Children.—Poor little F.[2] looked heavy.—We saw the whole Party.—Aunt Har^t:[3] hopes Cassy will not forget to make a pincushion for Mrs Kelly—as *she* has spoken of its' being promised her several times.—I hope we shall see Aunt H.- & the dear little Girls here on Thursday.—So much for the morn^g; then came the dinner & Mr Haden who brought good Manners & clever conversation;—from 7 to 8 the Harp;—at 8 Mrs L. & Miss E. arrived— & for the rest of the Even^g the Draw^g-room was thus arranged, on the Sopha-side the two Ladies Henry & myself making the best of it, on the opposite side Fanny & Mr Haden in two chairs (I *beleive* at least they had *two* chairs) talking together uninterruptedly.—Fancy the scene! And what is to be fancied next?—Why that Mr H. dines here again tomorrow.—To day we are to have Mr Barlow.—Mr H. is reading Mansfield Park for the first time & prefers it to P&P.—A Hare & 4 Rabbits from G^m yesterday, so that we are stocked for nearly a week.—Poor Farmer Andrews! I am very sorry for him, & sincerely wish his recovery.—A better account of the Sugar than I could have expected. I should like to help you break some more.—I am glad you cannot wake early, I am sure you must have been under great arrears of rest.—Fanny & I have been to B. Chapel,[4] & walked back with Maria Cuthbert.—We have been very little plagued with visitors this last week, I remember only Miss Herries [*p. 3*] the Aunt, but I am in terror for to day, a fine bright Sunday, plenty of Mortar[5] & nothing to do.—Henry gets out in his Garden every day, but at present his inclination for doing more seems over, nor has he now any plan for leaving London before Dec: 18, when he thinks of going to Oxford for a few days;[6]—to day indeed, his feelings are for continuing where he is, through the next two months. One knows the uncertainty of all this, but should it be so, we must think the best & hope the best & do the best—and my idea in that case is, that when *he* goes to Oxford *I* should go home & have nearly a week of you before *you* take my place.[7]—This is only a silent project you know, to be gladly given up, if better things occur.—Henry calls himself stronger every day & Mr H. keeps on approving his Pulse—which seems generally better than ever—but still they will not let him be well.—The fever is not yet quite removed.—The Medicine he takes (the same as before you went) is cheifly to improve his Stomach, & only a little aperient. He is so well, that I cannot think why he is not perfectly well.—I should not have supposed his Stomach at all disordered but *there* the Fever speaks probably;—but he has no headake, no sickness, no pains, no Indigestions!—Perhaps when Fanny is gone, he will be allowed to recover faster.—I am not disappointed, I never thought the little girl at Wyards[8] very pretty, but she will have a fine complexion & curling hair & pass for a beauty.—We are glad the Mama's cold has not been worse—& send her our Love & good wishes by every convenient opportunity. Sweet amiable Frank! why does *he* have a cold too? Like Capt. Mirvan to M^de Duval,[9] "I wish it well over with him." [*p. 4*] Fanny has heard all that I have said to you about herself & Mr H.—Thank you very much for the sight of dearest Charles's Letter to yourself.—How pleasantly & how naturally he writes! and how perfect a picture of his Disposition & feelings, his style conveys!—Poor dear Fellow!—not a Present!—I have a great mind to send him all the twelve Copies which were to have been dispersed among my near Connections—beginning with the P. R. & ending with Countess Morley.—Adeiu.—Y^rs affec^ly

J. Austen

Give my Love to Cassy & Mary Jane.—Caroline will be gone when this reaches you.

Miss Austen

[*Letter of Wednesday 29 November 1815 missing*]

129. *To Cassandra Austen*

Saturday 2 December 1815

Hans Place, Saturday Dec: 2.

My dear Cassandra

Henry came back yesterday, & might have returned the day before if he had known[1] as much in time. I had the pleasure of hearing from Mr T.[2] on wednesday night that Mr Seymour thought there was not the least occasion for his absenting himself[3] any longer.—I had also the comfort of a few lines on wednesday morn^g from Henry himself—(just after your Letter was gone) giving so good an account of his feelings as made me perfectly easy. He met with the utmost care & attention at Hanwell, spent his two days there very quietly & pleasantly, & being certainly in no respect the worse for going, we may beleive that he must be better, as he is quite sure of being himself.—To make his return a complete Gala, Mr Haden was secured for dinner—I need not say that our Even^g was agreable.—But you seem to be under a mistake as to Mr H.—You call him an Apothecary; he is no Apothecary, he has never been an Apothecary, there is not an Apothecary in this Neighbourhood— the only inconvenience of the situation perhaps, but so it is—we have not a medical Man within reach—he is a Haden, nothing but a Haden, a sort of wonderful nondescript Creature on two Legs, something between a Man & an Angel—but without the least spice of an Apothecary.—He is perhaps the only Person *not* an Apothecary hereabouts. —[*p. 2*] He has never sung to us. He will not sing without a P. Forte accompaniment. Mr Meyers gives his three Lessons a week—altering his days & his hours however just as he chuses, never very punctual, & never giving good Measure.—I have not Fanny's fondness for Masters, & Mr Meyers does not give me any Longing after them. The truth is I think, that they are all, at least Music Masters, made of too much consequence & allowed to take too many Liberties with their Scholar's time. We shall be delighted to see Edward on Monday—only sorry that you must be losing him. A Turkey will be equally welcome with himself.—He must prepare for his own proper bedchamber here, as Henry moved down to the one below last week; he found the other cold.—I am sorry my Mother has been suffering, & am afraid this exquisite weather is too good to agree with her.—*I* enjoy it all over me, from top to toe, from right to left,[4] Longitudinally, Perpendicularly, Diagonally; —& I cannot but selfishly hope we are to have it last till Christmas;— nice, unwholesome, Unseasonable, relaxing, close, muggy weather!— Oh!—thank you very much for your long Letter; it did me a great deal of good.—Henry accepts your offer of making his nine gallon of Mead, thankfully. The mistake of the Dogs rather vexed him for a moment, but he has not thought of it since.—To day, he makes a third attempt at his strengthening Plaister,[5] & as I am sure he will now be getting out a great deal, it is to be wished that he may be able to keep it on.—He sets off this morning [*p. 3*] by the Chelsea Coach to sign Bonds & visit Henrietta S^t, & I have no doubt will be going every day to Henrietta S^t—Fanny & I were very snug by ourselves, as soon as we were satisfied about our Invalid's being safe at Hanwell.—By Manoeuvring & good luck we foiled all the Malings attempts upon us. Happily I caught a little cold on wednesday, the morn^g we were in Town, which we made very useful; & we saw nobody but our Precious, & Mr Tilson.—This Evening the Malings are allowed to drink tea with us.—We are in hopes, that is, we *wish* Miss Palmer & the little girls may come this morning. You know of course, that she could *not* come on Thursday; – & she will not attempt to *name* any other day.—I do not think I shall send down any more dirty Linen;—it will not answer when the Car^ge is to be paid each way.—I have got Anna's arrow-root, & your gloves.—

God bless you.—Excuse the shortness of this—but I must finish it now, that I may save you 2^d6—Best Love.—Y^rs affec^ly

J. A.

It strikes me that I have no business to give the P. R. a Binding,[7] but we will take Counsel upon the question.—

I am glad you have put the flounce on your Chintz, I am sure it must look particularly well, & it is what I had thought of.—

Miss Austen
Chawton
Alton
Hants

[*Letters missing here*]

130. *To John Murray*

Monday 11 December 1815

Hans Place, Dec: 11th

Dear Sir

As I find that *Emma* is advertized for publication as early as Saturday next, I think it best to lose no time in settling all that remains to be settled on the subject, & adopt this method of doing so, as involving the smallest tax on your time.—

In the first place, I beg you to understand that I leave the terms on which the Trade should be supplied with the work, entirely to your Judgement, entreating you to be guided in every such arrangement by your own experience of what is most likely to clear off the Edition rapidly. I shall be satisfied with whatever you feel to be best.—

The Title page must be, Emma, Dedicated by Permission to H. R. H. The Prince Regent.—And it is my particular wish that one Set should be completed & sent to H. R. H. two or three days before the Work is generally public—It should be sent under Cover to the Rev: J. S. Clarke, Librarian, Carlton House.—I shall subjoin a list[1] of those persons, to whom I must trouble you to forward also a Set each, when the Work is out;—all unbound,² with *From the Authoress*, in the first page.—

[*p. 2*] I return you, with very many Thanks, the Books you have so obligingly supplied me with.—I am very sensible I assure you of the attention you have paid to my Convenience & amusement.—I return also, Mansfield Park, as ready for a 2ᵈ Edit: I beleive, as I can make it.—

I am in Hans Place till the 16ᵗʰ.—From that day, inclusive, my direction will be, Chawton, Alton, Hants.

I remain dear Sir,
Yʳ faithful HumServᵗ,
J. Austen

I wish you would have the goodness to send a line by the Bearer, stating the *day* on which the set will be ready for the Prince Regent.—

[*No address*]

131(C). *To John Murray*

Monday 11 December 1815

Hans Place, December 11

Dear Sir

I am much obliged by yours, and very happy to feel everything arranged to our mutual satisfaction. As to my direction about the title-page, it was arising from my ignorance only, and from my having never noticed the proper place for a dedication. I thank you for putting me right. Any deviation from what is usually done in such cases is the last thing I should wish for. I feel happy in having a friend to save me from the ill effect of my own blunder.

Yours, dear Sir, &c,
J. Austen

[*No address*]

132(D). *To James Stanier Clarke*

Monday 11 December 1815

Dec: 11.

Dear Sir

My Emma is now so near publication that I feel it right to assure You of my not having forgotten your kind recommendation of an early Copy for Cⁿ H.—& that I have Mʳ Murray's promise of its being sent to

HRH. under cover to You, three days previous to the Work being really out.—

I must make use of this opportunity to thank you dear Sir, for the very high praise you bestow on my other Novels—I am too vain to wish to convince you that you have praised them beyond their Merit.—

My greatest anxiety at present is that this 4th work shd not disgrace what was good in the others. But on this point I will do myself the justice to declare that whatever may be my wishes for its' success, I am very strongly haunted by the idea that to those Readers who have pre-ferred P&P. it will appear inferior in Wit, & to those who have pre-ferred MP. very inferior in good Sense. Such as it is however, I hope you will do me the favour of accepting a Copy. Mr M. will have direc-tions for sending one. I am quite honoured by your thinking me capable of drawing such a Clergyman [*p. 2*] as you gave the sketch of in your note of Nov: 16. But I assure you I am *not*. The comic part of the Character I might be equal to, but not the Good, the Enthusiastic, the Literary. Such a Man's Conversation must at times be on subjects of Science & Philosophy of which I know nothing—or at least be occa-sionally abundant in quotations & allusions which a Woman, who like me, knows only her own Mother-tongue & has read very little in that, would be totally without the power of giving.—A Classical Education, or at any rate, a very extensive acquaintance with English Literature, Ancient & Modern, appears to me quite Indispensable for the person who wd do any justice to your Clergyman—And I think I may boast myself to be, with all possible Vanity, the most unlearned, & unin-formed Female who ever dared to be an Authoress.

Beleive me, dear Sir,

Your obligd & faith¹ Hum. Servt.

J. A.

[*No address*]

132(A). *From James Stanier Clarke*

Thursday ?21 December 1815

Carlton House Thursday, 1815

My dear Madam,

The Letter you were so obliging as to do me the Honour of sending, was forwarded to me in Kent, where in a Village, Chiddingstone near Sevenoaks, I had been hiding myself from all bustle and turmoil—and getting Spirits for a Winter Campaign—and Strength to stand the sharp knives which many a Shylock is wetting to cut more than a Pound of Flesh from my heart, on the appearance of James the Second.[1]

On Monday I go to Lord Egremonts at Petworth—where your Praises have long been sounded as they ought to be. I shall then look in on the Party at the Pavilion[2] for a couple of nights—and return to preach at Park Street Chapel Green St. on the Thanksgiving Day.

You were very good to send me Emma—which I have in no respect deserved. It is gone to the Prince Regent. I have read only a few Pages which I very much admired—there is so much nature—and excellent description of Character in every thing you describe.

Pray continue to write, & make all your friends send Sketches to help you—and Memoires pour servir—as the French term it. Do let us have an English Clergyman after *your* fancy—much novelty may be introduced—shew dear Madam what good would be done if Tythes were taken away entirely, and describe him burying his own mother— as I did—because the High Priest of the Parish in which she died—did not pay her remains the respect he ought to do. I have never recovered the Shock. Carry your Clergyman to Sea as the Friend of some distinguished Naval Character about a Court—you can then bring foreward like Le Sage[3] many interesting Scenes of Character & Interest.

But forgive me, I cannot write to you without wishing to elicit your Genius;—& I fear I cannot do that, without trespassing on your Patience and Good Nature.

I have desired Mr Murray to procure, if he can, two little Works[4] I ventured to publish from being at Sea—Sermons which I wrote & preached on the Ocean—& the Edition which I published of Falconers Shipwreck.

Pray, dear Madam, remember, that besides My Cell at Carlton House, I have another which Dr Barne procured for me at N° 37, Golden Square—where I often hide myself. There is a small Library there much at your Service—and if you can make the Cell render you any service as a sort of Half-way House, when you come to Town—I shall be most happy. There is a Maid Servant of mine always there.

I hope to have the honour of sending you James the 2^d when it reaches a second Ed:—as some few Notes may possibly be then added.

Yours dear Madam, very sincerely

J. S. Clarke.

[*No address*]

133. *To Charles Thomas Haden*

Thursday 14 December 1815

Dear Sir

We return these volumes with many Thanks. They have afforded us great amusement.—As we were out ourselves yesterday Even^g we were glad to find you had not called—but shall depend upon your giving us some part of *this* Even^g—I leave Town early on Saturday, & must say "Good bye" to you.—

Y^r obliged & faithful
J. Austen

Thursday.

C. Haden Esqr

134(A). *From the Countess of Morley*

Wednesday 27 December 1815

Saltram
27th Dec^r

Madam—

I have been most anxiously waiting for an introduction to Emma, & am infinitely obliged to you for your kind recollection of me, which will procure me the pleasure of her acquaintance some days sooner than I sh^d otherwise have [*p. 2*] had it—I am already become intimate in the Woodhouse family, & feel that they will not amuse[1] & interest me less than the Bennetts, Bertrams, Norriss & all their admirable predecessors—I *can* give them no higher praise—

I am
Madam
Y^r much obliged
F. Morley—

To
Miss J. Austin [*sic*]
Chawton
Alton
Hants.

134(D). *To the Countess of Morley*

Madam

Accept my Thanks for the honour of your note & for your kind Disposition in favour of Emma. In my present State of Doubt as to her reception in the World, it is particularly gratifying to me to receive so early an assurance of your Ladyship's approbation.—It encourages me to depend on the same share of general good opinion which Emma's Predecessors have experienced, & to beleive that I have not yet—as almost every Writer of Fancy does sooner or later—overwritten myself.—I am Madam,

Your obliged & faith:[1] Servt.

J. Austen

Dec: 31.—1815.

[*No address*]

134. *To the Countess of Morley*

Chawton Dec: 31.

Madam

Accept my Thanks for the honour of your note & for your kind disposition in favour of Emma. In my present state of doubt as to her reception in the World, it is particularly gratifying to receive so early an assurance of your Ladyship's approbation. It encourages me to depend on the same share of general good opinion which Emma's Predecessors have experienced, & to beleive that I have not yet—as almost every Writer of Fancy does [*p. 2*] sooner or later—overwritten myself.

I am Madam
Your Obliged & faithful Serv[t]

J. Austen

[*No address*]

135. *To Anna Lefroy*

?December 1815–January 1816

My dear Anna

As I wish very much to see *your* Jemima,[1] I am sure you will like to see *my* Emma, & have therefore great pleasure in sending it for your perusal. Keep it as long as you chuse; it has been read by all here.—

[*No address*]

136. *To Catherine Ann Prowting*

?early 1816

My dear Miss Prowting

Had our poor friend[1] lived these volumes would have been at her service, & as I know you were in the habit of reading together & have had the gratification of hearing that the *Works of the same hand* had given you pleasure, I shall make no other apology for offering you the perusal of them, only begging that, if not immediately disposed for such light reading, you would keep them as long as you like, as they are not wanted at home.

Yours very sincerely
J. Austen

Sunday Night—

[*No address*]

137. *To Caroline Austen*

Wednesday 13 March 1816

Chawton Wednesday
March 13.

My dear Caroline

I am very glad to have an opportunity of answering your agreable little Letter. You seem to be quite my own Neice in your feelings towards M^{de} de Genlis.[1] I do not think I could even now, at my sedate time of Life, read *Olimpe et Theophile* without being in a rage. It really is too bad!—Not allowing them to be happy together, when they *are* married.—Don't talk of it, pray. I have just lent your Aunt Frank the 1st vol. of Les Veillees du Chateau, for Mary Jane to read. It will be some time before she comes to the horror of Olympe.—We have had sad weather lately, I hope you have liked it.—Our Pond is brimfull & our roads are dirty & our walls are damp, & we sit wishing every bad day may be the last. It is not cold [*p. 2*] however. Another week perhaps may see us shrinking & shivering under a dry East Wind.

I had a very nice Letter from your Brother not long ago, & I am quite happy to see how much his Hand is improving.—I am convinced that it will end in a very gentlemanlike Hand, much above Par.—We have had a great deal of fun lately with Post-chaises stopping at the door; three times within a few days, we had a couple of agreable Visitors turn in unexpectedly—your Uncle Henry[2] & Mr Tilson, Mrs Heathcote & Miss Bigg, your Uncle Henry & Mr Seymour. Take notice, that it was the same Uncle Henry each time.

I remain my dear Caroline
Your affec: Aunt
J. Austen

Miss C. Austen
Steventon

138(A). *From James Stanier Clarke*

Wednesday 27 March 1816

Pavilion—March 27th 1816.

Dear Miss Austen,

I have to return you the Thanks of His Royal Highness the Prince Regent for the handsome Copy you sent him of your last excellent Novel—pray dear Madam soon write again and again. Lord St Helens and many of the Nobility who have been staying here, paid you the just tribute of their Praise.

The Prince Regent has just [*p. 2*] left us for London; and having been pleased to appoint me Chaplain and Private English Secretary to the Prince of Cobourg, I remain here with His Serene Highness & a select Party until the Marriage.[1] Perhaps when you again appear in print you may chuse to dedicate your Volumes to Prince Leopold: any Historical Romance illustrative of the History of the august house [*p. 3*] of Cobourg, would just now be very interesting.

Believe me at all times
Dear Miss Austen
Your obliged friend
J. S. Clarke

Miss Jane Austen
at Mr Murrays
Albemarle Street
London[2]

138(D). *To James Stanier Clarke*

Monday 1 April 1816

My dear Sir

I am honoured by the Prince's thanks, & very much obliged[1] to
yourself for the kind manner in which You mention the Work. I have
also to acknowledge a former Letter, forwarded to me from Hans Place.
I assure You I felt very grateful for the friendly Tenor of it, & hope my
silence will have been considered as it was truely meant, to proceed
only from an unwillingness to tax your Time with idle Thanks.—

Under every interesting circumstance which your own Talents &
literary Labours have placed you in, or the favour of the Regent bestowed, you have my best wishes. Your recent appointments I hope are
a step to something still better.[2] In my opinion, The service of a Court
can hardly be too well paid, for immense must be the sacrifice of Time
& Feeling required by it.[3]

You are very, very kind in your hints as to the sort of Composition
which might recommend me at present, & I am fully sensible that an
Historical [*p. 2*] Romance, founded on the House[4] of Saxe Cobourg
might be much more to the purpose of Profit or Popularity, than such
pictures of domestic Life in Country Villages as I deal in—but I could
no more write a Romance than an Epic Poem.—I could not sit seriously
down to write a serious Romance under any other motive than to save
my Life, & if it were indispensable for me to keep it up & never relax
into laughing at myself or other people, I am sure I should be hung
before I had finished the first Chapter.—No—I must keep to my own
style & go on in my own Way;[5] And though I may never succeed again
in that, I am convinced that I should totally fail in any other.—

I remain my dear Sir,
Your very much obliged & very sincere friend
J. Austen

Chawton near Alton[6] April 1st—
1816—

[*No address*]

139. *To John Murray*

Monday 1 April 1816

Dear Sir

I return you the Quarterly Reveiw with many Thanks. The Author-ess of *Emma* has no reason I think to complain of her treatment in it—except in the total omission of Mansfield Park.—I cannot but be sorry that so clever a Man as the Reveiwer of *Emma*,[1] should consider it as unworthy of being noticed.—You will be pleased to hear that I have received the Prince's Thanks for the *handsome* Copy I sent him of *Emma*. Whatever he may think of *my* share of the Work, *Yours* seems to have been quite right.—

In consequence of the late sad Event[2] in Henrietta S^t—I must request that if you should at any time have anything to communicate by Letter, you will be so good as to write by the post, directing to me (Miss J. Austen) Chawton near Alton—and that for anything of a larger bulk, you will add to the same direction,[3] *by Collier's Southampton Coach.*—

I remain, dear Sir,
Yours very faithfully
J. Austen

Chawton April 1.
1816.

[*No address*]

140. *To Caroline Austen*

Sunday 21 April 1816

Chawton Sunday April 21—

My dear Caroline

I am glad to have an opportunity of writing to you again, for my last Note was written so long before it was sent, that it seemed almost good for nothing. The note to your Papa, is to announce the death of that excellent woman Mrs Elizth Leigh; it came here this morning enclosed in a Letter to Aunt Cassandra.—We all feel that we have lost a most val-ued old freind, but the death of a person at her advanced age, so fit to die, & by her own feelings so *ready* to die, is not to be regretted.—She has been so kind as to leave a little remembrance of £20- to your Grandmama.—I have had a letter from Scarlets[1] this morning, with a very tolerable account of health there.—We have also heard from Godmersham, & the day of your Uncle & Fanny's coming is fixed; they leave home tomorrow senight, spend two days in Town & are to be with us on Thursday May 2ᵈ—We are to see your Cousin Edward likewise, [*p. 2*] but probably not quite so soon.—Your Uncle Henry talks of being in Town again on Wednesday. He will have spent a complete fortnight at Godmersham, & no doubt it will have done him good.—Tell your Mama that he came back from Steventon much pleased with his visit to her.—Your Grandmama is not *quite* well, she seldom gets through the 24 hours without some pain in her head, but we hope it is lessening, & that a continuance of such weather as may allow her to be out of doors & hard at work every day will gradually remove it.—Cassy has had great pleasure in working this—whatever it may be[2]—for you; I beleive she rather fancied it might do for a quilt for your little wax doll, but you will find a use for it if you can I am sure.— She often talks of you; & we should all be very glad to see you again— and if your Papa comes on Wednesday, as we rather hope, & it suited everybody that you should come with him, it wᵈ give us great pleasure.—Our Fair at Alton is next Saturday, which is also Mary Jane's Birthday, & you would be thought an *addition* on such a great day.— [*p. 3*] I shall say no more, because I know the[re ?may be] many circumstances to make it inconvenient at home.—We are almost ashamed to include your Mama in the invitation, or to ask *her* to be at the trouble of a long ride for so few days as we shall be having disengaged, for we *must* wash before the Gᵐ Party come & therefore Monday would be [the *omitted*] last day that our House could be comfortable for her; but if she does feel disposed to pay us a little visit & you could *all* come, so much the better.—We do not like to *invite* her to come on Wednesday, to be turned out of the house on Monday. . . .

[*The last five lines of the letter mentioned James-Edward, and the "sad weather" which they had for him at Easter, so that his ride on Saturday "could only be tolerable by its taking him home".*][3]

Miss Caroline Austen

141(C). *To Anna Lefroy*

Sunday 23 June 1816

My dear Anna

Cassy desires her best thanks for the book. She was quite delighted to see it: I do not know when I have seen her so much struck by anybody's kindness as on this occasion. Her sensibility seems to be opening to the perception of great actions. These gloves having appeared on the Piano Forte ever since you were here on Friday, we imagine they must be yours. Mrs Digweed returned yesterday through all the afternoon's rain and was of course wet through, but in speaking of it she never once said "It was beyond everything," which I am sure it must have been. Your Mama means to ride to Speen Hill tomorrow to see the Mrs Hulberts who are both very indifferent. By all accounts they really are breaking now. Not so stout as the old Jackass.

Yours affec^ately J. A.

Chawton, Sunday, June 23rd Uncle Charles's birthday.

[*No address*]

142. *To James-Edward Austen*

Tuesday 9 July 1816

Chawton Tuesday July 9. 1816[1]

My dear Edward

Many Thanks. A thank for every Line, & as many to Mr W. Digweed for coming. We have been wanting very much to hear of your Mother, & are happy to find she continues to mend, but her illness must have been a very serious one indeed.[2]—When she is really recovered, she ought to try change of air & come over to us.—Tell your Father I am very much obliged to him for his share of your Letter & most sincerely join in the hope of her being eventually much the better for her present Discipline. She has the comfort moreover of being confined in such weather as gives one little temptation to be out. It is really too bad,[3] & has been too bad for a long time, much worse than anybody *can* bear, & I begin to think it will never be fine again. This is a finesse of mine, for I have often observed that if one writes about the Weather, it is generally completely changed before the Letter is read. I wish it may

315

prove so now, & that when M[r] W. Digweed reaches Steventon tomorrow, he may find You have had a long series of hot, dry weather. [*p. 2*] We are a small party at present, only G. Mama, Mary Jane & myself.— Yalden's coach cleared off the rest yesterday. I suppose it is known at Steventon that Uncle Frank & Aunt Cassandra were to go to Town[4] on some business of Uncle Henry's—& that Aunt Martha had some business of her own which determined her to go at the same time;—but that Aunt Frank determined to go[5] likewise & spend a few days with her family, may not be known—nor that two other places in the Coach were taken by Capt. & M[rs] Clement.—Little Cassy[6] went also, & does not return at present. They are all going to Broadstairs again.—The Aunt Cass: & the Aunt Martha did not mean to stay beyond two whole days, but the Uncle Frank & his Wife proposed being pressed to remain till Saturday.

I am glad you recollected to mention your being come home. My heart began to sink within me when I had got so far through your Letter without its being mentioned.[7] I was dreadfully afraid that you might be detained at Winchester by severe illness, confined to your Bed perhaps & quite unable to hold a pen, & only dating from Steventon in order, with a mistaken sort of Tenderness, to deceive me.—But now, I have [*p. 3*] no doubt of your being at home,[8] I am sure you would not say it so seriously unless it actually were so.—We saw a countless number of Postchaises full of Boys pass by yesterday morn[g]—full of future Heroes, Legislators, Fools, & Vilains.—You have never thanked me for my last Letter, which went by the Cheese. I cannot bear not to be thanked. You will not pay us a visit yet of course, we must not think of it. Your Mother must get well first, & you must go to Oxford[9] & *not* be elected; after that, a little change of scene may be good for you, & Your Physicians I hope will order you to the Sea, or to a house by the side of a very considerable pond.[10]—Oh! it rains again; it beats against the window.—Mary Jane & I have been wet through once already today, we set off in the Donkey Carriage for Farringdon as I wanted to see the improvements M[r] Woolls is making, but we were obliged to turn back before we got there, but not soon enough to avoid a Pelter all the way home. We met M[r] Woolls—I talked of its' being bad weather for the Hay—& he returned me the comfort of its' being much worse for the Wheat.—We hear that M[rs] S- does not quit Tangier[11]—Why & Wherefore?—Do you know that our Browning is gone?—You must prepare for a William[12] when you come, a goodlooking Lad, civil & quiet, & seeming likely to do.—Good bye. I am sure M[r] W. D. will be astonished at my writing so much, for the Paper is so thin that he will be able to count the Lines, if not to read them.—Yours affec^ly

J. Austen

[*p. 4*]
My dear James

We suppose the Trial[13] is to take place this week, but we only feel sure that it cannot have taken place yet because we have heard nothing of it. A Letter from G^m today tells us that *Henry* as well as William K-goes to France with his Uncle.[14]—

Y^rs Ever—J. A.

Mr Edward Austen
Steventon
By favour of
Mr W. Digweed

143. *To Caroline Austen*

Monday 15 July 1816

My dear Caroline

I have followed your directions & find your Handwriting admirable. If you continue to improve as much as you have done, perhaps I may not be obliged to shut my eyes at all half a year hence.—I have been very much entertained by your story of Carolina & her aged Father, it made me laugh heartily, & I am particularly[1] glad to find you so much alive upon any topic of such absurdity, as the usual description of a Heroine's father.—You have done it full justice—or if anything *be* wanting, it is the information of the venerable old Man's having married when only Twenty one, & being a father at Twenty two.

I had an early opportunity of conveying your Letter to Mary Jane, having only to throw it out of [the *omitted*] window at her as she was romping [*p. 2*] with your Brother in the Back Court.—She thanks you for it—& answers your questions through me.—I am to tell you that she has passed her time at Chawton very pleasantly indeed, that she does not miss Cassy so much as she expected, & that as to Diana's Temple[2] she is ashamed to say it has never been worked at since you went away.—She is very glad that you found Fanny again.—I suppose you had worn her in your stays without knowing it, & if she tickled you, thought it only a flea.

Edward's visit has been a great pleasure to us. He has not lost one

good quality or good Look, & is only altered in being improved by
being some months older than when we saw him last. He is [*p. 3*] get-
ting very near our own age, for *we* do not grow older of course.
. . . [*Complimentary close and signature cut away*][3]
Chawton
Monday July 15—

Miss C. Austen
Steventon

---

144. *To Cassandra Austen*

Wednesday 4 September 1816

[*First leaf, pp. 1 and 2, missing, and also top of p. 3*]

[*p. 3*] . . . Letter today. His not writing on friday gave me some
[?worry but now its] coming makes me more than amends.—I know
you heard from Edward yesterday, Henry wrote to me by the same
post, & so did Fanny—I had therefore 3 Letters at once which I thought
well worth paying for! Yours was a treasure, so full of everything.—
But how very much Cheltenham is to be preferred in May![1]—Henry
does not write diffusely, but chearfully;—at present he wishes to come
to us as soon as we can receive him—is decided for Orders &c.[2]—I
have written to him to say that after this week, he cannot come too
soon.—I do not really expect him however immediately; they will hardly
part with him at G^m yet.—Fanny does not seem any better, or very
little; she ventured to dine one day at Sandling & has suffered for it
ever since.—I collect from her, that Mr Seymour is either married or on
the point of being married to Mrs Scrane.—She is not explicit, because
imagining us to be informed.—I am glad I did not know that you had
no possibility of having a fire on Saturday—& so glad that you have
your Pelisse!—Your Bed room describes more comfortably than I could
have supposed.—We go on very well here, Edward is a great pleasure
to me;—he drove me to Alton yesterday; I went principally to carry
news of you & Henry, & made a regular handsome visit, staying there
while Edwd went on to Wyards with an invitation to dinner;—it was
declined, & will be so again today probably, for I really beleive Anna
is not equal to the fatigue.—The Alton 4[3] drank tea with us last night,

& we were very pleasant:—Jeu de violon[4] &c—all new to Mr Sweney— & he entered into it very well.—It was a renewal of former agreable evenings.—We all (except my Mother) dine at Alton tomorrow—& perhaps may have some of the same sports again—but I do not think M^r & Mrs D. will add much to our wit.—Edward is writing a Novel— we have all heard what he has written—it is extremely clever; written with great ease & spirit;—if he can carry it on in the same way, it will be a firstrate work, & in a style, I think, to be popular.—Pray tell Mary how much I admire it.—And tell Caroline that I think it is hardly fair upon her & myself, to have him take up the Novel Line. . .

[*top of p. 4 missing*]. . . but the coldness of the weather is enough to account for their want of power.—The Duchess of Orleans, the paper says, drinks at my Pump. Your Library will be a great resource.— Three Guineas a week for such Lodgings!—I am quite angry.—Martha desires her Love—& is sorry to tell you that she has got some Chilblains on her fingers—she never had them before.—This is to go for a Letter.—

Y^{rs} affec^{ly} J. Austen

[*Postscript below address panel*]

I shall be perfectly satisfied if I hear from you again on Tuesday.

Miss Austen

[*No address*]

145. *To Cassandra Austen*

Sunday 8–Monday 9 September 1816

Chawton, Sunday Sept: 8.

My dearest Cassandra

I have borne the arrival of your Letter today extremely well; anybody might have thought it was giving me pleasure.—I am very glad you find so much to be satisfied with at Cheltenham. While the Waters agree, every thing else is trifling.—A Letter arrived for you from Charles last Thursday. They are all safe, & pretty well in Keppel S^t, the Children decidedly better for Broadstairs, & he writes principally to ask when it will be convenient to us to receive Miss P.-[1] the little girls & himself.— They w^d be ready to set off in ten days from the time of his writing, to pay their visits in Hampshire & Berkshire—& he would prefer coming to Chawton *first*. I have answered him & said, that we hoped it might suit them to wait till the *last* week in Sept:^{r}, as we could not ask them sooner, either on your account, or the want of room. I mentioned the 23^d, as the probable day of your return.—When you have once left Cheltenham, I shall grudge every half day wasted on the road. If there were but a coach from Hungerford to Chawton!—I have desired him to let me hear again soon.—He does not include a Maid in the list to be accomodated, but if they bring one, as I suppose they will, we shall have no bed in the house even then for Charles himself—let alone Henry—. But what can we do?—We shall have the G^t House quite at our command;—it is to be cleared of the Papillons Servants in a day or two;—they themselves have been hurried off into Essex to take possession—not of a large Estate left them by an Uncle—but to scrape together all they can I suppose of the effects of a Mrs Rawstorn a rich old friend & cousin, suddenly deceased, to whom they are joint Executors. So, there is a happy end of the Kentish Papillons coming here. [*p. 2*] No morning service to day, wherefore I am writing between 12 & 1 o'clock.—Mr Benn in the afternoon—& likewise more rain again, by the look & the sound of things. You left us in doubt of Mrs Benn's situation, but she has bespoke her Nurse.—Mrs F. A. seldom either looks or appears quite well.—Little Embryo is troublesome I suppose.— They dined with us yesterday, & had fine weather both for coming & going home, which has hardly ever happened to them before.—She is still unprovided with a Housemaid.—Our day at Alton was very pleasant—Venison quite right—Children well-behaved—& M^r & Mrs Digweed taking kindly to our Charades, & other Games.—I must also observe, for his Mother's satisfaction, that Edward at my suggestion, devoted himself very properly to the entertainment of Miss S. Gibson.— Nothing was wanting except Mr Sweney; but he alas! had been ordered away to London the day before.—We had a beautiful walk home by Moonlight.—Thank you, my Back has given me scarcely any pain for many days.—I have an idea that agitation does it as much harm as fatigue, & that I was ill at the time of your going, from the very circumstance of your going.—I am nursing myself up now into as beautiful a state as I can, because I hear that Dr White means to call on me before he leaves the Country.—*Even^g*.—Frank & Mary & the Child^n visited us this morn^g.—M^r & Mrs Gibson are to come on the 23^d—& there is too much reason to fear they will stay above a week.—Little George could tell me where you were gone to, as well as what you were to bring him, when I asked him the other day.—Sir Tho: Miller is dead. I treat you with a dead Baronet in almost every Letter.—So, you have C. Craven[2] among you, as well as the Duke of Orleans & M[r] Pococke. But it mortifies me that *you* have not added one to the stock of common acquaintance. Do pray meet with somebody belonging to yourself.— I am quite weary of your knowing nobody.—

M[rs] Digweed parts with both Hannah & old Cook, the former will [*p. 3*] not give up her Lover, who is a Man of bad Character, the Latter is guilty only of being unequal to anything.—Miss Terry was to have spent this week with her Sister, but as usual it is put off. My amiable friend knows the value of her company.—I have not seen Anna since the day you left us, her Father & Brother visited her most days.— Edward[3] & Ben called here on Thursday. Edward was in his way to Selborne. We found him very agreable. He is come back from France,[4] thinking of the French as one c[d] wish, disappointed in every thing. He did not go beyond Paris.—I have a letter from M[rs] Perigord, she & her Mother are in London again;—she speaks of France as a scene of general Poverty & Misery,—no Money, no Trade—nothing to be got but by the Innkeepers[5]—& as to her own present prospects, she is not much less melancholy[6] than before.—I have also a letter from Miss Sharp, quite one of her Letters;—she has been again obliged to exert herself—more than ever—in a more distressing, more harrassed state— & has met with another excellent old Physician & his Wife, with every virtue under Heaven, who takes to her & cures her from pure Love & Benevolence.—D[r] & M[rs] Storer are *their* M[rs] & Miss Palmer—for they are at Bridlington. I am happy to say however that the sum of the account is better than usual. Sir William is returned; from Bridlington they go to Chevet, & she *is* to have a Young Governess under her.— I enjoyed Edward's company[7] very much, as I said before, & yet I was not sorry when friday came. It had been a busy week, & I wanted a few days quiet, & exemption from the Thought & contrivances which any sort of company gives.—I often wonder how *you* can find time for what you do, in addition to the care of the House;—And how good M[rs] West[8] c[d] have written such Books & collected so many hard words, with all her family cares, is still more a matter of astonishment![9] Composition seems to me Impossible, with a head full of Joints of Mutton & doses of rhubarb.—*Monday.* Here is a sad morn[g].—I fear you may not have been able to get to the Pump. The two last days were very pleasant.—I enjoyed them the more for your sake.—[*p. 4*] But today, it is really bad enough to make you all cross.—I hope Mary will change her Lodgings at the fortnight's end; I am sure, if you looked about well, you would find others in some odd corner, to suit you better. Mrs Potter charges for the *name* of the High S^t—Success to the Pianoforte! I trust it will drive you away.—We hear now that there is to be *no Honey* this year. Bad news for us.—We must husband our present stock of Mead;—& I am sorry to perceive that our 20 Gal: is very nearly out.—I cannot comprehend how the 14 Gal: c^d last so long.—

We do not much like Mr Cooper's new Sermons;[10]—they are fuller of Regeneration & Conversion than ever—with the addition of his zeal in the cause of the Bible Society.—Martha's love to Mary & Caroline, & she is extremely glad to find they like the Pelisse.—The Debarys are indeed odious!—We are to see my Brother tomorrow, but for only one night.—I had no idea that he would care for the Races, *without* Edward.—Remember me to all. Yours very affec:^ly

J. Austen

Miss Austen
Post Office
Cheltenham

---

146. *To James Edward Austen*

Monday 16–Tuesday 17 December 1816

Chawton, Monday[1] Dec: 16.

My dear Edward

One reason for my writing to you now, is that I may have the pleasure of directing to you *Esqre*—I give you Joy of having left Winchester.—Now you may own, how miserable you were there; now, it will gradually all come out—your Crimes & your Miseries—how often you went up by the Mail to London & threw away Fifty Guineas at a Tavern, & how often you were on the point of hanging yourself—restrained only, as some illnatured aspersion upon poor old Winton has it, by the want of a Tree within some miles of the City.—Charles Knight & his companions passed through Chawton about 9 this morning; later than it used to be. Uncle Henry & I had a glimpse of his handsome face, looking all health & goodhumour.—

I wonder when you will come & see us. I know what I rather speculate upon, but I shall say nothing.—We think Uncle Henry in excellent Looks. Look at him this moment & think so too, if you have not done it before; & we have the great comfort of seeing decided improvement in Uncle Charles, both as to Health, Spirits & Appearance.—And they are each of them so agreable in their different way, & harmonize so well, that their visit is thorough Enjoyment.—Uncle Henry writes very [*p. 2*] superior Sermons.—You & I must try to get hold of one or two, & put them into our Novels;—it would be a fine help to a volume; & we could make our Heroine read it aloud of a Sunday Evening, just as well as Isabella Wardour in the Antiquary,[2] is made to read the History of the Hartz Demon in the ruins of St Ruth—tho' I beleive, upon re-collection, Lovell is the Reader.—By the bye, my dear Edward, I am quite concerned for the loss your Mother mentions in her Letter; two Chapters & a half to be missing is monstrous! It is well that *I* have not been at Steventon lately, & therefore cannot be suspected of purloining them;—two strong twigs & a half towards a Nest of my own, would have been something.—I do not think however that any theft of that sort would be really very useful to me. What should I do with your strong, manly, spirited Sketches, full of Variety & Glow?—How could I possibly join them on to the little bit (two Inches wide) of Ivory on which I work with so fine a Brush, as produces little effect after much labour?

You will hear from Uncle Henry how well Anna is. She seems per-fectly recovered.—Ben was here on Saturday, to ask Uncle Charles & me to dine with them, as tomorrow, but I was forced to decline it, the walk is beyond my strength (though I am otherwise very well) & this is not a Season for Donkey Carriages; & as we do not like to spare Uncle Charles, he has declined it too.—[*p. 3*] *Tuesday.*—Ah! ha!—Mr Edward, I doubt your seeing Uncle Henry at Steventon to day. The weather will prevent your expecting him I think.—Tell your Father, with Aunt Cass:'s Love & mine, that the Pickled Cucumbers are ex-tremely good, & tell him also—"tell him what you will";[3] No, don't tell him what you will, but tell him that Grandmama begs him to make Joseph Hall[4] pay his Rent if he can. You must not be tired of reading the word *Uncle*, for I have not done with it. Uncle Charles thanks your Mother for her Letter; it was a great pleasure to him to know the parcel was received & gave so much satisfaction; & he begs her to be so good as to give *Three Shillings* for him to Dame Staples, which shall be allowed for in the payment of her debt here.—

I am happy to tell you that Mr Papillon[5] will soon make his offer, probably next Monday, as he returns on Saturday.—His *intention* can be no longer doubtful in the smallest degree, as he has secured the refusal

of the House which Mrs Baverstock at present occupies in Chawton &
is to vacate soon, which is of course intended for Mrs Eliz^th Papillon.—
Adeiu Amiable!—I hope Caroline behaves well to you.

Yours affec^ly
J. Austen

James Edward Austen Esqre
Steventon

147(C). *To Anna Lefroy*

Thursday ?December 1816

My dear Anna
   Your Grandmama is *very* much obliged to you for the Turkey, but
cannot help grieving that you should not keep it for yourselves. Such
Highmindedness is almost more than she can bear.—She will be very
glad of better weather that she may see you again & so we shall all.

Yours affec^ately
J. Austen

Thursday.

148. *To Cassandra Esten Austen*

Wednesday 8 January 1817

Ym raed Yssac
   I hsiw uoy a yppah wen raey. Ruoy xis snisuoc emac ereh yadretsey,
dna dah hcae a eceip fo ekac.—Siht si elttil Yssac's yadhtrib,[1] dna ehs
si eerht sraey dlo. Knarf sah nugeb gninrael Nital. Ew deef eht Nibor
yreve gninrom.—Yllas netfo seriuqne retfa uoy. Yllas Mahneb sah tog
a wen neerg nwog. Teirrah Thgink[2] semoc yreve yad ot daer ot Tnua
Ardnassac.—Doog eyb ym raed Yssac.—Tnua Ardnassac sdnes reh
tseb evol, dna os ew od lla.

Ruoy Etanoitceffa Tnua
Enai Netsua

Notwahc, Naj: 8.

Capt: C. J. Austen RN.
22, Keppel Street
Russel Square
London

149. *To Caroline Austen*

Thursday 23 January 1817

Chawton Thursday Jan: 23. 1817—

My dear Caroline

I am always very much obliged to you for writing to me, & have now I beleive two or three Notes to thank you for; but whatever may be their Number, I mean to have this Letter accepted as a handsome return for all, for you see I have taken a complete, whole sheet of Paper, which is to entitle me to consider it as a very long Letter whether I write much or little.—We were quite happy to see Edward,[1] it was an unexpected pleasure, & he makes himself as agreable as ever, sitting in such a quiet comfortable way making his delightful little Sketches.—He is generally thought grown since he was here last, & rather Thinner, but in very good Looks.—We have used Anna as ill as we could, by not letting him leave us before tomorrow morning, but it is a Vile World, we are all for Self & I expected no better from any of us.—But though *Better* is not to be expected, *Butter* may, at least from Mrs Clement's Cow, for she has sold her Calf.—Edward will tell you of the [*p. 2*] Grand Evening Party he has come in for. We were proud to have a young Man to accompany us, & he acquitted himself to admiration in every particular except selling his Deals at Vingt-un.—He read his two Chapters to us the first Evening;—both good—but especially the last in our opinion. We think it has more of the Spirit & Entertainment of the early part of his Work, the first 3 or 4 Chapters, than some of the subsequent.—Mr Reeves is charming—& Mr Mountain—& Mr Fairfax—& all their day's sport.—And the introduction of Emma Gordon is very amusing.—I certainly *do* altogether like this set of People better than those at Culver Court.

Your Anne is dreadful—. But nothing offends me so much as the absurdity of not being able to pronounce the word *Shift*. I could forgive her any follies in English, rather than the Mock Modesty of that french word. She should not only place her Quilt in the Centre, but give its' Latitude & Longitude, & measure its Dimensions by a Lunar Observation if she chose.—Cook & Sally seem very properly pleased by your remembrance, & desire their Duty & Thanks. Sally has got a new red Cloak, which adds much to her happiness, in other respects she is [*p. 3*] unaltered, as civil & well meaning & talkative as ever.—Only think of your lost Dormouse being brought back to you!—I was quite

325

astonished.—No time is fixed for Cassy's return,[2] but *March* has always been her month hitherto for coming down. Aunt Cass:- had a letter from her very lately, extremely well written in a large hand, but as you may suppose containing little beyond her hope of every bodys being well at Chawton, & Harriet & Fanny's love. Uncle Charles, I am sorry to say, has been suffering from Rheumatism, & now he has got a great eruption in his face & neck—which is to do him good however—but he has a sad turn for being unwell.—*I* feel myself getting stronger than I was half a year ago, & can so perfectly well walk to Alton, *or* back again, without the slightest fatigue that I hope to be able to do both when Summer comes.—I spent two or three days with your Uncle & Aunt[3] lately, & though the Children are sometimes very noisy & not under such Order as they ought & easily might, I cannot help liking them & even loving them, which I hope may be not wholly inexcusable in their & ?[your affectionate Aunt,

J. Austen]

[*Postscript upside down at top of p. 1*]

The Piano Forte often talks of you;—in various keys, tunes & expressions I allow—but be it Lesson or Country dance, Sonata or Waltz, *You* are really its' constant Theme. I wish you c^d come & see us, as easily as Edward can.

Miss Caroline Austen

150(C). *To Alethea Bigg*

Friday 24 January 1817

Chawton Jany 24—1817

My dear Alethea

I think it time there should be a little writing between us, though I believe the Epistolary debt is on *your* side, & I hope this will find all the Streatham party well, neither carried away by the Floods nor rheumatic through the Damps. Such mild weather is, you know, delightful to *us*, & though we have a great many Ponds, & a fine running stream through the Meadows on the other side of the road, it is nothing but what beautifies us & does to talk of. We are all in good health [&] *I* have certainly gained strength through the Winter & am not far from being well; & I think I understand my own case now so much better than I did, as to be able by care to keep off any serious return of illness. I am more &

more convinced that *Bile* is at the bottom of all I have suffered, which makes it easy to know how to treat myself. You will be glad to hear thus much of me, I am sure, as I shall in return be very glad to hear that your health has been good lately. We have just had a few days' visit from Edward, who brought us a good account of his Father,[1] & the very circumstance of his coming at all, of his Father's being able to spare him, is itself a good account. He is gone to spend this day at Wyards & goes home to-morrow. He grows still, & still improves in appearance, at least in the estimation of his Aunts, who love him better & better, as they see the sweet temper & warm affections of the Boy confirmed in the young Man: I tried hard to persuade him that he must have some message for William,[2] but in vain. Anna has not been so well or so strong or looking so much like herself since her Marriage, as she is now; she is quite equal to walking to Chawton, & comes over to us when she can, but the rain & dirt divide us a good deal. Her Grandmama & I can only see her at Chawton as this is not a time of year for Donkey-carriages, & our Donkeys are necessarily having so long a run of luxurious idleness that I suppose we shall find that they have forgotten much of their Education when we use them again. We do not use two at once however; don't imagine such excesses. Anna's eldest child just now runs alone, which is a great convenience with a second in arms, & they are both healthy nice children—I wish their Father were ordained & all the family settled in a comfortable Parsonage house. The Curacy only is wanting I fancy to complete the Business. Our own new Clergyman[3] is expected here very soon, perhaps in time to assist Mr Papillon on Sunday. I shall be very glad when the first hearing is over. It will be a nervous hour for our Pew, though we hear that he acquits himself with as much ease & collectedness, as if he had been used to it all his Life. We have no chance I know of seeing you between Streatham & Winchester:[4] you go the other road & are engaged to two or three Houses; if there should be any change, however, you know how welcome you would be. Edward mentioned one Circumstance concerning you my dear Alethea, which I must confess has given me considerable astonishment & some alarm—Your having left your best Gown at Steventon. Surely if you do not want it at Streatham, you will be spending a few days with Mrs G. Frere, & must want it there. I would lay any wager that you have been sorry you left it. We have been reading the "Poet's Pilgrimage to Waterloo",[5] & generally with much approbation. Nothing will please all the world, you know; but parts of it suit me better than much that he has written before. The opening—the *Proem* I beleive he calls it—

is very beautiful. Poor Man! One cannot but grieve for the loss of the Son so fondly described. Has he at all recovered it? What do M^r and Mrs Hill know of his present state? I hear from more than one quarter that Miss Williams is really better, & I am very glad, especially as Charlotte's being better also must I think be the consequence of it. I hope your Letters from abroad are satisfactory. They would not be satisfactory to *me*, I confess, unless they breathed a strong spirit of regret for not being in England. Kind love & good wishes for a happy New Year to you all, from all our four here. Give our love to the little Boys, if they can be persuaded to remember us. *We* have not at all forgot Herbert's & Errol's fine Countenances. Georgiana is very pretty I dare say. How does Edward like school?—I suppose his holidays are not over yet.

Yours affec^ly

J. Austen

The real object of this Letter is to ask you for a Receipt, but I thought it genteel not to let it appear early. We remember some excellent orange Wine at Manydown, made from Seville oranges, entirely or chiefly— & should be very much obliged to you for the receipt, if you can command it within a few weeks.

Miss Bigg
The Rev^nd Herbert Hill's
Streatham
London

---

151. *To Fanny Knight*

Thursday 20–Friday 21 February 1817

Chawton Feb: 20.—

My dearest Fanny,

➤ You are inimitable, irresistable. You are the delight of my Life. Such Letters, such entertaining Letters as you have lately sent!—Such a description of your queer little heart!—Such a lovely display of what Imagination does.—You are worth your weight in Gold, or even in the new Silver Coinage.[1]—I cannot express to you what I have felt in reading your history of yourself, how full of Pity & Concern & Admiration & Amusement I have been. You are the Paragon of all that is Silly & Sensible, common-place & eccentric, Sad & Lively, Provoking & Interesting.—Who can keep pace with the fluctuations of your Fancy,

the Capprizios of your Taste, the Contradictions of your Feelings?—
You are so odd!—& all the time, so perfectly natural—so peculiar in
yourself, & yet so like everybody else!—It is very, very gratifying to
me to know you so intimately. You can hardly think what a pleasure it
is to me, to have such thorough pictures of your Heart.—Oh! what a
loss it will be,[2] when you are married. You are too agreable in your
single state, too agreable as a Neice. I shall hate you when your delicious play of Mind is all settled down into conjugal & maternal affections. [*p. 2*] M[r] J. W.[3] frightens me.—He will have you.—I see you at
the Altar.—I have *some* faith in M[rs] C. Cage's observation, & still more
in Lizzy's; & besides, I know it *must* be so. He must be wishing to
attach you. It would be too stupid & too shameful in him, to be otherwise; & all the Family are seeking your acquaintance.—Do not imagine
that I have any real objection, I have rather taken a fancy to him than
not,[4] & I like Chilham Castle for you;—I only do not like you sh[d]
marry anybody. And yet I do wish you to marry very much, because I
know you will never be happy till you are; but the loss of a Fanny
Knight will be never made up to me; My "affec: Neice F. C. Wildman"
will be but a poor Substitute. I do not like your being nervous & so apt
to cry;—it is a sign you are not quite well, but I hope M[r] Scud—as you
always write his name, (your M[r] *Scuds*: amuse me very much) will do
you good.—What a comfort that Cassandra should be so recovered!—
It is more than we had expected.—I can easily beleive[5] she was very
patient & very good. I always loved Cassandra, for her fine dark eyes
& sweet temper.—I am almost entirely cured of my rheumatism; just
a little pain in my knee now & then, to make me remember what it was,
& keep on flannel.—Aunt Cassandra nursed me so beautifully!—I enjoy
your visit to Goodnestone, it must be a great pleasure to you, You have
not seen Fanny Cage in any comfort so long. I hope she represents &
remonstrates & reasons with you, properly. Why should you be living[6]
in dread of his marrying somebody else?[7]—(Yet, how natural!)—You
did not chuse to have [*p. 3*] him yourself; why not allow him to take
comfort where he can?—In your conscience you *know* that he could not
bear a comparison with a more animated Character.—You cannot forget how you felt under the idea of its' having been possible that he
might have dined in Hans Place.—My dearest Fanny, I cannot bear You
should be unhappy about him. Think of his Principles, think of his
Father's objection, of want of Money, of a coarse Mother, of Brothers
& Sisters like Horses, of Sheets sewn across &c.—But I am doing no
good—no, all that I urge against him will rather make you take his part

more, sweet perverse Fanny.—And now I will tell you that we like your Henry to the utmost, to the very top of the Glass, quite brimful.—He is a very pleasing young Man. I do not see how he could be mended. He does really bid fair to be every thing his Father & Sister could wish; and William I love very much indeed, & so we do all, he is quite our own William.[8] In short we are very comfortable together—that is, we can answer for *ourselves.*—Mrs Deedes is as welcome as May, to all our Benevolence to her Son; we only lamented that we c^d not do more, & that the £50 note we slipt into his hand at parting was necessarily the Limit of our Offering.—Good Mrs Deedes!—I hope she will get the better of this Marianne,[9] & then I w^d recommend to her & Mr D. the simple regimen of separate rooms.—Scandal & Gossip; —yes I dare say you are well stocked; but I am very fond of Mrs C. Cage, for reasons good. Thank you for mentioning her praise of Emma[10] &c.—I have contributed the marking to Uncle H.'s shirts, & now they are a complete memorial of the tender regard of many.—*Friday.* I had no idea when I began this yesterday, of sending it before your B^r went back, but I have written away my foolish thoughts at such a rate that I will not keep them many [*p. 4*] hours longer to stare me in the face.—Much obliged for the *Quadrilles*, which I am grown to think pretty enough, though of course they are very inferior to the Cotillions of my own day.—Ben & Anna walked here last Sunday to hear Uncle Henry, & she looked so pretty, it was quite a pleasure to see her, so young & so blooming & so innocent, as if she had never had a wicked Thought in her Life—which yet one has some reason to suppose she must have had, if we beleive the Doctrine of Original Sin, or if we remember the events of her girlish days.[11]—

I hope Lizzy will have her Play. Very kindly arranged for her. Henry is generally thought very good-looking but not so handsome as Edward.—I think *I* prefer his face.—W^m is in excellent Looks, has a fine appetite & seems perfectly well.—You will have a great Break-up at G^m in the Spring, You *must* feel their all going. It is very right however. One sees many good causes for it.—Poor Miss C.[12]—I shall pity her, when she begins to understand herself.—Your objection to the Quadrilles delighted me exceedingly.—Pretty Well, for a Lady irrecoverably attached to [*continued below address panel*] *one* Person!—Sweet Fanny, beleive no such thing of yourself.—Spread no such malicious slander upon your Understanding, within the Precincts of your Imagination.—Do not speak ill of your Sense, merely for the Gratification of your Fancy.—Yours is Sense, which [*continued upside down at top of p. 1*] deserves more honourable Treatment.—You are *not* in love with him. You never have been really in love with him.—Y[rs] very affec[ly]

J. Austen

Uncle H. & Miss Lloyd dine at M[r] Digweed's to day, which leaves us the power of asking Uncle & Aunt F.- to come & meet their Nephews here.

Miss Knight
Godmersham Park
Faversham
Kent

152. *To Caroline Austen*

Wednesday 26 February 1817

You send me great News indeed my dear Caroline, about M[r] Digweed M[r] Trimmer, & a Grand Piano Forte. I wish it had been a small one, as then you might have pretended[1] that M[r] D.'s rooms were too damp to be fit for it, & offered to take charge of it at the Parsonage.—I am sorry to hear of Caroline Wiggetts being so ill. M[rs] Chute I suppose would almost feel like a Mother in losing her.—We have but a poor account of your Uncle Charles 2[d] Girl; there is an idea now of her having Water in her head. The others are well.—William was mistaken when he told your Mama we did not mean to mourn for M[rs] Motley Austen.[2] Living here [*p. 2*] we thought it necessary to array ourselves in our old Black Gowns, because there is a line of Connection with the family through the Prowtings & Harrisons of Southampton.—I look forward to the 4 new Chapters with pleasure.—But how can you like Frederick better than Edgar?—You have some eccentric Tastes however I know, as to Heroes & Heroines.—Good bye.

Y[rs] affec[ly]
J. Austen

Wed: Night.[3]

Miss Caroline Austen

153. *To Fanny Knight*

Thursday 13 March 1817

Chawton, Thursday March 13.

As to making any adequate return for such a Letter as yours my dearest Fanny, it is absolutely impossible; if I were to labour at it all the rest of my Life & live to the age of Methusalah, I could never accomplish anything so long & so perfect; but I cannot let William go without a few Lines of acknowledgement & reply. I have pretty well done with Mr Wildman. By your description he can*not* be in love with you, however he may try at it, & I could not wish the match unless there were a great deal of Love on his side. I do not know what to do about Jemima Branfill. What does her dancing away with so much spirit, mean?—that she does not care for him, or only wishes to *appear* not to care for him?—Who can understand a young Lady?—Poor Mrs C. Milles, that she should die on a wrong day at last, after being about it so long!—It was unlucky that the Goodnestone Party could not meet you, & I hope her friendly, obliging, social Spirit, which delighted in drawing People together, was not conscious of the division & disappointment she was occasioning. [*p. 2*] I am sorry & surprised that you speak of her as having little to leave, & must feel for Miss Milles, though she *is* Molly, if a material loss of Income is to attend her other loss.— Single Women have a dreadful propensity for being poor—which is one very strong argument in favour of Matrimony, but I need not dwell on such arguments with *you*, pretty Dear, you do not want inclination.—Well, I shall say, as I have often said before, Do not be in a hurry; depend upon it, the right Man will come at last; you will in the course of the next two or three years, meet with somebody more generally unexceptionable than anyone you have yet known, who will love you as warmly as ever *He* did, & who will so completely attach you, that you will feel you never really loved before.—And then, by not beginning the business of Mothering quite so early in life, you will be young in Constitution, spirits, figure & countenance, while Mrs Wm Hammond[1] is growing old by confinements & nursing. Do none of the Plumptres ever come to Balls now?—You have never mentioned them as being at any?—And what do you hear of the Gipps?—or of Fanny & her Husband?[2]—Mrs F. A. is to be confined the middle of April, & is by no means remarkably Large for *her*.—Aunt Cassandra walked to Wyards yesterday with [*p. 3*] Mrs Digweed. Anna has had a bad cold, looks pale, & we fear something else.[3]—She has just weaned Julia.— How soon, the difference of temper in Children appears!—Jemima has a very irritable bad Temper (her Mother says so)—and Julia a very sweet one, always pleased & happy.—I hope as Anna is so early sensible of its' defects, that she will give Jemima's disposition the early & steady attention it must require.—*I* have also heard lately from your Aunt Harriot,[4] & cannot understand their plans in parting with Miss S-whom she seems very much to value, now that Harriot & Eleanor are both of an age for a Governess to be so useful to;—especially as when Caroline was sent to School some years, *Miss Bell* was still retained, though the others were then mere Nursery Children.—They have some good reason I dare say, though I cannot penetrate it, & till I know what it is I shall invent a bad one, and amuse myself with accounting for the difference of measures by supposing Miss S. to be a superior sort of Woman, who has never stooped to recommend herself to the Master of the family by Flattery, as Miss Bell did.—I *will* answer your kind questions more than you expect.—Miss Catherine is put upon the Shelve for the present, and I do not know that she will ever come out;—but I have a something ready for Publication, which may perhaps appear about a twelvemonth hence. It is short, about the length of Catherine.—This is for yourself alone. Neither Mr Salusbury nor Mr Wildman are to know of it.

[*p. 4*] I am got tolerably well again, quite equal to walking about & enjoying the Air; & by sitting down & resting a good while between my Walks, I get exercise enough.—I have a scheme however for accomplishing more, as the weather grows springlike. I mean to take to riding the Donkey. It will be more independant & less troublesome than the use of the Carriage, & I shall be able to go about with A^t Cassandra in her walks to Alton & Wyards.—

I hope you will think W^m looking well. He was bilious the other day, & Aunt Cass: supplied him with a Dose at his own request, which seemed to have good effect.—I was sure *you* would have approved it.—W^m & I are the best of friends. I love him very much.—Everything is so *natural* about him, his affections, his Manners & his Drollery.—He entertains & interests us extremely.—Max: Hammond & A. M. Shaw are people whom I cannot care for, in themselves, but I enter into their situation & am glad they are so happy.—If I were the Duchess of Richmond, I should be very miserable about my son's choice. What can be expected from a Paget, born & brought up in the centre of conjugal Infidelity & Divorces?—I will *not* be interested about Lady Caroline. I abhor all the race of Pagets.[5]—Our fears increase for poor little Harriet; the latest account is that Sir Ev: Home is confirmed in his opinion of there being Water on the brain.—I hope Heaven in its mercy will take her soon. Her poor Father will be quite worn out by his feelings for her.—He cannot spare Cassy at present, she is an occupation & a comfort to him.

[*p. 5*] Adeiu my dearest Fanny.—Nothing could be more delicious than your Letter; & the assurance of your feeling releived by writing it, made the pleasure perfect.—But how could it possibly be any new idea to you, that you have a great deal of Imagination?—You are all over Imagination.—The most astonishing part of your Character is, that with so much Imagination, so much flight of Mind, such unbounded Fancies, you should have such excellent Judgement in what you do!—Religious Principle I fancy must explain it.—Well, good bye & God bless you.

Y^{rs} very affec^{ly}
J. Austen

[Miss Knig]ht
[Godmers]ham Park

154. *To Caroline Austen*

Friday 14 March 1817

My dear Caroline

You will receive a message from me Tomorrow; & today you will receive the parcel itself; therefore I should not like to be in that Message's shoes, it will look so much like a fool.—I am glad to hear of your proceedings & improvements in the Gentleman Quack. There was a great deal of Spirit in the first part. Our objection to it You have heard, & I give your Authorship credit for bearing Criticism so well.—I hope Edwd is not idle. No matter what becomes of the Craven Exhibition[1] [*p. 2*] provided he goes on with his Novel. In that, he will find his true fame & his true wealth. That will be the honourable Exhibition which no V. Chancellor can rob him of.—I have just rec^d nearly twenty pounds[2] myself on the 2^d Edit: of S & S-* which gives me this fine flow of Literary Ardour.—

Tell your Mama, I am very much obliged to her for the Ham she intends sending me, & that the Seacale will be extremely acceptable—*is* I should say, as we have got it already;—the future, relates only to our time of dressing it, which will not be [*p. 3*] till Uncles Henry & Frank can dine here together.—Do you know that Mary Jane went to Town with her Papa?—They were there last week from Monday to Saturday, & she was as happy as possible. She spent a day in Keppel S^t with Cassy;[3]—& her Papa is sure that she must have walked 8 or 9 miles in a morn^g with him. Your Aunt F.[4] spent the week with us, & one

Child with her,—changed every day.—The Piano Forte's Duty, & will be happy to see you whenever you can come.

Y^{rs} affec^{ly}

J. Austen

* Sense and Sensibility.[5]

Chawton
March 14.[6]

Miss Caroline Austen

155. *To Fanny Knight*

Sunday 23–Tuesday 25 March 1817

Chawton, Sunday March 23.

I am very much obliged to you my dearest Fanny for sending me Mr Wildman's conversation,[1] I had great amusement in reading it, & I *hope* I am not affronted & do not think the worse of him for having a Brain so very different from mine, but my strongest sensation of all is *astonishment* at your being able to press him on the subject so perseveringly— and I agree with your Papa, that it was not fair. When he knows the truth he will be uncomfortable.—You are the oddest Creature!—Nervous enough in some respects, but in others perfectly without nerves!— Quite unrepulsible, hardened & impudent. Do not oblige him to read any more.—Have mercy on him, tell him the truth & make him an apology.—He & I should not in the least agree of course, in our ideas of Novels & Heroines;—pictures of perfection as you know make me sick & wicked—but there is some very good sense in what he says, & I particularly respect him for wishing to think well of all young Ladies; it shews an amiable & a delicate Mind.—And he deserves better treatment than to be obliged to read any more of my Works.—Do not be surprised at finding Uncle Henry acquainted with my having another ready for publication. I could not say No when he asked me, but he knows nothing[2] more of it.—You will not like it, so you need not be impatient. [*p. 2*] You may *perhaps* like the Heroine, as she is almost too good for me.—Many thanks for your kind care for my health; I certainly have not been well for many weeks, & about a week ago I was very poorly, I have had a good deal of fever at times & indifferent nights, but am considerably better now, & recovering my Looks a little, which have been bad enough, black & white & every wrong colour. I must not depend upon being ever very blooming again. Sickness is a dangerous Indulgence at my time of Life.—Thank you for everything you tell me;—I do not feel worthy of it by anything I can say in return, but I assure You my pleasure in your Letters is quite as great as ever, & I am interested & amused just as you could wish me. If there is a *Miss* Marsden, I perceive whom she will marry. *Even*ᵍ.—I was languid & dull & very bad company when I wrote the above; I am better now—to my own feelings at least—& wish I may be more agreable.— We are going to have Rain, & after that, very pleasant genial weather, which will exactly do for me, as my Saddle will then be completed— and air & exercise is what I want.—Indeed I shall be very glad when the Event at Scarlets³ is over, the expectation of it keeps us in a worry, your Grandmama especially;—She sits brooding over Evils which cannot be remedied & Conduct impossible to be understood.—Now, the reports from Keppel Sᵗ are rather better; [*p. 3*] Little Harriet's headaches are abated, & Sir Ev:ᵈ is satisfied with the effect of the Mercury, & does not despair of a Cure. The Complaint I find is not considered Incurable nowadays, provided the Patient be young enough not to have the Head hardened. The Water in that case may be drawn off by Mercury.—But though this is a new idea to us, perhaps it may have been long familiar to you, through your friend Mʳ Scud:—I hope his high renown is maintained by driving away William's cough. Tell William that Triggs is as beautiful & condescending as ever, & was so good as to dine with us today, & tell him that I often play at *Nines* & think of him.—Anna has not a chance of escape;⁴ her husband called here the other day, & said she was *pretty well* but not *equal to so long* a walk; she *must come in* her *Donkey Carriage.*—Poor Animal, she will be worn out before she is thirty.—I am very sorry for her.—Mʳˢ Clement too is in that way again. I am quite tired of so many Children.—Mʳˢ Benn has a 13ᵗʰ—The Papillons came back on friday night, but I have not seen them yet, as I do not venture to Church. I cannot hear however, but that they are [the *omitted*] same Mʳ P. & his sister they used to be. She has engaged a new Maidservant in Mʳˢ Calker's room, whom she means to make also Housekeeper under herself.—Old Philmore was buried yesterday, & I, by way of saying something to Triggs, observed that it had been a very handsome Funeral, but his manner of reply⁵ made me suppose that it was not generally esteemed so.⁶ I can only be sure of *one* part being very handsome, Triggs himself, walking behind in his Green Coat.—Mʳˢ Philmore attended as cheif Mourner, in Bombasin, made very short, and flounced with Crape.

[*p. 4*] *Tuesday*. I have had various plans as to this Letter, but at last I have determined that Un:ᶜ Henry shall forward it from London. I want to see how Canterbury looks in the direction.⁷—When once Uncˡ H. has left us I shall wish him with you. London is become a hateful place to him, & he is always depressed by the idea of it.—I hope he will be in time for your sick. I am sure he must do that part of his Duty as excellently as all the rest. He returned yesterday from Steventon, & was with us⁸ by breakfast, bringing Edward with him, only that Edwᵈ staid to breakfast at Wyards.—We had a pleasant family-day, for the Altons⁹ dined with us;—the last visit of the kind probably, which *she* will be able to pay us for many a month;—Very well, to be able to do it so long, for she *expects* much about this day three weeks, & is generally very exact.—I hope your own Henry is in France & that you have heard from him. The Passage once over, he will feel all Happiness.— I took my 1ˢᵗ ride yesterday & liked it very much. I went up Mounters Lane, & round by where the new Cottages are to be, & found the exercise & everything very pleasant, & I had the advantage of agreable companions, as Aᵗ Cass: & Edward [*continued below address panel*] walked by my side.—Aᵗ Cass: is such an excellent Nurse, so assiduous & un-wearied!—But you know all that already.—Very affecˡʸ Yours

J. Austen

Miss Knight
Godmersham Park
Canterbury

156. *To Caroline Austen*

Wednesday 26 March 1817

Chawton Wedʸ March
26.

My dear Caroline
    Pray make no apologies for writing to me often, I am always very happy to hear from you, & am sorry to think that opportunities¹ for such a nice little economical Correspondence, are likely to fail now. But I hope we shall have Uncle Henry back again by the 1ˢᵗ Sunday in May.—I think you very much improved in your writing, & in the way to write a very pretty hand. I wish you could practise your fingering oftener.—Would not it be a good plan for you to go & live entirely at Mʳ Wᵐ [*p. 2*] Digweed's?—He could not desire any other remuneration

than the pleasure of hearing you practise. I like Frederick & Caroline better than I did, but must still prefer Edgar & Julia.—Julia is a warm-hearted, ingenuous, natural Girl, which I like her for;—but I know the word *Natural* is no recommendation to you.—Our last Letter from Keppel S^t was rather more chearful.—Harriet's headaches were a little releived, & Sir Ev: Hume does not despair of a cure.—*He* persists in thinking it Water on the Brain, but none of the others are convinced.— I am happy to say that your Uncle Charles [*p. 3*] speaks of himself as quite well. How very well Edward is looking! You can have nobody in your Neighbourhood to vie with him at all, except Mr Portal.—I have taken one ride on the Donkey & like it very much—& you must try to get me quiet, mild days, that I may be able to go out pretty constantly.— A great deal of Wind does not suit me, as I have still a tendency to Rheumatism.—[In] short I am a poor Honey at present. I will be bet-ter[2] when you can come & see us.—[*complimentary close and signature cut away*]

Miss Caroline Austen

157. *To Charles Austen*

Sunday 6 April 1817

Chawton Sunday April 6.

My dearest Charles

Many thanks for your affectionate Letter. I was in your debt before, but I have really been too unwell the last fortnight to write anything that was not absolutely necessary. I have been suffering[1] from a Bilious attack, attended with a good deal of fever.—A few days ago my com-plaint appeared removed, but I am ashamed to say that the shock of my Uncle's Will[2] brought on a relapse, & I was so ill on friday & thought myself so likely to be worse that I could not but press for Cassandra's returning with Frank after the Funeral last night, which she of course did, & either her return, or my having seen Mr Curtis, or my Disorder's chusing to go away, have made me better this morning. [*p. 2*] I live upstairs however for the present & am coddled. I am the only one of the Legatees who has been so silly, but a weak Body must excuse weak Nerves. My Mother has borne the forgetfulness of *her* extremely well;— her expectations for herself were never beyond the extreme of modera-tion, & she thinks with you that my Uncle always looked forward to surviving her.—She desires her best Love & many thanks for your kind feelings; and heartily wishes that her younger Child^n had more, & all her Child^n something immediately. My Aunt felt the value of Cassandras company so fully, & was so very kind to her, & is poor Woman! so miserable at present (for her affliction has very much increased since the first) that we feel more regard for her than we ever did before. [*p. 3*] It is impossible to be surprised at Miss Palmer's being ill, but we are truly sorry, & hope it may not continue. We congratulate you on Mrs P.'s recovery.³—As for your poor little Harriet, I dare not be sanguine for her. Nothing can be kinder than Mrs Cooke's enquiries after you & her, in all her Letters, & there was no standing her affectionate way of speaking of *your* Countenance, after her seeing you.—God bless you all. Conclude me to be going on well, if you hear nothing to the contrary.—Yours Ever truely

J. A.

Tell dear Harriet that whenever she wants me in her service again, she must send a Hackney Chariot all the way for me, for I am not strong enough to travel any other way, & I hope Cassy will take care that it is a green one. [*p. 4*] I have forgotten to take a proper-edged sheet of Paper.⁴

Captn C. J. Austen RN
22, Keppel S^t
Russell Sq^re

158. *Will & Testament*

I Jane Austen of the Parish of Chawton do by this my last Will & Testament give and bequeath to my dearest Sister Cassandra Eliz^th every thing of which I may die possessed, or which may be hereafter due to me, subject to the payment of my Funeral Expences, & to a Legacy of £50. to my Brother Henry, & £50. to M^de Bigeon—which I request may be paid as soon as convenient. And I appoint my said dear Sister the Executrix of this my last Will & Testament.

Jane Austen

April 27, 1817.
My Will.—
To Miss Austen

159. *To Anne Sharp*

Chawton May 22^d.

Your kind Letter my dearest Anne found me in bed, for inspite of my hopes & promises when I wrote to you I have since been very ill indeed. An attack of my sad complaint seized me within a few days afterwards—the most severe I ever had—& coming upon me after weeks of indisposition, it reduced me very low. I have kept my bed since the 13. of April, with only removals to a Sopha. *Now*, I am getting well again, & indeed have been gradually tho' slowly recovering my strength for the last three weeks. I can sit up in my bed & employ myself, as I am proving to you at this present moment, & *really* am equal to being out of bed, but that the posture is thought good for me.—How to do justice to the kindness of all my family during this illness, is quite beyond me!—Every dear Brother so affectionate & so anxious!—And as for my Sister!—Words must fail me in any attempt to describe what a Nurse she has been to me. Thank God! she does not seem the worse for it *yet*, & as there was never any Sitting-up necessary, I am willing to hope she has no after-fatigues to suffer from. [*p. 2*] I have so many alleviations & comforts to bless the Almighty for!—My head was always clear, & I had scarcely any pain; my cheif sufferings were from feverish nights, weakness & Languor.—This Discharge was on me for above a week, & as our Alton Apoth^{yr} did not pretend to be able to cope with it, better advice was called in. Our nearest *very good*, is at Winchester, where there is a Hospital & capital Surgeons, & one of them attended me, & *his* applications gradually removed the Evil.— The consequence is, that instead of going to Town to put myself into the hands of some Physician as I sh^d otherwise have done, I am going to Winchester instead, for some weeks to see what Mr Lyford can do farther towards re-establishing me in tolerable health.—On Sat^y next, I am actually going thither—My dearest Cassandra with me I need hardly say—and as this is only two days off you will be convinced that I am now really a very genteel, portable sort of an Invalid.—The Journey is only 16 miles, we have comfortable Lodgings engaged for us by our kind friend Mrs Heathcote who resides in W. & are to have the accomodation of my elder Brother's Carriage which will be sent over from Steventon on purpose. Now, that's a sort of thing which Mrs J. Austen does in the kindest manner!—But still she is in the main [*p. 3*] *not* a liberal-minded Woman, & as to this reversionary Property's amending that part of her Character, expect it not my dear Anne;—too late, too late in the day;—& besides, the Property may not be theirs these ten years.[2] My Aunt is very stout.—Mrs F. A. has had a much shorter confinement than I have—with a Baby[3] to produce into the bargain. We were put to bed nearly at the same time, & she has been quite recovered this great while.—I hope *you* have not been visited with more illness my dear Anne, either in your own person or your Eliza's.[4]—I must not attempt the pleasure of addressing her again, till my hand is stronger, but I prize her invitation to do so.—Beleive me, I was interested in all you wrote, though with all the Egotism of an Invalid I write only of myself.—Your Charity to the poor Woman I trust fails no more in effect, than I am sure it does in exertion. What an interest it must be to you all! & how gladly sh^d I contribute more than my good wishes, were it possible!—But how you are worried! Wherever Distress falls, you are expected to supply Comfort. Ly P-[5] writing to you even from Paris for advice!—It is the Influence of Strength over Weakness indeed.—Galigai de Concini[6] for ever & ever.—Adeiu.— Continue to direct to Chawton, the communication between the two places will be frequent.—I have not mentioned my dear Mother; she [*p. 4*] suffered much for me when I was at the worst, but is tolerably well.—Miss Lloyd too has been all kindness. In short, if I live to be an old Woman I must expect to wish I had died now, blessed in the tenderness of such a Family, & before I had survived either them or their affection.—*You* would have held the memory of your friend Jane too in tender regret I am sure.—But the Providence of God has restored me—& may I be more fit to appear before him when I *am* summoned, than I sh^d have been now!—Sick or Well, beleive me ever y^r attached friend

J. Austen

Mrs Heathcote will be a great comfort, but we shall not have Miss Bigg, she being frisked off like half England, into Switzerland.

Miss Sharp
South Parade
Doncaster

160. *To James Edward Austen*

Tuesday 27 May 1817

Mrs Davids, College St Winton
Tuesday May 27.—

I know no better way my dearest Edward, of thanking you for your most affectionate concern for me during my illness, than by telling you myself as soon as possible that I continue to get better.—I will not boast of my handwriting;[1] neither that, nor my face have yet recovered their proper beauty, but in other respects I am gaining strength very fast. I am now out of bed from 9 in the morn^g to 10 at night—Upon the Sopha t'is true—but I eat my meals with Aunt Cass: in a rational way, & can employ myself, & walk from one room to another.—Mr Lyford says he will cure me, & if he fails I shall draw up a Memorial & lay it before the Dean & Chapter, & have no doubt of redress from that Pious, Learned & disinterested Body.—Our Lodgings are very comfortable. We have a neat little Draw^g-room with a Bow-window overlooking Dr Gabell's Garden. Thanks to the kindness of your Father & Mother in sending me their Carriage, my Journey hither on Saturday was performed with very little fatigue, & had [*p. 2*] it been a fine day I think I sh^d have felt none, but it distressed me to see Uncle Henry & W^m K- who kindly attended us on horseback, riding in rain almost all the way.— We expect a visit from them tomorrow, & hope they will stay the night, and on Thursday, which is Confirmation & a Holiday, we are to get Charles[2] out to breakfast. We have had but one visit yet from *him* poor fellow, as he is in Sickroom, but he hopes to be out tonight.—

We see Mrs Heathcote every day, & William[3] is to call upon us soon.— God bless you my dear Edward. If ever you are ill, may you be as tenderly nursed as I have been, may the same Blessed alleviations of anxious, simpathizing friends be Yours, & may you possess—as I dare say you will—the greatest blessing of all, in the consciousness of not being unworthy of their Love.—*I* could not feel this.—Your very affec: Aunt

J. A.

Had I not engaged to write to you, you w^d have heard again from your Aunt Martha, as she charged me to tell you with her best Love.—
J. E. Austen Esqre
Exeter College
Oxford

161(C). To ?Frances Tilson

?Wednesday 28/Thursday 29 May 1817

[Mrs David's, College Street, Winchester]

. . . My attendant is encouraging, and talks of making me quite well. I live chiefly on the sofa, but am allowed to walk from one room to the other. I have been out once in a sedan-chair, and am to repeat it, and be promoted to a wheel-chair as the weather serves. On this subject I will only say further that my dearest sister, my tender, watchful, indefatigable nurse, has not been made ill by her exertions. As to what I owe to her, and to the anxious affection of all my beloved family on this occasion, I can only cry over it, and pray to God to bless them more and more.

[*She next touches with just and gentle animadversion on a subject of domestic disappointment. Of this the particulars do not concern the public. Yet in justice to her characteristic sweetness and resignation, the concluding observation of our authoress thereon must not be suppressed.*]

. . . But I am getting too near complaint. It has been the appointment of God, however secondary causes may have operated. . . .

[*The following and final extract will prove the facility with which she could correct every impatient thought, and turn from complaint to cheerfulness.*]

You will find Captain——[1] a very respectable, well-meaning man, without much manner, his wife and sister all good humour and obligingness, and I hope (since the fashion allows it) with rather longer petticoats than last year.

CEA/1. From Cassandra Austen to Fanny Knight

Sunday 20 July 1817

Winchester Sunday

My dearest Fanny—doubly dear to me now for her dear sake whom we have lost.

She *did* love you most sincerely, & never shall I forget the proofs of love you gave her during her illness in writing those kind, amusing letters at a time when I know your feelings would have dictated so different a style. Take the only reward I can give you in my assurance

343

that your benevolent purpose *was* answer'd, you *did* contribute to her enjoyment. Even your last letter afforded pleasure, I merely cut the seal & gave it to her, she opened it & read it herself, afterwards she gave it me to read & then talked to me a little & not unchearfully of its contents, but there was then a languor about her which prevented her taking the same interest in any thing, she had been used to do. Since Tuesday evening, when her complaint returnd, there was a visible change,[1] she slept more & much more [*p. 2*] comfortably, indeed during the last eight & forty hours she was more asleep than awake. Her looks altered & she fell away, but I perceived no material diminution of strength & tho' I was then hopeless of a recovery I had no suspicion how rapidly my loss was approaching.—I *have* lost a treasure, such a Sister, such a friend as never can have been surpassed,—She was the sun of my life, the gilder of every pleasure, the soother of every sorrow, I had not a thought concealed from her, & it is as if I had lost a part of myself. I loved her only too well, not better than she deserved, but I am conscious that my affection for her made me sometimes unjust to & negligent of others, & I can acknowledge, more than as a general principle, the justice of the hand which has struck this blow. You know me too well to be at all afraid that I should suffer materially from my feelings, I am perfectly conscious of the extent of my irreparable loss, but I am not at all overpowerd & very little indisposed, nothing but what a short [*p. 3*] time, with rest & change of air will remove. I thank God that I was enabled to attend her to the last & amongst my many causes of self-reproach I have not to add[2] any wilfull neglect of her comfort.[3] She felt herself to be dying about half an hour before she became tranquil & aparently [*sic*] unconscious. During that half hour was her struggle, poor Soul! she said she could not tell us what she sufferd, tho she complaind of little fixed pain. When I asked her if there was any thing she wanted, her answer was she wanted nothing but death & some of her words were "God grant me patience, Pray for me Oh Pray for me". Her voice was affected but as long as she spoke she was intelligible. I hope I do not break your heart my dearest Fanny by these particulars, I mean to afford you gratification whilst I am relieving my own feelings. I could not write so to any body else, indeed you are the only person I have written to at all excepting your Grandmama, it was to her not your Uncle Charles I wrote on Friday.—Immediately after dinner on Thursday I went into the Town to do an errand which your dear Aunt was anxious about. I returnd about a quarter before six & found her recovering from faint: [*p. 4*] :ness & oppression, she got so well as

344

to be able to give me a minute account of her seisure & when the clock struck 6 she was talking quietly to me. I cannot say how soon afterwards she was seized again with the same faintness, which was followed by the sufferings she could not describe, but M[r] Lyford had been sent for, had applied something to give her ease & she was in a state of quiet insensibility by seven oclock at the latest. From that time till half past four when she ceased to breathe, she scarcely moved a limb, so that we have every reason to think, with gratitude to the Almighty, that her sufferings were over. A slight motion of the head with every breath remaind till almost the last. I sat close to her with a pillow in my lap to assist in supporting her head, which was almost off the bed, for six hours,—fatigue made me then resign my place to M[rs] J. A. for two hours & a half when I took it again & in about one hour more she breathed her last. I was able to close her eyes myself & it was a great gratification to me to render her these last services.[4] There was nothing convulsed or which gave the idea of pain in her look, on the contrary, but for the continual motion of the head, she gave me the idea of a beautiful statue, & even now in her coffin, there is such a sweet serene air over her countenance[5] as is quite pleasant to contemplate. This day my dearest Fanny you have had the melancholly intelligence & I know you suffer severely, but I likewise know that you will apply to the fountain-head for consolation & that our merciful God is never deaf to such prayers as you will offer.

[*p. 5*] The last sad ceremony is to take place on Thursday morning, her dear remains are to be deposited in the Cathedral—it is a satisfaction to me to think that they are to lie in a Building she admird so much—her precious soul I presume to hope reposes in a far superior Mansion. May mine one day be reunited to it.—Your dear Papa, your Uncles[6] Henry & Frank & Edw[d] Austen instead of his Father will attend, I hope they will none of them suffer lastingly from their pious exertions.—The ceremony must be over before ten oclock as the Cathedral service begins at that hour, so that we shall be at home early in the day, for there will be nothing to keep us here afterwards.—Your Uncle James came to us yesterday & is gone home to day—Uncle H. goes to Chawton tomorrow morning, he has given every necessary direction here & I think his company there will do good. He returns to us again on Tuesday evening. I did not think to have written a long letter when I began, but I have found the employment draw me on & I hope I shall have been giving you more pleasure than pain.

Remember me kindly to M[rs] J. Bridges (I am so glad she is with you now) & give my best love to Lizzy & all the others. I am my dearest Fanny

Most affect^ly yrs
Cass. Elizth Austen

I have said nothing about those at Chawton because I am sure you hear from your Papa.

Miss Knight
Godmersham Park
Canterbury

CEA/2. *From Cassandra Austen to Anne Sharp*

Monday 28 July 1817

My dear Miss Sharp

I have great pleasure in sending you the lock of hair you wish for, & I add a pair of clasps which she sometimes wore & a small bodkin which she had had in constant use for more than twenty years. I know how these articles,[1] trifling as they are, will be valued by you & I am very sure that if she is now conscious of what is passing on earth it gives her pleasure they should be [*p. 2*] so disposed of. — I am quite well in health & my Mother is very tolerably so & I am much more tranquil than with your ardent feelings you could suppose possible. What I have lost, no one but myself can know, you are not ignorant of her merits, but who can judge how I estimated them? — God's will be done, I have been able to say so all along, I thank God that I have. — If any thing should ever bring you into attainable distance from me we must meet my dear [*p. 3*] Miss Sharp. —

Beleive me very truly

Y^r affect^te friend
Cass. Elizth Austen

Chawton July 28th
Miss Sharp

CEA/3. *From Cassandra Austen to Fanny Knight*

Tuesday 29 July 1817

Chawton Tuesday

My dearest Fanny,

I have just read your letter for the third time & thank you most sincerely for every kind expression to myself & still more warmly for your praises of her who I believe was better known to you than to any human being besides myself. Nothing of the sort could have been more gratifying to me than the manner in which you write of her & if the dear Angel is conscious of what passes here & is not above all earthly feelings, she may perhaps receive[1] pleasure in being so mourned. Had *she* been the survivor I can fancy her speaking of *you* in almost the same terms—there are certainly many points of strong resemblance in your characters—in your intimate acquaintance with each other & your mutual strong affection you were counterparts.

[*p. 2*] Thursday was not so dreadful a day to me as you imagined, there was so much necessary to be done that there was not time for additional misery. Every thing was conducted with the greatest tranquility, & but that I was determined I would see the last & therefore was upon the listen, I should not have known when they left the House. I watched the little mournful procession the length of the Street & when it turned from my sight & I had lost her for ever—even then I was not overpowered, nor so much agitated as I am now in writing of it.—Never was human being more sincerely mourned by those who attended her remains than was this dear creature. May the sorrow with which she is parted from on earth be a prognostic of the joy with which she is hailed in Heaven!—I continue very tolerably well, much better than any one could have supposed possible, because I certainly have had considerable fatigue of body as well as anguish of [*p. 3*] mind for months back, but I really am well, & I hope I am properly grateful to the Almighty for having been so supported. Your Grandmama too is much better than when I came home.—I did not think your dear Papa appeared unwell, & I understand that he seemed much more comfortable after his return from Winchester than he had done before. I need not tell you that he was a great comfort to me—indeed I can never say enough of the kindness I have received from him & from every other friend.—I get out of doors a good deal & am able to employ myself. Of course those employments suit me best which leave me most at leisure to think of her I have lost & I do think of her in every variety of circumstance. In our happy hours of confidential intercourse, in the chearful family party, which she so ornamented, in her sick room, on her death bed & as (I hope) an inhabitant of Heaven. Oh! if I may one day [*p. 4*] be reunited to her there!—I know the time must come when my mind will be less engrossed by her idea,[2] but I do not like to think of it. If I think of her less as on Earth, God grant that I may never cease to reflect on her as inhabiting Heaven[3] & never cease my humble endeavours (when it shall please God) to join her there.

In looking at a few of the precious papers which are now my property I have found some[4] Memorandums, amongst which she desires that one of her gold chains may be given to her God-daughter Louisa & a lock of her hair be set for you. You can need no assurance my dearest Fanny that every request of your beloved Aunt will be sacred with me. Be so good as to say whether you prefer a brooch or ring.

[*Continued below address panel*]

God bless you my dearest Fanny. Believe me most affect[ly] Yours
                                                    Cass Elizth Austen

Miss Knight,
Godmersham Park,
Canterbury.

ABBREVIATIONS AND CITATIONS

A.	Austen
AL	Austen-Leigh
AP	Richard-Arthur Austen-Leigh, *Austen Papers, 1704–1856* (London, 1942)
B.	Brabourne
Bellas MS	Mrs Louisa-Langlois Bellas, Bellas MS, containing copies of letters to and from Mrs Anna Lefroy and other family history notes, compiled 1872
Bellas Notes	Annotations made in a copy of Lord Brabourne's edition of the *Letters of Jane Austen*; these volumes were at one time in the possession of Mrs Bellas, and early this century were given to Miss C. Linklater Thomson, who referred to them in the preface to her *Jane Austen: A Survey* (London, 1929). Dr Chapman then saw the annotations, and quoted two of them in his first edition of *Jane Austen's Letters*; according to him, the volumes later went to a private collector in America
Brabourne	Edward, 1st Lord Brabourne, *Letters of Jane Austen* (London, 1884)
CEA	Cassandra-Elizabeth Austen
Chapman	R. W. Chapman (ed.), *Jane Austen's Letters to her sister Cassandra and others* (Oxford, 1932; 2nd edn., 1952)
CJA	Charles-John Austen
CMCA	Caroline-Mary-Craven Austen
DNB	*Dictionary of National Biography*
Doody and Murray	Margaret Anne Doody and Douglas Murray (eds), *Jane Austen: Catharine and Other Writings* (Oxford, 1993)
E	*Emma*
EAK	Edward Austen (Knight)
Family Record	Deirdre Le Faye and W. and R. A. Austen-Leigh, *Jane Austen: A Family Record* (London, 1989)
Mrs FA	JA's own short reference to Mary Gibson, her brother FWA's wife
FCK	Fanny-Catherine Knight

FCL	Fanny-Caroline Lefroy
FCL MS Family History	Fanny-Caroline Lefroy, MS Family History, written *c.*1880–5
FWA	Francis-William Austen
Mr GA	Revd George Austen
Mrs GA	Mrs George Austen
GM	*Gentleman's Magazine*
Heawood	Edward Heawood, *Watermarks mainly of the 17th and 18th centuries* (Hilversum, 1950)
HEIC	Honourable East India Company
HTA	Henry-Thomas Austen
Mrs HTA	Eliza de Feuillide, first wife of Henry-Thomas Austen
JA	Jane Austen
Mrs JA	JA's own short reference to Mary Lloyd, her brother James's second wife
JAMT	Jane Austen Memorial Trust
JASNA	Jane Austen Society of North America
JA Society	The Jane Austen Society
JEAL	James-Edward Austen-Leigh
Johnson	R. Brimley Johnson, *The letters of Jane Austen, selected and with an introduction by R. Brimley Johnson* (London, 1925)
Lefroy MS	Mrs Anna Lefroy, Lefroy MS, compiled *c.*1855–72
Life	William and Richard-Arthur Austen-Leigh, *Jane Austen, her Life and Letters* (London, 1913)
Lock	F. P. Lock and D. J. Gilson, *Five Letters from Jane Austen to her Sister Cassandra, 1813* (Brisbane, 1981)
Mr LP	Mr James Leigh-Perrot
Mrs LP	Mrs Leigh-Perrot
MAAL	Mary Augusta Austen-Leigh
MAJA	Caroline-Mary-Craven Austen, *My Aunt Jane Austen*, JA Society (Chawton, 1952)
Memoir	James-Edward Austen-Leigh, *A Memoir of Jane Austen* (1870; ed. R. W. Chapman, Oxford, 1926)
Modert	Jo Modert, *Jane Austen's Manuscript Letters in Facsimile* (Carbondale and Edwardsville, Ill., 1990)
MP	*Mansfield Park*

Abbreviations and Citations

MW	*Minor Works*
NA	*Northanger Abbey*
NA&P	*Northanger Abbey* and *Persuasion*
N&Q	*Notes and Queries* (Oxford, continuing)
OFA	Oscar Fay Adams
P	*Persuasion*
P&P	*Pride and Prejudice*
RAAL	Richard-Arthur Austen-Leigh
Report(s)	*Report of the Jane Austen Society* (1949, continuing)
RES	*Review of English Studies* (Oxford, continuing)
RWC	Dr R. W. Chapman
SB	J. H. and Edith C. Hubback, *Jane Austen's Sailor Brothers* (London, 1906)
S&S	*Sense and Sensibility*
TLS	*Times Literary Supplement*
Vine Hunt	James-Edward Austen-Leigh, *Recollections of the Early Days of the Vine Hunt* (London, 1865)

In the numeration of the letters, the addition of **(A)** signifies that the text was not composed by JA, but was either a letter which she received and preserved, or else was something copied out by her; **(C)** is one of JA's own letters where the original MS is now missing and the text is known only from a copy made by some member of the Austen family in later years; **(D)** is a draft by JA, the fair copy of which may or may not also exist; **(S)** is a section cut from a letter, the descent of which may be different from that of the remainder of the MS.

NOTES

THE first object of these notes is to enable the reader to distinguish persons or places ambiguously named, so that reference can be made to the Biographical or Topographical Indexes if more information is wanted. It may be borne in mind that 'my Uncle' and 'my Aunt' always mean Mr and Mrs Leigh-Perrot; that 'Mary' may be either Mrs James or Mrs Frank Austen (often also referred to as 'Mrs J. A.' and 'Mrs F. A.'); 'Elizabeth' either Mrs Edward Austen (her daughter is always 'Lizzy') or Elizabeth Bigg, Mrs Heathcote; 'Eliza' either Mrs Henry Austen or Mrs Fowle; 'Edward' either JA's brother, or his eldest son, or James's son James-Edward.

The second object is to show the omissions, additions, and alterations that JA herself made in her texts; and the third object is to give background information, wherever possible, on some of the now obscure references to contemporary persons, places, and events.

1. *To Cassandra Austen. From Steventon to Kintbury. Saturday 9–Sunday 10 January 1796.*

Description. Unknown; original MS untraced since first publication.
Provenance. Bequeathed by CEA to Fanny, Lady Knatchbull, in 1845; inherited by Lord Brabourne 1882; probably in the Puttick & Simpson sale of 26–8 June 1893.
Publication. Brabourne i. 125; *SB* 42 (extract); *Life* 87, 98 (extracts); Johnson 27; Chapman (1st and 2nd).

1. *very near of an age.* Tom Lefroy was born on 8 Jan. 1776 and CEA on 9 Jan. 1773—JA is joking about the day, not the year.
2. *Mary.* Lloyd.
3. *Elizabeth.* Bigg.
4. *my Irish friend.* Tom Lefroy. [RWC]
5. *Henry goes to Harden.* Harden, now spelt Harpsden, near Henley-on-Thames, Oxon.
6. *Alethea.* Bigg.
7. *Charles.* Fowle, as letter 2 shows. [RWC]
8. *pink persian.* A thin plain silk fabric, often used for petticoats or dress-linings.

9. *adjutancy of the Oxfordshire.* The project was successfully revived, see letter **12**. [RWC]

10. *Cape of Good Hope.* The 86th Regt. was then stationed at Portsmouth, and embarked in June 1796 for the Cape, and thence in 1799 to India.

11. *well-behaved now.* George Lefroy was not yet 14.

12. *Tom Jones. The History of Tom Jones, a Foundling,* 6 vols. (1749), by Henry Fielding (1707–54); Book VII, ch. XIV. 'As soon as the sergeant was departed, Jones rose from his bed, and dressed himself entirely, putting on even his coat, which, as its colour was white, showed very visibly the streams of blood which had flowed down it.' [RWC]

13. *Charles.* CJA—then a midshipman under Capt. Thomas Williams, RN, on HMS *Unicorn*, at Portsmouth.

14. *Tom.* CEA's fiancé Revd Tom Fowle, on the verge of departing for the West Indian campaign with his kinsman Lord Craven; the vessel with the *funny name* may have been the *Ponsborne*.

15. *Miss M. . . . Eliza.* Miss Murden; Mrs Fowle.

2. *To Cassandra Austen. From Steventon to Kintbury. Thursday 14–Friday 15 January 1796.*

Description. Two leaves quarto.

Postmark. JA 16 96. This gives the month and year date for the letter.

Provenance. Bequeathed by CEA to Fanny, Lady Knatchbull, in 1845; inherited by Lord Brabourne 1882; probably in the Puttick & Simpson sale of 26–8 June 1893; in Sir Alfred Law's collection by 1931; Sir Alfred died unmarried in 1939 and bequeathed his estate to his cousin Emma Dixon and her descendants; the present ownership and location of his collection is unknown.

Publication. Brabourne i. 130 (misdated 16 Jan.); *SB* 42 (extract); *Life* 88, 99 (extracts); Johnson 30; Chapman (1st and 2nd). In Oct. 1931 Davidson Cook was able to inspect the original letter in the Law collection, but by then RWC's text for his first edition, copied from Brabourne, was already in proof, and consequently no corrections were made. The text now shows the changes in punctuation and capitalization marked up in MS by Davidson Cook on a copy of RWC's proof.

1. *Jane.* Williams, née Cooper.

2. *Edward.* Revd Edward Cooper.

3. *Anna.* James Austen's elder daughter.

4. *Mr & Mrs Fowle.* Revd Thomas Fowle the elder and his wife Jane.

5. *Tom.* Revd Tom Fowle.

6. *cold Souse.* Lightly pickled pork brawn.

7. *Tom.* Chute.

3. *To Cassandra Austen. From London to ?Steventon. Tuesday 23 August 1796.*

Description. One leaf quarto, wove; watermark ELGAR & SON.

Postmark. None.

Provenance. Bequeathed by CEA to Fanny, Lady Knatchbull, in 1845; inherited by Lord Brabourne 1882; Lord B. attempted to sell it to Messrs J. Pearson & Co., of Pall Mall, London, in June 1889, but later that year gave it to Oscar Fay Adams; given to the Boston Authors Club, Mass., at OFA's death in 1919; given by the Club to the Boston Public Library 1966 (BAC. MS.101).

Publication. Brabourne i. 133; O. F. Adams, 'In the Footsteps of Jane Austen', *New England Magazine*, NS 8 (1893), 594-608, facsimile; also shown facsimile in O. F. Adams, *The Story of Jane Austen's Life* (2nd edn., Boston, 1897)—the facsimile as prepared by Adams is however misleading, as it shows the letter reduced to approximately half-size and on one page only, whereas in fact it is written on both sides of the leaf; *Life* 99; Johnson 33; Chapman (1st and 2nd, from Brabourne); Modert F-1 and F-2.

1. *23 August 1796.* The date of 'Aug. 1796' has been added by another hand in the top left corner of the first page; the full date can be ascertained by the reference given below to the Canterbury races. See *N&Q* 232:4 (Dec. 1987), 478-81.

2. *Cork Street.* The young Austens had probably stayed overnight with Mr Benjamin Langlois—see *Family Record* 43-4.

3. *Edward & Frank.* 'Frank' superscript above 'Henry' cancelled.

4. *Astley's.* Astley's Amphitheatre, near Westminster Bridge; an equestrian circus, originally opened by Philip Astley (1742-1814) in 1770. See *Emma*, chs. XVIII and XIX.

4. *To Cassandra Austen. From Rowling to Steventon. Thursday 1 September 1796.*

Description. Unknown; original MS untraced since first publication.

Provenance. Bequeathed by CEA to Fanny, Lady Knatchbull, in 1845; inherited by Lord Brabourne 1882; possibly in the Puttick & Simpson sale of 26-8 June 1893.

Publication. Brabourne i. 134; *Life* 100 (extracts); Johnson 34; Chapman (1st and 2nd).

1. *Yarmouth.* Great Yarmouth, Norfolk, not Yarmouth in the Isle of Wight; HTA's regiment, the Oxfordshire Militia, was then guarding the East Anglian coast.

2. *Godmersham.* For a visit only—EAK and his young family were still living at Rowling, and did not take up permanent residence at Godmersham until Nov. 1797.

3. *Fanny.* EAK's eldest daughter.

4. *Camilla. Camilla, or a Picture of Youth,* 5 vols. (1796), by Frances (Fanny) Burney (1752–1840). The name of 'Miss J. Austen, Steventon' is in the list of subscribers to *Camilla.* The reference here is to Book IV, chs. II–III.

5. *Charles.* CJA, as letter 6 shows.

6. *Fanny.* Mrs Cage.

7. *Louisa.* Bridges; stout = strong, healthy, or robust, not fat.

8. *Mary Robinson.* Possibly the same 'Mary' as in letter 7.

5. *To Cassandra Austen. From Rowling to Steventon. Monday 5 September 1796.*

Description. One leaf quarto, wove, pp. 1–2 of the letter; second leaf missing; no watermark.

Postmark. None.

Provenance. Bequeathed by CEA to Fanny, Lady Knatchbull, in 1845; inherited by Lord Brabourne 1882; probably in the Puttick & Simpson sale of 26–8 June 1893; Sotheby's 1 Mar. 1909; Harold Murdock; Houghton Library of Harvard University 1935 (Autograph File).

Publication. Brabourne i. 138 (the second leaf, pp. 3–4 of the letter, was already missing at this date); facsimile (slightly reduced) W. H. Helm, *Jane Austen and her Country-House Comedy* (London, 1909), 129; *Life* 101 (extracts); Chapman (1st and 2nd); Modert F-3 and F-4.

1. *Michael.* Probably Michael Terry of the Dummer family.

2. *how.* Inserted superscript.

3. *the Marys.* Lloyd and Harrison. [RWC]

4. *the other couples.* Lewis Cage and Harriet Bridges, Frank Austen and Louisa Bridges, Fanny Cage and George Bridges.

5. *Eliz:th . . . Lady Bridges.* JA first wrote 'Eliz:th played one Country dance, to her Lady Bridges', then cancelled 'to her'.

6. *Henry.* Bridges.

7. *Miss Bridges.* Presumably the 'Marianne' mentioned in the following sentence, who was then the oldest unmarried daughter of Sir Brook Bridges III, just 21, but already in poor health.

8. *tomorrow.* Superscript above 'on Thursday' cancelled.

9. *Henry.* Austen.

10. *without fayl.* The misspelling was presumably a family joke.

11. *Richis.* A servant at Rowling.

12. *Crixhall ruff*. Not, as has naturally enough been assumed, a church, but a wood, which today has some fine oaks. [RWC]

13. *Dr Marchmont*. For his respectable meddling between Camilla and her young man see that work *passim*, and especially the last page of the last volume, where we are told that he at last 'acknowledged its injustice, its narrowness, and its arrogance'.

JA's copy of *Camilla* was presented to the Bodleian in 1930 by Capt. Ernest Austen, RN, a grandson of Sir Francis Austen. It contains in each volume the inscriptions, in CEA's hand, 'Cass. Eliz. Austen' (presumably to mark the change of ownership after JA's death) and 'Given to Lady Austen May 1837'. Lady Austen is best known to us as Martha Lloyd; she became Lady Austen in Feb. 1837 when her husband Francis was knighted, and perhaps *Camilla* was a gift from CEA to mark the occasion of the knighthood. In the lower margin of the last page of the last volume is a pencil inscription which I have no doubt was written by the first owner. She, as a subscriber, (see letter **4**, note 4) received the volumes in boards, uncut, and probably she wrote her comment when she finished the book in 1796. Later it was half-bound (CEA's signature is on the endpaper) and the inscription was mutilated, slightly in the outer margin, but more severely in the lower margin, where I think it has lost a line or two lines. The inscription is also faint, but I read it thus:

> Since this work went to the Press a
> Circumstance of some Importance to the
> happiness of Camilla has taken place,
> namely that Dr Marchmont has at last . . .

and I conjecture that in the missing conclusion JA pleased herself with the intelligence of Dr Marchmont's death. [RWC]

6. *To Cassandra Austen. From Rowling to Steventon. Thursday 15–Friday 16 September 1796.*

Description. Two leaves quarto, laid; watermark device coronet over escutcheon containing post-horn (see Heawood Nos. 2752–62), GR below, no date; mark of blue wafer.

Postmarks. SE B 17 .96   02 WINGHAM

Provenance. Bequeathed by CEA to Fanny, Lady Knatchbull, in 1845; inherited by Lord Brabourne 1882; probably in the Puttick & Simpson sale of 26–8 June 1893; Alfred Morrison; Sotheby's 10 Dec. 1918; J. P. Morgan 1920; Pierpont Morgan Library, New York (MA 977–1).

Publication. Brabourne i. 141; *Life* 102 (extracts); Chapman (1st and 2nd); Modert F-5 to F-8.

1. *Mr Claringbould's Funeral.* The Goodnestone parish register shows that John Claringbould was buried on 11 Sept. 1796, aged 56.
2. *told you.* Superscript above 'mentioned' cancelled.
3. *Lucy.* Lefroy.
4. *my Aunt Fielding.* Members of JA's family and others have been puzzled by places in the letters where 'my aunt' or 'my cousin' is applied to persons not so related to the writer. In most of these places it is clear that the personal pronoun is quoted as from a third person. Mrs Fielding's husband was half-brother to Sir Brook Bridges III, and she would naturally be called aunt by Sir Brook's children. See also letter 73: 'our cousin Marg^t. Beckford . . . my aunt Harding . . . my cousin Flora Long'; and 85: 'my cousin Caro*line*'. Miss Maria Beckford, sister-in-law of the then tenant of Chawton Great House, Mr Middleton, was a cousin of Miss Margaret Beckford; Mrs Harding and her niece Flora Long were connections of the Terrys; 'my cousin Caro*line*' was Mrs Tilson's cousin—the italics indicate her pronunciation.
5. *who is already.* 'is' written over 'has' partly erased.
6. *Jane.* Lady Williams, née Cooper.
7. *[she].* Lost underneath wafer.
8. *Fly.* A family nickname for Frank.
9. *In one particular.* JA first wrote 'In one particular indeed', then cancelled 'indeed'.
10. *Frank.* Superscript after 'he' cancelled.
11. *[J. A.]* There is no part of the paper missing, and yet no trace of a signature or even initials can be found; JA was presumably so busy adding in postscripts that she forgot she had never put her name to the main text.

7. *To Cassandra Austen. From Rowling to Steventon. Sunday 18 September 1796.*

Description. Two leaves quarto, laid; watermark FLOYD & CO, date partially obscured by seal—?1794; red seal.
Postmarks. SE B 19 .96   O2 WINGHAM
Provenance. Bequeathed by CEA to Fanny, Lady Knatchbull, in 1845; inherited by Lord Brabourne 1882; probably in the Puttick & Simpson sale of 26–8 June 1893; Alfred Morrison; Sotheby's 10 Dec. 1918; J. P. Morgan 1920; Pierpont Morgan Library, New York (MA 977–2).
Publication. Brabourne i. 146; *Life* 103 (extracts); Chapman (1st and 2nd); Modert F-9 to F-12.

1. *commanded by the Triton.* A playful inversion, as also in the postscript to the letter.
2. *Mary.* Pearson.

3. *walk the Hospitals . . . St James.* i.e. become a medical student, a law student, or a soldier.

4. *some fat Woman.* JA was probably thinking of Hogarth's set of prints *The Harlot's Progress*, in plate 1 of which an innocent country girl, just arrived in London by the York Wagon, is being enticed by a stout procuress.

5. *Mary.* ?Robinson—see letter 4.

6. *new 32 Frigate.* '32' inserted superscript.

8. *To Philadelphia Walter. From Steventon to Seal. Sunday 8 April 1798.*

Description. One leaf quarto, laid; watermark PORTAL & CO., no date; '1798' added in pencil by another hand; second leaf missing.

Postmark. Nil.

Provenance. Presumably sent on by Philadelphia Walter to her brother the Revd James Walter, incumbent of Market Rasen, Lincs.; by descent to his great-grandson John Charles Guy Nicholson of Castlefield House, Sturton-by-Scawby, Brigg, Lincs., who died unmarried in 1925; some of his effects were purchased at auction by the Revd R. G. Binnall of Manton, Lincs., and this letter was found amongst them; inherited by Canon Peter Binnall; Mrs Stephanie Binnall, and given by her to the British Library 1993 (BL Add. MSS 71,155).

Publication. Chapman (1st and 2nd); Modert F-13 and F-14.

1. *My dear Cousin.* Although the second leaf is missing, which would have borne the name and address, the content makes it clear that the recipient was JA's cousin Philadelphia Walter. In 1919 Mr Nicholson confirmed to RAAL that the letter had been sent to Philadelphia Walter, and that it was the only JA letter preserved in his family.

2. *Mrs Humphries.* A Kentish neighbour of the Walter family—*recte* Humphry.

3. *a Parent.* Philadelphia's father William-Hampson Walter died on 6 Apr. 1798.

4. *Seal, Sevenoaks, Kent.* Other family correspondence shows that the Walters had lived at Seal since at least 1785, and William-Hampson Walter was buried there on 12 Apr. 1798.

9. *To Cassandra Austen. From Dartford to Godmersham. Wednesday 24 October 1798.*

Description. Unknown; original MS untraced since first publication.

Provenance. Bequeathed by CEA to Fanny, Lady Knatchbull, in 1845; inherited by Lord Brabourne 1882; probably in the Puttick & Simpson sale of 26–8 June 1893.

Publication. Brabourne i. 153; *Life* 109 (extracts); Chapman (1st and 2nd).

1. *Daniel.* The Godmersham coachman, who would have taken the Austens to Sittingbourne in EAK's own carriage; possibly the Daniel Boys who was buried at Godmersham on 22 Dec. 1835 aged 73.

2. *Cax.* Unexplained—possibly a family joke.

3. *Harry's deputation.* Harry Digweed, of Steventon Manor; the right of shooting over an estate could be 'deputed' by its owner, so EAK is here providing a 'deputation' in order to give his tenant the privilege of shooting game on Steventon land. See *Persuasion*, ch. III.

4. *'Midnight Bell'. The Midnight Bell, a German Story, Founded on Incidents in Real Life,* by Francis Lathom (1798). See *Northanger Abbey*, ch. VI. [RWC]

5. *and mother.* I think JA wrote *& my mother.* [RWC].

6. *itty Dordy.* EAK's second son George had been born in 1795; no doubt this is his own phraseology.

10. *To Cassandra Austen. From Steventon to Godmersham. Saturday 27–Sunday 28 October 1798.*

Description. Two leaves foolscap, laid; watermark device a seated Britannia, between initials P and B (similar to Heawood Nos. 207–20); countermark monogram of P & B over date 1794; red seal.

Postmarks. OC 29 98   OVERTON

Provenance. Bequeathed by CEA to Fanny, Lady Knatchbull, in 1845; inherited by Lord Brabourne 1882; probably in the Puttick & Simpson sale of 26–8 June 1893; Sotheby's 4 July 1917; Mrs Raymond Hartz, New Jersey, 1943.

Publication. Brabourne i. 156 (with some passages suppressed); *Life* 111 (extracts); Johnson 37; Chapman (1st and 2nd—restoring in the latter edition the passages suppressed by Brabourne); Modert F-15 to F-18.

1. *uncommonly large.* She was eight months pregnant.

2. *Japan Ink.* A superior kind of black writing ink, generally glossy when dry; presumably it could be used to touch up a black ?straw hat.

3. *chose to do it.* 'it' inserted superscript; this servant 'Nanny' is probably Mrs Hilliard, née Anne Knight.

4. *Battleridge.* Mrs Austen's cousin, Mrs Cooke of Great Bookham, had just written *Battleridge, an historical tale founded on facts. By a lady of quality.* It was eventually published by Cawthorn(e) & Hutt, 24 Cockspur Street, London, in 1799.

5. *about Mr W.* 'about' superscript above 'over' [?] cancelled; Martha Lloyd had been disappointed in her hopes of marriage to a certain 'Mr W.'—see *Family Record* 92.

6. *which Molly found.* 'found' inserted superscript.

7. *your Patients.* Edward's wife Elizabeth and her latest baby, William, born 10 Oct. 1798.

8. *his brother's deputation.* See letter **9**, note 3.

9. *to Bath again.* Mrs Austen and her daughters had stayed with Mrs Leigh-Perrot in Bath in Nov. 1797—see *Family Record* 95.

11. *To Cassandra Austen. From Steventon to Godmersham. Saturday 17–Sunday 18 November 1798.*

Description. Unknown; original MS untraced since first publication.

Provenance. Bequeathed by CEA to Fanny, Lady Knatchbull, in 1845; inherited by Lord Brabourne 1882; possibly in the Puttick & Simpson sale of 26–8 June 1893.

Publication. Brabourne i. 162; *Life* 84, 113 (extracts); Johnson 42; Chapman (1st and 2nd).

1. *[1798].* JA did not normally include the year when dating her letters—this is probably an addition by Lord B.

2. *Miss Debary comes.* To Deane parsonage, to manage the household while Mary-Lloyd was in childbed.

3. *we shall do as much.* There is nothing to indicate how much text is missing here, and also at the end of the letter, nor whether the excisions were by CEA or Lord B.

4. *her nephew.* Tom Lefroy. [RWC]

5. *her friend.* Revd Samuel Blackall.

6. *the carriage.* The Austens had kept a carriage for only the last year or so— evidently it had proved too expensive a luxury for the family. See *Family Record* 96.

7. *baby grows.* William, at Godmersham.

8. *a fine little boy.* JA announces the birth of her first biographer, James-Edward Austen(-Leigh). [RWC]

9. *Betty Londe.* The name 'Londe' does not appear in the Steventon or Deane parish registers; this may be a misreading for the Elizabeth *Lovell* who was buried 9 Mar. 1808.

12. *To Cassandra Austen. From Steventon to Godmersham. Sunday 25 November 1798.*

Description. Unknown; original MS untraced since first publication.

Provenance. Bequeathed by CEA to Fanny, Lady Knatchbull, in 1845; inherited by Lord Brabourne 1882; possibly in the Puttick & Simpson sale of 26–8 June 1893.

Publication. Brabourne i. 167; *Life* 113 (extracts); Chapman (1st and 2nd).

1. *the qualification.* HTA had joined the Oxfordshire militia as a lieutenant in 1793, and by now had become Captain, Paymaster, and Adjutant.
2. *Mr Mowell.* Probably a misreading for *Morrell.*
3. *the Colonel.* Gore-Langton. [RWC]
4. *Nanny.* Mrs Hilliard.
5. *Nanny Littlewart.* Several members of the Littleworth (the spelling varied) family were servants to the Austens—see 'The Austens and the Littleworths', *Report* for 1987, 15–21.
6. *Oxford smack.* Unexplained.
7. *Overton Scotchman.* A 'scotchman' (not necessarily Scottish), was a pedlar carrying fabrics and drapery goods round the countryside for doorstep sales.
8. *The Irish.* Irish linen.
9. *Fitz-Albini.* Arthur *Fitz-Albini: a Novel* (1798), by (Sir) Samuel Egerton Brydges (1762–1837). 'The hopes and disappointments of his early years are disclosed in his Novel, called "Arthur Fitz-Albini", in which he clothed a fictitious personage with his own sentiments and aspirations, and at the same time depicted with the utmost freedom the foibles not only of his neighbours and acquaintants, but even those of his own family and relations' (*GM* (1837), ii. 535).
10. *Burdon's hands.* Either John Burdon, bookseller, College Street, or Thomas B., bookseller and wine-merchant, Kingsgate Street, both of Winchester. *Journal of a Tour to the Hebrides* (1785), and *Life of Johnson* (1791; probably the 2nd edn. 1793, published at 24*s.*), both by James Boswell (1740–95). William Cowper (1731–1800)—either the 6th edn. of his poems 1797, or the new edn. 1798.
11. *[J. A.]* The complimentary close and signature may have been removed before the letter came into Lord B.'s possession.

13. *To Cassandra Austen. From Steventon to Godmersham. Saturday 1– Sunday 2 December 1798.*

Description. Unknown; original MS untraced since first publication.
Provenance. Bequeathed by CEA to Fanny, Lady Knatchbull, in 1845; inherited by Lord Brabourne 1882; probably in the Puttick & Simpson sale of 26–8 June 1893.
Publication. Brabourne i. 171; *Life* 115 (extracts); Johnson 47; Chapman (1st and 2nd).

1. *East India Directors.* After signing off from HMS *Dispatch* in the East Indies on 23 June 1793, FWA had returned to England aboard an HEIC ship, and was still hoping that the Company would refund his passage money from India. His letter to which JA refers here was laid before the

Court of Directors on 5 Dec. 1798, only to be referred to their Committee for Government Troops and Stores; after another letter and further referral in Feb. 1801, FWA's application was eventually disallowed at the Court held on 4 Mar. 1801.

2. *You and my mother.* This is, I think, an error for *You and my Brother*; *Br* in JA's hand need not be very unlike *M.* It would be much more natural to 'address this advice' to two persons then in the same place than to one at a distance and one under the same roof as the writer; and the description 'tender-hearted' fits EAK and CEA particularly well. [RWC]

3. *the dressing-room.* See *Family Record* 69.

4. *action to-day.* There is no indication as to how much text has been omitted here, nor whether the excision was by CEA or Lord Brabourne.

5. *his mother and child.* James Austen's mother-in-law Mrs Lloyd, at Ibthorpe, to whom Anna (now aged 5) had evidently been sent to keep her out of the way during this period of domestic upheaval; *the child* in the next sentence is the new baby at Deane, JEAL.

6. *Letty.* Mary Lloyd seems to have had a maidservant named Charlotte (see letters **24** and **26**), and 'Letty' here may perhaps be a misreading for 'Lotty'.

7. *Kintbury . . . Eliza.* Mrs Eliza Fowle was pregnant; Elizabeth-Caroline F. was born 6 Dec. 1798.

8. *Mr May . . . Mr Deane.* Probably Thomas May, brewer, of Basingstoke, and Thomas Deane, brewer and brandy-merchant, of Winchester.

9. *a relation of Edward.* It seems from the context that 'Robert' is the husband of Nanny Hilliard née Knight; but according to the parish register, her husband's Christian name was John. To call him 'Robert' might have been a family joke—see letter **61**, 'his name shall be R., if you please', and also *Family Record* 153.

10. *ale for the Bishop.* Farnham Castle was one of the official residences of the Bishops of Winchester.

14. *To Cassandra Austen. From Steventon to Godmersham. Tuesday 18–Wednesday 19 December 1798.*

Description. Two leaves quarto, laid; watermark device only (Heawood Nos. 2752–62), no date; mark of red seal or wafer.

Postmarks. DE 20 .98   OVERTON

Provenance. Bequeathed by CEA to Fanny, Lady Knatchbull, in 1845; inherited by Lord Brabourne 1882; Sotheby's 11–14 May 1891; Alfred Morrison; Sotheby's 10 Dec. 1918; J. P. Morgan 1920; Pierpont Morgan Library, New York (MA 977–3).

Publication. Brabourne i. 176; *Life* 116 (extracts); Chapman (1st and 2nd); Modert F-19 to F-22.

1. *your Business.* Connected perhaps with her legacy from her fiancé Tom Fowle. But his will was proved in May 1797. [RWC]

2. *[as].* Cancelled by JA.

3. *my ten pounds.* Either Mr Austen's Christmas allowance to his daughters, or perhaps a present to each of them from Mrs Knight.

4. *Admiral Gambier.* CJA was hoping to transfer to a larger ship with more scope for active service.

5. *Sir Thoˢ. Williams.*

6. *I ever was born.* 'ever' may perhaps have been lightly cancelled by JA.

7. *a dish of Tea.* In honour of her birthday on 16 Dec.

8. *he has been.* 'he' inserted superscript.

9. *Lady Conyngham.* Elizabeth, daughter of J. Denison, married 1794 Baron Conyngham (1766–1832), who became 1816 1st Marquis and 1821 Baron Minster of Minster Abbey, Kent; Lady C. 'possessed great influence over George IV'. [RWC]

10. *but for your letter.* These words superscript above an illegible longer phrase, heavily cancelled by JA.

11. *to go with Mʳˢ Russell.* 'go' inserted superscript.

15. *To Cassandra Austen. From Steventon to Godmersham. Monday 24–Wednesday 26 December 1798.*

Description. Two leaves quarto, laid; watermark device only (Heawood Nos. 2752–62), no date; mark of red wafer.

Postmarks. ——98 (part missing) OVERTON

Provenance. Bequeathed by CEA to Fanny, Lady Knatchbull, in 1845; inherited by Lord Brabourne 1882; probably in the Puttick & Simpson sale of 26–8 June 1893; Frederick R. Koch Foundation, New York, Nov. 1983 (and on deposit at Pierpont Morgan Library (FRK 268)); Christie's New York 7 June 1990; Jeffrey R. Young, Esq., London, 1990; Louise Ross & Co, Bath, 1993; private collection, Surrey, 1993.

Publication. Brabourne i. 182; *Life* 118 (extracts); Johnson 51; Chapman (1st and 2nd); Modert F-23 to F-26.

1. *happiness to Martha.* It has been confidently assumed (e.g. by the authors of *Sailor Brothers*) that CEA and JA were making a match between Frank and Martha (who were actually married thirty years later). It seems more likely, however, that the sisters were hoping Martha would find someone else to replace the faithless 'Mr W.' in her affections—see letter 10.

2. *torment myself.* 'torment' written over the erasure of some other word.

3. *& only.* Inserted superscript.

4. *however.* Inserted superscript.

5. *Ashford Balls.* JA wrote 'Ashfords' and cancelled the 's'. She was probably last at an Ashford ball in Sept. 1798—see *Family Record* 99.

6. *imagine.* Written over an erasure—? 'believe'.

7. *supped with the Prince.* HRH Major-General Prince William-Frederick (1776–1834, second Duke of Gloucester 1805), whose military duties brought him into Kent.

8. *does not seem unlikely.* JA wrote 'likely' and then inserted 'un' superscript.

9. *often thought of.* 'of' inserted superscript above a cancellation—? 'over'.

10. *the Christening.* That of JEAL—JA herself made the entry in the Deane parish register.

11. *that kind of Youth.* Harriot Bridges's three elder sisters had all married straight from the schoolroom, and thereby assumed domestic and maternal responsibilities at a very early age.

16. *To Cassandra Austen. From Steventon to Godmersham. Friday 28 December 1798.*

Description. Two leaves quarto, laid; watermark device an elaborate crown; mark of red seal or wafer.

Postmarks. DE 29 98   OVERTON

Provenance. Bequeathed by CEA to Fanny, Lady Knatchbull, in 1845; inherited by Lord Brabourne 1882; with Banks MSS at Sotheby's 14 Apr. 1886; Oliver R. Barrett of Chicago, by 1932; Roger W. Barrett of Chicago.

Publication. Brabourne i. 190; *Life* 121; Chapman (1st and 2nd); Modert F-27 to F-29.

1. *the General.* Gen. Mathew, father of James Austen's first wife; his niece Louisa was the wife of Adm. Lord Gambier.

2. *India House.* See letter **13**, note 1. FWA's later relations with the Company were happier. In 1808 and 1809 substantial sums were voted to him 'for the Purchase of a Piece of Plate', or without such appropriation, with the Company's thanks for various services. [RWC]

3. *now.* Inserted superscript.

4. *a draft for the amount.* Mr Austen's account at Hoare's Bank shows that CEA received £12. 19s. 6d. (£12.97½ in modern decimal coinage).

5. *strength . . . forgive.* 'of' and 'never' both inserted superscript.

17. *To Cassandra Austen. From Steventon to Godmersham. Tuesday 8– Wednesday 9 January 1799.*

Description. Two leaves quarto, laid; watermark device (Heawood Nos. 2752– 62) above monogram [?]JP, no date; mark of red wafer.

Postmarks. D JA 10 99   OVERTON

Provenance. Bequeathed by CEA to Fanny, Lady Knatchbull, in 1845; inherited by Lord Brabourne 1882; probably in the Puttick & Simpson sale of 26–8 June 1893; Mrs Hester Forbes-Julian (1861–1934); bequeathed by her to the Torquay Natural History Society and rediscovered in their archives 1989 (L.1.).

Publication. Brabourne i. 191; *Life* 122 (extracts); Chapman (1st and 2nd); Modert F-29.1 to F-29.4.

1. [*1799*]. Although JA did not normally include the year when dating her letters, on this occasion the handwriting may possibly be hers—unless CEA added these figures upon receipt of the letter.

2. *for her.* Inserted superscript.

3. *a Mamalouc cap.* Printed as 'mamalone' by Lord Brabourne, but guessed to be 'mamalouc' by Constance Hill: 'The battle of the Nile, fought in the preceding August, had set the fashion in ladies' dress for everything suggestive of Egypt and of the hero of Aboukir. In the fashion-plates of the day we find Mamalouc cloaks and Mamalouc robes of flowing red cloth. Ladies wear toupees, somewhat resembling a fez, which we recognise as the "Mamalouc cap." Their hats are adorned with the "Nelson rose feather," and their dainty feet encased in "green morocco slippers bound with yellow and laced with crocodile-coloured ribbon." (p. 76).

4. *going to . . . some time.* 'Bookham', 'Theo' ', and 'at Baliol' were cancelled by CEA, presumably because she did not wish JA's rather unflattering thoughts concerning their Cooke cousins to be seen by anyone else. Lord Brabourne guessed the first name as 'Brighton', despite the fact that there is clearly no sign of a 'g' in the word. A study of the rediscovered MS enables the three names to be deciphered beneath the cancellations.

5. *lie awake in.* 'in' inserted superscript.

6. *W—W—'s Mama.* These dashes are JA's own—possibly she was joking about some member of the Wither family, as a descendant of theirs commented later: 'It was the custom of the Wither clan to fuss and talk a great [deal] about bad health.' (F. Awdry, *A Country Gentleman of the Nineteenth Century* (Winchester, 1906), 82).

7. *giving her name to a set.* JA means that she has called this house-party 'the Biggs', though only Catherine B. was strictly so named; for her father and brother were Bigg-Wither and her sister had become Mrs Heathcote. [RWC]

8. *act of Generosity.* Mrs Knight's abdication in favour of her adopted son was subject to an annuity for herself of £2,000. [RWC]

9. *little moveable apartment.* 'moveable' inserted superscript.

10. *Mr South.* The Bishop's name was North. [RWC]

11. *first impressions.* The first surviving mention in JA's letters of her adult literary work; this prototype of *Pride and Prejudice* had been finished in Aug. 1797—see *Family Record* 94–5.

12. *Jefferys Toomer & Legge*. A banking partnership in Basingstoke, evidently on the verge of bankruptcy.

13. *not filling my Sheet*. The fourth page of this letter was not fully used, so CEA was paying postage for rather less text than usual.

18. *To Cassandra Austen. From Steventon to Godmersham. Monday 21–Wednesday 23 January 1799.*

Description. Unknown; original MS untraced since first publication.

Provenance. Bequeathed by CEA to Fanny, Lady Knatchbull, in 1845; inherited by Lord Brabourne 1882; Sotheby's 11–14 May 1891.

Publication. Brabourne i. 198; *Life* 124 (extracts); Chapman (1st and 2nd).

1. *Mr Marshall . . . postage*. Mr Marshall was the innkeeper and postmaster at The George, Sittingbourne.

2. *Elizabeth Caroline*. Fowle.

3. *Our first cousins*. They had three—one on their father's side, Eliza Hancock (de Feuillide) who 31 Dec. 1797 became Mrs HTA, and two on their mother's, Edward Cooper and his sister Jane, Lady Williams, who had died in a driving accident 9 Aug. 1798. They also had three surviving Walter cousins—Weaver, James, and Phylly—but as these were the offspring of Mr GA's *half*-brother JA was perhaps discounting them in this context.

4. *the other living*. The Fowles' kinsman, Lord Craven, was patron of three livings in Shropshire—Wistanstow near Craven Arms, West Felton, and Onibury near Ludlow. While CEA had been engaged to Revd Tom Fowle, the Austens had hoped that one day the young couple might be given one of these family livings—see *Family Record* 92. At this date the Revd Mr Johnson held Wistanstow from Lord Craven as well as Hamstall Ridware from the Leigh family.

5. *talobert skin*. Either a family joke, or perhaps a misreading of 'rabbit skin'.

6. *Our own particular little brother*. A joking misquotation from *Camilla* (1802 edn., vol. III, Bk. VI, ch. X, p. 197).

7. *Charles being a crop*. i.e. wearing his hair cut short and unpowdered.

8. *shirk . . . who will be*. There is no indication as to whether this gap is an editorial omission by Lord Brabourne or an earlier excision of part of the text by CEA.

9. *Yours affectionately, Jane*. Complimentary close and signature as given by Lord Brabourne; but when this letter appeared in the Sotheby's sale of May 1891 it was catalogued (Lot 1102) as 'signature cut off'.

19. *To Cassandra Austen. From Bath to Steventon. Friday 17 May 1799.*

Description. Two leaves quarto, laid; watermark device only (Heawood Nos. 2752–62); red seal.

Postmark. BATH Endorsed 'Missent to Whitchurch'.

Provenance. Bequeathed by CEA to Fanny, Lady Knatchbull, in 1845; inherited by Lord Brabourne 1882; with Banks MSS at Sotheby's 14 Apr. 1886; in Frederick Locker-Lampson's Rowfant Library before his death in 1895; Samuel B. Grimson; deposited by him in the Houghton Library, Harvard University, 1953; bequeathed to the Houghton Library by Mrs Grimson 1960 (fMS Eng 870 (83A)).

Publication. Brabourne i. 206; *Life* 127 (extracts); Chapman (1st and 2nd, from Brabourne text, as MS not seen by RWC till 1959); Modert F-31 to F-34.

1. *John.* Littleworth—James A.'s coachman, who had presumably driven the party as far as Andover.
2. *Asparagus & a Lobster.* 'a' inserted superscript.
3. *the children.* EAK's two eldest children, Fanny and Edward jr., were of the party; the 'three little boys' mentioned later in the letter were George, Henry, and William, left at home in the Godmersham nursery.
4. *Frank.* The Leigh-Perrots' ?negro servant.
5. *Carpenters ... at Devizes.* William Fowle had married Miss Maria Carpenter of Devizes in July 1792.
6. *Garden of the last house.* 'Garden of the' inserted superscript.

20. *To Cassandra Austen. From Bath to Steventon. Sunday 2 June 1799.*

Description. Two leaves quarto, laid; no watermark; mark of red wafer; a section cut away at the top of the second leaf, causing the loss of about seven lines of writing at the beginning of p. 3 and a similar amount at the beginning of p. 4.

Postmark. BATH

Provenance. Bequeathed by CEA to Fanny, Lady Knatchbull, in 1845; inherited by Lord Brabourne 1882; Sotheby's 11–14 May 1891; Alfred Morrison; Sotheby's 10 Dec. 1918; J. Pierpont Morgan 1920; Pierpont Morgan Library, New York (MA 977-4).

Publication. Brabourne i. 211; *Life* 129 (extracts); Johnson 57; Chapman (1st and 2nd); Modert F-35 to F-38.

1. *at Steventon.* 'at' inserted superscript.
2. *does not cost.* 'cost' inserted superscript.
3. *this ... dearest Shops.* 'at' inserted superscript.
4. *Eliza's.* Could be either Mrs Fowle or Mrs HTA.
5. *Evelina, or a Young Lady's Entrance into the World;* by Fanny Burney (1778).
6. *Martha's Uncle.* Probably Revd John Craven, but could also possibly be Revd Thomas Fowle sr.

21. *To Cassandra Austen. From Bath to Steventon. Tuesday 11 June 1799.*

Description. Two leaves quarto, laid; watermark device (Heawood Nos. 2752–62) above initials PB, no date; red seal.

Postmark. BATH

Provenance. Bequeathed by CEA to Fanny, Lady Knatchbull, in 1845; inherited by Lord Brabourne 1882; with Banks MSS at Sotheby's and purchased by Edward Augustus Petherick, 14 Apr. 1886; presented by him to National Library of Australia, 1911 (MS 760/18/12).

Publication. Brabourne i. 215: *Life* 130 (extracts); Chapman (1st and 2nd); Modert F-39 to F-42.

1. *M*ʳˢ *Piozzi.* Hester Lynch Piozzi (1741–1831)—Dr Johnson's Mrs Thrale: *Letters to and from the late Samuel Johnson* (1788).
2. *lately.* Inserted superscript.
3. *think.* Inserted superscript.
4. *EA.* Child's initials scrawled in the corner.
5. *their elder Sisters company.* Probably Jane Bigg (1770–1855), married 1795 John Awdry of Notton, Wilts; but possibly the eldest of the sisters, Margaret (1768–1842), married 1792 Revd Charles Blackstone of Andover, Hants.

22. *To Cassandra Austen. From Bath to Steventon. Wednesday 19 June 1799.*

Description. Two leaves quarto, laid; watermark device only (Heawood Nos. 2752–62), no date; mark of wafer.

Postmarks. The dated postmark virtually absent; BATH

Provenance. Bequeathed by CEA to Fanny, Lady Knatchbull, in 1845; inherited by Lord Brabourne 1882; probably in the Puttick & Simpson sale of 26–8 June 1893; Alfred Morrison; Sotheby's 10 Dec. 1918; J. Pierpont Morgan 1920; Pierpont Morgan Library, New York (MA 977-5).

Publication. Brabourne i. 220; *Life* 131 (extracts); Chapman (1st and 2nd); Modert F-43 to F-46.

1. *a Yahoo.* See *Gulliver's Travels* (1726), by Jonathan Swift (1667–1745).
2. *a Physician.* 'a' inserted superscript.
3. *Play on Saturday.* Kotzebue's *The Birthday Day* and the 'romance' *Bluebeard*.
4. *after all that had passed.* 'had' inserted superscript. HTA's engagement to Mary Pearson was broken off in the summer of 1796—see *Family Record* 88–91, 95.

23. *To Cassandra Austen. From Steventon to Godmersham. Saturday 25–Monday 27 October 1800.*

Description. Two leaves quarto, laid; watermark device only (Heawood Nos. 2752–62), no date; red wafer.

Postmarks. D OCT 28 1800   OVERTON

Provenance. Bequeathed by CEA to Fanny, Lady Knatchbull, in 1845; inherited by Lord Brabourne 1882; probably in the Puttick & Simpson sale of 26–8 June 1893; Alfred Morrison; Sotheby's 10 Dec. 1918; J. Pierpont Morgan 1920; Pierpont Morgan Library, New York (MA 977–6).

Publication. Brabourne i. 230; *Life* 141 (extracts); Chapman (1st and 2nd); Modert F-47 to F-50.

1. *some.* 'some' repeated at beginning of p. 2, and cancelled by JA.
2. *Heathcote & Chute for ever.* An election cry. [RWC]
3. *Sandling.* Sandling Park, near Hythe, Kent.

24. *To Cassandra Austen. From Steventon to Godmersham. Saturday 1 November 1800.*

Description. Two leaves quarto, laid; watermark device only (Heawood Nos. 2752–62), no date; seal cut out.

Postmarks. D NOV 3 1800   OVERTON

Provenance. Bequeathed by CEA to Fanny, Lady Knatchbull, in 1845; inherited by Lord Brabourne 1882; probably in the Puttick & Simpson sale of 26–8 June 1893; Alfred Morrison; Sotheby's 10 Dec. 1918; J. Pierpont Morgan 1920; Pierpont Morgan Library, New York (MA 977–7).

Publication. Brabourne i. 235; *Life* 143 (extracts); Chapman (1st and 2nd); Modert F-51 to F-54.

1. *not.* Inserted superscript.
2. *not.* Inserted superscript.
3. *Jos: Wakeford.* The Deane parish register shows that he was buried on 30 Oct. 1800.
4. *Mrs Cooper.* Their aunt, Mrs Austen's sister, who had died in 1783; see *Family Record* 45–6.

25. *To Cassandra Austen. From Steventon to Godmersham. Saturday 8–Sunday 9 November 1800.*

Description. Two leaves quarto, laid; watermark device only (Heawood Nos. 2752–62), no date; seal cut out.

Postmarks. D NOV 11 1800   OVERTON

Provenance. Probably bequeathed by CEA to CMCA in 1845; descended in junior line of Austen-Leigh family and placed on deposit in British Museum Dept. of MSS by Miss Lois AL, 1936; now Joan AL (Mrs Denis Mason Hurley) and British Library, Loan No. 19(i).

Publication. Memoir (2nd) 58; *Life* 145 (extracts); Chapman (1st and 2nd); Modert F-55 to F-58.

1. *les Veillees du Chateau.* By Madame de Genlis (1746–1830), 1784; translated as *Tales of the Castle* (?1785). [RWC]
2. *in.* Inserted superscript.
3. *felicity.* Superscript above 'happiness' cancelled.
4. *Turkish Ship.* See *SB* 98–101.
5. *am.* Superscript above 'have' cancelled.

26. *To Martha Lloyd. From Steventon to Up Hurstbourne. Wednesday 12–Thursday 13 November 1800.*

Description. Two leaves quarto, laid; watermark device (Heawood Nos. 2752–62) above initials JB, no date; seal cut out.

Postmark. OVERTON .

Provenance. Remained in FWA's possession following Martha Lloyd's (by then Lady Austen) death in 1843; given by him to Miss Eliza Susan Quincy of Boston, Mass., in 1852; descended through the Quincy family to Mrs M. A. DeWolfe Howe; Massachusetts Historical Society, Boston, Mass. (John Quincy Papers II, 1800, Nov. 12, Austen, Jane).

Publication. Memoir (2nd 61, from a copy supplied to JEAL by Miss Q.); *Life* 148; *Yale Review*, 15 (1925–6), 319–35; Johnson 125; Chapman (1st and 2nd); Modert F-59 to F-62.

1. *You & I.* '& I' inserted superscript.
2. *Our invitations.* For the Hurstbourne ball. Lord Portsmouth had been a pupil at Steventon Rectory for a short time in his childhood; in later life his unpleasant eccentricities became notorious and he was eventually declared insane—see *Family Record* 23–4.
3. *Manydown.* The illness of both father and son has been mentioned in earlier letters; but they survived until 1813 and 1833 respectively. [RWC]
4. *Henry's History of England.* Robert Henry (1718–90): *History of Great Britain* (1771–93), published in six volumes quarto. The portion for Saturday is 'the history of the manners, virtues, vices, remarkable customs, language, dress, diet and diversions of the people'. [RWC]
5. *your's.* JA originally wrote 'your part', then cancelled 'part' and added an apostrophe 's' to 'your'.

371

27. *To Cassandra Austen. From Steventon to Godmersham. Thursday 20–Friday 21 November 1800.*

Description. Two leaves quarto, laid; watermark device only (Heawood Nos. 2752–62), no date; seal cut out.

Postmarks. D NOV 22 1800   OVERTON

Provenance. Bequeathed by CEA to Fanny, Lady Knatchbull, in 1845; inherited by Lord Brabourne 1882; probably in the Puttick & Simpson sale of 26–8 June 1893; Alfred Morrison; Sotheby's 10 Dec. 1918; J. Pierpont Morgan 1920; Pierpont Morgan Library, New York (MA 977–8).

Publication. Brabourne i. 241; *Life* 150 (extracts); Johnson 60; Chapman (1st and 2nd); Modert F-63 to F-66.

1. *twelve dances . . . nine.* 'twelve' superscript above 'ten', and 'nine' superscript above 'seven', cancelled by JA.

2. *with.* Inserted superscript.

3. *poor Rosalie.* In 1788 their cousin Eliza de Feuillide had had a maid called Rosalie; it would seem that this Rosalie had attracted Sir Thomas's attention.

4. *Anne.* The first Mrs James Austen; the Maitland girls were her nieces.

5. *The General.* General Mathew, father of Mrs Maitland and of the deceased Anne Austen.

6. *finishing his house.* Brooklands, near Southampton, Hants.

7. *Rice & Lucy.* Revd Henry Rice and Lucy Lefroy.

8. *Mrs Augusta.* Bramston.

9. *Dr Jenner's pamphlet.* Edward Jenner (1749–1823): pamphlets on cowpox, 1798–1800; a second edition of the original *Inquiry* was dedicated to the King in 1800. [RWC]

10. *love with you.* 'with' inserted superscript.

11. *George.* Presumably EAK's second son, born 1795.

12. *Lady S&S . . . daughter.* Lady Saye and Sele and her divorced daughter Mary-Cassandra Twisleton.

28. *To Cassandra Austen. From Ibthorpe to Godmersham. Sunday 30 November–Monday 1 December 1800.*

Description. Two leaves quarto, laid; watermark device only (Heawood Nos. 2752–62), no date; remains of plain wafer.

Postmarks. E DEC 2 1800   ANDOVER

Provenance. Possibly bequeathed by CEA to CMCA in 1845; descended in the junior line of the Austen-Leigh family and placed on deposit in the British Museum Dept. of MSS by Miss Lois AL, 1936; purchased by British Library 1990 (BL Add. MSS 70,625).

Publication. *Life* 153 (extracts); Chapman (1st and 2nd); Modert F-67 to F-70.

1. *Mrs Hastings . . . Maria.* The wife of Warren Hastings; the Austens' cousin Miss Maria Payne seems to have been almost permanently resident at Daylesford, presumably as Mrs Hastings's companion, and could well be described as 'faithful'.

2. *Shrewsbury Clock.* See *1 Henry IV*, v. iv; presumably the clock in the parish church of St Alkmund's.

3. *too dirty . . . Martha.* JA first wrote 'too dirty for such desperate Walkers as even Martha & I'; then cancelled 'even' and replaced it superscript earlier in the sentence.

4. *an.* Inserted superscript.

5. *Painter & Redding.* Thomas Painter, haberdasher; Grace Redding, linen and woollen draper.

6. *Staircase . . . Drawing room.* This house is now the Andover Museum, in Church Close.

7. *truth, . . . farther.* '&' and 'any' inserted superscript.

8. *the Eldest daughter.* JA is herself strict in observing this and similar rules; in writing to her niece Anna she always calls her husband 'Mr Ben Lefroy', because he had an elder brother. [RWC]

9. *to have a nice black frost.* JA actually wrote 'half' for 'have'.

10. *Delmar . . . rooms.* The *Kentish Gazette* of 4 Nov. 1800 announces 'A Ball at Delmar's Rooms', the first of a series, to be held on 6 Nov. The subscription for six balls was a guinea (£1.05). [RWC]

11. *various observations.* 'various' superscript above 'different' cancelled.

29. *To Cassandra Austen. From Steventon to Godmersham. Saturday 3–Monday 5 January 1801.*

Description. Two leaves quarto, laid; watermark device only (Heawood Nos. 2752–62), no date; seal cut out.

Postmarks. D JAN 6 1801   OVERTON

Provenance. Bequeathed by CEA to Fanny, Lady Knatchbull, in 1845; inherited by Lord Brabourne 1882; probably in the Puttick & Simpson sale of 26–8 June 1893; Alfred Morrison; Sotheby's 10 Dec. 1918; J. Pierpont Morgan 1920; Pierpont Morgan Library, New York (MA 977–9).

Publication. Brabourne i. 248; *Life* 156 (extracts); Chapman (1st and 2nd); Modert F-71 to F-74.

1. *she.* Inserted superscript.

2. *our Pictures.* The 'Battlepeice' was remembered by Anna Lefroy as hanging over the chimney-piece in the rectory dining-room—it apparently depicted a battle between the Swedes and the Poles in 1565; 'Mr Nibbs' and 'Sir Wm East' were presumably the family nicknames for pictures given by these gentlemen in appreciation of Mr GA's successful tutoring of their

respective sons into university; the 'paintings on tin' may have been either a decorative category (flowers, etc.) or small oil portraits, bigger than miniatures, such as Downman painted in the 1790s; the 'French agricultural prints' may have been souvenirs of EAK's Grand Tour in 1786–90.

3. *how.* Inserted superscript.

4. *Miss Walter.* Their Kentish cousin Phylly Walter.

5. *Miss Foote.* Presumably Harriet, younger sister of the reigning Lady Bridges. Her cousin Frederick I have not identified. [RWC]

6. *in for it!* She was now pregnant with her first child.

7. *good fortune.* Capt. Sir Richard Pearson's promotion to Lt.-Gov. of Greenwich Hospital for Seamen.

8. *It brings them.* Superscript above 'They have' cancelled.

9. *often.* Inserted superscript.

10. *Act of Parliament.* The reference is probably (as Professor Veitch suggests) to one of the measures proposed to meet the distress of the winter of 1800–1. One of these was the fixing of a maximum price of 10s. a bushel for wheat. This was proposed by Lord Warwick, but met with vigorous opposition. *Parl. Hist.* XXXV. 833–5. [RWC]

30. *To Cassandra Austen. From Steventon to Godmersham. Thursday 8–Friday 9 January 1801.*

Description. Two leaves quarto, laid; watermark device only (Heawood Nos. 2752–62), no date; blue wafer.

Postmarks. D JAN 10 1801   OVERTON

Provenance. Bequeathed by CEA to Fanny, Lady Knatchbull, in 1845; inherited by Lord Brabourne 1882; probably in the Puttick & Simpson sale of 26–8 June 1893; Alfred Morrison; Sotheby's 10 Dec. 1918; J. Pierpont Morgan 1920; Pierpont Morgan Library, New York (MA 977–10).

Publication. Brabourne i. 255; *Life* 158 (extracts); Chapman (1st and 2nd); Modert F-75 to F-78.

1. *Mr Payne.* One of the Austens' maternal cousins.

2. *many.* Inserted superscript.

3. *Peter.* Black Peter is the knave of spades, in a childish card game so called. [RWC]

4. *fixtures of the house.* Deane Parsonage—Egerton Brydges and Mrs Lloyd had both previously been Mr Austen's tenants here.

5. *Mrs Lawrel . . . Mr Hinchman.* The Lawrel or Laurel family were neighbours of Mrs Cooke at Great Bookham; the bridegroom may be Mr Thomas Henchman (1748–1804). JA goes on to joke by deliberately confusing this Mr H. with a maternal cousin of Mary Lloyd, a Mr John Hinx-, Hinch-, or Henchman, who lived in Gloucestershire.

6. *the wedding-day.* The anniversary of James Austen's marriage to Mary Lloyd on 17 Jan. 1797.

7. *Hugh Capet ... Mr Skipsey.* The former, I suppose, a horse; Mr S. I do not recognize, but he may be a horse too. [RWC]

31. *To Cassandra Austen. From Steventon to Godmersham. Wednesday 14–Friday 16 January 1801.*

Description. Two leaves quarto, laid; watermark device only (Heawood Nos. 2752–62), no date; mark of wafer.

Postmarks. D JAN 17 . . . (part missing)   OVERTON

Provenance. Bequeathed by CEA to Fanny, Lady Knatchbull, in 1845; inherited by Lord Brabourne 1882; probably in the Puttick & Simpson sale of 26–8 June 1893; Alfred Morrison; Sotheby's 10 Dec. 1918; J. Pierpont Morgan 1920; Pierpont Morgan Library, New York (MA 977-11).

Publication. Brabourne i. 261; *Life* 159 (extracts); Chapman (1st and 2nd); Modert F-79 to F-82.

1. *Galinies.* Domestic hens—from the Latin *gallina*, a hen. The neighbouring ladies were calling with a view to buying up Mrs Austen's poultry-yard.

2. *Mrs Welby ... Prince of Wales.* Mrs W. (née Wilhelmina Spry) was a niece of Mrs LP. The *Morning Post* of 12 Jan. reports: 'H. R. H. . . . now on a visit to Sir Hy. Featherstonhaugh in Hampshire . . . , a large party . . . sports of the field'. Sir Henry lived at Up Park, which is in Sussex, but very near the Hampshire border. Sir Alfred Welby tells me that he has a recollection of hearing that his ancestress *was* musical. [RWC]

3. *Major Byng.* From *The Times* of 13 Jan. 1801: 'We are extremely sorry to learn, by private letters received yesterday, the confirmation of the death of Mr Byng, a cousin of Mr Wickham, who was killed in the battle of the 14th near Salzburg. This gentleman was a Volunteer in the Austrian Service', &c. No previous notice has been found, and the Christian name is not given. *The Times* notice suggests that Mr B. was *not* a member of the Torrington family—the only Edmund of that family who can be found died in 1854. [RWC]
    JA's interest in this report, however, would suggest that her family were acquainted with the diarist, the Hon. John Byng (1743–1813), later very briefly the 5th Viscount Torrington. As Mr Byng was a kinsman of the Bramstons of Oakley Hall (see *The Torrington Diaries*, I. 107) perhaps he had met the Austens there in earlier years.

4. *Mr Doricourt ... best.* See Hannah Cowley, *Belle's Stratagem* (1780), V. v. [RWC]

32. *To Cassandra Austen. From Steventon to Godmersham. Wednesday 21–Thursday 22 January 1801.*

Description. Two leaves quarto, laid; watermark PORTAL &. CO 1797; mark of wafer.

Postmarks. D JAN 23 1801   OVERTON

Provenance. Bequeathed by CEA to Fanny, Lady Knatchbull, in 1845; inherited by Lord Brabourne 1882; probably in the Puttick & Simpson sale of 26–8 June 1893; Alfred Morrison; Sotheby's 10 Dec. 1918; J. Pierpont Morgan 1920; Pierpont Morgan Library, New York (MA 977–12).

Publication. Brabourne i. 266; *Life* 161 (extracts); Chapman (1st and 2nd); Modert F-83 to F-86.

1. *Fulwar was unsuccessful.* Fowle family tradition recalls that Fulwar F. was irascible, especially where losing a game was concerned.
2. *Caroline.* Cooper.
3. *Mrs G.* Mrs Girle, Caroline Cooper's grandmother.
4. *the Square.* Queen's Square, Bath.
5. *J. D.* James Digweed.
6. *the Boarding-school.* This would appear to be one of JA's own childhood storybooks, now being lent to little Fanny; in which case, it may have been Sarah Fielding's *The Governess, or, Little Female Academy* (1741, and reprinted up to 1768), or else Dorothy Kilner's *Anecdotes of a Boarding School* (*c.*1782). The anonymous *The Governess; or Evening Amusements at a Boarding-School* (1800) would be too late in this context.
7. *[J. A.]* No part of the letter is missing, but there is no complimentary close or signature.

33. *To Cassandra Austen. From Steventon to Godmersham. Sunday 25 January 1801.*

Description. Unknown; original MS untraced since first publication.

Provenance. Bequeathed by CEA to Fanny, Lady Knatchbull, in 1845; inherited by Lord Brabourne 1882; probably in the Puttick & Simpson sale of 26–8 June 1893.

Publication. Brabourne i. 272; *Life* 162 (extracts); Chapman (1st and 2nd).

1. *very cross.* Fulwar F. being a bad loser again.
2. *M. Halavant.* HTA's French chef.

34. *To Cassandra Austen. From Manydown to London. Wednesday 11 February 1801.*

Description. Two leaves quarto, laid; watermark device (Heawood Nos. 2752–62) above indecipherable monogram, no date; green wafer; endorsed faintly in pencil [?by JEAL] 'Feby 1801 From | C. Esten A.'

Postmarks.—FEB 13 1801 (part illegible)   BASINGSTOKE

Provenance. Bequeathed by CEA to CJA in 1845; descended to CJA's grand-daughters; purchased from them by RWC, probably in 1925; sold by him to British Museum Dept. of MSS 1925; now British Library Add. MSS 41,253.A, fos. 1–2.

Publication. *Memoir* (1st 81; 2nd 64 (extract)); *Life* 163 (extract); Chapman (1st and 2nd); Modert F-87 to F-90.

1. *Wednesday.* Written over 'Thursday' partly erased.
2. *Royal Passenger.* The Duke of Sussex, sixth son of George III, had contracted a morganatic marriage in 1793 with Lady Augusta Murray, daughter of the Earl of Dunmore.
3. *Elephants & Kangaroons.* CEA had probably told JA that she had visited the menagerie at Exeter Change, one of the well-known sights of London.
4. *Cath:* Catherine Bigg.
5. *into Hampshire.* Inserted superscript.
6. *sunday-chaise.* Unexplained.

35. *To Cassandra Austen. From Bath to Ibthorpe. Tuesday 5–Wednesday 6 May 1801.*

Description. Two leaves quarto, laid; watermark device (Heawood Nos. 2752–62) above monogram P&P[?], no date; plain wafer, cut out to open; endorsed [?by CEA or JA] 'May 5th 1801'.

Postmark. BATH

Provenance. Bequeathed by CEA to Fanny, Lady Knatchbull, in 1845; inherited by Lord Brabourne 1882; with Banks MSS Sotheby's 14 Apr. 1886; Lord Ashcombe; presented by him to the Fitzwilliam Museum Library, Cambridge, 1917.

Publication. Brabourne i. 278; *Life* 165 (extracts); Chapman (1st and 2nd); Modert F-91 to F-94.

1. *a magnificent manner.* JA first wrote 'magnificent a manner', then cancelled this 'a' and inserted it superscript before 'magnificent'.
2. *my stomach.* Lord B. printed this as 'me', and RWC did not correct it.
3. *Martha triumphs.* Unexplained—the successful outcome of some legal problem, perhaps?
4. *in Gloucestershire.* See *Family Record* 81.
5. *he.* Inserted superscript above 'the former' cancelled.
6. *accustomary.* Inserted superscript.
7. *Meat . . . cheese 9½d.* This sentence has been altered in two places; JA first wrote: 'Meat is only 8½d. a pound . . . & cheese 9d.'—then cancelled the '½d.' at 'meat' and added it to 'cheese', writing it over the dash and full point with which she had first finished her sentence.

36. *To Cassandra Austen. From Bath to Ibthorpe. Tuesday 12–Wednesday 13 May 1801.*

Description. Two leaves quarto, laid; watermark PORTAL [&] CO 1797; mark of wafer; endorsed [?by CEA or JA] 'May 12th 1801'.

Postmark. BATH

Provenance. Bequeathed by CEA to Fanny, Lady Knatchbull, in 1845; inherited by Lord Brabourne 1882; probably in the Puttick & Simpson sale of 26–8 June 1893; Alfred Morrison; Sotheby's 10 Dec. 1918; J. Pierpont Morgan 1920; Pierpont Morgan Library, New York (MA 977–13).

Publication. Brabourne i. 284; *Life* 166 (extracts); Johnson 66; Chapman (1st and 2nd); Modert F-95 to F-98.

1. *Mary.* Mrs J. A.—FWA was not yet married to his Mary Gibson.

2. *the Cassoon.* 'The deviation of a few hundred yards from the road to Combhay, leads us to the hydrostatical lock, called the *caisson*, the bason of which now alone remains. This plan for conveying boats from a higher to a lower level (a fall of about sixty feet) was the invention of Mr Weldon . . . the caisson . . . bade fair to be a most useful and important machine, and of course greatly excited and interested the public attention; . . . Unfortunately, however, for the inventor, the subscribers to the canal, and the public in general, the cistern . . . was not rendered sufficiently tight to hold the water necessary for its operations . . . the machine, therefore, was consigned to destruction, but not to oblivion, since it will ever remain a memorable proof of the superior mechanical abilities of its very ingenious inventor' (Revd Richard Warner, *Excursions from Bath* (1801)).

3. *the W. Kent scheme.* 'scheme' inserted superscript.

37. *To Cassandra Austen. From Bath to Kintbury. Thursday 21–Friday 22 May 1801.*

Description. Two leaves quarto, laid; watermark device only (Heawood Nos. 2752–62), nò date; seal or wafer cut out; endorsed [?by CEA or JA] 'May 21st 1801'.

Postmark. BATH

Provenance. Bequeathed by CEA to Fanny, Lady Knatchbull, in 1845; inherited by Lord Brabourne 1882; probably in the Puttick & Simpson sale of 26–8 June 1893; Alfred Morrison; Sotheby's 10 Dec. 1918; J. Pierpont Morgan 1920; Pierpont Morgan Library, New York (MA 977–14).

Publication. Brabourne i. 289; *Life* 168 (extracts); Chapman (1st and 2nd); facsimile (slightly reduced) of pp. 2–3 in *British Literary Manuscripts*, II (1981), facing 17; Modert F-99 to F-102.

1. *Weston.* 'The Promenade to Weston; the Hyde-Park, or Kensington-Gardens, of Bath . . . attractive from the shortness of its distance, which

does not exceed a mile and a half. . . . At the bottom of *Sion-Hill* . . . the Village of Weston . . . which is occupied by numerous laundresses, has altogether a superior appearance. . . . The Church is a small erection; but the numerous monuments in its Burying-Ground are highly attractive and interesting. . . . The visitor . . . can diversify the scene by turning off into *Barton's Fields'* (Pierce Egan, *Walks through Bath* (1819)). [RWC]

2. *been.* Inserted superscript.

3. *Dodsley's Poems.* Robert Dodsley (1703–64), *A Collection of Poems in Six Volumes by Several Hands* (1758).

4. *day.* Inserted superscript above 'Journey' cancelled.

5. *Disciple of Godwin.* William Godwin (1756–1836); JA was probably acquainted with his *Caleb Williams* (1794) and *St Leon* (1799).

38. *To Cassandra Austen. From Bath to Kintbury. Tuesday 26– Wednesday 27 May 1801.*

Description. Two leaves quarto, laid; watermark device (Heawood Nos. 2752– 62) above monogram TB[?], no date; mark of red wafer; endorsed [?by CEA or JA] 'May 26th 1801' and [?by CEA or JEAL] 'C. Esten A.'

Postmark. BATH

Provenance. Bequeathed by CEA to CJA in 1845; descended to CJA's granddaughters and sold by them in 1920s; E. Byrne Hackett; Charles Beecher Hogan by 1966; presented by him to JAMT 1974.

Publication. Memoir (1st 83; 2nd 65 (extract)); *Life* 169 (extracts); Chapman (1st and 2nd); Modert F-103 to F-106.

1. *the Harrison family.* This obscure allusion may be connected with the reference to Mary H. in letter **5**.

2. *my Master.* This suggests a quotation from Mrs Piozzi (cf. letter **21**) but it does not seem to be in her Johnsonian writings. [RWC]

3. *out of sight.* 'of sight' inserted superscript.

4. *Topaze crosses.* These two crosses accompanied letter **38** in its later wanderings, and were also purchased by Mr C. B. Hogan and presented by him to the JAMT in 1974; see *Reports* for 1966, 4–6, and 1974, 213–14. The ownership of the crosses was identified by Mr G. H. Tucker, see *Report* for 1978, 76–7.

5. *4th of June . . . fireworks.* The usual celebrations for the King's birthday.

39. *To Cassandra Austen. From Lyme Regis to Ibthorpe. Friday 14 September 1804.*

Description. Two leaves quarto, laid; watermark HVG 1803; mark of seal or wafer; endorsed [?by CEA or JA] 'From Lyme | Sept. 1804'.

Postmark. None.

Provenance. Bequeathed by CEA to CJA in 1845; descended to CJA's grand-daughters and sold by them in 1920s; Frederick R. Lovering; Sotheby's 3 May 1948; Mrs Alberta H. Burke; bequeathed by her to Pierpont Morgan Library, New York, 1975 (MA 2911).

Publication. *Memoir* (1st 89; 2nd 68 (extracts)); *Life* 177 (extracts); Chapman (1st and 2nd, from a copy made by RAAL in 1909); Modert F-107 to F-110.

1. *fine striped paper.* The paper of this letter is rather thin, so that the laid lines are slightly more visible than usual.

2. *the Royal Family.* Mr C. Wanklyn, the local historian of Lyme Regis, sent RWC an extract from the *Western Flying Post* for 10 Sept. 1804: 'Weymouth Sept. 8th. Arrived here this town's original patron, his Royal Highness the Duke of Gloucester on a visit to the Royal Family, all of whom we are happy to observe, enjoy good health and spirits. The King rises very early and visits the camps before breakfast, then embarks with the family for a cruise in the Royal Sovereign yacht, attended by the two others, the frigates, and a fleet of yachts of every description, returns to an evening parade and lastly visits the theatre. This is making the most of his time. The town was never known to be fuller of company than this season, since the Royal Family has been here.'
The *Morning Post* describes the embarkation on Tuesday: 'Weymouth Sept. 11. At half-past ten the Royal Family left the Lodge, and went to the shore in their carriages, when two boats were waiting to receive them, and convey them on board the Royal Yacht.'

3. *already.* Inserted superscript.

4. *Gloucester.* i.e. Gloucester House, in Weymouth, where the King and Queen had previously stayed during their visit in 1789.

5. *should have . . . had.* JA first wrote 'a little fever & indisposition, as I had', then cancelled 'a' and 'as', replacing them by 'the' and 'which' superscript.

6. *We all of us.* JA wrote 'We have all of us', then cancelled 'have'.

7. *Le Chevalier.* Unidentified.

8. *uncle Toby's annuity.* Laurence Sterne (1713–68), *Tristram Shandy* (1760–5), III. 22.

9. *I fancy.* JA omitted 'fancy', and had to insert it superscript.

10. *in poor James Selby.* 'in' inserted superscript. See Samuel Richardson (1689–1761), *Sir Charles Grandison* (1753), VI. 59, 75—Harriet Byron's 'cousin James Selby', who was 'on a sudden very earnest to go abroad; as if, silly youth, travelling would make him a Sir Charles Grandison'. [RWC]

11. *infamous plate.* i.e. name-plate on the front door of 4 Sydney Place in Bath, just vacated by the Austens before their seaside holiday.

12. *in the room.* 'the' inserted superscript.

13. *Eliza.* Probably Mrs HTA.

14. *Robinson Crusoe.* Daniel Defoe (?1661–1731), *Robinson Crusoe* (1719).

40. *To Francis Austen. From Bath to Portsmouth. Monday 21 January 1805.*

Description. Two leaves quarto, laid; watermark MOLINEUX JOHNSTON & A. LEE[?] 1803; mark of black wafer; endorsed by JA 'January 22nd 1805'. The original address of 'Dungeness | New Romney' has been crossed out and 'Portsmouth' added, by another hand.

Postmarks. .JA C 25. .805 E JAN 25 1805 BATH NEW ROMNEY DEAL 74.

Provenance. Descended in FWA's family to his grandson Capt. Ernest Leigh Austen, RN, who presented it to the British Museum Dept. of MSS, 1930; now British Library Add. MSS 42,180, fos. 1–2.

Publication. SB 125; *Life* 181 (extracts); Johnson 127; Chapman (1st and 2nd); Modert F-111 to F-114.

1. *to get up.* JA first wrote 'to walk' and then cancelled 'walk'.

2. *Brompton.* The HTAs were now living at 16 Michael's Place, Brompton, near London.

41. *To Francis Austen. From Bath to Portsmouth. Tuesday 22 January 1805.*

Description. Two leaves quarto, laid; watermark IVC[?] 1803; mark of red wafer. Endorsed by JA 'January 23rd 1805'.

Postmark. None.

Provenance. Descended in FWA's family to his grandson Capt. Ernest Leigh Austen, RN, who presented it to the British Museum Dept. of MSS, 1930; now British Library Add. MSS 42,180, fos. 3–4.

Publication. SB 127; *Life* 180 (with omissions); Johnson 129; Chapman (1st and 2nd); Modert F-115 to F-118.

1. *we understood.* 'we' inserted above 'he' cancelled.

2. *him.* Inserted superscript.

42. *To Francis Austen. From Bath to Portsmouth. Tuesday 29 January 1805.*

Description. Two leaves quarto, laid; watermark device only (Heawood Nos. 2752–62), no date; black wafer; endorsed by JA 'January 29th 1805'.

Postmark. BATH

Provenance. Descended in FWA's family to his grandson Capt. Ernest Leigh Austen, RN, who presented it to the British Museum Dept. of MSS, 1930; now British Library Add. MSS 42,180, fos. 5–6.

Publication. *SB* 129; Johnson 131; Chapman (1st and 2nd); Modert F-119 and F-120.

43. *To Cassandra Austen. From Bath to Ibthorpe. Monday 8–Thursday 11 April 1805.*

Description. Two leaves quarto, laid; watermark IWG[?] 1794; plain wafer impressed by wafer seal; endorsed [?by CEA] 'From Gay St—Bath' and '1805'.
Postmark. BATH

Provenance. Probably bequeathed by CEA to CMCA in 1845; descended in junior line of AL family; placed on deposit in the British Museum Dept. of MSS by Miss Lois AL, 1936; Sotheby's 29–30 June 1982; Frederick R. Koch; placed on deposit at Pierpont Morgan Library, New York (FRK Personal Deposit TD-1, 8 Apr. 1805); Christie's New York 7 June 1990; S. Lerner, Redmond, Washington.

Publication. *Memoir* (2nd) 70; *Life* 183 (extracts); Chapman (1st and 2nd), Modert F-121 to F-124.

1. *such weather.* Superscript above 'it' cancelled.
2. *Ridinghouse . . . Miss Lefroy's.* There were two riding-houses (i.e. riding-schools combined with livery stables) in Bath—Ryles's in Monmouth Street, and Dash's in Montpelier Row, which also had a real tennis court on the premises. This latter building is now known as the Bath Industrial Heritage Centre, Camden Works, Julian Road.
   Miss Lefroy = Lucy, now Mrs Henry Rice.
3. *her end.* Mrs Lloyd died 16 Apr. 1805.
4. *seems . . . Susan's.* In this phrase both 'been' and 'sister' are inserted superscript.
5. *his appearance is exactly.* 'is' written over 'has' partially erased.
6. *enjoyment with her.* 'with' inserted above 'to' cancelled.
7. *a Lady . . . upper Crescent.* Miss Colbourne of Lansdown Crescent.
8. *I am sorry.* 'I' inserted superscript.
9. *Urania . . . Wallop race.* The surname of the Earls of Portsmouth was Wallop, and many of the ladies of that family were Camilla or Urania—the ships so named reminded JA of this.
10. *Miss Gibson's Letters.* FWA was now engaged to Mary Gibson.
11. *Expedition.* A 44-gun ship, built at Chatham 1784.

44. *To Cassandra Austen. From Bath to Ibthorpe. Sunday 21–Tuesday 23 April 1805.*

Description. Two leaves quarto, laid; watermark device 3 fleurs-de-lis above a shield, CR below; no date; black seal; endorsed [?by CEA] 'From Bath—April 1805'.

Postmark. BATH (almost illegible)

Provenance. Bequeathed by CEA to CJA in 1845; descended to CJA's grand-daughters and sold by them in 1920s; Jerome Kern 1927; Anderson Galleries 7–10 Jan. 1929; Robert H. Taylor; placed on deposit at Princeton University Library 1971 and bequeathed to Princeton 1985.

Publication. *Memoir* (1st 93; 2nd 74 (extracts)); *Life* 185 (extracts); Chapman (1st and 2nd); Modert F-125 to F-128.

1. *actually.* Superscript above 'exactly' cancelled.
2. *attention.* Superscript above 'regard' cancelled.
3. *famous Saunders.* I have not traced this author, who may be fabulous. [RWC]
4. *whenever . . . of late.* 'whenever' superscript above 'whether' cancelled, and 'of late' superscript above 'now' cancelled.
5. *have sent word.* 'sent' inserted superscript.
6. *Lady Roden.* Robert Jocelyn, 2nd Earl, had married 5 July 1804 as his second wife Juliana-Anne, youngest daughter of John Orde of Weetwood, Northumberland, and the 2nd Earl's sister, Lady Louisa, was already married to another Orde of the Weetwood family; still more Ordes had previously come south and intermarried with the Hampshire Powletts; so there would be a strong neighbourhood connection to warrant the Austens calling upon the Rodens while they were both in Bath. An alternative reason would be that the Earl's second son, James-Bligh Jocelyn, was in the Navy (born 1790, Lt. 1811, died unmarried 1812), and may perhaps have been serving under either FWA or CJA.

45. *To Cassandra Austen. From Godmersham to Goodnestone Farm. Saturday 24 August 1805.*

Description. Two leaves quarto, wove; watermark WS, no date; remains of red seal.

Postmark. FEVERSHAM 47

Provenance. Bequeathed by CEA to Fanny, Lady Knatchbull, in 1845; inherited by Lord Brabourne 1882; probably in the Puttick & Simpson sale of 26–8 June 1893; Amy Lowell *c.*1905; bequeathed by her to Houghton Library of Harvard University 1925 (Lowell Autograph, rev. 1925).

Publication. Brabourne i. 298; *Life* 189 (extracts); Chapman (1st and 2nd); Modert F-129 to F-132.

1. *he said.* 'he' inserted superscript.
2. *private message.* 'private' inserted superscript.
3. *quite Palmerstone.* Mrs Rachel Hunter (1754–1813), *Letters from Mrs Palmerstone to her Daughters, inculcating Morality by Entertaining Narratives* (1803).

4. *other party*. JA first wrote 'other party concerned' and then cancelled the final word.
5. *defy her*. 'her' inserted superscript.
6. *Henry's picture*. HTA.
7. *from Henry*. HTA.

46. *To Cassandra Austen. From Goodnestone Farm to Godmersham. Tuesday 27 August 1805.*

Description. Unknown; original MS untraced since first publication.
Provenance. Bequeathed by CEA to Fanny, Lady Knatchbull, in 1845; inherited by Lord Brabourne 1882; probably in the Puttick & Simpson sale of 26–8 June 1893.
Publication. Brabourne i. 303; *Life* 190 (extract); Chapman (1st and 2nd).

1. *his patient*. Marianne Bridges.
2. *Duke of Gloucester's death*. The brother of George III; died 25 Aug. 1805. His death meant the cancellation of the ball at Deal on Friday.
3. *Sophie*. Cage.
4. *John*. Bridges.
5. *Henry*. Bridges.

47. *To Cassandra Austen. From Goodnestone Farm to Godmersham. Friday 30 August 1805.*

Description. Unknown; original MS untraced since first publication.
Provenance. Bequeathed by CEA to Fanny, Lady Knatchbull, in 1845; inherited by Lord Brabourne 1882; probably in the Puttick & Simpson sale of 26–8 June 1893.
Publication. Brabourne i. 307; *Life* 191 (extract); Chapman (1st and 2nd).

1. *Our Worthing scheme*. See *Family Record* 134.
2. *The evil intentions of the Guards*. Sir John Fortescue tells me that on Friday 30 Aug. (partridge shooting began on the Monday following) the First and Second Grenadier Guards marched from Deal for Chatham, the First Coldstreams and First Scots Guards from Chatham for Deal. A movement on such a scale might well disturb the birds; and Mr Edward Bridges may have apprehended that (in spite of the efforts of their officers) some of the men might do a bit of poaching. 'Yet (Sir John adds) the danger of invasion was only just past. Napoleon's orders for the march from Boulogne to the Danube were not issued until 22 August, and the camp at Boulogne was not finally evacuated until that same fateful 30 August.' [RWC]

3. *Gisborne*. Thomas Gisborne (1758–1846), *An Enquiry into the Duties of the Female Sex* (1797).

48(C). *To Fanny Austen (Knight). From Clifton to Godmersham. ?Thursday 24 July 1806.*

Description. Unknown; original MS possibly destroyed later in 19th cent.
Provenance. Copied by Anna Lefroy into her Lefroy MS, *c.*1855.
Publication. TLS (20 Feb. 1987), 185; Doody and Murray 275.

1. FWA and Mary Gibson were married at Ramsgate on Thursday, 24 July 1806, and came to Godmersham for their honeymoon on 26 July. FCK noted in her diary, under the date Tuesday, 29 July 1806: 'I had a bit of a letter from Aunt Jane with some verses of hers'.

49. *To Cassandra Austen. From Southampton to Godmersham. Wednesday 7–Thursday 8 January 1807.*

Description. Unknown; original MS untraced since first publication.
Provenance. Bequeathed by CEA to Fanny, Lady Knatchbull, in 1845; inherited by Lord Brabourne 1882; probably in the Puttick & Simpson sale of 26–8 June 1893.
Publication. Brabourne i. 312; *Life* 198 (extracts); Chapman (1st and 2nd).

1. *our guests.* James A., his wife Mary, and their toddler CMCA, staying in Southampton over the New Year. See *Family Record* 140–1.
2. *Mrs Foote's baby's name.* JA had forgotten that Captain Foote already had a Caroline—a daughter by his first wife.
3. *the Williams.* Sir Thomas and his second wife.
4. *'Alphonsine' . . . 'Female Quixotte'.* Mme de Genlis, *Alphonsine, ou la Tendresse maternelle* (1806); trans. as *Alphonsine, or Maternal Affection* (2nd edn., 1807).
   Charlotte Lennox (1720–1804), *The Female Quixote, or, the Adventures of Arabella* (1752).
5. *the family treaty.* The financial arrangements between Mr Leigh Perrot and the Leighs of Adlestrop regarding the Stoneleigh inheritance—see *Family Record* 138–9.
6. *meadows by the beach.* Not 'beech' as Lord Brabourne printed; Southampton had no beach, but in and after 1769 the path eastwards along the sea embankment from the Platform round the southernmost tip of the city to the Itchen Ferry was improved, planted with trees, and laid out as a marine walk which became known as the Beach.

7. *their house.* For information on the development of small estates on the outskirts of Southampton, see Jessica Vale, 'The Country Houses of Southampton', in *Proc. Hants Field Club*, 39 (1983), 171–90.

8. *fainting fit.* Mrs FA was now pregnant with her first child.

50. *To Cassandra Austen. From Southampton to Godmersham. Sunday 8–Monday 9 February 1807.*

Description. Two leaves quarto, laid; watermark device (Heawood Nos. 2752–62), 1803; mark of seal.

Postmarks. C FEB 10 1807   SOUTHAMPTON 80

Provenance. Bequeathed by CEA to Fanny, Lady Knatchbull, in 1845; inherited by Lord Brabourne 1882; probably in the Puttick & Simpson sale of 26–8 June 1893; Alfred Morrison; Sotheby's 10 Dec. 1918; J. Pierpont Morgan 1920; Pierpont Morgan Library, New York (MA 977–15).

Publication. Brabourne i. 320; *Life* 199 (extracts); Chapman (1st and 2nd); Modert F-133 to F-136.

1. *Queen Mary's Lamentation.* JA had copied this song into her MS book 'Songs & Duetts', now owned by the JAMT. See Patrick Piggott, *The Innocent Diversion* (London, 1979), 152–3.

2. *even for Harriot.* Harriot Bridges was now married to the Revd Mr Moore.

3. *if you are not.* 'if' inserted superscript.

4. *Our Garden.* At the Castle Square house.

5. *Cowper's Line. The Task*, 'The Winter Walk at Noon', vi, lines 149–50: '. . . Laburnum, rich | In streaming gold; syringa, iv'ry pure.'

6. *Catherine . . . Caroline.* Children of Captain Foote, RN.

7. *not so well-looking.* 'so' inserted superscript.

8. *Mrs W. K.* Mrs Wyndham Knatchbull.

9. *Hastings . . . H. Egerton.* Probably Hastings de Feuillide (1786–1801), the sickly little son of Mrs HTA by her first marriage; Henry Egerton was a friend of Mrs HTA.

10. *as not . . . Benefaction.* 'as' inserted superscript; JA first wrote 'Benefit', then cancelled '-it' and inserted '-action' superscript.

11. *M^de Duval.* See *Evelina*, II, letter 3.

12. *understanding of the Business.* HTA's broken engagement to Miss Mary Pearson seems to have left resentment on her side.

13. *Edward.* EAK's eldest son.

14. *Clarentine.* Sarah Harriet Burney (1770?–1844), *Clarentine, a Novel* (1798).

15. *Sir Tho.* Sir Thomas Williams.

16. *Gentlemen only.* 'only' inserted superscript.

17. *Mary.* Mrs FA.

18. *Dr Johnson.* See Johnson's letter to Boswell of 4 July 1774. [RWC]

51. *To Cassandra Austen. From Southampton to Godmersham. Friday 20–Sunday 22 February 1807.*

Description. Two leaves quarto; plain wafer impressed by wafer-seal.

Postmarks. FEB 23 1807   SOUTHAMPTON 80

Provenance. Bequeathed by CEA to Fanny, Lady Knatchbull, in 1845; inherited by Lord Brabourne 1882; Sotheby's 11–14 May 1891; R. B. Adam; Mary and Donald Hyde 1948; Viscountess Eccles (previously Mrs Donald Hyde).

Publication. Brabourne i. 329; *Life* 201 (extracts); Chapman (1st and 2nd); Modert F-137 to F-140.

1. *Mr Austen . . . Mr M^y Austen's.* John A. of Broadford, and Francis Motley A. of Kippington.
2. *Mary.* Mrs FA.
3. *her Baby.* Mrs EAK's tenth child Cassandra Jane, born 16 Nov. 1806.
4. *them & Adlestrop.* See letter **49**, note 5.
5. *Caroline.* Elizabeth (not Caroline) Coleman was baptized 1807. [RWC]
6. *the 1st Lord.* Thomas Grenville. [RWC]
7. *but.* Inserted superscript.
8. *Mrs Grant's Letters.* Mrs Anne Grant (1755–1838) of Laggan, *Letters from the Mountains, being the real correspondence of a Lady, between the years 1773 and 1807* (1807).
9. *speaks of them.* 'them' superscript above 'it' cancelled.
10. *the book.* Superscript above 'it' cancelled.
11. *Baretti's other book . . . Mr Sharpe.* Joseph Baretti (1719–89), *Account of the Manners and Customs of Italy* (1768—the 2nd edn. 1769 has an *Appendix added, in Answer to Samuel Sharp, Esq.*); *Journey from London to Genoa* (1770).
    Samuel Sharp (1700?–1778), *Letters from Italy* (1766).
12. *William.* Fowle.
13. *remedy.* Winchester College slang for a holiday.
14. *her Sister.* Mrs JA.
15. *Lady B.* Eleanor Foote (1778–1806), first wife of Sir Brook B., 4th baronet.
16. *want of subject.* 'subject' superscript above 'matter' cancelled.

52. *To Cassandra Austen. From Godmersham to Southampton. Wednesday 15–Friday 17 June 1808.*

Description. Unknown; original MS untraced since first publication.

Provenance. Bequeathed by CEA to Fanny, Lady Knatchbull, in 1845; inherited by Lord Brabourne 1882; probably in the Puttick & Simpson sale of 26–8 June 1893.

Publication. Brabourne i. 341; *Life* 204 (extracts); Chapman (1st and 2nd).

1. *coach at five.* A coach left the Cross Keys, Gracechurch Street, London, daily at 5 a.m., arriving at Dover (71 miles by this route) in 15 hours. [RWC]

2. *Our two brothers.* The journey to Canterbury was 55 miles, so James had arrived before the carriage party.

3. *since last year.* EAK had brought his family to Hampshire in Sept. 1807 for a holiday—see *Family Record* 144–5.

4. *John.* Bridges.

5. *little Edward.* JEAL, not yet 10 years old.

6. *Edward.* EAK's eldest son, aged 14.

7. *at that time.* Elizabeth was once again pregnant and the child expected in Sept.

8. *child of three.* James A.'s younger daughter, CMCA.

9. *Louisa.* Bridges—as also the next two references.

10. *Mary.* Mrs FA.

11. *Huxham.* From John Huxham, physician, (1692–1768), whose tincture of cinchona bark is in the British Pharmacopoeia. An advertisement (*London Chronicle*, 31 Dec. 1807) of Newbery & Sons, proprietors of Dr James's Powder, includes 'Huxham's Tinct. of Bark'. [RWC]

12. *one copy of the work.* Revd T. Jefferson of Tunbridge, *Two Sermons* (1808); the list of subscribers includes Mr and Mrs Edward Austen of Godmersham and Miss Jane Austen. [RWC]

13. *Miss Maria.* Cuthbert.

14. *in the Palace.* Sackree may have been admitted by favour of Mrs Charles Fielding, who was related to the Goodnestone family and was an inmate of the Palace. [RWC]

15. *Louisa.* EAK's daughter.

53. *To Cassandra Austen. From Godmersham to Southampton. Monday 20–Wednesday 22 June 1808.*

Description. Two leaves quarto, laid; watermark device (Heawood Nos. 2752–62) above monogram, no date; plain wafer.

Postmarks. A JUN 23 1808   FEVERSHAM 47

Provenance. Bequeathed by CEA to Fanny, Lady Knatchbull, in 1845; inherited by Lord Brabourne 1882; Puttick & Simpson 26–8 June 1893; Alfred Morrison; Sotheby's 10 Dec. 1918; J. Pierpont Morgan 1920; Pierpont Morgan Library, New York (MA 977–16).

Publication. Brabourne i. 350; *Life* 206 (extracts); Chapman (1st and 2nd); Modert F-141 to F-144.

1. *Mary Jane.* FWA's eldest daughter, then at Southampton.

2. *Caroline.* Mr Moore's daughter by his first marriage.

3. *Edward Junr.* EAK's eldest son.

4. *agreable present.* Mrs Knight's 'fee'.

5. *mysteries of Inman-ism.* 'Mrs Inman was the aged widow of a former clergy-man at Godmersham, who lived at the park-keeper's house ("Old Hills"), and it was one of the "treats" of the Godmersham children to walk up to her with fruit after dessert. She was blind, and used to walk about the park with a gold-headed walking-stick, and leaning on the arm of her faithful servant Nanny Part. She died in September, 1815'. (Brabourne i. 338).

6. *the noonshine.* A dialect word, especially in southern England, meaning any snack or small quantity of food consumed outside regular meal-times; several variant spellings, of which 'nuncheon' is the most common.

7. *unhappiness in her.* 'in' superscript above 'about' cancelled.

8. *the Dean.* Powys.

9. *It went off.* 'off' inserted superscript.

10. *Ought I.* 'I' inserted superscript.

11. *Marmion.* Sir Walter Scott (1771–1832), *Marmion* (1808).

12. *Mrs Powlett.* The scandal cannot be found in the London *Courier*, but see *Morning Post*, 18 and 21 June 1808. 'Another elopement has taken place in high life. A Noble Viscount, Lord S., has gone off with a Mrs P., the wife of a relative of a Noble Marquis' [of Winchester]. 'Mrs P.'s *faux pas* with Lord S——e took place at an inn near Winchester.' Col. P. was awarded £3,000 damages. [RWC]

54. *To Cassandra Austen. From Godmersham to Southampton. Sunday 26 June 1808.*

Description. Two leaves quarto, laid; watermark device (Heawood Nos. 2752–62) above monogram, no date; wafer impressed by wafer-seal.

Postmarks. A JUN 27 1808   FEVERSHAM 47

Provenance. Bequeathed by CEA to Fanny, Lady Knatchbull, in 1845; inherited by Lord Brabourne 1882; probably in the Puttick & Simpson sale of 26–8 June 1893; Alfred Morrison; Sotheby's 10 Dec. 1918; J. Pierpont Morgan 1920; Pierpont Morgan Library, New York (MA 977–17).

Publication. Brabourne i. 358; *Life* 207 (extracts); Chapman (1st and 2nd); Modert F-145 to F-148.

1. *young Edward.* EAK's eldest son.

2. *our Friends' visit.* Catherine and Alethea Bigg were due to come to Southampton. The *secrecy* of the explanation to EAK and his wife may be a reference to Harris Bigg-Wither's brief and unsuccessful courtship of JA in 1802; JA may have felt that to stay on at Godmersham would look like a deliberate attempt to avoid meeting his sisters.

3. *accompanying Edward.* EAK's eldest son, returning from Winchester for the Christmas holidays.

4. *Mrs M. of Nackington*. Milles.
5. *& Charles Graham*. '&' inserted superscript.
6. *Mrs Moore*. Widow of the Archbishop and mother-in-law of Harriot (Bridges) Moore.
7. *have had any leisure*. 'had' inserted superscript.
8. *was very particular*. 'was' inserted superscript.
9. *must keep it two*. Presumably letters from Godmersham were not sent to the post every day.
10. *whose object I imagine*. 'imagine' superscript above 'fancy' cancelled.
11. *her namesake*. Mrs FA.
12. *Seale*. Home of their Walter cousins.

55. *To Cassandra Austen. From Godmersham to Southampton. Thursday 30 June–Friday 1 July 1808.*

Description. Two leaves quarto, laid; watermark THIN[ ]ST 1807; plain wafer impressed with wafer-seal.

Postmarks. A JUL 2 1808   FEVERSHAM 47

Provenance. Bequeathed by CEA to Fanny, Lady Knatchbull, in 1845; inherited by Lord Brabourne 1882; Sotheby's 11–14 May 1891; Alfred Morrison; Sotheby's 10 Dec. 1918; J. Pierpont Morgan 1920; Pierpont Morgan Library, New York (MA 977–18).

Publication. Brabourne i. 366; *Life* 207 (extracts); Chapman (1st and 2nd); Modert F-149 to F-152.

1. *glad to go home*. See CMCA's *Reminiscences*, 20.
2. *I assure you*. 'you' inserted superscript.
3. *Fanny Austen's Match*. With Captain Holcroft, RA; possibly a shot-gun wedding?
4. *Smallbone*. Jenny S.'s daughter Mary was CMCA's nursemaid.
5. *brings intelligence*. JA first wrote 'brings the intelligence' and then cancelled 'the'.
6. *as her Papa*. 'as' inserted superscript.
7. *voyage down the Ganges*. In 1782 Warren Hastings's wife Marian made a hasty and dangerous voyage down the stormy Ganges, travelling 400 miles in three days, to nurse him when he had fallen seriously ill. After their return to England a few years later Hastings commissioned William Hodges to illustrate this event, and a large canvas known as *Mrs Hastings at the Rocks of Colgong* was the result. This, with other Indian scenes by Hodges, was hung in the 'picture room' at Daylesford. See Isabel Stuebe, 'William Hodges and Warren Hastings: A Study in Eighteenth-Century Patronage', in *The Burlington Magazine* (Oct. 1973), 659–66.

8. *now fool enough to keep it.* JA first wrote 'no wonder that he is fool enough to keep it'—then cancelled 'no wonder that', and inserted 'now' superscript.
9. *Mrs D.* Deedes.
10. *three little Bridgeses.* JA inserted 'but' and 'also' superscript into this phrase.
11. *Vulgar Economy.* JA first wrote 'Vulgar Economy & Cares', then cancelled the last two words.

56. *To Cassandra Austen. From Southampton to Godmersham.*
Saturday 1–Sunday 2 October 1808.

Description. Two leaves quarto, wove; watermark GATER 1808; plain wafer impressed by wafer-seal.

Postmarks. C OCT 3 1808   SOUTHAMPTON 80

Provenance. Bequeathed by CEA to Fanny, Lady Knatchbull, in 1845; inherited by Lord Brabourne 1882; probably in the Puttick & Simpson sale of 26–8 June 1893; Alfred Morrison; Sotheby's 10 Dec. 1918; J. Pierpont Morgan 1920; Pierpont Morgan Library, New York (MA 977–19).

Publication. Brabourne ii. 4; *Life* 210 (extracts); Chapman (1st and 2nd); Modert F-153 to F-156.

1. *birth of the Child.* EAK's sixth son, Brook-John, born 28 September 1808.
2. *Shalden and Neatham.* Part of the Chawton estate.
3. *Eliza.* Miss Maitland.
4. *Eliza.* Mrs HTA.
5. *giving it.* 'it' inserted superscript.
6. *but poor Woman . . . breeding again?* This sentence roughly cancelled—probably by Lord Brabourne—but still legible.
7. *perfectly* unexceptionable. HTA's bank now had a branch in Alton, hence he could provide local information on the housing situation.
8. *Our Yarmouth Division.* FWA and his family, on the Isle of Wight.
9. *Espriella's Letters.* Robert Southey (1774-1843), *Letters from England; by Dom Manuel Alvarez Espriella* (1807). An account of English life, written in the guise of letters assigned to a fictitious Spanish traveller.
10. *Miss B.* Bailey.
11. *probably to make.* 'probably' inserted superscript.
12. *till friday or Saturday.* JA first wrote 'Saturday or Sunday', then cancelled the last two words and inserted 'friday or' superscript.
13. *my little Goddaughter.* Louisa Austen (Knight).
14. *the Marquis.* Of Lansdowne.

57. *To Cassandra Austen. From Southampton to Godmersham. Friday 7–Sunday 9 October 1808.*

Description. Two leaves quarto, wove; watermark GATER 1808; mark of small plain wafer impressed with wafer-seal.

Postmarks. C OCT 10 1808   SOUTHAMPTON 80

Provenance. Bequeathed by CEA to Fanny, Lady Knatchbull, in 1845; inherited by Lord Brabourne 1882; probably in the Puttick & Simpson sale of 26–8 June 1893; Alfred Morrison; Sotheby's 10 Dec. 1918; J. Pierpont Morgan 1920; Pierpont Morgan Library, New York (MA 977–20).

Publication. Brabourne ii. 11; *Life* 212 (extracts); Chapman (1st and 2nd); Modert F-157 to F-160.

1. *your Winchester Correspondent.* EAK's eldest son Edward.
2. *a very proper day.* His father's birthday.
3. *his 30th year.* JA must have been joking—EAK was in fact 40, and this birthday made him 41.
4. *Eliza.* Maidservant in the Southampton household.
5. *Mrs E. K.* Possibly 'Mrs' Elizabeth Knight, the sister of Thomas Knight II, who was buried at Godmersham on 4 March 1809.
6. *dyed black.* JA first wrote 'dyed at black', then cancelled 'at'.
7. *those at Lyme.* There was a big fire at Lyme Regis on 5 Nov. 1803; this reference implies that the Austens had visited the town before their holiday there in the summer of 1804.
8. *were alarmed.* JA first wrote 'were a little alarmed', and then cancelled 'a little'.
9. *my two companions.* Mrs A. and Martha Lloyd.
10. *my best Love.* 'my' inserted superscript.
11. *the three boys.* Edward and George Austen (Knight), and Fulwar-William Fowle, all now at Winchester College.
12. *Harriot.* Moore.
13. *her son Edward's.* Had Edward Bridges's 'invitation' been a proposal of marriage to JA, possibly in the summer of 1805? See letters **46** and **55**.
14. *Catherine.* Bigg, soon to become Mrs Hill.
15. *can have mistaken it.* 'can' inserted superscript.
16. *Miss Foote.* Probably Catherine Foote, sr.
17. *to do with her long.* Presumably JA meant to write 'without'.
18. *Dr Percival of Manchester.* Thomas Percival, MD (1740–1804), *A Father's Instructions; consisting of Moral Tales, Fables, and Reflections, designed to promote the Love of Virtue* (1768).

58. *To Cassandra Austen. From Southampton to Godmersham.
Thursday 13 October 1808.*

Description. Two leaves quarto, wove; watermark GATER 1808; mark of blue
wafer.

Postmarks. C OCT 14 1808   SOUTHAMPTON 80

Provenance. Bequeathed by CEA to Fanny, Lady Knatchbull, in 1845; inherited
by Lord Brabourne 1882; probably in the Puttick & Simpson sale of 26–
8 June 1893; Alfred Morrison; Sotheby's 10 Dec. 1918; J. Pierpont Morgan
1920; Pierpont Morgan Library, New York (MA 977–21).

Publication. Brabourne ii. 18; *Life* 213 (extracts); Johnson 71; Chapman (1st
and 2nd); Modert F-161 to F-164.

1. *the sad news.* EAK's wife Elizabeth had died very suddenly on 10 Oct.
   1808.
2. *it came.* JA first wrote 'in came', and changed 'in' to 'it'.
3. *Henry.* HTA, who went to Godmersham on 12 Oct. to comfort his brother.
4. *the poor Boys.* Edward jr. and George, collected from Winchester College
   by Mrs JA.
5. *amusement there.* 'there' inserted superscript.
6. *Catherine.* Bigg.

59. *To Cassandra Austen. From Southampton to Godmersham.
Saturday 15–Sunday 16 October 1808.*

Description. Two leaves quarto, laid; no watermark; black wax seal with image
of a tall ship.

Postmarks. C OCT 17 1808   SOUTHAMPTON 80

Provenance. Bequeathed by CEA to Fanny, Lady Knatchbull, in 1845; inherited
by Lord Brabourne 1882; probably in the Puttick & Simpson sale of 26–
8 June 1893; Simon Gratz; given by him to The Historical Society of
Pennsylvania, Philadelphia, *c.*1925 (Simon Gratz Collection, Case 10, Box
26).

Publication. Brabourne ii. 21; *Life* 214 (extracts); Johnson 73; Chapman (1st
and 2nd—but leaving text uncorrected); Modert F-165 to F-168.

1. *you see the Corpse.* It was the custom of the period for relatives to take a last
   farewell look at the body before the coffin was closed prior to the funeral;
   it was also the custom that very few mourners should actually attend the
   interment.
2. *Henry & John.* HTA and John Bridges.
3. *Mr Fowle.* As Revd Thomas F. sr. had died in 1806, JA was now punctili-
   ous in referring to his son Fulwar (so called in her earlier letters) as 'Mr'
   Fowle, in accordance with his dignity as the new head of the family.

4. *the Palmers.* Tom Fowle jr. (Fulwar's second son) was now a midshipman aboard CJA's sloop HMS *Indian*; and CJA had married Fanny Palmer in 1807; hence items for TF could be sent to him via FP's parents in London.

60. *To Cassandra Austen. From Southampton to Godmersham. Monday 24–Tuesday 25 October 1808.*

Description. Unknown; original MS untraced since first publication.

Provenance. Bequeathed by CEA to Fanny, Lady Knatchbull, in 1845; inherited by Lord Brabourne 1882; probably in the Puttick & Simpson sale of 26–8 June 1893.

Publication. Brabourne ii. 25; *Life* 216 (extracts); Chapman (1st and 2nd).

1. *Mr Wise.* 'Old Wyse, a civil, respectful mannered, elderly man, exceedingly fond of hunting, who drove Roger's coach every day, Sundays excepted, from Southampton to Popham Lane in the morning, and back to Southampton in the afternoon. He arrived at the Flower Pots, Popham Lane, soon after ten o'clock, and left it between three and four.' JEAL, *Vine Hunt*, 66.

2. The italicized phrases in this letter (as printed by Brabourne) may represent underlining by another hand—perhaps Fanny Knight.

3. *bilbocatch.* Anglicized form of the French name for the cup-&-ball game—bilboquet.

4. *Catherine.* Bigg.

5. *our plans to ourselves.* Their proposed move from Southampton; *Fanny's letter* to her brothers must have referred to it, and *this proposal* is EAK's offer of the cottage at Chawton.

6. *Their aunt.* Mrs JA.

7. *Lake of Killarney.* By Anna Maria Porter (1780–1832), published 1804.

8. *looked into the 74.* The naval warship in course of construction.

61. *To Cassandra Austen. From Southampton to Godmersham. Sunday 20 November 1808.*

Description. Two leaves quarto, wove; watermark GATER 1808; black wafer.

Postmarks. C NOV 21 1808   SOUTHAMPTON 80

Provenance. Bequeathed by CEA to Fanny, Lady Knatchbull, in 1845; inherited by Lord Brabourne 1882; probably in the Puttick & Simpson sale of 26–8 June 1893; Alfred Morrison; Sotheby's 10 Dec. 1918; J. Pierpont Morgan 1920; Pierpont Morgan Library, New York (MA 977–22).

Publication. Brabourne ii. 32; *Life* 219 (extracts); Chapman (1st and 2nd); Modert F-169 to F-172.

1. *Harriet.* Foote.

2. *John & Lucy.* This would have been a third Bridges–Foote match—but the marriage did not in fact occur.

3. *Edward's Manservant.* For occasions when EAK might wish to stay briefly at the Cottage rather than open up the Great House.

4. *His name shall be Robert.* See *Family Record* 153.

5. *from nothing.* JA first wrote 'from nothing probably', and then cancelled 'probably'.

6. *Chambers.* Mrs Leigh Perrot had had an old maidservant of this name years ago, and was evidently still capable of repining her death—see *AP* 194.

7. *spoken of.* 'of' inserted above 'away' cancelled.

8. *Our Brother.* Presumably James.

9. *Mary Jane.* FWA's daughter; her parents had left Southampton a few days before.

62. *To Cassandra Austen. From Southampton to Godmersham. Friday 9 December 1808.*

Description. Two leaves quarto, wove; watermark GATER 1808; black wafer; piece cut away from bottom of second leaf.

Postmarks. C DEC 10 1808   SOUTHAMPTON 80

Provenance. Bequeathed by CEA to Fanny, Lady Knatchbull, in 1845; inherited by Lord Brabourne 1882; probably in the Puttick & Simpson sale of 26–8 June 1893; Alfred Morrison; Sotheby's 10 Dec. 1918; J. Pierpont Morgan, 1920; Pierpont Morgan Library, New York (MA 977–23).

Publication. Brabourne ii. 38; *Life* 221 (extracts); Chapman (1st and 2nd); Modert F-173 to F-176.

1. *Mrs Piozzi. Letters to and from the late Samuel Johnson* (1788), i. 270; the quotation is substantially accurate. [RWC]

2. *so many matters.* 'many' inserted superscript.

3. *The Bracelets.* Possibly some memento from Elizabeth's effects.

4. *Connections in West Kent.* The Austens of Broadford and elsewhere.

5. *I may have.* JA first wrote 'I may to', and then cancelled the 'to'.

6. *Our Ball.* On Tuesday, 6 Dec., at the Dolphin Inn.

7. *that Sunday.* Unexplained.

8. *English Language.* He was probably a French-speaking Jerseyman.

9. *Sir Robert.* Sloper.

10. *Hampstead living.* See CMCA's *Reminiscences*, 18–19.

11. *Mrs Hill.* Not Catherine Bigg, but the wife of Dr Hill, Rector of Holy Rood, Southampton, and also of Church Oakley near Deane.

12. *previously struck herself.* JA first wrote 'my Mother', then cancelled this and inserted 'herself' superscript.

63. *To Cassandra Austen. From Southampton to Godmersham. Tuesday 27–Wednesday 28 December 1808.*

Description. Two leaves quarto, wove; watermark GATER 1808; plain wafer impressed with wafer-seal.

Postmarks. C DEC 29 1808   SOUTHAMPTON 80

Provenance. Bequeathed by CEA to Fanny, Lady Knatchbull, in 1845; inherited by Lord Brabourne 1882; probably in the Puttick & Simpson sale of 26–8 June 1893; John Boyd Thatcher, Albany, NY; Anderson Auction Co. 13 May 1915; Robert H. Taylor; placed by him on deposit at Princeton University Library 1971 and bequeathed to Princeton 1985.

Publication. Brabourne ii. 46; *Life* 223 (extracts); Chapman (1st and 2nd); Modert F-177 to F-180.

1. *the party.* Probably Mr and Mrs James A.
2. *Eliza.* The maidservant.
3. *Sir B-.* Sir Brook Bridges, still a widower.
4. *Black Butter.* A conserve also known as 'apple butter'.
5. *his Godson.* JEAL.
6. *it will probably.* 'will' inserted superscript.
7. *at Bermuda.* CJA and his wife Fanny Palmer—now expecting her first child.
8. *a day of sad remembrance.* The anniversary of EAK's marriage in 1791.
9. *Corinna.* Mme de Stael (1766–1817), *Corinne, ou l'Italie* (1807); two translations into English published in 1807. [RWC]
10. *useless silver.* JA first wrote 'useless silver by her', and then cancelled the last two words.
11. *shall not tell.* 'not' inserted superscript.
12. *Eliza.* Mrs HTA.
13. *your God Mother.* 'Mrs' Elizabeth Leigh of Adlestrop.

64. *To Cassandra Austen. From Southampton to Godmersham. Tuesday 10–Wednesday 11 January 1809.*

Description. Two leaves quarto, wove; no watermark; mark of plain wafer.

Postmarks. C JA 12 1809   SOUTHAMPTON 80

Provenance. Bequeathed by CEA to Fanny, Lady Knatchbull, in 1845; inherited by Lord Brabourne 1882; probably in the Puttick & Simpson sale of 26–8 June 1893; Dr John S. H. Fogg, ante-1896; bequeathed to the Maine Historical Society by Mrs Fogg *c.*1906 (Fogg Coll. No. 420, vol. 26).

Publication. Brabourne ii. 53; *Life* 224 (extracts); Chapman (1st and 2nd); Modert F-181 to F-184.

1. *our poor Army.* Sir John Moore's heroic twelve days' retreat to Corunna was now in progess, and the battle was fought there on 16–17 January. It is mentioned again in the next two letters. The news on this occasion seems to have come very quickly. HMS *St Albans* (under the command of FWA) was at Spithead, and there took charge of the disembarkation of the remnants of Sir John Moore's forces.

2. *The Regency.* The Portuguese Regent, Prince John of Braganza, had been rescued from Napoleon's forces by the British fleet and taken to Rio de Janeiro in Nov. 1807. In Apr. 1809 the Regent announced that he would place the Portuguese army under British training and discipline; his decree to this effect, appointing Wellington Principal Member of the Regency and C.-in-C. of all the forces, was received in Lisbon on 7 Oct. 1809. Presumably some rumour of Prince John's intentions in this regard was circulating as early as Jan. 1809.

3. *to be at Godmersham.* In fact these plans had to be changed, as Mrs A. fell ill during Mar. 1809. See *Family Record* 152–3.

4. handsome *present.* 'present' inserted superscript.

5. *The American Lady.* Mrs Anne Grant of Laggan, *Memoirs of an American Lady* (Catalina Schuyler) (1808).

6. *Margiana.* Mrs S. Sykes, *Margiana, or Widdrington Tower*, 5 vols. (1808). For a resumé of the plot, see M. H. Dodds, *N&Q*, 11th ser., vol. 7 (1913), 233–4.

7. *very well indeed.* 'indeed' inserted superscript.

8. *this sister is not.* 'sister is' inserted superscript.

9. *very generous.* The first edition of *Marmion*, in quarto, cost £1. 11s. 6d. (£1.57½), but several octavo editions appeared in 1808, so we need not suppose that JA laid out more than 12s. (£0.60). [RWC]

10. *your little Namesake.* EAK's daughter Cassandra Jane.

11. *many happy returns.* Of CEA's birthday, 9 Jan. 1773.

65. *To Cassandra Austen. From Southampton to Godmersham. Tuesday 17–Wednesday 18 January 1809.*

Description. Two leaves quarto, wove; watermark GATER 1808; mark of plain wafer.

Postmarks. C JAN 19 1809   SOUTHAMPTON 80

Provenance. Bequeathed by CEA to Fanny, Lady Knatchbull, in 1845; inherited by Lord Brabourne 1882; probably in the Puttick & Simpson sale of 26–8 June 1893; Alfred Morrison; Sotheby's 10 Dec. 1918; J. Pierpont Morgan 1920; Pierpont Morgan Library, New York (MA 977–24).

Publication. Brabourne ii. 59; *Life* 226 (extracts); Chapman (1st and 2nd); Modert F-185 to F-188.

1. *her new Aunt.* Mrs Brownlow Mathew.
2. *Mrs Esten . . . Mrs C. A.* Mrs Esten was the wife of James Christie Esten, Chief Justice of Bermuda, and the eldest sister of Mrs CJA. This sentence has been lightly cancelled, presumably by Lord Brabourne, but is still quite legible.
3. *William . . . Mary Jane.* Fowle.
4. *Miss Owenson.* Sydney Owenson, Lady Morgan (1783?–1859), *The Wild Irish Girl* (1806); *Woman, or Ida of Athens* (1809).
5. *sermons from Hamstall.* Revd Edward Cooper, *Examination of the Necessity of Sunday-drilling* (1803); *Sermons, chiefly designed to elucidate . . . Doctrines* (1804); *Practical and Familiar Sermons; designed for parochial and domestic Instruction* (1809).
6. *my nephew Edwd* 'Edwd' inserted superscript.
7. *The Queen's Birthday.* Queen Charlotte was actually born on 19 May 1744, but 'as Her Majesty's birthday came within three weeks of that of the King, it was deemed advisable, for the benefit of trade, and public convenience, to celebrate the former on the 18th of January following, and ever after on the same day. That day was accordingly kept with great state and splendour at Court, the nobility and gentry vying with each other in richness of dress and grandeur of equipage' (J. Watkins, *Memoirs of Her Most Excellent Majesty Sophia Charlotte, Queen of Great Britain, from Authentic Documents* (1819), 152). The Southampton Assembly Balls were normally held fortnightly on Tuesdays from the beginning of November until the end of April; in 1809 Tuesday fell on 17 Jan., hence the ball being moved to the following day.

66. *To Cassandra Austen. From Southampton to Godmersham. Tuesday 24 January 1809.*

Description. Two leaves quarto, wove; watermark GATER 1808; mark of plain wafer impressed with wafer-seal.

Postmarks. C [JA]N 25 [18]09 SOUTHAMPTON 80

Provenance. Bequeathed by CEA to Fanny, Lady Knatchbull, in 1845; inherited by Lord Brabourne 1882; probably in the Puttick & Simpson sale of 26–8 June 1893; Alfred Morrison; Sotheby's 10 Dec. 1918; J. Pierpont Morgan 1920; Pierpont Morgan Library, New York (MA 977-25).

Publication. Brabourne ii. 66; *Life* 227 (extracts); Chapman (1st and 2nd); Modert F-189 to F-192.

1. *Miss Beverleys.* Miss B. is the heroine of *Cecilia, or Memoirs of an Heiress*, 5 vols. (1782), by Fanny Burney.
2. *a small prize.* CJA had captured *La Jeune Estelle*, a small privateer.

3. *giving.* JA first wrote 'in putting a final e'; then cancelled 'putting' and inserted 'giving' superscript.
4. *Mary.* Cooke.
5. *will not turn.* 'not' inserted superscript.
6. *Caleb.* See letter **67**, note 2.
7. *Propria que Maribus.* One of the first lessons in Pote's *Introduction to the Latin Tongue* (the Eton Latin Grammar).

> Propria quae maribus tribuuntur, mascula dicas;
> ut sunt Divorum; Mars, Bacchus, Apollo [*etc.*]

8. *Miss C.* Curling.
9. *Mother.* JA invariably writes 'my Mother', and no doubt regarded 'Mother' as a vulgarism. [RWC]
10. *complacency of her Mama.* As Mr Hammond was a bachelor, Mrs JA had acted as his hostess for the ball.
11. *Dr M.* Dr Mant.
12. *such a son's death.* Sir John Moore.
13. *The Portsmouth paper. Hampshire Telegraph*, 23 Jan. 1809.

67. *To Cassandra Austen. From Southampton to Godmersham. Monday 30 January 1809.*

Description. Two leaves quarto, wove; watermark GATER 1808; mark of red seal.
Postmarks. C JAN 31 1809   SOUTHAMPTON 80 (imperfectly printed)
Provenance. Bequeathed by CEA to Fanny, Lady Knatchbull, in 1845; inherited by Lord Brabourne 1882; Puttick & Simpson 26–8 June 1893; Alfred Morrison; Sotheby's 10 Dec. 1918; J. Pierpont Morgan 1920; Pierpont Morgan Library, New York (MA 977–26).
Publication. Brabourne ii. 72; *Life* 228 (extracts); Chapman (1st and 2nd); Modert F-193 to F-196.

1. *their Journey.* Lizzy and Marianne Austen (Knight) were sent to a boarding-school in Wanstead, Essex, for a few months, till Fanny could engage a governess for them.
2. *Coelebs.* Hannah More (1745–1833), *Coelebs in Search of a Wife* (1809).
3. *at that time.* 'at' inserted superscript.
4. *Mrs E. L.* 'Mrs' Elizabeth Leigh.
5. *Caroline.* Cooper.
6. *Miss B.* Bailey.
7. *do so too.* 'so' inserted superscript.
8. *Aunt Fatty.* This was the Bridges family nickname for Miss Isabella Fielding. JA first wrote 'Fanny', no doubt from force of habit, and then added

two ts heavily over the two ns. The fire was at St James's Palace on Saturday, 21 Jan. 1809.

9. *Sir J. Moore.* I think 'no one nearer than Sir John himself' implies *some* family connexion; but some take the meaning to be that there was no connexion. None has been traced.

Miss C. L. Thomson (*Jane Austen, a Survey* (1929), 275) thinks the reference to *Christian* and *Hero* 'not only conventional, but an offence against good taste'. But we do not know all that was in JA's mind.

Sir Charles Oman writes: 'What Jane was thinking of with regard to Sir John's deathbed—of which a rather full narrative survives—was that he is reported to have said nothing about God and the other world, but a good deal about public opinion in England, and his hope that it would acquit him; as well as some messages to Lady Hester Stanhope and other friends in London. I think she was hinting that it was not a very "Christian" end, and that her words have no further meaning.'

Miss Lascelles suggests a reminiscence of *Rambler* 44 (Elizabeth Carter): 'The christian and the hero are inseparable'. [RWC]

10. *back into.* JA wrote 'back in' and added 'to' superscript.

11. *the Child.* FWA's Mary Jane.

68(D). *To R. Crosby & Co. From Southampton to London. Wednesday 5 April 1809.*

Description. Approximately three-quarters of a quarto leaf, laid; watermark 1808; the scrap is the partly unused second leaf of a letter, and bears the name 'Miss Austen' heavily cancelled, and mark of a red wafer. Endorsed by JA 'Copy of a Letter to Messrs Crosbie [*sic*] & Co'; and by CEA[?] '& Mr Crosbie's reply'. The draft, though scribbled very hastily, is unmistakably JA's autograph.

Postmark. None.

Provenance. Bequeathed by CEA to CJA in 1845; descended to CJA's granddaughters and sold by them in the 1920s; J. Pierpont Morgan 1925; presented by him to the British Museum Department of MSS, 1925; now British Library Add. MSS 41,253.B, fo. 12.

Publication. Life 230; Chapman (1st and 2nd); Modert F-197 and F-198.

1. *Seymour.* Mr William Seymour, HTA's lawyer.

2. *particular circumstances.* The Austens were now packed up and on the verge of leaving Southampton for a long visit to Godmersham before moving to Chawton.

68(A). *To Jane Austen. From London to Southampton. Saturday 8 April 1809.*

Description. One leaf quarto, wove; no watermark; yellow wafer.

Postmark. .AP C 10. .809

Provenance. Bequeathed by CEA to CJA in 1845; descended to CJA's grand-daughters and sold by them in the 1920s; J. Pierpont Morgan 1925; presented by him to British Museum Department of MSS, 1925; now British Library Add. MSS 41,253.B, fo. 13.

Publication. *Life* 231; Chapman (1st and 2nd).

69(D). *To Francis Austen. From Chawton to [China]. Wednesday 26 July 1809.*

Description. One leaf octavo, wove; no watermark.

Postmark. None.

Provenance. Bequeathed by CEA to CJA in 1845; descended to CJA's grand-daughters and sold by them in the 1920s; Frederick R. Lovering; Sotheby's 3 May 1948; T. Edward Carpenter and bequeathed by him to JAMT, 1969.

Publication. Modert F-203 and F-204.

1. *a boy.* FWA jr. was born at Rose Cottage, Alton, on 12 July 1809.
2. *Our Chawton home.* Mrs A. and her daughters took up residence in the Cottage on 7 July 1809.
3. *over-right us.* i.e. staying in the Great House. FWA returned in 1810, but CJA and his family did not arrive in England until 1811.

69. *To Francis Austen. From Chawton to [China]. Wednesday 26 July 1809.*

Description. Two leaves quarto, wove; watermark GATER 1808; small red wafer.

Postmark. None.

Provenance. Descended in FWA's family to his grandson Capt. Ernest Leigh Austen, RN, and presented by him to the British Museum Department of MSS, 1930; now British Library Add. MSS 42,180, fos. 7–8.

Publication. *Times* 16 Dec. 1930 (extracts); Chapman (1st and 2nd); Modert F-199 to F-202.

70. *To Cassandra Austen. From London to Godmersham. Thursday 18– Saturday 20 April 1811.*

Description. Two leaves quarto, laid; watermark device (Heawood Nos. 2752–62) above monogram, no date; mark of seal or wafer. A thin strip cut out across the middle of the first leaf, in order to excise text on p. 2, some of which is also cancelled.

Postmark. .AP A 20. .811

Provenance. Bequeathed by CEA to Fanny, Lady Knatchbull, in 1845; inherited by Lord Brabourne 1882; probably in the Puttick & Simpson sale of 26–8 June 1893; Alfred Morrison; Sotheby's 10 Dec. 1918; J. Pierpont Morgan 1920; Pierpont Morgan Library, New York (MA 977–27).

Publication. Brabourne ii. 82; *Life* 244 (extracts); Chapman (1st and 2nd); Modert F-205 to F-208.

1. *Liverpool Museum.* Of natural history exhibits, then on display at 22 Piccadilly.
2. *British Gallery.* Gallery of the British Institution, Pall Mall.
3. *[to some].* Words missing here due to excision of strip across page.
4. *Manon.* Mrs HTA's maidservant.
5. *Grafton House.* Probably the premises of the drapers Wilding & Kent, which were on the corner site of Grafton Street and 164 New Bond Street.
6. *green cruels.* Cruel or crewel was a loosely twisted fine two-ply worsted yarn, especially suited to embroidery as it easily pulled through cloth. It would therefore appear that CEA had been hoping JA would find muslin embroidered with a design in green crewel yarn.
7. *I took . . . for you.* 'I took' and 'for you' have been cancelled, and the words in between cut out. However, parts of the missing words can still be seen, and, taken in the context of executing shopping commissions, the sentence seems to have read as now printed. The (?)two words before 'for you' are completely missing; CEA's anxiety to censor this phrase suggests it concerned some rather personal matter.
8. *at 2/4^d.* Inserted superscript.
9. *Mr Moore.* Of Wrotham, no doubt. [RWC]
10. *Miss Beaty.* Presumably a Miss Beatrice Smith.
11. *Henry Walter.* A younger cousin of both JA and Mrs HTA.
12. *the W. Friars.* i.e. to Mrs Knight in Canterbury.
13. *'mais le moyen'.* Occurs in a letter of Chesterfield, 23 Oct. 1749. [RWC]
14. *Mary.* Mrs FA.
15. *Mrs Hill.* Their old friend Catherine Bigg, now married and living in Streatham, near London.
16. *James's verses.* James A. often wrote verses, and a number of them were collected and transcribed into albums by JEAL in the 1830s.
17. *Mrs K.* Mrs Knight—presumably James had written something that JA felt would particularly appeal to her.

71. *To Cassandra Austen. From London to Godmersham. Thursday 25 April 1811.*

Description. Two leaves quarto, laid; watermark device (Heawood Nos. 2752–62) over monogram, no date; black wafer.

Postmarks. .AP B2. .[8]11   [. . .] Clock 25 AP   Also a large oval, very faint, possibly the 'Two P^y Post | Unpaid | Sloane Street' which appears on letter **84**.

Provenance. Bequeathed by CEA to Fanny, Lady Knatchbull, in 1845; inherited by Lord Brabourne 1882; Puttick & Simpson 26–8 June 1893; Sotheby's 5–7 July 1900; British Museum Dept. of MSS; now British Library Add. MSS 36,525, fos. 7–8.

Publication. Brabourne ii. 89; facsimile *English Literature*, IV (1903), between 93–4; *Life* 246 (extracts); Chapman (1st and 2nd); Modert F-209 to F-212.

1. *Our new nephew.* Henry Edgar A., FWA's second son, born Portsmouth 21 Apr. 1811.

2. *my Brother.* FWA.

3. *S&S. Sense and Sensibility.*

4. *W's first appearance.* Willoughby—i.e. I, ch. IX.

5. *Mrs K.* Mrs Knight.

6. *lordly Company.* The adjective is squeezed in at the very edge of the paper, and could equally well be read as 'lowly'.

7. *connecting Passage.* For a description of the interior of 64 Sloane Street see Winifred Watson's *Jane Austen in London* (Chawton, 1960).

8. *The Music.* For what follows I am indebted to Mr Archibald Jacob. A chorus by Sir Henry Rowley Bishop (1786–1855) begins:

> Strike the harp in praise of my love
> The lovely sunbeam of Dunseaith,
> Strike the harp in praise of Bragela.

'In peace love tunes the shepherd's reed' is a glee by J. Attwood; *Lay of the Last Minstrel*, iii. 2.

'Rosabelle', a glee by John Wall Callcott (1766–1821); no doubt *Lay of the Last Minstrel*, vi. 23.

'The Red Cross Knight', a glee by Callcott, 1797, 'the words from Evans's Old English Ballads' ('Blow, Warder! blow thy sounding horn').

'Poor Insect': 'The May Fly', a glee by Callcott, 'Poor insect, poor insect'. [RWC]

9. *Prike pe Parp.* JA and her niece Fanny had a nonsense language between themselves, putting a P in front of every word—see also letter **72**, note 5.

10. *the Hypocrite.* Isaac Bickerstaffe (fl. c.1735–c.1782), *The Hypocrite* (1768), adapted from Cibber's version of *Tartuffe*.

11. *Mrs Siddons.* Mr C. B. Hogan tells me that *King John*, with Mrs Siddons as Constance, had been announced at Covent Garden for Saturday, 20 Apr.; but, a day or two before, the play was changed for *Hamlet*, and Mrs S. made her first appearance (since Dec. 1810) in *Macbeth* on the following

Monday. JA was in London till May; but other engagements may have prevented her seeing Mrs S. in *The Gamester* (27 Apr.) or *Douglas* (1 May). [RWC]

12. *dislike in.* 'in' inserted superscript.

13. *this morning's paper.* 'On Tuesday, Mrs H. AUSTIN [*sic*] had a musical party at her house in Sloane-street' (*Morning Post*, 25 Apr.).

14. *my God-daughter.* Louisa Austen (Knight).

72. *To Cassandra Austen. From London to Godmersham. Tuesday 30 April 1811.*

Description. Two leaves quarto, laid; watermark device (Heawood Nos. 2752–62) above monogram, no date; the letter travelled inside a franked wrapper, hence there is no seal or wafer.

Postmark. None.

Provenance. Bequeathed by CEA to Fanny, Lady Knatchbull, in 1845; inherited by Lord Brabourne 1882; probably in the Puttick & Simpson sale of 26–8 June 1893; Alfred Morrison; Sotheby's 10 Dec. 1918; J. Pierpont Morgan 1920; Pierpont Morgan Library, New York (MA 977–28).

Publication. Brabourne ii. 97; *Life* 251 (extracts); Chapman (1st and 2nd); Modert F-213 to F-215.

1. *Mr W. K.* Wyndham Knatchbull.

2. *Self-Controul.* Mary Brunton (1778–1818), *Self-Control, a Novel* (1810).

3. *Miss Allen.* The new governess at Godmersham; she arrived 27 Apr. 1811 and lasted till 11 Nov. 1812.

4. *Emma Plumbtree . . . Henry Gipps.* They became engaged on 18 Sept. 1811.

5. *Pery pell.* 'Very well—or are they? or no—or at the most, I hope they like it.' See letter **71**, note 9.

6. *Mrs Dundas's day.* ?For coming to London—see letter **67**.

7. *inviting Anna.* To come and stay in Sloane Street.

73. *To Cassandra Austen. From Chawton to Godmersham. Wednesday 29 May 1811.*

Description. Two leaves quarto, laid; no watermark; seal or wafer missing.

Postmark. .MA B 30. .811

Provenance. Bequeathed by CEA to Fanny, Lady Knatchbull, in 1845; inherited by Lord Brabourne 1882; sold to dealer Pearson June 1889; Ferdinand Dreer; given by him or by his estate to The Historical Society of Pennsylvania, Philadelphia, 1890 or later (Dreer Collection, English Prose Writers, 103:1 p. 29).

Publication. Brabourne ii. 100; *Life* 251 (extracts); Chapman (1st and 2nd); Modert F-216 to F-219.

1. *Gloucester House.* Presumably that in Weymouth—see letter **39**, note 3.
2. *The Papers say.* The circumstances of the elopement are known, but RWC could not trace this newspaper scandal.
3. *at Cowes.* FWA and family.
4. *distress of the Family.* Marianne Bridges had died on 12 Apr. 1811, and John B. was probably now seriously ill, as he died on 3 July 1812 'after a most lingering illness'.
5. *Maria M.* Middleton.
6. *H^t B.* Harriet Benn.
7. *away from the family.* Anna A. had engaged herself to Michael Terry during the winter of 1809-10 (see *Family Record* 161-2); the engagement and its termination had caused embarrassment to Austens and Terrys alike.
8. *we have had.* 'had' inserted superscript.
9. *Mrs Harding . . . Mrs Toke.* They were sisters.
10. *Diana.* JA is presumably quoting Miss Harding.
11. *her Cottage.* 'her' inserted superscript.
12. *a Gravel pit.* The grounds of the house still known as 'Prowtings' adjoin those of the Cottage, but the approach road has been diverted in recent years. A rough hillock close to the old entrance gateway is probably the remains of this gravel-working.

74. *To Cassandra Austen. From Chawton to Godmersham. Friday 31 May 1811.*

Description. Two leaves quarto, laid; watermark RUSES TURNERS 1807; mark of wafer.

Postmarks. D 1 JU 1 1811   ALTON 50

Provenance. Bequeathed by CEA to Fanny, Lady Knatchbull, in 1845; inherited by Lord Brabourne 1882; probably in the Puttick & Simpson sale of 26-8 June 1893; Alfred Morrison; Sotheby's 10 Dec. 1918; J. Pierpont Morgan 1920; Pierpont Morgan Library, New York (MA 977-29).

Publication. Brabourne ii. 105; *Life* 252 (extracts); Chapman (1st and 2nd); Modert F-220 to F-223.

1. *to Mrs Lloyd.* 'to' inserted superscript.
2. *Gaieties of Tuesday.* Celebrations of George III's birthday (1738) on 4 June.
3. *Harriot B.* Benn.
4. *Mary.* Cooke.
5. *two Curates.* Revd George Hanway Standert, curate of Great Bookham 1808 and of Little Bookham 1809; Revd John Collinson Bissett, curate of Great Bookham 1809.

6. *so many killed.* The *Hampshire Telegraph* of Monday, 27 May, reported a battle at Almeida a few days previously, with some casualties given; then on Monday, 3 June, carried a special supplement 'London Gazette Extraordinary', with a full account of the battle, named 'Albuera' by the Duke of Wellington.

7. *recent publication. Practical Piety* (1811).

8. *Quickset hedge.* Made on 28 Jan. 1811, according to EAK's Chawton Estate Account Book: Hampshire County Record Office, 79M78MB211.

75. *To Cassandra Austen. From Chawton to Godmersham. Thursday 6 June 1811.*

Description. Two leaves quarto, laid; watermark device (Heawood Nos. 2752–62) above initials R & T; no date; mark of seal or wafer.

Postmarks. D 7 JU 7 1811   ALTON 50

Provenance. Bequeathed by CEA to Fanny, Lady Knatchbull, in 1845; inherited by Lord Brabourne 1882; Sotheby's 11–14 May 1891; Alfred Morrison; Sotheby's 10 Dec. 1918; J. Pierpont Morgan 1920; Pierpont Morgan Library, New York (MA 977–30).

Publication. Brabourne ii. 111; *Life* 254 (extracts); Chapman (1st and 2nd); Modert F-224 to F-227.

1. *directly.* i.e. from Leicestershire, rather than via London.

2. *to Cowes.* FWA and his family.

3. *Lady B.* Lady Bridges; *the proposed party*—some of the Goodnestone family, no doubt.

4. *Harriot.* Moore.

5. *the Common.* Selborne Common.

6. *any regret.* 'any' inserted superscript.

7. *Lady of the Lake.* Sir Walter Scott, *The Lady of the Lake* (1810). JA was presumably thinking of either canto II, stanza XVII, lines 7–12, or else canto III and the whole of stanza XXIV.

8. *Abingdon S^t* Presumably Mrs Dundas's London address.

9. *the King's death.* George III was seriously ill during May 1811, though he did not in fact die until 1820.

10. *does not seem.* 'does' inserted superscript.

11. *Harry.* EAK's third son.

76(C). *To Anna Austen. From Chawton to Steventon. ?Between Thursday 29–Saturday 31 October 1812.*

Description. Unknown; original MS untraced.

Provenance. At least four copies of this text exist, all differing slightly in content and punctuation. Anna Lefroy herself copied it out twice, for JEAL's benefit when he was composing the *Memoir*; her daughter Fanny-Caroline Lefroy also copied it out twice. The descent of the original, and of these copies, is distinguished as follows:

76(C.1). Anna Lefroy's rough draft of a letter to JEAL, Dec. 1864.

76(C.2). Anna Lefroy's fair copy of her letter to JEAL, Dec. 1864.

The **original MS of letter** 76 was inherited in 1872 by Fanny-Caroline Lefroy (1820–85), who gave it to her cousin Cholmeley Austen-Leigh (1829–99); this cannot now be found in the AL archive.

76(C.3). FCL's copy, in her MS volume of Family History, with some differences from both **C.1** and **C.2**.

76(C.4). FCL's copy, on a loose sheet of paper (two leaves octavo, laid, no watermark), headed: 'Copy of Note written by Jane Austen to her niece Anna Austen (Mrs B. Lefroy) and given by me (F. C. Lefroy) to Cholmeley [Leigh *deleted*] Austen Leigh for his Collection of Autographs.' This copy differs again from **C.3**.

76(C.1) was Lot 269 at Sotheby Parke Bernet 13 Dec. 1977, as 'the property of a great-great-nephew of JA'; James M. W. Borg, Lake Forest, Illinois.

76(C.2) and **76(C.3)** remain in the Austen-Leigh archive.

76(C.4) was Lot 268 at Sotheby Parke Bernet 13 Dec. 1977, as 'the property of a great-great-nephew of JA'; Pierpont Morgan Library, New York (MA 3611).

Publication. Hill 195–6 (using **76(C.3)**); Chapman (1st and 2nd, using **76(C.4)**—the original MS was presumably already lost by that date; he described it as unpublished, having failed to notice it in Hill); Mary Gaither Marshall, *Jane Austen's Sanditon, together with 'Reminiscences of Aunt Jane'* (Chicago, 1983), 155–63 (using **76(C.1)**); Deirdre Le Faye, 'Anna Lefroy's Original Memories of Jane Austen', *RES*, NS 39: 155 (Aug. 1988), 417–21 (using **76(C.2)**). The text given here is that of **76(C.2)**, with one additional sentence—see note 4 below.

1. *?29–31 October 1812.* For the dating of this letter, see Deirdre Le Faye, 'Jane Austen: More Letters Redated', *N&Q*, 236:3 (Sept. 1991), 306–8.

2. *Nicholson or Glover.* Francis Nicholson (1753–1844) and John Glover (1767–1849), two well-known landscape painters of the day.

3. *Tarefield Abbey.* Anna first wrote 'Tarefield Hall', then cancelled 'Hall' and continued with 'Abbey'.

4. *It is . . . complete.* This sentence does not appear in Anna Lefroy's two copies, but only in those made by Fanny-Caroline Lefroy. It is impossible to determine whether this was an omission by Anna or an invention by FCL.

5. *the Flint family.* The book about which JA and Anna were joking was *Lady Maclairn, the Victim of Villainy* (1806), by Mrs Rachel Hunter of

Norwich (1754–1813). See Deirdre Le Faye, 'Jane Austen & Mrs Hunter's Novel', in *N&Q*, NS 32:3 (Sept. 1985), 335–6.

6. *Car of Falkenstein.* The Alton coach was known both as 'Collier's [or Collyer's] Southampton coach' and as 'Falknor's coach'—perhaps Collier/Collyer was the owner and Falknor the coachman, or vice versa. JA herself refers to it as 'Falknor'—see letter **79**.

In **76(C.1)** Anna wrote: 'The Car of Falkenstein, Collier's, but at that time called Falknor's coach relates to some former nonsence [*sic*] of mine—' This 'former nonsense' was 'a mock heroic story', written by Anna under encouragement from JA, which 'had no other foundation than their having seen a neighbour passing on the coach, without having previously known that he was going to leave home'. See CMCA, *MAJA*, 8.

In **76(C.4)** FCL added a final paragraph: 'The Car of Falkenstein was a nonsensical name for the Alton Coach. The rest of the note refers to a voluminous and most tiresome & prosy novel the Aunt & Niece had been reading & laughing over, together. It was in eight volumes and the tears of the heroine were for ever flowing—.

'The note is addressed—
Miss Austen
Steventon.'

77. To Martha Lloyd. From Chawton to Kintbury. Sunday 29–Monday 30 November 1812.

Description. Two leaves quarto, laid; watermark JOHN HAYES 1809; mark of seal; endorsed by JA: 'Chawton Novr. 29'.
Postmark. None.
Provenance. Descended in FWA's family to one of his granddaughters (probably Mrs J. R. Saunders); W. T. H. Howe 1920; Sotheby's 14–17 Apr. 1930; Owen D. Young; Henry W. & Albert A. Berg, 1941; New York Public Library, NY, 1941.
Publication. Chapman (1st and 2nd); Modert, F-228 to F-231.

1. Martha Lloyd was then at Barton with her friend Mrs Dundas, who died there on 1 Dec. *Mrs D. D.* was the latter's daughter Mrs Deans Dundas. [RWC]
2. *sim.* i.e. *seem*; the short vowel occurs in many dialects. [RWC]
3. *Sally.* Maidservant at the Cottage.
4. *Edward & his Harem.* EAK, with his daughters Fanny and Lizzy and his wife's niece Mary Deedes.
5. *change of name.* EAK's change of name from 'Austen' to 'Knight' was officially registered on 10 Nov. 1812.

6. *William*. EAK's fourth son, now leaving his prep school at Eltham to start at Winchester.

7. *Miss W.* Urania Wallop. This verse on Miss Wallop, who married 26 Mar. 1813 an elderly curate, the Revd Henry Wake, was passed down in the AL family; and many years later, after Anna Lefroy's fourth daughter Georgiana-Brydges had married Seymer Terry of the Dummer family, Anna and Seymer's father Stephen Terry were both in Southampton to visit their children. Stephen Terry records the verse in his diary, under the date Friday, 13 Apr. 1860 (*not* 11 Apr. 1866, as erroneously given by Stirling in *The Diaries of Dummer*):

> Camilla good humoured & merry & small
> For a Husband it happend was at her last stake;
> & having in vain danced at many a ball
> Is now very happy to Jump at a Wake.

He adds: 'These lines given to me this day by Mrs Ben Lefroy here, Georgies Mother; they were written by her very clever Relation Miss Jane Austen, the celebrated Novelist, about the beginning [of] the Century.' Terry Diaries, Hampshire Record Office, 24M49/19. The *Memoir* (2nd, 88) calls the lady Maria; her mother's name was Camilla.

8. *Mary Jane*. Fowle.

9. The letter had no direction; doubtless it was enclosed in a cover to Mr Dundas, who, being a Member of Parliament, would receive it free. [RWC]

78. *To Cassandra Austen. From Chawton to Steventon. Sunday 24 January 1813.*

Description. Two leaves quarto, laid; watermark JOHN HAYES 1809; last leaf, or wrapper, missing.

Postmark. None.

Provenance. Bequeathed by CEA to CJA in 1845; descended to his granddaughters and sold by them probably in 1924; Frederick R. Lovering; Sotheby's 3 May 1948; T. Edward Carpenter and bequeathed by him to the JAMT 1969.

Publication. Memoir (1st 133–9, 2nd 99–101, where extracts from this and from letter **81** are printed as one letter (of Feb. 1813)); *Life* 258 (extracts); Chapman (1st and 2nd, from MS copy made by RAAL 1909); Lock; Modert F-232 to F-235.

1. *Travels in Spain.* Sir John Carr (1772–1832), *Descriptive Travels in the Southern and Eastern Parts of Spain and the Balearic Isles, in the year 1809* (1811).

2. *Society-Octavo.* i.e. a book from the Chawton Book Society, or reading club.

3. *Capt. Pasley.* Sir Charles William Pasley, RE (1780–1861), *Essay on the*

Military Policy and Institutions of the British Empire (1810). It is *Military Policy* on the title-page, but the *OED* has *police* in that sense at an even later date. [RWC]

4. *Clarkson or Buchanan.* Thomas Clarkson (1760–1846), *History of the Abolition of the African Slave Trade* (1808).
Claudius Buchanan (1766–1815), probably *Christian Researches in Asia* (1811), a very popular book.

5. *two Mr Smiths.* James Smith (1775–1839) and his brother Horatio (1779–1849), *Rejected Addresses: or the new Theatrum Poetarum* (1812).

6. *the Commissioner's.* See *MP* II, ch. VI.

7. *Tax-cart.* More correctly 'Taxed' cart; the *OED* defines it as: 'a two-wheeled (originally springless) open cart drawn by one horse, and used mainly for agricultural or trade purposes, on which was charged only a reduced duty (afterwards taken off entirely)'.
'1795 (Act 35 Geo. III, *c.*109 section 2): For and upon every Carriage with less than four Wheels, ... which shall have the Words "A taxed Cart", and also the Owner's Name and Place of Abode, there shall be charged and paid the yearly Sum of ten Shillings.'

8. *Thomas.* Thomas Carter, manservant at Chawton Cottage.

9. *Miss P. T.* Miss Patience Terry.

10. *what she meant.* Mrs Digweed may not have expressed herself very clearly, but in fact she was remembering one of the poems in the *Rejected Addresses* better than JA was; her reference is to the opening lines of 'The Theatre', the parody of Crabbe.

11. *round table.* Eleven, less four for whist, and JA, leaves six. The round table in *MP* consisted of Lady Bertram and Edmund, two Prices, and two Crawfords (*MP* II, ch. VII). [RWC]

12. *Biglands . . . Mackenzies.* John Bigland (1750–1832), perhaps *History of Spain* (1810) or *System of Geography and History* (1812); Sir John Barrow (1764–1848), editor of *Journal of the Embassy to China* (by Lord Macartney (1737–1806)) (1807); Sir George Steuart Mackenzie (1780–1848), *Travels in Iceland* (1811).

13. *her well-behaved . . . children.* 'her' inserted superscript.

14. *Bank Stock.* i.e. Miss P., as the representative of the rector of Chawton, gave some money to this (?widowed) villager.

15. *in a Cover.* The letter did not go through the post (if it had, a cover would have doubled the charge). No doubt it was in the parcel collected from Alton by John Bond (see letter **79**), and the remainder of the text was written inside the cover.

16. *hunt away the rogues.* Are these imaginary burglars, as in *Cranford*, ch. 10? Or did Martha allow the Cottage's watch-dogs (normally tended by the manservant, see letter **81**) to sleep under her bed?

17. *Mrs Leigh's.* Probably 'Mrs' Elizabeth Leigh, CEA's godmother.
18. *Brother Michael.* Presumably Michael Terry.

79. *To Cassandra Austen. From Chawton to Steventon. Friday 29 January 1813.*

Description. One leaf quarto, laid; watermark 1809; no seal or wafer; second leaf (pp. 3–4) missing.
Postmark. None.
Provenance. Bequeathed by CEA to CJA in 1845; descended to his grand-daughters and sold by them probably in 1924; Frederick R. Lovering; Sotheby's 3 May 1948; T. Edward Carpenter and bequeathed by him to the JAMT 1969.
Publication. Memoir (1st 131; 2nd 97 (extracts)); *Life* 260 (extracts); Chapman (1st and 2nd, from copy made by RAAL 1909); Lock; Modert F-236 and F-237.

1. *own darling Child.* JA's first copy of *P&P.*
2. *our paper to day.* There is no advertisement for the book in either the *Hampshire Chronicle* or the *Hampshire Telegraph* of 29 Jan. 1813, but it is mentioned in the *Morning Chronicle* of Thursday, 28 Jan., under the heading 'Books Published This Day'; presumably the London papers would reach Chawton the following day.
3. *my stupidest of all.* JA looks forward to a crescendo of price and stupidity. In the event she feared that *Emma* would be thought 'inferior in good sense' to *MP.* We do not know where she would have ranked *Persuasion* in point of stupidity. [RWC]
4. *two such people.* JA and her mother.
5. *I do not write.* Marmion, vi. 38.

> I do not rhyme to that dull elf
> Who cannot image to himself . . .

6. *The 2^d vol.* The number of pages is: i. 307, ii. 239, iii. 323. This compares with *S&S:* i. 317, ii. 278, iii. 301; 25 more pages overall.
7. *Ordination.* Over-hasty reading of this letter in the past has led some critics to believe that JA was only just now deciding to compose *MP* and that 'ordination' would be her theme for the novel. As her comments in letter **78** make clear, she was in fact by this date already half-way through *MP.* Her request to CEA for 'enquiries' was no doubt concerning the time necessary for the process of ordination—i.e. how long Edmund Bertram might be kept away from Mansfield Park for this purpose. CEA was then staying with James Austen, the cleric of the family, who would obviously be in the best position to provide the details of his own ordination in 1787.

8. *Country of Hedgerows*. RWC assumed this enquiry meant that JA thought of using in *MP* the device which she later used in *Persuasion* (the dialogue presumably would have been between Edmund and Mary, overheard by Fanny) and that she did not do so because CEA told her there were *no* hedgerows in Northamptonshire. Professor Treitel points out to me that JA could equally well have been asking CEA to check that the reference to hedgerows which she *had* made already in vol. ii, ch. IV was correct— where Fanny, sitting with Mary Crawford in Mrs Grant's shrubbery, says; 'Three years ago, this was nothing but a rough hedgerow . . .'

9. *your Charades*. A collection of *Charades &c written a hundred years ago by Jane Austen and her family* was published by Spottiswoode & Co. in 1895.

10. *beyond anything & everything*. Quoting Mrs H. Digweed's favourite expression.

11. *Betsy*. Maidservant at Chawton.

12. *she desired me*. 'she' inserted superscript.

80. *To Cassandra Austen. From Chawton to Steventon. Thursday 4 February 1813.*

Description. One leaf quarto, laid; watermark fragmentary, top part of device (Heawood Nos. 2752–62), no date; no seal or wafer; 2nd leaf (pp. 3–4) missing.

Postmark. None.

Provenance. Bequeathed by CEA to CJA in 1845; descended to his grand-daughters and sold by them probably in 1924; Frederick R. Lovering; Sotheby's 3 May 1948; T. Edward Carpenter and bequeathed by him to the JAMT 1969.

Publication. *Memoir* (1st 133; 2nd 99 (extracts)); *Life* 261 (extracts); Chapman (1st and 2nd, from a copy made by RAAL in 1909); Modert F-238 and F-239.

1. *fits of disgust*. A much less strong expression then than now. Dr Johnson has lost reputation by describing *Lycidas* as disgusting. [RWC]

2. *Mrs D.* Digweed.

3. *John M.* Middleton.

4. *the Harwoods*. 'On the death of the old man sad disclosures came to light, and ruin stared them in the face. The property at Deane was worth about £1,200 a year and it had descended through a squirearchy of John Harwoods, fathers and sons, for five or six generations, but it was *so* to descend no longer. Old Mr Harwood had contracted debts, quite unsuspected by his family. He had borrowed and mortgaged so freely, that it seemed as if the estate itself could scarcely pay its own liabilities. There was nothing for his widow, and his sister's small portion had been left in his hands, and had

gone with the rest of the money, so that both ladies were dependent on the heir' (CMCA, *Reminiscences*, 27).

5. *M.T.* Revd Michael Terry, who had become rector of Dummer in 1811. It is not clear who *Fanny* is, nor how her faith was unsettled. If it was religious faith, it may be worth while to mention that Michael Terry is described in the Powlett correspondence as 'poor blundering Michael Terry'. [RWC] Fanny Knight was not staying at Steventon at the time, but she had been going through a phase of teenage piety and possibly CEA had been writing to her on the subject of religious faith.

6. *the Wedding.* Their manservant Thomas Carter married Ann Trimmer at Chawton on 30 Jan. 1813.

7. *Edward's information.* EAK—the 'information' was presumably that Henry had gone to Oxford.

8. *was correct.* 'was' inserted superscript.

9. *S. & P.* Steventon and Portsmouth.

81. *To Cassandra Austen. From Chawton to Manydown. Tuesday 9 February 1813.*

Description. Two leaves quarto, laid; watermark device (Heawood Nos. 2752–62) above a florid letter H[?], no date; red wax seal, impressed with oval device but design indistinct.

Postmark. None.

Provenance. Bequeathed by CEA to CJA in 1845; descended to his grand-daughters and sold by them probably in 1924; Frederick R. Lovering; Sotheby's 3 May 1948; T. Edward Carpenter and bequeathed by him to the JAMT in 1969.

Publication. Memoir (1st 133–9; 2nd 99–101, where extracts from this and from letter **78** are printed as one letter (of Feb. 1813)); *Life* 262 (extracts); Chapman (1st and 2nd, from copy made by RAAL in 1909); Lock; Modert F-240 to F-243.

1. *your last visit there.* Old Mr Bigg-Wither was now very close to his end (he died on 24 Feb. 1813), and in accordance with the etiquette of the period his two single daughters would be expected to leave Manydown when the heir, their brother Harris (presently living elsewhere in Hampshire), brought his wife and children to take over the family home. In the event the wid-owed Mrs Heathcote and the unmarried Alethea Bigg went to live in Winchester, and JA and CEA continued to visit them there. See for ex-ample the opening chapters of *S&S*.

2. *Mrs Heathcote.* 'It was generally supposed, I believe I might say, it was generally known amongst his intimate friends, that he [John Harwood] had formed an attachment to a lady of good position in his own

neighbourhood. It was also believed, though not of course with equal certainty, that this lady, a widow, and quite her own mistress, would be willing to accept him. Nor could it have been considered a bad match for *her*, if, on his father's death he could have offered her, as he had a right to expect, a home in the family mansion with an estate of at least £1,000 a year around it. But, as I have said before, he then found himself a ruined man, and bound to provide as best he could for his mother and aunt' (CMCA, *Reminiscences*, 27–8).

Maria may perhaps be a reference to Maria Bertram in *MP*.

3. *the Boys.* EAK's sons, and some of their cousins, all now at Winchester—see letter **82**.

4. *I shall tell Anna.* The secret of authorship of *S&S* and *P&P*?

5. *but she has.* 'but' inserted superscript.

6. *Pulteney S^t.* The Leigh-Perrots had given up renting 1 Paragon, and purchased 49 Pulteney Street during the winter of 1810–11.

7. *Lady W.* Williams.

8. *work for one evening more.* To finish reading aloud *P&P*.

9. *Miss Edgeworth.* Probably *Tales from Fashionable Life* (2nd series, 1812); by Maria E. (1767–1849).

82. *To Martha Lloyd. From Chawton to Kintbury. Tuesday 16 February 1813.*

Description. Two leaves quarto, laid; watermark JOHN HAYES 1809; remains of blue wafer. Endorsed [?by JA] 'Chawton Feb. 16.'

Postmark. None.

Provenance. Descended in FWA's family; sold, 'the property of a Lady' (probably FWA's granddaughter Mrs Janet Saunders), Sotheby's 31 July–1 Aug. 1933; Mrs Henry Burke 1939 or later; bequeathed by her to Pierpont Morgan Library, New York, 1975 (MA 2911).

Publication. Chapman (2nd); Modert F-244 to F-247.

1. *account from Sloane S^t.* Mrs HTA was now terminally ill.

2. *Mrs D. D.* Deans Dundas.

3. *about her.* 'her' inserted superscript.

4. *Northamptonshire.* HTA was accustomed to visit Northamptonshire in the course of his financial business, as Sir James Langham of Cottesbrooke was related to Mr James Tilson, one of HTA's banking partners.

5. *do not wish you.* 'you' inserted superscript.

6. *Princess of Wales's Letter.* The Princess of Wales had written to her estranged husband, stating her grievances, on 14 Jan. 1813, and this letter was subsequently published in the *Morning Chronicle* of Monday, 8 Feb. 1813; the *Hampshire Telegraph* reprinted it in its issue of Monday, 15 Feb.

83. *To ?Francis Austen. From Chawton to ?Deal. Wednesday 17 February 1813.*

Description. Scrap only, possibly cut from a quarto leaf; laid.

Provenance. Given by FWA to Lord William FitzRoy, at the request of Mr William Upcott, who passed it on to Miss Catherine Hutton (1756–1846) for her autograph collection, 1841; William Clay, of Rochester, NY, *c.*1940; Mrs Edith Lank, Rochester, NY, *c.*1980.

Publication. Modert F-248 and pp. 34–5.

1. As this scrap came from FWA, presumably the letter itself had been addressed to him in his new lodgings at Deal (see letter **82**); it might, however, have been primarily addressed to his first wife, Mary Gibson. In his covering letter to Lord William FitzRoy FWA wrote:

   > The individual whose Autograph your friend is desirous to obtain was my Sister. I have several letters of hers in my possession, but not one that I could feel justified in parting with. I send you however her Signature such as she usually wrote it when she used (which she rarely did) more than her initials. The year is not affixed to the date, but I know it to have been 1813. She scarcely ever wrote her Christian name at full length except when writing to some of her most intimate friends, when she did not use her Sirname [*sic*].

2. *Lord William FitzRoy.* A younger brother (1782–1857) of the 3rd Duke of Grafton. An Isabella FitzRoy (probably Lord William's niece) owned a copy of the 2nd edition of *S&S* and pencilled at the beginning of vol. iii:

   > What a pity that the characters had not been touched up a little before publication of this pretty novel—Mrs Jennings made less vulgar—and the fortunes of her daughters shd. be mentioned as their beauty—and tho' Colonel Brandon was grave why was he to be silent—the best is done to make E. Ferrars seem a mean looking man—and Col. B. must have been good looking, or Marianne never cd. have married him.

   Charles W. Traylen of Guildford—sales cat. No. 106, 1990.

84. *To Cassandra Austen. From London to Chawton. Thursday 20 May 1813.*

Description. Two leaves quarto, laid; watermark device (Heawood Nos. 2752–62) above monogram HW, no date; black wafer impressed with wafer-seal. Endorsed [?by JA or CEA] 'From Sloane St | May 1813'

Postmarks. .MA 20. .813 . . . Clock 20.My. . . (part-printed only)   Two Pʸ Post Unpaid Sloane St.

Provenance. Bequeathed by CEA to CJA in 1845; descended to his granddaughters and sold by them probably in 1924; Frederick R. Lovering;

Sotheby's 3 May 1948; T. Edward Carpenter and bequeathed by him to the JAMT 1969.

Publication. Memoir (2nd 102 (extracts)); *Life* 265 (extracts); Chapman (1st and 2nd); Lock; Modert F-249 to F-252.

1. *the Hog's-back.* A narrow ridge of bare chalk hills between Farnham and Guildford; the road runs along the summit and gives extensive views over six counties.

2. *little Cass . . . Betsies.* In this context 'little Cass' is CJA's eldest daughter (born Dec. 1808) and her nursemaid Betsy; there was also a maidservant Betsy currently employed at the Cottage. 'Cassy' is EAK's fifth daughter (born Nov. 1806)—he and his family had recently arrived at Chawton Great House for a summer holiday.

3. *the Water-coloured Exhibition.* That currently on display in Spring Gardens—see letter **85**.

4. *a 16th of the £20,000.* Martha Lloyd had evidently received a legacy, perhaps from Mrs Dundas—see letters **102** and **106**.

85. *To Cassandra Austen. From London to Chawton. Monday 24 May 1813.*

Description. Two leaves quarto, laid; watermark device (Heawood Nos. 2752–62) above florid monogram WR[?]; no date; mark of wafer impressed by wafer-seal; endorsed [?by JA or CEA] 'May 1813 From Sloane St'. A few words cut out of line 3 on p. 2, not affecting the text on p. 1.

Postmark. None.

Provenance. Bequeathed by CEA to Fanny, Lady Knatchbull, in 1845; inherited by Lord Brabourne 1882; probably in the Puttick & Simpson sale of 26–8 June 1893; Alfred Morrison; Sotheby's 10 Dec. 1918; J. Pierpont Morgan 1920; Pierpont Morgan Library, New York (MA 977-31).

Publication. Brabourne ii. 139; *Life* 267 (extracts); Johnson 77; Chapman (1st and 2nd); Modert F-253 to F-256.

1. *Remnants . . . Laytons.* T. Remnant, glover, 126 Strand; Christian & Son, linen-drapers, 11 Wigmore Street; Layton & Shears, mercers, Bedford House, 11 Henrietta Street.

2. *No. 10.* Henrietta Street, now being prepared for HTA's home as well as his office. See Watson, *Jane Austen in London.*

3. *Exhibition in Spring Gardens.* Held by the Society of Painters in Oil and Water Colours.

4. *Mrs Bingley.* The most likely identification of this picture seems to be catalogue No. 27, 'Portrait of a Lady' by J. F. M. Huet-Villiers. See Martha M. Rainbolt, 'The Likeness of Austen's Jane Bennet: Huet-Villiers' "Portrait of Mrs Q."' in *English Language Notes* (Dec. 1988), 35–43. However,

the three miniatures by Charles John Robertson in the same exhibition, of Lady Nelthorpe (No. 246) and her sisters-in-law Lady Anderson (No. 15), and Mrs Clarke of Welton [not Weston] Place (No. 116), cannot be completely ruled out as alternatives.

5. *the Great Exhibition.* The British Academy exhibition at Somerset House, which opened 3 May.

6. *Sir Joshua Reynolds's.* 'The Managers of the British Institution, as a tribute to the memory of Sir Joshua Reynolds, have borrowed 130 of his performances, which are now on exhibition for the benefit of Students' (*GM* (May 1813), 48).

7. *My cousin Caro*line. JA is quoting Mrs Tilson's words and pronunciation.

8. *drive to Hampstead.* Mrs HTA had been buried in the churchyard of St John-at-Hampstead (now London NW3) on 1 May.

9. *a wild Beast.* The secret of authorship was leaking out. [RWC]

10. *come to bide.* A quotation from FWA's childhood, as letter **69** shows.

11. *We are to go.* 'to' inserted superscript.

12. *at all sure.* 'all' inserted superscript.

13. *sort of Letter that Miss D. would write.* On Friday 21 May Fanny Knight had written to JA as Miss Darcy, evidently hoping that her aunt would answer in character.

86. *To Francis Austen. From Chawton to the Baltic Ocean.*

Saturday 3–Tuesday 6 July 1813.

Description. Two leaves quarto, laid; watermark device (Heawood Nos. 2752–62), no date; black wafer impressed with wafer-seal.

Postmark. None.

Provenance. Descended in FWA's family to his grandson Capt. Ernest Leigh Austen, RN, and presented by him to the British Museum Dept. of MSS, 1930; now British Library Add. MSS 42,180, fos. 9–10.

Publication. SB 233; *Life* 85, 270; Johnson 131; Chapman (1st and 2nd); Modert F-257 to F-260.

1. *Gustavus-Vasa . . . Linneus.* Gustavus-Vasa (1496–1560): Swedish nobleman who delivered Sweden from Danish rule, and was elected King of Sweden in 1523; Charles XII of Sweden (1682–1718): another warrior king; Queen Christina (1626–89): preferred intellectual study to a crown, and abdicated in 1654; Charles Linnaeus (1707–78): naturalist and originator of the Linnaean system of botanical classification.

2. *have a strong resemblance.* 'a' inserted superscript.

3. *has had better luck.* 'had' inserted superscript.

4. *a new Garden.* Chawton House faces west; in front of it, at some distance and at a lower level, is the Alton–Southampton road. The Rectory is on

the other side of the road. The present garden, which is large and enclosed by a beautiful brick wall, is 'at the top of the lawn' behind the house, and is no doubt of Edward's making. Mrs Montagu Knight tells me that the old garden was in the church meadow. [RWC]

5. *to have the new.* 'have' inserted superscript.

6. *dishonourable accomodation.* I suppose because the boy's keep was saved. [RWC]

7. *Deputy Receiver.* HTA had been promoted to Receiver-General for Oxfordshire. [RWC]

8. *his nephew.* Edward Knight jr. went with HTA.

9. *worthless Nephews & Neices.* JA was thinking here of Mr Leigh's relations on the Saye and Sele side of the family—see Biographical Index.

10. *Mrs L. P.* Leigh Perrot.

11. *vile compromise.* See letter **49**, note 5.

12. *Mr Blackall's marriage.* For his previous appearance see letter **11**. His marriage was reported in the *Hampshire Telegraph* of Monday, 11 Jan. 1813.

13. *to sweeten it.* i.e. to allow time for the fumes from the new paint to evaporate; 'painter's colic' is a mild form of lead poisoning caused by such fumes.

14. *not all off.* Sir Francis in extreme old age had still a quantity of hair. [RWC]

15. *not half so entertaining. MP.*

16. *your old Ships.* The ships borrowed for *MP* were *Cleopatra, Elephant, Endymion.*

87. *To Cassandra Austen. From London to Chawton. Wednesday 15– Thursday 16 September 1813.*

Description. Four leaves quarto; about six lines and signature cut away from top of fourth leaf. [RWC]

Postmark. None.

Provenance. Bequeathed by CEA to Fanny, Lady Knatchbull, in 1845; inherited by Lord Brabourne 1882; probably in the Puttick & Simpson sale of 26–8 June 1893; Sir Alfred Law, by 1931; Sir Alfred died unmarried in 1939 and bequeathed his estate to his cousin Emma Dixon and her descendants; the present ownership and location of his collection is unknown.

Publication. Brabourne ii. 145; *Life* 273 (extracts); Johnson 82; Chapman (1st and 2nd). In Oct. 1931 Davidson Cook was able to inspect the original letter in the Law collection, but by then RWC's text for his first edition, copied from Brabourne, was already in proof, and consequently no corrections were made. The text now shows the changes in punctuation and capitalization marked up in MS by Davidson Cook on a copy of RWC's proof.

1. *W^m*. William, HTA's servant.
2. *Edward finds his quarters.* He was staying at a hotel nearby.
3. *Mr Crabbe.* René Huchon, *Crabbe and his Times* (Engl. trans. (1907; new imp. 1968), 375) states that the Crabbes were in London from July until just before Mrs C.'s death in Sept. [RWC]
   For JA's interest in Mr Crabbe see *Family Record* 158.
4. *Lady Robert.* Kerr.
5. *Mrs H. and Miss B.* Mrs Heathcote and her sister Alethea, who became *Miss* Bigg on her elder sister Catherine's becoming Mrs Hill. [RWC]
6. *Clandestine Marriage &* Midas. George Colman the elder (1732–94), *The Clandestine Marriage* (with Garrick, 1766); Kane O'Hara (1714(?)–82), *Midas: An English Burletta* (1764, and often revived).
7. *Don Juan. Don Juan, or the Libertine Destroyed* (1792, a pantomime founded on Shadwell's *Libertine*).
8. *Five hours at Brighton.* Samuel Beazley (1786–1851), *The Boarding House; or, Five Hours at Brighton* (1811).
9. *The Beehive.* A musical farce attributed to Millingen. [RWC]
10. *Harriet Byron's feather. Sir Charles Grandison,* letter 22: 'A white Paris sort of cap, glittering with spangles, and encircled by a chaplet of artificial flowers, with a little white feather perking from the left ear, is to be my headdress.' [RWC]
11. *Mrs Fra. A.* The reading is not certain; presumably the wife of Francis Motley Austen, or possibly the wife of his eldest son, Francis Lucius A. [RWC].
    Davidson Cook thought the cramped abbreviation might also be read as 'Mrs Tho. A', in which case it would refer to Margaretta, wife of Col. Thomas A.—see letter **86.**
12. *M^de B.* Bigeon.
13. *crimson velvet.* Perhaps JA was thinking here of Crabbe's *Tales* (1812), p. 45, *The Gentleman Farmer*: 'In full festoons the crimson curtains fell.'
14. *remembrances connected with Midas.* There is no clue as to when or where JA and CEA had seen this entertainment previously.
15. *November collection.* As Receiver-General for Oxfordshire, HTA was personally responsible for collecting the monies due.
16. *Nothing has been done.* I guess that there was a question of sending *S&S* to Warren Hastings, who had read and admired *P&P*. This would require the mediation of HTA. In the idiom of the time, which is not quite that of today, 'books' may mean either the set of three volumes or, as we say, 'copies', and especially presentation copies. 'Do not let us teize one another about books', wrote Dr Johnson to his publisher. [RWC]
17. *sent down to Alton.* To work at Austen, Gray & Vincent, HTA's branch partnership.

18. *Mr H.* Warren Hastings.

19. *Poor F. Cage.* The combination of the White Hart and susceptibility to noise reminds us of Louisa Musgrove's accident and subsequent nerves. I can find no report of the accident in the Bath newspapers [RWC].

At Godmersham, FCK noted in her diary, under the date Sunday, 12 Sept: 'Papa heard from Aunt Louisa of their safe arrival at Bath, & of dearest Fannys escape from harm in a bad accident.'

20. *Mr Bridges.* Revd Henry B.

21. *By favour of Mr Gray.* The letter went to Alton in 'the parcel' and Mr G. conveyed it thence to Chawton. [RWC]

88. *To Cassandra Austen. From London to Chawton. Thursday 16 September 1813.*

Description. Two leaves quarto, laid; watermark device (Heawood Nos. 2752–62), 1810; traces of red wax above address, and a black wafer below address. Endorsed [?by CEA]: 'Henrietta St Autumn | of 1813'

Postmark. None.

Provenance. Bequeathed by CEA to Fanny, Lady Knatchbull, in 1845; inherited by Lord Brabourne 1882; Sotheby's 11–14 May 1891; Anderson Gallery, New York, Dec. 1909; Cleveland H. Dodge; The Cleveland H. Dodge Foundation, Inc., New York.

Publication. Brabourne ii. 154; *Life* 276 (extracts); Chapman (1st and 2nd—a collation of the text was sent to him by Cleveland H. Dodge in May 1925); Modert F-261 to F-264.

1. *found you all well.* 'well' inserted superscript.

2. *in need of Leeches.* For headaches—see letter **89.**

3. *perhaps may delay his visit.* 'may' inserted superscript.

4. *Mrs T.* Tilson.

5. *within 3 or 4 days.* A daughter was born shortly afterwards.

6. *from the Compting House.* Mr T. was a partner in the bank, and HTA was now living 'over the shop'. [RWC]

7. *bought her Irish.* Linen.

8. *good enough for your purpose.* 'good' inserted superscript.

9. *the Stockings.* JA wrote 'the the Stockings', then cancelled the first 'the'.

10. *We then went.* 'went' inserted superscript.

11. *Hook's Lessons.* James Hook (1746–1827), *Guida di Musica, being a complete book of instruction for the Harpsichord or Pianoforte* (1790; new edn., 1810). Robert Birchall was a music seller and publisher at 133 New Bond Street.

12. *Triggs.* EAK's gamekeeper for the Chawton estate.

89. *To Cassandra Austen. From Godmersham to Chawton. Thursday 23–Friday 24 September 1813.*

Description. Two leaves quarto, laid; watermark device (Heawood Nos. 2752–62), no date; red wax seal.

Postmarks. FEVER[SHAM]   dated pm illegible.

Provenance. Bequeathed by CEA to Fanny, Lady Knatchbull, in 1845; inherited by Lord Brabourne 1882; probably in the Puttick & Simpson sale of 26–8 June 1893; Alfred Morrison; Sotheby's 10 Dec. 1918; J. Pierpont Morgan 1920; Pierpont Morgan Library, New York (MA 977–32).

Publication. Brabourne ii. 159; *Life* 276 (extracts); Chapman (1st and 2nd); Modert F-265 to F-268.

1. *her little Boy.* Benjamin Clement (1813–73).
2. *sister in Lucina.* Lucina was the Roman goddess who presided over the birth of children.
3. *Mary P.* Plumptre.
4. *Ben.* Lefroy.
5. *dinner-invitation.* See letter **90.**
6. *The Mr Ks.* Brothers and nephew of the deceased Mrs Knight: Mr Wyndham K., his son Wadham, and Capt. Charles K., RN.
   The *Inscription.* For Mrs Knight's memorial tablet in Godmersham church.
7. *with the two Seniors.* 'the' inserted superscript.
8. *the two others.* Edward Knight jr., and George.
9. *T'is Night.* James Beattie (1735–1803), *The Hermit*, line 25.
10. *Tyldens & double Tyldens.* Presumably a reference to the fact that one branch of this family had taken the additional name of Pattenson in 1799.
11. *Colleges at Cambridge.* Probably R. B. Harraden's *Cantabrigia Depicta: A Series of Engravings* (1809). [RWC]
12. *Dame L.* Presumably Dame Lipscombe.
13. *empty Pew.* EAK and his family had been at Chawton since 21 Apr. 1813, so that on Sunday, 19 Sept., their pew in Chawton church was empty for the first time for months. [RWC]
14. *Bentigh.* (Pronounced to rhyme with *high*). A wooded hill in Godmersham park. A map of 1769 shows, within a few miles, a *Clovertigh* and an *Ollantigh*. [RWC]
15. *not much upon.* JA first wrote 'not much of', and then cancelled 'of'.
16. *Mary O. nor Mary P.* Oxenden, Plumptre.
17. *Fanny C.* Cage.
18. *Modern Europe.* Perhaps John Bigland's *Letters on the Modern History and Political Aspect of Europe* (1804).
19. Thing *for measuring Timber with.* Probably the particular version of a slide

rule invented by Henry Coggeshall in 1677 and still known today by that name.

20. *Mrs Driver.* The new housekeeper at Godmersham.
21. *new Novel.* Fanny Burney, *The Wanderer, or Female Difficulties,* 5 vols. (1814).
22. *Mr Twisleton.* For the chequered career of the Hon. and Revd Dr Thomas James Twisleton, see Biographical Index.
23. *Mistress of all I survey.* William Cowper, *Verses supposed to be written by Alexander Selkirk.*

90. *To Francis Austen. From Godmersham to the Baltic Ocean. Saturday 25 September 1813.*

Description. Two leaves quarto, laid; watermark device (Heawood Nos. 2752–62), 1810; mark of green or yellow wafer.

Postmark. None.

Provenance. Descended in FWA's family to his grandson Capt. Ernest Leigh Austen, RN, and presented by him to the British Museum Dept. of MSS, 1930; now British Library Add. MSS 42,180, fos. 11–12.

Publication. SB 243; *Life* 278; Johnson 136; Chapman (1st and 2nd); Modert F-269 to F-272.

1. *St Paul's Shipwreck. Acts* 27:44.
2. *The Clerk.* John Hogben (1772–1841).
3. *my application.* To use the names of his old ships in *MP*—see letter **86.**
4. *I can of it.* 'by' deleted, 'of' inserted superscript.
5. *in the Son's hands.* The Trimmer family of Alton were EAK's lawyers for his Hampshire property.

91. *To Cassandra Austen. From Godmersham to Chawton. Monday 11– Tuesday 12 October 1813.*

Description. Two leaves quarto, laid; watermark device (Heawood Nos. 2752–62), 1810; plain wafer.

Postmarks. A 13 OC 13 1813 FEVERSHAM 47

Provenance. Bequeathed by CEA to Fanny, Lady Knatchbull, in 1845; inherited by Lord Brabourne 1882; probably in the Puttick & Simpson sale of 26–8 June 1893; Alfred Morrison; Sotheby's 10 Dec. 1918; J. Pierpont Morgan 1920; Pierpont Morgan Library, New York (MA 977–33).

Publication. Brabourne ii. 169; *Life* 282 (extracts); Chapman (1st and 2nd); Modert F-273 to F-276.

1. *Mr J. P.* John Plumptre.
2. *very last week perhaps.* JA first wrote 'very last week of Octr.', then partly erased the last two words and wrote 'perhaps' over the erasure.

3. *Weyhill week.* Weyhill, near Andover, Hants. A week-long fair was held there—see Hardy's *The Mayor of Casterbridge*, ch. 1.

4. *Tollard Royal.* Wiltshire; at that time the home of Anna's future brother- and sister-in-law, Revd Henry Rice and his wife Lucy (Lefroy).

5. *triennial bliss.* JA was guilty of a malapropism—she seems to have meant to coin the word 'triunal'.

6. *in my last.* This letter, presumably written during the week beginning Sunday, 3 Oct. 1813, was no doubt destroyed by CEA for this reason.

7. *disgust me again.* See letter **80**, note 1.

8. *Self Control.* By Mary Brunton.

9. *Such a long Letter!* Refers to CEA's; the second page of JA's own has only 36 lines. [RWC]

10. *Harriot Byron.* See *Sir Charles Grandison*, letter 33: 'What shall I do with my gratitude! O my dear, I am *overwhelmed* with my gratitude; I can only express it in silence before them' (before Sir Charles who had rescued her from abduction, and his sister who had sheltered her). [RWC]

11. *Johncock.* The Godmersham butler.

12. *Mrs. H- & Alethea.* Mrs Heathcote and Miss Bigg.

13. *naming a Heroine.* The heroine of *Sanditon* is Charlotte.

14. *Miss Yates & her companions.* See *MAJA* 8.

15. *Life of Nelson.* By Robert Southey, 1813. Nelson himself wrote very favourably of FWA, but the latter is not mentioned in Southey's text.

16. *one Brother . . . Wife.* CJA at the Nore, and Mrs FWA at Deal.

17. *whether Mrs Tilson has ever lain-in.* 'has' inserted superscript above 'had' cancelled; for Mrs T.'s pregnancy see letter **88**, note 5.

18. *dined upon Goose.* I am referred to *British Apollo* (1708), i. 74:

> . . . pray tell me whence
> The Custom'd Proverb did commence,
> That who eats Goose on Michael's Day,
> Shan't Money lack, his Debts to pay.

Old Michaelmas Day was 11 Oct.; the 2^d *Edition* was that of *S&S*. [RWC]

19. *Uncle Edward.* Bridges.

20. *she does not like it.* No doubt because JA did not wish FCK to see her comments on Fanny's brothers and her admirer Mr Plumptre.

92. *To Cassandra Austen. From Godmersham to Chawton. Thursday 14–Friday 15 October 1813.*

Description. Three leaves quarto, laid; watermark device (Heawood Nos. 2752– 62), 1810; red wax seal with imprint of ship.

Postmarks. [OC] 16 1813   FEVER[SHAM]

Provenance. Bequeathed by CEA to Fanny, Lady Knatchbull, in 1845; inherited by Lord Brabourne 1882; probably in the Puttick & Simpson sale of 26–8 June 1893; Amy Lowell, and bequeathed by her to The Houghton Library, Harvard University, Cambridge, Mass., 1925 (Lowell Autograph, rev. 1925).

Publication. Brabourne ii. 177; *Life* 283 (extracts); Johnson 89; Chapman (1st and 2nd); Modert F-277 to F-282.

1. *room for the seal.* A franked letter could be enclosed in an 'envelope', so that the seal need not be on the same piece of paper as the text. JA left a space on her third page and also again on the fifth, as that leaf would be the 'envelope' and carry the seal.

2. *Foresters or the Franfraddops.* Are these fabulous families, perhaps a reference to some item of JA's juvenilia that has not survived?

3. *either House.* Chilham Castle (Wildman), and the vicarage (Tylden).

4. *Lady B.* The Dowager Lady Bridges.

5. *Hooper.* Holder.

6. *Fanny is to be put.* 'be' inserted superscript.

7. *Fanny may spend.* 'may' inserted superscript.

8. *Miss Austen of a Wiltshire Family.* 'of' inserted superscript; apart from Kentish Austens, there were at this time other families of Austens/Austins in Devon, Dorset, Gloucestershire, Durham, London, and Ireland; this Miss Austen is in fact from Dorset, not Wiltshire—see Biographical Index.

9. *on board.* i.e. living on HMS *Namur*, at Sheerness.

10. *her B^r.* Tom Fowle, also serving on the *Namur*.

93. *To Cassandra Austen. From Godmersham to London. Thursday 21 October 1813.*

Description. Unknown; original MS untraced since first publication.

Provenance. Bequeathed by CEA to Fanny, Lady Knatchbull, in 1845; inherited by Lord Brabourne 1882; probably in the Puttick & Simpson sale of 26–8 June 1893.

Publication. Brabourne ii. 189; *Life* 285 (extract); Chapman (1st and 2nd).

1. *Miss Floyd.* 'It was my grandmother who changed the pronunciation of Lloyd into Floyd as it was always spoken in my recollection. They said *that* was the true Welsh pronunciation of double L, but a Welshman and a scholar has assured me it was useless to try and imitate their accent, the English tongue could not give it, and that we had therefore better say Lloyd' (CMCA, *Reminiscences*, 10).

2. *Key Street.* Not a street but a Kentish village.

3. *Harriot.* Mrs Moore.

4. *Mrs Crabbe.* Sarah C., wife of the poet, died 21 Sept. 1813.

5. *one of his prefaces.* To *The Borough* (1810); in the third paragraph Crabbe likens an author's partiality for his manuscript to a parent's for his child, showing some familiarity with 'manuscripts in the study' and 'children in the nursery'. [RWC]

6. *I will comfort* him. For JA's joke about marrying Crabbe see *Family Record* 158.

94. *To Cassandra Austen. From Godmersham to London. Tuesday 26 October 1813.*

Description. Two leaves quarto, laid; watermark W TURNER & SON 1810; red wax seal with impression of tall ship.

Postmarks. A 27 OC 27 1813   FEVERSHAM 47

Provenance. Bequeathed by CEA to Fanny, Lady Knatchbull, in 1845; inherited by Lord Brabourne 1882; probably in the Puttick & Simpson sale of 26–8 June 1893; Maggs Bros. 1918; William Randolph Hearst; Henry G. & Alberta H. Burke 1938; bequeathed by Alberta H. Burke to Pierpont Morgan Library, New York, 1975 (MA 2911).

Publication. Brabourne ii. 194; *Life* 285 (extracts); Chapman (1st and 2nd); Modert F-283 to F-286.

1. *I guess Caroline.* The latest Tilson baby was baptized Caroline-Jane on 26 Nov. 1813.

2. *little George.* Moore.

3. *& we had.* 'we' inserted superscript.

4. *Wyndham Knatchbull's son.* Wyndham K. jr., in the Army.

5. *to his Servant.* These three words inserted superscript.

6. *spoil their Boy.* JA originally wrote 'spoil their Boy at all', and cancelled the last two words.

7. *one infallible Pope.* JA had in mind Pope's *Essay on Man*, line 284: 'One truth is clear, Whatever is, is right'.

8. *was not in raptures.* FCK was then cherishing a sentimental admiration for Mr George Hatton, and had perhaps mentioned something of this to JA.

9. *what he does not approve.* JA first wrote 'what he does not approve it', and cancelled the last word.

10. *as soon as she can.* 'My father although deeply attached to my mother was far too high-principled and conscientious to take Holy Orders for the sake of being immediately married. Possibly he had not yet quite decided on his profession, at all events he was not ordained until three years afterwards. As to my mother's reluctance to go to Chawton, sent away as she was to mark my Gd Mother's anger with him, it was not possible she should go with any other feelings' (Bellas Notes). [RWC]

11. *Lady Elizabeth.* Finch-Hatton.

95. *To Cassandra Austen. From Godmersham to London. Wednesday 3 November 1813.*

Description. Two leaves quarto, laid; watermark W TURNER & SON 1810; small red wax seal, design not clear.

Postmarks. A 4 NO 4 1813   FEVERSHAM 47.

Provenance. Bequeathed by CEA to Fanny, Lady Knatchbull, in 1845; inherited by Lord Brabourne 1882; Puttick & Simpson 26-8 June 1893; Alfred Morrison; Sotheby's 10 Dec. 1918; J. Pierpont Morgan 1920; Pierpont Morgan Library, New York (MA 977-34).

Publication. Brabourne ii. 200; *Life* 287 (extracts); Johnson 99; Chapman (1st and 2nd); Modert F-287 to F-290.

1. *this celebrated Birthday.* Janice Kirkland, 'Jane Austen and the Celebrated Birthday', *N&Q* 232:4 (Dec. 1987), 477-8, suggests that of Princess Sophia, the fifth of George III's daughters (3.11.1777). Kirkland also suggests that the Lord Howard mentioned at the end of this letter was Lord Howard of Effingham (1748-1816), Secretary and Comptroller to Queen Charlotte.

2. *unless you know.* 'unless' inserted superscript.

3. *Lady B. . . . Dr P.* The Dowager Lady Bridges; Dr Parry.

4. *all the Panoramas.* Henry Aston Barker's Panorama in Leicester Square. 'These pictures may be fairly entitled *the Triumph of Perspective*. There are two circles, an upper and a lower, in which are constantly exhibited views of great cities, of battles, &c, &c. The illusion is so complete, that the spectator may imagine he is present at the display of the real objects. The price of admission is 1s. to each picture.' *Mr Ogle* was perhaps a friend of the proprietor.

5. *a* ready money *house.* 'a' inserted superscript.

6. *Bru of feu the Archbishop.* (French)—the daughter-in-law of the late Archbishop = Harriot Moore.

7. *Lady B.* This Lady Bridges is Dorothy (Hawley), second wife of Sir Brook B. IV.

8. *Mrs Harrison.* Sister of JA's deceased friend Madam Lefroy of Ashe, and therefore aunt to Ben Lefroy.

9. *five tables . . . two fires.* The main entrance of Godmersham Park is on the north, and opens on the large hall. The room in which JA sat with these tables and chairs is probably what is now called the south drawing-room. It might escape identification today; for Lady Lewisham tells me that 'in putting up the old Adams bookcase at the end of this room, when we redecorated it, we closed up a second fireplace'. The *library* was probably a smaller room on the same side of the house. The *hall chamber* is above the hall, and the *yellow room* adjoins it.

The house is described in Zechariah Cozens, *Tour through the Isle of Thanet* (1793), as 'a modern building of a centre and two wings; one of which, the Eastern, contains a most excellent library; in the centre are some good apartments, particularly on the back front, which command exceeding delightful prospects of the hill and pleasure grounds'. [RWC]

10. *William.* HTA's manservant.

11. *Tame Hares . . . Charing Cross.* Cowper, *Epitaph on a Hare*; Boswell's *Life of Johnson* (2 Apr. 1775).

12. *all white & red, with my Head on one side.* JA was no doubt thinking of Sir Joshua Reynolds's female portraits—see letter **85.**

13. *young M^r D'arblay.* Fanny Burney's son.

14. *Money for Printing &c.* Because the second edition of *S&S* was produced at the author's expense. [RWC]

15. *How he does cry about it!* JA first wrote 'How it does cry about it!', then cancelled the first 'it' and inserted 'he' superscript.

96. *To Cassandra Austen. From Godmersham to London. Saturday 6– Sunday 7 November 1813.*

Description. Two leaves quarto, laid; watermark W. TURNER & SON 1810; red wax seal, design indecipherable.

Postmarks. Dated postmark illegible;   FEVERSHAM 47.

Provenance. Bequeathed by CEA to Fanny, Lady Knatchbull, in 1845; inherited by Lord Brabourne 1882; Puttick & Simpson, 26–8 June 1893; Alfred Morrison; Sotheby's 10 Dec. 1918; J. Pierpont Morgan 1920; Pierpont Morgan Library, New York (MA 977–35).

Publication. Brabourne ii. 209; *Life* 288 (extracts); Johnson 105; Chapman (1st and 2nd); Modert F-291 to F-294.

1. *the famous Ball.* Perhaps that at which CEA was present in Jan. 1801—see letters **30** and **31.**

2. *a sort of Chaperon for I am put on the Sofa.* JA wrote 'short' and crossed out the 'h'; 'for' inserted superscript.

3. *about seeing dear Fanny.* 'seeing' inserted superscript.

4. *la Mere Beauté.* Mme de Sévigné (1626–96), *Lettres* (1726, in English 1758).

5. *Letter from Mary.* Mrs JA.

6. *my 2^d Edit.* Of *S&S*, not *P&P.* The second edition of the latter was published at nearly the same time; but JA had sold the copyright to Egerton, and there is no evidence that she was consulted. The second edition (unlike those of *S&S* and *MP*) contains no correction due to her. See my article, 'Jane Austen and her Publishers', in *London Mercury* (Aug. 1930). [RWC]

7. *Eliza.* Mrs Fowle.

8. *Fyfield Estates.* The Fowle family had owned an estate at Fyfield, near Marlborough, Wilts., since the end of the seventeenth century; in 1812 this was offered for sale by Revd Fulwar-Craven Fowle.

9. *given to Miss Hamilton.* Elizabeth Hamilton (1758–1816); JA had probably read *The Cottagers of Glenburnie* (1808), and 'respectable' suggests knowledge of *Popular Essays on the Elementary Principles of the Human Mind* (1812), at least of the reputation of that and similar works. [RWC]

10. *what news!* The Address was moved in both Houses on 4 Nov.; when the Marquis Wellesley 'concurred in the language of Mr Pitt, that England had saved herself by her firmness and energies, and had saved other countries by her example'. On 8 Nov. Lord Bathurst 'in a neat speech' moved the thanks of the House of Lords to the Marquis of Wellington for the eminent skill and ability displayed in the operations succeeding the battle of Vittoria. [RWC]

11. *Black & red letter.* i.e. the crossing of the text was written in red ink, to assist its legibility.

12. *Mrs H.* Heathcote, staying with her sister Mrs Hill at Streatham.

13. *you did came.* 'you' inserted superscript; the phrase evidently dates to FWA's infancy.

14. *Mr Hampson's scheme.* Unidentified.

97. To Cassandra Austen. From London to Chawton. *Wednesday 2– Thursday 3 March 1814.*

Description. Two leaves quarto, laid; watermark device (Heawood Nos. 2752– 62), 1810; red wax seal, device possibly a tall ship. Endorsed [probably by CEA] 'From Hen:^{ta} St | March 1814'; and in pencil 'C. Esten A.' There is also a seven-line list, in very faint pencil, on the seal panel, part of which gives a name and address 'Mrs Carbonel | 4 Hynd St | Manchester Sqre.' The present-day Hinde Street is on the east side of Manchester Square.

Postmark. None.

Provenance. Bequeathed by CEA to CJA in 1845; descended to CJA's granddaughters and sold by them in the 1920s; Frederick R. Lovering; Sotheby's 3 May 1948; Eric G. Millar; T. Edward Carpenter 1952 and bequeathed by him to the JAMT 1969.

Publication. Memoir (2nd 104 (extracts)); *Life* 291 (extracts); Chapman (1st and 2nd); Modert F-295 to F-298.

1. *John.* HTA's coachman.

2. *We did not begin reading.* This must be the proof-sheets of *MP*; no doubt JA had arranged publication with Egerton during her visit to London at the end of Nov. 1813, and had corrected the proofs during the spring of 1814, as publication was originally expected before the end of Apr. (see

letter **100**). There is no mention of any work on proof-correction during this present London visit, even though the book did not in fact appear until 9 May 1814.

3. *but does not appear.* 'does' inserted superscript.

4. *the Heroine.* Eaton Stannard Barrett (1786–1820), *The Heroine, or Adventures of Cherubina* (1813).

5. *Miss P.* Prowting or Papillon?

6. *seeing Keen.* The Shakespearean actor Edmund Kean (1787–1833) had made his first appearance at Drury Lane on 26 Jan. 1814 and had immediately taken the town by storm.

7. *the Willow.* 'Willow sheets' or 'willow squares'—pieces of plaited willow sold ready prepared for hat-making.

8. *Frederick.* Maj.-Gen. (Tilson) Chowne's Christian name was Christopher; but see also letters **98** and **99**, where he is referred to again as 'Frederick'. Could it be that CEA and JA had once seen an amateur performance of *Lovers Vows,* with a much younger Mr (Tilson) Chowne taking the part of 'Frederick' that JA later allocated to Henry Crawford in *MP*? Mrs Inchbald's translation of *Lovers Vows* was first performed in London at Covent Garden on Thursday, 11 Oct. 1798, and versions of the text were published 1798–1800.

9. *little Cassandra.* CJA's daughter.

10. *Dr Syntax.* William Combe (1741–1823), *The Tour of Dr Syntax in Search of the Picturesque* (1812).

11. *Gogmagoglicus.* A legendary giant; one version has it that he lived near Cambridge and was transformed into Gogmagog Hill, another says that he and his brother were captured and made to serve as porters at the Guildhall in London. As proof of the latter version, two great wooden effigies, one holding a long staff with a ball stuck with spikes hanging at the end of it, and the other holding a halberd, were on display in the Guildhall from at least the early fifteenth century.

98. *To Cassandra Austen. From London to Chawton. Saturday 5– Tuesday 8 March 1814.*

Description. Four leaves quarto, laid; watermark device (Heawood Nos. 2752– 62), 1810; red wax seal. About five words cut out on p. 2, not affecting text on p. 1; p. 6 mostly unused; p. 7 blank, p. 8 blank except for address and short shopping-list added faintly in pencil. Endorsed [?by CEA] 'March 1814'.

Postmark. None.

Provenance. Bequeathed by CEA to Fanny, Lady Knatchbull, in 1845; inherited by Lord Brabourne 1882; Puttick & Simpson 26–8 June 1893; Alfred

Morrison; Sotheby's 10 Dec. 1918; J. Pierpont Morgan 1920; Pierpont Morgan Library, New York (MA 977–36).

Publication. Brabourne ii. 222; *Life* 294 (extracts); Chapman (1st and 2nd); Modert F-299 to F-304.

1. *the Corsair.* Lord Byron (1788–1824), *The Corsair* (1814).

2. *Young Wyndham.* Knatchbull, second son of Sir Edward, 8th Bt. FCK did better in marrying his elder brother, afterwards Sir Edward, 9th Bt. But JA in Mar. 1814 could not foresee the death of that gentleman's first wife, later in the year. [RWC]

3. *Mrs L. & Miss E.* Latouche and her daughter East.

4. *Miss H. Moore.* Miss Harriet M., of Hanwell—she and her sister Miss Eliza were HTA's friends.

5. *a second prosecution.* This is evidently part of *the Baigent business* later in the letter. There was a Baigent family of yeomen farmers in Chawton at the time, and *the Boy* may be one of the sons.

6. *Illusion. Illusion, or the Trances of Nourjahad* ('a melodramatic spectacle').

7. *This 6 weeks mourning.* For the Queen's brother, the Duke of Mecklenburg-Strelitz. [RWC]

8. *Mr Richard Snow.* Jack Frost and Dick Snow—mythical personifications of winter weather.

9. *Catherine.* Mrs Hill.

10. *you have not heard that.* 'heard that' inserted superscript.

11. *escaping his Lawsuit.* Presumably an early reference to the lawsuit formally commenced against EAK by the Hinton/Baverstock family in Oct. 1814, laying claim to the Chawton estate as heirs-at-law of the extinct Knight family.

12. *the Devil to pay.* Charles Coffey (d. 1745), *The Devil to Pay* (1731).

13. *Artaxerxes.* An Italian opera translated from Metastasio.

14. *Rich^d.* HTA's manservant, successor to William.

15. *have it enquired for.* 'it' inserted superscript.

16. *the Farmers Wife.* Charles Dibdin (1745–1814), *The Farmer's Wife* (1814).

99. *To Cassandra Austen. From London to Chawton. Wednesday 9 March 1814.*

Description. Two leaves quarto, laid; watermark device (Heawood Nos. 2752–62), 1810; red wafer. Endorsed [?by CEA] 'March 1814'.

Postmark. None.

Provenance. Bequeathed by CEA to Fanny, Lady Knatchbull, in 1845; inherited by Lord Brabourne 1882; Sotheby's 11–14 May 1891; Puttick & Simpson, 26–8 June 1893; Alfred Morrison; Sotheby's 10 Dec. 1918; J. Pierpont Morgan 1920; Pierpont Morgan Library, New York (MA 977–37).

Publication. Brabourne ii. 231; *Life* 295 (extracts); Johnson 112; Chapman (1st and 2nd); Modert F-305 to F-308.

1. *the Indian Jugglers.* A troupe of Indians who gave daily performances at 87 Pall Mall. Miss Berry saw them in 1813: 'I was very much amused. The figures, dress, language, and the movements of these two men, all transport one into another quarter of the globe; their skill seemed almost supernatural.'

2. *Mathews, Liston & Emery.* Three popular actors of the day: Charles Mathews (1776–1835); John Liston (1776?–1846); John Emery (1777–1822).

3. *decided attachment.* FCK first met John Plumptre in 1811 and indeed came very close to marrying him—see letters **109** and **114.**

4. *Young in Richard.* Charles Mayne Young (1777–1856), actor; *Richard III.*

5. *your little companion.* CJA's daughter Cassy-Esten.

6. *Lord Portsmouth . . . Miss Hanson!* See Biographical Index.

7. *my Letter to night.* 'to night' inserted superscript.

100. *To ?Francis Austen. From London to ?Spithead. Monday 21 March 1814.*

Description. Scrap, cut from the top of a quarto leaf, approximately 7″ wide by 1″ deep, laid; no watermark or mark of seal or wafer.

Postmark. None.

Provenance. Found in a scrapbook with no related material and no sign of previous ownership, and sold as No. 920 in Maggs Bros. Winter Catalogue 1969; Dr Sidney Ives, Gainesville, Florida.

Publication. Dr Ives published most of the verso (*MP* reference) as an epigraph for 'The Trial of Mrs Leigh Perrot, wife of James Leigh Perrot, Esq.', a paper delivered before the Club of Odd Volumes on 17 May 1978; the Grolier Club on 29 Sept. 1978; and subsequently published as a limited edition at The Stinehour Press for the Club of Odd Volumes, Boston, 1980; Modert, F-309.

Too little remains of this letter for the recipient to be identified with certainty. By elimination, however, FWA and CJA are the likeliest addressees; FWA was then aboard HMS *Elephant* at Spithead, and CJA alternating between HMS *Namur* at Sheerness and his Palmer in-laws in London. Either of them would appreciate news of JA's novels and of what she and CEA were doing in London while staying with HTA. As JA had already discussed with FWA the question of using his ships' names in *MP*, it seems most likely that she would have continued to keep him advised of its progress through the press.

101. *To Cassandra Austen. From Chawton to London. Tuesday 14 June 1814.*

Description. Two leaves quarto, laid; watermark device (Heawood Nos. 2752–62) above monogram, no date; mark of wafer; p. 3 blank, p. 4 blank except for the address.

Postmark. None.

Provenance. Bequeathed by CEA to Fanny, Lady Knatchbull, in 1845; inherited by Lord Brabourne 1882; in the Banks MSS sale, Sotheby's 14 Apr. 1886; Richard Bentley II and Mrs Bentley; Hodgsons 8 July 1938; Henry G. and Alberta H. Burke; bequeathed by Alberta H. Burke to Pierpont Morgan Library, New York, 1975 (MA 2911).

Publication. Brabourne ii. 234; *Life* 303 (extracts); Chapman (1st and 2nd); Modert F-310 to F-312.

1. *any other trouble.* JA first wrote 'another trouble', then cancelled 'an-' and inserted 'any' superscript.
2. *dawdled away an hour.* 'an hour' inserted superscript.
3. *the Emperor.* Alexander I of Russia.

102. *To Cassandra Austen. From Chawton to London. Thursday 23 June 1814.*

Description. Two leaves quarto, laid; watermark L MUNN KENT 1810; mark of seal or wafer.

Postmark. None.

Provenance. Bequeathed by CEA to Fanny, Lady Knatchbull, in 1845; inherited by Lord Brabourne 1882; probably in the Puttick & Simpson sale of 26–8 June 1893; Charles Roberts; presented by his widow to Haverford College Library, Haverford, Penn., in 1902 (Charles Roberts Autograph Letters Collection, File No. 145).

Publication. Brabourne ii. 236; *Life* 304 (extracts); Chapman (1st and 2nd); Modert F-313 to F-316.

1. *drinking tea.* 'tea' inserted superscript.
2. *no Bavins.* 'Bavins for heating the oven, and making a sudden but transient fire, are purchased in the woods and different parts of the county, so low as 6s. and so high as 15s. per hundred' (Charles Vancouver, *General View of the Agriculture of Hampshire* (1813)). Mrs GA normally received all her firewood free, from the Chawton estate.
3. *Henry at Whites!* White's Club in London had arranged a magnificent ball to celebrate the end of the war—see *Family Record* 191.
4. *Miss B.* Probably Miss Burdett.
5. *still a swelling.* 'a' inserted superscript.

6. *Marquis of Granby.* George-John-Frederick Manners, heir of the Duke of Rutland, had been baptized on 4 Jan. 1814. The godparents were the Prince Regent and the Duke of York, in person, and the Dowager Duchess of Rutland as proxy for the Queen; the Archbishop of Canterbury had performed the ceremony; and fifteen cannon were fired from Belvoir Castle to announce the event, followed by other prolonged festivities—see the *Morning Chronicle* for 6 Jan. 1814. Unfortunately the baby died on 15 June 1814.

7. *Sir W. P.'s, in Yorkshire.* Sir William Pilkington; 'in' inserted superscript.

8. *as* Under. i.e. as Under Cookmaid (assistant cook).

103. *To Anna Austen. From Chawton to Steventon. ?mid-July 1814.*

Description. One leaf quarto, wove; no watermark; plain wafer, impressed by wafer-seal; endorsed [?by Anna] '1814'. This single leaf is pp. 3–4 of the letter only, which was primarily written by Mrs GA; the other leaf, pp. 1–2, was apparently not preserved.

Postmark. None.

Provenance. Descended in Anna Lefroy's family; bequeathed by her granddaughter Miss Mary Isabella Lefroy to St John's College, Oxford, 1939 (MS St John's College 279). Also **copied** by FCL into her MS Family History, with a number of errors.

Publication. Brabourne ii. 304 (probably from a copy by FCL); *Life* 354; Johnson 166; Chapman (1st and 2nd); Modert F-317 and F-318.

1. *?mid-July 1814.* For the suggested date see Deirdre Le Faye: 'Jane Austen: Some Letters Redated', in *N&Q* 232:4 (Dec. 1987), 478–81.

2. *sending your MS.* 'The story to which most of these letters of Aunt Jane's refer was never finished. It was laid aside for a season because my mother's hands were so full she lacked the leisure to continue it. Her eldest child was born in October [1815], and her second in the Sept. following [1816] and in the longer interval that followed before the birth of the third [1818] her Aunt died and with her must have died all inclination to continue her writing. With no Aunt Jane to read, to criticise and to encourage it was no wonder the MS every word of which was so full of her, remained untouched. Her sympathy which had made the real charm of the occupation was gone and the sense of the loss made it painful to write. The story was laid by for years and then one day in a fit of despondency burnt. I remember sitting on the rug and watching its destruction amused with the flames and the sparks which kept breaking out in the blackened paper. In later years when I expressed my sorrow that she had destroyed it she said she could never have borne to finish it, but incomplete as it was Jane Austen's criticisms would have made it valuable' (Fanny-Caroline Lefroy, MS Family History).

By these 'later years', however, Anna had evidently forgotten that she did make an attempt to continue with her story, for in a letter to JEAL, dated 26 Oct. 1818, she says: 'I am in the middle of a scene between Mrs Forrester & Mrs St Julian—I hope I shall do it tolerably well, because it requires to be done so—I want to get a good parcel done to read to you at Christmas but you know how little time I have for any thing of that sort—'

3. *Lord Orville.* In Fanny Burney's *Evelina.*

104. *To Anna Austen. From Chawton to Steventon. Wednesday 10–Thursday 18 August 1814.*

Description. Two leaves quarto, laid; watermark device (Heawood Nos. 2752–62) above monogram EJB[?], no date; no seal or wafer. Endorsed [?by FCL] 'Augst 10th'.

Postmark. None.

Provenance. Descended in Anna Lefroy's family; bequeathed by her granddaughter Miss Mary Isabella Lefroy to St John's College, Oxford, 1939 (MS St John's College 279). Also **copied** by FCL into her MS Family History, with several errors and some omissions.

Publication. Memoir (1st 119; 2nd 91 (extract)); Brabourne ii. 305 (probably from a copy by FCL); *Life* 354; Johnson 167; Chapman (1st and 2nd); D. J. Gilson, *TLS* (11 Sept. 1973), 1372–3, adding a postscript overlooked by Chapman; Modert F-319 to F-322.

1. *"Enthusiasm".* This title was perhaps relinquished on the discovery that Mme de Genlis had written *Les Voeux Temeraires ou L'Enthousiasme* (1799 or earlier). [RWC]

2. *Desborough.* A barony of this name was created in 1905.

3. *W. D. . . . H. D.* Digweed.

4. *Portman family.* A barony of this name was created in 1837.

5. *100 miles apart.* 'apart' inserted superscript.

6. *from one set of people.* JA first wrote 'change of people', then inserted 'from one set of' superscript, and cancelled the previous 'of'.

105. *To Cassandra Austen. From London to Chawton. Tuesday 23–Wednesday 24 August 1814.*

Description. Two leaves quarto, laid; watermark device (Heawood Nos. 2752–62) above florid initial D, no date; mark of seal or wafer. Endorsed by CEA: 'From Hans Place | Augt 1814 | For Lady K.'

Postmark. None.

Provenance. Bequeathed by CEA to Fanny, Lady Knatchbull, in 1845; inherited by Lord Brabourne 1882; probably part of Lot 1104, Sotheby's 11–14 May

1891; Alfred Morrison; Sotheby's 10 Dec. 1918; J. Pierpont Morgan 1920; Pierpont Morgan Library, New York (MA 977–38).

Publication. Brabourne ii. 240; *Life* 305 (extracts); Chapman (1st and 2nd); Modert F-323 to F-326.

1. For confirmation of the date of this letter, see Le Faye 'Jane Austen: Some Letters Redated', *N&Q* 232:4 (Dec. 1987), 478–81.

2. *in his way* from *Woolwich.* Percy Benn was a cadet at the Royal Military Academy, Woolwich.

3. *my own Coach.* See 'Love and Freindship', *MW* 105.

4. *M*ʳ *J. P.* The initials have been cancelled, perhaps by Lord Brabourne.

5. *no Lady Charlottes.* Kirby was the Northamptonshire seat of Lord Winchilsea, so the reference is to the Finch-Hattons of Eastwell. Young George F.-H. married in 1814 Lady Charlotte Graham. [RWC could not identify any other Lady Charlotte in the Finch-Hatton family, and JA's use of the plural may have been only in jest.]

6. *a delightful Place.* For a description of Hans Place, and of No. 23, see Watson, *Jane Austen in London.*

7. *Patronage.* By Maria Edgeworth (1814).

8. *his Hanwell favourite.* Miss Harriet Moore.

9. *in the mor*ⁿᵍ. Inserted superscript.

10. *the Parcel is made up.* From Henrietta Street to the Alton branch bank. The letters sent 'by favour of Mr Gray' would be enclosed therein.

11. *Nunna Hat's love to George.* JA herself, no doubt, but the etymology is unknown. [RWC] *George* here is FWA's third son, b. 1812.

11. *M*ʳˢ *C.* Probably Mrs Craven, as this is Steventon news; 'farther & farther from Poverty' may be ironical. [RWC]

12. *Ben . . . Edward.* Lefroy; JEAL.

106. *To Martha Lloyd. From London to Bath. Friday 2 September 1814.*

Description. Two leaves quarto; some words lost beneath the seal; irregular portion torn off bottom of second leaf, losing text in last four lines on p. 3 and in last two lines on p. 4 together with signature. Endorsed [? by JA or Martha Lloyd] 'Hans place Sep. 2. | 1814'.

Postmark. 3 SE .814

Provenance. Descended in FWA's family to his great-granddaughter Mrs Rosemary Mowll, and thence to her daughter Mrs Peter Wilson, of Woodstock, Vermont.

Publication. Chapman (2nd); Modert F-327 to F-330.

1. *much more.* JA wrote 'much before', then cancelled 'before' and inserted 'more' superscript.

2. *I am extremely pleased.* 'am' inserted superscript.

3. *an American war*. This reference is puzzling: America had already declared war on Britain on 17 June 1812, and this was ended by the Treaty of Ghent on 24 Dec. 1814; the Battle of New Orleans occurred on 8 June 1815, as the news of the Treaty had still not reached the combatants. Perhaps at the time of this letter there had been a temporary lull in the fighting, and public opinion considered that hostilities were likely to recommence rather than totally cease.

4. *I am in some hope*. 'in' inserted superscript.

5. *Egerton's account*. For the first edition of *MP*.

6. *melancholy disproportion*. Mr Hill was considerably older than his wife, and more of an age to be grandfather to his children.

7. *Gratitude as an Author*. Had Capt. Deans Dundas provided JA with naval information?

8. *with a Girl*. CJA's fourth daughter, Elizabeth—born 31 Aug. and died 20 Sept. 1814.

107. *To Anna Austen. From Chawton to Steventon. Friday 9–Sunday 18 September 1814.*

Description. Two leaves quarto, wove; watermark W TURNER & SON, no date; plain wafer impressed by wafer-seal. Endorsed [?by FCL] 'Sept. 9'.

Postmark. None.

Provenance. Descended in Anna Lefroy's family to her granddaughter Miss Mary Isabella Lefroy, and bequeathed by her to St John's College, Oxford, 1939 (MS St John's College 279). Also **copied** by FCL into her MS Family History.

Publication. *Memoir* (1st 120; 2nd 91 (extract)); Brabourne ii. 310 (probably from a copy by FCL); *Life* 357 (extracts); Johnson 170; Chapman (1st and 2nd); Modert F-331 to F-334.

1. *would not be likely*. 'not' inserted superscript.

2. *very natural*. 'natural' inserted superscript above 'good' cancelled.

3. *Newton Priors*. Newton Valence and Priors Dean, both in the Chawton neighbourhood, may have suggested NP. [RWC]

4. *this sad Event*. The death of CJA's wife Fanny Palmer, on Tuesday, 6 Sept., following her latest childbirth.

5. *M^r D*. Digweed.

108. *To Anna Austen. From Chawton to Steventon. Wednesday 28 September 1814.*

Description. Two leaves quarto, wove; watermark C WILMOTT 1812; mark of plain wafer. Endorsed [?by FCL] 'Sept. 28'.

Postmark. None.

Provenance. Descended in Anna Lefroy's family to her granddaughter Miss Mary Isabella Lefroy, who bequeathed it to St John's College, Oxford, 1939 (MS St John's College 279). Also **copied** by FCL into her MS Family History.

Publication. Memoir (1st, 111, 120; 2nd, 85, 91 (extracts)); Brabourne ii. 315 (probably from a copy by FCL); *Life* 359; Johnson 174; Chapman (1st and 2nd); Modert F-335 to F-338.

1. *Waverley.* Published 7 July 1814. JA had no more doubt as to who was the author than Miss Mitford had. [RAAL]
2. *not to be pleased.* 'be' inserted superscript.
3. *Alicia de Lacy. Alicia de Lacy, an Historical Romance* (1814) by Mrs Jane West (1758–1852).
4. *in an old great Coat.* This phrase inserted superscript.
5. *place as yours.* JA wrote 'place as yourself', and then cancelled '-elf'.
6. *Sherlock's Sermons.* Thomas Sherlock (1678–1761), *Several Discourses preached at the Temple Church* (1754–97; new edn., Oxford, 1812).

109. *To Fanny Knight. From Chawton to Goodnestone. Friday 18– Sunday 20 November 1814.*

Description. Two leaves quarto, laid; watermark J BUDGEN 1813; black wax seal impressed with wafer-seal. Endorsed [?by FCK] 'No. 6. Novr. 1814'.
Postmarks. D 21 NO . . . 181. (part unprinted)   ALTON 50
Provenance. Inherited by Lord Brabourne 1882 and remains in possession of the Brabourne family; deposited by them in Kent Archives Office, Maidstone, 1962 (U951 C112/1).
Publication. Brabourne ii. 277; *Life* 308, 342 (extracts); R. W. Chapman (ed.), *Five Letters from Jane Austen to her Niece Fanny Knight* (Oxford, 1924); Johnson 144; Chapman (1st and 2nd); Modert F-339 to F-342.

1. *Mr J. P.* John Plumptre.
2. *as to make.* 'to' inserted superscript.
3. *meet in one person.* JA wrote 'meet with', then cancelled 'with' and inserted 'in' superscript.
4. *do not know how I could have accounted for the parcel.* 'know' inserted superscript; 'for' inserted superscript above 'by' cancelled.
5. *Host & Hostess.* EAK had lent the Great House to FWA, and was now his brother's guest in his own house. [RWC]
6. *Aunt Louisa.* Bridges.
7. *Fanny C.* Cage.

110. *To Anna Lefroy. From Chawton to Hendon. Tuesday 22 November 1814.*

Description. One leaf quarto, laid; watermark L MUNN, no date; seal or wafer cut out, leaving a hole in the text. Verso badly blotched with ink or dirt, also bearing some scribbles by Anna: 'Mrs B. Lefroy | Mrs | Mrs | Mrs Lefroy'

Postmarks. 8 o'Clock 24 NO 1814 M.^{g} 10 o'Clock NO^v 24 1814 FN^n Third postmark illegible.

Provenance. Descended in Anna Lefroy's family and eventually bequeathed by her granddaughter Miss Louisa-Langlois Lefroy to the Bodleian Library in 1954 (MS Eng. Lett. d. 147, fo. 2). Also **copied** by FCL into her MS Family History.

Publication. Brabourne ii. 320 (probably from a copy by FCL); Chapman (1st and 2nd); Modert F-343 to F-344.

1. *Brother & Cousins.* William AK, plus any of their Bridges and Deedes cousins who were also at the College.

2. *the Wen.* This name for London is associated with Cobbett, who, however, does not seem to have it earlier than 1821. Dean Tucker, 1783, writing of London, has: 'no better than a wen or excrescence upon the body politic'. [RWC]

111. *To Anna Lefroy. From Chawton to Hendon. ?Thursday 24 November 1814.*

Description. Scrap cut from quarto leaf, approximately 7¼″ × 2½″, giving eight lines of text each side.

Postmark. None.

Provenance. Probably given by Anna Lefroy to JEAL in the late 1860s for use in his *Memoir.* In Mar. 1926 RAAL told RWC that it was 'in a copy of N.A. 1833', but this volume cannot now be found in the AL archive. RWC saw and measured the scrap, and the layout of the lines is given in his working notes for his first edition.

Publication. Memoir (1st 173; 2nd 131); Chapman (1st and 2nd).

1. For suggested date, see Le Faye: 'Jane Austen: Some Letters Redated', *N&Q* 232:4 (Dec. 1987), 478–81. Further research, however, has shown that the fragment beginning *We have got 'Rosanne' in our Society* must date to the spring of 1815—see letter **118** below. It is still possible that these two fragments, letters **111** and **118**, belong together, in which case **111** should also be dated spring 1815.

2. *Mrs Creed's opinion.* See 'Opinions of MP', *MW* 435.

112. *To Anna Lefroy. From London to Hendon. Tuesday 29 November 1814.*

Description. Two leaves octavo, laid; watermark fragment of device, no date; seal.

Postmark. B [NO]V 29 .814

Provenance. Remained in Anna Lefroy's possession, and post-1869 was divided into at least **5 sections**:

112 (S.1). Pp. 1 and 2 of the letter, one leaf octavo; p. 1 begins *I am very much obliged* and ends *one remove from Br & Sr.*; p. 2 begins *We all came away* and ends *hugs Mr Younge delightfully.*

112 (S.2). Scrap, one sentence only, top of p. 3: *I am going this morning to see the little girls in Keppel Street.*

112 (S.3). Scrap, middle of p. 3, begins *Cassy was excessively* and ends *Benjamin was born in?"* This section carried the seal, and also some repetitive scribbles, presumably by Anna testing her quill for a reply: 'Mrs | . .ss J. Austen | . .ss J. Austen | Hans Place | Sloane Street | Miss J. Austen'.

112 (S.4). Scrap, lower part of p. 3, begins *If your Uncle were at home* and ends *23 Hans Place.* This section has the address on the verso.

112 (S.5). Tiny scrap 2″ × 1″, cut presumably from the bottom corner of p. 3, giving only the date, *Tuesday Nov: 29.* '1814' has been added below, but this last is not in JA's hand. This section has a fragment of the watermark and also bears the postmark on the verso.

Section 112 (S.1) passed to the Austen-Leigh family; it was at one time in an envelope endorsed 'Part of a letter of Jane Austen's addressed to her niece Mrs B. Lefroy who gave it in 1869 to her niece Mary A. Austen-Leigh'; the letter itself was endorsed at the top in pencil 'From Hans Place | Nov. 29, 1814'. In 1926 RAAL lent this section to RWC, who copied it to its exact size and also noted that there was an undated watermark on the leaf. In later years it seems to have become one of the several fragmentary letters which were 'momentarily mislaid' by RAAL, and has not so far reappeared.

Section 112 (S.2) was possibly removed and destroyed by some Lefroy descendant towards the end of the nineteenth century.

Section 112 (S.3) descended to Anna's granddaughter Miss Mary Isabella Lefroy, and was seen by RWC and collated by him with **Section 112 (S.1)**; thereafter this section too seems to have disappeared. FCL **copied** pp. 2–3 into her MS Family History (with some omissions), but made no mention of p. 1.

Sections 112 (S.4) and **112 (S.5)** were possibly in the Sotheby's sale of 2 July 1917; Lady Charnwood by 1918; The Charnwood Trust, deposited at the British Library, 1965 (Loan In No. 60, Vol. 2, 43(4) and 43(5)).

Publication. Memoir (1st 116; 2nd 88 (extract)); Brabourne ii. 321; *Life* 361; Chapman (1st and 2nd); Modert F-346 **Sections (S.4) and (S.5)** only. **Section (S.2)** was published by Brabourne as: *I am going this morning to see the girls in Keppel Street.* FCL in her MS Family History copied it as: *I am going this morning to see the little girls in——Street.* It may therefore have been either FCL or Mary Isabella Lefroy who removed this sentence before dividing the letter still further.

1. *Susan & Maria.* Middleton.
2. *Your Uncle & Edwd.* EAK and his eldest son, who had brought JA up from Chawton.
3. *Isabella.* David Garrick (1717–79), *Isabella, or the Fatal Marriage* (1776; a tragedy adapted from Southerne's *Fatal Marriage*).
4. *your Uncle.* HTA.

113. To Anna Lefroy. From London to Hendon. Wednesday 30 November 1814.

Description. One leaf octavo, laid; watermark fragmentary device (Heawood Nos. 2752–62), no date; no seal or wafer. Second leaf of letter (pp. 3–4) lost or destroyed during the nineteenth century.

Postmark. None.

Provenance. Descended in Anna Lefroy's family to her granddaughter Miss Mary Isabella Lefroy, who bequeathed it to St John's College, Oxford, 1939 (MS St John's College 279). Also **copied** by FCL into her MS Family History.

Publication. Memoir (1st 121; 2nd 92 (extract)); Brabourne ii. 322 (the concluding paragraph he prints does not belong here but to letter **118**); *Life* 361; Johnson 178; Chapman (1st and 2nd); Modert F-352 and F-353.

1. *Hans Place, Wednesday.* For the dating of this letter, see Le Faye, 'Jane Austen: Some Letters Redated', in *N&Q* 232:4 (Dec. 1987), 478–81.
2. *Aunt or other.* 'other' inserted superscript.
3. *St Julian's early.* FCL in her copy of this letter in her MS Family History provides a conclusion to this sentence, which may or may not be correct.

114. To Fanny Knight. From London to Godmersham. Wednesday 30 November 1814.

Description. Two leaves quarto, laid; watermark device (Heawood Nos. 2752–62) above monogram JB [?], no date; black wax seal with imprint of wafer-seal. Endorsed by FCK: 'No. 7. Novr. 1814'.

Postmark. B DE 2. .814

Provenance. Descended in the Brabourne family, and placed by them on deposit in Kent Archives Office, Maidstone, 1962 (U. 951/C. 112/2).

Publication. Brabourne ii. 284; *Life* 308, 345 (extracts); facsimile in Chapman (ed.), *Five Letters from Jane Austen to Fanny Knight;* Johnson 149; Chapman (1st and 2nd); Modert F-348 to F-351.

1. *give them* both *Pleasure.* 'When first my father and mother married, they lived at Hendon with his next elder brother Edward who at that time had a house there. This will explain *why* Aunt Jane was glad she had the power of asking her friends to it and also that the "both" to whom it was "so proper that her visit should give pleasure" referred to the two gentlemen' (Bellas Notes). [RWC]

2. *think you* very *capable.* 'you' inserted superscript.

3. *I shall hope.* 'shall' inserted superscript.

4. *a 2^d Edition.* Of *MP*; the second edition was published in 1816 by Murray. [RWC]

5. *well as anybody.* 'as' inserted superscript.

115. *To Caroline Austen. From Chawton to Steventon. ?Tuesday 6 December 1814.*

Description. One leaf octavo, folded to make 2 leaves 3½″ × 4½″, laid; no watermark, no seal or wafer; part torn away from second leaf, not affecting text.

Postmark. None.

Provenance. Descended in the junior line of the Austen-Leigh family to Joan AL (Mrs Denis Mason-Hurley).

Publication. *Life* 363; Johnson 180; Chapman (1st and 2nd); Modert F-382 and F-383.

1. For the suggested redating of this letter, see Le Faye, 'Jane Austen: More Letters Redated', in *N&Q* 236:3 (Sept. 1991), 306–8.

116. *To ?Anna Lefroy. From ?Chawton to ?Hendon. ?late December 1814.*

Description. Scrap cut from quarto leaf, laid; no watermark; no seal or wafer; mounted and bound into a copy of vol. I of the Winchester Edition of the novels (reissue 1911–12). Approximately six lines of text each side.

Postmark. None.

Provenance. M. V. Whitmore, Esq.; Sotheby's 9–10 Nov. 1964; A. G. Thomas; Sotheby's 29 Oct. 1968; J. H. Salby; Mabel Hicking; Sotheby's New York, 17–18 June 1992; Heritage Book Shop Inc., Los Angeles; Mrs Lucy Magruder, La Canada, California, 1992.

Publication. Sotheby's catalogue entries (recto only); Modert p. 66.

In 1964 the scrap was described in the sale catalogue as being 'lightly mounted on part of an album leaf'; in 1968 the catalogue description added that the mounting partially obscured the text on the verso and that a detached signature of JA was mounted below; between 1968 and 1992 the mount was changed and the 'detached signature' now no longer accompanies the scrap—it may perhaps have been only a facsimile.

It seems probable that this scrap comes from a letter to Anna Lefroy. JA was at Grafton House by herself in 1811, and with Fanny Knight in 1813, so Fanny would not need to write any description of the shop to her aunt. On the other hand, Anna had never been to London before her marriage in the autumn of 1814, and could well have sent JA an amusing pen-picture of her first shopping expedition into central London.

117. *To Anna Lefroy. From ?Chawton to Hendon. ?between February–July 1815.*

Description. Scrap cut from quarto leaf, laid; no watermark; no seal or wafer. Four lines of text on recto (p. 4) with some shaved words of fifth line; three lines on verso (p. 3) with some shaved words of fourth line.

Postmark. None.

Provenance. Descended to Anna Lefroy's daughter FCL, who gave the scrap to Euphemia ('Effie') Lefroy, the wife of FCL's cousin Clement George Lefroy (1850–1917), as the latter was the son of the 'little Charles Lefroy' (1810–61) mentioned in the text, on 5 Feb. 1877. Mrs Effie Lefroy immediately passed it on, with a covering letter, to Frederick Locker-Lampson (1821–95) for the 'Great Album' in his Rowfant Library; E. Dwight Church, 1905; Dodd, Mead & Co.; Paul M. Warburg, c.1908; bequeathed to his son-in-law and daughter, Mr and Mrs Samuel B. Grimson; deposited by Mr Grimson in The Houghton Library, Harvard University, Cambridge, Mass., 25 June 1953; presented to Harvard by his widow, 1960 (The Locker-Lampson-Warburg-Grimson Album, bMS Eng 870 (83B)).

FCL also **copied** both sides of the scrap (with some inaccuracies and omissions) on to an octavo leaf, wove, watermark indecipherable, adding at bottom: 'Copy of the Scrap of Aunt Jane's Writing I sent Mrs Clement Lefroy Feb 5/77'. This copy (**117(C)**) was part of Lot 268 Sotheby's 13 Dec. 1977; Pierpont Morgan Library, New York (MA 3611).

Publication. Recto in *A Catalogue of the Printed Books, Manuscripts, Autograph Letters, Drawings and Pictures, collected by Frederick Locker-Lampson* (London, 1886); recto and verso given by Modert, in *St Louis Post-Dispatch* (18 Dec. 1983), p. 4E; Modert F-354 and pp. 48–9.

JA and CEA stayed at Ashe Rectory in Jan. 1815 (*Family Record* 199) and may have suffered from little Charles Lefroy's undisciplined behaviour during this visit. As the text mentions 'uncles' in the plural, the child must have been staying in Hendon while Ben and Anna were living there with C. Edward Lefroy—i.e. before the end of July 1815.

118. *To Anna Lefroy. From Chawton to Hendon. ?late February–early March 1815.*

Description. Two interlocking scraps, cut from a quarto leaf, parts of pp. 3–4 of a letter; laid; no watermark; no seal or wafer.

Postmark. None.

Provenance. Probably given by Anna Lefroy to JEAL in the 1860s for use in his *Memoir,* as the subdivision of the text seems to have occurred thereafter. **Section S.1** begins at approximately the middle of p. 3: *We have got Rosanne* and ends on a shaved and incomplete line *Miss Ormesdens, introduced just at last? Very flat and un:* The verso of this section contained the address panel and a postscript.

Section S.2 has approximately seven lines text, beginning with the shaved line *Miss Ormesdens, . . .* [next line] *:natural.—Mlle. Cossart is rather my passion.—*and ends at the bottom of p. 3 . . . [*kind*] *wishes.* Part of the last line is missing where the end of p. 4 has been cut away.

The verso of **S.2**, the last quarter of p. 4, has approximately eight lines text, beginning *which is quite against my skin & conscience.* and ending *not to be in print.* The complimentary close and signature have been cut away; there are traces of the postscript on the address panel at the top right-hand corner of the scrap.

S.1 seems to have been lost post-*Memoir,* as FCL **copied** only the verso of **S.2** into her MS Family History, referring to that as a 'scrap'; **S.2** itself descended to Anna's granddaughter Miss Mary Isabella Lefroy; given by her to RWC 1931; Mrs RWC; David Gilson, Oxford, 1979.

Publication. Memoir (1st 173; 2nd 131) begins *We have got Rosanne* and ends *rather my passion;* Memoir (1st 116; 2nd 89) begins (incorrectly) *So, Miss B. is actually married* and ends *not to be in print.;* Brabourne ii. 323 (misplaced) begins *We shall see nothing* and ends *not to be in print.;* Life 362 (misplaced) begins (incorrectly) *Mrs Heathcote writes me word* and ends *not to be in print.;* Chapman (1st and 2nd); Modert F-345 (**S.2** only, recto and verso).

1. *Rosanne.* Laetitia Matilda Hawkins (1760–1835), *Rosanne; or a Father's Labour Lost* (1814). The avowed purpose of *Rosanne* was 'to point out— though better illustrated by her Ladyship's example—the inestimable advantages attendant on the practice of pure Christianity'. (Her Ladyship, to whom the book was dedicated, was the Countess of Waldegrave.) [RWC]

2. *I cannot flourish in this east wind.* This phrase is given only by FCL in her MS Family History; it was presumably the last line of the first doubledown on p. 4, just above the address panel.

3. *lye-in of a Daughter.* A prediction falsified by the event, as Alfred Hill was born 14 Mar. 1815. [RWC]

4. *Miss Blachford* is *married.* Winifred, the eldest Miss Blachford, was married to Revd J. Mansfield, rector of Rowner, Hants, on 18 Feb. 1815. The marriage may not have been mentioned in the newspapers, but was recorded by the *GM* for 1815, I. 274.

119. *To Caroline Austen. From Chawton to Steventon. ?Thursday 2 March 1815.*

Description. Scrap cut from quarto leaf, laid; approximately four lines of text; laid down on the mount of a copy of the engraved portrait of JA used in the *Memoir*, framed and glazed, overall size 16″ × 14″.

Postmark. None.

Provenance. The mounting of the scrap may have been done by Caroline Austen herself, probably in later years (between 1860–80) when she lived at Frog Firle, Sussex, with her two bachelor nephews Charles and Spencer Austen-Leigh. The picture remained at Frog Firle, which later became the home of Edward Chenevix Austen-Leigh (1865–1949). On 6 Aug. 1936 Miss Emma AL (1868–1940), sister of both ECAL and RAAL, wrote from Frog Firle to RWC: 'I am staying here & have just noticed these words in Jane Austen's handwriting pasted at the foot of an engraving of her—. . . I am away from my books for a time & wonder if I may ask if they occur in your book of Jane Austen's Letters—& if so where.' The picture descended to RAAL (1872–1961) and so to his widow Mrs Margaret AL, who died 26 Aug. 1986; it then left the AL archive and appeared at Sotheby's 23–4 July 1987; Mrs Constance Camner, Hopewell, NJ.

Publication. Chapman (2nd); Modert F-402.

For the suggested date, see Le Faye, 'Jane Austen: More Letters Redated', *N&Q* 236:3 (Sept. 1991), 306–8.

120. *To Anna Lefroy. From Chawton to Wyards. Friday 29 September 1815.*

Description. One leaf quarto, laid; watermark J JELLYMAN, no date; no mark of seal or wafer. Second leaf missing, but no text lost.

Postmark. None.

Provenance. Descended in Anna Lefroy's family and eventually bequeathed by her granddaughter Miss Louisa-Langlois Lefroy to the Bodleian Library in 1954 (MS Engl. Lett. d. 147, fo. 3). Also **copied** by FCL into her MS Family History.

Publication. Brabourne ii. 324; facsimile (but showing text as if on one page only) Hill, facing 230; Chapman (1st and 2nd); Modert F-355 and F-356.

1. *Wyards.* Anna and Ben had now moved from Hendon to a house called Wyards, just outside Chawton. 'It was a large farmhouse belonging to an Alton shopkeeper, one end of which was occupied by a sort of bailiff or foreman with his family, and they rented the remainder' (FCL, MS Family History).

2. *she has preferred.* 'has' inserted superscript.

121. *To Cassandra Austen. From London to Chawton. Tuesday 17– Wednesday 18 October 1815.*

Description. Two leaves quarto, laid; watermark J JELLYMAN 1813; seal torn out, with loss of one or two words.

Postmarks. C .OC 18. .815   Two Py P[ost] Unpaid Sloane St   7 o'Clock 18.OC 1815 N

Provenance. Bequeathed by CEA to CJA in 1845; descended to CJA's granddaughters and sold by them in 1920s; Frederick R. Lovering; Sotheby's 3 May 1948; Mrs Henry Burke; bequeathed by her to Pierpont Morgan Library, New York, 1975 (MA 2911).

Publication. *Life* 309 (extracts); Chapman (1st and 2nd, from a copy made by RAAL in 1909); Modert F-357 to F-360.

1. *he is a Rogue.* See the autobiography *Samuel Bagster of London 1772–1851* (1972), 168–9.

2. *M^r or Miss P.* Probably Papillon; HTA's second wife was a Jackson, and her mother was a Papillon. [RWC]

3. *comical consequence.* It is believed that Mr S. had at some time proposed marriage [RWC].
   This may be a family tradition passed on from RAAL to RWC, as no information at all on the subject can be found in the present AL archive.

4. *Cleveland Row.* Mr Gordon of Cleveland Row was connected with HTA's friends the Misses Moore of Hanwell.

5. *Henry's illness.* HTA grew worse, and on Sunday, 22 Oct., JA wrote by express post to CEA, James, and EAK. EAK set off immediately for London on 23 Oct.; James collected CEA from Chawton and they arrived in London on 25 Oct. See CMCA's *Reminiscences*, 46–7, and FCK's diary for 1815.

6. *& he is certainly.* 'he' inserted superscript.

7. *Henry is an excellent Patient.* 'Henry' superscript above 'He' cancelled.

8. *It will be mostly dirty Cloathes.* 'be' inserted superscript.

9. *in his Cause.* EAK's impending lawsuit with the Hintons.

122(A)(D). *To John Murray. From London, Hans Place, to London, Albemarle Street. ?Friday 20/Saturday 21 October 1815.*

Description. One leaf quarto, laid; no watermark, seal, or wafer. JA's autograph, as also the endorsement.

Postmark. None.

Provenance. Bequeathed by CEA to CJA in 1845; descended to CJA's granddaughters and sold by them 1925; Bodleian Library, Oxford (MS Autogr. d. 11, fo. 224).

Publication. *Life* 310; Modert F-361 and F-362.

1. *so small an Edit:*. The first edition of *S&S* was 750 or 1,000 copies; that of *MP* probably 1,250; and of *E* 2,000.

This draft was composed in Oct.; the fair copy, or some similar text, was probably sent to John Murray early in Nov. 1815 to confirm the terms of publication of *Emma*. It may have been sent even as late as Monday, 20 Nov., if it was the 'note' referred to by JA in letter **126.**

123. *To Caroline Austen. From London to Chawton. Monday 30 October 1815.*

Description. Two leaves octavo, wove; no watermark or seal; most of second leaf missing, hence no address shown. Endorsed twice '1815', not in JA's hand.

Postmark. None.

Provenance. Descended in junior line of AL family to Joan AL (Mrs Denis Mason Hurley).

Publication. *Life* 365; Chapman (1st and 2nd); Modert F-363 and F-364.

1. *you should be at Chawton.* CMCA and her mother Mrs JA were staying at the Cottage—see CMCA's *Reminiscences* 46–7.

2. *the Hermit.* Probably Tommaso Giordani's very popular setting of Beattie's poem. [RWC]

3. *become an Aunt.* Anna Lefroy's first child, Anna-Jemima, was born at Wyards on 20 Oct. 1815.

124(D). *To John Murray. From London, Hans Place, to London, Albemarle Street. Friday 3 November 1815.*

Description. One leaf quarto, wove; watermark 1815; written in pencil; outside fold faded and dirty.

Postmark. None.

Provenance. Bequeathed by CEA to CJA in 1845; descended to CJA's granddaughters and sold by them 1925; Bodleian Library, Oxford (MS Autogr. d. 11, fo. 225).

Publication. Chapman (1st); Modert F-366.

1. *in the Even^g or any in the Morn^g.* This phrase inserted superscript.
2. *a copy of Waterloo.* Scott's *The Field of Waterloo* (1815).

124. *To John Murray. From London, Hans Place, to London, Albemarle Street. Friday 3 November 1815.*

Description. One leaf quarto, wove; watermark W TURNER & SON, no date; no seal or wafer; no address. Endorsed, no doubt by Murray's clerk, '1815 Nov. | Austen, Miss J.'. In the lower left-hand corner of the recto there are also some faint notes in ink (?perhaps a scribbled *aide-mémoire* by Murray concerning some other business of the day): 'as a Librarian | Castle Street | opposite ye Mews' and 'Mr Ward | Nerots Hotel | Clifford Street'.

Postmark. None.

Provenance. Remained in Murray's archives until 1870, when it was given by John Murray III (1808–92) to the historian 5th Earl Stanhope (1805–75) — a covering note to this effect is preserved with the letter; descended in the Stanhope family to the 7th and last Earl (1880–1967); Administrative Trustees of the Chevening Estate, Sevenoaks, Kent, and on deposit at the Kent Archives Office, Maidstone (Chevening Collection, U.1590/C.474/Autograph Letters Miscellaneous, 1).

Publication. Chapman (2nd—corrected from **124 (D)** given in first edition, after seeing the MS at Chevening at some time post-1932); Modert F-365.

125(D). *To James Stanier Clarke. From London, Hans Place, to London, Carlton House. Wednesday 15 November 1815.*

Description. Scrap, irregularly trimmed, wove; no watermark.

Postmark. None.

Provenance. Bequeathed by CEA to CJA in 1845; descended to CJA's granddaughters and sold by them 1925; J. Pierpont Morgan; Pierpont Morgan Library, New York (MA 1034-9).

Publication. *Memoir* (1st 149; 2nd 112); *Life* 312; R. W. Chapman (ed.), *Plan of a Novel* (Oxford, 1926), 25; Chapman (1st and 2nd); Modert F-367.

125(A). *To Jane Austen. From London, Carlton House, to London, Hans Place. Thursday 16 November 1815.*

Description. Two leaves quarto, wove; watermark W TURNER & SON, no date; p. 4 blank; accompanied by remains of wrapper, part of folded quarto sheet.

Postmarks. Two Py Post Unpaid Jermyn St   10 o'Clock 16.NO 1815 F.N^n.

Provenance. Bequeathed by CEA to CJA in 1845; descended to CJA's granddaughters and sold by them 1925; J. Pierpont Morgan; Pierpont Morgan Library, New York (MA 1034–10 and –11).

Publication. *Life* 312; R. W. Chapman (ed.), *Plan of a Novel* (Oxford, 1926), 26; Chapman (1st and 2nd).

1. *Beatties Minstrel.* James Beattie (1735–1803) *The Minstrel; or, the Progress of Genius* (1771–4), Book I, lines 140–2.

2. *Tableau de Famille.* This is *Leben eines armes Landpredigers*, by August Heinrich Julius Lafontaine, 1801, of which a French translation by Mme de Montholieu, *Nouveaux Tableaux de Famille, ou la vie d'un pauvre ministre de village allemand et ses enfants*, was reprinted in London, 1803. *Tableaux de Famille* is the first title of the same translator's version of *Karl Engelmanns Tagebuch*, by the same author, 1800, but Mr Clarke clearly intended the *Nouveaux Tableaux*. [RWC]

126. *To John Murray. From London, Hans Place, to London, Albemarle Street. Thursday 23 November 1815.*

Description. Two leaves octavo, laid; watermark fragmentary device (Heawood Nos. 2752–62), 1813; plain wafer impressed by wafer-seal. Endorsed, no doubt by Murray's clerk: '1815 Nov. 23 | Austen Miss'.

Postmark. None.

Provenance. John Murray archive, Albemarle Street, London.

Publication. *Memoir* (2nd 122, from a copy provided to JEAL by John Murray III); *Life* 314; Chapman (1st and 2nd—from the JM III copy, as the original MS was then mislaid); Modert F-368 and F-369.

1. *delays of the Printers.* Roworth, who printed vols. i–ii of *Emma.* The paper has a watermark dated 1815. [RWC]

2. *Scott's account of Paris.* Walter Scott, *Paul's Letters to his Kinsfolk* (Murray, 1815).

127. *To Cassandra Austen. From London to Chawton. Friday 24 November 1815.*

Description. Two leaves quarto, laid; watermark device (Heawood Nos. 2752–62), 1813; red wax seal.

Postmark. None.

Provenance. Bequeathed by CEA to Fanny, Lady Knatchbull, in 1845; inherited by Lord Brabourne 1882; probably in the Puttick & Simpson sale of 26–8 June 1893; Alfred Morrison; Sotheby's 10 Dec. 1918; J. Pierpont Morgan 1920; Pierpont Morgan Library, New York (MA 977–39).

Publication. Brabourne ii. 249; *Life* 315 (extracts); Chapman (1st and 2nd); Modert F-370 to F-373.

1. *Miss Williams.* Helen Maria Williams (1762–1827), *A Narrative of the Events which have lately taken place in France* (1815).
2. *We shall live upon Pheasants.* 'live' inserted superscript above 'leave' cancelled.
3. *little Herbert.* FWA's sixth child and fourth son, born 8 Nov. 1815 at Chawton Great House.
4. *every sort of Wickedness.* Mr Haden must have been quoting or paraphrasing *Merchant of Venice*, v. i:

> The man that hath no music in himself,
> Nor is not moved with concord of sweet sounds,
> Is fit for treasons, stratagems, and spoils,
> The motions of his spirit are dull as night,
> And his affections dark as Erebus.
> Let no such man be trusted.

128. *To Cassandra Austen. From London to Chawton. Sunday 26 November 1815.*

Description. Two leaves quarto, laid; watermark device (Heawood Nos. 2752–62), 1813; mark of wafer.

Postmark. None.

Provenance. Bequeathed by CEA to Fanny, Lady Knatchbull, in 1845; inherited by Lord Brabourne 1882; Puttick & Simpson 26–8 June 1893; Bernard Buchanan McGeorge; Sotheby's 1 July 1924; H. V. Marrot; Owen D. Young; Henry W. & Albert A. Berg 1941; New York Public Library, New York (The Berg Collection).

Publication. Brabourne ii. 253; *Life* 316 (extracts); Johnson 115; Chapman (1st and 2nd—collation of text provided by Sotheby's June 1924); Modert F-374 to F-377.

1. *any other good.* 'other' inserted superscript.
2. *Poor little F.* CJA's Fanny.
3. *Aunt Har^t:* Harriet Palmer, CJA's sister-in-law and (later) second wife; CJA's Cassy-Esten was then at the Cottage.
4. *B. Chapel.* Belgrave.
5. *plenty of Mortar.* No plausible explanation of this has been suggested [RWC].
6. *to Oxford for a few days.* 'for' inserted superscript.
7. *before* you *take my place.* 'take' inserted superscript above 'took' cancelled.
8. *little girl at Wyards.* Probably a child of Mr Marshal, the bailiff/foreman who also lived at Wyards—see letter **120,** note 1.
9. *Md^e Duval. Evelina,* i., letter 21.

129. *To Cassandra Austen. From London to Chawton. Saturday 2 December 1815.*

Description. Two leaves quarto, laid; watermark JOHN HALL 1814; blue wafer; last page blank except for address. Endorsed [?by CEA]: 'Decr 2 | 1815' and also with a pencilled list of trees: '2 Oaks | 8 Chestnuts | 3 Sycamores | 2 Limes | 1 Elm'.

Postmark. B DE 2. .815

Provenance. Bequeathed by CEA to Fanny, Lady Knatchbull, in 1845; inherited by Lord Brabourne 1882; probably in the Puttick & Simpson sale of 26–8 June 1893; Alfred Morrison; Sotheby's 10 Dec. 1918; J. Pierpont Morgan 1920; Pierpont Morgan Library, New York (MA 977–40).

Publication. Brabourne ii. 258; *Life* 317 (extracts); Johnson 119; Chapman (1st and 2nd); Modert F-378 to F-381.

1. *if he had known.* 'he' inserted superscript above 'it' cancelled.
2. *Mr T.* Tilson.
3. *absenting himself.* HTA's impending bankruptcy (the Alton branch of Austen, Gray & Vincent was on the verge of collapse) might make a temporary absence from the head office prudent.
4. *from right to left.* 'from' inserted superscript.
5. *strengthening Plaister.* 'Plaister' is an obsolete spelling for 'plaster'; HTA was probably trying to wear external medication that would provide local warmth—e.g. a Burgundy pitch plaster, which was 'warmed and spread upon linen or leather, and applied over the chest in cases of catarrh, difficult breathing and hooping-cough; over the loins in debility or lumbago; and over any part that it is desirable to excite a mild degree of inflammation in'.
6. *save you 2d.* JA probably finished her letter hurriedly so that HTA could take it with him to Henrietta Street to start on its journey to Chawton from there, thus saving CEA the extra 2*d.* for the local post from Hans Place to central London.
7. *give the P.R. a Binding.* This was settled—no doubt on Mr Murray's advice—in favour of a binding; see letters **138(A)** and **139**. The other presentation copies were sent 'unbound', that is, in publishers' boards. [RWC]

130. *To John Murray. From London, Hans Place, to London, Albemarle Street. Monday 11 December 1815.*

Description. One leaf quarto, laid; watermark fragmentary device (Heawood Nos. 2752–62) above monogram PJC[?], no date; second leaf missing; no sign of any wafer or seal. Endorsed, no doubt by Murray's clerk: '1815 Dec. 12 | Austen Miss'; and in another hand, in pencil: 'The Novelist'.

Postmark. None.

Provenance. John Murray archive, Albemarle Street, London.

Publication. Memoir (2nd 122, from a copy provided to JEAL by John Murray III); *Life* 318; Chapman (1st and 2nd); Modert F-386 and F-387.

1. *subjoin a list.* JA probably wrote this on the second leaf of her paper, which was therefore torn off for the despatch clerk's work.

2. *all unbound.* Collectors will note that presentation copies of *Emma* with 'From the Authoress' in a clerkly hand need not be suspected on that account. [RWC]

131(C). *To John Murray. From London, Hans Place, to London, Albemarle Street. Monday 11 December 1815.*

Description. Unknown; original MS untraced.

Provenance. Remained in the Murray archive till at least 1870, as John Murray III was able to send a copy to JEAL for use in the *Memoir*, but apparently lost between then and 1932.

Publication. Memoir (2nd 124, from a copy provided by John Murray III); *Life* 319; Chapman (1st and 2nd, from the *Memoir*).

132(D). *To James Stanier Clarke. From London, Hans Place, to London, Carlton House. Monday 11 December 1815.*

Description. One leaf quarto, laid; watermark JOHN HALL, no date; no seal or wafer.

Postmark. None.

Provenance. Bequeathed by CEA to CJA in 1845; descended to CJA's granddaughters and sold by them in 1920s; Frederick R. Lovering; Sotheby's 3 May 1948; T. Edward Carpenter and bequeathed by him to the JAMT 1969.

Publication. Memoir (1st 152; 2nd 114); *Life* 319; Chapman (1st and 2nd); Modert F-384 and F-385.

132(A). *To Jane Austen. From London, Carlton House, to [London, Hans Place]. Thursday ?21 December 1815.*

Description. Two leaves quarto plus single quarto leaf, wove; watermark C WILMOTT 1814; no seal or wafer; no address.

Postmark. None.

Provenance. Bequeathed by CEA to CJA in 1845; descended to CJA's granddaughters and sold by them in 1925; J. Pierpont Morgan; Pierpont Morgan Library, New York (MA 1034–12).

Publication. Life 320; Chapman (1st and 2nd).

1. *James the Second. Life of King James II* (1816); there seems to have been no second edition. [RWC]
2. *the Pavilion.* The Prince Regent's seaside palace at Brighton.
3. *Le Sage.* Alain-Rene Lesage (1668–1747), French novelist and playwright; Mr Clarke was probably thinking of his *Gil Blas* (1715–35), English translation by Smollett 1749.
4. *two little Works. Sermons preached in the Western Squadron during its services off Brest, on board HM ship Impetueux* (1798), and Mr Clark's edition of William Falconer's poem *The Shipwreck* (1804).

133. *To Charles Thomas Haden. From London, Hans Place, to London, Sloane Street. Thursday 14 December 1815.*

Description. Scrap, perhaps cut from octavo leaf, wove; fragment of watermark—LOWS—12; no seal or wafer.

Postmark. None.

Provenance. Found in an album once the property of Miss K. H. Gordon, granddaughter of George Huntley Gordon, protégé and amanuensis of Sir Walter Scott; Sotheby's 16 Dec. 1940; Henry and Alberta Burke 1941; bequeathed by Mrs Burke to Pierpont Morgan Library, New York, 1975 (MA 2911).

Publication. Chapman (2nd); Modert F-388 and F-389.

134(A). *To Jane Austen. From Saltram to Chawton. Wednesday 27 December 1815.*

Description. Two leaves octavo (2nd leaf blank), wove; no watermark. Accompanied by wrapper, one leaf quarto, wove; no watermark; remains of red wax seal. Wrapper endorsed: 'favord by | Mr Trimmer' and (in JA's hand): 'Lady Morley'.

Postmark. None.

Provenance. Bequeathed by CEA to CJA in 1845; descended to CJA's granddaughters and sold by them 1925; J. Pierpont Morgan; given by him to Cambridge University Library 1925 (Add. 4251 (B) 987).

Publication. *Memoir* (1st 139; 2nd 125); Chapman (1st and 2nd).

1. *they will not amuse.* 'not' inserted superscript.

134(D). *To Lady Morley. From Chawton to Saltram. Sunday 31 December 1815.*

Description. Scrap, laid; watermark fragmentary device (Heawood Nos. 2752–62), above monogram JB[?], no date; no seal or wafer.

Postmark. None.

Provenance. Bequeathed by CEA to CJA in 1845; descended to CJA's grand-daughters and sold by them 1925; J. Pierpont Morgan; given by him to Cambridge University Library 1925 (Add. 4251 (B) 38).

Publication. *Memoir* (1st 140; 2nd 126); *Life* 326 (extract); Chapman (1st and 2nd); Modert F-392.

This draft was originally written in pencil, but JA then rewrote it in ink. The ink version was at first actually over the pencil, then after a few lines she placed it slightly above the pencil, and finally the pencilled text, where it still showed between the inked lines, was almost entirely erased.

134. *To Lady Morley. From Chawton to Saltram. Sunday 31 December 1815.*

Description. One leaf, approximately octavo irregularly trimmed, wove; frag-mentary watermark—DGEN—813; no seal or wafer; no address.

Postmark. None.

Provenance. Mrs D. Hicks, Oxford; Sotheby's 5–7 June 1944; Henry G. Burke; bequeathed by Mrs Alberta H. Burke to Pierpont Morgan Library, New York, 1975 (MA 2911).

Publication. Modert F-390 and F-391.

135. *To Anna Lefroy. From Chawton to Wyards. ?December 1815–January 1816.*

Description. Scrap, laid; no watermark visible; no seal or wafer; tipped in to a copy of 1833 edn. of *Emma*. On the verso is 'Remaining in hand' and a few figures—presumably some domestic calculation by either JA or Anna.

Postmark. None.

Provenance. AL archive; also **copied** by FCL into her MS Family History.

Publication. *Memoir* (1st 203; 2nd 148 (paraphrased)); Chapman (1st and 2nd, from MS); Modert F-393.

1. your *Jemima*. Anna-Jemima Lefroy was born at Wyards 20 Oct. 1815, but due to winter weather JA had not yet been able to see her first great-niece.

136. *To Catherine Ann Prowting. From Chawton to Chawton. ?early 1816.*

Description. Two leaves octavo; watermark 1813.

Postmark. None.

Provenance. Descended in Prowting family to the recipient's great-niece Miss Lilias Edith (Lily) Clement (1860–95); given by her to Edith Mendham; given by E. M. to Miss Anne Tucker; lent by A. T. (then living in Tewkesbury), via a friend R. M. A. Owen, to RWC in 1926 and presum-ably returned by him thereafter; now untraceable.

Publication. Chapman (1st and 2nd).

1. *our poor friend.* Probably Miss Mary Benn, who was buried at Chawton, aged 46, on 3 Jan. 1816. *These volumes* may perhaps be the set of *Emma* previously lent to Anna Lefroy—see letter **135**.

137. *To Caroline Austen. From Chawton to Steventon. Wednesday 13 March 1816.*

Description. Two leaves octavo, laid; watermark fragmentary device (Heawood Nos. 2752–62), no date; red wax seal, design indistinct. Text only on pp. 1–2; p. 3 blank, p. 4 address only.

Postmark. None.

Provenance. Descended in junior line of AL family and placed on deposit in British Museum Dept. of MSS by Miss Lois AL in 1936; now Joan AL (Mrs Denis Mason Hurley) and British Library Loan No. 19(iii).

Publication. *Life* 365 (misdated 1815); Chapman (1st and 2nd); Modert F-394 to F-396.

1. *M^{de} de Genlis.* 'de' inserted superscript. *Les Veillées du Château* (1784), contains as one of its parts *Olympe et Théophile*, translated as *Theophilus and Olympia; or the Errours of Youth and Age.* [RWC]

2. *your Uncle Henry.* 'Henry' inserted superscript.

138(A). *To Jane Austen. From Brighton Pavilion to London, Albemarle Street. Wednesday 27 March 1816.*

Description. Two leaves quarto, laid; watermark J WHATMAN 1811. Separate wrapper, quarto sheet, laid; watermark fragmentary device (Heawood Nos. 2752–62), no date; large red wax seal with Royal Arms, franked 'Clarence' and endorsed 'Brighton March twenty seventh 1816'.

Postmarks. 28 MR 28 1816   MR 29 816

Provenance. Bequeathed by CEA to CJA in 1845; descended to CJA's grand-daughters and sold by them in 1920s, when the letter and its wrapper became separated. The letter went to Frederick R. Lovering; Sotheby's 3 May 1948; T. Edward Carpenter and bequeathed by him to the JAMT 1969. The wrapper went to J. Pierpont Morgan 1925; Pierpont Morgan Library, New York (MA 1034-13).

Publication. *Life* 322; Chapman (1st and 2nd).

1. *the Marriage.* Prince Leopold of Saxe-Cobourg (1790–1865) to the Prince Regent's daughter the Princess Charlotte of Wales (1796–1817).

2. *London.* The letter was readdressed to Henrietta Street, and again to Chawton.

138(D). *To James Stanier Clarke. From Chawton to Brighton Pavilion. Monday 1 April 1816.*

Description. One leaf quarto, laid; watermark J JELLYMAN, no date; no seal or wafer.

Postmark. None.

Provenance. Bequeathed by CEA to CJA in 1845; descended to CJA's grand-daughters and sold by them in 1920s; Frederick R. Lovering; Sotheby's 3 May 1948; T. Edward Carpenter and bequeathed by him to the JAMT 1969.

Publication. Memoir (1st 156; 2nd 116); *Life* 323; Chapman (1st and 2nd); Modert F-397 and F-398.

1. *very much obliged.* JA first wrote 'am very much obliged', and then cancelled 'am'.
2. *something still better.* 'still' inserted superscript.
3. *In my opinion . . . required by it.* JA's first version of this sentence was: 'In my opinion not more surely should They who preach the Gospel, live by the Gospel, than They who live *in* a Court, live by it—& live well by it too; for the sacrifices of Time & Feeling they must make are immense.' This was cancelled and the second version inserted superscript.
4. *Romance . . . House.* JA first wrote: 'Romance, on the History of the House . . .', then cancelled 'on the History of' and inserted 'founded on' superscript.
5. *go on in my own Way.* 'in' inserted superscript.
6. *near Alton.* Inserted superscript.

139. *To John Murray. From Chawton to London, Albemarle Street. Monday 1 April 1816.*

Description. One leaf quarto, laid; watermark fragmentary device (Heawood Nos. 2752–62), no date; address presumably on missing second leaf. Endorsed, no doubt by Murray's clerk: '1816 April 1 | Austen G Esq' [*sic*].

Postmark. None.

Provenance. Remained in Murray archive until at least 1870; thereafter probably given by some member of the Murray family to either the 6th or 7th Earl Beauchamp of Madresfield Court, Great Malvern (both of whom had literary interests), and placed in album with other autographs; Sotheby's 25 June 1975; Mrs Dorothy Warren; given by her to King's College Library, Cambridge, 1990.

Publication. Memoir (2nd 124, from a copy provided by John Murray III); *Life* 327; Chapman (1st and 2nd, from the *Memoir*); Modert F-399.

1. *the Reveiwer of* Emma. Sir Walter Scott—see C. B. Hogan, in *Publications of the Modern Language Association of America*, 45 (1929), 1264. [RWC]

2. *the late sad event.* HTA's bankruptcy, declared 15 Mar. 1816.
3. *the same direction.* JA first wrote 'the same direction, with', then cancelled 'with' and inserted superscript 'you will add to' earlier in the sentence.

140. *To Caroline Austen. From Chawton to Steventon. Sunday 21 April 1816.*

Description. Two leaves quarto, laid; watermark 1813. Endorsed by CMCA on p. 4: 'The corresponding page dated Chawton Sunday April 21st sent to Miss Le Marchant Sep^t 20th 1852'.
Postmark. None.
Provenance. The letter remained in CMCA's possession and was divided by her into **3 sections**, 1852 or thereafter.
140 (S.1). First leaf, pp. 1–2, sent to Miss Helen Augusta Le Marchant (died 1924, a niece by marriage of JEAL) in 1852; appeared at Sotheby's 13 Dec. 1990, but remains in Le Marchant family. **A separate scrap**, bearing the words: *Yours affec:^ly | J. Austen* and with the mark of a green wafer, has been tipped on to the bottom left-hand corner of p. 1. This complimentary close and signature may have been cut from letter **143** (15 July 1816), as the scrap bears a trace of a descending letter which could be the tail of the 'g' in *do not grow older* at the end of that text.
FCL also **copied** this section into her MS Family History.
140 (S.2). Second leaf, top of pp. 3 and 4, from *I shall say no more* to *out of the house on Monday*, descended in junior line of AL family to Joan AL (Mrs Denis Mason Hurley). The verso of this section bears the endorsement by CMCA, and *Austen* with part of the *A* cut away.
140 (S.3). Second leaf, bottom of pp. 3 and 4, containing last five lines of text and signature, was Lot 562, 'Property of a Lady', Sotheby's 18 July 1967; Mrs Diana Parikian, now (1990) mislaid. The verso bore *Miss Caroline* with part of the succeeding *A* of *Austen*, thus linking it firmly to **140 (S.2).**
Publication. **Section(S.1).** Chapman (1st and 2nd), from a **copy** probably made by Charles Edward AL (1832–1924) and apparently preserved in junior line of AL family. This copy evidently did not specify that the complimentary close and signature did not belong to the original MS, hence RWC treated this single page as if it were the whole letter. RWC mentioned that **another copy**, made (according to him) by Mrs Bellas, was in the possession of Miss Isabel Lefroy. The present location of this is unknown.
Section(S.2). Chapman (1st and 2nd, from MS); Modert F-400 and F-401.
Section(S.3). Known only from Sotheby's catalogue for 18 July 1967 sale.

1. *letter from Scarlets.* i.e. the Leigh-Perrots.
2. *whatever it may be.* 'be' inserted superscript.
3. *taking him home.* Mrs JA's diary for 1816 mentions JEAL's return home on Saturday, 13 Apr.; 14 Apr. was Easter Sunday.

141(C). *To Anna Lefroy. From Chawton to Wyards. Sunday 23 June 1816.*

Description. Unknown; original MS untraced.

Provenance. Inherited by FCL 1872, and **copied** by her into her MS Family History; she may have sent the original MS to Lord Brabourne and possibly it was never returned to her. FCL apparently made another **separate copy** (as punctuation and capitalization differ) which came to Miss Mary Isabella Lefroy and was used by RWC in the 1920s, collated with the Brabourne text; ownership and location of this copy is unknown. The text given here is that of Brabourne/Chapman, which seems more likely to be accurate than the Family History version.

Publication. Brabourne ii. 326; Chapman (1st and 2nd).

142. *To James Edward Austen. From Chawton to Steventon. Tuesday 9 July 1816.*

Description. Two leaves quarto, wove; no watermark; mark of red wafer.

Postmark. None.

Provenance. Descended in junior line of AL family and placed on deposit in British Museum Dept. of MSS by Miss Lois AL in 1936; now Joan AL (Mrs Denis Mason Hurley) and British Library Loan No. 19(iv).

Publication. *Memoir* (1st 208; 2nd 151); *Life* 371; Chapman (1st and 2nd); Modert F-403 to F-406.

1. *July 9. 1816.* JA did not normally give the year when dating her letters, but this '1816' does seem to be in her hand.
2. *very serious one indeed.* See CMCA's *Reminiscences* 48.
3. *It is really too bad.* JA first wrote 'It is really is too bad', and cancelled the second 'is'.
4. *go to Town.* 'to Town' inserted superscript.
5. *Aunt Frank determined to go.* JA first wrote 'Aunt Frank also determined to go', then cancelled 'also'.
6. *Little Cassy.* In this context, CJA's daughter.
7. *without its being mentioned.* 'its' inserted superscript.
8. *your being at home.* In the *Memoir* JEAL commented on his youthful self: 'It seems that her young correspondent, after dating from his home, had

been so superfluous as to state in his letter that he was returned home, and thus to have drawn on himself this banter.'

9. *must go to Oxford.* JA first wrote 'must not go to Oxford' and then cancelled 'not':

10. *very considerable pond.* The pond at the road junction outside the Cottage was finally drained in the 1920s, but is shown on earlier maps.

11. *M^{rs} S- does not quit Tangier.* Mrs Sclater; 'does' inserted superscript.

12. *William.* Littleworth.

13. *the Trial.* Perhaps the 'Baigent business'.

14. *with his Uncle.* HTA.

143. *To Caroline Austen. From Chawton to Steventon. Monday 15 July 1816.*

Description. Two leaves octavo, signature cut away from second leaf; no watermark; p. 4 blank except for address.

Postmark. None.

Provenance. Descended in junior line of AL family to Joan AL (Mrs Denis Mason Hurley).

Publication. Life 364; Johnson 180; Chapman (1st and 2nd); Modert F-407 and F-408.

1. *I am particularly.* 'I' inserted superscript.

2. *Diana's Temple.* Probably Mary Jane's story, picture, or piece of needlework.

3. The missing complimentary close and signature may be that now tipped on to the lower edge of letter **140 (section 1).**

144. *To Cassandra Austen. From Chawton to Cheltenham. Wednesday 4 September 1816.*

Description. Approximately three-quarters of a quarto leaf, laid; no watermark; mark of seal or wafer. Possibly as many as eight lines of text are missing at the top of each side of the leaf, as well as some of the remaining words being shaved, otherwise it contains pp. 3–4 of a letter. Endorsed [?by CEA]: 'Dated | Chawton Sept 4th, 1816', and in pencil: 'For Caroline'.

Postmark. None.

Provenance. Presumably bequeathed by CEA to CMCA in 1845; descended in junior line of AL family to Joan AL (Mrs Denis Mason Hurley); Sotheby Parke Bernet 12 Dec. 1984; Frederick Koch Foundation and placed on deposit at Pierpont Morgan Library, New York (Koch Deposit 382); Christie's New York 17–18 May 1991; present owner and location unknown.

Publication. Life 374; Chapman (1st and 2nd); Modert F-409 and F-410.

1. *Cheltenham ... May!* JA and CEA had visited Cheltenham in May 1816, and CEA was now staying there again with Mrs JA and CMCA.
2. *decided for Orders &c.* See *Family Record* 212.
3. *The Alton 4.* FWA and his wife, Miss S. Gibson, and FWA's naval friend Lt. Mark Halpen Sweny.
4. *Jeu de violon.* Apparently some parlour game.

145. *To Cassandra Austen. From Chawton to Cheltenham. Sunday 8– Monday 9 September 1816.*

Description. Two leaves quarto, laid; watermark RUSS & TURNERS 1815; wafer cut out. Endorsed [?by CEA]: 'Sept: 1816 | For Lady K.'
Postmarks. D 10 SE 10 [part unprinted]   ALTON 50
Provenance. Bequeathed by CEA to Fanny, Lady Knatchbull, in 1845; inherited by Lord Brabourne 1882; Sotheby's 11–14 May 1891; Alfred Morrison; Sotheby's 10 Dec. 1918; J. Pierpont Morgan 1920; Pierpont Morgan Library, New York (MA 977–41).
Publication. Brabourne ii. 262; *Life* 375 (extracts); Chapman (1st and 2nd); Modert F-411 to F-414.

1. *Miss P.-* Palmer.
2. *C. Craven.* The Cheltenham *Chronicle* of 1 Aug. mentions the Duke and Duchess of Orléans, and the issue of 8 Aug. mentions Charlotte Craven. But the Public Librarian, who kindly searched the files, could not find Miss Austen or Mr Pococke. [RWC]
3. *Edward.* Ben's elder brother Christopher Edward Lefroy. [RWC]
4. *come back from France.* 'from France' inserted superscript.
5. *to be got but by the Innkeepers.* 'but' inserted superscript.
6. *she is not much less melancholy.* 'she' inserted superscript.
7. *Edward's company.* JEAL.
8. *good Mrs West.* Mrs Jane West (1758–1852), a prolific authoress of novels, poetry, and plays.
9. *astonishment!* Inserted superscript above some other word cancelled and illegible.
10. *new Sermons.* Revd E. Cooper, *Two Sermons preached at Wolverhampton* (1816).

146. *To James Edward Austen. From Chawton to Steventon. Monday 16–Tuesday 17 December 1816.*

Description. Two leaves quarto, wove; watermark KENT 1812; seal or wafer cut out.
Postmark. None.

Provenance. Descended in junior line of AL family and placed on deposit in British Museum Dept. of MSS by Miss Lois AL in 1936; now Joan AL (Mrs Denis Mason Hurley) and British Library Loan 19(v).

Publication. Biographical Notice in *NA* 1818 (extract, misquoted); *Memoir* (1st 212; 2nd 153); *Life* 377; Chapman (1st and 2nd); Modert F-415 to F-418.

1. *Monday.* 'Monday' written following 'Tuesday' cancelled.
2. *the Antiquary.* Sir Walter Scott, *The Antiquary* (1816).
3. *"tell him what you will".* Hannah Cowley (1743–1809), *Which is the Man? a Comedy* (1783), iv. 1.
4. *Joseph Hall.* Mrs GA's tenant at Steventon, renting 'a little land' there at £6 p.a. See *AP* 264.
5. *Mr Papillon.* JA repeats the family joke that she should marry him—see letter **62**. '*Mrs Eliz^{th} P*' is his (unmarried) sister.

147(C). *To Anna Lefroy. From Chawton to Wyards. Thursday ?December 1816.*

Description. Unknown; original MS untraced.

Provenance. Given probably by Anna Lefroy to her grandson William Chambers Lefroy (1849–1915); **copied** (? before or after Anna's death in 1872) by FCL into her mother's volume of family history notes (Lefroy MS), with the explanatory comment: 'This note was written the winter of 1816 & the original is in the possession of W. Chambers Lefroy the Grandson of the Receiver.' The note apparently was not preserved, as Chapman saw only the copy in the Lefroy MS, which was then in the possession of Miss Mary Isabella Lefroy. FCL also **copied** it into her own MS Family History.

Publication. Chapman (1st and 2nd).

148. *To Cassandra Esten Austen. From Chawton to London, Keppel Street. Wednesday 8 January 1817.*

Description. One leaf quarto, wove; watermark GATER 1815; mark of wafer. This leaf is pp. 3–4 of the whole letter, pp. 1–2 of which was for CJA.

Postmark. D 9 JA 9 1817   ALTON 50

Provenance. Descended in CJA's family to his granddaughters and sold by them *c.*1925; J. Pierpont Morgan; Pierpont Morgan Library, New York (MA 1034–7). FCL also **copied** it into her MS Family History.

Publication. Brabourne ii. 327; Chapman (1st and 2nd); Modert F-419 and F-420.

1. *little Cassy's birthday.* FWA's second daughter Cassandra-Elizabeth, born 8 Jan. 1814.

2. *Harriet Knight.* There were several Knight families among the Chawton villagers; this is probably H.-Frances K., daughter of Abraham and Olive K., baptized 15 Apr. 1804. See *Family Record* 158.

149. *To Caroline Austen. From Chawton to Steventon. Thursday 23 January 1817.*

Description. Two leaves quarto; watermark 1815; red seal; complimentary close and signature cut out of second leaf.

Postmark. None.

Provenance. Descended in junior line of AL family to Joan AL (Mrs Denis Mason Hurley).

Publication. *Memoir* (2nd 160 (extract)); *Life* 366; Chapman (1st and 2nd); Modert F-421 to F-424.

1. *to see Edward.* JEAL arrived at the Cottage on Tuesday, 21 Jan. 1817, and left on Friday, 24 Jan., to return via Wyards to Steventon.

2. *Cassy's return.* CJA's daughter.

3. *your Uncle & Aunt.* FWA and family, in Alton.

150(C). *To Alethea Bigg. From Chawton to Streatham. Friday 24 January 1817.*

Description. Unknown; original MS untraced.

Provenance. **Copied** by JEAL's daughter Mary Augusta Austen-Leigh (1838–1922); copied from this copy by RAAL. Alethea Bigg died unmarried in 1847, and her sister Mrs Heathcote, with whom she lived, died in 1855; presumably the letter descended to Sir William Heathcote, JEAL's boyhood friend, who may have lent it for use in the *Memoir*; it is not, however, in the surviving Heathcote archive deposited in the Hampshire Record Office.

Publication. *Memoir* (2nd 158 (extracts)); *Life* 379 (extracts); Chapman (1st and 2nd, from RAAL's copy).

The text given here is taken from **MAAL's copy** (in AL archive), which differs slightly from that made by RAAL, and seems more likely to be accurate.

1. *a good account of his Father.* James A. was by now in poor health, and died in 1819.

2. *William.* Heathcote, the future 5th baronet.

3. *Our own new Clergyman.* HTA.

4. *Streatham & Winchester.* Miss Bigg lived in Winchester with her widowed sister Mrs Heathcote, and was presently visiting their other sister Mrs Hill at Streatham.

5. *'Poet's Pilgrimage to Waterloo'.* Robert Southey (1816). Southey, who was Mr Hill's nephew, lost his elder (and at that date, only) son Herbert in Apr. 1816, and the *proem* contains an affectionate description of the boy. [RWC].

151. *To Fanny Knight. From Chawton to Godmersham. Thursday 20– Friday 21 February 1817.*

Description. Two leaves quarto, wove; watermark GATER 1815; mark of red wafer; endorsed [?by FCK]: '3 Feb. 20 | 1816' [*sic*].

Postmarks. D 22 . . 22 1 . . . (part unprinted) ALTON 50

Provenance. Inherited by Lord Brabourne 1882; descended in Brabourne family and placed on deposit at Kent Archives Office (Centre for Kentish Studies), Maidstone, 1962 (U.951/C.112/3).

Publication. Brabourne ii. 290; *Life* 348, 383 (extracts); facsimile in Chapman (ed.), *Five Letters from Jane Austen to Fanny Knight*; Johnson 154; Chapman (1st and 2nd); Modert F-425 to F-428.

1. *the new Silver Coinage.* Announced by proclamation of 12 Feb.; it replaced a debased currency. [RWC]
2. *it will be.* JA first wrote 'it will be, to me, when you are married', then cancelled 'to me,'.
3. *Mr. J. W.* James Wildman.
4. *fancy to him than not.* 'not' inserted superscript above 'otherwise' cancelled.
5. *easily beleive.* 'beleive' inserted superscript.
6. *Why should you be living.* 'you' inserted superscript.
7. *his marrying somebody else?* This refers to the Mr John Plumptre of the 1814 letters.
8. *your Henry . . . William.* FCK's brothers, both now visiting their grandmother at the Cottage; also one of their Deedes cousins, still at Winchester.
9. *this Marianne.* Mrs Deedes's eighteenth child.
10. *her praise of Emma.* See *MW* 'Opinions of Emma', 439.
11. *her girlish days.* See *Family Record* 161–2.
12. *Poor Miss C.* Clewes.

152. *To Caroline Austen. From Chawton to Steventon. Wednesday 26 February 1817.*

Description. Two leaves octavo, laid; no watermark; remains of black seal.

Postmark. None.

Provenance. Descended in junior line of AL family to Joan AL (Mrs Denis Mason Hurley).

Publication. Life 367; Johnson 181 (extracts); Chapman (1st and 2nd); Modert F-429 and F-430.

1. *you might have pretended.* 'might' inserted superscript.
2. *William . . . Mrs Motley Austen.* W. Knight, visiting Steventon from Chawton; Elizabeth, widow of Mr Francis Motley Austen of Kippington, died Monday, 17 Feb. 1817.
3. *Wed: Night.* For the dating of this letter, see Le Faye, 'Jane Austen: Some Letters Redated', *N&Q* 232:4 (Dec. 1987), 478–81.

153. *To Fanny Knight. From Chawton to Godmersham. Thursday 13 March 1817.*

Description. Two leaves quarto, laid; watermark device (Heawood Nos. 2752–62) above monogram RT[?], no date; no seal or wafer; endorsed [?by FCK]: 'No 4 March 13'. Also a separate scrap, approximately half a quarto leaf, of thinner paper, laid; watermark fragment of monogram JT[?], no date.

Postmark. None.

Provenance. Inherited by Lord Brabourne 1882; descended in Brabourne family and placed on deposit at Kent Archives Office (Centre for Kentish Studies), Maidstone, 1962 (U.951/C.112/4).

Publication. Brabourne ii. 295 (but omitting the separate leaf); *Life* 351, 383 (extracts); facsimile in Chapman (ed.), *Five Letters from Jane Austen to Fanny Knight*; Johnson 158; Chapman (1st and 2nd); Modert F-431 to F-436.

1. *Mrs Wm Hammond.* FCK's débutante friend Mary Oxenden.
2. *Fanny & her Husband.* Probably F. Plumptre, who married Robert Ramsden the previous year.
3. *we fear something else.* Anna must have miscarried, as her third child was not born till 1818.
4. *Aunt Harriot.* Mrs Moore.
5. *the race of Pagets.* The elopement of Henry, Lord Paget (later Earl of Uxbridge and first Marquis of Anglesey) with the Duke of Wellington's sister-in-law Lady Charlotte Wellesley in 1808 had caused great scandal. 'He seduced this woman, then the mother of four children, and a verdict against him for £24,000, the full amount claimed in an action for *crim. con.*, a duel between him and her brother Capt Cadogan, and two divorces, were the results of this misconduct.' Lady Paget divorced her husband in 1810 and married the Duke of Argyll; Sir Henry Wellesley divorced Charlotte and in 1810 Lord Paget married her. It was Lord Paget's eldest daughter by his first marriage, Caroline, who was now engaged to the young Earl of March, heir to the Richmond dukedom.

154. *To Caroline Austen. From Chawton to Steventon. Friday 14 March 1817.*

Description. Two leaves octavo, laid; watermark fragmentary device, no date; mark of green wafer. Endorsed in pencil [?by a dealer]: 'Jane Austen (Novelist)'.

Postmark. None.

Provenance. Presumably descended in junior line of AL family; Sotheby's 12 June 1939; Lady Charnwood; The Charnwood Trust, on deposit at the British Library, 1965 (Loan No. 60/2, 43(1)).

Publication. Chapman (2nd); Modert F-437 and F-438.

1. *Craven Exhibition.* Mrs JA's diary for 1817 shows that JEAL went to Oxford on Thursday, 13 Mar., to apply for this scholarship. See also CMCA's *Reminiscences* 49–50.

2. *nearly twenty pounds.* JA noted that on 7 Mar. 1817 she had received £19. 13s. 0d. [£19.65] profits from the second edition of *S&S*. See Chapman (ed.), *Plan of a Novel*, 35 (MS now in Pierpont Morgan Library).

3. *Mary Jane . . . Cassy.* Daughters of FWA and CJA respectively. CJA's diary for 1817 confirms the visit by FWA and MJA to Keppel Street on Tuesday, 4 Mar.

4. *Your Aunt F.* Mrs FWA.

5. **Sense and Sensibility.* JA added this footnote in pencil at the bottom of p. 2 of the letter.

6. *March 14.* Another hand has added '1815' here in pencil; but the correct date can be ascertained by the internal references.

155. *To Fanny Knight. From Chawton to Godmersham. Sunday 23– Tuesday 25 March 1817.*

Description. Two leaves quarto, laid; watermark device (Heawood Nos. 2752–62) above monogram RT[?], no date; red wax seal. Endorsed [?by FCK]: '5 March 23 1816 [year lightly crossed through] | 1817'. On the seal panel are the remains of FCK's shopping-list: 'Long Gloves Lsa | Calico &c Miss C | Bowers Locket | Loadstone | Good Poetry | Flannel . . . | Toothpaste . . . | Epsom Salts | Pipe . . . | Salvolatile | Salts of Harts. | Budden &c | . . . Lsa | Bobbin Tapes | . . . & India ink [?] | 1 yd. Jact. mus.'

Postmark. A MR 25. 1817

Provenance. Inherited by Lord Brabourne 1882 and remains in Brabourne family; deposited Kent Archives Office (Centre for Kentish Studies), Maidstone, 1962 (U.951/C.112/5).

Publication. Brabourne ii. 299; *Life* 352, 383 (extracts); facsimile in Chapman (ed.), *Five Letters from Jane Austen to Fanny Knight*; Johnson 162; Chapman (1st and 2nd); Modert F-439 to F-442.

1. *Mr Wildman's conversation.* This is not recorded in the 'Opinions' on *MP* and *Emma.* Perhaps he was made to begin at the beginning with *S&S.* [RWC]

2. *but he knows nothing.* 'he' superscript above 'it' cancelled.

3. *Event at Scarlets.* Mr Leigh-Perrot's impending death.

4. *a chance of escape.* But see letter **153**, note 3.

5. *manner of reply.* 'of' written over 'in'.

6. *generally esteemed so.* 'So' added superscript.

7. *in the direction.* Mr E. V. Hewkin of the GPO kindly informs me that: '... there is no trace in the records here, of the route which would be taken by letters in transit between Chawton, Hants, and Godmersham, Kent, in the year 1817. In all probability such letters would circulate via London. Although "Feversham" was the correct address for letters for Godmersham, it appears to have been the practice of residents in the district to have their correspondence addressed "Canterbury" in spite of the fact that this entailed an extra penny postage. The advantage of the arrangement was that while letters addressed "Canterbury" were conveyed to addressees on the road to Ashford by a private van, those addressed "Feversham" had to be sent for.' [RWC]
Cassandra's two letters to Fanny from Winchester (**CEA/1** and **CEA/3**) are directed to Canterbury.

8. *& was with us.* 'was' inserted superscript.

9. *the Altons.* FWA and his wife Mary, the latter (*she*) now heavily pregnant.

156. *To Caroline Austen. From Chawton to Steventon. Wednesday 26 March 1817.*

Description. Two leaves octavo, laid; no watermark; red wax seal; signature cut out of second leaf.

Postmark. None.

Provenance. Descended in junior line of AL family to Joan AL (Mrs Denis Mason Hurley).

Publication. Life 367; Johnson 182 (extracts); Chapman (1st and 2nd); Modert F-443 and F-444.

1. *opportunities.* HTA had been taking occasional duty at Steventon, for James's health was failing.

2. *I will be better.* JA's use of *shall* and *will* is strict. This is a promise. [RWC]

157. *To Charles Austen. From Chawton to London. Sunday 6 April 1817.*

Description. Two leaves quarto, laid; watermark device (Heawood Nos. 2752–62) above monogram TCP[?], no date; seal cut out. Endorsed: 'My last letter | from | Dearest Jane | C-JA'.

Postmarks. D 7 AP 7 1817   ALTON 50

Provenance. Descended to CJA's granddaughters and sold by them to RWC 1925; he in turn sold it to the British Museum Dept. of MSS 1925; now British Library Add. MSS 41,253.A, fos. 3–4.

Publication. Memoir (1st 207; 2nd 150 (short extract)); *Life* 385 (extracts); Johnson 143; Chapman (1st and 2nd); Modert F-445 to F-448.

1. *I have been suffering.* 'been' inserted superscript.
2. *my Uncle's Will.* Mr LP left everything to his wife for her lifetime, with the reversion of a large sum to James Austen and his heirs, and of £1,000 each to those of Mrs Austen's younger children who should survive Mrs LP. See also *Family Record* 222.
3. *Mrs P.'s recovery.* During Mar. 1817 CJA's daughter Harriet-Jane continued to be seriously ill, and in addition his mother- and sister-in-law Mrs and Miss Harriet Palmer both fell ill; his diary entries reveal his worries in this situation.
4. *proper-edged sheet of Paper.* i.e. the paper did not have the black edge used to denote mourning.

158. *To Cassandra Austen. From Chawton to Chawton. Sunday 27 April 1817.*

Description. One leaf quarto, laid; watermark fragmentary device (Heawood Nos. 2752–62), no date.
Provenance. Public Record Office, London (PROB/1/78).
Publication. Life 384 (extract); Chapman (1st and 2nd).

The Will itself is endorsed with notes of probate being granted to CEA on 10 Sept. 1817. As it was unwitnessed, CJA's in-laws Mr John Grove Palmer and Miss Harriet Ebel Palmer also attended on 10 Sept. to swear to the authenticity of the handwriting and signature, and the Will is accompanied by separate foolscap sheets bearing their depositions and signatures to this effect.

159. *To Anne Sharp. From Chawton to Doncaster. Thursday 22 May 1817.*

Description. Two leaves quarto, wove; watermark KINGSFORD 1814; black wax seal.
Postmarks. D 23 MY 23 1817   ALTON 50
Provenance. Miss Anne Sharp died 1853; this letter previously given by her to Dr Zechariah Sillar (1796–ante-1875), sometime Physician to the Northern Hospital, Liverpool; descended to his granddaughter Miss A. L. Sillar (born c.1855) and in her possession 1926; Mrs Winifred Bavington of Budleigh Salterton, and her sisters, by 1953; Sotheby's 8 Feb. 1954; Henry G. and

Alberta H. Burke; bequeathed by Mrs Burke to Pierpont Morgan Library, New York, 1975 (MA 2911).

Publication. *The Times* (1 Feb. 1926), 13–14; Chapman (1st and 2nd, from photographs of the MS); Modert F-449 to F-452.

1. *our Alton Apothy.* Mr Curtis.
2. *these ten years.* In fact Mrs LP survived until 1836, so that her husband's property finally passed to James-Edward Austen, who then added '-Leigh' to his surname in consequence.
3. *a Baby.* FWA's seventh child, Elizabeth, born Alton 15 Apr. 1817.
4. *your Eliza.* One of Miss Sharp's pupils, the eldest Miss Pilkington.
5. *Ly. P-.* Lady Pilkington.
6. *Galigai de Concini.* Eléonore G., a maid of honour to Marie de Médicis, married Concino Concini, and was burned as a sorceress in 1617. When one of her judges asked her what charm she had put on her mistress, she replied: 'Mon sortilège a été le pouvoir que les âmes fortes doivent avoir sur les esprits faibles' (Voltaire, *Essai sur les Moeurs*, ch. 175. I owe the reference to Mr L. F. Powell). JA may have owed her knowledge to Lord Chesterfield: see his letter of 30 Apr. (OS) 1752; or to *The Absentee*, ch. III (M. Edgeworth). [RWC]

160. *To James Edward Austen. From Winchester to Oxford. Tuesday 27 May 1817.*

Description. Two leaves quarto, wove; watermark KINGSFORD 1814; remains of black wax seal.

Postmarks. WINCHESTER MY 27 181[7] 58 E 28 MY 28 1817

Provenance. Descended in junior line of AL family and placed on deposit by Miss Lois AL in the British Museum Dept. of MSS, 1936; now Joan AL (Mrs Denis Mason Hurley) and British Library Loan No. 19(vi).

Publication. *Memoir* (2nd 163); *Life* 389; Johnson 183; Chapman (1st and 2nd); Modert F-453 to F-455.

1. *my handwriting.* In this and in letter **157** the uneven writing betrays JA's weakness.
2. *Charles.* EAK's fifth son, at Winchester College.
3. *William.* Heathcote.

161(C). *To ?Frances Tilson. From Winchester to ?London, Hans Place. ?Wednesday 28 or Thursday 29 May 1817.*

Description. Unknown; original MS probably not preserved.

Provenance. Only known by HTA's use of extracts from it in his *Biographical Notice.*

Publication. Biographical Notice in *NA* 1818; *Memoir* (1st 207, 224; 2nd 150, 164); *Life* 391; Chapman (1st and 2nd).

For a discussion of the suggested recipient and the dating, see Le Faye, 'Jane Austen: More Letters Redated', *N&Q* 236:3 (Sept. 1991), 306–8.

1. *Captain* ——. HTA suppressed the name for the purposes of his publication; it was most probably Capt. Benjamin Clement, RN, with his wife and sister-in-law Miss Catherine-Ann Prowting.

CEA/1. *To Fanny Knight. From Winchester to Godmersham. Sunday 20 July 1817.*

Description. Three leaves quarto, laid; watermark device (Heawood Nos. 2752–62) above florid initial or monogram, no date; black wax seal.

Postmarks. WINCHESTER JY 20 1817   E [21] JY 21 1817

Provenance. Inherited by Lord Brabourne 1882; Puttick & Simpson sale of 26–8 June 1893; Colbeck Radford & Co, London, Cat. no. 12, Nov. 1930; Sotheby's 23 June 1947; Mrs Alberta H. Burke and bequeathed by her to Pierpont Morgan Library, New York, 1975 (MA 2911).

Publication. Brabourne ii., 333; Chapman (1st and 2nd).

1. *a visible change.* 'visible' inserted superscript.
2. *I have not to add.* 'to' inserted superscript.
3. *neglect of her comfort.* 'her' written over 'any' partly erased.
4. *these last services.* CEA first wrote 'these last services myself.', and cancelled the final word.
5. *serene air over her countenance.* 'over' inserted superscript above 'in' cancelled.
6. *your Uncles.* CJA was in Eastbourne, Sussex, with his children and Palmer in-laws, and so was too far away to be able to attend the funeral; he had already taken leave of JA in June. See *Family Record* 226.

CEA/2. *To Anne Sharp. From Chawton to Doncaster. Monday 28 July 1817.*

Description. Two leaves octavo, laid; watermark fragmentary device (Heawood Nos. 2752–62), no date; black wax seal.

Postmark. None.

Provenance. Miss Anne Sharp died 1853; this letter previously given by her to Dr Zechariah Sillar (1796–ante-1875), sometime Physician to the Northern Hospital, Liverpool; descended to his granddaughter Miss A. L. Sillar (born c.1855) and in her possession 1926; Mrs Winifred Bavington of Budleigh Salterton, and her sisters, by 1953; Sotheby's 8 Feb. 1954; Henry G. and

Alberta H. Burke; bequeathed by Mrs Burke to Pierpont Morgan Library, New York, 1975 (MA 2911).

Publication. The Times (1 Feb. 1926), 13; JA Society *Report* for 1977, 47–50; published here by permission of The Pierpont Morgan Library, New York.

  1. *these articles.* Unfortunately they did not survive with the letter.

CEA/3. *To Fanny Knight. From Chawton to Godmersham. Tuesday 29 July 1817.*

Description. Two leaves quarto, laid; watermark device (Heawood Nos. 2752–62), no date; mark of black wafer. Endorsed in pencil by FCK: 'At. Cassandra 1817'.

Postmarks. D 30 JY 30 1817   ALTON 50

Provenance. Inherited by Lord Brabourne 1882; Puttick & Simpson sale of 26–8 June 1893; 'an American collector'; his widow Mrs Florence Martin; given by her to Professor Caroline Spurgeon, *c.*1934; bequeathed by Prof. C. S. to Helen Waddell (the authoress) *c.*1946; given by H. W. to her niece Miss Mollie Martin; Sotheby's 19 Nov. 1974; Michael M. Kloss. Esq, London.

Publication. Brabourne ii. 338; Chapman (1st and 2nd).

  1. *she may perhaps receive.* 'may perhaps' inserted superscript above 'must' cancelled.

  2. *her idea.* 'idea' inserted superscript.

  3. *inhabiting Heaven.* CEA first wrote 'inhabiting the Heaven', and cancelled 'the'.

  4. *I have found some.* CEA first wrote 'I have a found', then cancelled 'a'.

GENERAL NOTES ON THE LETTERS

Of the 135 letters or fragments of letters in this collection which bear some form of signature by JA, 60 are signed 'J. Austen', 57 initialled 'J. A.', 12 are 'Jane' by itself, and only 6 are signed in full 'Jane Austen'; see FWA's comments, note 1 to letter **82**.

WATERMARKS

Not all the letters bear watermarks, but the following papermakers can be identified:

J BUDGEN. Dartford Mill, Kent.

ELGAR & SON. Little Ivy Mill, Loose, Kent.

FLOYD & CO. Eynsford Mill, Kent; later mark was FLOYD & FELLOWS.

GATER. John and William Gater, Up Mills, West End, South Stoneham, Hants.

JOHN HALL. Cotton Mill, Ringstead, Northamptonshire.

JOHN HAYES. Padsole Mill, Maidstone, Kent.

J JELLYMAN. Joseph Jellyman, Downton Mill, Salisbury, Wilts.

KINGSFORD. William Kingsford, Buckland Mill, near Dover, Kent.

MOLINEUX JOHNSTON & A LEE. Joseph Molineux, Thomas Johnston, and Arthur Lee, Isfield Mill, near Lewes, Sussex.

L MUNN KENT. Lewis Munn, Ford Mill, Little Chart, Kent.

PORTAL & CO. Laverstoke, Hants.

RUSES TURNERS. Ruse and Turner, later Ruse Turner & Welch, Upper Tovil Mill, Maidstone, Kent.

W TURNER & SON. William Turner & Son, Chafford Mill, Penshurst, Kent.

J WHATMAN. Turkey and Poll Mills, Kent.

C WILMOTT. Charles Wilmott, Sundridge Mill, Kent.

The device which appears on many of the letters of a coronet above an elaborate escutcheon upon which is a post-horn, sometimes with initials or monogram below (Heawood Nos. 2752–62), was used by a number of different papermakers at the end of the eighteenth century, including some of those named above.

General Notes on the Letters

OWNERSHIPS

At the time of compilation (1993), the bulk of JA's letters are in the collections of libraries or institutions, and so unlikely to circulate further. These can therefore be listed as under:

Australian National Library: **21**.

Bodleian Library, Oxford: **110, 120, 122(A)(D), 124(D)**.

Boston Public Library, Mass.: **3**.

The British Library, London: **8, 28, 34, 40, 41, 42, 68(A), 68(D), 69, 71, 86, 90, 157**.

Cambridge University Library: **134(A), 134(D)**.

Fitzwilliam Library, Cambridge: **35**.

King's College, Cambridge: **139**.

Houghton Library of Harvard University: **5, 19, 45, 92, 117**.

Haverford College, Haverford, Penn.: **102**.

The Jane Austen Memorial Trust: **38, 69(D), 78, 79, 80, 81, 84, 97, 132(D), 138(A), 138(D)**.

Maine Historical Society: **64**.

Massachusetts Historical Society: **26**.

New York Public Library, NY: **77, 128**.

St John's College, Oxford: **103, 104, 107, 108, 113**.

Historical Society of Pennsylvania: **59, 73**.

The Pierpont Morgan Library, New York: **6, 7, 14, 20, 22, 23, 24, 27, 29, 30, 31, 32, 36, 37, 39, 50, 53, 54, 55, 56, 57, 58, 61, 62, 65, 66, 67, 70, 72, 74, 75, 76(C.4), 82, 85, 89, 91, 94, 95, 96, 98, 99, 101, 105, 117(C), 121, 125(A), 125(D), 127, 129, 132(A), 133, 134**, wrapper of **138(A), 145, 148, 159, CEA/1, CEA/2**.

Princeton University, NJ: **44, 63**.

Public Record Office, London: **158**.

Torquay Natural History Society: **17**.

Of the remaining letters, some are in private ownership and so will change hands again in the future; others are missing (and in some cases must be presumed lost or destroyed, e.g. **131, 136, 141**) but may yet reappear in the salerooms. In this last category may be noted the 14 letters which have never been seen since Lord Brabourne published them in 1884: **1, 4, 9, 11, 12, 13, 18, 33, 46, 47, 49, 52, 60**, and **93** of the present edition.

SELECT BIBLIOGRAPHY

MANUSCRIPT SOURCES

Austen, Charles-John, Diaries and journals, 1815–17. National Maritime Museum (AUS/101-/109).

Austen, Mrs Charles-John (Fanny Palmer), Letters 1810–14. Gordon N. Ray Collection, The Pierpont Morgan Library, New York (MA 4500).

Austen, Francis-William, Letterbooks, 1801–14. National Maritime Museum (AUS/7-/9).

Austen, Henry-Thomas, Letters to 2nd Marquis of Hastings, 1839. Huntington Library, San Marino, California (HA. 348–51).

Austen, James, Collected Verses. Quarto volume, compiled and copied out c.1834–40 by James-Edward Austen-Leigh. Two copies of this collection exist, with some slight differences in content and wording; (A) in Austen-Leigh archive, and (B) at Jane Austen's House, Chawton. The bulk of the AL archive is now in the Hampshire Record Office (23M93).

Austen, Mrs James (Mary Lloyd), Diaries for 1810–17. AL archive.

Bath Rate Books, 1766–1812. Guildhall, Bath.

Bellas, Mrs Louisa-Langlois, Bellas MS. Octavo volume, containing copies of letters to and from her mother Mrs Anna Lefroy, and other miscellaneous family history notes, compiled 1872. Lefroy archive.

Bellas Notes. Annotations made in a copy of Lord Brabourne's edition of the *Letters of Jane Austen*; these volumes were at one time in the possession of Mrs Bellas, and early this century were given to Miss C. Linklater Thomson, who referred to them in the preface to her *Jane Austen: A Survey* (London, 1929). Dr R. W. Chapman then saw the annotations, and quoted two of them in his first edition of *Jane Austen's Letters*; according to him, the volumes later went to a private collector in America.

Butler-Harrison family history. Southampton City Record Office (D/Z/676/1).

Chapman, Dr R. W., Miscellaneous papers and working notes for first edition. Bodley (MSS Eng. lett. c.759–61 and 924–5).

Chute, Mrs William (Elizabeth Smith), of The Vyne. Diaries for 1790, 1792–4, 1797–1800, 1802, 1804, 1807, 1813, 1815–17, 1819. AL archive.

Clerus List. Oxfordshire Record Office.

Craven archive. Reading University Library (BER. 27.4).

Hales, Caroline (Mrs Gore), Diaries for 1788, 1789, 1791, 1792, 1799, 1800. Jane Austen's House, Chawton.

Heathcote archive. Hampshire Record Office (63M84).

HEIC archive. India Office Library and Records, London.

Hoare's Bank, London. Ledgers 1765 onwards, containing accounts of several members of the Austen family.

Irby Collection. Canterbury Diocesan Record Office.

Knatchbull, Lady (Fanny Knight), Diaries, 1804–72. Centre for Kentish Studies, Maidstone (U951 F24/1–69).

—— Letters to Miss Chapman. Centre for Kentish Studies (U951 C102–9).

Knight, Edward Austen, Chawton Estate Account Book, 1808–19. Hampshire Record Office (79M78MB211).

Lefroy, Mrs Anna, Lefroy MS. Quarto volume of notes on family history, compiled c.1855–72. Great-grandsons of Adm. Sir Francis Austen.

Lefroy, Fanny-Caroline, FCL MS Family History, written c.1880–5. AL archive.

Papillon archive. Centre for Kentish Studies (U1015).

Powlett archive. Hampshire Record Office (72M92).

Powys, Mrs Philip-Lybbe, Diaries and journals, 1757–1808. British Library Add. MSS 42160–73.

Rainey, S. R., The Letters of Mary White 1759–1833 to her Brother Thomas Holt White 1763–1841. M.Phil. thesis, CNAA, Chichester, 1990.

Messrs Ring, of Basingstoke, Account books, 1785–96. Hampshire Record Office (8M62/14 and /15).

Sawtell, George, 'The Kintbury Family' (MS Fowle family history).

Terry, Stephen, Journals, etc., 1841–62. Hampshire Record Office (24M49).

Walter, Mrs James (Frances-Maria Walter), Reminiscences, 1809. Original MS untraceable, as also typescript copy made therefrom in early twentieth century; MS copy of typescript made by Dr F. Henthorn, Brigg, Lincolnshire.

Wiggett, Caroline (Mrs Thomas Workman), Reminiscences, 1869. National Trust, The Vyne.

Parish registers, bishops' transcripts, rate books, etc., for London, Hampshire, Kent, and Surrey parishes.

PRINCIPAL PUBLISHED SOURCES

Adams, O. F., *The Story of Jane Austen's Life*, 2nd edn., (Boston, 1897).

Altick, R. D., *The Shows of London* (London, 1978).

Andrews, C. Bruyn, *The Torrington Diaries* (London, 1934–8).

The Monthly Army List (London, 1798–1817).

Austen, Caroline-Mary-Craven, *My Aunt Jane Austen*, JA Society (Chawton, 1952, and new edn., 1991).

—— *Reminiscences*, introd. and ed. Deirdre Le Faye, JA Society (Chawton, 1986).

Austen, James, *The Loiterer* (Oxford, 1789–90).

Austen, Jane, *Sense and Sensibility* (Oct. 1811) ed. R. W. Chapman (Oxford, 1967).

—— *Pride and Prejudice* (Jan. 1813) ed. R. W. Chapman (Oxford, 1967).

—— *Mansfield Park* (May 1814) ed. R. W. Chapman (Oxford, 1966).

—— *Emma* (Dec. 1815) ed. R. W. Chapman (Oxford, 1966).

—— *Northanger Abbey* and *Persuasion* (Dec. 1817) ed. R. W. Chapman (Oxford, 1965).

—— *Minor Works* ed. R. W. Chapman (Oxford, 1963).

—— *Catharine and Other Writings*, ed. Margaret Anne Doody and Douglas Murray (Oxford, 1993).

Austen-Leigh, Emma, *Jane Austen and Steventon* (London, 1937).

—— *Jane Austen and Bath* (London, 1939).

Austen-Leigh, James-Edward, *Recollections of the Early Days of the Vine Hunt* (London, 1865).

—— *A Memoir of Jane Austen* (1st edn., London, 1870; 2nd edn. (enlarged), London, 1871); ed. R. W. Chapman (Oxford, 1926; repr. 1951).

Austen-Leigh, Mary-Augusta, *James Edward Austen-Leigh, a Memoir by His Daughter*, privately printed (1911).

Austen-Leigh, Richard-Arthur, *Pedigree of Austen* (London, 1940).

—— *Austen Papers, 1704–1856* (London, 1942).

—— *Jane Austen and Lyme Regis* (London, 1946).

—— *Jane Austen and Southampton* (London, 1949).

—— *The Eton College Register, 1753–1790* (Eton, 1921).

Austen-Leigh, William, and Knight, Montague George, *Chawton Manor and its Owners* (London, 1911).

—— and Austen-Leigh, Richard-Arthur, *Jane Austen, her Life and Letters* (London, 1913).

Awdry, F., *A Country Gentleman of the Nineteenth Century* (Winchester, 1906).

Bagster, Samuel, *Samuel Bagster of London, 1772–1851* (London, 1972).

Baigent, F. J., and Millard J. E., *A History of Basingstoke* (Basingstoke, 1889).

Balleine, G. R., *The Tragedy of Philippe d'Auvergne* (Chichester, 1973).

Bamford, Francis (ed.), *Dear Miss Heber* (London, 1936).

Barrett, Charlotte (ed.), *The Diary and Letters of Madame D'Arblay* (London, 1842–6).

Barrett, Philip, 'Philip Williams—The Acceptable Face of Pluralism', in *Winchester Cathedral Record*, 57 (1988), 13–26.

Berkshire Federation of Women's Institutes, *The New Berkshire Village Book* (Newbury and Reading, 1985).

Bettany, Lewis (ed.), *Diaries of William Johnston Temple, 1780–1796* (Oxford, 1929).

Bigg-Wither, Revd R. F., *Materials for a History of the Wither Family* (Winchester, 1907).

Bignell, Alan, *The Kent Village Book* (Newbury, 1986).

Birch, Mrs, *Letters written by the late Mrs Birch of Barton Lodge, in the Ninety-ninth and Hundredth years of her age*, privately printed (n.d., ?1837).

Blake, Mrs Warrenne (ed.), *Memoirs of a Vanished Generation, 1813–1855* [Knox family, Earls of Ranfurly] (London, 1909).

—— *An Irish Beauty of the Regency* [Hon. Mrs Calvert] (London, 1911).

Blanch, Lesley, *The Game of Hearts* (London, 1957).

Bloomfield, Peter, *Kent and the Napoleonic Wars*, Kentish Sources X (Gloucester, 1987).

Boyle, Eliza, *Court and Country Guide* (London, 1815).

Brabourne, Edward, 1st Lord, *Letters of Jane Austen*, 2 vols. (London, 1884).

Brannon, G., *Views of the Isle of Wight* (1824; repr. Wakefield, 1972).

Broadley, A. M., and Melville, Lewis (eds), *The Beautiful Lady Craven* (London, 1914).

Brode, Anthony, *The Hampshire Village Book* (Newbury, 1980).

Brydges, Egerton, *The Autobiography, Times, Opinions and Contemporaries of Sir Egerton Brydges* (London, 1834).

Burke, Bernard, John, John B., and others, *Portrait Gallery of Distinguished Females* (London, 1833).

—— *Commoners* (London, 1834–8; repr. Baltimore, 1977).

—— *Extinct Baronetcies* (London, 1838).

—— *Extinct Peerages* (London, 1846).

—— *Landed Gentry* (London, 1846).

—— *Anecdotes of the Aristocracy* (London, 1849 and 1850).

—— *Peerage and Baronetage* (London, 1857, 1963).

—— *Vicissitudes of Families* (London, 1859, 1860, 1863).

—— *Landed Gentry of Ireland/Irish Family Records* (London, 1976).

Carlton House: The Past Glories of George IV's Palace, catalogue of exhibition at The Queen's Gallery, Buckingham Palace (1991–2).

Cary, John, *New Itinerary . . . of the Great Roads*, 6th edn. (London, 1815).

Chapman, R. W. (ed.), *Jane Austen's Letters to her Sister Cassandra and Others* (Oxford, 1932; 2nd edn., 1952).

—— *Five letters from Jane Austen to her Niece Fanny Knight, Printed in Facsimile* (Oxford, 1924).

—— *Plan of a Novel [etc]* (Oxford, 1926).

Clanchy, V. A., 'Jane Austen and the Williams Family', in *Hampshire*, 17:2 (Dec. 1976), 56–8.

Cokayne, G. E., *The Complete Peerage* (London, 1887–98; repr. Gloucester, 1982).

Collyer, Graham, *The Surrey Village Book* (Newbury, repr. 1990).

Corney, A., *Fortifications in Old Portsmouth* (Portsmouth, 1980).

Course, E., *The Itchen Navigation* (Southampton, 1983).

Crook, John (ed.), *The Wainscot Book: The Houses of Winchester Cathedral Close and their Interior Decoration, 1660–1800* (Winchester, 1984).

Cumberland, Richard, *Memoirs* (London, 1807).

Curtis, William, *History of Alton* (Winchester, 1896).

—— *The Town of Alton, with the Adjacent Villages* (Winchester, 1906).

Curtis, W. H., *Quaker Doctor and Naturalist* (London, 1961).

Dictionary of National Biography.

Ditchfield, G. M., and Keith-Lucas, Bryan (eds), *A Kentish Parson*, Kent Arts and Libraries (Maidstone, 1991).

Doody, Margaret Anne, and Murray, Douglas (eds), *Jane Austen: Catharine and Other Writings* (Oxford, 1993).

Draper, Jo, *Hampshire, the Complete Guide* (Wimborne, 1990).

Egerton, J., *George Stubbs, 1724–1806*, catalogue of exhibition at the Tate Gallery (London, 1984).

Egremont, Lord, *Wyndham and Children First* (London, 1969).

von Erffa, Helmut, and Staley, Allen, *The Paintings of Benjamin West* (New Haven, Conn., and London, 1986).

Finch, W., *A Historical Sketch of the County of Kent* (Canterbury, 1803).

Finlay, Michael, *Western Writing Implements in the Age of the Quill Pen* (Carlisle, 1990).

Fortescue, S. E. D., *The Story of Two Villages* (Great Bookham, 1975).

—— *People and Places, Great and Little Bookham* (Great Bookham, 1978).

Foster, Joseph, *Alumni Oxonienses 1715–1886* (London, 1887).

Fraser, Sir William, *The Melvilles, Earls of Melville, and the Leslies, Earls of Leven* (Edinburgh, 1890).

Gentleman's Magazine (London, 1731 onwards).

Gibson, J. S. W., *Monumental Inscriptions in Sixty Hampshire Churches* (Basingstoke, 1958).

Gill, R., *Trials for Adultery, 1799–1802* (London, ?1802).

Gilson, David, *A Bibliography of Jane Austen* (Oxford, 1982).

Grant, Mrs Elizabeth, *Memoirs of a Highland Lady, 1797–1827* (London, 1967).

Grant, G. L., *The Standard Catalogue of Provincial Banks and Banknotes* (London, 1977).

Greig, James (ed.), *The Farington Diary* (London, 1922 onwards).

A Guide to all the Watering and Sea Bathing Places (London, n.d., post-1815).

Hammond, Nigel, *The Oxfordshire Village Book* (Newbury, 1983).

The Hampshire Directory (Winchester, 1784).

Hart, W. G., *The Register of Tonbridge School from 1553 to 1820* (London, 1935).

Hawkins, C. W., *The Story of Alton* (Alton, 1973).

Heathcote, E. D., *Account of Families of the Name of Heathcote* (Winchester, 1899).

Heawood, Edward, *Watermarks Mainly of the 17th and 18th Centuries* (Hilversum, 1950).

Helm, W. H., *Jane Austen and her Country-House Comedy* (London, 1909).

Hemlow, Joyce (ed.), *The Journals and Letters of Fanny Burney* (Oxford, 1972 onwards).

Hett, Francis P. (ed.), *Memoirs of Susan Sibbald, 1783–1812* (London, 1926).

Hibbert, Christopher, *George IV, Regent and King, 1811–1830* (Newton Abbot, 1975).

Hicks Beach, Mrs William, *A Cotswold Family: Hicks and Hicks Beach* (London, 1909).

Hill, Constance, *Jane Austen, her Homes and her Friends* (London, 1902; new edn., 1904).

Holden's Triennial Directory (London, 1811).

Holt-White, Rashleigh, *Life and Letters of Gilbert White* (London, 1901).

Hubback, J. H., and Edith C., *Jane Austen's Sailor Brothers* (London, 1906).

Ison, Walter, *Georgian Buildings of Bath* (rev. edn., Bath, 1980).

Jane Austen Society, Chawton, Hampshire, *Collected Reports*, I (1949–65), II (1966–75), III (1976–85), and individual annual *Reports* (1986 continuing).

Jane Austen Society of North America (JASNA), North Vancouver, B.C., Canada, *Persuasions*, (1979 continuing).

—— *Occasional Papers*, 2 (1986): Deirdre Le Faye, 'Fanny Knight's Diaries: Jane Austen through her Niece's Eyes'.

Johnson, R. Brimley, *The Letters of Jane Austen, Selected and with an Introduction by R. Brimley Johnson* (London, 1925).

Kaye, Sir J. W. (ed.), *Autobiography of Miss Cornelia Knight* (London, 1861).

Keith-Lucas, B., 'Francis and Francis Motley Austen, Clerks of the Peace for Kent', in A. Detsicas and N. Yates (eds), *Studies in Modern Kentish History* (Maidstone, 1983).

Kemble, Fanny, *Record of a Girlhood* (London, 1878).

Klinkenborg, V., Cahoon, H., and Ryskamp, C., *British Literary Manuscripts, Series II, from 1800 to 1914* (The Pierpont Morgan Library, New York, 1981).

Knatchbull-Hugessen, Sir Hughe, *Kentish Family* (London, 1960).

Le Faye, Deirdre, and Austen-Leigh, W. and R. A., *Jane Austen: A Family Record* (London, 1989).

Lefroy, J. A. P., 'Jane Austen's Irish Friend: Rt. Hon. Thomas Langlois Lefroy, 1776–1869', in *Proceedings of the Huguenot Society of London*, 23: 3 (1979).

Le Neve, John, *Fasti Ecclesiae Anglicanae, 1541–1857*, III. Canterbury, Rochester, and Winchester Dioceses, comp. Joyce M. Horn (London, 1974).

Lewis, Samuel, *A Topographical Dictionary of England*, 4th edn. (London, 1840).

Lewis, Lady Theresa (ed.), *Journals and Correspondence of Miss Berry* (London, 1865).

Lloyd, David W., *Historic Towns of Kent & Sussex* (London, 1991).

Lock, F. P., and Gilson, D. J., *Five Letters from Jane Austen to her Sister Cassandra, 1813* (Brisbane, 1981).

Lowe, J. A., (ed.), *Records of the Portsmouth Division of Marines, 1764–1800* (Portsmouth, 1990).

Lysons, Daniel and Samuel, *Magna Britannia, Berkshire* (1806; repr. Wakefield, 1978).

Madge, Canon F. T., *Hampshire Inductions* (Winchester, 1918).

[Marsh, Catherine], *The Life of the Rev. William Marsh, DD, by his Daughter* (London, 1873).

Marshall, John, *Royal Naval Biography* (London, 1824–35).

Marshall, Mary Gaither (ed.), *Jane Austen's Sanditon: A Continuation, with 'Reminiscences of Aunt Jane' by Anna Austen Lefroy* (Chicago, 1983).

Middlesex Federation of Women's Institutes, *The Middlesex Village Book* (Newbury, 1989).

Modert, Jo, *Jane Austen's Manuscript Letters in Facsimile* (Carbondale and Edwardsville, Ill., 1990).

Montgomery-Massingberd, Hugh, *Burke's Family Index* (London, 1976).

Moore, Doris Langley, *Lord Byron Accounts Rendered* (London, 1974).

479

Mornington, Gerald, *Southampton's Marquis* (Sherborne, 1984).

National Maritime Museum, *The Commissioned Sea Officers of the Royal Navy, 1660–1815* (London, n.d.).

Notes and Queries (Oxford, continuing).

O'Byrne, William R., *A Naval Biographical Dictionary* (London, 1849; also revised enlarged edn., 1859–61).

Oliver, Vere Langford, *History of the Island of Antigua* (London, 1894–9).

Oman, Carola, *Ayot Rectory* (London, 1965).

Parker, Eric, *Highways and Byways in Surrey* (London, repr. 1925).

Patterson, A. Temple, *A History of Southampton 1700–1914* (Southampton, 1966).

Pevsner, Nikolaus, and others (eds), *The Buildings of England* (Harmondsworth, dates as below).

> *Berkshire* (1966; repr. 1988).
>
> *South Devon* (1952).
>
> *Dorset* (1972).
>
> *Gloucestershire, The Cotswolds* (1979).
>
> *Hampshire and the Isle of Wight* (1967; repr. 1990).
>
> *London* (1957).
>
> *North-East and East Kent* (1983).
>
> *West Kent and the Weald* (1976; repr. 1991).
>
> *Northamptonshire* (1973).
>
> *Oxfordshire* (1974).
>
> *North Somerset and Bristol* (1958).
>
> *Surrey* (1971).
>
> *Warwickshire* (1966).
>
> *Wiltshire* (1975).
>
> *Worcestershire* (1968).

Phillips, Richard, *The Picture of London* (London, various early 19th cent. eds).

—— *A Morning's Walk from London to Kew* (London, 1817).

Piggott, Patrick, *The Innocent Diversion: A Study of Music in the Life and Writings of Jane Austen* (London, 1979).

Plowden, Francis, *Crim. Con. Biography* (London, 1830).

Pope, E. B., *History of Wargrave* (Hitchin, 1929).

A Genuine Report of the Proceedings in the Portsmouth Case (London, 1823).

Post Office Annual Directory (London, 1810, 1815).

Quaritch, Bernard, *A Catalogue of the Printed Books, Manuscripts, Autograph Letters, Drawings and Pictures, collected by Frederick Locker-Lampson* (London, 1886).

Read, D. H. Moutray, *Highways and Byways in Hampshire* (London, 1923).

Reilly, Emily, *Historical Anecdotes ... of the ... Jocelyns* (n.p., 1839).

Richardson, John, *Covent Garden* (New Barnet, Herts., 1979).

Robbins, G., *Bath Directory* (Bath, 1801).

Romilly, S. H. (ed.), *Letters to 'Ivy' from the First Earl of Dudley* (London, 1905).

Rosenfeld, Sybil, *Temples of Thespis* (London, 1978).

Rothstein, Natalie (ed.), *Barbara Johnson's Album of Fashions and Fabrics* (London, 1987).

Russell-Barker, G. F., and Stenning, A. H., *Westminster School: The Record of Old Westminsters* (London, 1928).

Scott, James Renat, *Memorials of the Family of Scott of Scot's Hall* (London, 1876).

Shaw, W. A., *The Knights of England* (London, 1906; repr. 1971).

Shorter, A. H., *Paper Mills and Paper Makers in England 1495–1800* (Hilversum, 1957).

Simmons, Jack, *Southey* (London, 1945).

Smithers, Sir David Waldron, *Jane Austen in Kent* (Westerham, 1981).

Catalogue of Exhibition of Society of Painters in Oil & Watercolours, at Spring Gardens (London, 1813).

The Southampton Guide (Southampton, 1774).

Directory for Town of Southampton (Southampton, 1803).

Stanley, Diana, *Within Living Memory* (Basingstoke, 1968).

Stovold, J., *Bygone Southampton* (Chichester, 1984).

Thorne, James, *Handbook to the Environs of London* (1876; repr. Bath, 1970).

Thoyts, Revd F. W., *A History of Esse or Ashe* (London, 1888).

Tilson, Revd W. T. M. Lushington, *Home Light: The Life & Letters of Maria Chowne, Wife of the Rev. William Marsh, DD* (London, 1858; repr. 1885).

Tucker, George Holbert, *A Goodly Heritage: A History of Jane Austen's Family* (Manchester, 1983).

The Universal British Directory of Trade, Commerce and Manufacture (London, 1791).

Vancouver, Charles, *A General View of the Agriculture of Hampshire* (London, 1813).

Venn, J. A., *Alumni Cantabrigienses* (Cambridge, 1922).

Verey, D. (ed.), *The Diary of a Cotswold Parson: Rev F. E. Witts, 1783–1854* (Gloucester, 1979).

Victoria County History of Berkshire (London, 1907).

Victoria County History of Gloucestershire (London, 1907).

Victoria County History of Hampshire (London, 1900).

Vipont, Elfrida, *A Little Bit of Ivory: A Life of Jane Austen* (London, 1977).

Walford, Edward, *The County Families of the United Kingdom* (London, 1860).

Walker, Annabel, and Jackson, Peter, *Kensington & Chelsea* (London, 1987).

Warner, Revd Richard, *Excursions from Bath* (Bath and London, 1801).

Watson, Winifred, *Jane Austen in London*, JA Society (Chawton, 1960).

Whyman, John, *The Early Kentish Seaside (1736–1840)*, Kentish Sources VIII (Gloucester, 1985).

Willis, Arthur J. (comp.), *Winchester Ordinations, 1660–1829* (Folkestone, 1964–5).

Wilson, Margaret, *Almost Another Sister*, Kent Arts and Libraries (Maidstone, 1990).

Wood and Cunningham, *The New Bath Directory, corrected to May 1812* (Bath, 1812).

Woodworth, Mary Katherine, *The Literary Career of Sir Samuel Egerton Brydges* (Oxford, 1935).

Miscellaneous information has been gathered from ephemeral local history publications on churches, parishes, and villages.

BIOGRAPHICAL INDEX

Abercromby, General Sir Ralph (1734–1801). (Not 'Abercrombie' as JA wrote.) Appointed 1800 to the command of the British troops in the Mediterranean, and died 28 March 1801 of wounds received a week earlier at Alexandria.

Adams, the. Chawton villagers: presumably the Andrew Adams and Sophia Whiten who were married 1 September 1811.

Allen, Miss. Governess at Godmersham, from 27 April 1811 to 11 November 1812.

Amos, Will. Godmersham villager, buried 11 February 1819 aged 71.

Anderdon, Edmund. (Not 'Anderton' as JA wrote.) Apothecary, of 4 Queen Square, Bath.

Andrews, Farmer. There were several Andrews families in Chawton and the neighbouring villages; the one JA refers to is James Andrews, who married Jane Baigen(t) in 1801 and had several children. In June 1814 their latest baby, John, was probably ailing, as he was buried, aged six months, on 12 July. The Mrs Browning mentioned in the same context is probably Sarah (née Andrews) the wife of James Browning, who had a daughter Elizabeth born in 1808; by the standards of the time even so young a child as this would have been considered quite suitable as a nurse-companion for a babe in arms. Farmer Andrews himself survived his illness in November 1815, as another child of his was baptized in 1818.

Anne. There are three maidservants of this name mentioned by JA: (1) 'late of Manydown', who died in childbirth 1798; (2) from Wales, with the Austens in Bath ante 1805; (3) leaving her employment in 1808 to get married.

Anning, Richard. Carpenter at Lyme Regis (died 1810); father of Mary Anning (1799–1847), who became the first fossil hunter to excavate methodically the deposits in the Lyme Regis cliffs and so led the way towards the scientific study of fossils.

Armstrong family. Residents or visitors in Lyme Regis 1804; Miss Armstrong renews acquaintance with JA in Bath the following spring. The Bath directory for 1801 shows a Sarah Armstrong, Lamp & Oil Warehouse, 1 Barton Street—could this be Miss Armstrong's less than genteel family?

Arnold family. 'Gentry' at Chippenham; at least three Misses Arnold, also a Sam Arnold; friends or connections of the Cookes (q.v.), the Leighs of Adlestrop (q.v.) and the Leigh-Perrots (q.v.); they also visit Bath.

Atkinson, the Misses. Presumably daughters of Revd Arthur Atkinson, rector of Knight's Enham with Upton Grey, Hants, 1782–1814.

Austen families. There were and are many families of the name of Austen/ Austin in Kent; *Pedigree of Austen* traces one line of the Austens back definitely to John Austen I of Horsmonden (?1560–1620), and this John Austen was very probably descended from the William Astyn of Yalding who died in 1522. In this index only those Austens, or their connections, of contemporary or future relevance to the novelist and her works will be discussed in any detail; their names are shown in **bold** for easy identification.

By JA's time the **Steventon Austens**, other Austen relatives whom she mentions in her correspondence, and the **Knights of Godmersham**, had a common ancestor in **John Austen III** (1629–1705). He married Jane Atkins and had several children, of whom only **John IV** and **Jane** concern us: **Jane** married 1680 Stephen Stringer of Goudhurst, and from this marriage descended the **Knights** (q.v.).

John Austen IV (?1670–1704) of Broadford and Horsmonden married 1693 Elizabeth Weller of Tonbridge. This couple had six sons and one daughter, of whom only the four elder sons concern us: (1) **John V** (1696–1728), (2) **Francis** (1698–1791), (3) **Thomas** (1699–1772), and (4) **William** (1701–37).

(1) **John Austen V** of Broadford married his cousin Mary Stringer of Goudhurst, and had one son and two daughters: **John VI** (?1716–1807), Jane (1724–70), and Elizabeth, who married John Fermor of Sevenoaks.

(1a) **John Austen VI** of Broadford married 1759 Joanna Weeks of Sevenoaks, and had only one daughter, Mary (1760–1803), who died unmarried. John Austen VI therefore left the Broadford estate to his cousin **John Austen VII**, grandson of **Francis Austen** (see below).

(2) **Francis Austen** practised as a solicitor in Sevenoaks. He married (1) 1747 Anne Motley of Dulwich, who died later that year in childbirth, leaving one son, **Francis-Motley Austen** (1747–1815); (2) 1758 Jane Chadwick (died 1782), widow of Samuel Lennard of West Wickham, by whom he had another two sons, Sackville (1759–86) and **John** (1761–1831). Francis Austen assumed responsibility for the upbringing of his brother William's children, following the latter's early death; his second wife was one of JA's godmothers.

(2a) **Francis-Motley Austen** married 1772 Elizabeth (died 1817), daughter of Sir Thomas Wilson of West Wickham, purchased the Kippington estate on the outskirts of Sevenoaks, and had eleven children: **Francis-Lucius** (1773–1815), **Thomas** (1775–1859), **Jane** (1776–1857), **John VII** (1777–1851) who inherited Broadford, Henry (1779–1850), Elizabeth (1780–1858), Marianne (1781–96), George-Lennard (1782–1844), **Frances** (1783–18??), Edward (1785–1815), **William** (1787–1854).

Of these eleven children, **Francis-Lucius** married 1805 Penelope Cholmeley (q.v., a kinswoman of Mrs Leigh-Perrot), but had a mental breakdown and died insane in 1815 leaving only two young daughters. The Kippington estate therefore passed to his next brother **Colonel Thomas Austen**, who had been abroad for many years on Army service; he resigned his commission and returned to Kent in 1817 following his mother's death that year, but despite two marriages (1803 Margaretta Morland (died 1825), and 1826 Caroline Manning) he died childless and Kippington passed to his nephew **John-Francis Austen** (1817–93) eldest son of **John Austen VII**. **William** married 1814 his cousin **Elizabeth-Matilda Harrison** of Southampton (q.v.). FMA's eldest daughter **Jane** (an almost exact contemporary of her second cousin JA of Steventon) married 1797 William-John Campion of Danny, Sussex, and had a large family; **Frances** married 1808 Capt. William Holcroft, RA (later a partner in Francis Austen's legal firm in Sevenoaks) and had issue.

(**2b**) **John Austen** married Harriet Hussey of Burwash, Sussex, and had one son **John-Thomas** (1794–1876) and one daughter Anne. This **John-Thomas Austen** took Holy Orders, and was rector of Aldworth, Berks., 1832–48, of West Wickham 1848–76, and Hon. Canon of Canterbury 1873–6; he married Charlotte-Sophia Tilson (q.v.) and had one daughter, Frances-Eliza (1836–64).

Frances-Eliza Austen married Revd Dr James Cartmell, Master of Christ's College, Cambridge, and had a son James (1862–1921), who in later life added Austen- to his surname. James Austen-Cartmell recorded the family tradition that his grandparents had been introduced to each other by HTA.

(**3**) **Thomas Austen** was an apothecary at Tonbridge and married Elizabeth Burgess; they had one son **Henry**, known as **'Harry'** (1726–1807).

(**3a**) **Harry Austen** was Head Boy of Tonbridge School 1743; Queen's College, Cambridge, 1743; BA 1747, MA 1750, Fellow of Queen's and Fellow of Clare College 1748–60; vicar of Shipbourne 1747–54, rector of Steventon, Hants, 1754–61, rector of West Wickham 1761–85; he married 1763 Mary Hooker of Tonbridge and had three surviving children: **Elizabeth-Matilda** (1766–1855), **Harriet-Lennard** (1768–1839), Francis-Edgar (1774–1804). **Elizabeth-Matilda** married **John Butler Harrison II** of Southampton (q.v.), and in 1814 their daughter **Elizabeth-Matilda Harrison** married her cousin **William Austen** (see above). **Harriet-Lennard Austen** never married, and lived with the Harrisons in Southampton.

(**4**) **William Austen** practised as a surgeon at Tonbridge. He married (1) 1727 **Rebecca**, daughter of **Sir George Hampson**, Bt. (q.v.), and widow of **William Walter**, MD (q.v.) of Frant, Sussex. Rebecca had one son by her first marriage, **William-Hampson Walter** (1721–98), and four children by **William Austen**: Hampson (1728–30, a daughter), **Philadelphia**

(1730–92), **George** (1731–1805), Leonora (1732—post-1769). Rebecca died soon after the birth of Leonora, and William Austen married (2) 1736 Susanna Kelk of Tonbridge, who died 1768 without issue.

(4a) **Philadelphia Austen** went to India in 1752 and married Tysoe Saul Hancock, physician, at Cuddalore in 1753; they had one daughter **Elizabeth** (see below). Mr Hancock died in India 1774; Mrs Hancock, who had previously returned to Europe, spent some years in France with her daughter and then came back to London, where she died and was buried in Hampstead, NW3.

    Elizabeth ('Eliza') Hancock (22 December 1761–25 April 1813): born in Calcutta and a god-daughter of Warren Hastings (q.v.), married (1) in France 1781 **Jean Capot de Feuillide**, who was guillotined in Paris 22 February 1794, and by whom she had one son **Hastings de Feuillide** (1786–1801), a sickly child who died young; (2) 1797 her cousin **Henry-Thomas Austen** (see below), but had no further issue. Buried with her mother and son in Hampstead NW3.

(4b) **George Austen** (1 May 1731–21 January 1805): Tonbridge School 1741–7; St John's College, Oxford, 1747; BA 1751, MA 1754, BD 1760, Fellow 1751–60; ordained 1754; perpetual curate 1754–7 of Shipbourne and Usher (Second Master) at Tonbridge School; rector of Steventon, Hants, from 1761, and of Deane, Hants, from 1773; married 26 April 1764 at Walcot, Bath, **Cassandra Leigh** (q.v.); retired to Bath 1801 and died there 1805; buried at Walcot.

    After her husband's death Mrs GA lived in Southampton 1806–9 and in Chawton thereafter; died 17 January 1827 and buried at Chawton.

    George and Cassandra had six sons and two daughters: **James** (1765), **George** (1766), **Edward** (1767), **Henry-Thomas** (1771), **Cassandra-Elizabeth** (1773), **Francis-William** (1774), **Jane** (1775), **Charles-John** (1779).

(1) **James Austen**, born Deane 13 February 1765; scholar and Fellow of St John's College, Oxford, 1779; MA 1788; curate of Stoke Charity, Hants, 1788, and of Overton, Hants, 1790; vicar of Sherborne St John, Hants, 1791; curate of Deane 1792; vicar of Cubbington, War., 1792 and perpetual curate of Hunningham, War., 1805; curate of Steventon 1801, then rector 1805–19; died 13 December 1819 and buried at Steventon. He married (1) 27 March 1792 at Laverstoke, Hants, **Anne Mathew** (died 3 May 1795, q.v.), and had one daughter; (2) 17 January 1797 at Hurstbourne Tarrant, Hants, **Mary Lloyd** (died 3 August 1843, q.v.), and had one son and one daughter.

    James's children were: **Jane-Anna-Elizabeth** (1793, known as 'Anna') by his first marriage; **James-Edward** (1798) and **Caroline-Mary-Craven** (1805) by his second. (For details of this generation see below.)

(2) **George Austen**, born Deane 26 August 1766; epileptic from childhood and possibly deaf and dumb, he was never able to take his place in the family circle. He was boarded out locally, under the supervision of first his parents and later his brothers; died 17 January 1838 and buried at Monk Sherborne, Hants. He is not mentioned in Jane's letters.

(3) **Edward Austen**, born Deane 7 October 1767; adopted 1783 by his distant cousin, **Thomas Knight II** (q.v.) of Godmersham, and from him inherited three estates—Steventon and Chawton in Hampshire, Godmersham in Kent; went on the Grand Tour 1786–90; married 27 December 1791 **Elizabeth Bridges** (died 10 October 1808, q.v.) and lived first at Rowling, near Goodnestone, Kent; moved to Godmersham 1797; six sons and five daughters; following his wife's death spent more time at Chawton, and provided a house in that village for his mother and sisters; took the name of **'Knight'** officially in 1812; died 19 November 1852 and buried at Godmersham.

Edward's children were: **Fanny-Catherine** (1793), **Edward** (1794), **George-Thomas** (1795), **Henry** (1797), **William** (1798), **Elizabeth** (**'Lizzy'**) (1800), **Marianne** (1801), **Charles-Bridges** (1803), **Louisa** (1804), **Cassandra-Jane** (1806), and **Brook-John** (1808). (For details of this generation see below.)

(4) **Henry-Thomas Austen**, born Steventon 8 June 1771; scholar and Fellow of St John's College, Oxford, 1788; MA 1796; joined the Oxfordshire Militia as a Lieutenant 1793; Captain and Adjutant 1797; army agent and banker 1801; Receiver-General for Oxfordshire 1813; bankrupt March 1816; took Holy Orders and became curate of Chawton 1816; chaplain to the British Embassy in Berlin 1818 and delivered a series of *Lectures upon . . . the Book of Genesis*; when these were published in 1820 HTA described himself on the title-page as being Domestic Chaplain to HRH the Duke of Cumberland and also Domestic Chaplain to the Earl of Morley; rector of Steventon 1820–2; curate of Farnham, Surrey, 1822–7, and Master of the Grammar School there 1823–7; perpetual curate of Bentley, Hants, 1824–39; then lived in Colchester, Essex, and Tunbridge Wells, Kent; died 12 March 1850 and buried at Tunbridge Wells.

HTA married (1) 31 December 1797 at St Marylebone, London, his cousin **Eliza de Feuillide** (see above); (2) 11 April 1820 at Chelsea **Eleanor Jackson** (died 3 May 1864, q.v.), but had no children by either marriage.

HTA's London banking partnership began as Austen, Maunde & Austen (when FWA was initially associated with him), and later became Austen, Maunde & Tilson. The bank premises were in Cleveland Court, St James, 1801–4, then at 1 The Courtyard, Albany, Piccadilly, 1804–7, and finally at 10 Henrietta Street, Covent Garden, 1807–16. HTA had other branch partnerships in the country: Austen, Gray & Vincent at No. 10 High Street, Alton, Hants, 1806–15, and also Austen, Louch & Co, of the same address, *c.*1814–15; Austen, Vincent & Clement in The Square, Petersfield, Hants (this changed later to Austen, Blunt & Clement, and changed again to Austen, Blunt & Louch) 1810–14; Austen & Louch in Hythe, Kent, 1810–14. His partners were Henry Maunde and James Tilson in London, and William Blunt, Henry Clement, Edward-William Gray, William-Stevens Louch, and William Vincent in the provinces.

Apart from his business addresses, in London HTA lived at 24 Upper Berkeley Street, Portman Square, 1801–4; 16 Michael's Place, Brompton, 1804–9; 64 Sloane Street, Chelsea, 1809–13; 10 Henrietta Street 1813–14; 23 Hans Place, Chelsea, 1814–16.

HTA was instrumental in getting his sister Jane's novels published, and was the first person to provide any biographical information about her, in the form of his introduction to the posthumous publication of *Northanger Abbey* and *Persuasion* 1817/18.

(5) **Cassandra-Elizabeth Austen**, born Steventon 9 January 1773; educated The Abbey School, Reading, 1785–6; 1792 engaged to **Revd Tom Fowle** (q.v.) of Kintbury, but following his death in the West Indies in 1797 remained single; lived at Steventon till 1801; at Bath 1801–6; at Southampton 1806–9; at Chawton thereafter; died 22 March 1845 while on a visit to FWA at Portsdown, but buried at Chawton.

CEA was Jane's heiress and executrix, and was responsible for the preservation and subsequent distribution to her brothers, nephews, and nieces of Jane's letters, manuscripts, and memorabilia.

(6) **Francis-William ('Frank') Austen**, born Steventon 23 April 1774; educated Royal Naval Academy, Portsmouth, 1786–8; midshipman 1791, Lieutenant 1792, Commander 1798, Post-Captain 1800; commanding North Foreland unit of Sea Fencibles, Ramsgate, Kent, 1803; on active service again 1804–15; Rear-Admiral 1830, KCB 1837, Vice-Admiral 1838, Admiral 1848, and C.-in-C. the N. America and West India station, Admiral of the Fleet 1863; when on shore after the end of the Napoleonic wars in 1815 lived at Chawton, Alton, and Portsdown near Portsmouth, Hants; died at Portsdown 10 August 1865, and buried at Wymering, Hants. (For details of his naval service, see William R. O'Byrne, *A Naval Biographical Dictionary* (London, 1849; rev. edn., 1859–61).

FWA married (1) 24 July 1806 **Mary Gibson** of Ramsgate (died 15 July 1823, q.v.) and had by her six sons and five daughters; (2) 24 July 1828 **Martha Lloyd** (died 24 January 1843, q.v.) but had no further issue.

Some of Jane's letters and memorabilia were preserved by Frank and descended in his family, and later in the nineteenth century he also gave away other letters to autograph collectors.

Frank's children were: **Mary-Jane** (1807), **Francis-William** (1809), **Henry-Edgar** (1811), **George** (1812), **Cassandra-Eliza** (1814), **Herbert-**

Grey (1815), **Elizabeth** (1817), **Catherine-Anne** (1818), **Edward-Thomas** (1820), **Frances-Sophia** (1821), and **Cholmeley** (1823). (For details of this generation see below.)

(7) **Jane Austen**, born Steventon 16 December 1775; educated The Abbey School, Reading, 1785–6; wrote the several short pieces now known as the *Juvenilia* 1787–93; *Lady Susan* ?1794; *Elinor and Marianne* ?1795; *First Impressions* 1796—rejected unseen by publisher Cadell 1797; *Elinor and Marianne* converted into *Sense and Sensibility* 1797; *Susan* 1798; moved to Bath 1801; *Susan* revised 1803, and accepted by Crosby, but never published; *The Watsons* ?1804 (abandoned); moved to Southampton 1806; attempted unsuccessfully to secure publication of *Susan* 1809; later in 1809 moved to Chawton; *S&S* accepted by Egerton 1810 and published 1811; *First Impressions* converted into *Pride and Prejudice* 1811–12 and published by Egerton 1813; *Mansfield Park* published by Egerton 1814; *Emma* published by John Murray 1815; HTA bought back *Susan* from Crosby 1816, and JA considered publication elsewhere but did not offer it again, perhaps because she was busy finishing *Persuasion* this year; *Sanditon* begun in January 1817 but left unfinished in March; died unmarried in Winchester 18 July 1817 and buried in the Cathedral.

HTA arranged publication of *Persuasion* and *Northanger Abbey* (the latter apparently his choice of a new title for *Susan*) by Murray, at the end of December 1817 (volumes actually dated 1818).

(8) **Charles-John Austen**, born Steventon 23 June 1779; educated Royal Naval Academy, Portsmouth, 1791–4; midshipman 1794, Lieutenant 1797, Commander 1804, Post-Captain 1810; coastguard service in Cornwall 1820–6; Rear-Admiral 1846, C.-in-C. of East India and China Station 1850; died of cholera 7 October 1852 while on active service in Burmese waters, and buried at Trincomalee. (For details of his naval service, see O'Byrne, *Naval Biographical Dictionary*.)

CJA married (1) in Bermuda 19 May 1807 **Frances-Fitzwilliam Palmer** (died at Sheerness 6 September 1814, q.v.), by whom he had four daughters; (2) in London 7 August 1820 her elder sister **Harriet-Ebel Palmer** (died at Penzance 5 December 1867, q.v.), by whom he had three sons and one daughter.

Charles's children were: **Cassandra-Esten** (1808), **Harriet-Jane** (1810), **Frances-Palmer** (1812), **Elizabeth** (1814); by his second marriage **Charles-John** (1821), **George** (1822), **Jane** (1824), **Henry** (1826). (For details of this generation see below.)

Some of JA's letters and memorabilia were given by CEA to Cassandra-Esten, and from her descended to the daughters of Charles-John jr.

The grandchildren of Revd George Austen, JA's nephews and nieces, were the children of four of his sons:

James Austen's children were:

(1) **Anna,** born Deane 15 April 1793 and died Reading, Berks., 1 September 1872. She married at Steventon 8 November 1814 **Benjamin,** youngest son of **Revd Isaac-Peter-George Lefroy** (q.v.) and had one son and six daughters.

Anna preserved some of the letters she had received from JA, and these descended to her granddaughters (see below under **Lefroy**). She also provided information for JEAL to use in his *Memoir of Jane Austen* (see below).

(2) **James-Edward,** born Deane 17 November 1798 and died Bray, Berks., 8 September 1874. Commoner of Winchester 1814–16; Exeter College, Oxford, 1816, MA 1826; ordained 1823 and curate of Newtown near Burghclere, Berks.; vicar of Bray 1852–74. He married 16 December 1828 Emma Smith (q.v.), niece of Mrs William-John Chute (q.v.) of The Vyne, and had ten children: **Cholmeley** (1829–99), Emma-Cassandra (1831–1902, 'Amy'), Charles-Edward (1832–1924), Spencer (1834–1913), **Arthur-Henry** (1836–1917), **Mary-Augusta** (1838–1922), Edward-Compton (1839–1916), Augustus (1840–1905), George-Raymond (1841–42), and **William** (1843–1921). He became the heir of his great-aunt **Mrs Leigh-Perrot**, and assumed the additional surname of **Leigh** in 1837; he also inherited the Leigh-Perrot house at Scarlets, Berks., which he sold in 1863.

JEAL wrote the *Memoir* of his aunt in 1869; his youngest son **William** and grandson **Richard-Arthur** (son of Cholmeley) collaborated in 1913 to write *Jane Austen, her Life and Letters, a Family Record*; his daughter **Mary-Augusta** wrote *Personal Aspects of JA* in 1920. Some of JA's letters and other Austeniana have remained with the senior branch of the family, the descendants of JEAL's eldest son **Cholmeley Austen-Leigh.**

(3) **Caroline-Mary-Craven,** born Steventon 18 June 1805 and died unmarried Frog Firle, Alfriston, Sussex, 12 November 1880. Goddaughter of CEA. CMCA lived with her mother Mary Lloyd until the latter's death in 1843, and thereafter remained near her brother JEAL and assisted in looking after his large family; she spent the last twenty years of her life at Frog Firle, acting as hostess for two of his bachelor sons, Charles-Edward and Spencer.

In 1867 CMCA wrote down her memories of JA, which were used by JEAL in his *Memoir*; she treasured the letters she had received from JA and gave them to her brother's children; they have now passed to a junior branch of the family, the descendants of JEAL's fourth son **Arthur-Henry Austen-Leigh.**

Edward Austen Knight's children (NB they were all born **Austen** and did not officially become **Knight** until 1812) were:

(1) **Frances-Catherine (Fanny)**, born Rowling 23 January 1793; married as his second wife 24 October 1820 **Sir Edward Knatchbull**, 9th Bt. (q.v.) of Mersham-le-Hatch, Kent; nine children; died Provender, Kent, 24 December 1882. Their eldest son **Edward** (1829–93), 1880 first **Lord Brabourne**, edited the *Letters of Jane Austen* (1884) from those he found amongst his mother's possessions.

(2) **Edward**, born Rowling 10 May 1794; commoner of Winchester 1807–11; St John's College, Oxford, 1811. Lived at Chawton Great House from 1826; married (1) May 1826 Mary-Dorothea Knatchbull (q.v., his sister Fanny's stepdaughter) and had seven children; (2) 3 March 1840 Adela Portal (q.v.) and had another nine children; sold Godmersham 1874; died Chawton 5 November 1879. Chawton Great House is still owned by Edward's descendants.

(3) **George-Thomas**, born Rowling 22 November 1795; commoner of Winchester 1809–12; St John's College, Oxford, 1813; married 1837 Hilaire, Lady Nelson, but had no issue; travelled widely on the Continent; died 1867. 'He was one of those men who are clever enough to do almost anything, but live to their lives' end very comfortably doing nothing' (Brabourne i. 26).

(4) **Henry**, born Rowling 27 May 1797; commoner of Winchester 1810–14; Army 1818–37, retiring as Major in 8th Light Dragoons; married (1) his cousin Sophia Cage (q.v.), (2) Charlotte Northey, and had issue by both wives; developed epilepsy in later life and died 31 May 1843.

(5) **William**, born Godmersham 10 October 1798; commoner of Winchester 1813–14; Exeter College, Oxford; ordained June 1823; curate and then rector of Steventon 1823–73; married (1) 1825 Caroline Portal (q.v., died 1837) and left issue, (2) c.1840 Mary Northey (died 1854), (3) Jane Hope; died 5 December 1873.

(6) **Elizabeth (Lizzy)**, born Godmersham 27 January 1800; married 6 October 1818 Edward Royd **Rice** (q.v.) of Dane Court, Kent; fifteen children; died 27 April 1884.

(7) **Marianne**, born Godmersham 15 September 1801; known as 'Aunt May' to later generations; never married, but lived at Godmersham till her father's death, then with brother Charles-Bridges at Chawton, and later with brother Brook-John at Bentley; finally joined her niece Cassandra Hill at Ballyvar, Gweedore, Co. Antrim, 1878; died 4 December 1896.

(8) **Charles-Bridges**, born Godmersham 11 March 1803; commoner of Winchester 1816–20; Trinity College, Cambridge; ordained 1828; curate of West Worldham, Hants; rector of Chawton 1837–67; died unmarried 13 October 1867.

(9) **Louisa**, born Godmersham 13 November 1804 and god-daughter of JA; married 11 May 1847 in Denmark Lord George-Augusta Hill of Ballyvar House, Gweedore, Co. Antrim (see below); died 29 July 1889.

(10) **Cassandra-Jane**, born Godmersham 16 November 1806; married 21 October 1834 Lord George-Augusta Hill, fifth son of 2nd Marquess of Downshire; died at birth of her fourth child, 14 March 1842. Her elder sister Louisa went to Gweedore to care for the orphaned children, and subsequently became Lord George's second wife (see above).

(11) **Brook-John**, born Godmersham 28 September 1808; commoner of Winchester 1822–6; Army 1826, retiring as Captain 1860; married 24 May 1853 Margaret Pearson, but left no issue; died 10 January 1878.

Francis-William Austen's children were:

(1) **Mary-Jane**, born Southampton 27 April 1807; married 10 June 1828 Cdr. George-Thomas-Maitland Purvis, RN, of Blackbrook Cottage, Fareham, Hants, and left issue; died 29 December 1836.

(2) **Francis-William**, born Alton 12 July 1809; RN 1823, Flag-Captain 1846 (for details see O'Byrne, *Naval Biographical Dictionary*); married 13 July 1843 his cousin **Frances-Palmer Austen** (see below), but had no children; died 13 December 1858.

(3) **Henry-Edgar**, born Portsmouth 21 April 1811; St John's College, Oxford, 1829; barrister of Inner Temple; died unmarried 21 October 1854.

(4) **George**, born Deal, Kent, 20 October 1812; commoner of Winchester 1827–30; St John's College, Oxford, 1830; RN Chaplain 1837–48 or later; rector of St John's, Redhill, Havant, Hants, 1856–97; married 9 July 1851 Louisa-Lane Tragett, and left issue; died 13 June 1903.

Some of JA's letters descended to George's son **Capt. Ernest-Leigh Austen, RN**, who gave them to the British Museum in the 1930s.

(5) **Cassandra-Eliza**, born Portsmouth 8 January 1814, died unmarried 6 May 1849.

(6) **Herbert-Grey**, born Chawton 8 November 1815; RN 1830, Captain 1864 (for details see O'Byrne, *Naval Biographical Dictionary*); married 12 June 1862 Louisa-Frances Lyus and left issue; died 31 March 1888.

Some Austenian memorabilia have descended in this branch of the family.

(7) **Elizabeth**, born Alton 15 April 1817; died 22 May 1830.

(8) **Catherine-Anne**, born Chawton 7 July 1818; married 24 August 1842 **John Hubback**, barrister of Lincoln's Inn, and had three sons; the two younger, Edward and Charles, emigrated to America *c*.1870, and CAH eventually followed them there and died in Virginia 25 February 1877.

Between 1850–63 CAH wrote ten novels, the first one, *The Younger Sister*, being a completion of JA's fragment *The Watsons*. Her eldest son **John-Henry Hubback** (1844–1939) wrote *JA's Sailor Brothers* (1906) in collaboration with his daughter **Edith-Charlotte** (later **Mrs J. F. L. Brown**).

(9) **Edward-Thomas**, born Chawton 28 January 1820; St John's

College, Oxford, 1842; rector of Barfreston, Kent, 1855–1908; married June 1855 Jane Clavell, and left issue; died 1 June 1908.

Some Austenian memorabilia have descended in this branch of the family.

(10) **Frances-Sophia**, born Ryde, Isle of Wight, 12 December 1821; in later years lived with her brother Edward-Thomas at Barfreston and died unmarried March 1904.

Some of JA's letters descended to her, and after her death passed to her brother George's family.

(11) **Cholmeley**, born Gosport 8 July 1823, died 11 January 1824.

Charles-John Austen's children were:

(1) **Cassandra-Esten**, born Bermuda 22 December 1808; CEA's goddaughter; died unmarried Plymouth 11 September 1897.

Cassandra-Esten assisted her father in executing CEA's Will in 1845, and thereby became possessed of memorabilia of JA which CEA had always preserved; Cassandra-Esten in turn left them to her nieces, the five daughters of Charles-John Austen jr. (see below). She was also able to assist JEAL in the composition of his *Memoir*.

(2) **Harriet-Jane**, born Bermuda 19 February 1810; JA's god-daughter; died unmarried West Cowes, Isle of Wight, 30 March 1865.

(3) **Frances-Palmer**, born London 1 December 1812; married 13 July 1843 her cousin **Francis-William Austen jr.** (see above), and died without issue 1882.

(4) **Elizabeth**, born Sheerness 31 August and died 20 September 1814; buried in Kentish Town, London NW5.

(5) **Charles-John**, born 28 May 1821; RN service 1833–48 (for details see O'Byrne, *Naval Biographical Dictionary*); coastguard service 1851–6 and 1859–65; naval agent in charge of mails 1865; married 6 September 1848 Emma de Blois of Nova Scotia, Canada; died at sea 22 January 1867; one son (left issue) and five daughters.

CJA jr.'s daughters were: **Jane** (1849–1928, unmarried), **Emma-Florence** (1851–1939, unmarried), **Frances-Cecilia** (1853–1923, married Capt. L. P. Willan, RN, and left issue), **Edith** (1857–1942, married Capt. Stokes, RN, and left issue), **Blanche-Frederica** (1859–1924, unmarried). Their aunt Cassandra-Esten (see above) left her Austenian letters and memorabilia amongst the five girls, and it was the three spinsters who sold most of these items in the 1920s.

(6) **George**, born 12 December 1822, died 1824.

(7) **Jane**, born 12 August 1824, died 18 August 1825; buried in Kentish Town, London NW5.

(8) **Henry**, born 16 April 1826; RN 1840, then changed to Army; Ensign, Lieutenant, and Captain in 81st Regt. of Foot, 1843–8; transferred to

73rd Regt. of Foot 1850; died unmarried 21 October 1851 ('killed by a fall') while at the Cape of Good Hope with his regiment.

Austen, Miss, 'of a Wiltshire family'. JA was misinformed; this was Miss Cooth-Ann Austen, youngest daughter of the late William Austen (died 1791), of Ensbury, a village in Dorset, near Bournemouth. No connection with the Steventon Austens can so far be traced, but *Pedigree of Austen* shows a number of collateral Austen families in Kent during the seventeenth century, any one of which may have moved to Dorset thereafter.

Awdry family. John Awdry of Notton House, Wilts. (1766–1844), barrister and Receiver of Land Tax; married 15 January 1795 Jane (died 1855), second daughter of Lovelace Bigg of Chilton Foliat, Wilts. (who later became Bigg-Wither of Manydown Park, Hants, q.v.); eight children.

Badcock, Mr and Mrs. Probably William Badcock (1774–3 April 1802), amateur actor, of 5 Burlington Street, Bath, who married Sophia, second daughter of the dramatist Richard Cumberland (1732–1811), and, in his father-in-law's words, 'died a victim to excess in the prime of life'.

Another possibility might be Thomas-Stanhope Badcock of Little Missenden, Bucks. (died 1821 and buried in Bath Abbey), and his wife Anne.

Baigent. Chawton villagers—several families of this name were living there in the eighteenth and nineteenth centuries.

Bailey, Mr. Lieutenant Bailey of the Royal Marines, then stationed at Portsmouth, and a friend of Earle Harwood. Perhaps a member of the Bailey family at Dummer; Miss Eliza Bailey is possibly his sister.

Bailey, Miss. Of Hinckley, Leics.; Miss Sharp (q.v.) became her companion.

Bailey, Harriet. See under Graham family.

Baker, Misses. In Southampton 1803 a Mrs Baker was a milliner, at Above Bar, and a Miss Baker of the same address was a mantua-maker; another Miss Baker was a mantua-maker in Chapel Street.

Balgonie, Lord (1785–1860); afterwards (1820) Earl of Leven and Melville (q.v.).

Ballard, Misses, of Southampton. Related to the Harrisons (q.v.).

Barker, Mrs. Unidentified; perhaps some connection of the deceased Mr Barker who had recently owned an estate at Stanford Dingley, near Newbury, Berks.

Barlowe, Mr. One of HTA's employees in the London bank.

Barnewall, the Hon. Mr. (Not 'Barnwall' as JA wrote.) Possibly John-Thomas Barnewall (1773–1839), heir to the Irish barony of Trimlestown and later (1813) 15th baron; but more probably his distant kinsman Mathew

Barnewall (died 1834), who for some years past had been a claimant to the viscountcy of Kingsland, and whose claim was eventually admitted by the House of Lords in 1814. Mathew Barnewall had been a 'missing heir', and his past life as an illiterate potboy in the slums of Dublin could well account for JA's description of him. See *Vicissitudes of Families*, 3rd ser. (1863), 16-21.

Baskerville, Mrs. Shopkeeper in Canterbury; probably the wife or widow of William Baskerville, hairdresser and perfumer.

Bather, Revd Edward (1780-1847); Oriel College, Oxford, 1798; BA 1803, MA 1808; vicar of Meol Brace, near Shrewsbury, 1804-47; Archdeacon of Shropshire and Prebendary of Lichfield; married April 1805 Emma Hallifax.

Battys, the. Possibly the Steventon villagers Peggy and Thomas Batt, who died respectively 1808 and 1813.

Baverstock, Mrs. Jane (born 1751), eldest daughter of Revd John Hinton (q.v.); married 1769 James Baverstock (1741-1815) of Alton. Their son James-Hinton Baverstock (born 1785), a 'clever and rather scampish brewer of Alton', was the chief claimant in the lawsuit brought by the Hintons, Baverstocks, and Dusautoys against EAK in 1814 for possession of his Hampshire estates.

Ba(y)le, James. Cabinet-maker, etc., in Winchester.

Beach family. In the mid-eighteenth century Charles Wither, of Oakley Hall, Hants, had two daughters: Henrietta-Maria (1713-90) who married Edmund Bramston (q.v.) and inherited Oakley Hall, and Anne (1718-88) who married William Beach of Keevil and Fittleton, Wilts. The Beaches had one son and two daughters: the son, William-Wither Beach (1747-1829), made some mark as a poet when he was at New College, Oxford; later on he was reputedly disappointed in love, and never recovered from this depression, which unbalanced his mind. The elder daughter, Anne, eloped with the fortune-hunting curate of Keevil, Revd William Wainhouse, and died very soon after her marriage. The younger daughter Henrietta-Maria (1760-1837) married 1779 Michael Hicks, and from 1790 the family was known as Hicks-Beach. As well as Keevil and Fittleton, they had an estate at Netheravon, Wilts., and another at Williamstrip Park, Glos. Four of their nine children died in infancy; a surviving son, William Hicks-Beach (1783-1836), inherited Oakley Hall in 1832, following the death of his cousin Wither Bramston. The wit and writer Revd Sydney Smith was for a time curate of Netheravon and tutor to the Hicks-Beach sons.

Beatrice. A maidservant to someone in the Chawton district?

Beaty, Miss. Apparently connected with Mr and Mrs Smith, in London, so perhaps a Miss Beatrice Smith; or is this JA's misspelling of a different surname, Beattie?

Beckford family. Francis Beckford of Basing Park, Hants (uncle of William Beckford of Fonthill, the author of *Vathek*), married 1755 Susannah Love of Basing. His son Francis-Love Beckford inherited Basing Park; his elder daughter Charlotte married John Middleton (q.v.) and had several children, and after her early death her unmarried sister Maria lived with the Middleton family as hostess for her brother-in-law. When in London for the season Miss Beckford lived at 17 Welbeck Street.

William Beckford of Fonthill married 1783 Lady Margaret Gordon, and had two daughters, Margaret-Maria-Elizabeth (1785–1818) and Susanna-Euphemia (1786–1859). Margaret Beckford married 15 May 1811 Col. James Orde (q.v.), to her father's great annoyance; Susanna married 26 April 1810 the Marquess of Douglas, heir to the dukedom of Hamilton.

Becky. Probably Rebecca Cadwallader, maidservant to Miss Elizabeth Leigh of Adlestrop.

Bell, Miss. Governess at Wrotham to the Revd George Moore's children; perhaps a poor relation of his sister-in-law Mrs Robert Moore née Bell.

Bendish, Mr and Miss. Perhaps Mr Richard Bendyshe of 8 Henrietta Street, and later 10 Grosvenor Place, Bath; they may also be part of the Bendyshe family of Barrington, Cambs.

Benham, Sally. Chawton village girl; baptized 21 November 1802, daughter of Charles and Elizabeth Benham.

Benn family. Revd John Benn (1766–1857), rector of Farringdon, Hants, 1797, married 1790 Elizabeth-Thornton Heysham (1772–1861). His children were: Harriet-Anne-Bridget (1793), John (1795), Henry-Clavering (1797), Piercy (1799), Margaret-Elizabeth (1801), William-Wilshere (1803), Robert-Joseph-Charles (1805), Frances-Mary (1807), Isabella-Jane (1809), George-Thomas (1811), Anthony (1813), Edward (1815), and Philip (1817). Piercy went to Woolwich Academy and ended his career as a Major-General in the Royal Artillery.

Mr Benn also had a younger sister, Mary, unmarried and living in very poor circumstances in Chawton, who was buried there aged 46 on 3 January 1816.

Bent, Mr. Presumably a local auctioneer/valuer.

Bertie families. There were two families of this name living in Southampton, not officially related to each other:

(1) **Sir Albemarle Bertie** (1755–1824); Rear-Admiral 1804, Vice-Admiral 1808, Admiral 1814; first and last baronet 1812. Illegitimate son of Lord Albemarle Bertie the brother of 3rd and 5th Dukes of Ancaster; married 1782 Emma Heywood, who died 1805; of Hill, near Southampton. Catherine Brownlow Bertie, his second daughter, died at Hill 17 April 1808.

(2) **Sir Thomas Bertie** (né Hoar) (1758–1825); brother of George

Hoar and of Mrs Dickens (qq.v.); married 1788 Catherine-Dorothy, daughter of Peregrine Bertie (a junior branch of the ducal family of Ancaster), and took her name. Rear-Admiral 28 April 1808, Admiral and knighted 1813; lived at The Polygon, Southampton, where Lady Bertie died 1823.

Best, Miss Dora (Dorothy). Daughter of George Best of Chilston Park, Kent, and married Revd Joseph-George Brett.

Betsy. One girl of this name was maidservant at Chawton Cottage; another was nursemaid to Fanny Palmer, Mrs CJA.

Bickerton. Sir Richard Bickerton was Port Admiral at Plymouth and died February 1792; Admiral Sir Richard Hussey Bickerton, Bt. (1759–1832), was C.-in-C. at Portsmouth 1812, and has a memorial in Bath Abbey. Perhaps the schoolboy Bickerton and ?his sister Amelia were members (?godchildren) of this family and known to the Austens through the naval connection.

Bigeon, Mme/Mrs. HTA's housekeeper, and presumably a French emigrant; Mme/Mrs Perigord (q.v.) is probably her daughter.

Bigg/Bigg-Wither family. Of Manydown Park, Wootton St Lawrence, Hants. This estate, owned by the Bishopric of Winchester, had been tenanted by the Wither family for four centuries, but when the last William Wither died without issue in 1789 the heir was Lovelace Bigg (4 August 1741–24 February 1813), of Chilton Foliat, Wilts., whose grandmother had been a Wither. He and his male descendants added Wither to their surname, but his daughters did not.

From 1789, therefore, the family at Manydown consisted of Lovelace Bigg-Wither and his children: Margaret (1768), Jane (1770), Dorothy (1771–93), Elizabeth (1773), Catherine (1775), Alethea (1777), Lovelace-Wither (1780–94), Harris (1781), Mary-Ann (1783, died in infancy). Mr Bigg-Wither was a widower, as his second wife Margaret Blachford, the mother of these children, had died in 1784.

Of the surviving children, Margaret married 1792 Revd Charles Blackstone (q.v.) and died 1842; Jane married 1795 John Awdry of Notton, Wilts (q.v.) and died 1855; Elizabeth married 1799 Revd William Heathcote (q.v.) and died 1855; Catherine married 1808 Revd Herbert Hill (q.v.) and died 1848; Alethea died unmarried 1847; Harris married 1804 Anne-Howe Frith, and till his father's death lived at Wymering, near Cosham, Hants, where seven of his ten children were born; he returned to Manydown 1813 and lived there till his own death in 1833.

Elizabeth, Catherine, and Alethea Bigg were particular friends of JA and CEA in their girlhood days, and it was perhaps encouragement from these elder sisters which had emboldened the shy, stammering young Harris Bigg-Wither to propose marriage to JA in December 1802. The fact that JA accepted Harris one evening, only to withdraw her consent the next morning, did not rupture her friendship with his sisters. See *Family Record* 121–2.

Alethea gave JA her honest opinion that although *MP* was superior in a great many points to the two preceding novels, it did not have the spirit of *P&P*; later on she commented that *Emma* was not equal to either *P&P* or *MP*.

Binns, John. Manservant, presumably in the Scarlets neighbourhood, who did not accept employment with the Leigh-Perrots.

Birch, Mrs. Mary, daughter of Thomas Newell, of Henley Park, Henley, Oxon; married 22 December 1770 George Birch (died 1805), barrister, of the Middle Temple and St Leonard's Hill, near Windsor, Berks.; three sons; lived later at Barton Lodge, Windsor, and died 29 March 1837, aged 99; MI in Clewer church, Berks. Up to five days before her death she was still writing letters that were 'most remarkable instances of clearness of intellect, vivacity of mind, and warmth and vividness of feeling and affection'. Mrs Birch was a girlhood friend of Mrs GA, and also knew the Cooper and Powys families (qq.v.).

Birchall, Robert. Music-seller and publisher, 133 New Bond Street, London.

Blachford family, of Osborne House, Isle of Wight. Margaret Blachford (1739–84), daughter of Brydges Blachford of Osborne, married 1766 as his second wife Lovelace Bigg-Wither (q.v.). Her brother Robert-Pope Blachford (1742–90) had one son and three daughters; the daughters in particular often visited their Bigg-Wither cousins at Manydown. The eldest daughter, Winifred, married 18 February 1815 Revd J. Mansfield, rector of Rowner, Hants; the second, Anne, married a Col. Campbell and went out to India; the youngest, Jane, married at Rowner 30 December 1817 Philip Williams (q.v.), of the Inner Temple.

Blackall, Revd Samuel (1770–1842). Fellow of Emmanuel College, Cambridge, 1794; rector 1812 of North (Great) Cadbury, Somerset; married 5 January 1813 Susannah Lewis (q.v.).

Blackstone family. Margaret (1768–1842) eldest daughter of Lovelace Bigg-Wither (q.v.), married 1792 Revd Charles Blackstone (1759–1800) vicar 1789 of Andover, Hants.

Mrs H. Blackstone was Jane-Dymock, née Brereton, of Winchester, the widow of Revd Henry Blackstone (1722–76), Fellow of New College, Oxford, vicar of Adderbury, Oxon, and uncle of Revd Charles Blackstone. Mrs Henry Blackstone had two daughters, Alethea and Harriet.

Blairs, the. In Canterbury, friends or connections of the Oxenden family.

Blake, Capt. Perhaps of 13 Lower Grosvenor Place, London.

Blount, Mr and Mrs. Perhaps Edward Walter Blunt (1779–1860) of Kempshott Park, Hants, and his wife Janet Shirley; or perhaps Joseph Blount of the Mapledurham family (born 1779) and his wife Jane Satterthwaite.

Blunt, William. HTA's partner in the Petersfield bank.

Bolton, Lord. Thomas Orde (1746–1807, q.v.) married 1778 Jane-Mary Powlett, illegitimate daughter and ultimately heiress of the 5th Duke of Bolton, and added her name to his in 1795 when she inherited the Bolton estates; he was created Baron Bolton 20 October 1797; of Hackwood Park, Basingstoke, Hants. His eldest son William (1782–1850) married 1810 Maria, the eldest daughter of Lord Dorchester (q.v.), but had no issue.

Bond, Miss. Perhaps of Upper Park Street, or possibly a daughter or sister of Sir James Bond, Bt., of 6 Henrietta Street, Bath.

Bond, John. Revd GA's farm bailiff at Steventon. Born Laverstoke *c.*1738, married 1772 Anne Naishon/Nation of Deane, and had four children: Hannah (1773), George (1776), John (1780), Elizabeth (1782); John and his wife both died in 1825. Lizzie Bond married Joseph Beale of Overton, at Steventon, in 1809. See JA Society *Report* for 1992, 9–13.

Bonham, Mr F. Possibly Francis Bonham, who matriculated at Corpus Christi, Oxford, in January 1804 aged 18, and subsequently entered Lincoln's Inn 1808. The Miss Bonham whom JA met in Lyme Regis may be related to him.

Booth, Mr, and sisters. Residents of Southampton in 1808.

Bourne, Robert (1761–1829). Professor of medicine at Oxford, and consultant to Miss Elizabeth Leigh of Adlestrop.

Bowen, William (1761–1815). Spry & Bowen, apothecaries, 1 Argyle Buildings, Bath.

Boyle, Courtenay (1770–1844). Third son of the 7th Earl of Cork; married 1799 Carolina-Amelia, daughter of William Poyntz; of Midgham, Berks.; Capt. RN, later Vice-Admiral and Commissioner of the Navy Board.

Boys, Daniel. Coachman at Godmersham, and buried there 22 December 1835 aged 73.

Bradshaws, the. Perhaps of 13 The Vineyards, Bath.

Bramston family of Oakley Hall. The senior line of the Bramstons lived at Skreens, Essex; a member of a younger branch, Edmund Bramston (1708–63), married 1746 Henrietta-Maria Wither (1713–90), daughter and co-heiress of Charles Wither of Oakley Hall, and had three children: Augusta (1747–1819), Henrietta (1751–71) who both died unmarried, and Wither (1753–1832) who married 1783 Mary Chute (q.v.) but had no issue. Oakley Hall was then inherited by his cousin William Hicks-Beach (q.v. under **Beach**).

The diarist Hon. John Byng (1742–1813), who was a cousin of Edmund Bramston, paid a visit to the West Country in the summer of 1782, and on his return journey rode through Overton without calling at Oakley Hall, commenting to himself: 'I allways pass with regret a house at a small distance from the road, whose late owner (Mr B.) I much esteem'd, and where I have been well receiv'd; but now I ride by.—Tho' I am as zealous of relationship as can be, and wou'd go as far as cou'd be to serve one: but the present dowager possessor, an artful worldly woman, of a notable self-sufficient capacity, is not selon mon gout; and her son is little better than a blockhead.' *Torrington Diaries*, I. 107.

Mrs Wither Bramston enjoyed *MP*, but her sister-in-law 'Mrs' Augusta Bramston found the first three of JA's published novels boring and nonsensical.

Branfill, Jemima-Elizabeth. Daughter of Champion Branfill of Upminster Hall, Essex (died 1792) and Charlotte Brydges (q.v.).

Brecknell, Joseph. Married 9 October 1810 Lady Catherine Colyear, daughter of the 3rd Earl of Portmore (q.v.).

Brecknell & Twining. JA may have been confusing different tradesmen here, either accidentally or deliberately. William Brecknel was a furnishing ironmonger at 13 Fenchurch Street; Brecknell & Turner were wax and tallow chandlers at 31 Haymarket; and Twinings had their tea-warehouse at 216 Strand.

Breton, Revd Dr Moyle (1744–1821). (Not 'Britton', as JA wrote.) 'He was a gentleman little in stature, somewhat odd in appearance, and eccentric in character.' He was also described as a man of extensive learning, one 'who has left no path of science or literature unexplored'. He inherited property in Boughton Aluph and Kennington near Ashford, Kent, and served as incumbent of Kenardington and Kennington 1777–85; married 1803 Sarah Billington, widow of John Billington of Bybrook, near Kennington; no issue.

Brett family, of Spring Grove, near Wye, Kent. Thomas Brett practised as an attorney in Wye, and succeeded to the estate at Spring Grove upon the death of his father, Revd Nicholas Brett (1713–76). The Revd Joseph-George Brett who married Dora Best (q.v.) may also be a member of this family. The house is now used as a school.

Bridges family, baronets of Goodnestone Park, Goodnestone-next-Wingham, Kent. Sir Brook Bridges, 3rd Bt. (1733–91) married 1765 Fanny (1747–1825), daughter of Edmund Fowler of Graces, Essex, and had thirteen children: Brook (1766), Brook-William (1767), Brook-Henry (1770), Fanny (1771), Sophia (1772), Elizabeth (1773), Marianne (1774), Charles (1776),

Louisa (1777), Brook-Edward (1779), Harriot-Mary (1781), Brook-John (1782), Brook-George (1784). Apart from the two who died young (see below) all the others were known to JA and are mentioned in her letters.

(1) Brook (1766–9 July 1781) died at Eton as the result of a playground accident.

(2) Sir Brook-William, 4th Bt. (1767–1829), married (1) 1800 Eleanor Foote (1778–1806, q.v.), and had by her four children: Brook-William (1801), Brook-George (1802), Brook-John (1804–5), and Eleanor (1805). He married (2) 1809 Dorothy-Elizabeth Hawley (1778–1816, q.v.) who died after having a stillborn child.

(3) Revd Brook-Henry (1770–1855), rector of Woodham Ferrers and of Danbury, Essex; married 1795 Jane Hales (q.v.), and had two sons and two daughters.

(4) Fanny (1771–May 1805), married 1791 Lewis Cage (q.v.) of Milgate, and had two daughters, Fanny and Sophia.

(5) Sophia (1772–1844), married 1791 William Deedes (q.v.) of Sandling, and had nineteen children.

(6) Elizabeth (1773–10 October 1808), married 1791 Edward **Austen** later **Knight** (q.v.) of Godmersham, and had eleven children; she died suddenly a fortnight after the birth of the last.

(7) Marianne (1774–12 April 1811), was an invalid from an early age, and died unmarried.

(8) Charles (1776–7), died in infancy.

(9) Louisa (1777–1856), died unmarried. She bought a first edition of *Emma* in January 1816, and signed her name in all three volumes.

(10) Revd Brook-Edward (1779–1825), perpetual curate of Goodnestone 1802–9, rector of Orlingbury, Northants, 1805–7, rector of Bonnington, Kent, 1807–25, Prebendary of Lichfield 1810, vicar of Lenham, Kent, 1810–25, perpetual curate of Wingham, Kent, 1817–25; married 1809 Harriet Foote (q.v.) and had a large family.

(11) Harriot-Mary (1781–1840), married 1806 as his second wife Revd George Moore (q.v.) of Wrotham, Kent, and had several children.

(12) Revd Brook-John (1782–3 July 1812), rector 1808 of Saltwood and Hythe, Kent; married 1810 Charlotte Hawley (q.v.), no issue. Mrs J. Bridges preferred *Emma* to all JA's preceding novels.

(13) Brook-George (1784–August 1807), Lieutenant RN 1805 and died of wounds received in action while aboard HMS *Canopus*.

The Bridges daughters were educated at the select boarding-school in Queen Square, London, known as the 'Ladies' Eton' (see JA Society *Report* for 1989, 23–5). Fanny, Sophia, and Elizabeth all became engaged in 1791, and Fanny married first, on 14 December of that year; Sophia and Elizabeth had a double wedding on 27 December 1791, and this was followed by a double christening at Goodnestone on 28 February 1793 of their respective first children—Sophia Deedes born 31 January 1793 and Fanny Austen born 23 January 1793.

During her widowhood, Fanny, Lady Bridges, lived at the dower house, Goodnestone Farm, with her unmarried daughters Marianne, Louisa, and Harriet, and (post-1805) her orphaned granddaughters Fanny and Sophia Cage (q.v.).

Briggs, Mr. Perhaps Revd John Briggs (1771–1840), an Eton contemporary of John Lyford (q.v.).

Bromley, Mrs Ann. Lodging-house keeper, 12 and 13 Queen Square, Bath.

Brown(e) families, in Bath. The *Bath Directory* for 1801 shows several Brown(e)s: Admiral Brown of 26 Brock Street; the Hon. Mrs Brown, of 3 Burlington Street; Dr Brown, FRCP Edin., of 6 Brunswick Place; Mrs Brown of 2 Queen Square; Mrs Mary Brown of 33 Bathwick Street; Miss Brown of 17 Russell Street; Dr Browne, physician, of 37 Marlborough Buildings.

Brown(e), Capt. and Mrs, in Southampton. There were numerous naval officers named Brown(e); the one JA met may be Capt. Edward-Walpole Browne, RN.

Brown, Bob. Perhaps a manservant at Godmersham.

Browning. There were a number of Browning families in Chawton and the surrounding villages at this date. A Browning youth, who had been in domestic service previously, was manservant at Chawton Cottage from February 1813 until approximately July 1816; this may be Thomas, son of John and Mary Browning, who was baptized in Chawton 1791, and perhaps referred to by his surname to distinguish him from the other Thomas, Thomas Carter (q.v.), who had just left the Austens' service. Thomas Browning's younger brother Solomon, baptized 1794, is another possibility.

Brydges family. Mrs Jemima Brydges (1727–1809, née Egerton), of the Precincts, Canterbury, was the widow (1780) of Edward Brydges of Wootton Court, Kent, and 'a lively, witty person who surrounded herself with merry company and became known in Kent for her brilliant though modest salon'. She was the mother of eight children: Edward-Tymewell (1748–1807); Anne (1749–1804) married Revd I. P. G. Lefroy (q.v.); Jemima ('Miss Brydges' in 1808, died unmarried 1819); Jane (died unmarried 1788); Deborah-Jemima (1755–89) married Henry Maxwell of Ewshot House, Crondall, Hants; Sir Samuel-Egerton Brydges (1762–1837); John-William (1764–1839); Charlotte (1765–1849) married (1) Champion Branfill and had one son and one daughter Jemima-Elizabeth (q.v.), and (2) John Harrison of Denne Hill, Kent, but had no further issue.

Samuel-Egerton Brydges was a shy and moody young man, with literary and antiquarian interests. He was very fond of his elder sister Anne

Lefroy, and when she and her husband moved to Ashe he followed them and rented the parsonage at Deane from Mr Austen for a couple of years, before returning to London in 1788 to pursue his researches. He married (1) 1786 Elizabeth Byrche (died 1796), had five children, and settled at Denton Court, near Wootton, Kent; (2) 1797 Mary Robinson (q.v.) and had another ten children. From 1789 onwards he published a number of works on a variety of topographical, genealogical, and poetical subjects, including the novels *Mary de Clifford* (1792) and *Arthur Fitz Albini* (1798) to which JA refers. In later years he laid claim to the Barony of Chandos of Sudeley, and became obsessed by his grievances when his claim was eventually rejected. In 1810 he moved to Lee Priory near Canterbury, where he was able to indulge his literary interests to the full, setting up his own private Lee Priory Press in the servants' quarters of his new home. In 1814 a baronetcy was bestowed upon him; but he was always extravagant and in 1818 had to flee to the Continent to avoid his creditors. He was never able to live in England thereafter, and a plan to raise money whereby part of the trust estates of Lee Priory were sold at an inflated price ended in a disastrous lawsuit that ruined the family. Sir Egerton died in Switzerland 8 September 1837.

His second daughter Jemima-Anne-Deborah married February 1817 Edward Quillinan of the 3rd Dragoon Guards, and died 1822.

Budd, Mrs. Possibly Martha, née Browning, wife of Henry Budd of Newton Valence, the neighbouring parish to Chawton. A John Budd was vestryman of Chawton Church in 1748.

Buller family. Revd Richard (1776–19 December 1806); son of William Buller (*c.*1736–96), Dean of Exeter 1784, of Canterbury 1790, Prebendary of Winchester 1763–92, and Bishop of Exeter 1792–6, and Anne, daughter of John Thomas, Bishop of Winchester 1761–81; born at Wonston, Hants, and pupil of Revd GA at Steventon 1790–5; Oriel College, Oxford, 1795, BA 1798 and MA 1801; married Anna Marshall 1800 and had issue; vicar of Colyton, Devon, 1799–1806.

Susanna-Catherine Buller (1769–1840), sister of Richard, married 1808 Sir John Duckworth, Bt.

Bulmore, Capt. In the *Southampton Directory* for 1803 a John Bulmore, mariner, is shown at 26 High Street; perhaps he skippered a ferry service to the Isle of Wight.

Burdett family. Sir Francis Burdett, Bt. (1770–1844), MP, of 78 Piccadilly, London; rich and radical, and frequently at odds with the Establishment. His sister Elizabeth married 1801 Sir James Langham, Bt. (q.v.), of Cottesbrooke, Northants; the Miss Burdett whom JA mentions, and who did not like *MP* so well as *P&P*, was probably his other sister Frances (died 1846).

Burdon. Either John Burdon, bookseller of College Street, or Thomas Burdon, bookseller and wine merchant of Kingsgate Street, Winchester. In April 1803 the *Hampshire Chronicle* reported the death of John Burdon—'who for more than forty years lived in College-street and was an eminent bookseller. In the trade he was a man of industry, probity and punctuality. It will always reflect honour on his memory, as it afforded consolation to his mind, that he would never expose to sale works of vicious or immoral tendency.' See Helen Lefroy, JA Society *Report* for 1991, 32.

Burton, Miss. Perhaps a daughter of H. Burton, haberdasher, of 38 George Street, Manchester Square, London.

Busby, Mrs. Probably Mrs Sarah Busby, of 5 King Street, Bath.

Bushell, Dame. Of Oakley parish; Elizabeth, wife of Thomas Bushell of Steventon (died 1821), and buried at Steventon 8 April 1823. 'Sukey' was presumably either her daughter or granddaughter.

Butcher, Samuel. Born 1770; Lieutenant RN 1794; appointed to HMS *Sans Pareil* 9 October 1795; Rear-Admiral 1840; friend of Lt. Frank Temple, RN (q.v.).

Butler, Mr and Mrs John. Possibly the Capt. Butler of the Wilts. Militia who had married in Guernsey 16 November 1812 Eliza, only child of Capt. Dobree, RN.

Butler, Richard. Hairdresser, of Basingstoke.

Byng, Edmund. Probably Edmund-John-Shanson Byng of the Royal Fusiliers, promoted from Captain to Major July 1797; *not* the son of the diarist Hon. John Byng.

Cage family, of Milgate, Kent. Lewis Cage (died 11 January 1805) married 1791 Fanny (1771–May 1805), eldest daughter of Sir Brook Bridges III (q.v.), thereby becoming brother-in-law to **Edward Austen Knight**; they had two daughters: Fanny (1793–1874) who married 1834 her cousin Sir Brook Bridges V, and Sophia (1799–1833) who married her cousin Henry Austen Knight. After their parents' early and almost simultaneous deaths the two little girls lived with their grandmother the Dowager Lady Bridges at Goodnestone Farm. In later life Fanny Cage did not much care for *MP*, but liked *Emma* very much indeed.

Revd Charles Cage (died 1848), younger brother of Lewis; incumbent of Bensted and Bredgar, lived at Chrismill, near Milgate, and later at Leybourne; married Miss ?Charlotte Graham (q.v.). Mrs Cage wrote to FCK praising *Emma* most enthusiastically.

Revd Edward Cage (died 1835), younger brother of Lewis; rector of Eastling; had a daughter Annetta, who later married as his second wife General Sir Henry-Tucker Montresor (q.v.).

Calker, Mrs. Maidservant to the Revd Mr Papillon at Chawton.

Calland, Revd John (1763–12 September 1800). Rector of Bentworth near Alton, Hants, 1791–1800 and buried there 20 September 1800. Mr Calland's attachment to his hat was well known to the Austens—see *Family Record* 79–80, where Mrs Austen comments on his attendance at a Basingstoke ball in 1794. He appears again in a letter from Nancy Powlett to her husband (Powlett correspondence, 5 April 1799; now (1993) in Hampshire Record Office): 'You know my dear Love the Beaux always find out your absence immediately—no sooner had you mounted your Horse than one made his appearance—he was let in, and exerted himself to entertain me for near an Hour; when I tell you this said Beau was *Mr Calland* you will not be surprised that all his exertions were unsuccessful. . . . At last he took his leave. Perhaps for the sake of my vanity I ought to conceal that his motive for calling, I believe, was to ask your assistance next Sunday.' [RWC]

Canterbury, Archbishop of. Charles Manners Sutton (1755–1828), Archbishop 1805–28.

Canterbury, Dean of. See **Powys**.

Carnarvon, Earl of. Henry George Herbert, 2nd Earl (1772–1833), of Highclere, Hants.

Carpenter, Mr. Physician at Lyme Regis, 1804.

Carrick, Mrs. Perhaps Charity, daughter of Pierse Creagh of Dangan, Co. Clare, Ireland, who married Gerald Carrick. She thought *MP* was to be preferred to the two preceding novels.

Carter, Thomas. Manservant at Chawton Cottage; married 30 January 1813 Ann Trimmer of Chawton.

Cawthorn. Cawthorn & Hutt, publishers, of 24 Cockspur Street, London.

Chalcraft, Lucy. Presumably a village child in Alton or Chawton.

Chamberlayne family. There were several branches of the Chamberlayne family in Oxfordshire, Warwickshire, and Gloucestershire; the couple to whom JA refers were probably Revd John Chamberlayne of Maugersbury House, Glos., and his wife Martha Doughty; or possibly their son Edmund-John Chamberlayne (died 1831) and his wife Cecil Talbot.

Chambers. A former maidservant to Mrs Leigh-Perrot.

Chambers, William. Silk-dyer, Canal Place, Southampton.

Champneys, Sir Thomas (1745–1821). First baronet (1767) of Orchardleigh, Somerset. His daughter Catherine-Harriet (1776–1812) married J. Butcher.

Chaplin, Miss. Presumably a London shopkeeper: perhaps Mary Chaplin, lace-dealer, 61 Grosvenor Street; or perhaps Chaplin & Smith, warehousemen for Manchester goods (i.e. stockists of assorted cotton fabrics), 8 Ave Maria Lane.

Chapman, Mrs and Miss Laura. From Margate; perhaps related to the Revd Mr Chapman who was schoolmaster there in the 1790s.

Chard, Mr. George William Chard (1765–1849), assistant organist at Winchester Cathedral, and also JA's visiting music master at Steventon. See H. Neville Davies, 'More light on Mr Chard', in JA Society *Report* for 1989, 12–14.

Charlotte. Maidservant to Mary Lloyd at Deane.

Charteris, the Misses. Daughters of Lord Elcho and sisters of Francis, 8th Earl of Wemyss; the Elcho family rented the Great House at South Warnborough, Hants, from at least February 1797 until October 1800. The eldest daughter Henrietta had already married 1797 the 6th Earl of Stamford, so the Misses Charteris present at the ball in January 1799 would have been Susan, Catherine, and Augusta, or any two of these three.

Chessyre, Mr. Physician to Miss Bailey in Hinckley?

Children family, of Ferox Hall, Tonbridge, Kent. John-George Children (1777–1852) married July 1798 at Pinner Miss Holwell (q.v.).

Chisholme, Revd Charles. Rector 1812 of Eastwell, Kent.

Choles. The Austens' manservant at Southampton.

Cholmeley family, baronets of Easton Hall, Lincolnshire. James Cholmeley (died 1735) had three children: John, Robert, and Catherine. John's grandson Mountague (1772–1831) was created a baronet in 1806, and the latter's sister Penelope married **Francis-Lucius Austen** (q.v.). Robert went to Barbados and married Ann Willoughby, by whom he had three children: James, Jane, and Katherine; **Jane** (1744–1836) was sent back to England in 1750 for education, and in 1764 married **James Leigh-Perrot** (q.v.); Katherine married William Spry, Governor-General of Barbados 1767–71, and their daughter Wilhelmina Spry married her cousin Sir William Welby (q.v.), grandson of the elder Catherine Cholmeley's marriage to William Welby. After returning to England as a child, Mrs Leigh-Perrot never saw her brother James again, but she retained very fond memories of him and left legacies to his descendants. The Cholmeleys themselves are not mentioned in JA's letters.

Chowne. See **Tilson.**

Christian's. Probably Christian & Son, linen-drapers, of 11 Wigmore Street, London.

Chute family, of The Vine/Vyne, Sherborne St John, Hants. The Chutes had owned the ancient house since 1653, but in 1776 the male line of descent failed and the estate passed to Thomas Lobb of South Pickenham, Norfolk, whose mother had been a Chute. He changed his name to Chute, and had, amongst other children who died unmarried, William-John (1757), Mary (1763), and Thomas-Vere (1772).

(1) William-John Chute (1757–1824), MP for Hants 1790–1806 and 1807–1820; Master of the Vine foxhounds; inherited the estate 1791; married 1793 Elizabeth Smith (q.v.) but had no issue. In 1803 the Chutes adopted as a daughter a distant cousin, Caroline Wiggett (q.v.); her elder brother William eventually inherited The Vyne in 1827 and became known as Wiggett-Chute.

(2) Mary Chute (1763–1822) married 1783 Wither Bramston of Oakley Hall (q.v.), but had no issue.

(3) Revd Thomas-Vere Chute (1772–1827); Pembroke College, Cambridge, 1790, BA 1794, MA 1801; in the Hants Fencible Cavalry and early in 1798 stationed at Deal and New Romney, Kent; ordained 1804 and occupied the Lobb family livings of Great Moulton St Michael and South Pickenham, in Norfolk, till his death; inherited The Vyne 1824; died unmarried at South Pickenham Hall, 22 January 1827. He owned copies of *S&S*, *P&P*, and *NA&P*, and signed his name in the volumes.

Claringbould. Farming family, at Goodnestone, Kent. John Claringbould was buried 11 September 1796.

Clarke, Revd James-Stanier (1767–4 October 1834). Author, biographer, naval chaplain 1795–9; Domestic Chaplain 1799 and Librarian 1805 to the Prince of Wales; Historiographer to the King 1812, Deputy Clerk of the Closet to the King 1816; rector of Preston-cum-Hove, Sussex 1790–1834, Canon of Windsor 1808–34, rector of Tillington, near Petworth, Sussex, 1816; MI at Tillington. He purchased the first edition of *NA&P*, and signed his name in the volumes.

Amongst his other literary pursuits Mr Clarke started in 1799 the *Naval Chronicle* which ran for twenty years. Having failed to interest JA in his ideas for romantic novels, he had better success in patronizing Jane Porter (1776–1850), who accepted his suggestion of the theme for her fourth and last novel, *Duke Christian of Luneberg*: 'Clarke supplied Miss Porter with authorities; it was published in three volumes in 1824, and dedicated to the king, who expressed satisfaction with it.'

Clarke family. John Clarke (1759–1842) of Worting, Hants; married Anne, second daughter of Carew Mildmay and sister of Lady Mildmay (q.v.). The Clarkes were old friends of Mr and Mrs George Hoar (q.v.).

Clayton, Mr. Probably George Clayton (died 1828), son of Sir William and Lady Louisa (née Fermor) Clayton of Harleyford, Bucks., and 79 Gloucester Place, Portman Square, London; maternal cousin of Mrs Fielding (q.v.).

Clement family, of Alton and Chawton. Thomas Clement (1745–13 October 1826) of Alton, attorney, married 1780 Jane White (1755–3 January 1831, q.v.), and had nine children.

Of these nine, his daughter Mary-Anne (1783) married 1809 Frederick Gray (q.v.) of Alton; and his younger son Benjamin (1785–5 November 1835), Capt. RN, married 1811 Ann-Mary Prowting (q.v.) of Chawton, and had three children: Benjamin (1813), William-Thomas (1821), and Anne-Mary (1824).

Of these three, Revd Benjamin (1813–27 November 1873) was for thirty-four years a Minor Canon of Winchester; William-Thomas (1821–13 January 1864) had an only daughter, Lilias-Edith (Lily) (1860–2 February 1895) who died unmarried; Anne-Mary (1824–22 February 1893) married George Wolfe, but had no issue.

The Henry Clement who was HTA's banking partner in Petersfield was probably a member of this Alton family.

Clewes, Miss. Governess at Godmersham from 1813 to 1820. She agreed (perhaps sycophantically?) with FCK's opinions of *MP*.

Cobourg, Prince of. See under **Royal Family.**

Colbourne, or (more phonetically) **Cooban, Miss.** Owner of the girls' boarding-school at 10 Upper [Lansdown] Crescent, Bath.

Cole, Benjamin. The next tenant of 4 Sydney Place, Bath, following the Austens' residence there.

Coleby, B. H. Draper in Alton; CEA paid him £20 in January 1817.

Coleman family. Richard (1777–1832) and Mary-Anne Coleman, of Court Lodge, Godmersham; their daughter Elizabeth was baptized 14 January 1807.

Collier or **Collyer.** Coachman or coachmaster at Alton.

Colyear, Lady Catherine. Daughter of the 3rd Earl of Portmore (q.v.), married 9 October 1810 Mr Joseph Brecknell (q.v.).

Conyngham, Lady. Elizabeth, daughter of J. Denison, married 1794 Baron Conyngham (1766–1832), who became 1816 1st Marquis Conyngham, and 1821 Baron Minster of Minster Abbey, Kent.

Cooke family, of Great Bookham. Revd Samuel Cooke (1741–1820), rector of Cotsford, Oxon., and vicar of Great Bookham, Surrey, 1769–1820; married 16 June 1768 Cassandra Leigh (27 January 1743/4–1826, q.v.), first cousin, namesake, and almost exact contemporary of Mrs GA; godfather to JA. The Cookes had eleven children, of whom only three survived:

(1) Revd Theophilus-Leigh Cooke (13 April 1778–11 October 1846); Balliol College, Oxford, 1794, then Fellow of Magdalen College, Oxford;

perpetual curate of Beckley, Northants, 1803, and Little Ilford, Essex; rector of Brandeston, Norfolk, 1815; died unmarried, buried Beckley.

(2) Revd George-Leigh Cooke (1 July 1779–1853); Balliol College, Oxford, 1797 and Fellow of Corpus Christi College, Oxford, 1800–15; Sedleian Professor of Natural Philosophy 1810–53; Keeper of the Archives 1818–26; vicar of Rissington Wick, Glos., vicar of Cubbington and perpetual curate of Hunningham, War., 1820; married Anne Hay (1786–1869) and had issue; buried Beckley.

(3) Mary (14 March 1781–post-1818), died unmarried.

When Fanny Burney married Gen. d'Arblay in 1793 the couple lived first in Great Bookham till 1797, and then in the nearby village of West Humble till 1801. During this period, and also for some years afterwards, there are a number of references to the Cookes in Fanny's correspondence, beginning straightaway on 30 August 1793:

> Mr Cooke, our vicar, a very worthy man, & a goodish—though by no means a marvellously *rapid* Preacher—tells me he longs for nothing so much as a Conversation with Dr Burney, upon the subject of Parish Psalm singing.—He complains that the Methodists run away with the regular Congregations, from their superiority in Vocal devotion, & he wishes to remedy this evil by a little laudable emulation. . . . His Wife, Mrs Cooke, is a very sensible & benevolent woman, & excessively kind to me.

> December 1797: We quitted Bookham with one single regret—that of leaving our excellent neighbours, the Cookes. I do not absolutely include the fair young Lady in my sorrow!—but the Father is so worthy, & the Mother so good, so deserving, so liberal & so infinitely kind, that the world certainly does not abound with people to compare with them. . . . The eldest son, too, is a remarkably pleasing young man: the younger seems as sulky as the sister is haughty.

> March 1799: An excellent, though new friend of ours, the wife of our Bookham vicar, Mrs Cooke, is now at Bath: & if you can set aside the prejudice her appearance & solemnity of Manner may give rise to, you will find her a cultivated, well bred woman, as well as scrupulously honourable, & warmly zealous for those she loves. . . . Her Daughter is sensible, but stiff & cold, & by no means equally amiable in her disposition *now*, though I think improving, & opening into something better. (Joyce Hemlow (ed.), *The Journals and Letters of Fanny Burney* (Oxford, 1972–), iii. 2–3 and iv. 50, 262).

Fanny Burney preserved seven letters from Mrs Cooke, written between 1796–1819 (British Library Egerton MSS 3698, fos. 127–136*b*).

The curates with whom Mary Cooke did *not* fall in love were Revd George-Hanway Standert (Great Bookham 1808 and Little Bookham thereafter), Revd John-Collinson Bissett (Great Bookham 1809), and their neighbour Revd John Warneford of Dorking (q.v.).

Mrs Cooke was herself an authoress, having published a novel *Battleridge, an historical tale founded on facts* in 1799. When *MP* appeared, the Cookes told JA that they were very much pleased with it, 'particularly with the Manner in which the Clergy are treated'—and Mr Cooke called it 'the most sensible Novel he had ever read'. Mary Cooke was quite as much pleased with it as her parents.

Cooper family. Revd Dr Edward Cooper (1728–27 August 1792), son of Gislingham Cooper of Phyllis Court, Henley, Oxon.; Queen's College, Oxford, 1743/4 and Fellow of All Souls 1747–68; Holcombe Prebendary of Bath and Wells 1770; rector of Hill Deverill, Wilts., 1781–4; rector of Whaddon near Bath 1782–4; vicar of Sonning, Berks., 1784–92; married 1768 Jane Leigh (q.v.), sister of Mrs GA; lived for a time at Southcote near Reading, Berks., and later at Bath; after his wife's sudden death in October 1783 moved to Sonning; one son Edward and one daughter Jane; buried at Whaddon, with his wife.

Jane Cooper (29 June 1771–9 August 1798) married at Steventon 11 December 1792 Capt. Thomas Williams, RN (q.v.); killed in a road accident in the Isle of Wight, and left no issue.

Revd Edward Cooper jr. (1 July 1770–20 February 1833); Eton and Fellow of All Souls, Oxford; married 14 March 1793 Caroline-Isabella Powys (died 1838, q.v.) and had eight surviving children; curate at Harpsden near Henley, Oxon., 1793–9; rector of Hamstall Ridware, Staffs., 1799 and of Yoxall, Staffs., 1809; buried Hamstall Ridware. He wrote hymns and also published a number of sermons. Edward Cooper's children were:

(1) Edward-Philip (27 October 1794–29 November 1864), born Harpsden; godson of HTA; married 1825 his cousin Caroline-Louisa Powys and had issue; vicar of Long Itchington, War., and of Little Dalby, Leics., 1852–64.

(2) Isabella-Mary (29 November 1795–31 January 1859), born Harpsden; married 9 April 1834 Revd Thomas Arden and had issue; died Walton-on-Trent, Derbyshire.

(3) Cassandra-Louisa (24 May 1797), born Harpsden.

(4) Jane-Elizabeth (8 March 1799), born Harpsden.

(5) Frederick-Leigh (7 January 1801), born Hamstall Ridware; married, no issue.

(6) Henry-Gisborne (28 April 1802–10 July 1876), born Hamstall Ridware; married Elizabeth Palmer, no issue; vicar of Burton-under-Needwood, Staffs., 1838–76.

(7) Philip-Arden (25 December 1803–30 April 1879), born Hamstall Ridware; married his cousin Amelia-Frances Powys, no issue; vicar of Orton on the Hill, Leics., 1834–73.

(8) Warren (5 March 1805–18 March 1844), born Hamstall Ridware; married Frances Pugh; no surviving issue.

Cope, Revd Sir Richard, 9th Bt. (1719–1806). Of Bramshill Park, and rector of Eversley, Hants.

Corbett. Farm bailiff at Steventon; Mary Corbett, maidservant at Ashe Park, is probably his daughter. Perhaps the William Corbet who was buried at Ashe, aged 70, in 1826.

Cottrell family. Charles Cottrell (1765–25 February 1829), of Hadley, Middx., died unmarried. His younger brother Revd Clement Cottrell (died 26 July 1814) was rector 1800 of North Waltham, Hants, and had six children, the eldest of whom, Charles-Herbert Cottrell, succeeded to his uncle's property in Hadley; Clement's daughter Sophia married Revd J.-H.-George Lefroy (q.v.).

A senior branch of the Cottrell family added Dormer to their name in the eighteenth century upon inheriting the property of a cousin.

Coulthard family. Probably the Thomas Coulthard (1756–1811) who was creating an estate for himself by buying land in the parish of Bentworth, and living in large rented houses elsewhere in Hampshire while doing so. He was at Farleigh ante-1792, Alresford, Basing Park 1797, and tenant of Chawton Great House 1800–7; in 1802 a Chawton village girl, Sarah Andrews, had her illegitimate child baptized Thomas-Coulthard. He married (1) 1778 Mary Battin (1751–82), and (2) 1784 Frances Barlow (1764–1829); five sons and one daughter; his second son James-Battin Coulthard (1782–1856) was living in Alton 1815. The second wife is presumably the Mrs Coulthard who was at 13 Sydney Place, Bath, in 1805, and moving to live at Oakley 1813; the Mrs Coulthard who died in childbed 1798 does not seem to be connected to this family.

Courtenay, Capt. Thomas. Married 1799 Sarah Lefroy (q.v.).

Cove, Mrs and Miss Anna. Visitors or residents at Lyme Regis, 1804.

Cox, the Misses. Perhaps daughters or sisters of Revd George Coxe (1756–1844), curate of Houghton, Hants, 1786, and rector of St Michael's, Winchester, 1810–44.

Crabbe, Revd George (1754–1832). For details of his life and poetic publications see *DNB*; JA knew of and referred to his visit to London in July 1813; his wife Sarah died 21 September 1813 after their return home; Mr Crabbe became incumbent of Trowbridge, Wilts., 1814; visited London again in 1817.

Craven family. In JA's time the senior line of the Cravens was represented by William Craven (1770–1825), 7th baron and 1801 1st Earl of the 2nd creation, of Hampstead Marshall and Ashdown Park, Berks. Lt.-Colonel of the 3rd Foot ('The Buffs') and on active military service in the West Indies 1795–6; Aide-de-Camp to the King 1798–1805; Major-General 1805, Lt.-General 1811, General 1825; Lord Lieutenant of Berkshire. In 1803 he was encamped with The Buffs at Brighton, and so bored his 15-year-old mistress Harriette Wilson with tales of his campaigns in the West Indies (not to mention her disapproval of his 'ugly cotton nightcap') that she soon ran away from him to the protection of Frederick Lamb (1782–1853), later 3rd Viscount Melbourne.

In 1805 Lord Craven saw Louisa Brunton (?1785–1860), daughter of John Brunton (a greengrocer turned actor and theatre manager in Norwich), and now making a name for herself as a Shakespearean actress at Drury Lane—her principal parts included Celia in *As You Like It*, Anne Boleyn in *Henry VIII*, and Lady Anne in *Richard III*. In 1807 Mrs Calvert watched her perform in Brighton, and commented in her diary: 'She is certainly a very handsome woman, but I don't think her looks pleasing. She has prodigious fine black eyes, but she rolls them about too much. Lord Craven is supposed to be very much in love with her, and many think he will marry her.' Fanny Kemble's mother remembered Louisa Brunton as 'a very eccentric as well as attractive and charming woman, who contrived, too, to be a very charming actress, in spite of a prosaical dislike to her business, which used to take the peculiar and rather alarming turn of suddenly, in the midst of a scene, saying aside to her fellow-actors, "What nonsense all this is! Suppose we don't go on with it." This singular expostulation my mother said she always expected to see followed up by the sudden exit of her lively companion, in the middle of her part. Miss Brunton, however, had self-command enough to go on acting till she became Countess of Craven, and left off the *nonsense* of the stage for the *earnestness* of high life.'. . . 'Miss Brunton, at the beginning of December 1807, with characteristic modesty, made her final curtsey on the stage'—and married Lord Craven on 12 December at his town house in London. Later gossip-writers recalled her as 'tall and commanding and of the most perfect symmetry, and her face the perfection of sweetness and expression'.

In 1816 the Countess admired *Emma* very much, but did not think it equal to *P&P*.

The Earl was one of the founder-members of the Royal Yacht Squadron, and in 1809 named his yacht *Louisa*. He was patron of several livings, including Hampstead Marshall and Enborne in Berkshire, and Wistanstow, West Felton, and Onibury in Shropshire.

A Craven family of a junior line was known personally to JA and is mentioned frequently in her letters; their descent is as follows:

Charles Craven (1682–1754), youngest brother of William, 2nd Lord Craven; known in the family as 'Governor Craven', as he had been Governor of the state of South Carolina 1711–16; married *c.*1720 Elizabeth Staples and had six surviving children; within a few months of Charles Craven's death his widow married Mr Jemmet Raymond of Barton Court, Kintbury, Berks., and died there in 1773. Of her Craven children only Margaret, Jane, Martha, and John concern us.

(1) Margaret (*c.*1723–1815), eloped *c.*1750 with Robert Hinch- or Hinxman (q.v.), and had issue.

(2) Jane (1727–98), married 18 July 1763 Revd Thomas Fowle II (q.v.), and had issue.

(3) Martha (1729–1805), married 2 June 1763 Revd Nowis or Noyes Lloyd (q.v.), and had issue.

(4) John (1732–1804): St Mary Hall, Oxford, and took Holy Orders; curate of Laverstoke, Hants, 1755; rector of Wolverton, Hants, 1759–1804; went to live at Barton Court, Kintbury, 1774; in 1776 cited in a *crim. con.* case brought by Mr John Potter Harris of Baughurst, Hants, for adultery with Mrs Harris during 1774–5, and had to pay £3,000 damages; married (1) ?1756 Elizabeth Raymond of Barton Court, younger half-sister of his mother's second husband ('She had a good fortune, with more in prospect; but she was a young woman of weak intellect'), who died without issue; (2) 1779 Catherine Hughes, daughter of James Hughes of Letcombe, Berks., and had two sons and one daughter; lived at Barton Court and also at Chilton Foliat, Wilts.; died 'after an hour's illness' 19 June 1804, 'many years an acting magistrate for Berks, Wilts, Glos and Hants'. His widow lived later at Speen Hill and died 31 March 1839.

Revd John Craven's children were: Fulwar (1782–1860), leaving issue; Charles-John (1784–1864), leaving issue; and Charlotte-Elizabeth (1798–7 October 1877), married 9 September 1819 Sir John Walter Pollen, 2nd Bt., of Redenham near Andover, Hants, but had no issue. Charlotte-Elizabeth Craven was at school in London in 1813, and later on owned a first edition of *Emma*, signing her name in all three volumes. She and her mother liked it, but not so much as the preceding novels.

Crawford, Mr. Visitor or resident in Lyme Regis, 1804.

Creed, Mrs, of Hendon. Catherine Herries (q.v.) married 1813 Henry Knowles Creed (1785–1855), who took Holy Orders 1826 and became vicar of Corse, Glos., 1828. Mrs Creed preferred *S&S* and *P&P* to *MP*. A Mr William Creed and daughter were living in Hampstead, near Hendon, in 1795; and in 1815 a Mr H. Creed was living at 19 Hans Place, Chelsea, who may be the same HKC.

Criswick family. Mrs Criswick of Highclere seems to have been employed at some time by Governor Craven, father of Revd John Craven; the Mr Criswick mentioned in 1808 is possibly her son, and perhaps the same as the

James Criswick whose infant daughter Anna was buried at Newbury in January 1816.

Crook and Besford's. John Crook, Son, and Besford, haberdashers and hosiers, 104 Pall Mall, London.

Crooke, Mr, and sisters. Mr John-Crosse Crooke purchased the Kempshott Park estate near Worting, Hants, in 1788, and these three young people are no doubt his children.

Crosby, Richard. Crosby & Co, publishers, of 4 Stationers' Court, Ludgate Street, London.

Croucher, Mary. Godmersham villager, buried 11 September 1814 aged 79.

Crutchley family. Mr Jeremiah Crutchley, who had purchased Sunninghill Park, Berks., in 1769, died in 1805 leaving a young son; it was presumably his widow whom HTA was now considering as a possible second wife for himself.

Cure family. George Cure, an upholsterer in the Haymarket, London (with royal appointment to the Prince of Wales), married *c.*1730 Elizabeth Hampson, daughter of Sir George Hampson, 4th Bt. (q.v.). She died childless 1733; George Cure married 1735 Catherine Payne (q.v.), and had two sons; the Mr Cure whom JA met in 1811 was probably the younger one, Capel Cure (1746–1820), of Blake Hall near Ongar, Essex, and also 37 Great George Street, London.

Curling, Miss and Miss Eliza. Cousins of Mary Gibson, Mrs FWA.

Curtis. For nearly three hundred years, up to the 1950s, the prolific Curtis family played an important part in the life of the town of Alton. They were Quakers and medical practitioners, and the apothecary William Curtis who attended JA in her last illness was already the fourth generation of this profession; his son, another William (1803–81), founded the Museum in Alton which bears his name, and lived in the house opposite, now 4 High Street. The botanist William Curtis (1746–99), author of the *Flora Londinensis* and of the *Botanical Magazine*, was also a member of the family.

Unfortunately the medical notes which Mr Curtis presumably made on his patients were not preserved by his descendants, nor is there any Curtis archive which refers to the Austens.

Cuthbert family. Miss Cuthbert, her sister Maria, and their brother, lived at Eggerton House near Godmersham, where they looked after Elizabeth, sister of Mr Thomas Knight (q.v.).

D'Antraigues, Comte Emmanuel-Louis (1756–22 July 1812). An accomplished scholar who was also a professional spy, forger, and double agent; married a beautiful French opera singer, Anne de St Huberti, and had one son Julien (1792–1861), who later lived at 27 Montague Place, Russell Square,

London; came to England 1806 with credentials purporting to be from the Tsar of Russia; lived at Queen Ann Street West [Queen Anne Street] in London, and also at 27 The Terrace, Barnes, Surrey; he and his wife were both murdered in their Barnes house one evening by their Italian servant, possibly on account of a personal grievance or possibly for political reasons.

D'Arblay, Alexander (1794–1837), son of Fanny Burney and General D'Arblay. From 1793–7 the D'Arblays lived at Great Bookham, and were in frequent contact with Revd Samuel Cooke (q.v.) and his wife; it is not known whether JA ever actually met Fanny Burney, but Mrs Cooke no doubt passed on information to Steventon concerning these new and interesting parishioners.

D'Auvergne, Corbet-James. Commander RN 1807 and appointed to the sloop HMS *Autumn* in September 1810, Post-Captain 1811; died 1825; a Jerseyman, and younger half-brother of Admiral Philip D'Auvergne, RN, who was briefly the Prince de Bouillon.

Davis, Miss. Professional singer in London.

Davis, Mrs. Draper in Basingstoke.

Dawes, Miss. Possibly the Sophia Dawes (1774–1820) of Ditcheat, Somerset, who married Andrew Christie, MD.

Dawkins, Betty. Steventon villager, buried 16 April 1810.

Day, Mrs. Perhaps the wife of John Day, baker, at 145 High Street, Southampton.

Daysh, George. Clerk in the Ticket Office, Navy Office, London, 1778–1821.

Deane family. Mrs Deane and her daughters Harriet and Augusta, of Monk (West) Sherborne, Hants. They may perhaps be part of the prolific Deane family who were prominent in the civic affairs of Reading, Berks., at this period. A Deane boy, either George or Henry, was one of Revd GA's pupils at Steventon Rectory *c.*1779. There was also a Mr Thomas Deane, brewer and brandy-merchant of Winchester, who may be related.

Debary family. Revd Peter Debary (1725–January 1814), vicar 1755–1814 of Hurstbourne Tarrant, Hants, and 1772 of Burbage, Wilts.; married Ann Hayward (1727–1809) and had two sons and four daughters: Ann (1763–1834); Revd Peter Debary jr. (1764–1841), curate 1804 and rector January 1807–24 of Eversley, Hants, vicar of Aisgarth, Yorks., and rector of Orwell, Cambs., 1830; Mary (1766–1854); Richard (1767–1829); Susannah (1768–1852); Sarah (1770–1823).

Deedes family, of Sandling Park, near Hythe, Kent. William Deedes (1761–1834) married 27 December 1791 Sophia Bridges, second daughter of Sir Brook Bridges III (q.v.), and thus became a brother-in-law of **Edward**

Austen Knight. The Deedes had nineteen children, all but the last of whom were known to JA: Sophia (1793), Mary (1794), Fanny (1795), William (1796), Julius (1798), Isabella (1799), Henry (1800), Edward (1801), John (1803), Harriett (1805), George (1806), Elizabeth (1807), Charles (1808), Robert (1809), Lewis (1811), Edmund (1812), Louisa (1813), Marianne (1817), Emily (1818); Harriett, Elizabeth, Louisa, and Emily died young.

William Deedes was Colonel of the South Kent Volunteers—'when the coast was threatened with invasion, he remained in his post in the fearless discharge of all his public and private duties'—and MP for Hythe 1807-12. On 26 June 1814 the Tsar of Russia passed through Hythe during his visit to England for the peace celebrations, and the 'fair and accomplished daughter' of Mr Deedes helped to serve him coffee at the Swan—this presumably would have been the eldest, Sophia.

Dering family, of Surrenden-Dering, near Ashford, Kent. Sir Edward, 6th Bt. (1732–8 December 1798), succeeded by his son Edward, 7th Bt. (1757–1811).

Dewar family. Penelope-Susanna Mathew (q.v.) married 1787 her first cousin David Dewar (died 1794) of St Christopher's, West Indies, and of Enham House, Hants, and had three children: Jane-Charlotte (1791), George (1792), David (1794); a descendant George Bertie Albemarle Dewar was a naturalist and writer in the Edwardian era. Mrs Dewar married (2) 1799 Charles Cumberland (died 1835), third son of the dramatist Richard Cumberland, and had another five children; their debts obliged them to live abroad.

Dickens, Mrs. Mary, née Hoar, married 1785 Col. Richard-Mark Dickens of the 34th Regt.; sister of George Hoar and Adm. Sir Thomas Bertie (qq.v.).

Dickson, Mrs. There were numerous naval officers named Dickson in the eighteenth and nineteenth centuries; this is possibly Jane Dickson, who married 1801 her cousin Capt. (later Admiral) Archibald Dickson, RN (1772–1836) and died 1856. She did not much like *Emma*, and thought *MP* not equal to *P&P*.

Digweed family. The Digweeds had been tenants of the Steventon manor-house and estate since at least the early eighteenth century. In JA's time there was a Richard Digweed (c.1733–1805) and his wife Amy (c.1739–84), who had one daughter Mary (1761–1825, married William Webb (q.v.)); this family lived later on at Baughurst and Hannington, Hants, leaving the manor house to be inhabited by Hugh Digweed (1738–98) and his wife Ruth (1740–91) and their six children. Of these six, two died young, leaving four sons whom JA knew:

(1) John Digweed (1766), succeeded to other family estates at Ecchinswell, Hants, and is not mentioned in JA's letters.

(2) Harry Digweed (1771–1848), from 1798 till his marriage joint tenant of Steventon with his brother William-Francis; married 3 March 1808 Jane Terry (died 1860, q.v.) and had four children; lived at Greywell, Alton, and later on the Continent—both he and his wife died in Paris and were buried there. Mrs Digweed found *Emma* very dull and was barely able to read it through.

Harry's children were: Mary-Jane (1809–24, buried in Brussels); William-Henry (1810–81), who inherited the Ecchinswell property, became JP for Hants and Lt.-Colonel of the Hants Militia, and had only one daughter who predeceased him; Thomas-Frederick (died 1868, buried in Paris); John (died London 1887, 'late of Paris').

(3) James Digweed (1774–1862), ordained 1797 and became curate of Steventon 1798, but never actually held a benefice; married 1803 Mary-Susannah Lyford (1772–1840, q.v.), and lived at Worting and Dummer, Hants.

James had five children: a son John-James (1807–81) who took Holy Orders, succeeded as tenant of Steventon manor-house upon the death of his uncle William, moved to West Meon in 1877 and died there unmarried; three daughters who died unmarried, and one daughter Susannah (died 1847) who married and left issue.

(4) William-Francis (1776), remained at Steventon when his brother Harry married and moved away; apparently died unmarried.

Dinah. Maidservant to the Fowles at Kintbury, and aunt of Mary Lloyd's maidservant Jenny Jennings (q.v.) at Deane.

Doe, Mary. Maidservant at Chawton Great House; probably Mary, daughter of William and Sarah Doe, baptized 17 August 1796 and married William Garnett 30 November 1816.

Dolphin family. John-Vernon Dolphin, High Sheriff of Gloucestershire 1798; of Eyford House, Glos.

Dorchester, Lord. Guy Carleton (1724–1808); Colonel of 4th Dragoons, served in the Guards at the battle of Fontenoy 1745, defended Quebec 1775 and saved Canada; C.-in-.C. in America 1781–3, first Baron Dorchester 1786; of Kempshott Park, Hants. Married 1772 Maria Howard (died 1836), daughter of 2nd Earl of Effingham; nine sons and two daughters. Two of the sons died in infancy, six were in the armed forces and died on active service between 1793 and 1820, and the youngest, Richard, became rector of the family living of Nately Scures, Hants. Of the two daughters, Maria (1779–1863) married William, 2nd Lord Bolton (q.v.); Frances (1785–1812) married Revd John Orde (q.v.).

Dormer, Mrs. Perhaps a member of the Cottrell-Dormer family (q.v. Cottrell).

Dowdeswell, 'Mrs' Dorothy (1741–1804). Daughter of Revd Bernard Dowdeswell of Westwell, Oxon., and so cousin of Mrs Foley (q.v.); of 17 Marlborough Buildings, Bath.

Downes, the. Visitors or residents in Lyme Regis, 1804.

Dowton, William. Actor (1764–1851); had been performing at Canterbury and Tunbridge Wells since 1791; made his debut at Drury Lane 1796 and became a celebrated comedian.

Drew, Mrs. Resident in the boarding-house No. 17 High Street, Southampton.

Driver, Mrs. Housekeeper at Godmersham.

Duer, Mrs. Of Southampton; wife or widow of John Duer of Antigua, and grandmother of Sir George Henry Rose, MP for the city of Southampton.

Duncan family. Mr, Mr John, and their sisters; perhaps children of Lady Mary Duncan of 44 Great Pulteney Street, Bath; or of the Revd Dr John Duncan who was rector of South Warnborough, Hants, 1788.

Dundas family. Charles Dundas (1751–1832), MP for Berkshire 1794–1832; created Baron Amesbury 1832; married Ann Whitley (1752–1 December 1812), heiress of Barton Court, Kintbury, Berks.; their only daughter Janet-Whitley Dundas married April 1808 her first cousin Capt. James Deans, RN (born 1785), who became known as Capt. Whitley-Deans-Dundas and was later Rear-Admiral and Naval Aide-de-Camp to King William IV. Mrs Deans-Dundas thought *Emma* very clever, but did not like it so much as the preceding novels.

Durham, Sir Philip (1763–1845). Captain RN, Admiral and GCB 1830; appointed to HMS *Endymion* February 1801. (For details of his naval career see John Marshall, *Royal Naval Biography* (London, 1824–35).)

Dusautoy/du Sautoy family. According to a letter received by RWC in 1954 from a Mr P. du Sautoy, then living in Africa, this family were not Huguenots but originated in England with Pierre-François du Sautoy, known to his descendants as the 'Old Frenchman'. He was born 1731 at Liège, ward of Comte de Clermont, and obtained a commission in the French army; fought at Fontenoy and subsequently came over to Scotland to join the army of Prince Charles Edward, the Young Pretender; apparently captured by the English at Culloden and released on parole at Basingstoke. In 1758 he married at Basingstoke Mary Abbot, and had four sons; married twice more, his third marriage being in 1775 to Mary Bourchier or Boucher, in Southampton; taught in Winchester; died 1819 and buried at Buriton, Hants.

The eldest son of his first marriage, Peter-John Du Sautoy, became curate of Chawton, and performed the marriage in 1789 of JA's second cousin, Elizabeth-Matilda Austen of Tonbridge (q.v.), to John-Butler Harrison II of

Southampton (q.v.). Another son, James Du Sautoy, married in 1793 Mary Hinton (q.v.); James had been in the Marines, and ended his military career as barrack-master in Totnes, Devonshire, and later Taunton, Somerset, dying in Taunton in 1859 at the age of 97; he had numerous children, of whom the 'Miss Dusautoy' JA mentions is probably his eldest daughter Mary (1795–1818), and her 'youngest sister' Fanny (1813–1913). See W. A. W. Jarvis, 'The Dusautoys' in JA Society *Report* for 1984, 302–4.

According to the *Southampton Directory* for 1803, a Louis Dusautoy was a French teacher, living (appropriately) in French Street; while a Charles Dusautoy was a cabinet-maker and upholsterer at 132 High Street.

William-Stevens Dusautoy (born 1783), son of Revd Peter-John, became curate of Monk Sherborne, Hants, 1806.

Dyson family. Henry Dyson (1765–1846), third son of Jeremiah Dyson, Cofferer to HM Household; King's College, Cambridge, 1784, BA 1789, MA 1792, Fellow 1787–92; ordained 1790, curate of Baughurst, Hants, 1793, then rector of Baughurst 1796–1842 and vicar of Wexham, Bucks., 1814–46. Married 1792 Elizabeth ?Wilcocks, and had twelve children: Henry (1793), Elizabeth (1794), John (1795), George (1797), Frederick (1798), Mary (1800), William (1801), Charlotte (1803), Francis (1805), Jeremiah (1807), Alfred (1809), Edward (1810). When JA called at Baughurst in February 1801, Mrs Dyson was pregnant with William.

Many years later, JEAL remembered Mr Dyson: 'The old rector of Baughurst, a gentleman of the most wooden and inexpressive countenance imaginable. He seldom spoke, unless spoken to; and was rarely seen within a field or two of hounds; but he loved hunting in his own way, and went quite as well in the vale as on the hills.'

There was also Revd Henry's elder brother Jeremiah Dyson and his wife Elizabeth Collins, living at Compton, Hants; Revd Philip Williams (q.v.), was brother-in-law to this couple.

East, Miss. Martha (died unmarried 17 June 1854), daughter of Edward East of Whitehall, Jamaica; Mrs Latouche (q.v.) was her mother.

East, Sir William (1738–1819). First baronet 1766 of Hall Place, Hurley, Berks., and 38 Welbeck Street, London; his eldest son Gilbert (1764–1828) was one of Revd GA's pupils c.1779.

Eden, the Misses. The Rt. Revd John Moore, Archbishop of Canterbury 1783–1805 (q.v.) had married 1770 as his second wife Catherine, second daughter of Sir Robert Eden, Bt.; the Misses Eden to whom JA refers may have been her nieces.

Edwards, Mr and daughter. Perhaps Revd Mr Edwards of 7 Gay Street, Bath.

Edwards, Mrs. Perhaps the wife of William Edwards of Alton, wealthy butcher and churchwarden in 1814.

Edwin, Mrs John jr. (1769–1854). Actress, but evidently not a star performer.

Egerton, Henry. Eliza de Feuillide (Mrs HTA) had in past years stayed with her friends Revd Charles Egerton and his wife, at Washington, Co. Durham, where Mr Egerton was rector 1786–1819; this Henry is probably their son.

Egerton, Thomas. Of the Military Library, Whitehall. JA's first publisher, who brought out *S&S* and *P&P* and the first edition of *MP*.

Egremont, Lord. George Wyndham (1751–1837), 3rd Earl of Egremont, of Petworth, Sussex. A very wealthy, amiable, and sociable landowner, who kept open house at Petworth for anyone who liked to visit him. 'He would wander through the great rooms, his hat on his head, his hands in his pockets and little dogs at his heels, exchanging civilities whenever he felt obliged to do so.' He was also a generous patron of the arts, and especially of J. M. W. Turner, who lived at Petworth from 1809. See Lord Egremont, *Wyndham and Children First* (London, 1968), 27–39.

Ekins, Anne. Younger daughter of Revd Jeffery Ekins, Dean of Carlisle; living with her mother at 7 Upper [Lansdown] Crescent, Bath; married 1812 as his second wife John-Hooper Holder (q.v.). Miss Ekins 'had nothing to commend her except her dulcet tones', and Mr Holder's mother was so disgusted at his choice that she would not go to the wedding. See Carola Oman, *Ayot Rectory* (London, 1965), 62.

Eliza. The Austens' maidservant in Southampton.

Elliot, Revd William (born 1773). Curate 1796 of Tangley, Hants, a village 5 miles west of Hurstbourne Tarrant; friend of Revd William Lance of Netherton.

Elliott, Mrs. Perhaps Mrs Elliott of 33 New King Street, or else Mrs Grace Elliott of 4 Seymour Street, Bath.

Ellis, Charles Rose. Owned Claremont Park, Esher, Surrey, from 1807 to 1816.

Elliston family. Robert William (1774–1831), actor, of the Bath Theatre and 39 Milsom Street; later a theatrical manager in London and the provinces; married 1796 Elizabeth Rundall, a teacher of dancing in Bath, who 'in the height of his success continued her occupation'. Her Dancing Academy was at 2 Trim Street in 1801, and by 1812 at 21 Milsom Street.

Revd Dr William Elliston (1732–1807), Master of Sidney College, Cambridge; 'uncle to Mr Elliston the dramatic performer, to whom he has left considerable property, Report says 17,000£'.

Elrington, Major. Either Major Francis, of the 122nd Foot, or Major Thomas-Gerard of the 115th Foot.

Elton, James. Presumably at one time employed by the Austens, but his name is not in the Deane or Steventon parish registers.

Emery, John. Actor (1777–1822); excelled in playing the parts of comic rustics.

Esten, Mrs. Née Palmer (q.v.); wife of Mr James Christie Esten, Chief Justice of Bermuda, and sister-in-law of CJA.

Estwick, Mrs. Cassandra-Julia, elder daughter of 2nd Lord Hawke (q.v. under Turner) and niece of Lady Saye and Sele (q.v. under Twisleton); married (1) 1793 Samuel Estwick of Barbados (1770–97), (2) September 1800 Revd Stephen Sloane (q.v.), and (3) post-1812 Thomas Green.

Evelyn family. William-Glanvill Evelyn (1734–1 November 1813), of St Clere near Ightham, Kent, and 10 Queen's Parade, Bath; Sheriff of Kent 1757 and MP for Hythe 1768–96; died at Bath; his equestrian portrait by Stubbs is in the Tate Gallery. Married 1760 Susanna Barret and had one son William and one daughter Frances. This son died in 1788; Frances married 1782 Col. Alexander Hume, who later changed his name to Evelyn.

A cousin, John Evelyn, lived for a time at 23 Marlborough Buildings, Bath.

Fagg, Revd Sir John, 6th Bt. (?1760–1822), of Mystole near Canterbury, and rector of Chartham, Kent. Married 1789 Anne Newman of Canterbury; four sons and five daughters: Elizabeth, Sarah-Anne, Augusta, Lucy, Jemima. In 1806 the 13-year-old Fanny Knight wrote to her former governess Miss Dorothy Chapman: 'I think I quite agree with you, as to Miss Faggs plainness, poor thing! To be sure, she is unfortunately ugly!'

Sir John Fagg's sister Helen married 1795 as his second wife Revd Philip Williams (q.v.).

Falknor. The coach service between London and Southampton was officially referred to as 'Collier's Southampton Coach' (sometimes spelt 'Collyer'); perhaps Falknor was the local Alton manager or coachman.

Fe(a)ver. John Fever, of Woolland, Dorset married Catherine Page and left an only child and heiress, Catherine, who married (1) Capt. Sch(u)yler and (2) George-Colby Loftus.

Fellow(e)s, Dr. Physician Extraordinary to the Prince of Wales; at 4 Bladud's Buildings, and later at Axford's Buildings, Bath.

Fendall, William (1758–?1813). Of Matson, Glos.; barrister of the Inner Temple 1783; widower, married 1801 at Baughurst, Hants, Mrs Jane Lyford (q.v.); Fendall, Evans & Jelf were a banking partnership in Gloucester 1800–13.

Fielding family. Earlier in the eighteenth century Miss Anne Palmer married (1) Sir Brook Bridges II of Goodnestone, and by him had one son, Sir Brook Bridges III (born 1733); she married (2) 1737 Col. the Hon. Charles Fielding (sometimes also spelt Feilding), and by him had a daughter Isabella and a son Charles. This younger Charles, Commodore RN (died 1783), married 1772 Sophia, daughter of William and Lady Charlotte Finch (née Fermor) and sister of the 8th Earl of Winchilsea; she is the 'Mrs Fielding' to whom JA refers in 1796; she had also a maternal cousin, George Clayton (q.v.).

Mrs Charles Fielding lived for a time with her mother at the royal residences of Windsor and St James's, since Lady Charlotte Finch (died June 1813) was governess to the children of George III.

As soon as the Prince of Wales was born she took her station by his cradle, on being appointed governess to the royal infant and his future brothers and sisters . . . never was anyone in a similar employment more sincerely or more justly esteemed and beloved. Her judgement was clear, and her manners perfect. I have always thought it equally honourable to her royal pupils and to herself, that, however differing in pursuits and disposition, they were all warmly attached to Lady Charlotte Finch, and never varied in their affection for her. (Sir J. W. Kaye, *Autobiography of Miss Cornelia Knight*, (London, 1861), ii. 167–8).

Miss Isabella Fielding, known affectionately as 'Aunt Fatty' to the Godmersham children, and godmother to Marianne Austen Knight, died unmarried in 1812.

Filmer family, baronets of East Sutton, Kent. The Revd Sir Edmund Filmer was 1751 rector of Crundale, Kent, and moved from there to East Sutton when he became 6th Bt. 1806; he died 1810. His sixth son Revd Francis (1773–1859) (who also became rector of Crundale) married 1806 Mary-Anne Close, daughter of Revd Henry-Jackson Close, rector of Bentworth, Hants.

Finch and Finch-Hatton family. George Finch (1747–1823) of Eastwell Park near Ashford, Kent; added -Hatton to his name 1764; cousin of 8th Earl of Winchilsea; MP for Rochester 1772–84, and patron of the living of Wye; married 1785 Lady Elizabeth Murray, daughter of 2nd Earl of Mansfield, and had five children: Louisa-Anne (*c.*1786), George-William (1791), Daniel-Heneage (1795), Anna-Maria (died 1837), Emily-Mary.

(1) Louisa married 1807 Major-Gen. the Hon. Charles Hope, and died 1875.

(2) George (1791–1858), married (1) 1814 Lady Georgiana-Charlotte Graham (died 1835), daughter of 3rd Duke of Montrose, whom FCK noted in her diary as being a 'sweet little perfection'; (2) 1837 Emily Bagot (died

1848); (3) 1849 Fanny-Margaretta Rice, eldest daughter of FCK's sister Lizzy, Mrs Rice (q.v.); succeeded his cousin as 9th Earl of Winchilsea 1826.

(3) Daniel (1795–1866); 1819 rector of Great Weldon, Northants, and later Chaplain to Queen Victoria; married 1825 Lady Louisa Greville.

JA also refers to a Mr E. Hatton, who was presumably the resoundingly named John-Emilius-Daniel-Edward Finch-Hatton (1755–1841), younger brother of George Finch-Hatton of Eastwell.

The Misses Anne and Mary Finch (who did not add -Hatton) were the unmarried sisters of George Finch-Hatton of Eastwell; a third sister, Harriet, married 1781 Sir Jenison-William Gordon, Bt. (q.v.).

Fitzhugh family. Valentine Fitzhugh, of Bitterne Manor, Southampton, had three children: William (1758–1842), Mary (died 1835), and Valentine (died 1811). William went to China and made a fortune, and upon his return became an MP, with a London address at 18 Orchard Street, and rebuilt the old Banister Court farmhouse on the outskirts of Southampton into an elegant country villa; Mary married 1789 David Lance (q.v.); the younger Valentine, afflicted as he was by deafness, died 17 June 1811, 'of an atrophy', at his boarding-house, 17 High Street, Southampton.

Fletcher, Miss. Cecilia Scott, eldest daughter of George Scott of Bombay, married (1) Brice Fletcher (died 1776) and had three children: Hinwood, Brice, and Cecilia. Mrs Fletcher married (2) c.1777 her cousin Francis-Talbot Scott (q.v.), and had two sons: George and Francis-Peach.

Fletcher, Mrs. Wife of William Fletcher, of Trinity College, Dublin, and Judge of Common Pleas, Ireland.

Floor, Mr. ?Tradesman in Southampton—perhaps a dyer?

Foley, Mrs Anne (1726–1802). Daughter of Revd William Dowdeswell, rector of Kingham, Oxon., 1712; cousin of Dorothy Dowdeswell (q.v.); married 1749 Revd Dr Robert Foley (1720–83), vicar of Newent, Glos., 1762, rector of Kingham, Dean of Worcester 1778; of 17 Marlborough Buildings, Bath.

Fonnereau, Miss. A family of this name were in Reading, Berks., in the 1780s, and from the middle of the eighteenth century until at least the 1820s they or perhaps another branch owned the Bear Hill estate at Wargrave, Berks. Two of them had London addresses in 1815: Mrs Fonnereau at 9 Baker Street, and Mr M. Fonnereau at 1 Clifford Street.

Foote family. John Foote, a banker in London (died ante-1800), had five daughters: Eleanor, Harriet, Lucy, Anne, and Mary. Of these Eleanor married 1800 Sir Brook Bridges IV and died 1806; Harriet married 1809 Revd Brook-Edward Bridges; and Lucy did *not* marry Revd Brook-John Bridges (q.v. the Bridges family).

John Foote had a cousin Edward-James Foote (1767–1833), Captain RN, Vice-Admiral 1821, KCB 1831; of Highfield House, Southampton. He married (1) 1793 Nina, illegitimate daughter of Sir Robert Herries, whom he divorced in 1803 (children Francis, Catherine (Kitty, 1797–1813), Caroline); (2) 1803 Mary eldest daughter of Admiral Patton (children Mary, Helena, Anne, Elizabeth (baptized 27 January 1807)). It was this second marriage which inspired Mr Leigh-Perrot's epigram:

> Through the rough ways of Life, with a patten your Guard,
> May you safely and pleasantly jog;
> May the ring never break, nor the Knot press too hard,
> Nor the Foot find the Patten a Clog.

Captain Foote had had a sister Caroline who died 1778; the Miss Foote mentioned by JA in 1808 may perhaps be another sister, Catherine, or possibly one of the Misses Foote from London.

Captain (Admiral) Foote was surprised that JA was able to draw the Portsmouth scenes of *MP* so well.

Forbes, Lady, of Dover. Elizabeth, wife of Maj.-Gen. Lord Forbes, Lt.-Colonel of the Coldstream Foot Guards, two battalions of which were then on garrison duty in Kent.

Foresters, the. Perhaps a fictional family.

Fowle family of Kintbury, Berks. The Fowle family can be traced back to a John Fowle, who died at Stanton Berners, Wilts., in 1613. The first Fowle to come to Berkshire seems to have been Revd Thomas Fowle I (1697–1762), who was vicar of Upavon, Wilts., 1723, and vicar of Kintbury 1741. He had several children, including Revd Thomas II, Christiana, and Jane; Christiana (1723–1808) married a Mr Murden, had one daughter Jane Murden (q.v.), and died at Kintbury; Jane died at Kintbury unmarried in 1807.

Revd Thomas Fowle II (1726–7 February 1806) succeeded his father as vicar of Kintbury 1762; also became rector of Hampstead Marshall, Berks., 1771, and of Allington, Wilts., 1797. He married 18 July 1763 Jane Craven (died 1798, q.v.), and had four sons: Fulwar-Craven (1764), Thomas (1765), William (1767), Charles (1770).

(1) Revd Fulwar-Craven Fowle (14 May 1764–9 March 1840). Pupil of Revd GA at Steventon 1778–81; St John's College, Oxford, 1781; MA 1788; married 15 September 1788 his cousin Eliza Lloyd (died 1839, q.v.); received the rectory of Elkstone, Glos., from his kinsman 7th Lord Craven and resided there 1789–94; returned to Kintbury 1794 and took over the incumbency of Kintbury in 1798, though his father continued to live at the vicarage; had eight children: Fulwar-William (1791), Mary-Jane (1792), Thomas (1793), Caroline-Elizabeth (born and died 1794), Elizabeth-Caroline (1798), Isabella (1799), Charles (1804), Henry (1807); buried at Kintbury. (For details of his children see below.)

Fulwar-Craven Fowle was remembered by his descendants as being physically rather short and slight, with fair hair, very blue eyes, and a long nose, and also as having an impatient and rather irascible nature; he was an excellent horseman and a most successful Lt.-Colonel of the local volunteer force, the Kintbury Riflemen, 1805. He did not bother to read anything of *Emma* except the first and last chapters, because he had heard it was not interesting.

(2) Revd Tom Fowle (1765–13 February 1797). Pupil of Revd GA at Steventon 1779–83; St John's College, Oxford, 1783, MA 1794; curate of East Woodhay, Hants, 1788–9, and of Welford, Berks.; received the rectory of Allington, Wilts., 1793 from his kinsman Lord Craven, and was also appointed one of Lord Craven's domestic chaplains; went with him in this capacity to the campaign in the West Indies 1795 and died of fever at San Domingo 1797.

Tom Fowle had become engaged to Cassandra Austen probably late in 1792, but the young couple could not afford to marry then due to Tom's very limited income; they had hopes of eventually receiving one of Lord Craven's more valuable livings in Shropshire. See W. A. W. Jarvis, 'Some Information on JA's Clerical Connections', in JA Society *Report* for 1976, 11–17.

(3) William Fowle (9 May 1767–1801). Probably a pupil of Revd GA at Steventon in the early 1780s; apprenticed to his uncle William Fowle in London to study medicine, and became MD of Leyden University 1791; married 19 July 1792 Maria Carpenter of Devizes and had two children, Marianne (1796) and Charles (1797); joined the army 1795 as a physician and served in the West Indies; went with the army to Egypt in 1800 and died there 1801.

(4) Charles Fowle (24 October 1770–12 February 1806). Probably a pupil of Revd GA at Steventon in the 1780s; Lincoln's Inn January 1790, called to the Bar 1800, and practised law in Newbury; married 1799 Honoria Townsend of Newbury (died 1823) and had children; Major in the Hungerford Pioneers 1798 and Major again when this volunteer unit was re-formed 1802 as the Hungerford Infantry; fell ill in 1805 and spent a few months in Bath, but returned to Kintbury to die; both he and his father were buried there on 17 February 1806.

The children of Fulwar-Craven Fowle (see above) were:

(1) Fulwar-William Fowle, born Deane 15 April 1791; Winchester scholar 1803–9, where he was nicknamed 'Gentleman Fowle'; Merton College, Oxford, and BA 1813; rector of Allington 1816 and of Amesbury 1818, and Prebendary of Salisbury; married 1819 Emily Hallett and had eleven children; died 28 June 1876.

(2) Mary-Jane Fowle, born Kintbury September 1792; educated at Mrs Nunes's boarding-school in Overton; married Lt. Christopher Dexter and went with him to India; he died at Madras on their return journey and she died at Kintbury 1883; no issue.

(3) Thomas Fowle, baptized Upper Hurstbourne December 1793; joined the Navy and was with CJA in the West Indies by December 1808; Lieutenant 1812; died in France *c*.1822.

(4) Caroline-Elizabeth, born and died at Upper Hurstbourne April 1794.

(5) Elizabeth-Caroline, born 6 December 1798 at Kintbury; died unmarried at Kintbury 1860.

(6) Isabella, born December 1799 at Kintbury; married 23 October 1845 John Lidderdale, MD, and died 1884.

(7) Charles, born Kintbury 1804; entered the HEIC in adulthood.

(8) Henry, born Kintbury 1807; entered the HEIC in adulthood.

Fowler, Miss. Perhaps a sister or daughter of Robert Fowler, Captain RN 1811.

Frances. Maidservant at Godmersham.

Franfraddops, the. Probably a fictional family.

Frank. Mr Leigh-Perrot's manservant in Bath.

Franklyn, Mrs. Of 3 Montpelier, Bath.

Freeman, Mrs. Possibly a connection by marriage of JA, on the Hampson side (q.v.); *c*.1723 John-Cope Freeman married Catherine-Margaret Hampson and had four children: John-Cope jr. (?1724–88), Mary-Clementina (?1726), Stella-Frances (?1728) who married 1799 an elderly widower Admiral Allen of Devonshire Place, London (died 2 October 1800), and Catherine-Margaretta (?1730) who married (1) 1746 Charles Stanhope of Westminster (died *c*.1770) and had one son Philip-Dormer Stanhope (born 1753), and married (2) *c*.1772 a Mr Jones of Yateley, Hants.

Philip-Dormer Stanhope grew up a wild wastrel and was expelled from King's College, Cambridge, in 1773; went to India and quarrelled with everyone there; married 1780 Elizabeth Hughes of London, and had one daughter Stella-Eloisa; Cornet of 7th Regt. of Dragoon Guards 1780 and Ensign 12th Foot 1781, but his name disappears from the Army List after 1784.

John-Cope Freeman jr. lived at Abbots Langley, Herts.; Sheriff of Herts. 1763; married 1756 Susannah Tophill of Rickmansworth (died 1803); at least one son, Henry-Thomas-Cope Freeman (*c*.1757–76). Mr Freeman left an annuity in his Will to his nephew Philip-Dormer Stanhope, but later revoked this bequest, evidently in view of the young man's bad behaviour.

Although Revd GA had been sufficiently in touch with his cousin to ask him to become godfather to CJA in 1779, presumably the connection had weakened thereafter, for CJA is not mentioned in Mr Freeman's Will.

French, Peter William. Of St Lawrence parish, Reading; chemist, married 1799 Mary Skeete, widow, of Basingstoke.

Frere, Mrs G. Elizabeth, née Grant, who married 1806 George Frere, and lived at 33 Brunswick Square, London.

Fust, Lady. Philippa, daughter of John Hamilton of Chilson, Kent, and widow of Sir John Fust, Bt. (1725–99), of Hill Court, Glos.; died 1803.

Gabell, Dr Henry-Dyson (1764–1831). Rector of St Lawrence, Winchester, 1788–1818, rector of Avington, Hants, 1796–1820, and of Ashow, War., 1812; Second Master of Winchester College 1793–1810, and Headmaster 1810–23.

Gambier, James (1756–1833). Brother of Samuel Gambier (see below); Admiral and first Baron; one of the Lords of the Admiralty; married Louisa, daughter of Daniel Mathew (q.v.).

Gambier, Samuel (died 11 May 1813). Brother of James Gambier (see above); Secretary of the Navy Board 1795–6, Commissioner 1796–1813; married Jane, youngest daughter of Daniel Mathew (q.v.).

Gardiner, Revd Dr John (1757–1838). Of 10 Paragon Buildings and Minister of the Octagon Chapel, Bath, 1796; married at St Michael's, Bath, June 1799 Mrs J. Piersy.

Garnett, Dame. Chawton villager; probably the Jane Ewens who married 1792 William Garnett.

Garrett, Miss. Unidentified; apparently a friend of the Harwoods and the Terrys, and normally resident in Kent.

Gauntlett, Mr. Possibly Revd Samuel Gauntlett (1745–1822), who held the Hampshire livings of Lainston, Hursley, Otterbourne, and Portsea from 1788; or else either Revd Carew Gauntlett, curate of Bishops Sutton 1793, or Revd Henry Gauntlett, curate of Bishops Sutton 1803; apparently connected to the Coulthard family.

Gaylards. (Not 'Gayleard' as JA wrote.) James Gaylard & Son, hatters and habit-makers, 82 New Bond Street, London.

George III and his consort Queen Charlotte. See under **Royal Family.**

Gibb(e)s, Dr. FRS and physician, of 28 Gay Street and later 11 Laura Place, Bath.

Gibson family. Mr John Gibson, of the High Street, Ramsgate, Kent, and his children: Mary (married 24 July 1806 at Ramsgate FWA (q.v.) and died at Gosport 14 July 1823 following the birth of her eleventh child), Eliza, Julia, John-Edgar (born 1789, St John's College, Oxford, 1806, MA 1813); JA also refers to a Miss S. Gibson, who may be another daughter or perhaps a cousin; the 'young Gibson' at Holybourne in 1814 may be from a different family.

Gipps, Revd Henry. St John's College, Cambridge; LLB 1810; ordained 1815 and vicar of SS Peter and Owen, Hereford, 1824–32; married June 1812 Emma-Maria, second daughter of John Plumptre (q.v.); three sons; died 1832.

Girle, Mrs (1712–8 January 1801). Barbara Slaney, married 1734 John Girle, MD, of London; mother of Caroline Girle (1738–1817) who married Philip-Lybbe Powys (q.v.), and grandmother of Revd Edward Cooper's wife Caroline Powys.

Gloucester, Dukes of. See under **Royal Family.**

Glyn, Miss. Probably daughter of Sir James Glynne of Bugle Hall, Southampton.

Goddard, Revd Dr William-Stanley (1757–1845). Second Master of Winchester 1784–93 and Headmaster 1793–1809; rector of Bepton, Sussex, and vicar of Wherwell, Isle of Wight; Prebendary of Salisbury and of St Paul's Cathedral.

Goodchild, Mary. 'Under' [assistant] cook to the FWA family while they were living at Chawton Great House; later married Mrs GA's manservant William Littleworth (q.v.).

Gordon, Mr. A business friend of HTA; of Cleveland Row, London, and also connected with the Misses Moore of Hanwell (q.v.).

Gordon, Sir Jenison-William (1748–1831). Second baronet, of Haverholm Priory, Lincolnshire; married 1781 Harriet Finch, sister of George Finch-Hatton (q.v.). Lady Gordon was enthusiastic in her praise of JA's novels.

Gore, Mrs Caroline. Fifth and youngest daughter (born 1772) of Sir Thomas-Pym Hales (q.v.) of Bekesbourne, Kent, and younger sister of Mrs Brook-Henry Bridges (q.v.); married 1798 Col. the Hon. William-John Gore, second son of the Earl of Arran. Six of her pocket-books (for the years 1788, 1789, 1791, 1792, 1799, and 1800 only) have survived and are now preserved at Jane Austen's House, Chawton; see JA Society *Report* for 1977, 34–6.

Gore, Capt. John, RN. Sir John Gore, Captain 1794, knighted 1805, Rear-Admiral 1813.

Gore-Langton, William (1760–1847). Of Kidlington, Oxford, and Newton Park, Somerset; Lt.-Colonel of the Oxfordshire Militia, 4 October 1798.

Gould, Revd John (1780–1866). Of Trowbridge, Wilts.; Trinity College, Oxford, BD 1814; vicar of New Shoreham 1816 and rector of Beaconsfield, Bucks., 1818.

Graham family. Col. John Graham, sometime Governor of Georgia and later living at St Lawrence near Canterbury, Kent, had at least three daughters and one son. The son, Charles-Clarke Graham (1778–1837), was vicar of Petham with Waltham, Kent, 1808 and also rector of Barham. Of his sisters, Frances married 1785 as his second wife Sir Edward Knatchbull, 8th Bt. (q.v.); Mary married 1795 or earlier Sir Henry Oxenden (q.v.); and another Miss Graham (?possibly Charlotte) married Revd Charles Cage (q.v.). The Harriet Bailey to whom JA refers as being a cousin of Charlotte Graham, may therefore belong to this family.

Graham, Lady Georgiana-Charlotte. Eldest daughter of the 3rd Duke of Montrose; married 7 August 1814 George-William Finch-Hatton (q.v.), later Earl of Winchilsea, and died 13 February 1835.

Granby, Marquis of. George-John-Frederick Manners, heir of Duke of Rutland; baptized 4 January and died 15 June 1814.

Grant family. Sir Alexander Grant of Dalvey, 7th Bt. (*c.*1750–1825); married 1780 Sarah Cray of Ibsley, Hants, and lived at Malshanger House near Worting, Hants.

Granville, Mrs, and son. Visitors or residents in Lyme Regis, 1804.

Gray family. The Gray family had been connected with Berkshire for centuries, and one branch became prominent in Newbury when Joseph Gray, cheesefactor and mealman in Bartholomew Street, married 1771 Ruth Tinsley and had thirteen children. Three of the sons, Frederick, Charles-Henry, and Edward-William (born 1786, ninth and youngest son), migrated across the county border to Alton, Hants, and the first two of them set up in their father's trade of cheesefactor, *c.*1800; Frederick married 1809 Mary-Anne Clement (q.v.), and Charles-Henry died unmarried the same year. Edward-William Gray joined HTA 1806–15 in the banking partnership of Austen, Gray & Vincent, with offices at 10 High Street, Alton; following the firm's bankruptcy at the end of 1815 he returned to his father's business in Newbury; he never married, but became a keen topographer and local historian and was noted for his involvement in public service in Newbury—JP, Alderman, and Mayor 1839—and died rich and respected at the age of 74 in 1860.

Greaves. In 1801 there were four Greaves shown in the Bath directory: Admiral Greaves of 15 Burlington Street; Capt. Greaves of 18 Henrietta Street; Mrs Martha Greaves of 74 Great Pulteney Street; Mrs Margaret Greaves of 15 New [Lansdown] Crescent.

Gregory, Mrs and Miss. Perhaps related to Revd Francis Gregory, Minor Canon of Canterbury Cathedral.

Gregorys, the young. Presumably members of a family resident at Speen Hill, Berks.

Grenville, Rt. Hon. Thomas (1755–1846). First Lord of the Admiralty 1806–April 1807.

Guillemarde, Mr. Probably John-Lewis Guillemarde (1765–1844), of St John's College, Oxford, and of 27 Gower Street, London.

Gunthorpe, William (1785–ante-1843). Son of William Gunthorpe (1755–1807) of St John's, Antigua, and Bugle Hall, Southampton; Christ Church, Oxford 1803; married 28 January 1807 Alicia Jackson (q.v.) and had four children.

Hacker, John. Gardener and seedsman, of Basingstoke.

Hacket, Pierce, MD. Of 170 High Street, Southampton.

Haden, Charles-Thomas (1786–1824). (Not 'Haydon' as JA wrote). Surgeon, of 62 Sloane Street, Chelsea, and also surgeon 1814 to the Chelsea and Brompton Dispensary, on the corner of Sloane Square; died of tuberculosis at Malta, leaving a son Francis-Seymour (born 1818) who also became a surgeon and practised at the same address. Mr Haden was *'quite delighted'* with *Emma*. See W. Watson, 'The Austens' London Doctor', in JA Society *Report* for 1961, 194–7.

Halavant, Monsieur. The HTAs' French chef while they were living at 24 Upper Berkeley Street.

Hales family, baronets, of Bekesbourne, Kent. Lady Hales (died 1803), widow 1773 of Sir Thomas-Pym Hales, 4th Bt.; her daughters Mary-Anne (1765); Jane (1766) married 1795 Revd Brook-Henry Bridges (q.v.); Elizabeth (1769) married John Calcraft; Harriet (1770); Caroline (1772) married 1798 Col. the Hon. William-John Gore (q.v.).

Hall, Mr. Hairdresser in London—perhaps connected with the J. B. Hall who was a Patent-Violet-Soap manufacturer at Jubilee Place, Chelsea, 1815.

Hall, Mrs. ?Maidservant to the Austens at Castle Square, Southampton.

Hall, Revd Dr Henry (1749–1829). Son of Richard Hall of Penrith, Cumberland; Queens College, Oxford, 1768; DD 1793; Vicar of Monk (West) Sherborne and Pamber, Hants, 1793; his widow died at Basingstoke, January 1846.

Hall, Joseph. Steventon villager, renting a field there from Mrs GA at £6 p.a.; buried 2 December 1821 aged 54.

Hallett, James. Of Higham, near Bridge, on the Canterbury–Folkestone road, and also of 11 North Audley Street, London.

Hallifax, Emma. Married April 1805 Revd Edward Bather (q.v.).

Hamilton, Mrs. Of Canterbury, a friend of the Fagg family.

Hammond family, of St Alban's Court, near Wingham, Kent. William Hammond (1752–1821) married 1785 Elizabeth Beauvoir and had seven children: William-Osmund (1790), Maximilian (1792), Elizabeth, Mary, Charlotte, Julia, and Jemima.

William-Osmund (1790–1863); Christ Church, Oxford, 1809; married 1815 Mary-Graham eldest daughter of Sir Henry Oxenden, Bt. (q.v.); seven children; JP, DL, and High Sheriff for Kent 1846.

Maximilian-Dudley-Digges (born 1792) took the surname of Dalison upon inheriting the estates of that family in 1819; married 8 May 1819 Anne-Maria Shaw (q.v.).

The 'Miss Hammond' to whom JA referred was presumably Elizabeth, if she was still unmarried at that time.

Hammond, Revd Arthur-Atherley (1772–1852). Son of Arthur Hammond of Southampton; St John's College, Oxford, 1789, MA 1796; curate of Deane 1806–15. It is probably this Mr Hammond who gave the ball in January 1809 for which Mary Lloyd acted as hostess.

Hampson family, baronets. Sir George Hampson, 4th Bt. and MD, who died in Gloucester 1724, had five surviving children: George, Rebecca, Elizabeth, Jane, and Catherine-Margaret.

(1) George (died 1754), succeeded his father as 5th Bt.; his son George-Francis 6th Bt. (1738–74); his son Thomas-Philip (1763–1820) held republican views and therefore did not like to be known as the 7th Bt.; his son George-Francis 8th Bt. (1788–1833); and all later Hampson baronets. Sir Thomas-Philip ('Mr') Hampson had two addresses in London: 10 Great Cumberland Place, and 9 Hinde Street, Manchester Square.

(2) Rebecca (died 1733), married (1) c.1720 William Walter, MD (died 1726, q.v.) and had one son William-Hampson Walter; married (2) 1727 William Austen (q.v.) and left two surviving children, **Philadelphia** and **George Austen**.

(3) Elizabeth (died 1733), married George Cure (q.v.), but left no issue.

(4) Jane married c.1728 Capel Payne (q.v.) and had a son George and a daughter Catherine.

(5) Catherine-Margaret married c.1723 John-Cope Freeman (q.v.), and had a son John and daughters Mary, Stella-Frances, and Catherine-Margaretta.

By virtue of their common ancestor in **Sir George Hampson**, 4th Bt., the **Hampsons**, **Paynes**, and **Freemans** were all cousins in some degree of the **Steventon Austens** and the **Kentish Walters**.

Hancock, Mrs. Perhaps connected with Thomas Hancox, woollen-draper, of 411 Oxford Street, London.

Hanson, Miss. Mary-Anne, daughter of John Hanson, lawyer, of 29 Bloomsbury Place and 65 Chancery Lane, London, and also of Farleigh House near Basingstoke, Hants; married 7 March 1814 as his second wife the lunatic 3rd Earl of Portsmouth (q.v.).

Harding family. Robert Harding of Upcott, Devon, married 1780 Dyonisia, second daughter of Sir Bourchier Wrey, Bt. (q.v.); six children, including a daughter also called Dyonisia ('Diana').

Robert Harding's sister Elizabeth (1751–1811) married Thomas Terry (q.v.) of Dummer, Hants.

Hare, Miss. Milliner in London—perhaps connected with Richard Hare, hatter, 71 Strand.

Harrison, Mrs. Charlotte (1765–1849), fifth daughter of Jemima Brydges (q.v.) and sister of (amongst others) Mrs Anne Lefroy (q.v.) and Sir Egerton Brydges (q.v.); married (1) Champion Branfill of Upminster Hall, Essex, and had one son and one daughter Jemima-Elizabeth; and (2) John Harrison (died 1818) of Denne Hill near Canterbury, but had no further issue.

Harrison family, of Overton. Revd William Harrison (1768–1846), son of Revd John Harrison of Croydon; curate and 1796 vicar of Overton, Hants, vicar 1811 of Fareham, Hants, sinecure rector of Overton 1818, Prebendary of Winchester 1820. His sister Mary married September 1797 as his second wife Philip-Henry Poore (q.v.).

Harrison family, of Southampton. John-Butler Harrison I (1739–11 April 1767) of Amery near Alton, Hants, married (1) July 1764 at Southampton Elizabeth Ballard, who died 1765 at the birth of her daughter Elizabeth-Goring Harrison; married (2) August 1766 at Chawton her cousin Frances Ballard, who died 30 May 1767 after giving birth to John-Butler Harrison II (6 May 1767); died of smallpox and buried at Southampton.

John-Butler Harrison I had a sister, Jane, who married Revd John Hinton (q.v.).

John-Butler Harrison II (1767–1850) was brought up by his uncle Robert Ballard, who sold the Amery property; thereafter the Harrisons lived at St Mary's, a rural suburb of Southampton. John-Butler Harrison II married 1789 at Chawton Elizabeth-Matilda Austen (1766–1855, q.v.), and had ten children: John-Butler III (1790), Henry-Austen (1791), Elizabeth-Matilda (1793), Mary-Hooker (1795), Charles (1797), Edward (1799), Jane (1801), William-Francis (1802), Frances-Sarah (1805), George-Augustus (1808). He was Sheriff of Southampton in 1790 and Mayor in 1794 and 1811; buried with his wife at Pear Tree Green, Southampton.

The spinster Harriet-Lennard Austen, sister of Elizabeth-Matilda, lived with the Harrisons in Southampton; and it seems that the spinster Elizabeth-Goring Harrison also lived with her half-brother's family.

Of John-Butler Harrison II's ten children, Elizabeth-Matilda (1793–1855), who was JA's god-daughter, married 15 December 1812 her cousin Revd William Austen (q.v.), rector of Horsted Keynes, Sussex, and had three children; of her nine siblings, only three others left issue.

Harvey, Mr and Mr Richard. Probably Richard Harvey sr., of Eastry, Kent, with his son, also Richard. Richard jr. (1766–1816) was at Trinity College, Cambridge, 1783; curate of Swingfield with Acrise, Kent, 1788, and of Littlebourne, Kent, 1792; vicar of Leatherhead, Surrey, and of Warnham, Surrey, 1798, and rector of Ham, Kent, 1809.

Harwood family. The squirearchal family of Harwood had been living at Deane House, next door to the church, for several generations during the seventeenth and eighteenth centuries. In the Austens' time the family consisted of John Harwood VI (24 November 1747–11 January 1813), his wife Anne (1750–1842), and their three sons: John VII (1770), Earle (1773), and Charles (1783); Mr Harwood's spinster sister Betty-Anna-Maria (1751–18 March 1838) also lived with them. At Mr Harwood's death in 1813 it was discovered that he had 'contracted debts, quite unsuspected by his family. He had borrowed and mortgaged so freely, that it seemed as if the estate itself could scarcely pay its own liabilities. There was nothing for his widow, and his sister's small portion had been left in his hands, and had gone with the rest of the money, so that both ladies were dependent on the heir. He found himself a ruined man on his father's death, blighted in all his hopes and prospects of life . . .'

(1) The unfortunate heir was Revd John Harwood VII (1770–1846); curate 1794–8 of Wolverton near Basingstoke, Hants; rector of Ewhurst 1799, of Laverstoke 1820, and of Sherborne St John 1825. He had previously been an unsuccessful suitor of Elizabeth Bigg (q.v.), and following the early death of her husband Revd William Heathcote in 1802 it had become understood amongst their friends that she would marry Revd Mr Harwood once he had come into his inheritance; in the event, however, he could not afford to marry anyone, but spent the rest of his life struggling to pay off his father's debts in order to retain the family property and support his dependants.

(2) Earle Harwood (1773–1811); attempted to set up in business as a coal merchant 1794; joined the Royal Marines and was a Lieutenant in 1796; married 2 August 1797 at Stoke Damerel, Devon, Sarah Scott, a girl of apparently doubtful reputation; appointed 27 December 1798 to the prison ship HMS *Prothee*, moored at Portsmouth; on HMS *Gladiator* 1800; served in the West Indies, taking part in the capture of Curacao 1805, and Commanding Officer of Fort Amsterdam at that place 1807; back in England by 1809; by the time of his death in 1811 he was Captain in the Woolwich Division of Marines; buried at Deane; no issue.

(3) Charles Harwood (1783–1855); married 1810 Eliza Terry (1788–23 August 1841, q.v.) of Dummer; three surviving children: John-Terry (1811), Charles-Earle (1812), Anne (1816). He and his family lived in a farmhouse at Deane, and later in the nineteenth century he was referred to only as 'yeoman', no longer 'esquire' or 'gentleman'.

JA noted that all the members of the Harwood family enjoyed *MP*.

Hastings, Warren (1732–1818), of Daylesford, Glos., and Governor-General of Bengal. For details of life and career see *DNB*. In his private capacity Hastings had several connections of enduring friendship with the Austens: he had known Mrs GA's Leigh family since his boyhood days as their neighbour in Gloucestershire; on the strength of this he had sent his little son George (1757–64) back from India to be the Austens' foster-child and pupil at Deane. In India Hastings had also been the friend and business partner for a number of years of Tysoe-Saul Hancock, husband of Philadelphia Austen (q.v.), and was godfather to their daughter Elizabeth (later Eliza de Feuillide, Mrs HTA); and finally, Revd GA's cousin Miss Maria Payne (q.v.) seems to have lived for some years at Daylesford as companion to Mrs Hastings.

Hawker, Revd Mr (not 'Harpur'). Friend and neighbour of Revd Brook-Edward Bridges, at Lenham.

Hawkins, Mrs. Wife of Thomas Hawkins of Nash Court, Boughton-under-Blean, near Faversham, Kent, and mother of Mary Hawkins (died 1850), third wife of Sir Edward Knatchbull, 8th Bt. (q.v.).

Hawley family, baronets, of Leybourne, Kent, and 4 Harley Street, London. Sir Henry Hawley (1746–1826): barrister of the Inner Temple 1769, High Sheriff of Kent 1783–4, baronet 1795. His eldest daughter Dorothy-Elizabeth married 1809 as his second wife Sir Brook-William Bridges IV (q.v.) and died in childbirth 1816; his younger daughter Charlotte married 1810 Revd Brook-John Bridges (q.v.), but had no issue; JA also met the second daughter Harriot Hawley.

Hayter, Sir William (1792–1878). For many years Patronage Secretary of the Treasury in several Liberal governments.

Heartley, Mr. Possibly a member of the Hartley family, of Bucklebury, Berks.

Heathcote family, baronets, of Hursley Park, Hants. Sir William (1746–1819) 3rd Bt. 1787; married 1768 Frances Thorpe (1742–1816) and had eight children: Thomas (1769), Frances (1770–81), William (1772), Samuel (1773), Harriet (1775), Henry (1777), Gilbert (1779), Maria (1787).

(**1**) Thomas (1769–1825), 4th Bt.; MP for Hants 1808–20; married 1799 but had no issue.

(**3**) Revd William (1772–1802), rector of Worting, Hants, and Prebendary of Winchester, married 11 January 1798 Elizabeth Bigg (q.v.) and had one son, William (1801; see below). After her husband's early death Mrs Heathcote returned with her little boy to her father's house at Manydown and lived there till 1814; she and her unmarried sister Alethea Bigg then moved to Winchester and lived at 12 The Close. Mrs Heathcote had copies of all JA's novels.

(5) Harriet (1775–1850), in 1796 the eldest surviving daughter of the 3rd Bt.; married 1798 Langford Lovell.

(7) Gilbert (1779–1831), Capt. RN; married 1809 Anne Lyell (q.v.).

(8) Maria-Frances (1787–1859), married 1824 Charles Wyndham.

Revd William Heathcote's son William (17 May 1801–17 August 1881) was a schoolmate of JEAL at Winchester, and the two remained close friends thereafter. William succeeded his uncle in 1825 as 5th Bt.; married (1) 1825 Caroline Perceval (died 1835) and had four children; married (2) 1841 Selina Shirley and had another eight children; MP for Hampshire 1826–32 and 1837–49, and for the University of Oxford 1854–68; also other public offices.

In August 1824 Mrs Charles Smith (q.v.) of Suttons went to a party where William Heathcote was also present, and afterwards described him to her sister Mrs Chute (q.v.) of The Vyne as 'lively & merry without ever being wild or vulgar, obliging in heart & manner; seeming quite unconscious of his merits & his charms, equally agreeable as the companion of a grave or a merry hour: I think he is quite captivating.' (Hampshire County Record Office, Heathcote archive (63M84/233/p. 59.*b*)).

Herington, Mr. Tradesman, probably grocer, at Guildford.

Herries family. Catherine and Isabella, sisters of John Charles Herries, of 21 Cadogan Place, Sloane Street. Catherine married 1813 Henry-Knowles Creed (q.v.); Isabella (died 1870) disapproved of *Emma*.

Hey, Revd Dr Thomas. Rector of Wickhambreux, vicar of Eastchurch, Prebendary of Rochester.

Heywood, Mrs (1732–1824). Of Above Bar, Southampton, and widow of Lt.-Col. Heywood, Mayor of Southampton 1800–1.

Hibbs, John. Hosier and milliner, 152 High Street, Southampton.

Hill, Revd Herbert (1749–1828). Uncle of the poet Robert Southey (q.v.). Chaplain to the British factory at Oporto, Portugal, 1774–1801; rector of Staunton-on-Wye, Hereford, 1801, of Streatham, Surrey, 1810 and of Worting, Hants, 1815; Chancellor of the Choir of Hereford Cathedral; married 25 October 1808 Catherine Bigg (died 1848, q.v.); children Edward (1810), Herbert (1811, who married Robert Southey's daughter Bertha), Errol (1812), Alfred-Wither (14 March 1815), Georgiana (1816), and Robert-Southey (1817).

Hill, Revd Dr Hugh. Rector of Holy Rood, Southampton, and of Church Oakley near Deane, 1792–1824.

Hilliard, Nanny. Maidservant at Steventon rectory: Anne Knight, married 1795 John Hilliard; one daughter Hannah born 1796. It may be this Hannah Hilliard who was Mrs Digweed's unsatisfactory servant in 1816. John Hilliard was perhaps nicknamed 'Robert' by the Austens, to distinguish him from their other servant John Littleworth (q.v.).

Hinchman, Mr. JA was probably referring to Thomas Henchman (1748–1804), a rich nabob, of New Burlington Street, London, who may perhaps have married as his second wife Mrs Lawrel or Laurel (q.v.) in 1801.

Hinch-, Hincks-, or Hinxman, Robert. Yeoman farmer, of Sevenhampton, Glos. Eloped with Margaret Craven (died January 1815, q.v.) and had one son, John; this son died 1828, and left his property to his surviving cousins on the Craven side, who at that date were Mr and Mrs Fowle, Mary Lloyd (Mrs James Austen), Martha Lloyd (by then FWA's second wife), Lady Pollen, and her brothers Fulwar and Charles Craven.

Hinton family, of Chawton. Revd John Hinton (1720–1802), rector of Chawton 1744–1802, married (1) 1745 his cousin Martha Hinton, 'sole representative of the Knights of Chawton' (died 1761), and had one daughter Jane (1751) who married 1769 James Baverstock (q.v.). Revd John Hinton married (2) post-1761 Jane Harrison (died 1799), sister of John-Butler Harrison I (q.v.) of Amery near Alton, and had four children: Mary (died 1851), Elizabeth, another Jane (1771–1856), and John-Knight ('Jack') (1774–1846). Mr Hinton received a long eulogistic obituary in the *GM* for 1802, I. 471–2.

Of these four children by the second marriage, Mary married 1793 James Dusautoy (1762–1859, q.v.) and went to live in the West Country; Elizabeth married Revd George Wells and had a daughter Elizabeth who married 1825 Arthur Loveday, and their son Revd Arthur Loveday (1826–85) married 1859 Elizabeth-Lucy Lefroy (1827–96), youngest daughter of Anna and Ben Lefroy (q.v.); Jane II (the 'Miss Hinton' mentioned by JA in 1813) married 1816 Revd Dr James Ventris, vicar of Beeding, Sussex (died 1841); John-Knight Hinton lived at Chawton Lodge, and his sister Mrs Ventris returned to live with him during her widowhood.

Both Revd John Hinton and his first wife, Martha Hinton, were kinsfolk of the Knights of Chawton, and on this score their grandson James-Hinton Baverstock (q.v.) commenced a lawsuit against EAK in 1814 for possession of his Hampshire estates, aided in his efforts by his uncle John-Knight Hinton; this lawsuit was not settled until 1818, when the Hintons agreed to be bought off for £15,000.

Hoar, Mr George. (Not 'Hoare' as JA wrote.) Brother of Adm. Sir Thomas Bertie and of Mrs Dickens (qq.v.). Married 1787 Elizabeth Cook, and went to India in 1790 as paymaster of the British forces; returned to England 1793 and lived at Worting and also Twyford Lodge, Hants; Mrs Hoar left her husband in 1800 to join a friend of theirs from Indian days, Major Allen; Mr Hoar sued for divorce in December 1800. Mr John Clarke (q.v.) was an old friend of the Hoars, and gave evidence in the divorce case.

Hoblyn family. Perhaps Thomas Hoblyn of 125 Sloane Street; there was also a Mrs Houblon at 36 Baker Street, Portman Square, London.

Hogben/Hogbin, John (1772–1841). Parish clerk of Godmersham.

Holder family. William Holder of Lincoln's Inn Fields (died in Barbados 1752) had two sons: William-Thorpe (1745) and James (1747). These two young men took the tenancy of Ashe Park, Hants, in 1770, and, after William married a year or two later, James lived on there as a bachelor until his West Indian fortune failed in the latter part of his life (probably *c.*1804), and he died senile and in poverty.

William-Thorpe Holder (1745–87); High Sheriff of Dorset 1768; married ante-1772 Philippa-Elliot —— (died ?September 1813), and had four children: John-Hooper, William-Philip (1772–97), Margaret-Dehany (died 1809), and Philippa-Harbin (died ante-1801). During her widowhood Mrs Holder lived at Bathford and at 16 St James Square, Bath.

John-Hooper Holder, of Cerney House, Glos., married (1) 1808 Elizabeth (died January 1810) younger daughter of Hon. William Hewitt, and had one daughter Elizabeth-Philippa; in 1811 he paid some court to Miss Eliza Sneade, sister of Mrs Joseph-Thomas Brown of Winifred House, Sion Hill, Bath, but instead married (2) 1812 Anne Ekins (q.v.). See Oman, *Ayot Rectory*, 62.

Holder, Joseph. Deane villager, married 1805 Mary Tolfree of Ashe.

Holwell, Miss ?Anne. Married July 1798 at Pinner, Middx, John-George Children (q.v.); daughter of Lt.-Col. Holwell of Southborough, and granddaughter of Governor Holwell of Bengal. Gov. Holwell was one of the survivors of the Black Hole of Calcutta, and in 1758 published his *Genuine Narrative* of that event.

Home, Sir Everard (1746–1832). Of 30 Sackville Street, London; Serjeant-Surgeon to the King; baronet 1813.

Honywood family, baronets of Evington, Kent. Sir John, 5th Bt. (1787–1832); married 1808 Mary-Anne, daughter of Revd Sir William-Henry Cooper, Bt. Sir John's sister Annabella-Christiana (died 1814) was the first wife of Sir Edward Knatchbull, 9th Bt. (q.v.).

Hook, Miss M. (died 1816). Daughter of Brig.-Gen. Hook.

Hookey, Mrs. Widow, chemist, and lodging-house keeper in Southampton.

Hope, Mrs. Née Louisa Finch-Hatton (q.v.).

Hore, Mrs. ?One of HTA's neighbours in Hans Place, 1815.

Howard, Lord. Probably Richard Howard (1748–1816), 4th and last Earl of Effingham; Secretary and Comptroller of the Household to Queen Charlotte, 1784–1814, and Treasurer 1814–16. See J. Kirkland, 'JA and the Celebrated Birthday', in *N&Q* 232:4 (Dec. 1987), 477–8.

Hughes, Mrs and children. Probably part of the Hughes family of Betshanger, Kent.

Hulbert, the Misses. Of Speen Hill, Berks. Miss Elizabeth Hulbert died at 32 Gay Street, Bath, 17 December 1819; her sister died 21 January 1840 aged 96.

Humphry family. Revd William Humphry was the incumbent of Seal, Kent, and consequently his family were neighbours of the Walters (q.v.); it was no doubt his wife who wrote to the Austens in 1798 to announce the death of William-Hampson Walter.

Hunter, Mrs Rachel (1754–1813). Of Norwich, authoress; for details of her works see *DNB*.

Husket, Mr. Servant of Lord Lansdown, living in the Castle, Southampton.

Hussey, Edward (died 1817). Of Scotney Castle, Kent; also lived at Pett Place, near Charing, Kent, ante-1813.

Hutchins, Mary. Steventon villager; Mary Bennet who married John Hutchins 1763.

Inglis, Capt. RN. Charles Inglis, Commander 1800 and Captain 1802, died 1833.

Inman, Rebecca (1738–10 September 1815). Of Ashford, buried 20 September in the centre passage of the nave of Godmersham church; the floor of the nave was raised in 1865–6 and the gravestone is now covered over.

Iremonger, Miss. Presumably Miss Elizabeth Iremonger (died 1826), younger daughter of Joshua Iremonger (died 1804) of Wherwell Priory near Andover, Hants.

Irvine, Mrs and Miss. Of 19 Lansdown Crescent, Bath.

Isaac. Apparently the Austens' manservant in Bath.

Isham, Revd Dr Edmund (1745–1817). Warden of All Souls, Oxford, 1793–1817.

Jackson, Alicia. Daughter of Josiah Jackson of Belle Vue, Southampton; married 1807 at the age of 18 William Gunthorpe (q.v.), and had four children; died 28 February 1843 in London, described as the relict of Revd William Gunthorpe of Antigua.

Jackson family. Henry Jackson of 9 Sloane Terrace, Chelsea, and his wife Sarah Papillon (q.v.); their three daughters: Eleanor (married 1820 as his second wife HTA, and died 1864), Henrietta, and Sarah. A Charles Jackson succeeded HTA as perpetual curate of Bentley in 1839, and may also be part of this family. See W. Midgley, 'The Revd Henry and Mrs Eleanor Austen', in JA Society *Report* for 1978, 86–91.

James. The Austens' manservant in Lyme.

Jefferys, Toomer & Legge. Banking partnership in Basingstoke.

Jefferson, Revd Thomas (*c*.1760–18 February 1829). Curate 1784 of Appledore with Ebony, Kent, but lived in Tonbridge; married twice and had eight children; published by subscription 1808 *Two Sermons . . . also an Essay*. See W. A. W. Jarvis, 'Mr Jefferson's Case', in JA Society *Report* for 1989, 15–18.

Jenkins, Mr. Probably the Revd Stiverd Jenkins (born 1766), curate of Hannington, Hants, in 1794.

Jennings family, servants to the Austens. Jane (Jenny) Jennings, baptized 16 December 1781, was JEAL's nursemaid at Deane; her brother John was firstly a labourer on Steventon Manor Farm and later a gamekeeper to the Digweeds and to James Austen; Dinah, maidservant to the Fowles at Kintbury, was their aunt.

Jenny. From Ecchinswell, Hants; the Austens' maidservant at Lyme, Bath, and perhaps Southampton as well.

Jervoise family, of Herriard, Hants. Col. George-Purefoy Jervoise (1770–1847) married (1) 1798 Elizabeth Hall of Preston Candover (died 1821) and (2) Anna-Maria Locke, but died without issue; his brother Richard-Purefoy, Major 1st Royal Dragoons, married 1809 Anna-Victoria Story and died 1811, leaving one daughter; his sister Mary-Purefoy married Revd Francis Ellis, rector of Lasham, Hants, and vicar of Long Compton, War., and this family eventually succeeded to the Herriard estate and took the name of Jervoise.

John. HTA's coachman in London.

Johncock. Butler at Godmersham.

Johnson, Revd Robert-Augustus (1745–99). Married 1773 a sister of the 6th Lord Craven; described by his sister-in-law the 'Beautiful Lady Craven' as 'a mild and good man, but entirely governed by his wife'; rector of the Craven living of Wistanstow, Shropshire, and also rector 1791–9 of the Leigh living of Hamstall Ridware, Staffs, as there had been a Leigh-Craven marriage in an earlier generation.

In 1799 the Wistanstow living was given to a George Nott, and then in 1806 to Robert-Henry, son of Revd Robert-Augustus Johnson. See W. A. W. Jarvis, 'Some Information about JA's Clerical Connections', in JA Society *Report* for 1976, 11–17; and also *Barbara Johnson's Album of Fashions and Fabrics*, 9–15.

Jordan, Mrs. Dorothy ('Dolly') Jordan (1762–1816); famous comedy actress and mistress 1790–1811 of the Duke of Clarence (q.v. under **Royal Family**), presenting him with a large family of FitzClarences; made her last appearance on the English stage 1814 and died in France two years later. For details of her career see the *DNB*.

Kean, Edmund (1789–1833). Famous tragedian, especially in Shakespearean roles; first appeared at Drury Lane as Shylock in January 1814, and took the town by storm. For details of his career see *DNB*.

Keith, Lord. Admiral George Keith Elphinstone (1746–1823), Baron Keith 1797; his wife was Hester-Maria Thrale (1764–1857), eldest daughter of Dr Johnson's Mrs Thrale; of Purbrook Park near Havant, Hants, and also 45 Harley Street, London.

Kelly, Mrs. Probably the wife of James Kelly, of 59 Gower Street, Bloomsbury, London.

Kemble, Mr. Unidentified; CEA's dancing partner at Chilham in January 1801 and apparently in the militia; probably *not* related to the famous Kemble/Siddons dynasty of actors and actresses.

Kendall, young. Perhaps Thomas Kendall, Lieutenant RN 8 February 1815.

Kennet, Mrs. New laundress at Godmersham, 1808.

Kennet, Richard. Perhaps a servant of the Gibson family, in Ramsgate.

Kerr, Lady Robert. Mary Gilbert, of Cornwall; married 1806 Lord Robert Kerr (1780–1843), younger son of 5th Marquis of Lothian, and died 1861. She very much enjoyed *P&P* and *MP*.

Kew, Dame. Steventon villager; Elizabeth, wife of William Kew, whose four children were baptized at Steventon between 1753–62.

Knatchbull family, baronets of Mersham Hatch, Kent. The Knatchbulls can be traced back with certainty to at least the early fifteenth century; those whom JA met or mentioned had a common ancestor in Sir Edward Knatchbull, 4th Bt. (died 1730).

By JA's time the senior line was represented by Sir Edward Knatchbull, 8th Bt. (1759–1819); MP for Kent 1790–1802, and 1806–19; he married (1) 1780 Mary Hugessen, co-heiress of Provender, Kent (died 1784) and had two sons; (2) 1785 Frances Graham (died 1799, q.v.) and had seven children; (3) 1801 Mary Hawkins (died 1850, q.v.) and had eight children.

Sir Edward Knatchbull (1781–1849), was the eldest son by his first marriage of Sir Edward Knatchbull, 8th Bt., whom he succeeded in 1819 as 9th Bt. Married (1) 1806 Annabella-Christiana Honywood (died 1814, q.v.) and had six children, of whom the eldest daughter, Mary-Dorothea, eloped 1826 with Edward Knight II of Godmersham (q.v. under Austen); (2) 1820 JA's niece Fanny Knight (q.v.), and had nine children; their eldest son Edward (1829–93) became 1880 the first **Lord Brabourne.**

Revd Dr Wyndham Knatchbull (1786–1868), Laudian Professor of Arabic at Oxford, and rector of Smeeth, Aldington, and Westbere, Kent, was the eldest son of Sir Edward, 8th Bt., by his second wife.

A junior line derived from Revd Dr Wadham Knatchbull (1707–60), fourth son of Sir Edward, 4th Bt.; Chancellor and Prebendary of Durham, Dean of Canterbury, rector of Chilham, Kent; his children were Charles (1747), Wyndham (1750), and Catherine (1753).

(1) Charles Knatchbull (1747–1826), Captain RN; married 1785 his cousin Frances Knatchbull (daughter of Revd Dr Wadham Knatchbull's younger brother Norton) and heiress of Babington, Somerset (died 1818); no issue.

(2) Wyndham Knatchbull (1750–1833), merchant, of 16 Russell Place, London; married 1790 his cousin Catherine-Maria Knatchbull (sister of Sir Edward Knatchbull, 8th Bt., died 1807); their children included Revd Wadham (1794–1876) Prebendary of Wells, and Wyndham (1795–1813) Ensign in 1st Regt. of Foot Guards. His mercantile firm was presumably that of Knatchbull, Rule, Cunningham & Paterson, of 52 Gracechurch Street, London.

(3) Catherine Knatchbull (1753–14 October 1812); married 1779 Thomas Knight II of Godmersham (died 1794, q.v.); no issue; later in her widowhood Mrs Knight retired to White Friars, Canterbury.

An old Miss ('Mrs') Joan-Elizabeth Knatchbull (died 1801), of Canterbury, was a granddaughter of the 4th Bt. and therefore another cousin of Sir Edward Knatchbull, 8th Bt.

Knight family of Chawton, Steventon, and Godmersham. The original Knight family had been living in Chawton since at least the middle of the sixteenth century, but the male line came to an end in 1679 when Sir Richard Knight died childless. He left his estate to the grandchildren of his aunt Dorothy Martin, and they took the name of Knight; however, they in turn all died childless and the estate passed to a maternal cousin of theirs, Thomas Broadnax of Godmersham.

The mother of Thomas Broadnax had been a Miss Anne May, and in 1727 her son changed his name to May in order to inherit the property of his cousin Sir Thomas May; in 1738 he changed his name again to Knight, when he inherited the Chawton estate. Mr Thomas Broadnax-May-Knight (1701–80), married 1729 Jane Monk (died 1765), and had at least five children: Anne (1734–73), Thomas (1735–94), Jane (died 1793), Sarah (1745–60), and Elizabeth (died 1809).

Of these children, all the daughters died unmarried; Elizabeth was feeble-minded and had a separate establishment of her own at Eggerton House near Godmersham, looked after by the Misses Cuthbert (q.v.). Thomas Knight II was MP for New Romney 1761–8 and for Kent 1774–80; married 1779 Catherine Knatchbull (died 1812, q.v.), but had no issue; he therefore looked to his maternal relatives for an heir, and adopted his distant cousin **Edward Austen** (q.v.).

The **Austens** and **Knights** had a common ancestor in **John Austen III** (died 1705, q.v.); his daughter Jane Austen married Stephen Stringer of

Goudhurst; their daughter Hannah Stringer married William Monk; and their daughter Jane Monk was the mother of **Thomas Knight II.**

Knight families in Hampshire. By JA's time there were many other groups of Knights in the villages of north-east Hampshire, including several families of this name in Chawton, Deane, and Steventon—in a much humbler rank of life, but perhaps originally all connected to the squires of Chawton. For example, in Steventon the Austens' maidservant Mrs Nanny Hilliard had been born Knight; and in Chawton the girls Hannah (baptized May 1798) and Harriet (baptized April 1804) were part of the large family of Abraham and Olive Knight.

Lambould, Mr. Postmaster at Overton.

Lance family. Revd William Lance was rector of Faccombe, Hants, 1792–1848, but his rectory was actually a mile away at Netherton. Both Faccombe and Netherton were hamlets not far from Hurstbourne Tarrant, and no doubt the Austens had met him through the Lloyd connection (q.v.).

His brother David entered the HEIC, and was a factor at Canton in 1775, where one of his partners in private trading enterprises was William Fitzhugh, son of Valentine Fitzhugh sr. (q.v.). David Lance made his fortune in the East and returned to Hampshire in January 1789, married his partner's sister, Mary Fitzhugh, and had six children: Mary (1790–1866), twins Eliza and Emma (1791—Eliza died later that year, Emma died 1810), William (January 1793–1822, died unmarried in India), Revd John-Edwin (December 1793–1885, leaving issue), Frances (born and died 1801). David Lance built Chessel (Chiswell) House in 1797, on the Bitterne side of Southampton, and the road in its vicinity became known as Lance's Hill. He was Sheriff of Hampshire in 1807, and travelled widely on the Continent with his family before dying c.1819. Mrs Lance and Mary lived on in Paris, where Mrs Lance died in 1835. Mary eventually married Revd W. H. Turner; one of the highlights of her life was attending the Duchess of Richmond's ball in Brussels on 15 June 1815, the eve of Waterloo.

Lane, Mr Edward. Of Worting; a connection of the Bigg-Wither family, and executor to the last Mr William Wither who died in 1789.

Langham baronets, of Cottesbrooke, Northants, and 22 Manchester Square, London. Sir James Langham, 10th Bt. (1776–1833), married 1800 Elizabeth Burdett (q.v.) and had eight children. Sir James's maternal grandmother Catherine Musgrave (née Chichester) had married secondly Revd John Sanford (q.v.); due to her two marriages, the Sanfords and Tilsons (q.v.) known to JA were all in some degree related to the Langham family. The Langhams are not mentioned in JA's letters, but she recorded Sir James's opinions of *MP* and *Emma*.

Langley, Miss. Perhaps daughter of John Langley, attorney, of 18 Green Street, and later 14 Charles Street, Bath.

Lansdowne, Marquis of. John-Henry Petty (1765–1809), known earlier as Lord Wycombe. A widely travelled but rather solitary man, who settled in Southampton in order to indulge his passion for yachting. He lived initially at Peartree Green just outside Southampton, but in 1804 bought the old ruined castle within the city walls and enlarged it into a Gothic fantasy, selling off his father's library and art collection at Bowood House to pay for the rebuilding. He succeeded as 2nd Marquis in 1805, and then married Mary-Arabella, daughter of Revd Hinton Maddox and widow of Sir Duke Gifford, who had been his mistress for some years; she was described by Lady Bessborough as a fat and 'vulgar Irish woman near fifty'. Lady Gifford had children by her first marriage, but none by the Marquis; after his death she lived on at the Castle for a few years, but eventually left Southampton in 1814.

On 24 October 1811 Lady Bessborough visited the Castle, and wrote afterwards: 'We went this morning to see the strange house Ld. Lansdowne built here, and with it, its stranger Mistress, who with her three daughters following her, wrapt in thin lace veils, blue silk shoes, and bare-headed, not only braved the wind and the rain, but the sharp stones and muddy streets of Southampton, and the astonished gaze of the passengers.'

From his boyhood visits to his grandmother's house, JEAL remembered another of the Marchioness's whimsies: '[She] had a light phaeton drawn by six, and sometimes by eight little ponies, each pair decreasing in size, and becoming lighter in colour, through all the grades of dark brown, light brown, bay and chestnut, as it was placed further away from the carriage. The two leading pairs were managed by two boyish postillions, the two pairs nearest to the carriage were driven in hand. It was a delight to me to look down from the window and see this fairy equipage put together; for the premises of this Castle were so contracted that the whole process went on in the little space that remained of the open square.'

The title and estates passed to Lord Henry Petty, half-brother of the 2nd Marquis. It was this 3rd Marquis (who devoted himself to re-establishing the dispersed family collections at Bowood) who admired JA's works and was 'grieved and affected' in 1817 to hear of her death.

Latouche, Mrs. Mary Wilkins, who married (1) 1774 as his second wife Edward East and had three children, including Martha East (q.v.); married (2) post-1785 John-James Digges-Latouche of Jamaica; later of 14 Portman Street, Portman Square, London.

Laurel(l), Mrs. Neighbour of the Cooke family (q.v.), as Lord Howard had sold the manor of Great Bookham to James Laurell in 1801.

Layton & Shears. Mercers, of Bedford House, 11 Henrietta Street, Covent Garden.

Ledger, the two Misses. Unidentified; at the Manydown ball in January 1796.

Lee, Miss. Probably a sister of Richard Lee, who married 1801 Elizabeth Prowting (q.v.); perhaps Jane, daughter of the late R. Lee, Esq., of Mile End, London, who married *c*.May 1811 the Revd Charles Laprimaudaye, vicar of Leyton, Essex. Not the same as the Miss Lee staying at Chilham Castle, Kent, in 1813.

Lefevre, Mrs. Helena, daughter of John Lefevre, and heiress of Heckfield Place, Hants; her husband Charles Shaw of Reading added her name to his upon their marriage in 1789. Mr Shaw-Lefevre was subsequently MP for Reading and died 1823; between 1790 and 1860 he and his son, Charles Shaw-Lefevre II, bought up all the land in the Heckfield area to achieve an estate of over 4,000 acres, and in 1857 the son was created Viscount Eversley.

Lefroy families. The earliest English Lefroys were Huguenots, who came to this country in the late sixteenth century and settled in Kent. The families whom JA knew had a common ancestor in Anthony Lefroy (1703–79); he was a banker, in partnership with Peter Langlois of Leghorn, Italy, and in 1738 married his partner's daughter Elizabeth (1720–82). They had two surviving sons: (1) Anthony-Peter (1740) and (2) Isaac-Peter-George (1745, known in the family as 'George'), who were sent back to England to be educated at King's School, Canterbury. (For details of these sons see below.)

  Mrs Lefroy had several unmarried brothers, of whom Benjamin Langlois (1727–1802) in particular took a keen interest in his sister's family. Mr Langlois was Secretary of the British Embassy at Vienna, and, after returning to England, became a Member of Parliament, Secretary of the Board of Ordnance, and Under-Secretary of State. He had a house in Cork Street, Burlington Gardens, London, but for the last few years of his life came to live with his younger nephew at Ashe, and was buried there in November 1802. Sir Egerton Brydges (q.v.), who met him in the 1780s, described him as 'a good and benevolent old man, with much diplomatic experience, but most fatiguingly ceremonious, with abilities not much above the common'.

  (1) Anthony-Peter Lefroy (1740–1819) went into the Army, as his Langlois uncles purchased a commission for him in the 33rd Regiment; it was then stationed in Ireland, and by force of this circumstance Anthony-Peter became the ancestor of the Irish branch of the Lefroy family. He married in 1765 Anne Gardiner and had eleven children, of whom only three concern us: Sarah (1773), Thomas-Langlois (1776), and Anthony (1777). Anthony-Peter Lefroy retired as a Colonel in the 9th Dragoons in 1791, and lived in Limerick thereafter.

(**1a**) Sarah Lefroy (1773–1836) married 9 May 1799 Capt. Thomas Courtenay of Grange, Co. Antrim; she was not in fact the 'third Miss Irish Lefroy', as JA wrote, but the fourth daughter.

(**1b**) Thomas-Langlois Lefroy (1776–1869, the 'Tom Lefroy' of JA's correspondence) was educated at the expense of his great-uncle Benjamin Langlois. Tom went to Trinity College, Dublin, in 1790, entered Lincoln's Inn 1793, was called to the Irish Bar 1797, and thereafter practised law in Dublin, becoming Lord Chief Justice of Ireland in 1852; he lived in Leeson Street, Dublin, and also bought the Carrigglas estate in Co. Longford, where his descendants still live. He married in 1799 Mary Paul, sister of a college friend, and had nine children.

(**1c**) Anthony Lefroy (1777–1857) became a Captain in the 65th Regiment, the commission being purchased for him by his Langlois great-uncles. Unfortunately, Anthony married in 1798 Elizabeth Wilkin, who was considered in some way undesirable, and the Langlois family refused to provide any further financial assistance. Tom Lefroy was eventually able to obtain for his brother the position of Barrack-Master, first in Arundel and later in York, where this branch of the family therefore remained. One of their sons, Thomas-Edward-Preston Lefroy (1815–87), married in 1846 his cousin Anna-Jemima Lefroy (daughter of Anna Austen and Benjamin Lefroy; see below).

(**2**) I.-P.-George Lefroy (1745–13 January 1806); Fellow of All Souls, Oxford; took Holy Orders; 1777 vicar of Compton near Guildford, Surrey (a Brydges family living); Benjamin Langlois also bought for him three presentations of the living of Ashe in Hampshire. George Lefroy married 1778 Anne Brydges (1749–16 December 1804, q.v.), and they took up residence in Ashe in 1783. 'Madam Lefroy', as she was known locally, became the great friend and mentor of the youthful JA; and in 1808 JA wrote her poem 'To the Memory of Mrs Lefroy' on the fourth anniversary of her sudden death in a riding accident. The Lefroys had seven children: Jemima-Lucy (1779), John-Henry-George (1782), Julia-Elizabeth (1783), Anthony-Brydges (1784), Christopher-Edward (1785), William-Thomas (1787), and Benjamin (1791).

(**2a**) Jemima-Lucy (1779–11 March 1862) married 20 July 1801 Henry Rice (q.v.), and had issue.

(**2b**) John-Henry-George (12 January 1782–5 September 1823) married 1806 Sophia Cottrell (q.v.) and had eleven children (see below). He succeeded his father as rector of Ashe and vicar of Compton in 1806; in 1818 he inherited from his maternal uncle Henry Maxwell (q.v. under Brydges) Ewshott House (later known as Itchel Manor) at Crondall near Farnham, Surrey, and following his early death in 1823 his widow Sophia brought up her eight surviving children there. Sophia's opinions of JA's works were very lukewarm.

(**2c**) Julia-Elizabeth (August 1783–6 September 1783) was buried in Basingstoke, where the Lefroys seem to have been living temporarily before moving into Ashe parsonage.

(**2d**) Anthony-Brydges (21 September 1784–27 January 1800), died as a result of a riding accident two years previously.

(**2e**) Christopher-Edward (24 November 1785–2 July 1856, known as 'Edward') entered the law, and in 1819 became British Commissary Judge for the suppression of the slave trade in Surinam; he never married, and in later years returned from Surinam in order to support his brother Benjamin's family; buried at Westham near Basingstoke, Hants.

(**2f**) William-Thomas (9 October 1787–15 August 1791).

(**2g**) Benjamin (13 May 1791–27 August 1829), married 8 November 1814 at Steventon **Anna Austen** (q.v.), and had seven children (see below). The young couple lived with C.-Edward Lefroy in Hendon, Middx., November 1814–August 1815, and then returned to Hampshire, renting part of a farmhouse called Wyards just outside Chawton. Ben Lefroy eventually took Holy Orders in 1817 and became curate of Lasham, near Alton; he held the family living of Compton 1819–23, and then succeeded his brother as rector of Ashe in 1823. Following his early death in 1829 Anna and her children lived in various rented houses in Westham, Oakley, Basingstoke, Winchester, Monk Sherborne, and Reading; she died in Reading 1 September 1872 and was buried in Ashe.

At some time in her middle age—approximately 1855 onwards—Anna composed a manuscript volume of family history notes, which is now known as the **Lefroy MS**. This later came into the possession of her daughter Fanny-Caroline Lefroy (see below), together with letters which Anna had received in her girlhood from JA.

(**2b**) The children of John-Henry-George Lefroy and Sophia Cottrell were:

(**1**) George (1807–24) died at school at Winchester.

(**2**) Anne (1808–89) married 1829 John McLintock, 1st Baron Rathdonnell; no issue.

(**3**) Charles-Edward (1810–61, the 'little Charles Lefroy' of JA's correspondence) married 1845 Janet Walker, and left two sons: Charles-James-Maxwell and Clement-George. It was Clement Lefroy's wife Euphemia ('Effie') who begged a scrap of one of JA's letters from her husband's cousin Fanny-Caroline Lefroy (see below).

(**4**) Frances-Phoebe (1811–59) married 1842 Sir George Kettleby Rickards, barrister and Counsel to the Speaker in the House of Commons; in 1861 he married Julia-Cassandra, daughter of Anna and Ben Lefroy (see below).

(**5**) Revd Anthony-Cottrell (1812–84) married 1841 Miss Rickman.

(**6**) Sophia-Ann (1814–97) married 1852 Revd Ernest Hawkins, Canon of Westminster.

(7) Gen. Sir John-Henry (1817–90) became a distinguished soldier, explorer, and scientist, and founded the Canadian branch of the Lefroys.

(8) Henry-Maxwell (1818–79) founded the Australian branch of the Lefroys.

(9) Lucy-Jemima (1819–27).

(10) Frederick-William (1821–8).

(11) Isabella-Elizabeth (1823–87) married 1854 Revd Charles-Frederick Seymour, rector of Winchfield.

(2g) The children of **Benjamin Lefroy** and **Anna Austen** were:

(1) Anna-Jemima (20 October 1815–23 October 1855, known as 'Jemima'); married 1846 at Church Oakley, Hants, her Yorkshire cousin Thomas-Edward-Preston Lefroy (see above) and had three children, dying at the birth of the third: Jemima-Anne (1847), William-Chambers (1849–1915), and Mary-Georgina-Langlois (1855).

(2) Julia-Cassandra (27 September 1816–1884) married 1861 as his second wife Sir George Kettleby Rickards, widower of her cousin Frances-Phoebe Lefroy (see above).

(3) George-Benjamin-Austen (18 May 1818–1910) married 1853 Emma Cracroft and had six children: Revd Edward-Cracroft (1855–91, leaving issue); Florence-Emma (1857–1926, married her cousin Augustus Austen-Leigh (q.v.) but had no issue); Mary-Isabella ('Isabel', 1860–1939, died unmarried); Franklin-George (1861–1936, married but no issue); Jessie (died 1941 unmarried); and Louisa-Langlois ('Louie', 1864–1954, unmarried). Miss Jessie Lefroy lived in Winchester, and her sisters Isabel and Louie lived together at Bentworth, Hants, where RWC called upon them in the 1920s and saw the JA letters then in their possession (see below). Miss Louie Lefroy lived on to become a founder-member of the JA Society.

(4) Fanny-Caroline (4 July 1820–1885). FCL was the only one of Anna's children who never married, and so lived with her mother till the latter's death in 1872. FCL dabbled in literature, publishing anonymously some small pious Sunday School novels, and also contributing stories to Charlotte M. Yonge's magazine for girls, the *Monthly Packet*. At some time towards the end of her life—probably in the late 1870s—she composed her manuscript volume of **Family History,** which was subsequently given by her sister Mrs Bellas (see below) to their cousin Cholmeley Austen-Leigh in 1886. FCL used for this work her mother's **Lefroy MS**, the original letters from JA to Anna, and also information contained in other letters and papers collected by her sister Mrs Bellas, referred to by RWC as the **Bellas MS**.

(5) Georgiana-Brydges (14 April 1822–1882) married 1847 Alured-John-George-Seymer Terry, youngest son of Stephen Terry of Dummer (q.v.), and had issue.

(6) Louisa-Langlois (5 November 1824–1910) married 28 July 1859 Revd

Septimus Bellas, vicar of Monk Sherborne, and had issue. After her mother's death, and probably in 1872, Mrs Bellas copied out into a notebook (the **Bellas MS**, see above) a few extracts from Anna's diaries and also two small collections of letters—the first group being some which Anna herself had received in the earlier part of her life and kept for sentimental reasons, and the second group some which Mrs Bellas had received from her mother in more recent years.

The Lefroy MS, the Bellas MS, and the JA letters to Anna, descended to the unmarried daughters of G.-B.-A. Lefroy (see above), apart from those few items given away to other relatives by FCL.

(7) Elizabeth-Lucy (22 July 1827–1896) married 10 May 1859 Revd Arthur Loveday (a descendant of Revd John Hinton of Chawton, q.v.), curate of Monk Sherborne and later of Corhampton near Bishops Waltham and Goring Heath, Oxon., and had issue.

Leigh families. Mrs GA, the Leighs of Adlestrop, the Cookes (q.v.) of Great Bookham, the Coopers (q.v.) of Hamstall Ridware, the Turner baronets (q.v.), and Lady Saye and Sele (q.v. under Twisleton), had a common ancestor in Theophilus Leigh (*c.*1643-1725) of Adlestrop, Glos., who married November 1689 as his second wife Mary Brydges (sister of James Brydges, 1st Duke of Chandos), and had by her twelve children. Of these twelve, only three concern us: (1) William (1691), (2) Theophilus (1693), and (3) Thomas (1696).

(1) William (1691-1757) married Mary Lord (1695-1756) and had several children, of whom only four concern us: Cassandra (1723), James (1724), Thomas (1734), and Elizabeth (17??).

(1a) Cassandra (1723-70) married September 1739 Sir Edward Turner (q.v.), 2nd Bt. of Ambrosden, Oxon., and had several children.

(1b) James (1724-74) married 1755 his cousin Lady Caroline Brydges (born 1730, daughter of 2nd Duke of Chandos), and had a son James-Henry (1765-1823), who married 1786 his cousin Julia-Judith Twisleton (q.v., daughter of Lady Saye and Sele), and eventually inherited Stoneleigh Abbey in 1813. Their son Chandos (1791-1850) became 1839 Lord Leigh of 2nd creation.

(1c) Revd Thomas (1734-26 June 1813), rector of Adlestrop and of Broadwell, married 1762 his cousin Mary (1731-97), daughter of Revd Dr Theophilus (see below) but had no children. In 1806 Revd Thomas Leigh inherited Stoneleigh Abbey from the senior branch of the Leighs (see below).

(1d) Elizabeth (17??-1816), never married, but lived with her brother Revd Thomas at Adlestrop Rectory; she was CEA's godmother, and is referred to in JA's correspondence as 'Mrs' Elizabeth Leigh in accordance with her age, even though single.

(2) Revd Dr Theophilus (1693–1784) married 1728 Anne Bee (died 1766), and had six children, of whom only two survived: Mary (1731) and Cassandra (1744). He was Master of Balliol College, Oxford for many years, and was renowned for his witty sayings.

(2a) Mary (1731–97) married 1762 her cousin Revd Thomas Leigh of Adlestrop (see above), but had no children. After her death her husband commented: 'She wrote some novels highly moral and entertaining, on which she spent more time than accorded with her health'—but it does not seem that any of her literary works were ever published. She was also very proud of her ancestry, and left a short manuscript history of the Leigh family, completed in 1788.

(2b) Cassandra (1744–1826) married 1768 Revd Samuel Cooke (q.v.), and had issue.

(3) Revd Thomas (1696–1764); Fellow of All Souls, Oxford; rector of Harpsden near Henley-on-Thames, Oxon., 1731–64. He married 1732 Jane Walker (1704–68) and had four surviving children: James (1735), Jane (1736), Cassandra (1739), and Thomas (1747).

(3a) James (1735–28 March 1817) added -Perrot to his name in 1751 in order to inherit the estate of his maternal great-uncle Thomas Perrot. Married 9 October 1764 Jane Cholmeley (died 1836, q.v.); of Scarlets near Maidenhead, Berks.; also rented 1799–1810 No. 1 Paragon Buildings, Bath, then purchased 1810 No. 49 Great Pulteney Street, Bath; died at Scarlets and buried at Wargrave, Berks.; no issue.

(3b) Jane (1736–83) married 1768 Revd Dr Edward Cooper (q.v.) and left issue.

(3c) Cassandra (1739–1827) married 1764 in Bath Revd George Austen (q.v.), and became JA's mother.

(3d) Thomas (1747–1821) was 'imbecile' and in accordance with the custom of the time presumably did not live in the Harpsden rectory. It seems that in later years both he and Mrs GA's second son, the handicapped George Austen jr. (q.v.), were living together at Monk Sherborne, cared for by the Culham family of that parish.

The Leighs of Adlestrop in Gloucestershire and the Leighs of Stoneleigh Abbey near Kenilworth in Warwickshire had a common ancestor in Sir Thomas Leigh, Lord Mayor of London, who died 1571. In 1643 a Thomas Leigh of the Warwickshire line was created Baron Leigh of Stoneleigh, but this family came to an end with Edward, 5th Lord Leigh (1742–86), who was single and in 1774 declared lunatic. His unmarried sister Hon Mary Leigh died in July 1806, when the Stoneleigh estate devolved upon Revd Thomas Leigh of Adlestrop (see above).

Leven and Melville, Earls of. Alexander Leslie-Melville, 7th Earl of Leven and 6th Earl of Melville (1749–1820); married 1784 Jane Thornton (died

1818); their portraits agree with JA's description of them. Of their eight children the eldest son David (1785–1860), styled Viscount Balgonie until he succeeded as 8th and 7th Earl, was in the Navy—Lieutenant 1806, Captain 1812, and Rear-Admiral 1846; the youngest daughter, 'pretty little Lady Marianne', married 1822 Abel Smith, MP, and died 1823.

Despite—or perhaps because of—his naval service, Viscount Balgonie seems to have been frequently unwell; as late as 1814 he was described as 'a good-humoured, pleasing young man, but seems in bad health'. However, he survived to the reasonable age of 75, and remained a constant friend of CJA to the end of the latter's life.

In 1818 Lord Balgonie met Miss Beaujolois Campbell and her sisters in Italy; the 15-year-old Beaujolois summed him up in her journal in truly Austenian style: 'He has a good countenance and is very near being handsome. He is not rich and was a sailor for many years which has as usual affected his walk. He is one of those men whom any body could marry for the trouble of making love to him. He liked us very much and I beleive was rather inclined towards Eleanor, but he was here too short a time and she giving no encouragement it naturally ended in nothing. He is poor and is not what I should wish for as a husband. At the same time he is of good rank and might make one very happy.'

Lewis, Susannah (1780–1844). Daughter of James Lewis of Clifton and formerly of Jamaica (not Antigua); married 1813 Revd Samuel Blackall (q.v.).

Lillingston, Mrs. Of 10 Rivers Street, Bath; died 1806 and buried at Charlcombe.

Limbrey, Mr (Not 'Limprey' as JA wrote.) Probably Mr John Limbrey of Hoddington House, Upton Grey, Hants; or possibly a member of the Limbrey-Sclater family, who lived at Tangier Park, near Manydown, during the eighteenth and nineteenth centuries.

Lipscombe, Dame. (Not 'Libscombe', as JA wrote.) Chawton villager; Hannah, widow 1807 of Thomas Lipscombe; the 'deaffy child' was probably her illegitimate granddaughter Mary-Winter Lipscombe (baptized 1809), whose mother Mary married another man in 1813.

Liston, John (1776–1846). Actor; first appeared on the London stage 1805 and became a popular comedian 1807, noted especially for his double-act with Charles Mathews (q.v.); retired 1837.

Littlehales, Dr John, FRCP (1754–1810). Physician at Winchester Hospital, and lived in Southgate Street.

Littleworth family. Deane villagers, and the foster-family of Mr GA's children. See Deirdre Le Faye, 'The Austens and the Littleworths', in JA Society *Report* for 1987, 15–21. Anne ('Nanny') Littleworth was one of the

Austens' maidservants at Steventon (perhaps the cook or dairymaid), her husband John was coachman to James Austen, and JA was godmother to their eldest daughter Eliza-Jane. A cousin of theirs, William Littleworth of Alton, was manservant at Chawton Cottage and later married Mary Goodchild (q.v.).

Lloyd family, of Enborne, Deane, and Ibthorpe. Martha Craven (1729–16 April 1805, q.v.), married 1763 Revd Nowis or Noyes Lloyd (1719–89), rector of Little Hinton, Wilts., and also 1771 of Enborne near Newbury, Berks; three daughters: Martha (1765–1843) who became 1828 the second wife of FWA, and died at Portsdown; Eliza (1768–1839) who married 1788 her cousin Revd Fulwar-Craven Fowle (q.v.) and died at Kintbury; and Mary (1771–1843) who became 1797 the second wife of James Austen, and died at Speen. After Mr Lloyd's death his widow and her two unmarried daughters lived in Mr GA's parsonage at Deane, moving in 1792 to Ibthorpe, a hamlet near Hurstbourne Tarrant, Hants.

Lloyd, Mrs. Friend of Miss Sharp (q.v.); not apparently connected with the Lloyds above.

Lock(y)er, Capt., RN. Lt.-Governor of Greenwich Hospital for Seamen, succeeded 1801 by Capt. Sir Richard Pearson (q.v.).

Lodge, Jane. Daughter of John Lodge of Great Blakenham near Ipswich, Suffolk; married (1) 1799 John Lyford (q.v.), and (2) 1801 William Fendall (q.v.).

Long, Flora. Younger daughter of Florentina Wrey (q.v.), who married Richard-Godolphin Long of Rood (or Rowde) Ashton, Wilts.

Louch, William-Stevens. HTA's banking partner in Alton and Hythe.

Lovell, Betty. Probably 'Lovell' rather than Lord Brabourne's reading 'Londe'; the Steventon parish register shows that an Elizabeth Lovell was buried on 9 March 1808—'died in consequence of the fire which took place at the house where she lived'.

Lovett, Mr. John Lovett of Overton, Hants.

Lucan, Earl of. Richard Bingham (1764–1839), succeeded as 2nd Earl 1799. He married in 1794 Lady Elizabeth Belasyse, whom he had seduced from her husband Bernard-Edward Howard (later Duke of Norfolk), and by whom he had six children. In 1804 they separated—'More from disagreement of temper and extreme absurdity on both sides than any other cause. How extraordinary after giving up the world for each other, and living happily near 10 years! At the end of that time they went to Brighthelmstone, where he had the gout. She took to racketing and neglected him, he grew low-spirited and scolded her. Incessant wranglings ensued, mix'd up with accusations of flirtation on one side and stinginess on the other. This continued for near two years . . . ' — so it is perhaps not surprising that the Earl took a mistress in 1807.

Ludlow, Mr. Arnold, widower, of Andover, married January 1799 Sal Pugh of Andover.

Lushington, Stephen-Rumbold (1776–1868). Of Norton Court, Kent, and 4 Cleveland Square, London; fourth son of Revd James-Stephen Lushington of Rodmersham, Kent; married 1798 Anne-Elizabeth, daughter of 1st Lord Harris; MP for Rye 1807–12 and for Canterbury 1812–30; Governor of Madras 1827–32; MP again for Canterbury 1835–7; his portrait is in Canterbury Art Gallery.

Lyddy. Maidservant in Southampton.

Lyell, Mrs. Widow of Charles Lyell, of Kinnordy, Forfarshire; settled in Southampton 1808 with her son and two daughters Mary and Anne, the latter of whom married Gilbert Heathcote (q.v.).

Lyford family, of Basingstoke and Winchester. John Lyford (1740–1829), surgeon of Basingstoke; probably the son of Giles Lyford (1700–83, four times mayor of Basingstoke); married 1766 Mary Windover and had three children: Revd John (1769–12 June 1799) of Queen's College, Oxford, 1786, Lincoln's Inn 1789, curate of Basing and Nately 1793, married 19 April 1799 at Great Blakenham, Jane Lodge (q.v.), died suddenly and buried at Basingstoke; Mary Susannah (1772–1840) married June 1803 Revd James Digweed (q.v.); Charles (1778–1859), partner and successor to his father. See W. A. W. Jarvis, 'Who was John Lyford?' in JA Society *Report* for 1962, 216–18.

Charles Lyford (1743–1805), brother of the elder John Lyford, practised as a surgeon in Winchester, living in Peter Street; his son Giles-King Lyford (1764–1837) was Surgeon-in-Ordinary at the County Hospital, Winchester, and attended JA in her last illness; his daughter Louisa married September 1798 Mr Marsh, surgeon of the Wilts. Supplementary Militia. There was also a third Charles Lyford (? son of the above Charles), who was an apothecary and druggist in Southampton 1791.

Lynch, Revd Dr John (1735–1803). Rector of Adisham, Kent, and also 1781 Prebendary and 1788 Archdeacon of Canterbury.

Lysons, Mrs. Wife of Dr Lysons of 3 Paragon Buildings, Bath.

Mackays, the. Perhaps the family of Donald-Hugh Mackay, Captain RN January 1806.

Maitland families. Thomas Maitland of Lyndhurst (died 1797) married Jane Mathew (1759–1830), daughter of General Mathew (q.v.); five sons and three daughters; the widowed Mrs Maitland lived in Albion Place, Southampton. Her eldest daughter Jane married 25 March 1800 Lt.-Col.

Warren of the 3rd Foot Guards (q.v.); Caroline (1782–1830) married 1812 Capt. William Roberts, RA; Eliza married post-1812 Revd Mr Rankin.

The eldest son, Sir Peregrine Maitland (1777–1854), who commanded the Guards at Waterloo, eloped October 1815 with the Duke of Richmond's daughter Lady Sarah Lennox, as the Duke had refused his consent to their marriage on account of Sir Peregrine's poverty. 'Sir P, who was extremely handsome, afterwards became Governor of the Cape [of Good Hope, South Africa]. But the Duchess of Richmond always spoke contemptuously of her daughter as "Barrack Sal". Lady Sarah died in 1873.'

The Mr Maitland whom JA met in Bath—Mrs Busby's nephew—may perhaps be Charles Barclay Maitland, whose son Charles (born in Bath *c.*1786) became rector of Little Longford, Wilts. This family does not appear to be related to the Lyndhurst/Southampton Maitlands.

Malings, the. Probably Mrs Maling of 21 Hans Place, or C. T. Maling of 146 Sloane Street.

Manon. Eliza de Feuillide's French maidservant.

Mant, Mr Henry. Attorney, of 23 Gay Street and 4 Green Park Buildings, Bath; Lieutenant of Infantry in the Bath Military Association.

Mant, Revd Dr Richard (1745–1817). Master of King Edward's Free Grammar School, Southampton, 1770–95; Rector 1793 of All Saints, Southampton, and of Fonthill Bishop, Wilts.

Mapleton family. Dr Mapleton, physician, of 14 Belmont, and also 12 The Circus, Bath; his daughters Jane, Marianne (died 18 May 1801), and Christian(a).

March, Charles, Earl of. Eldest son of the Duke of Richmond; married 10 April 1817 Lady Caroline Paget (q.v.).

Marlow, Revd Dr Michael (1759–1828). Vicar of St Giles, Oxford, and rector of Handborough; President 1795–1828 of St John's College, Oxford; Vice-Chancellor of the university 1798–1802; Prebendary of Canterbury 1808.

Marriott, Mrs. Perhaps wife or daughter-in-law of Revd Dr James Marriott (1743–1809), patron and rector of Horsmonden, Kent, 1785–1809.

Marshal, Mr. Chawton yeoman; shared the Wyards farmhouse with Anna and Ben Lefroy.

Marshall, Mr and Mrs. Landlords of the George, Sittingbourne, Kent.

Martha. Sometime maidservant to Mrs Leigh-Perrot.

Martin, Mrs. Probably the Mary Martin who was landlady of the Maidenhead Inn and also held the Excise Office at Basingstoke 1791.

Mascall, Robert-Curteis (1795–1816). Oriel College, Oxford, 1811 and BA 1815; Lincoln's Inn 1814; died at Nice.

Mathew family. Edward Mathew (1728–1805), born in Antigua; of Argyll Street, London, and Clanville Lodge near Andover, Hants. Equerry to George III 1783; Governor of Grenada 1783 and C.-in-C. of the Windward and Leeward Isles; General 1797. Married at Bath Abbey January 1753 Lady Jane Bertie (died 1793) daughter of the 2nd Duke of Ancaster and had four children: Jane (1759, later Mrs Maitland, q.v.); Anne (1759, twin with Jane, later Mrs James Austen, q.v.); Brownlow (1760–1826) of Clanville Lodge and later of Shrubshill near Lyndhurst, Hants, married 1807 Henrietta Taylor and in 1819 took the additional surname Bertie; Penelope-Susannah (Mrs Dewar, q.v., later Mrs Cumberland).

Daniel Mathew (1730–77), of Felix Hall, Essex, brother to Gen. Edward; his daughter Louisa married Adm. Lord Gambier, and his daughter Jane married Samuel Gambier (qq.v.).

Mathews, Charles (1776–1835). Actor; a comedian and mimic, performing in London and the provinces, and noted for his double-act with John Liston (q.v.).

Maunde, Henry. One of HTA's banking partners; probably the Mr Maunde of 5 York Buildings, New [Euston] Road, Marylebone; died before 1822.

Mawhood, Collet and Mrs. Of 10 Belmont, Bath.

Maxwell, Mr. Perhaps James Maxwell, of Lewes, Sussex, who entered Trinity College, Cambridge, 1804 aged 18; ordained 1811 and went to a Norfolk living.

May, Mr. Either Thomas May (1765–1843) or his brother Charles (1767–1844); the May family had lived in Basingstoke for many generations, and became brewers c.1750. Thomas and Charles were very prominent in local affairs in the later eighteenth and early nineteenth centuries, and Thomas was Mayor of Basingstoke eleven times.

Meyer, Mr. Harp teacher, of Upper Marylebone Street. Presumably Philip-James Meyer (1732–1820) from Strasbourg, who was the first musician to play the pedal harp in this country.

Middleton, John-Charles (1755–1826). Mr Middleton seems to have had no fixed home or estate of his own, but moved constantly from one rented property to another throughout his life. He was at Hinton Ampner and Twyford in Hampshire, and Weybridge in Surrey; at Chawton Great House 1795 and again 1808–13; and finally at Hildersham House, Cambridge, 1824–6. Married 1793 Charlotte Beckford (died 1803, q.v.) and had six children: John (born c.1794, perhaps the JM who joined the RN as a First-Class Volunteer 1804, and was midshipman 1805 and Lieutenant 1811); Susan;

Charlotte-Maria (married 1831 her cousin Revd Charles-Douglas Beckford); Lucy; Charlotte-Lydia-Elizabeth (married 1824 Septimus Burton); and Frederick-Graeme (1803, later incumbent of Bembridge, Isle of Wight). His wife's sister, Miss Maria Beckford, lived with him as his hostess.

Middleton, Mrs. Perhaps Mrs Robert Middleton—see under **Woodd.**

Mildmay family. Jane Mildmay, eldest daughter and co-heiress of Carew Mildmay of Shawford, Hants, married 1786 Sir Henry-Paulet St John (q.v.) of Moulsham, Essex, 3rd Bt., who took 1790 the additional surname of Mildmay; her eldest son was Henry-Paulet St John-Mildmay, afterwards (1808) 4th Bt., of Dogmersfield, Hants. Her sister Anne married Mr John Clarke (q.v.) of Worting, Hants.

Miller, Robert. Pastry-cook, 143 High Street, Southampton.

Miller, Sir Thomas, 5th Bt. (*c.*1735–4 September 1816). Of Froyle Place near Alton, Hants; MP for Portsmouth 1806–16.

Milles family, of Nackington. Richard Milles (1736–1820), MP for Canterbury 1761–80; married 1765 Mary-Elizabeth, daughter of Revd Thomas Tanner, Prebendary of Canterbury; their only daughter Mary married (1) 2nd Baron Sondes (q.v.) and (2) Sir Henry Montresor (q.v.).

Milles, Mrs Charles (1723–6 March 1817). Widow (1749) of Charles Milles, uncle of Richard Milles of Nackington; her daughter 'Molly' or 'Moy'; lived in Canterbury.

Millman, Dr. Kentish ?physician, attending EAK; could this be Dr Thomas Milner, MD, of Maidstone?

Mitchell, Sarah. Probably the Chawton village girl Sarah (baptized 1790), daughter of William and Mary Mitchell, who had an illegitimate daughter Frances (baptized 1816).

Moira, Lord (1754–1826). Francis Rawdon, succeeded his father as Earl of Moira 1793; appointed 1812 Governor-General of Bengal and C.-in-C. of the forces in India, and left England in 1813; created first Marquis of Hastings 1817; died heavily in debt.

Between 1806–13 HTA, as his banker, had lent Lord Moira a total of £6,000, but despite numerous promises to do so repayment was never made, which in part contributed to HTA's bankruptcy in 1816. In 1839 HTA approached the 2nd Marquis (1808–44) with an appeal to him to honour his father's debts; but the young man was interested only in hunting, had married an extravagant wife in 1831, and already had six children, and it seems that this appeal was similarly ignored.

Molly. The Austens' maidservant at Steventon, who followed them to Bath and Southampton—if the references are to one and the same person.

Montresor family of Nash Court, Kent. General Sir Henry-Tucker Montresor (1767–1837), KCB; married (1) January 1809 Lady Sondes (q.v.), and (2) Annetta Cage (q.v.), and had issue. His sister Maria-Lucy married September 1801 Lt.-Gen. Sir F. W. Mulcaster.

Moore families. There are three separate Moore families mentioned in JA's correspondence:

(**1**) **Rt. Revd John Moore** (1730–1805). Dean of Canterbury 1771–5, Bishop of Bangor 1775–83, Archbishop of Canterbury 1783–1805. Married 1770 as his second wife Catherine Eden (q.v.) and had several children; she lived at the Oaks, Canterbury, during her widowhood.

The Archbishop's eldest son by his second marriage, Revd George Moore (1771–1845), was Prebendary of Canterbury 1795, rector of Brasted, Kent, 1795–1800, rector of Wrotham, Kent, 1800, vicar of East Peckham, Kent, 1805, rector of Ladock, Cornwall, 1814, and of Owmby, Lincs., 1823; he married (1) 1795 Lady Maria-Elizabeth Hay, seventh daughter of the 14th Earl of Errol and had a daughter Caroline (born *c*.1800); (2) 1806 Harriot-Mary Bridges (q. v.) and had several children by her—JA mentions Eleanor, George, and Harriot.

Edward Hasted, having published his *History and Topographical Survey of the County of Kent* between 1778–99, continued to keep notes on local events, perhaps with a view to a new edition. Under 'Wrotham' he recorded, 11 October 1806: 'The Rector Mr Moore is so universally hated here that when he made his first appearance at Church, on his marriage with Miss Bridges, to shew it the clerk put up & they sung the funeral hymn instead of the usual Nuptial Psalm'. Canterbury Diocesan Record Office, Irby Collection (U.11, V/514).

The Archbishop's third son, Revd Robert Moore, married 1800 a Miss Bell, daughter of the late Matthew Bell of Wolsington, Northumberland; the Miss Bell mentioned by JA as having been governess to Revd George Moore's daughter Caroline, may perhaps be a poor relation of Mrs Robert Moore.

(**2**) **The Misses Harriet and Eliza Moore,** of Hanwell; perhaps nieces or granddaughters of Mr Gordon of Cleveland Row (q.v.). Harriet admired *Emma* very much, but *MP* was her favourite of all.

(**3**) **Dr John Moore** (1729–1802), MD, and writer, and his wife Jane; lived in Surrey and attended the Lock family at Norbury, and so known to Fanny Burney and her circle and also to the Cooke family at Great Bookham; parents of Gen. Sir John Moore (1761–killed at Corunna 1809).

Morgan, Revd Nathaniel. Master of the Grammar School, Broad Street, Bath.

Morgan, Miss. Unidentified; she was presumably ailing in December 1798.

Morley, Countess of. Frances Talbot (1782–1857), daughter of a surgeon at Wymondham, Norfolk; married August 1809 as his second wife John Parker (1772–1840), 2nd Lord Boringdon, created 30 September 1815 1st Earl of Morley; his estate was at Saltram, near Plymouth, Devon.

Lord Boringdon's first wife, Lady Augusta Fane, whom he had married in 1804, objected to sharing her husband's favours with his mistresses, and eloped with Sir Arthur Paget (q.v.) in 1808, whom she married in February 1809 as soon as her divorce from Lord Boringdon was finalized. Frances Talbot, however, was able to make the Earl into a good husband, and their marriage lasted thirty-one years.

Lady Morley was an attractive and witty woman, with literary interests, and for a time some people believed her to be the authoress of both *S&S* and *P&P*. It is not known how JA became acquainted with her, but the likeliest explanation is that it was through HTA, with his many contacts in London society. Although Lady Morley thanked JA warmly for the gift of *Emma*, in her letters to her sister-in-law Mrs George Villiers she spoke of it less than enthusiastically, rating it below *P&P* and *MP*. See W. A. W. Jarvis, 'JA and the Countess of Morley', in JA Society *Report* for 1986, 9–16; and C. Viveash, 'Lady Morley and the "Baron so Bold" ', in JASNA, *Persuasions*, 14 (1992), 53–6.

Morley family. Mr James Morley (1743–98), an East India merchant, had briefly owned the Kempshott Park estate, near Basingstoke, 1787–8; these girls are presumably his daughters, and probably living in Winchester.

Morrell family. Mr James Morrell, of 1 St Giles, Oxford, was the father of Revd Deacon Morrell (1775–1854). Deacon Morrell was perhaps one of Revd GA's pupils at Steventon, *c.*1791–2; Christ Church, Oxford, 1792, MA 1799; Lincoln's Inn 1796; of Streatley and Henley, Oxon., also of Moulsford, Berks., and finally of 35 Sackville Street, London; although ordained it seems that he never actually held a living.

Deacon Morrell never married, but his younger brother Baker did, and one of the latter's descendants was the Philip Morrell who married Lady Ottoline Cavendish-Bentinck of the Bloomsbury Set.

Morrice family, of Betshanger, Kent. (Not 'Morris' as JA wrote.) The Revd James Morrice was rector of Betshanger, and the 'two Morrises' who came to Godmersham in 1808 to play with young JEAL were probably his children.

Morton, Mr. Martha Lloyd's friend, perhaps living in Harrogate.

Mulcaster, Lt.-Gen. Sir F. W. Married September 1801 Maria-Lucy Montresor (q.v.); his sister Miss Mulcaster.

Murden, Jane (17??–1820). Daughter of——Murden and Christiana Fowle (q.v.); lived most of the time at Kintbury Rectory, and died at Hungerford, Berks. She thought *Emma* was inferior to all the other of JA's novels.

Murray, John (1778–1843). Of Albemarle Street, London; publisher. Brought out *Emma*, *NA*, and *P* and also the second edition of *MP*.

   Described by the 1st Earl of Dudley as '. . . the excellent Murray. He is the prince of all booksellers and publishers—liberal-minded, well-educated and well-mannered, and of a pleasing aspect . . .' JA's assessment of him as 'a rogue of course, but a civil one' is unwittingly corroborated by a fellow publisher, Mr Samuel Bagster, who records in his autobiography (168–9) an anecdote which shows Mr Murray in a rather equivocal light.

Musgrove, Miss. Apparently did *not* marry Mr Richard Harvey in 1796.

Mussell, Mrs. Dressmaker/milliner, wife of William Mussell, hairdresser, of 9 Queen Street and later 7 Pulteney Bridge, Bath.

Newton, Isaac. Linen-draper, 14 Leicester Square, London.

Nibbs, James-Langford (1738–95). Of Antigua, and later of Devonshire; matriculated at St John's College, Oxford, 1758; godfather to James Austen. His son George (1765–1832) was one of Revd GA's pupils c.1781–3; Oriel College, Oxford, 1783, BA 1787; vicar of Cutcombe with Luxborough, Somerset, 1791. The picture to which JA refers jokingly as 'Mr Nibbs' may be a portrait of either the father or the son—or perhaps just any picture given to the Austens by this family.

North, Rt. Revd Brownlow (1741–1820). Bishop of Winchester 1781–1820.

North, Miss. Visitor or resident in Bath, 1799.

Nottley, George (or perhaps 'Knottley'). Landlord of the Bull & George in Dartford.

Nunes, Mrs. Mistress of a boarding-school in Overton, Hants, where Mary-Jane Fowle (q.v.) was educated.

Nutt, Mr. A connection of the Pearson family (q.v.), and apparently a military cadet at Woolwich Academy.

Ogle, Mr. The *Court Guide* for 1815 shows four gentlemen of this name in London: Henry Ogle of 12 Stratton Street; H. M. Ogle, MP, 13 John Street, Adelphi; J. Ogle of Southampton Street, Bloomsbury; Richard Ogle of 65 Great Russell Street, Bloomsbury; there was also a Miss Ogle in Kensington Gore.

O'Neil, Mr. Drawing-master to Fanny Cage jr.

O'Neill, Eliza (1791–1872). (Not 'O'Neal'. as JA wrote.) A tragedy actress and classic beauty; first appeared on the London stage in 1814, and was a reigning favourite until her retirement in 1819: 'Her face is not expressive, perhaps, but her actions are most graceful, her voice melodious, and her manners so natural that you can scarcely believe she is not the person she means to represent. I believe there was not a dry eye in the house'. —Mrs

Calvert, describing her in the part of Mrs Haller, June 1815; Miss Berry, later that year, met her offstage and reported: 'Miss O'Neil is in society what she is on the stage—gentle, pleasing, and interesting.' Miss O'Neill married 1819 Sir William Wrixon-Becher of Ballygiblin, Co. Cork, Ireland (1st baronet 1831), and had five children; in 1849 Carlyle visited Ballygiblin, and wrote to his sister: 'This house is the mansion of Sir Wm. Beecher [*sic*], whose "Lady Beecher" my present hostess was the once celebrated actress Miss O'Neil. She is now an elderly, austerely religious, stately and I really think worthy tho' not very lovable woman.'

Orde family. Of Northumbrian origin, with branches at Nunnykirk and Weetwood Hall, but several had come south to Hampshire:

(1) Thomas Orde (1746–1807) of Nunnykirk married 1778 Jean Powlett, illegitimate daughter of Charles, 5th Duke of Bolton (q.v.).

(2) A kinsman of Thomas Orde, Lt.-Gen. Leonard-Shafto Orde (died 1820) of Weetwood Hall, married 1800 as his second wife Lady Louisa Jocelyn (died 1807), daughter of Robert, 1st Earl of Roden (q.v.).

(3) Revd John Orde (1771–1850, brother of Leonard-Shafto); vicar of Kingsclere, Hants, 1796–1817, of Winslade, Hants, 1811–29, of Itchenstoke and Abbotstone, Hants, 1817–29, and rector of Wensley, Yorks., 1829; married 1802 Frances Carleton, second daughter of Guy, 1st Lord Dorchester (q.v.) and had six daughters.

(4) Lt.-Col. James Orde (brother of Leonard-Shafto and Revd John) married 15 May 1811 Margaret Beckford (died 1818, q.v.).

(5) Juliana-Anne, daughter of John Orde of Weetwood, married as his second wife 1804 the 2nd Earl of Roden (q.v.).

(6) William Orde, described by JA as 'a cousin of the Kingsclere man'— perhaps William Orde of Nunnykirk, who died unmarried in 1843.

Orléans, Duke and Duchess of. Members of the French Royal Family who had sought refuge in England—Louis-Philippe (1773–1850), eldest son of the Duc d'Orléans, Egalité (1747–93), and his wife 1809 Marie-Amelie; Louis-Philippe was King of the French 1830–48.

Osborne, Mr and Mrs. Probably connections of the Tylden family; there had been an Osborne/Tylden marriage earlier in the eighteenth century.

Owen, Mrs. Either Mrs Owen of 14 Portland Place, or Mrs Maria Owen of 7 Axford Buildings, Bath.

Oxenden family, baronets, of Deane Park, Wingham, and Broome House, Kent. Sir Henry (1756–1838) 7th Bt. 1803; married 1793 Mary Graham (q.v.), and had twelve children; his portrait is in Canterbury Art Gallery. His daughter Mary-Graham (born ?1794) married 15 July 1815 William-Osmund Hammond (q.v.).

Oxford, Lady. Edward Harley, 5th Earl of Oxford (1773–1848) married 1794 Jane Elizabeth (1773–1824), daughter of James Scott, vicar of Itchen Stoke, Hants. Her notoriously free lifestyle after her marriage resulted in her children being referred to as the Harleian Miscellany.

Paget family, of Beaudesert, Staffs., and Plas Newydd, Anglesey. JA's comments in 1817 on the immorality of the Paget family were no more than the truth: Henry-William Paget (1768–1854), previously Lord Uxbridge and 1815 created 1st Marquess of Anglesey, married 1795 Lady Caroline Villiers (1774–1835) and had eight children, before eloping in 1808 with Lady Charlotte Wellesley, sister-in-law of the Duke of Wellington, who herself had four children. Both marriages ended in divorce, and in 1810 Lady Caroline married the Duke of Argyll while her erstwhile husband married Lady Charlotte and had a further ten children by her. The 1st Marquess's younger brother Sir Arthur Paget (1771–1840) seduced in 1808 Lady Boringdon (q.v. under Morley), whom he married in 1809 when her divorce was finalized and six weeks before their child was born.

The Lady Caroline Paget who married the Earl of March in 1817 was the eldest daughter of the Marquess of Anglesey's first marriage.

Paget, Revd Mr, and wife. William Paget, of Queen's College, Cambridge; ordained deacon in Winchester diocese 10 March 1805, with letters dimissory from Canterbury diocese.

Painter, Thomas. Haberdasher in Andover.

Palmer family. John Grove Palmer (died 1832), sometime Attorney-General of Bermuda and later of 22 Keppel Street, Bloomsbury, London; married Dorothy Ball; sons John, R—. I—. (with whom he was on bad terms), and Charley; daughters Esther (married John-Christie Esten, q.v.); Harriet (died 1867) and Frances (died 1814) both married CJA (q.v.) and had issue.

The Mrs and Miss Palmer mentioned in 1816 may be different people.

Papillon family. Thomas Papillon (1757–1838), of Acrise Place, Kent, was a distant connection of the Knights (q.v.) of Chawton, due to a Papillon/Broadnax marriage in the mid-seventeenth century; another child of this marriage, Sarah Papillon, married Samuel Rawstorn (q.v.) of Lexden, Essex. Thomas Papillon's younger brother Revd John-Rawstorn (1763–1837 unmarried) was vicar of Tonbridge, Kent, 1791–1804 and rector of Chawton 1801–37, and their spinster sister Elizabeth lived with him in Chawton as his hostess; another sister, Sarah, married 1791 Henry Jackson (q.v.). Revd John-Rawstorn Papillon owned a first edition of *S&S* and signed his name in it. The Papillon archive (U.1015) is at the Centre for Kentish Studies, Maidstone.

Parry, Caleb Hillier, MD (1755–1822). Physician, of 27 The Circus, Bath; daughters Maria, Sarah, and Caroline, and son Sir William-Edward Parry (1790–1855), the Arctic explorer.

Payne family, of Brooklands, Weybridge, Surrey. Cousins of Revd GA and his family through their common Hampson ancestry: Jane, daughter of Sir Thomas Hampson, 4th Bt. (q.v.), married *c.*1728 Capel Payne, Town Clerk of Gloucester, and had two children, George and Catherine; she became one of the Women of the Bedchamber to the Princess of Wales, and died in Gloucester 1786.

George Payne (1729–7 December 1800) entered Merton College, Oxford, 1746; barrister-at-law of the Inner Temple 1753; bencher of the Inner Temple 1791. He built a house on Crown land at Brooklands *c.*1764; married Elizabeth——and had five children: Maria, Harriet (1759), Amelia (1767), Louisa (1770), and one son George jr. (1777). George Payne seems to have maintained his mother's court connections, and was sent as Ambassador to the Emperor of Morocco in 1784—unfortunately his expenses for this service were never reimbursed. He was also 'Patentee of the Lion Office in the Tower' (i.e. keeper of the royal menagerie in the Tower of London); and when he died suddenly and intestate in 1800 his widow had to pay for the upkeep of these animals until his estate was eventually settled in 1807.

George Payne was also an old friend of Warren Hastings (q.v.), and in later years George's eldest daughter Maria seems to have lived almost permanently at Daylesford as a companion to Hastings's wife Marian. In Surrey the Paynes were neighbours of the 3rd Earl of Portmore (q.v.).

Mr Payne was buried at Walton-on-Thames 15 December 1800; his widow Elizabeth moved to Thames Place, Shepperton, where she died in 1818 but was also buried at Walton. The house at Brooklands was purchased 1803 by the Duke of York and demolished 1834; early this century the estate became the Brooklands motor-racing track. Payne family letters are in the Hastings Papers, British Library.

The Catherine Payne who married 1735 George Cure (q.v.) was probably a sister of Capel Payne of Gloucester.

Peach, Revd Isaac (1754–1816). Pembroke College, Cambridge, 1773; BA 1777 and MA 1786; curate of Wootton St Lawrence, Hants, 1779 till his death in 1816.

Pearson, Miss. Mary Pearson, elder daughter of Capt. Sir Richard Pearson, RN (1731–1805), Lt.-Gov. of the Greenwich Hospital for Seamen 1801, succeeding Capt. Lock(y)er. See *Family Record* 88, 90–1.

Pellew, Adm. Sir Edward (1757–1833). First Viscount Exmouth; for details of his career see *DNB*.

Penlington. Tallow-chandler at the Crown & Beehive, Charles Street, Covent Garden, and later at 15 Hanway Street, Oxford Street.

Percival, Edward (1783–1819), MB. Physician at Southampton, and son of Dr Thomas Percival of Manchester (1740–1804) who wrote *A Father's Instructions to his Children* (1768).

Perigord, Mme/Mrs Mary. One of HTA's servants, probably daughter of Mme/Mrs Bigeon.

Peters, Mr. Perhaps Charles Peters, of St Clement's, Cornwall, who entered Queen's College, Oxford, 1786 aged 18, and died 1824. Mr Peters (whether this Charles or not) seems to have been a clergyman (probably a curate) at Tichborne and later at Ovington, Hants. The Powlett correspondence contains letters from Anne Powlett (q.v.) to her friend Miss Peters in Truro, in which reference is frequently made to this clergyman, her brother. A letter of 1 November 1800 speaks of talk about him and Miss Lyford; but a later letter, 5 August 1801, reports that 'we have ceased to talk of your Brother and Miss Lyford'.

Phebe. The Austens' maidservant in Southampton.

Philips, Mr. Proprietor of 12 Green Park Buildings, Bath; perhaps William Phil(l)ips, builder, of 12 Portland Place, Bath.

Phil(l)ips, Mr. One of HTA's bank clerks in London.

Phillott, Ven. Dr James (1749–1815). Archdeacon and rector of Bath 1798, vicar of Lyncombe and Widcombe, rector of Stanton Prior, Somerset, Prebendary of Wells 1791, and Chaplain to the Bath Military Association; of Parsonage House, Upper Borough Walls, Bath; married October 1808 Lady Frances St Lawrence (q.v.).

Philmore, John (1736–17 March 1817). Chawton villager; widower of Mary (died 1809); buried by HTA 22 March 1817; his son John jr. (baptized 1772) married 1809 Rachel Stubbington; other members of the family are also buried in Chawton churchyard.

Pickford, Mr and Mrs. Visitors to Bath 1801.

Piersy, Mrs J. (Not 'Percy' as JA wrote.) Married June 1799 Revd Dr Gardiner (q.v.) of Bath.

Pilkington family, baronets of Chevet near Wakefield, Yorks. Sir Thomas Pilkington, 7th Bt. (1773–1811), married 1797 Elizabeth-Anne Tufnell of Langleys, Essex (died 1842); four daughters: Eliza (married 1819), Anne (married 1822), Louisa (married 1830), Catherine (married 1831), to whom Miss Sharp (q.v.) was governess. The baronetcy was inherited by Sir Thomas's younger brother William (1775–1850), who married 1825 Mary Swinnerton.

Pinckards, the. Perhaps Dr George Pinckard, of 18 Bloomsbury Square, London; see *DNB*.

Plumptre family, of Fredville, Kent. John Plumptre (*c.*1760–1827), married 1788 Charlotte Pemberton, and had eleven children, including John-Pemberton, Henry-Western, Charlotte-Sophia, Emma-Maria, Mary-Louisa, and Frances-Matilda.

(1) John-Pemberton (1791–1864); St John's College, Cambridge, 1808, BA 1813, MA 1816; Lincoln's Inn 1813 and called to the bar 1817; MP for East Kent 1832–52. FCK nearly became engaged to him *c.*1814, but his 'very serious disposition' and his religious views which eventually 'induced him to think dancing and other social amusements of the same sort things which ought to be eschewed and avoided by Christian people' made her change her mind (Brabourne ii. 269–72); he married 2 April 1818 Catherine-Matilda Methuen, of Corsham House, Wilts., and had three daughters. Mr Plumptre approved of *MP* and especially of Sir Thomas Bertram: 'his conduct proves admirably the defects of the modern system of Education'.

(2) Revd Henry-Western, rector of Eastwood, Notts., married 1828 Eleanor Bridges, only daughter of Sir Brook-William Bridges (q.v.).

(3) Charlotte-Sophia died unmarried 1809.

(4) Emma-Maria married 1812 Revd Henry Gipps (q.v.).

(5) Mary-Louisa married Capt. John Smyth, RE, and died 1833 in Demerara.

(6) Frances-Matilda married 29 July 1816 Robert Ramsden (q.v.).

Pococke, Mr. Perhaps George Pocock (1765–1840) MP; of 39 Charles Street, Berkeley Square, London, and also of Hallwood, Kent.

Pollens, the two Mrs. Of Above Bar, Southampton.

Poore family, of Andover. Philip-Henry Poore (1764–1847), surgeon, apothecary, and man-midwife; originally at Littleton near Winchester, but moved to Andover and 1788 became a Capital Burgess of the Corporation; *c.*1800 he bought a house in New Street; his descendants were prominent in Andover civic affairs. By his first wife Mr Poore had several children, of whom the two eldest sons William and John went into the Navy; he married September 1797 as his second wife Mary Harrison (q.v.), and their daughter Mary-Anne was born March 1799.

Portal family. Of Huguenot origin; the senior line lived in Hampshire and owned the mills at Laverstoke which made paper for the Bank of England notes, and a junior branch lived in London.

William Portal (1755–1846) of Laverstoke, also owned Ashe Park, tenanted for many years by James Holder (q.v.); one daughter, Sophia. Mrs Portal admired *MP* very much.

John Portal (1764–1848), younger brother of William; of Freefolk Priors and later of Ashe Park, Hants; married twice and had several children. A daughter by his first marriage, Caroline, married 1825 William Knight; a daughter by his second marriage, Adela, married 1840 as his second wife Edward Knight II of Godmersham and Chawton (qq.v. under **Austen**).

Revd Benjamin-William Portal (1768-1812), elder son of William Portal of London; Scholar and Fellow of St John's College, Oxford, 1785-1812; BA 1789, MA 1795, BD 1798, Select Preacher 1804; rector of Wasing, Berks., and vicar of Sandford, Oxon. Contributed some articles to James Austen's magazine *The Loiterer*.

Portman, Mr and Mrs. Edward-Berkeley Portman (1771-1823), of Bryanston, Dorset, and Orchard Portman, Somerset; married at Bath 28 August 1798 Lucy Whitby (q.v.); their son Edward-Berkeley (born 1799) was created 1837 Baron Portman of Orchard Portman, and 1873 Viscount Portman of Bryanston.

Portmore, Earl of. William-Charles Colyear, 3rd Earl (1745-1823); of Ham Haw Park near Chertsey, Surrey, and 13 Foley Place, London; a neighbour of Mr George Payne (q.v.); his youngest daughter Lady Catherine-Caroline Colyear married 1810 James Brecknell (q.v.).

Portsmouth, Earl of. John-Charles Wallop (1767-1853), 3rd Earl 1797; of Hurstbourne Park near Andover, Hants. He had been Revd GA's pupil for a few months in 1773, when Mrs Austen noted that he stammered and was very backward for his age (see *Family Record* 23-4); although he was not ineducable, by the time he reached manhood his family knew his mental state was such that he would be unable to live a normal life, and in 1790 appointed trustees to supervise him and manage the estate; a marriage was also arranged for him in 1799 with a much older woman, Hon. Grace Norton, who was able to control him and make him play a reasonably decent part in society, until her death in 1813. The Earl's lawyer and trustee Mr John Hanson (q.v.) then cynically married off his daughter Mary-Anne to his ward, who by now was obviously a sadistic and necrophiliac lunatic. The marriage took place on 7 March 1814 at St George's, Bloomsbury, and Lord Byron was persuaded—possibly bribed—by Hanson to give away the bride. Mary-Anne herself was under no illusion as to her husband's mental condition, and lost no time in bringing her lover William-Rowland Alder to join her at Hurstbourne Park, where they together had three children and maltreated the wretched Earl—perhaps unwittingly with poetic justice— just as he had maltreated his servants and animals in previous years. Mr Hanson, for his part, took over control of the Wallop estates and occupied Farleigh House rent free, supposedly in lieu of his legal fees. Eventually the Earl's younger brother, Hon. Newton Wallop Fellowes, rescued him from his wife's family, and then brought a lawsuit for a Commission in Lunacy; in 1823 the Commission decided that the Earl had been insane since 1809, and the marriage with Miss Hanson was accordingly annulled. The Earl lived on at Hurstbourne Park for many years, and was eventually succeeded by his brother; Miss Hanson married her lover in 1828 and disappeared into obscurity.

Potter, Mrs. Lodging-house keeper, High Street, Cheltenham.

Pottinger, Mrs. Probably a member of the Pottinger family, squires of the village of Compton, Berks. A Miss Eliza-Head Pottinger married 1807 Revd James-Wilkes Best of Chieveley, Berks.; it may perhaps be this Mr Best's elderly father Charles Best (1732-1813) who did *not* escort Martha Lloyd to Harrogate in 1806—see 'Lines to Martha Lloyd' in *MW* 445, and also D. Greene, 'New Verses by JA', in *Nineteenth Century Fiction*, 30 (1975-6), 257-60.

Powlett families. Charles, 3rd Duke of Bolton, had three sons by his mistress Lavinia Beswick or Fenton (an actress who was the original 'Polly Peachum' in *The Beggar's Opera*): Charles (1728-1809), Percy (*c*.1734), and Lt.-Col. Horatio-Armand. Percy Powlett became a Lieutenant in the Navy and died young, leaving one son Charles, born *c*.1765. This child was brought up by his elder uncle, Charles, largely at the ducal home of Hackwood Park, where 'he became acquainted with rank and fashion in abundance, which somewhat unsettled him for the sphere to which his ill-starred fortunes destined him'. He entered Trinity College, Cambridge, in 1781, but did not graduate; held various Bolton family livings: rector of St Martin-by-Looe, Cornwall, 1790-1807, rector of Winslade, Hants, 1789-94, rector of Blackford, Somerset, 1794-6, back to Winslade 1796-1811, rector of Itchenstoke, Hants, 1796-1817, perpetual curate of Swingfield, Kent, 1817-26, and finally rector of High Roding, Essex, 1817-34; Chaplain-in-Ordinary to the Prince of Wales 1790. For some years he took pupils, one of whom, Lord Roden, presented him to the High Roding living. He married in November 1796 Anne ('Nancy') Temple (q.v.) and had several children; his extravagant habits obliged him to flee to France in 1827, following his wife's death, and he died at Brussels in 1834.

A premature obituary notice for Revd Charles Powlett appeared in the *GM* for 1830, ii. 471; while acknowledging that he was 'cheerful, benevolent, conscientious, and virtuous', the anonymous biographer added that 'His person was diminutive, and his limbs not well formed. He had a quick apprehension, and an excellent memory; but he was somewhat deficient in judgment and profundity. His opinions were apt to run to extremes, and to be lightly taken up, and lightly abandoned. He was a little too free of his advice, which was given with a self-sufficiency not always well received.'— and so on for several further candid comments, adding up to a general picture of an affable but foolish man.

Although a number of his letters written between 1789-1801 survive in the Powlett archive, in which the Lefroys and Lyfords are mentioned, unfortunately there are no references to the Austens.

Powlett, Lt.-Col. Thomas-Norton. A distant kinsman of the above, being descended from a junior but legitimate branch of the family, one of whom became 1794 the 12th Marquess of Winchester; Lt.-Colonel 1802, Colonel 1811, Major-General 1815, died 1824. Married 1798 at Ashbourne, Derbyshire, Letitia-Mary Percival; while they were living at Albion Place in Southampton she eloped with the 2nd Viscount Sackville (q.v.), later (1815) the last Duke of Dorset—meeting him at the White Hart in Winchester. Col. Powlett won £3,000 damages in his *crim. con.* case against Lord Sackville in 1808.

Powys family. Caroline Girle (1738–1817, q.v.), married 5 August 1762 Philip-Lybbe Powys (1734–1809) of Hardwick House, Oxfordshire, and had three children: Philip-Lybbe (1765), Thomas (1768), Caroline-Isabella (1775); the latter married 1793 Revd Edward Cooper (q.v.) and had eight children.

Thomas Powys (1736–1809), younger brother of Philip-Lybbe Powys of Hardwick; St John's College, Oxford, 1753; BA 1757, MA 1760, BD and DD 1795; rector of Fawley, Bucks., 1762 and of Silchester, Hants, 1769; Prebendary of Hereford 1769, Dean of Bristol 1779, Chaplain to the King 1781, Canon of Windsor 1796–7, Dean of Canterbury 1797–1809; unmarried.

Mrs Lybbe Powys kept diaries and journals (most of which are now in the British Library, Add. MSS 42160–173), and in 1899 Mrs Emily J. Climenson, wife of the vicar of Shiplake, Oxon., edited these under the title of *Passages from the diaries of Mrs Philip Lybbe Powys of Hardwick House, Oxon, A.D. 1756 to 1808.* While this volume has undoubtedly been of use in making the diaries known to historians, unfortunately Mrs Climenson's editing was often inaccurate, so that her version of Mrs Lybbe Powys's text must be used with caution.

Prince of Wales/Prince Regent, Princess of Wales. See under **Royal Family**.

Prowting family, of Chawton. The Prowtings had been copyholders and then freeholders in the parish of Chawton since the sixteenth century, and had gradually risen in local importance. The family whom JA knew were William Prowting (1754–1821), JP, DL, and his wife Elizabeth (1752–1832), who had five children: Elizabeth (1778); Catherine-Ann (1783–1848, unmarried); William (1784–99); Ann-Mary (1787–1858); and John-Rowland (1791–1800).

Elizabeth married 1801 Richard Lee (q.v.) but apparently had no children, as the Prowting property in Chawton passed to her sister Ann-Mary, who had married 1811 Capt. Benjamin Clement, RN (q.v.), and to their descendants.

Pugh, Miss. Of Andover, married 1799 Arnold Ludlow (q.v.).

Pyne, Mr. Owner of the lodgings in Lyme Regis which the Austens rented in 1804; possibly the cottage in Lyme High Street known now as Pyne House.

Rawstorn, Miss Anne. Of Lexden, Essex, and 29 Bedford Row, London; a cousin of the Papillon family (q.v.) of Acrise, as a Sarah Papillon of an earlier generation had married Samuel Rawstorn of Lexden; the Papillons inherited Lexden Manor at her death in 1816.

Rebecca. Maidservant at Godmersham.

Redding, Grace. Linen and woollen draper in Andover.

Remmington, Wilson & Co. Silk manufacturers, 30 Milk Street, London.

Remnant, T. Glover, etc., 126 Strand, London.

Reynolds, Sir Joshua (1723–92). Artist; President of the Royal Academy; for details of his career see *DNB*.

Rice family, of Kent. Henry Rice, of Bramling near Canterbury, was a commander in the HEIC's merchant service 1770–81, captain of the East Indiaman *Dutton*, and an Elder Brother of Trinity House; he married Sarah Sampson of Dover (1755–1841) and had three sons: Henry (1776), John-Adamson (1778), and Edward-Royd (1790); died 1797.

(1) Henry Rice was cheerful and amusing but a hopeless spendthrift and gambler, forever expecting his widowed mother to pay the debts he constantly incurred. He entered Christ's College, Cambridge, 1796 and resided till 1800, but did not graduate; married 20 July 1801 Jemima-Lucy Lefroy (q.v.) of Ashe, and had three children: Henry-George (1802–21), Sarah (1804–42), and Anne (died unmarried); curate of Ashe 1800–5, and of Deane 1801–5(?); by 1807 had moved to Cholderton near Salisbury, Wilts.; in 1809 his mother apparently bought the advowson and estate of Great Holland in Essex for him and he may have lived there for a time, as in 1812 he was instituted to the rectory; also in 1812 his brother-in-law C.-Edward Lefroy sued him for debt; in 1813 he was at Tollard Royal near Salisbury; in 1818 the Great Holland estate was sold, and in 1819 he had to flee to Dunkirk to avoid his creditors; he returned to England *c.*1822 and after receiving his share of his mother's estate in 1841 seems to have managed to avoid getting into debt again thereafter; eventually died 17 September 1860 at 10 Cavendish Place, Bath; his widow Jemima died 1 March 1862 at 2 St James Square, Bath; both buried Lansdown Cemetery. See M. Hammond, 'Mrs Henry Rice', in JA Society *Report* for 1986, 16–22, and also 'Jemima-Lucy Lefroy', in JASNA, *Persuasions*, 14 (1992), 57–61.

(2) John-Adamson Rice followed his father into the HEIC, and died unmarried in India 1804.

(3) Edward-Royd Rice (1790–1878) married October 1818 JA's niece Lizzy Knight (q.v.) and had fifteen children; old Mrs Rice bought Dane

Court near Dover for the young couple, and they lived there for the rest of their lives; Edward was MP for Dover for over twenty years.

Richard. HTA's manservant, successor to William.

Richis. Maidservant at Rowling.

Richmond, Duchess of. Mother of the Earl of March who married 1817 Lady Caroline Paget.

Rider (or Ryder), Mrs. Draper/haberdasher in Basingstoke, died ?December 1800.

Ripley, Revd Thomas (1752–20 October 1813). Rector of Wootton Bassett, Wilts.; married 1780 Sophia Pemberton; the 'young Ripley' at school in Bath 1805 may perhaps be his son.

Rivers family, baronets of Chafford, Kent. Revd Sir Peter, 6th Bt. and Prebendary of Winchester (died 1790), married 1768 Martha Coxe (died *c.*1835); seven children alive in 1796: sons Thomas (7th Bt., died 1805), James (8th Bt., accidentally killed 1805), and Revd Henry (9th Bt., died 1851), rector of Martyr Worthy, Hants., and daughters Mary, Emilia, Maria, and Louisa. The 'Sophy' Rivers whom JA mentions in 1813 may perhaps be fictional.

Robert. The Leigh-Perrots' manservant.

Robinson, Dr. Physician at Lyme Regis, 1804.

Robinson, Mary. Presumably a maidservant at Rowling.

Robinson, Revd Matthew (*c.*1775–1827). Rector 1800–27 of Burghfield near Reading, Berks.; cousin of Lord Rokeby and brother-in-law of Sir Egerton Brydges (q.v.), who had married his sister Mary.

Roden family. Robert Jocelyn (1756–1820), 2nd Earl of Roden, married (1) 1788 Frances-Theodosia Bligh (died 1802) and had six children; (2) 1804 Juliana-Anne, youngest daughter of John Orde (q.v.) of Weetwood, Northumberland, and had two sons. The second son of his first marriage, James-Bligh, was Lieutenant RN 1811, but died of asthma July 1812, aged 22.

Rogers, Mrs. Draper/haberdasher in Basingstoke, succeeding Mrs Rider, in 1801.

Roland, Mr. ?Hairdresser at Godmersham?

Rolle, the Misses. Lucilla (*c.*1757–1851) and Ann (*c.*1758–1842), sisters of Lord Rolle of Stevenstone, Devon (1756–1842); of 82 Gloucester Place, Portman Square, London; friends of the Cooke family (q.v.), and of the Locks of Norbury; rented Fanny Burney's 'Camilla Cottage' at West Humble 1802–3.

Roope, Mr. Tutor or music master to the Finch-Hatton family.

Biographical Index

Rosalie. Sometime maidservant to Eliza de Feuillide, Mrs HTA.

Roworth, C. Printer, at 38 Bell Yard, Temple Bar, London.

Royal Family. George III (1738–1820) ascended the throne 1760, and married 1761 Princess Charlotte of Mecklenburg-Strelitz (1744–1818); they had fifteen children (see below); later in life the King began to suffer bouts of illness which affected him mentally as well as physically, and in 1811 he became a hopeless invalid and so remained until his death in 1820. From the symptoms recorded by his doctors it is now believed that he was suffering from porphyria—a genetic disorder associated with abnormal metabolism of various pigments.

George III had a younger brother William-Henry (1743–1805), created Duke of Gloucester; his son William-Frederick (1776–1834) became the 2nd Duke in 1805 upon his father's death, and later married his cousin Mary, 4th daughter of George III.

George III's children were:

(1) George-Augustus-Frederick (1762–1830); Prince of Wales from his birth until 1811, when he became Prince Regent following his father's incapacitation; succeeded as King George IV in 1820. He married in 1795 his cousin, Princess Caroline of Brunswick (1768–1821)—a marriage which was immediately unhappy—and had one daughter, Charlotte, born 1796. Princess Charlotte married Prince Leopold of Saxe-Cobourg in 1816 and died in childbirth November 1817.

(2) Frederick (1763–1827), Duke of York; married 1791 Princess Frederica of Prussia (1767–1820), but died without issue.

(3) William-Henry (1765–1837), Duke of Clarence; lived with the actress Dorothy Jordan (q.v.) for many years and had ten children by her, all given the surname of FitzClarence; married 1818 Princess Adelaide of Saxe-Meiningen (1792–1849); succeeded as King William IV in 1830; no surviving legal issue.

(4) Charlotte-Augusta-Matilda (1766–1828), Princess Royal; married 1797 Prince Frederick of Wurttemberg (1754–1816); no issue.

(5) Edward-Augustus (1767–1820), Duke of Kent; married 1818 Princess Victoire of Saxe-Cobourg (1786–1861) and had one daughter, Alexandrina-Victoria (1819–1901), who succeeded in 1837 as Queen Victoria.

(6) Augusta-Sophia (1768–1840) died unmarried.

(7) Elizabeth (1770–1840), married 1818 Frederick, Landgrave of Hesse-Homburg (1769–1829); no issue.

(8) Ernest-Augustus (1771–1851), Duke of Cumberland; married 1815 Princess Frederica of Mecklenburg-Strelitz (1778–1841); 1837 ascended throne of Hanover as King Ernest; one son, King George of Hanover (1819–78).

(9) Augustus-Frederick (1773–1843), Duke of Sussex; married morganatically (1) 1793 Lady Augusta Murray (c.1762–1830), by whom he had two children; and (2) 1831 Lady Cecilia Buggin (1793–1873). Lady Augusta owned a first edition of *NA&P*.

(10) Adolphus-Frederick (1774–1850), Duke of Cambridge; married 1818 Princess Augusta of Hesse-Cassel (1797–1889) and had three children: George (1819–1904), Augusta (1822–1916), and Mary-Adelaide (1833–97).

(11) Mary (1776–1857); married 1816 her cousin William, 2nd Duke of Gloucester; no issue.

(12) Sophia (1777–1848) died unmarried.

(13) Octavius (1779–83).

(14) Alfred (1780–2).

(15) Amelia (1783–1810) died unmarried.

Russell. Manservant at Godmersham.

Russell, Mrs. Probably the widow 1794 of Francis Russell of Basingstoke, and therefore probably a connection by marriage of Revd Dr Richard Russell (1695–1783), vicar of Overton 1719–71 and rector of Ashe 1729–83. This Dr Russell, predecessor at Ashe of the Lefroy family, was the grandfather of Mary Russell Mitford, authoress, best known for her *Our Village* essays.

S., Miss. Governess to the Moore family at Wrotham.

Sa(y)ce, Mrs. Lady's-maid at Godmersham; niece of Mrs Sackree (q.v.); married a German in 1822 and died at Stuttgart 1844.

Sackree, Susannah (1761–1851, known as 'Caky'). Nursemaid at Godmersham 1793–1851; MI in Godmersham church. See JA Society *Report* for 1972, 174–6.

Sackville, Viscount. Charles Sackville-Germain (1767–1843), 2nd Viscount Sackville of Drayton, Northants; also of 46 Harley Street, London; 1815 succeeded his cousin as 5th and last Duke of Dorset; died unmarried. 'A little, smart-looking man, and a favourite with the ladies'—q.v. Powlett.

St Helens, Lord. Alleyne Fitzherbert, created 1791 Lord St Helens, died unmarried 1839.

St John families. Revd Ellis St John jr., of West Court, Finchampstead, Berks., had three sons: Henry-Ellis (1776–1842), rector 1800–9 of Winchfield, Hants; Edward (1778), vicar 1805–19 of Hartley Wintney, Hants, and rector of Winchfield 1839; also John, of Quidhampton near Overton.

At this period there were several other St Johns in Hampshire: Revd William (1749–97), vicar of Hartley Wintney 1786–97 and rector of Dogmersfield 1773–97; Revd Oliver-Goodyer (1741–1804), rector of Mottisfont 1775; and his son Revd Oliver-D'Oyley (1779) of Lockerley and East Dean, later following his father to Mottisfont. See also under Mildmay.

St Lawrence, Lady Frances. Third daughter of the 1st Earl of Howth; of 1 Russell Street, Bath; married October 1808 Ven. Dr James Phillott (q.v.); died 1842.

St Vincent, Lord. John Jervis (1735–1823), Earl of St Vincent. For details of his naval career see Marshall, *Royal Naval Biography*, and *DNB*.

Salkeld, Mrs. Housekeeper at Godmersham.

Sally. The Austens had one or more maidservants of this name.

Salusbury, Mr. Friend of FCK, in Kent.

Sanford family. Early in the eighteenth century Catherine Chichester, daughter of Sir John Chichester of Youlston, Devon, married (1) George Musgrave of Huish, Somerset; their daughter Juliana married 1767 Sir James Langham of Cottesbrooke, 7th Bt., and became the mother of Sir William, 8th Bt. and Sir James, 10th Bt. (q.v.). Mrs Musgrave married (2) Revd John Sanford of Welford, Somerset, and had another nine children; of these, her eldest son Henry-William Sanford had a son, also Henry, and a daughter Caroline; and her third son William had a daughter Frances (1777–8 August 1823) who married James Tilson (q.v.).

Henry Sanford was HTA's friend and business associate, and lived at apartment F.3 in Albany, Piccadilly; he was first cousin to Frances Sanford, and they were both also cousins, though only by half-blood, of the Langham baronets. Mr Sanford was very much pleased with *Emma*, but *MP* was still his favourite.

Sankey, Mr. Doctor or apothecary, attending Marianne Bridges.

Saunders, Mr. Mentioned only as a friend of the Austens' cousin Sir Thomas-Philip Hampson (q.v.); the *Court Guide* shows six gentlemen of this name in London: Mr D. of 19 Buckingham Street, Mr G. of 252 Oxford Street, Mr John of 4 Weymouth Street, Mr Thomas of 25 Howland Street, Mr W. of 19 Chapel Street, Grosvenor Place, and Mr William of 11 Charlotte Street, Fitzroy Square.

Sawbridge, Miss. Perhaps Elizabeth-Jane, sister of Revd Henry Sawbridge, rector of Welford near Newbury, Berks.

Saye and Sele, Lady. See under Twisleton.

Scarman, Mr. James Austen's London dentist.

Sch(u)ylers, the. Capt. Sch(u)yler and his wife Catherine, son-in-law and daughter of Mrs Fe(a)ver (q.v.).

Sclater family. Mrs Penelope Lutley-Sclater (1750–1840), tenant of Tangier Park, Hants; also her nephew, Mr Sclater of Hoddington, who in fact lived with his aunt at Tangier Park. Mrs Lutley-Sclater liked *Emma* very much, more than *MP*.

Biographical Index

Scott family, of Scot's Hall, Smeeth, Kent. Cecilia Scott, eldest daughter of George Scott of Bombay, married (1) Brice Fletcher (died 1776, q.v.) and had issue; (2) c.1777 her cousin Francis-Talbot Scott (1745–89), and had two sons: Revd George (1778–ante-1839), and Francis-Peach (1779). Francis-Talbot Scott was the last member of the family to live at their ancestral home Scot's Hall; when he left there in 1765 the income from the estate was reduced to £800 p.a. and the property was mortgaged for £12,000.

Scott, Sir Walter (1771–1832). In 1813 he was known to the reading public as a poet; *Waverley* and its successors were published anonymously 1814 onwards.

Scrane, Mrs. Probably Mrs Anne-Jane Skrine, of 9 Gloucester Place, New [Euston] Road, London, connected with the Maunde family (q.v.).

Scudamore, Edward. Of Canterbury; married 1813 Mary Toke (q.v.); physician, surgeon, and apothecary, and attended the Knights of Godmersham.

Seagraves, the. Perhaps a fictional family.

Serle, Mr. Of Bishopstoke; perhaps James Serle, Receiver-General of Hampshire, died 1809 aged 64, MI in St Lawrence's, Winchester.

Seward, Bridger. EAK's farm bailiff at Chawton, who died February 1808. He and his wife occupied the cottage at the crossroads in Chawton which EAK refurbished in 1809 for the use of Mrs GA and her daughters.

Seymer, Maria-Bridget. Daughter of Lt.-Col. Seymer of Hadford, Dorset; married 1805 Stephen Terry (q.v.).

Seymour, William. HTA's friend and lawyer; of 19 Margaret Street, Cavendish Square, London, with his office entrance round the corner at 12 Little Portland Street.

Sharp, Anne. Governess to FCK at Godmersham from 21 January 1804 to mid-January 1806, but had to resign owing to continued ill-health; in March 1806 she was with a Mrs Raikes as governess to one little girl aged 6; but even this was too much for her strength, and in May 1806 she moved to become companion to Mrs Raikes's sister, the crippled Miss Bailey, at Hinckley, Leics. In the summer of 1811 Miss Sharp left Miss Bailey and by October 1811 was governess to the four young daughters of the recently widowed Lady Pilkington (q.v.). It is not known when Miss Sharp left this employment; but by 1823 she was running her own boarding-school for girls at 14–15 Everton Terrace, Liverpool, where she remained until 1841; she retired to York Terrace, Everton, and died on 8 January 1853, leaving instructions for her burial in a vault in Everton churchyard. When JA wrote to her in 1817 at South Parade, Doncaster, Yorks., she may perhaps have been staying or even working at Miss Haugh's boarding-school there, perhaps gaining experience before starting up her own establishment. Miss

Sharp's opinions of JA's novels were that *MP* was excellent, but she preferred *P&P*, and rated *Emma* between these two.

It is not certain from JA's surviving letters whether Miss Sharp did eventually manage to visit Hampshire in the late summer of 1811, but she certainly was at Chawton in June 1815, and again for a longer visit in August–September 1820, when JEAL met her at the Cottage and told his sister Anna that she was 'horridly affected but rather amusing'.

The Miss Sharp whom JA mentions as being in Bath in 1805 is clearly not the same as this Miss Anne Sharp.

Shaw, Anne-Maria. Married 1819 Maximilian-Dudley-Digges Hammond (q.v.).

Sherer, Revd Joseph-Godfrey (1770–1824). Vicar of Blandford Forum, Dorset, 1800; vicar of Westwell, Kent, 1806–24, and vicar of Godmersham 1811–24. He liked *MP* best of all, and ranked *Emma* below that and *P&P*; he was in general displeased with JA's pictures of clergymen. His son Joseph entered the Navy as a First-Class Volunteer 1811, was midshipman 1813, Lieutenant 1822, Commander 1829, and Captain 1841.

Shipley, Conway (1782–1808). Son of Revd William-Davies Shipley, Dean of St Asaph, who lived at Twyford House, Hants. Entered RN on his eleventh birthday and was in battle the following year; Lieutenant 1800, Commander 1803, Captain 1804, and killed in action off the Portuguese coast April 1808.

Sibley, the Misses. Daughters of Joseph Sibley of Hall Place, West Meon, Hants.

Siddons, Mrs Sarah (1755–1831). The famous tragedy actress; for details of her career see *DNB*.

Simpson, Capt. RN, and his brother. Robert Simpson, Captain 1806, and John Simpson, Captain 1809.

Skeete, Mrs Mary. Widow, of Basingstoke; married 1799 Peter William French (q.v.) of Reading, Berks.

Sloane, Stephen. Married September 1800 Mrs Estwick (q.v.); Trinity Hall, Cambridge, 1801; BA 1805, MA 1809; sinecure rector of Gedney, Lincs., 1806–12; died at his father's house in Upper Harley Street, London, 16 April 1812.

Sloper, Mr. Probably Robert Orby Sloper, of 20 Montague Street, London, only legitimate son of General Sir Robert Sloper (1728–1802), of West Woodhay, Berks., who left five illegitimate children, three sons and two daughters.

Small, Miss. Dressmaker in ?Overton.

Smallbone families. Villagers of Steventon and Deane; Daniel Smallbone(s) married 1790 Jane ('Jenny') Read and had eight children; of these Mary (1792) was CMCA's nursemaid in 1808, married 1834 James Hutt, a widower from Longparish, and died at Deane 1859; Betsy (1794) replaced her sister as CMCA's attendant in 1809. There was also another Daniel Smallbone (presumably a cousin of the above), who married 1796 Sarah Tilbury (q.v.).

Smith, Miss. Actress; appeared in *Merchant of Venice* at Drury Lane, with Kean as Shylock, March 1814, and also as Desdemona to his Othello.

Smith, Mr and Mrs. Friends of the Tilsons and of HTA, in London; the 'Miss Beaty' who seems to be connected with them, is perhaps either a Miss Beatrice Smith, or a Miss Beattie, if JA misspelt her surname.

Smith, Col. and Mrs Cantelo. Probably jocular, in allusion to their singing; a Charles Cantelo had been performing in Bath in 1801.

Smith, Captain, RN. Either Matthew Smith, Commander February 1801 and Captain April 1808; or William-Richard Smith, Commander December 1808 and Captain January 1817.

Smith family, of Suttons and Tring. In the mid-eighteenth century Joshua Smith, MP, of Stoke Park, Wilts., had four daughters, of whom only two concern us: Elizabeth (c.1770–1842) and Augusta (1772–1845).

(1) Elizabeth married 1793 William-John Chute (q.v.) of The Vyne but had no children. She therefore paid much attention to the children of her younger sister Augusta (see below).

(2) Augusta married 1798 Charles Smith (1756–1814) of Suttons, Essex, and had nine children: Augusta (1799–1836), Charles-Joshua (1800–31), Emma (1801–76), Frances (1803–71), Spencer (1806–82), Sarah-Eliza (1808–94), Charlotte-Judith (1810–40), Drummond (1812–32), Maria-Louisa (1814–87). JEAL met this family when they came to visit their aunt Mrs Chute, and in 1828 he married Emma.

Joshua Smith's younger brother Drummond, of Tring Park, was created a baronet 1804, with special remainder to the male heirs of the Smiths of Suttons; Charles-Joshua therefore succeeded his great-uncle as 2nd Bt. in 1816.

Sir Drummond Smith married as his second wife Elizabeth (died 1835), daughter of 2nd Viscount Galway; Mrs Augusta Smith rented Tring Park from her in 1827, and when JEAL married Emma the young couple lived there with the rest of the Smith family till 1833.

Smith, James (1775–1839), and **Horace** (1779–1849). The 'two Mr Smiths of the City' who wrote 1812 the *Rejected Addresses*.

Smith, Robert. Apothecary, of 62 Sloane Street, Chelsea, London; employer of Mr Haden (q.v.).

Smithson, Mr. A friend of HTA; perhaps John Smithson, of 10 Montague Street, Portman Square, London.

Somerville, Mrs Maria. Perhaps a sister of Revd William Somerville of 21 Belvidere, Bath, and rector of Aston Somerville, Glos., 1774–1803.

Sondes, Lady. Mary-Elizabeth, only daughter of Richard Milles of Nackington (q.v.); married (1) 1785 2nd Baron Sondes of Lees Court (died 1806) and had six children; (2) January 1809 Gen. Sir Henry-Tucker Montresor (q.v.).

South, Mr, of Winchester. Possibly a younger brother of Revd Henry South, curate of Fawley, Hants, 1791, and of Dibden near Fawley 1792.

Southey, Robert (1774–1843). Nephew of Revd Herbert Hill (q.v.); poet and writer, Poet Laureate 1813; married 1795 Edith Fricker and had eight children: Margaret (1802–3), Edith-May (1804, married 1834), Herbert (1806–16), Emma (1808–9), Bertha (1809, married her cousin Herbert Hill jr.), Katharine (1810), Isabel (1812–26), Charles-Cuthbert (1819).

Southey visited the Hill family at Streatham in 1813, and they evidently told him of their friendship with JA, for in later years he wrote to Sir Egerton Brydges (q.v.): 'You mention Miss Austen; her novels are more true to nature, and have (for my sympathies) passages of finer feeling than any others of this age. She was a person of whom I have heard so well, and think so highly, that I regret not having seen her, nor ever having had an opportunity of testifying to her the respect which I felt for her.'

Spence, Mr. Either George Spence, dentist to George III, of 17 Old Bond Street, or Spence & Son of 1 Arlington Street, London.

Spencer, Mr and Miss. Friends of HTA; four Spencers are shown in the *Court Guide*: Mr F. of 4 Northumberland Street, Marylebone; Mr H. of 12 Great Marlborough Street; Mr J. of 2 Golden Square; and Mr R. L. of 53 Lambs Conduit Street.

Spencer, George John (1758–1834). 2nd Earl, and First Lord of the Admiralty 1794–1801.

Spicer, John. Owner 1805 of Esher Place, the manor-house of Esher, Surrey; also of 8 Hanover Square, London.

Stacey, Mary. There were several Stacey families amongst the Chawton villagers; this would appear to be the Mary Stacey who was buried 5 July 1819.

Stanhope, Adm. and Mrs. Sir Henry-Edwin Stanhope, Rear-Admiral 1801, Vice-Admiral 1805, Admiral 1812; of 10 Seymour Street, Bath.

Staples, Dame. Steventon villager; Elizabeth (1753–1828) wife of Thomas Staples, and her nine children, of whom Hannah was born 1791.

Steel & Meyer. Lavender Water warehouse, Catherine Street, Strand.

Steevens families. There were several Steevens amongst the Steventon villagers; Mary Pain (1738–1822) married 1759 Thomas Steevens, and John Steevens (1765–1816) was their son. Mary Tilbury (q.v.) married 1789 William Steevens.

Stent, Mary (died 24 December 1812). 'With Mrs Lloyd had also lived to the last Mrs Stent, an early friend, of rather inferior position in life, and reduced, from family misfortunes, to very narrow means. I remember her quite an old lady, lodging at Highclere in a small cottage, near to Mrs Criswick' (CMCA's *Reminiscences* 7).

Stephens, Catherine (1794–1882). Actress and singer; first appeared at Covent Garden in September 1813 as Mandane in *Artaxerxes*, and was an immediate success. She was held to have the sweetest soprano voice of the time, a natural manner, and a simple style; she retired from the stage in 1835 and three years later married at 5 Belgrave Square, London, the 5th Earl of Essex, an octogenarian widower, who died 1839. Lady Essex survived him forty-three years, dying in the house in which she was married.

Stockwell, Mrs. Perhaps Ann Stockwell, died 23 July 1820, daughter of Revd Thomas Stockwell, late rector of Dummer.

Storer, Dr and Mrs. Apparently a physician at Bridlington, Yorks.

Streatfeild, Henry (1757–1829). Of Chiddingstone, Kent; High Sheriff of Kent 1792.

Street, Mr. There are two men of this name mentioned in JA's letters: (1) her dancing-partner in 1799, who was probably Revd George Street, curate of Kingsclere, Hants, 1798; (2) of Key Street, Kent, who was Purser on CJA's ship HMS *Namur*.

Summers, Miss. Dressmaker in the Steventon area, 1800.

Sussex, Duke of. See under **Royal Family**.

Sweny, Mark-Halpen (born 1785). (Not 'Sweeney/Sweney', as JA wrote.) Lieutenant RN 1806, Commander 1821, Captain 1838; one of FWA's officers on HMS *St Albans* and HMS *Elephant*, and went with him to China 1809; twice severely wounded and lost a leg, for which in 1816 he received a pension and a place at Greenwich Hospital.

Taylor family, of Bifrons near Bridge, Kent. Revd Edward Taylor (1734–8 December 1798), patron and vicar of Patrixbourne; his son Edward (1774–1843), MP for Canterbury 1807–12, married 1802 Louisa Beckingham, *not* his cousin Charlotte.

Temple family. Revd William-Johnston Temple of St Gluvias, Cornwall (Boswell's correspondent), had eight surviving children, of whom his eldest daughter Anne (1772–1827) married November 1796 Revd Charles Powlett (q.v.). His second son Frank (1771–1863) was in the Navy: Lieutenant 1793,

Commander 1803, Captain 1805, Vice-Admiral 1847, and Admiral 1854. Frank and his friend Lt. Samuel Butcher, RN (q.v.), had stayed previously with the Powletts in March or April 1797. 'The horrid one of all' is probably one of Frank's next three brothers Robert, John, or Frederick, who at this date ranged in age from 20 to 24.

Terry family, of Dummer, Hants. Thomas Terry (1741–1829) married Elizabeth Harding (1751–1811, q.v.), and had thirteen children: Stephen (1774), Revd Michael (1775), Jane (1776), Mary (1778), Patience (1780–1860, 'Patty'), Col. Robert (1781–1869), Ann (1782), Thomas-Harding (1784), John (1786), Eliza (1788), Richard (1789–1872), Charlotte (1791), George (1793); two of the younger sons predeceased their parents.

(**1**) Stephen (1774–1867); King's College, Cambridge, 1794; BA 1802, Fellow 1797–1805; 1798 Lieutenant in North Hants Militia and stationed at Gosport; married 1805 Maria-Bridget Seymer (q.v.); five children, of whom his youngest son, Alured-John-George-Seymer Terry (1820–97) married 1847 Anna Lefroy's daughter Georgiana-Brydges (q.v.) and left issue.

(**2**) Revd Michael (1775–1848); St John's College, Cambridge, 1794, BA 1798; rector of Dummer 1811–48; engaged to Anna Austen during the winter of 1809–10. See *Family Record* 161–2.

(**3**) Jane (1776–1860) married 1808 Harry Digweed (q.v.) and had issue.

(**4**) 'Miss Terry'—presumably Mary—admired *Emma* very much.

(**5**) Patty (1780–1860) died at Bath Easton.

(**6**) Eliza (1788–1841) married 1810 Charles Harwood (q.v.) of Deane and had issue.

Stephen Terry kept a diary/journal, and twenty-nine miscellaneous volumes (including other notes and memoranda) are now in the Hampshire Record Office (24M49/1–29); they cover the period 1841–62, and deal mostly with his daily round of farming and fox-hunting. Occasionally he included reminiscences of events in his earlier years; but unfortunately his memory was no longer reliable, and his anecdotes of past times are demonstrably inaccurate. These journals were edited by A. M. W. Stirling as *The Diaries of Dummer* (1934), but to confound confusion still further, the editing was in itself very bad, so this work must be used with caution.

Terry, Daniel (?1780–1829). Actor and playwright; performed mature male roles, both tragedy and comedy, at Covent Garden 1813–22 and at Drury Lane thereafter.

Thistlethwaite, Thomas (born 1779). Of Southwick Park; High Sheriff of Hampshire 1806, and MP for Hants 1806–7; JP, DL.

Thomas. EAK's manservant.

Tickars, Mrs. Presumably a London staymaker or dressmaker.

Tilbury, Dame. In JA's time there were two Tilbury families amongst the Steventon villagers: (1) Mathew (1718–1800) and Susannah (1732–1824) married 1758 and had four children: Mary, Betty, William, and Mathew; (2) John (died 1812) and Anne (died 1809), probably married *c.*1765, who likewise had four children: Anne, Mary, Sarah, and William. One or other of the Mary Tilburys married 1789 William Steevens (q.v.); Sarah married 1796 Daniel Smallbone (q.v.); and an Elizabeth Tilbury (presumably the 'Betty' above) married at Church Oakley 1793 George Smith of Dummer— their daughter Charlotte Smith was baptized at Steventon on 5 September 1798.

Tilson family, of Watlington Park, Goring, Oxon. John Tilson (1722–79) married 1767 Maria Lushington (died 1805) and had five children: (1) John-Henry (1768), (2) George (1770), (3) Christopher (1771), (4) James (1773), and (5) Maria-Chowne (1776).

(1) John-Henry (1768–1836); Lt.-Colonel in Oxfordshire Militia 1803; married 1809 the widowed Mrs Sophia Langford (died 1829), and had seven children, of whom only the youngest daughter, Maria-Susan, survived to marry 1842 Thomas-Shaen Carter of Castle Martin, Kildare. The Carters lived on at Watlington Park till 1875.

(2) George (1770–95); Captain RN; died unmarried in Antigua.

(3) Christopher (1771–1834); in 76th Regt., Brigadier-General 1804, Major-General 1808, Lieutenant-General 1813, General 1830; 1812 changed his surname to Chowne in accordance with a cousin's Will and inherited an estate at Alfriston, Sussex; married *c.*1823 Jane Craufurd; no issue; she married (2) 1836 Revd Sir Henry-Robert Dukinfield.

(4) James (1773–1838); HTA's partner in the Austen, Maunde & Tilson bank in London; married February 1797 Frances Sanford (1777–8 August 1823, q.v.) and had at least eleven children: William (?1798–1804), George (1799–1828), Mary-Juliana (1801), Frances-Melesina (1802), Amelia (?or Emilia, *c.*1803), Charlotte-Sophia (1804–1902), another daughter 'G—' (*c.*1806), Anna (1808–23), Margaret-Augusta (1810), James-Henry (1812–post-1872), Caroline-Jane (1813).

(4a) George died unmarried at Goring, Oxon.

(4b) Mary-Juliana married 1834 Revd S. F. Morgan (died 1872) rector of All Saints, Birmingham, and later incumbent of Chepstow and of Creech St Michael.

(4c) Charlotte-Sophia married *c.*1835 Revd John-Thomas Austen (q.v.), and had one daughter.

(4d) Anna died 27 August 1823, a few days after her mother's death.

(4e) Margaret-Augusta married ante-1837 Revd Thomas Moseley (died 1882) rector of St Martin's, Birmingham.

(4f) James-Henry changed his surname to Chowne at his uncle's death in 1834; initially a Captain in the Bengal Infantry, but later took Holy Orders; married 1835 Mary Braddon, and had issue; living in Bath 1872.

The other Tilson daughters seem to have died in the 1820s.

When the James Tilsons were first married their elder children were born in the parishes of St George's, Hanover Square, and St Marylebone; between 1801 and' 1808 they were presumably elsewhere in London; between 1808 and c.1816 they were living at 26 Hans Place, Chelsea, and their four youngest children were baptized in that parish; they later moved to Foley Place, Marylebone; and following the deaths there of his wife and daughter Anna Mr Tilson returned to the family home at Watlington Park.

(5) Maria-Chowne (1776–1833); married November 1806 Revd Dr William Marsh (1775–1864), vicar of Basildon, Oxon., and had five children; from c.1814–1829 in Colchester, and c.1829 onwards in Birmingham; after her death in 1833 Revd Dr Marsh married twice more and ended his life as rector of Beckenham, Kent.

Maria Tilson became 'serious'—i.e. Evangelical—in her youth, and her husband was all his life a devoted and well-known Evangelical preacher. Under their influence all the other members of the Tilson family became Evangelical, and three of the James Tilson daughters 'established a Bible Association in their own house. Their father and mother are patron and patroness; the eldest is secretary, the others are collectors; the servants subscribe, and also procure subscriptions from their friends.' These strict religious views may account for the fact that Mrs Tilson preferred *MP* to *P&P*.

It may have been due to her friendship with the James Tilsons that JA was initially drawn towards Evangelicalism (see Letter **109**); however, by 1816 she seems to have found either their or else her cousin Revd Edward Cooper's enthusiastic piety rather excessive (see Letter **145**).

Tincton, Mr. Unidentified; a possible dancing-partner for CEA in Hampshire, September 1796.

Toke family, of Godinton near Ashford, Kent. Mr John Toke (1738–1819), High Sheriff of Kent 1770; married 1762 Margaretta Roundell (died 1780); his eldest son Nicolas-Roundell (1764–1837) married 1791 Anna-Maria Wrey (q.v.) and had one daughter; his second son Revd John Toke (1766–1820) was vicar of Bekesbourne and rector of Harbledown, Kent; his daughter Mary married 1813 Edward Scudamore, MD (q.v.).

Triggs, William. EAK's gamekeeper at Chawton.

Trimmer, Robert (1767–1813). Of Farnham, Surrey; attorney-at-law, came to Alton and married Elizabeth Bradly, and founded the legal partnership of Bradly Trimmer, which still has its offices in Alton High Street, though no members of the original families are now involved. Robert Trimmer had at least three sons, and his descendants were prominent in Alton civic affairs for several generations. He died in London 11 September 1813 and was buried in Alton on 20 September; EAK's lawyer for his Hampshire properties.

Turner, G. Chawton farm labourer; probably the George Turner who married 1810 Sarah Browning.

Turner, Mr. Presumably a naval agent or supplier. RWC was told by Geoffrey Callender, the then secretary of the Society for Nautical Research, that a William Turner was in business at 85 High Street, Portsmouth, until 1823. However, this identification is not confirmed by modern Portsmouth historians; according to recent research, a tailor's shop was at this address from *c.*1770 until at least the 1860s, but the proprietor was initially W. Morgan and later Thomas Sheppard; it may be perhaps that Turner was the manager or dispatch clerk for the business. Certainly in 1791 it was Morgan who advertised in nautical slang:

> MORGAN. Mercer and Sea-Draper, No. 85, opposite the Fountain Inn, High Street.
>
> Sailors rigged complete from stem to stern, *viz.*, chapeau, mapeau, flying-job and flesh-bag; inner pea, outer pea, and cold defender; rudder-case, and service to the same, up-haulers, down-treaders, fore-shoes, lacings, gaskets, etc.

Turner baronets, of Ambrosden, Oxon. Sir Edward Turner, 2nd Bt. (1719–66) married 1739 Cassandra (1723–70) daughter of William Leigh of Adlestrop (q.v.), and had five children: Elizabeth (1741), Gregory (1748), John (1752), William, and Cassandra.

(1) Elizabeth (1741–1816), married 1767 Thomas Twisleton (q.v.), 13th Lord Saye and Sele, and had issue.

(2) Gregory, 3rd Bt. (1748–1805), added 1775 the surname of Page, and became the ancestor of later Page-Turner baronets.

(3) John (1752–97), married 1781 Elizabeth Dryden and took her name; created a baronet 1795; ancestor of later Dryden baronets of Canons Ashby, Northants.

(4) William was alive in 1815, but presumably died unmarried thereafter.

(5) Cassandra (died 1813), married 1771 Martin Bladen, 2nd Lord Hawke (1744–1805), and had four children: Edward, Martin-Bladen, Annabella, and Cassandra-Julia. This last daughter married (1) 1793 Samuel Estwick (q.v.); (2) 1800 Revd Stephen Sloane (q.v.); and (3) post-1812 Thomas Green.

In 1788 Lady Hawke published a two-volume novel *Julia de Gramont* ('By the Right Honourable Lady H****').

Due to their common Leigh ancestry, the Turners, Drydens, and

Twisletons were all in some degree related to the Steventon Austens, the Cookes, and the Coopers.

Fanny Burney met Lord and Lady Saye and Sele, together with Sir Gregory Page-Turner and Lady Hawke, in 1782: '[Lady Saye and Sele] seems pretty near fifty—at least turned forty; her head was full of feathers, flowers, jewels, and gew-gaws . . . her dress was trimmed with beads, silver, persian sashes, and all sort of fine fancies; her face is thin and fiery, and her whole manner spoke a lady all alive. . . . Lady Hawke . . . is much younger than her sister, and rather pretty; extremely languishing, delicate, and pathetic; apparently accustomed to be reckoned the genius of her family, and well contented to be looked upon as a creature dropped from the clouds.' Lord Saye and Sele was 'a square man, middle-aged, and humdrum'; Sir Gregory Page-Turner was 'younger, slimmer, and smarter'. See Barrett, *Diaries and Letters of Madame D'Arblay*, ii. 116–22, for a full description of Fanny Burney's meeting with this family group.

Twining, Messrs R. J., R. G., and J. A. Tea-merchants, with their warehouse at 216 Strand, London.

Twisleton family, of Broughton Castle, near Banbury, Oxon. Elizabeth Turner (1741–1816, q.v.) married 1767 Thomas Twisleton (1735–1788) 13th Baron Saye and Sele (commonly but erroneously called the 10th Baron) and had four children: Gregory-William (1769), Thomas-James (1770), Julia-Judith (1771), and Mary-Cassandra (1774). Lord Saye and Sele committed suicide at his house in Harley Street, London—according to family tradition, this was because he had been told that a disease which gave him a violent pain in his head was incurable.

(1) Gregory-William (1769–1844) became the 14th (not 11th) Baron; his only son William-Thomas, 15th Baron (1798–1847) died unmarried, and the title descended to the latter's cousin Frederick-Benjamin (see below).

(2) Hon. and Revd Dr Thomas-James (1770–1824); in his boyhood became devoted to amateur dramatics, and while at Westminster School appeared with great success as Phaedria in Terence's comedy *The Eunuch*. In May 1788 he acted in a lavish private production of *Julia* opposite a Miss Charlotte Wattell, said to be a very beautiful young lady of very respectable connections, and four months later, while still a schoolboy, eloped to Gretna Green with her. The young couple maintained their theatrical interests for a time, in a semi-public fashion, until Mrs Twisleton decided she wished to become a professional actress, which gave her husband one reason for obtaining first a deed of separation in 1794 and then a divorce in 1798. They had had five children, of whom only one daughter survived to maturity; before their divorce, however, Mrs Twisleton had another son, 'the result of an affair with a merchant named Stein, who accepted paternity of the boy and helped educate him'. In later years it 'became necessary to

prove that Mrs Twisleton's son was not the rightful heir. Mr Stein was discovered still living, but over eighty, and prepared to admit the truth that he considered the son to be his; and the son, now a man of fifty-two, was also found, at some sea port on the eve of embarking as a sailor in the commercial marine. He readily confirmed the statement made by Stein whom he thought to be his father' (D. Verey, (ed.), *The Diary of a Cotswold Parson: Rev F. E. Witts, 1783–1854* (Gloucester, 1979), 169).

Thomas Twisleton returned to his studies, entering St Mary Hall, Oxford, 1789; BA 1794, MA 1796, and DD by decree 1819; received the family livings of Broadwell and Adlestrop, Glos., and Woodford and Blakesley, Northants; went to Ceylon as Secretary and Chaplain to the Colonial Government, 1802; Archdeacon of Colombo 1815 until his death there in 1824. He married (2) 1798 Anne Ashe, and had several more children, of whom the eldest son, Revd Dr Frederick-Benjamin (1799), became 1847 the 16th Lord Saye and Sele.

(3) Julia-Judith (1771–1843) married 1786 her cousin James-Henry Leigh (q.v.) of Adlestrop, and had issue.

(4) Mary-Cassandra (1774–1843) eloped 1790 with Edward-Jervis Ricketts (afterwards Viscount St Vincent) and had three children; she then committed adultery 1797 with Charles-William Taylor, the MP for Wells, at his London house; divorce finalized 1799; married (2) 1806 Richard-Charles Head-Graves (1782–1822), but had no further children.

Twitchen, Farmer Andrew, and wife Sarah. Of Warren Farm, Ashe.

Twyford, Revd Charles-Edward (born 1788). Curate 1812 of Great (East) Worldham, Hants.

Tylden family. Richard Tylden (*c.*1755–1832), of Milsted, Kent; sons Revd Richard-Osborne, vicar of Chilham, Kent, 1809–62, and Sir John-Maxwell (knighted 1812). His brother, Revd Richard-Cooke Tylden (died 1819), rector of Milsted, took the additional name of Pattenson 1799. See also under Osborne.

Utterson, Alfred (1792–1841). Son of John Utterson of Fareham, Hants; entered St John's College, Oxford, 1810; BA 1815, MA 1820; rector of Layer Marney, Essex, 1828–41.

Valentine, David. Lieutenant RN 1795, and apparently First Lieutenant of HMS *Endymion* 1801, Commander 1806.

Vincent, William. HTA's banking partner in the Alton branch.

W., Mr. Unidentified; Martha Lloyd had hoped to marry him.

Wake, Revd Henry. Married 26 March 1813 Urania Wallop (q.v.), and was presented to the family living of Over Wallop the following month.

Wakeford, Joshua. Deane villager, and buried there 30 October 1800.

Waller, Richard. Of Bevis Hill, Southampton; died 11 June 1808. A Mrs Waller called on Mrs Chute at The Vyne in 1793.

Wallop, family name of Earls of Portsmouth. The Hon. and Revd Barton Wallop (1744/5–81), brother of the 2nd Earl, married 1771 his cousin Camilla-Powlett Smith of Crux Easton, Hants (died 1820), and had a daughter Urania; Mrs Wallop and her daughter lived in Above Bar, Southampton, and Miss Wallop married at Southampton 26 March 1813 Revd Henry Wake (q.v.).

Hon. Coulson Wallop (1774–1807), younger brother of 3rd and 4th Earls of Portsmouth (q.v.); MP for Andover 1796–1802.

Walsby, Dr and Mrs. Dr Edward Walsby (1750–1815), Prebendary of Canterbury Cathedral 1793–1815.

Walter family, of Tonbridge, Kent. Rebecca Hampson (q.v.) married (1) *c.*1720 William Walter, MD (1697–1726) son of George Walter of New Trench in the parish of Tonbridge, and had one son, William-Hampson Walter (1721); she married (2) 1727 **William Austen** (q.v.), and by him had **George** and **Philadelphia Austen** (qq.v.).

William-Hampson Walter (1721–98) lived initially at Shipbourne near Tonbridge, Kent, and afterwards at other villages in the same area, finally settling at Seal; married *c.*1745 Susannah Weaver (1716–1811) of Maidstone, and had seven children: Weaver (1747), Susannah (1749, 'Sally'), William (1750), George (1754), John (1757, died young), James (1759), and Philadelphia (1761).

(1) Weaver (1747–1814). Head Boy of Tonbridge School 1764; Christ's College, Cambridge, 1764; BA 1767, MA 1770, Fellow 1779–1802; ordained 1776; under-usher at Newcastle-on-Tyne Grammar School 1767–78 and later took pupils at Penshurst; curate of Penshurst, Kent, 1779; obtained college livings of Brisley and Gately, Norfolk, 1801; married in Penshurst 1806 Sarah Pearch; then lived in Brisley till his death in 1814; no issue.

(2) Sally (1749–70) died suddenly when on the verge of marriage.

(3) William (1750–87) went to Jamaica and died there.

(4) George (1754–79) followed his brother to the West Indies and died there.

(5) James (1759–1845). Corpus Christi College, Cambridge, 1777; BA 1781, Fellow 1783; Assistant Master at Louth Grammar School, Lincs., 1783–7; Headmaster of the Free Grammar School, Brigg, Lincs., 1787–1834; rector of Market Rasen, Lincs., 1789–1845; married 1784 his distant cousin Frances-Maria Walter of London and had eighteen children, of whom only eight survived to maturity: Henry (1785), John-Charles (1787), Frances (1788), George (1792), Sarah (1795), Weever [*sic*] (1797), Anna-Maria-Philadelphia (1799), and Edward (1801).

(**5a**) Henry (1785–1859). St John's College, Cambridge, 1802; BA (2nd Wrangler and Smith's Prize) 1806, MA 1809, BD 1816, Fellow 1806–24; ordained 1809; Professor of Natural Philosophy and Mathematics at HEIC College, Haileybury, 1806–30; rector of Hazelbury-Bryan, Dorset, 1821–59; wrote a three-volume *History of England*.

(**5b**) John-Charles (1787). Grandfather of John-Charles-Guy Nicholson (died 1925), sometime owner of JA's Letter **8**.

(**5c**) Frances (1788) married Revd Joseph Stockdale, vicar of Kingerby, Lincs., and had twelve children.

(**5d**) George (1792) married twice; went to Tasmania and had a large family.

(**5e**) Sarah (1795) married 1822 Patteson Holgate; no surviving issue.

(**5f**) Weever (1797–1860) married twice and left issue; incumbent of Gate Burton, Lincs., 1828–35, and of Bonby, Lincs., 1835–60, Canon of Lincoln 1846.

(**5g**) Anna-Maria-Philadelphia (1799) unmarried; inherited family papers and other items from her aunt Philadelphia (see below).

(**5h**) Edward (1801–77) married 1828 and had issue; incumbent of Woodhall and of Langton-by-Horncastle, Lincs., 1828–77.

(**6**) Philadelphia (1761–1834) married 1811, at Brisley, George Whitaker of Pembury, Kent; no issue.

Waltham, Lady (1743–1819). Drigue-Billers Olmius, 2nd Baron Waltham of New Hall, Essex, married 1767 Miss Coe, and died 1787 without issue; she died at Goodnestone, Kent.

Wapshare family, of Salisbury, Wilts. The eldest daughter Mary (1778–1825) married 1800 as his second wife Capt. Sir Thomas Williams (q.v.) but had no issue; her brothers were Revd Charles (married 1802 Miss Dyneley of Bloomsbury Square, London) and Revd William-Sandford, vicar of Chitterne, Wilts. (who married November 1813 Miss Cooth-Ann Austen of Ensbury, Dorset (q.v.)).

Warneford, Revd John (born 1778). Son of Revd John Warneford of Dorking; ordained 1801; later vicar of St Bartholomew's, Winchester, and rector of Oakley, Hants.

Warren, John-Willing (1771–*c.*1831). Probably one of Mr GA's pupils at Steventon, *c.*1785; entered St John's College, Oxford, 1786, BA 1789; Fellow of Oriel College, Oxford, 1791; Inner Temple 1798; barrister-at-law and a Charity Commissioner; married 1807; of 13 Harcourt Buildings, London; cousin of Lt.-Col. Richard Warren (see below). He was one of the contributors to James Austen's Oxford magazine *The Loiterer*.

Warren, Lt.-Col. Richard (1763–1820). Entered Christ Church College, Oxford, 1781, but did not graduate; 3rd Regt. Foot Guards 1783–1800, retiring as Lt.-Colonel; Gentleman Usher and Daily Waiter to the Prince of Wales 1790; married 25 March 1800 Jane Maitland (q.v.); their daughter Mary-Jane was born 15 March 1801 at Houghton, Hants, and was followed by at least three sons; cousin of John-Willing Warren (see above).

There was also a Revd Thomas-Alston Warren (1769–1853), who entered St John's College, Oxford, 1787, BA 1791, MA 1795, BD 1800; Fellow until 1814 and Chaplain 1834–53; rector of the College living of South Warnborough, Hants, 1814–53; he too contributed to *The Loiterer*; perhaps related to the two Warrens above.

Watkins family. Revd George Watkins (died 1798), vicar of Odiham and rector of East Tisted, Hants; his sons Revd George-Nowell (1771–1844), curate of Odiham 1793, perpetual curate of Long Sutton, Hants, 1806–44; and Revd Charles-Kemeys (1777–1840), rector of Fenny Compton, War., 1821–40.

Weatherhead, Anne-Eliza. (Not 'Wethered' as JA wrote.) Daughter or sister of Robert Weatherhead, Collector of Excise, Southampton.

Webb family. Mrs Webb and daughters, living in Chawton May 1811–September 1814; perhaps Mary (née Digweed (q.v.) 1761–1825) who married William Webb of Kingsclere.

Webb, Thomas. Pastry-cook, 153 High Street, Southampton.

Wedgwood, Josiah. Ceramic manufacturer, of Staffordshire; his London showroom was in York-street, St James's.

Weippart. (Not Wiepart as JA wrote.) Professor of the harp, at 8 Foley Street, Portland Chapel, London.

Welby, Mrs. Wilhelmina (1773–1847), only daughter of William Spry, Governor of Barbadoes 1767–71, and his wife Katherine Cholmeley (q.v.); married 1792 William-Earle Welby (1768–1852), who became 1815 2nd baronet; of Denton Hall near Grantham, Lincs., and of Argyll Street, London; their eldest son William-Earle (1794–1806) died at Eton.

Wemyss, Miss. Perhaps a daughter of Revd James Wemyss of Bogie, Fife.

West, Benjamin (1738–1820). American artist, who settled in London 1763, and was patronized by George III thereafter. Amongst other works he exhibited two enormous canvases with religious themes—*Christ Healing the Sick* and *Christ Rejected by the Elders*—seen by JA in London respectively 1811 and 1814.

West, Jane (1758–1852). Wife of Thomas West, a yeoman farmer in Northamptonshire; self-educated authoress, producing many volumes of poems, plays, and novels, from 1780 onwards; see *DNB*.

Whitby family. Revd Thomas Whitby, of Creswell Hall, Staffs., and 3 Portland Place, Bath; his daughters Julia, Lucy, and Mary. Lucy married at Bath

28 August 1798 Edward-Berkeley Portman (q.v.); Mary married June 1809 Ayshford Wise, of Totnes Parva, Devon.

White family, of Hampshire and London. Revd Gilbert White (1720–93) of Selborne, Hants (author 1789 of *The Natural History of Selborne*) was a bachelor, but had numerous nephews and nieces (referred to in his writings as his 'nepotes'), several of whom either lived in Hampshire, or else came to visit their uncle.

Jane (1755–3 January 1831), daughter of Benjamin White (1725–94) of London; married 1780 Thomas Clement (q.v.) of Alton and had issue.

Edmund (1758–1838), son of Benjamin White of London; vicar of Newton Valence, Hants, 1785–1838, and rector of Greatham, Hants, 1785–1814; married Anne daughter of William Blunt of Petersfield and had issue.

John (1765–1855), son of Benjamin White of London; married Mary-Anne, daughter of Revd Gabriel Tahourdin of Hannington, Hants; lived for a time in Selborne after his uncle's death.

John (1759–1821), son of Revd John White (1727–80) Chaplain to the Gibraltar garrison; lived during his boyhood with his uncle Gilbert and nicknamed by him 'Gibraltar Jack'; became a surgeon and practised c.1785 in Alton and afterwards at Salisbury and elsewhere.

Gibraltar Jack's mother Barbara (1734–1802, née Freeman) in her widowhood joined Gilbert White in his Selborne home 'Wakes' as his housekeeper and lived there till his death; she herself was buried in Alton.

White, Mrs. Perhaps wife of Mr George White of Canterbury.

Whitfield, Revd Francis (1743–1810). Son of Francis Whitfield of Ashford, Kent, attorney; rector of Westbere and vicar of Godmersham 1778–1810.

Whitworth, Charles (1752–1825). Earl Whitworth; married 1801 Arabella-Diana (née Cope), widow of the 3rd Duke of Dorset, and lived with her at Knole, Sevenoaks; Lord Lieutenant and Viceroy of Ireland 1813–17.

Wickham, Mr. Probably the Hon. William Wickham, of Cottingley, Yorks., and Wyck, Hants—a hamlet 3 miles NE of Chawton; in 1814 he had an unmarried son, Henry-Louis, aged 25, which is perhaps why JA mentions FCK's name in her next sentence.

Wiggett, Caroline (1799–post-1869). Revd James Wiggett was a maternal cousin of William-John Chute (q.v.) of The Vyne; and upon his being left a widower with seven children, Mr and Mrs Chute adopted Caroline, the youngest daughter, in 1803; she married 1837 as his second wife Thomas Workman, surgeon of Basingstoke; no surviving issue. Caroline's younger brother William-Lyde Wiggett eventually inherited The Vyne in 1842, and his family became known as Wiggett-Chute.

Wigram, Sir Robert (1744–1830). Baronet 1805; of Belmont, Worcs., and also of Walthamstow, Essex, and 57 Portland Place, London. He owned a shipbuilding yard next door to the East India Docks on the river Thames, London. His obituary in the *GM* for 1830, ii. 563-4, credits him with twenty-one children by two marriages; the Henry-Loftus Wigram (1791–1866) whom JA met was the sixth son.

Wildman family, of Chilham Castle, near Godmersham. James Wildman (1747–1816) purchased Chilham Castle 1792; his son James-Beckford Wildman (1788–1867) married 1820 Mary-Anne Lushington and had ten children. When he succeeded his father in 1816 the estate was worth £20,000 a year, but 'over-generous provision for members of the family' combined with 'mortgages raised to provide funds to work the family estates in the West Indies by machinery, after the emancipation of the slaves' meant that the property had to be sold in 1861; Mr Wildman subsequently lived at Yotes Court, near Maidstone, until his death.

Wilkes, Mr. Presumably John-Golding Wilkes, of St John's College, Cambridge; LLB 1816.

William. HTA's manservant in London.

Williams, the Misses. Miss Williams and her sisters Grace and Mary, lodging with one or other of the Dusautoy families (q.v.) in Southampton.

Williams, Mrs. The Mrs Williams of Letter 22 (1799) seems to be in the Steventon area; the elderly Mrs Williams of Letter 54 (1808) may perhaps be the mother of the three Misses Williams of Southampton (see above).

Williams family, of Compton, Hants. Revd Philip Williams (1742–1830); Fellow of New College, Oxford, 1760-9; Fellow of Winchester College, Hants, 1769–1819; rector of Compton, Hants, 1781–1830; Canon of Lincoln 1783; Chaplain to the Speaker of the House of Commons 1784-7; Canon of Canterbury 1789-97; Canon of Winchester 1797; married (1) 1779 Sarah (c.1757–87), daughter of Thomas Collins, Second Master of Winchester College, and had four children: Elizabeth (born ?1779, 'Betsy'), Philip jr. (1780–1843), Charlotte (born c.1783), and Charles (1784–1866); married (2) 1795 Helen Fagg (q.v.) of Mystole, Kent, but had no further issue.

Betsy Williams had intellectual interests, but suffered from physical illnesses and mental depression, and both she and her sister Charlotte spent much time staying at health resorts such as Bath, Cheltenham, and Tunbridge Wells.

Mr Williams had a prebendal house in Winchester Cathedral Close, now known as No. 12; and as he preferred to reside in Compton it was available in 1813 to be rented by Mrs Elizabeth Heathcote and her sister Miss Alethea Bigg (qq.v.).

Philip Williams jr. became a successful barrister and Recorder of Winchester; married 30 December 1817 Jane Blachford (q.v.).

Jeremiah Dyson (q.v.) who lived for a time at Compton Rectory, was brother-in-law to Revd Philip Williams, as his wife was Elizabeth Collins, sister of Sarah.

Williams, Edmund. Employed by HTA in the London bank and later sent to the Alton branch partnership; perhaps the son of Thomas Williams of 1 Grosvenor Place, Knightsbridge.

Williams, Capt. (later Adm.) Sir Thomas (1761–1841). Knighted 1796; captain HMS *Endymion*; commanded the Sea-Fencibles of the Gosport division 1806–7; married (1) at Steventon 11 December 1792 Jane, daughter of Revd Dr Edward Cooper (q.v.), who was killed in a road accident 9 August 1798; (2) 1800 Mary Wapshare (q.v.) of Salisbury (died 1824); of Brooklands near Southampton and later of Burwood House, Walton-on-Thames; no issue; for details of his naval career see Marshall, *Royal Naval Biography*.

Willoughby, Lady (died 1828). Priscilla-Barbara-Elizabeth, Baroness Willoughby de Eresby in her own right, and wife of Lord Gwydyr; first cousin to Anne Mathew (q.v.) and therefore related to Anna Austen (q.v.). See R. Vick, 'Some Errors and Omissions in the Indexes to JA's Letters', in *N&Q* 237:2 (June 1992), 164.

Wilmot [or Wylmot], —. MD, of Ashford, Kent; with a wife and family.

Wilson, Mr. Probably John Wilson, innkeeper, of the Three Crowns in Basingstoke.

Winchester, Bishops of. In JA's time they were: Dr Benjamin Hoadly, 1734–61; Dr John Thomas, 1761–81; Dr the Hon. Brownlow North, 1781–1820.

Winstone, Miss, and the Winstones. Perhaps the family of Mr Hayward Winstone, of 10 Great Bedford Street, Bath, and Captain of Infantry of the Bath Military Association.

Wise, Mr. '. . . old Wyse, a civil, respectful-mannered, elderly man, exceedingly fond of hunting, who drove Rogers' coach every day, Sundays excepted, from Southampton to Popham Lane in the morning, and back to Southampton in the afternoon. He arrived at the Flower Pots, Popham Lane, soon after ten o'clock, and left it between three and four' (*Vine Hunt* 66).

Wood, Miss. There are two Misses Wood mentioned by JA: (1) Mrs Evelyn's companion, in Bath; (2) Mrs Rider's shop assistant, in Basingstoke.

Wood, Mr John. Unidentified; JA's dancing-partner in the winter of 1798–9.

Woodd, Miss. George-Basil Woodd (1724–84) married 1774 as his second wife Gertrude Ballard of Leatherhead, Surrey, and had six children; of these Susanna-Martha married 1801 Robert Middleton, and her younger sister

Maria died unmarried 1814. The family had Yorkshire connections, so it may be this Mrs Middleton and her sister who were the subject of the midwinter tragedy of 1808–9 to which JA refers in Letter **64**. The Woodds were also Evangelical and friends of the Tilsons (q.v.), which may be how the Austens came to know them.

Woodford, Captain A. G. Of the Coldstream Guards, Captain 11 December 1799, and garrisoned at Deal 1805.

Woodward, Revd James. Of Brasenose College, Oxford; married May 1801 at Queen Square Chapel, Bath, Miss Wroe (not 'Rowe' as JA wrote), daughter of the late Major Wroe of Calcutta.

Woolls, Mr and Miss. Living at Farringdon *c.*1813–16; perhaps connected with the Wooll family whose MIs were in St Thomas's, Southgate Street, Winchester.

Wren, Mr. Silk-dyer, 76 High Street, Southampton.

Wrey, Sir Bourchier, Bt., of Tawstock, Devon. Of his three daughters, Florentina married Richard-Godolphin Long (q.v.); Dyonisia married 1780 Robert Harding (q.v.); and Anna-Maria, the youngest, married 1791 Nicolas-Roundell Toke (q.v.). Sir Bourchier Wrey himself is not mentioned in JA's letters.

Wright, Mr and Mrs. Revd Robert Wright (born 1772), curate of Dummer 1797 and later rector of Ovington, Hants; his wife Elizabeth; their son Robert-John-William was born at Dummer 1803 and became curate to his father at Ovington 1826.

Wynne, Mr. Resident in the boarding-house 17 High Street, Southampton.

Yalden, Mr. Of Alton; owner of a private coach, which he drove from Alton to London one day and back the next.

Yates, Lady. Probably Elizabeth (née Baldwyn), widow of Sir Joseph Yates (1722–70), a Puisne Justice of the King's Bench and afterwards of the Common Pleas; one son Joseph (1764–1820) and one daughter; the Miss Yates of Letter **91** may perhaps be this daughter—see also *MAJA* 8.

York, Duchess of. See under **Royal Family**.

Young, Charles Mayne (1777–1856). Tragedian; appearing on the London stage 1809 onwards and considered as the successor to John-Philip Kemble. A well-educated man, noted for his dignity, good looks, and strong melodious voice.

TOPOGRAPHICAL INDEX

Adlestrop, Glos. Village 85 miles NW of London, just off the A 436 between Stow-on-the-Wold, Glos., and Chipping Norton, Oxon.; home of Mrs GA's Leigh family since 1553. James-Henry Leigh's Adlestrop House is now called Adlestrop Park, and Revd Thomas Leigh's rectory is now called Adlestrop House and is no longer used as a rectory. Edward Thomas's poem 'Adlestrop' gives a brief pen-picture of the countryside as it was early in this century.

Albany: see **London.**

Alton, Hants. Country town 51 miles SW of London on the A 31, and approximately 1 mile NE of Chawton; the coaching inns were the Swan and the Crown; post-town for Chawton. HTA's banking partnership of Austen, Gray & Vincent was at 10 High Street, Mr Curtis the apothecary at No. 4, and EAK's lawyer Mr Trimmer at No. 63; Harry Digweed and his wife Jane Terry also lived in the town. There was a Saturday market and two annual fairs, one on the last Saturday in April and the other on 29 September (Michaelmas).

The town has increased in size since the nineteenth century, and is now nearly joined to Chawton; the development, however, has been discreet and tactful and much of what remains would still be recognizable by JA.

Andover, Hants. Country town 68 miles SW of London and 22 miles from Basingstoke, on the A 30/A 303. It had a number of large coaching inns, of which only three survive: the White Hart (formerly the Star), the Danebury Hotel (formerly the White Hart, which also had the post-office and Excise Office), and the Angel (formerly the Lower Angel). Mrs Poore's house was later the residence for the Headmasters of the local grammar school, and is now 6 Church Close, the Andover Museum.

Appleshaw, Hants. Village 5 miles NW of Andover on the A 342.

Ashdown Park, near Lambourn, Newbury, Berks. Home of the Earls of Craven since the seventeenth century; the house is now owned by the National Trust and open to the public.

Ashe, Hants. Village 7 miles W of Basingstoke on the B 3400 (now a minor road but once part of the main coaching routes from London to the SW of England), and 2 miles N of Steventon.

Ashe Park was in JA's time owned by the Portals, and tenanted by the Holders.

Ashe Rectory was the home of the Lefroy family 1783–1829; now called

Ashe House and no longer used as a rectory. The church, Holy Trinity and St Andrew, was rebuilt 1877-9.

Ashford, Kent. Country town 55 miles SE of London on the A 20, and 7 miles S of Godmersham. The coaching inn was the Saracen's Head.

Astley's Amphitheatre: see **London.**

Bagshot, Surrey. Village and staging post, 27 miles SW of London on the A 30; at one time it had fourteen inns to cater for travellers, of which the King's Arms and the White Hart were the biggest.

Barnes, Surrey. Originally a separate Thames-side village, 8 miles upriver from London; now London SW13. The D'Antraigues's house, 27 The Terrace, facing the river, still survives.

Barton Court, Kintbury, Berks. A late eighteenth-century house, between Speen and Hungerford on the A 4; Revd John Craven inherited a life interest in the property from his mother, and after his death in 1804 it passed to the Dundas family.

Barton Lodge, St Leonard's Hill, near Windsor, Berks. Home of Mrs GA's old friend Mrs Birch.

Basingstoke, Hants. Market town and important staging post 49 miles SW of London on the A 30, and 9 miles NE of Steventon. The main coaching inns were the Crown, the Maidenhead, and the Wheatsheaf, and the Angel had a small ballroom built over the stables at the rear of the yard—see *Emma* ch. 29 for a similar arrangement at the Crown in Highbury. The assembly balls were held in the upper rooms of the Town Hall in the Market Place— see R. Vick, 'The Basingstoke Assemblies' in the JA Society *Report* for 1993, 22–5.

Practically all the centre of the town was demolished and redeveloped in a coarse and brutal manner in the 1960s, and since then there have been added on the outskirts tower-blocks of offices surrounded by tangled knots of motorway roundabouts, the whole now creating a huge and incongruous urban blot on the Hampshire landscape.

Bath, Somerset. Fashionable inland spa city, 116 miles W of London on the A 4, via Maidenhead, Reading, Hungerford, and Devizes. There are numerous books describing Bath's archaeology, history, Georgian architecture, and famous residents, so the following notes concern only the Austens and the references in JA's letters.

The Austen family lived at 4 Sydney Place 1801–4, then at 3 Green Park Buildings East 1804–5; after Revd GA's death there in January 1805 Mrs GA and her daughters lodged temporarily (probably April–June 1805) at 25 Gay Street, and also in Trim Street (probably January–June 1806). The Leigh-Perrots rented 1 Paragon from at least 1797, and then bought 49 Great Pulteney Street in 1810.

The whole row of Green Park Buildings East was destroyed in the Second World War and has been rebuilt in a different manner; the number of the lodging-house in Trim Street was not specified by Mrs GA in her surviving correspondence. The other houses in Bath associated with the Austens still survive.

There were two Assembly Rooms, in 1801 described as follows: the Old, or Lower Rooms,

> are situated on the Walks, leading from the Grove to the North-parade; the principal room is one of the pleasantest in the kingdom for a morning lounge, commanding a view of the adjacent hills, woods, the valley, and the river Avon. The card room is likewise large and convenient. There are two excellent billiard tables in adjoining apartments. The dress balls are on Friday nights, excepting in Lent, when they are changed to Thursdays; the fancy or cotillon balls are on Tuesday nights; the subscription to the former is one guinea the season for two tickets, transferable to ladies; to the fancy balls half-a-guinea, the tickets not transferable. The amusements at these rooms are conducted by James King, Esq. . . . The New Assembly Rooms are situated near the Circus, and are particularly spacious and elegant; they were opened in the winter of 1771. The ball room is 105 feet long 42 wide, and 42 high; there is a large concert or tea room, and an octagon tea room, with a coffee room attached, likewise billiard rooms, &c. The dress balls are on Monday night, the fancy or cotillon balls on Thursdays, excepting in Lent, when they are changed to Saturdays; the subscriptions the same as the lower rooms; the present master of the ceremonies is Richard Tyson, Esq.

The Lower Rooms closed in 1820; the Upper Rooms survive in use and also house a Museum of Costume.

The canal by which JA walked in 1801, was presumably the Kennet & Avon Canal, which was cut from the Avon just below Bath and ran eastwards to join the Kennet river at Hungerford, Berks. The 'cassoon' [caisson] was part of the construction works for another, abortive little canal to the SW of Bath, which was 'intended to convey the coals of the Timsbury, Paulton, Camerton, and Dunkerton pits to Bath'.

The chapel which the Austens attended was probably St Mary's (now demolished), just off Queen Square.

The Charitable Repository, Bath Street, 'opened in 1797, for the encouragement of industry in all descriptions of persons reduced to distress, by affording them a ready sale for their articles, and paying them the full value, when sold, without any deduction' (Directory for 1812).

The Crescent is now known as Royal Crescent, and the Crescent Fields as Victoria Park. JA's other aunt and uncle, Revd Dr Cooper and his wife Jane Leigh, had lived 1771–84 at 12 [Royal] Crescent.

The Hetling Pump, where EAK drank the waters, was so called after a successful wine-merchant who occupied old Hungerford House in Westgate

Buildings, and changed its name to Hetling House. The adjoining pump-room was opened about 1770.

Kingsmead fields lay between the two rows of Green Park Buildings East and West.

Lansdown Crescent was in JA's time referred to as either the 'New' or the 'Upper' Crescent.

'The two Riding-schools are kept by Mr. Dash and Mr. Ryles, the first is in Montpelier-row, above the New Rooms, and the other in Monmouth-street, no considerable distance from Queen's-square. Attendance from 10 till 4.'

Sydney Garden

> is beautifully situated East of Bath, facing Great Pulteney-street, in the front of which is a superb hotel, where families may be accommodated in the first stile. The amusements of these gardens begin early in the spring with public Breakfasts, Evening Promonades [*sic*], and temporary Illuminations, enliv-ened with music. There are generally four or five grand GALA NIGHTS in the course of the Summer Season, for brilliancy, taste, and elegance not sur-passed by any garden in the kingdom. It contains about sixteen acres, laid out in Serpentine-Walks, Water-falls, Pavillions, Alcoves, Grottos, Laby-rinth, Bowling-Greens, with Merlin and other Swings, and every requisite that can be conducive to health and pleasure; the whole surrounded by a spacious and pleasant ride. The beautiful situation of the garden is consid-erably heightened by the Kennet and Avon Canal passing through, over which two elegant cast iron bridges are thrown after the manner of the chinese. Terms of subscription for walking in the garden 7s.6d. per annum, or 2s. 6d. per month; more than one in a family subscribing 5s. each; sub-scription to the ride 15s. per annum.

Mr and Mrs GA had been married in 1764 at Walcot church, and Mr GA was buried there in January 1805.

The White Hart in Stall Street was one of the biggest coaching inns in the city, and therefore understandably noisy. It was demolished in 1867 and replaced by the Pump Room Hotel; this in its turn was demolished after the Second World War, and Arlington House, an office block, now occupies the site opposite the Abbey churchyard.

In the vicinity of Bath JA mentions: Beacon Hill, on the N side of the city, between Lansdown and Walcot; Charlcombe, a village to the N, still just separate from the city; Kingsdown, a hill to the NE on the main road from London into Bath; Lyncombe, a southern suburb of Bath, across the Avon; Sion Hill, on the NW going towards the village of Weston, which, like Charlcombe, is not quite overtaken by Bath; Twerton, originally a village on the W side, now a suburb; Widcombe, another southern suburb across the Avon.

Battersea, Surrey. Originally a separate Thames-side village 5 miles upriver from London; now London SW11.

Baughurst, Hants. Village 7 miles NW of Basingstoke; Mr Dyson was the incumbent in JA's time.

Beaulieu, Hants. Village near the coast, 4 miles from the Solent up the Beaulieu river. It has the ruins of the thirteenth-century Beaulieu Abbey, part of which was converted in the sixteenth century into Palace House, home of the Montagu family. The National Motor Museum is now in the Abbey grounds.

If the Austens did visit Beaulieu, they would probably have travelled by ferry across Southampton Water to Hythe and so inland. Earlier in the eighteenth century the 2nd Duke of Montagu had founded a shipyard and little port just below Beaulieu, called Buckler's Hard, and between *c.*1750 – 1820 twelve merchant vessels and fifty-two men-of-war were built there — an added incentive for a visit by a family with naval interests. The shipyards and buildings are now preserved as a maritime museum.

Beckenham, Kent. Originally a separate village, 12 miles SE of London, now part of Greater London. Mr Moore's maternal relatives, the Edens, lived there.

Bedfont, Middx. Originally a separate village 15 miles W of London, near Staines on the A 30; now part of Greater London.

Bentigh. One of the Godmersham woodlands.

Bentley, Hants. Village 5 miles NE of Alton on the A 31. HTA was perpetual curate of St Mary's, 1824–39, and was responsible for enlarging the church *c.*1835; it was however rebuilt *c.*1890.

Bifrons, Kent. Home of the Taylor family, near Bridge on the A 2; demolished 1945.

Bilting, Kent. A hamlet on the A 28, near Godmersham.

Birmingham, War. Commercial and manufacturing centre, 108 miles NW of London. In JA's time it had already developed a reputation for the production of light metalwork items of all kinds:

> To give a list of the manufacturers, even taking them alphabetically from awl-blade makers and bellows makers, down to steel *man-trap* makers, and wooden *mouse-trap* makers, would be an Herculean labour . . . the brass founderies . . . the gilt-toy manufactories . . . the pin manufacturers . . . the famous Soho works, belonging to Messrs. Boulton and Co., forming one of the most extensive manufactories in the kingdom . . . consists of four squares, with connecting ranges of shops like streets, capable of employing about 1000 workmen in all the varieties of the button, buckle, plated, or argent-molu, steel and trinket manufactory.

Bishopstoke, Hants. Originally a separate village, now nearly incorporated with Eastleigh; 73 miles SW of London on the A 335.

Blackheath, Kent. Originally a separate village 6 miles SE of London on the A 2, and notoriously dangerous for ambushes by highwaymen; now London SE3.

Blandford Forum, Dorset. Market town 107 miles SW of London, and 24 miles N of Weymouth on the A 354 via Dorchester.

Bookham, Great, Surrey. Village 22 miles SW of London and 2 miles from Leatherhead, off the A 246. Revd Samuel Cooke was incumbent of Great Bookham 1769–1820; the rectory was demolished in the 1960s and the site redeveloped. Little Bookham is half a mile W.

Brentford, Middx. Originally a separate small town, 7 miles W of London; now part of Greater London.

Bridlington, Yorks. Seaside resort, 228 miles N of London.

Brighton, Sussex. Originally a small fishing village called Brighthelmstone, but became a fashionable seaside town and had its name abbreviated when the Prince of Wales converted a farmhouse into his Marine Pavilion in the 1780s; 53 miles S of London on the A 23. The Pavilion is now a truly outstanding museum.

Bristol, Glos. Ancient city and seaport, on the river Avon, 120 miles W of London on the M 4/A 4, and 13 miles NW of Bath; at one time famous for its involvement in the slave, rum, sugar, and tobacco trade between England, Africa, America, and the West Indies.

Broadstairs, Isle of Thanet, Kent. Seaside resort, 79 miles SE of London, and 19 miles from Canterbury on the A 253.

Brompton, Middx. Originally a hamlet in Kensington parish, and famed for its market gardens which supplied London consumers; the HTAs lived 1804–9 at 16 Michael's Place; the site was redeveloped later in the nineteenth century and is now London SW3.

Brooklands, Sarisbury, Bursledon, Hants. Sir Thomas Williams's country villa, overlooking the Hamble river; in private ownership.

Broome Park, Barham, Kent. A seventeenth-century house, one of the seats of the Oxenden family; now divided into apartments in private ownership; a landscape view, taken *c.*1830, is in the Canterbury Art Gallery.

Buckwell. Part of the Godmersham estate.

Cadbury, Great (North), Somerset. Village 5 miles W of Wincanton and N of the A 303; Revd Samuel Blackall acquired the living 1812.

Cambridge, Cambs. Ancient university city, 60 miles NE of London on the A 10. JA's cousin Henry Walter studied there.

Canterbury, Kent. Archbishop's see and cathedral city; 61 miles SE of London and 16 from Dover on the A 2, and 8 miles from Godmersham.

Mrs Moore, the Archbishop's widow, lived in a house in the Oaks—an area on the east side of the Cathedral Precincts—and Mrs Brydges was also in the Precincts. Mrs Charles Milles lived in the Precincts at one time, but by 1808 had apparently moved into a house presumably in either Burgate Street or St George's Street, as to call on her provided JA with a short cut from the Oaks to Mrs Thomas Knight II at White Friars. White Friars was an urban mansion, dating back to its foundation as an Austin Friary in 1325; it was converted into a house post-Reformation, enlarged and improved in the 1790s; sold in 1879 to the Governors of the Simon Langton Schools, who demolished the house and built schoolrooms on the site; these schools were in turn outgrown, and the whole area has now been totally redeveloped as a modern shopping centre. The Precincts themselves suffered from bomb damage in the Second World War, and several of the houses were destroyed.

Balls were held in Delmar's Rooms, built over the Canterbury Bank; the large corner site, facing the High Street, has been rebuilt but is still used as a bank.

The Canterbury Gaol was built in Longport in 1791; the gatehouse is the only part now remaining.

Charlcombe, Somerset. Village 1 mile N of Bath, now nearly overtaken by the city's development.

Charmouth, Dorset. Village near the coast, 145 miles SW of London, and 3 miles E of Lyme Regis.

Chawton, Hants. Village 52 miles SW of London on the A 31 Winchester–Southampton road, and approximately 1 mile SW of Alton. The A 32 Fareham–Gosport road joined the A 31 outside the Austens' home, and a shallow but wide pond lay in the angle; this was eventually drained and filled in the 1920s. Chawton Great House is about 5 minutes walk beyond the village, on the A 32. Mounters Lane (now nearly disused) runs NW from the outskirts of the village to Chawton Park Wood and Ackender Wood.

A new bypass has taken away the through traffic from the village, and although there has been some modern development it remains overall very much as JA knew it. The new rectory that Mr Papillon built for himself is now in private ownership; St Nicholas church was rebuilt in 1871; Chawton Lodge, where the Hintons lived, seems unaltered; the house where the Prowtings lived has been enlarged and re-fronted, but is still known by this name.

Cheesedown Farm. Part of the Steventon estate.

Chelsea, Middx. Originally a separate Thames-side village 4 miles upriver of London; now London SW3.

Cheltenham, Glos. Inland spa town, 96 miles NW of London, on the A 40; developed 1770 onwards and by 1815 had more than 300 lodging-houses and several different wells and pumps.

Chessel (Chiswell) House, Southampton, Hants. Home of the Lance family; built 1796 and demolished *c.*1920.

Chevet, near Wakefield, Yorks. Home of the Pilkington baronets.

Chilham, Kent. Village 2 miles N of Godmersham on the A 252; in JA's time the early seventeenth-century Chilham Castle was owned by the Wildmans, and the Tyldens were at the vicarage. Both survive, in private ownership; Chilham Castle gardens, but not the house, are open to the public.

Chilton House, near Hungerford, Berks. On the A 419, on the Berks/Wilts border; home of Revd John Craven and his family.

Chippenham, Wilts. Country town 100 miles W of London, and 13 miles from Bath, on the A 4.

Clanville Lodge, near Weyhill, Andover, Hants. Rented 1793–1805 by Anna's grandfather Gen. Mathew, and again briefly in 1810 by his son Mr Brownlow Mathew.

Clapham, Surrey. Originally a separate village 6 miles S of London; now London SW4.

Claremont Park, Esher, Surrey. A new mansion was built, and the grounds improved by Brown, for Lord Clive in 1768; Viscount Galway 1774; Charles Rose Ellis 1807; sold by him to the Crown 1816 for the use of the newly married Princess Charlotte of Wales, who died in childbirth there the following year, at the age of 21. The gardens, but not the house, are now owned by the National Trust and open to the public.

Clifton, Bristol, Somerset. Originally a separate spa development on the hills to the W of Bristol, above the river Avon; now part of the residential suburbs of the city.

Cobham, Surrey. Village 20 miles SW of London at the junction of the A 3 and A 245; the best coaching inns were the George and the White Lion.

Colyton, Devon. Small town N of the A 35, between Sidmouth and Lyme Regis. Revd Richard Buller was the vicar 1799–1806.

Cowes, Isle of Wight. One of the three main towns, on the N tip of the Island and linked by ferry across the Solent to Southampton. FWA and his family lodged in Cowes in 1811.

Cranford Bridge, Middx. Originally a village 13 miles W of London on the A 4, now part of Greater London; the coaching inn was the White Hart.

Crixhall ruff. A wood near Rowling.

Croydon, Surrey. Originally a separate market-town 11 miles s of London on the A 23; now part of Greater London.

Crundale, Kent. Village approximately 2 miles E of Godmersham, just off the A 28; the thirteenth- to seventeenth-century Crundale House, which still survives, was the home of the Filmer family.

Danbury, Essex. Village approximately 40 miles NE of London, between Chelmsford and Maldon, on the A 414. Revd Brook-Henry Bridges was rector of Danbury and also of nearby Woodham Ferrers.

Dartford, Kent. Originally a market and manufacturing town 19 miles SE of London, and the first post-town on the Dover road; now nearly part of Greater London. There were several coaching inns in the town, but the best was the Bull (later called the Royal Victoria and Bull), opposite which was a smaller establishment, the Bull and George.

Dawlish, Devon. Originally a fishing village, but at the end of the eighteenth century it became a small seaside resort; 186 miles SW of London, and 15 miles s of Exeter on the A 379.

Daylesford, near Adlestrop, Glos. Home of Warren Hastings's ancestors, and sold by them in the seventeenth century; as a boy it became his ambition to buy back the property, and this he achieved in 1787; the house was then rebuilt for him by Cockerell with touches of Indian fantasy. The gardens, but not the house, are now sometimes opened to the public.

Deal, Kent. Seaside town and port, 80 miles SE of London and 18 miles from Canterbury, on the A 257/A 258; the coaching inns were the Hoop & Griffin, the Royal Exchange, and the Three Kings, and the Assembly Rooms were at the corner of Duke Street. The Downs anchorage lies offshore.

Deane, Hants. Village 55 miles SW of London, 5 miles W of Basingstoke, and 2 miles N of Steventon, just off the B 3400. Revd GA was the rector from 1773 till his death in 1805; the rectory in which the Austens lived was demolished later in the nineteenth century and by 1900 the only trace of it that Constance Hill could find was the old-fashioned mud wall surrounding the site; all that remains today is an overgrown plot of land on the corner of the lane which passes the church. Another house further down the lane was subsequently used as the rectory, but this is now in private ownership. All Saints church itself was totally rebuilt in 1818 at the expense of Mr Wither Bramston.

Deane House, a late seventeenth-century brick building, home of the Harwood family for several generations, is situated close to the church.

The Deane Gate Inn, just outside the village on the B 3400, was and is a stopping place for coaches, horse or petrol-powered, on the Basingstoke – Andover road.

Deane Park, near Wingham, Kent. One of the seats of the Oxenden family, demolished *c*.1830; a landscape view of it is in the Canterbury Art Gallery.

Deptford, Kent. Originally a separate naval shipbuilding town with victualling yards, on the Thames 4 miles downstream from London; now London SE8.

Devizes, Wilts. Country town 92 miles W of London and 27 miles NW of Andover on the A 342; the coaching inns were the Bear and the Castle.

Doncaster, Yorks. Market town 170 miles N of London; Miss Sharp was staying or living there in 1817.

Dorking, Surrey. Country town 25 miles SW of London on the A 24 and 13 miles from Guildford; the coaching inns were the White Horse, King's Head, and Bull's Head.

Dover, Kent. Ancient fortified seaport, 78 miles SE of London, and 16 miles from Canterbury on the A 2; the coaching inns were the City of London, Royal Hotel, Ship, and York House; the town is the nearest point to France, as the English Channel is here only 21 miles wide.

Downs, the. Areas of the English Channel, the Downs and the Small Downs, off the seaside towns of Ramsgate and Deal, used for safe anchorage by ships awaiting orders or fair winds.

Dummer, Hants. Village 5 miles SW of Basingstoke, just off the A 30; home of the Terry family, and Michael Terry held the living.

Eastling, Kent. Village 5 miles SW of Faversham, off the A 2. Edward Cage was the rector.

Eastwell Park, Kent. Home of the Finch-Hatton family until 1893; 3 miles N of Ashford on the A 20, and W of the A 251. Demolished, and rebuilt 1926 as a replica of another house, Markyate Cell, Herts.; now an hotel.

Ecchinswell, Hants. (Not 'Itchingswell' as JA wrote.) Village 10 miles NW of Basingstoke, close to the Berkshire border, between the A 34 and A 339.

Edinburgh. Capital of Scotland, 405 miles N of London.

Eggerton, Kent. House in Crundale parish; home of the Cuthbert family and the feeble-minded old 'Mrs' Elizabeth Knight. In later years EAK demolished it, as he felt it was too close to Godmersham itself to be tenanted by strangers.

Egham, Surrey. Country town 20 miles SW of London on the A 30; the coaching inns were the King's Head, Red Lion, Catherine Wheel, and Crown.

Elmsted, Kent. Village 8 miles S of Canterbury, and W of the Hythe road; Evington Place, the home of the Honywood family, was demolished in 1938.

Eltham, Kent. Originally a village 8 miles from London on the A 2; now London SE9. The preparatory school for EAK's sons was at Eltham.

Enham, Hants. Village 2 miles N of Andover on the A 343. Originally called Knight's Enham; enlarged after the First World War by the creation of an estate for disabled ex-servicemen, and enlarged still further for the same purpose after the Second World War, when the name was changed to Enham Alamein to commemorate the battle of El Alamein in North Africa. Revd Arthur Atkinson was the incumbent 1782–1814.

Enham Place was the home of the Dewar family, Anna Lefroy's maternal cousins.

Esher, Surrey. Small town 16 miles SW of London on the A 3; the coaching inns were the Bear and the White Lion.

Esher Place was the manor-house of the parish; bought by John Spicer 1805 and rebuilt, and remained in his family for some decades.

Claremont was another house and estate in the parish.

Eton College, Eton, near Slough, Bucks. The town is 22 miles W of London, and linked to Windsor by a bridge across the Thames. The boys' public and boarding-school was founded by Henry VI in 1440.

Everleigh, Wilts. (Not 'Everley' as JA wrote.) Village 12 miles NW of Andover on the A 342.

Eversley, Hants. Village on the Hants./Berks. border, 7 miles SE of Reading, Berks. and 10 miles NW of Basingstoke, on the A 327. The Revd Sir Richard Cope was rector till his death in 1806, followed by Revd Peter Debary 1807–24; Charles Kingsley, the author, was curate and then rector, 1844–75.

Evington, Elmsted, Kent. Village 8 miles S of Canterbury and W of the B 2068 Hythe road; in JA's time home of the Honywood baronets; the house was demolished 1938.

Exeter, Devon. The county town, 172 miles SW of London on the A 30, and 15 miles N of Dawlish.

Falmouth, Cornwall. Natural harbour and port, 282 miles SW of London.

Fareham, Hants. Originally a fishing village, but by 1805 had become a market town and small port, popular for the retirement homes of naval officers; on the N side of Portsmouth Harbour above Gosport and Portsmouth, 76 miles SW of London, and 12 miles from Southampton, at the junction of the A 32 and A 27 roads; the coaching inn was the Red Lion.

Farnham, Surrey. Market town, 39 miles SW of London, and 9 miles NE of Alton, on the A 31; one of the episcopal residences of the See of Winchester was at Farnham Castle. The coaching inns were the Bush and the Goat's Head.

Farringdon, Hants. Village E of the A 32, 1 mile S of Chawton and 2½ miles from Selborne. Revd John Benn was rector 1797–1857.

Faversham (earlier Feversham), Kent. Market town and river port; 53 miles SE of London on the A 2, and 10 miles from Canterbury; the post-town for Godmersham. The coaching inn was the Ship.

Folly Farm, Hants. Between Basingstoke and Kingsclere, just off the A 339.

Fredville, near Knowlton, Kent. Home of the Plumptre family; S of Sandwich and W of the A 256. The house was used as a school in the 1920s–30s, then commandeered by the Army in the Second World War and suffered fire damage; the remainder was demolished post-war.

Froyle, Hants. Village just off the A 31 and 5 miles N of Chawton; Froyle Place bought by Sir Thomas Miller, 5th Bt., 1770, and remained in the Miller family till 1949; in private ownership.

Fyfield, Wilts. Village 3 miles W of Marlborough, Wilts; an estate there was acquired by the Fowle family in 1697, which descended to Revd Fulwar-Craven Fowle, and he sold it to a Mr John Goodman *c.*1812.

Glencoe, Scotland. Historic site and beauty spot, 501 miles N of London.

Godinton Park, Ashford, Kent. Home of the Toke family; the sixteenth- to seventeenth-century house still survives.

Godmersham Park, Godmersham, Kent. EAK's main estate, 8 miles SE of Canterbury on the A 28 and 5 miles from Chilham. It was known originally as 'Ford Park', as the river Stour is fordable just below the church. The early eighteenth-century house was enlarged 1781 and again in the nineteenth century and was sold by Edward Knight II in 1874; now in private ownership, but the gardens are occasionally opened to the public. In JA's letters there are references to the interior of the house: the yellow room, white room, chintz room, library, hall and hall-chamber, dressing-room, breakfast-room, drawing-room, and billiard-room; but there have been modern alterations to this layout.

Various parts of the estate are named by JA or can be otherwise identified: Bentigh, Buckwell, Canterbury Hill Plantation, Eggerton, the limetree walk, Seaton Wood, Temple Plantation (so named from the Doric temple erected therein for use as a summerhouse), Winnigates. Another temple, Ionic in style, was erected in the grounds in 1935—this was in fact made from the S porch of the house, when that façade was remodelled.

The church of St Lawrence, overlooking the Stour, was restored in 1865–6 and looks considerably different from the building in which JA worshipped. The vicarage survives, though now a private residence. The thirteenth-century Court Lodge, also known as Godmersham Priory, where the Coleman family lived in JA's time, was demolished in 1955; a modern house, built in the style of Godmersham Park, is now called Court Lodge.

Goodnestone Park, Goodnestone-next-Wingham, Kent. Home of the Bridges baronets since 1700 and enlarged later in the eighteenth century; 7 miles from Canterbury and E of the B 2046; now the home of Lord and Lady FitzWalter (descendants of both the Plumptre and Bridges families), and the gardens are open to the public in summer. Goodnestone Farm was used by the Bridges family as the dower house; this also survives, in private ownership, renamed Well House.

The Goodnestone fair used to be held at Michaelmas.

Gosport, Hants. A naval town, on the W side of the entrance to Portsmouth Harbour and originating as an overflow service area to Portsmouth itself; 82 miles SW of London on the A 32, 31 miles from Alton via Fareham, and about 41 miles from Steventon via Winchester. The Red Lion and the India Arms, both in Middle Street, were the best coaching inns. The great Royal Naval Hospital at Haslar, just outside Gosport, was built 1746-62, and was then the largest hospital in Europe, with the capacity for 1,000 patients. The town was severely damaged in the Second World War and much of it has been rebuilt.

Gravesend, Kent. Market town and port on the S bank of the Thames estuary (first port on the Thames when approaching from the North Sea), 26 miles E of London and 7 miles E of Dartford on the A 226.

Greenwich, Kent. Originally a separate Thames-side village, 6 miles downstream from London; now London SE10. The village grew up round Greenwich Palace, which was a favourite country residence of Queen Elizabeth I; the Palace was rebuilt as a home/hospital for old seamen at the end of the seventeenth century and now houses the National Maritime Museum.

Guildford, Surrey. Market town, and originally the county town, 30 miles SW of London on the A 3, and 20 miles NE of Alton on the A 31. The Castle ruins, with bowling-green laid out inside them, are still there. The main coaching inns were the White Lion, Crown, and White Hart, but now only the Angel in the High Street survives.

Hackwood Park, 1 mile S of Basingstoke, Hants. Built by the 1st Duke of Bolton in the late seventeenth century, remodelled 1800-13 by Lewis Wyatt for the 1st and 2nd Lords Bolton. The gardens, but not the house, are opened to the public twice a year.

Hadley, Middx. Originally a village 13 miles N of London, now part of Greater London; the Cottrell family lived there.

Hampstead, Middx. Originally a village on the hills 4 miles N of London, now London NW3. Mrs Hancock, Eliza de Feuillide, and Hastings de Feuillide are buried together in the churchyard of St-John-at-Hampstead.

Hamstall Ridware, Staffs. Village 123 miles NW of London, 6 miles N of Lichfield and W of the A 515. Edward Cooper became rector of St Michael and All Angels 1799, and his rectory house still survives, now in private ownership.

Hamstead (or Hampstead) Marshall, Berks. Village 4 miles W of Newbury and 1 mile from Enborne. Lord Craven was patron of the living, and it was held by Revd Thomas Fowle II from 1771 till his death in 1806.

Hanwell, Middx. Originally a village 8 miles NW of London, on the Wycombe road; now part of Greater London. HTA's friends the Moore sisters lived there.

Harefield, Middx. Village 21 miles NW of London, 5 miles N of Uxbridge, and E of the A 412.

Harpsden, Oxon. (Previously spelt 'Harden'.) Village 1 mile S of Henley-on-Thames. Home of Mrs GA in her girlhood, as her father Revd Thomas Leigh was rector 1731–64. Her nephew Edward Cooper was curate there 1793–9. The old rectory survives, now in private ownership.

Hartford Bridge, Hants. (Sometimes written 'Hartfordbridge'.) Hamlet, continuation of Hartley Wintney, 10 miles NW of Basingstoke on the A 30; the coaching inn was the White Lion.

Hartley Wintney, Hants. Village and staging post, with numerous inns, 9 miles NW of Basingstoke on the A 30. Hartley Row was an almost separate terrace at one end of Hartley Wintney High Street.

Hatch: see under **Mersham.**

Hendon, Middx. Originally a village 7 miles NW of London, now London NW4; Anna and Ben Lefroy lived there for a few months following their marriage in November 1814, sharing a house with Ben's elder brother C.-Edward Lefroy. The coaching inn was the Bell.

Henley-on-Thames, Oxon. Riverside town, 36 miles W of London on the A 4/A 423. The diarist Mrs Philip-Lybbe Powys, mother-in-law of Revd Edward Cooper, spent the last few years of her life there, in a house which still survives, 55 New Street, close to the bridge.

Hinckley, Leics. Country town, 100 miles NW of London; home of Miss Bailey and her companion Miss Sharp, sometime governess at Godmersham.

Hog's Back, the. A long narrow ridge of bare downland hill on the Farnham-Guildford section of the A 31.

Holybourne, Hants. Originally a hamlet 2 miles E of Alton on the A 31, now largely overtaken by the growth of Alton.

Horsham, Sussex. Country town, 38 miles S of London on the A 264, and 20 miles SE of Guildford.

Hungerford, Berks. Country town 67 miles W of London, and 9 from Newbury, on the A 4.

Hurstbourne Priors, Hants. Village 5 miles E of Andover on the B 3400. Hurstbourne Park, home of the Earls of Portsmouth; a James Wyatt house, burnt down in 1870; rebuilt 1894 and demolished 1965.

Hurstbourne Tarrant, Hants. Village 5 miles N of Andover on the A 343; also known as Up or Upper Hurstbourne, or Uphusband. The Debary family lived there 1755–1814, when Revd Peter Debary sr. was vicar.

Hythe, Kent. Originally a seaside town and one of the Cinque Ports, 68 miles SE of London, 13 miles from Dover, and 12 miles from Ashford on the A 20/ A 261; coastal changes over the centuries mean it now lies inland. HTA's branch bank, Austen & Louch, was here 1810–14.

Ibthorpe, Hants. (Pronounced 'Ibtrop'.) Hamlet just to the W of Hurstbourne Tarrant. Mrs Lloyd and her two unmarried daughters moved there from Deane in 1792, and, after Mary Lloyd's marriage to James Austen in 1797, Martha and her mother stayed on together, with Mrs Stent as their companion, till Mrs Lloyd's death in 1805.

Ilford, Essex. Originally two adjacent villages, Great and Little Ilford, 11 miles NE of London, on the A 118; now part of Greater London. Theo-Leigh Cooke was perpetual curate of Little Ilford in 1803.

Itchen, River, Hants. The rivers Itchen and Test form a promontory as they debouch close together into Southampton Water, the Test on the W and the Itchen on the E, and the original Saxon settlement of Hamwic (Southampton) was on this naturally protected site. In JA's time there was a ferry across the Itchen, now replaced by a bridge.

Kempshott Park, Basingstoke, Hants. The estate, 4 miles S of Basingstoke, was purchased 1788 by Mr J. C. Crooke, who then let it 1788–95 to the Prince of Wales, and after him to Lord Dorchester; the house survived into this century, but all that now remains is the stable-block and part of the kitchen garden.

Kensington, Middx. Originally a separate village, 4 miles W of London; now London SW7. An early seventeenth-century house there was bought and enlarged by William III in 1690 as a country residence for himself outside the dirt and smoke of London, and succeeding monarchs rebuilt it still further; it is now a museum open to the public.

The grounds of Kensington Palace were also enlarged and laid out as gardens, and these were opened to the public at a very early date, so that by JA's time the guidebook to London could say:

> One of the most delightful scenes belonging to this great metropolis, and that which most displays its opulence and splendour, is formed by the company in Hyde Park and Kensington Gardens in fine weather, chiefly on Sundays, from March till July.

The spacious gravel roads, within the park, are, on a fine Sunday, covered with horsemen and carriages, from two till five o'clock in the afternoon. A broad foot-path, that runs from Hyde Park corner to Kensington Gardens, is frequently so crowded during the same hours, with well-dressed people passing to, or returning from the gardens, that it is difficult to proceed.

A noble walk, stretching from north and south, in Kensington Gardens, at the eastern boundary, with its gay company, completes this interesting scene. Numbers of people of fashion, mingled with a great multitude of well-dressed persons of various ranks, crowd the walk for many hours together.

Key Street, Kent. Village 2 miles W of Sittingbourne, on the A 2.

Kingsclere, Hants. Village 8 miles NW of Basingstoke, on the A 339. Revd John Orde was vicar 1796–1817.

Kingston upon Thames, Surrey. Originally a market town, and in recent years made the county town of Surrey, 10 miles SW of London on the A 3; the coaching inns were the Castle, Griffin, and Sun.

Kintbury, Berks. Village 64 miles W of London, between Hungerford and Newbury and just S of the A 4, on the river Kennet. Home of the Fowle family for a century, as three generations served as vicars of St Mary's Church 1741–1840; the vicarage JA knew was demolished and rebuilt later in the nineteenth century, and this Victorian replacement is now privately owned.

Barton Court, once the home of Revd John Craven and after him the Dundas family, lies across the river.

Kippington, near Sevenoaks, Kent. Home of Francis-Motley Austen and his family from 1796 to 1864. The estate was built over earlier this century, and the house has recently been used as an old people's home.

Kirby, Northants. Family seat of the Earls of Winchilsea.

Lake Katherine. Perhaps JA was thinking of the Scottish Loch Katrine.

Lenham, Kent. Small town 9 miles from Ashford on the A 20; Revd Brook-Edward Bridges was vicar 1810–25.

Litchfield, Hants. Village 3 miles N of Whitchurch on the A 34; alternatively, as JA was not always certain of the spelling of placenames, she may have meant the town of Lichfield in Staffordshire, 123 miles N of London.

London. There are countless books on the history and topography of London, so the following notes deal only with the places mentioned by JA. The codes for postal districts are of course a modern development, but are given within [ ] as an aid to location:

Abingdon Street [SW1]. Near the Houses of Parliament, and so convenient for Mr Dundas as an MP.

Albany, Piccadilly [w1]. A town mansion, with later extensions at the rear,

> on the site of the gardens belonging to the House, formerly the property of the Duke of York and Albany, whence the name. They contain upwards of 70 complete and distinct apartments, besides the Mansion House, and those situated in the courtyard. They are inhabited by many of the unmarried nobility and gentry, and by officers and professional men.

HTA's banking premises were at 1 The Courtyard 1804–7, and his friend Mr Henry Sanford lived at apartment F.3.

Albemarle Street [w1]. Described in 1708 as 'a street of excellent new Building inhabited by persons of Quality'. John Murray the publisher moved there from Fleet Street in 1812, and his office is still at No. 50.

Astley's Amphitheatre. An equestrian circus, open annually from Easter till October or November; it was situated off the Westminster Bridge Road, s of the Thames. The area has now been totally redeveloped.

Bath Hotel, on the corner of Arlington Street and Piccadilly [sw1].

Bedford House (Layton & Shears), 11 Henrietta Street, Covent Garden [wc2].

Belgrave Chapel. Unidentified; perhaps JA was giving a geographically descriptive nickname to what was otherwise called St George's Chapel, Five Fields, Chelsea [sw1]. This isolated little building lay on the fringe of the district now known as Belgravia, and was close enough to HTA's home to provide a pleasant, almost rural walk for JA.

Bentinck Street [w1]. The Cookes lodged here in 1811.

Bond Street [w1]. Then as now, a smart shopping district, with expensive lodgings above the shops.

British Gallery, the. More correctly called the Gallery of the British Institution, at [59] Pall Mall [sw1].

> This Institution was established in 1805, under the patronage of his majesty, for the encouragement and reward of the talents of British artists, and exhibits, during half of the year, a collection of the works of living artists for sale; and, during the other half year, it is furnished with pictures painted by the most celebrated masters, for the study of the academic and other pupils in painting.

Carlton House. Luxurious small palace, London home of the Prince of Wales from 1783; demolished by him in 1827. Waterloo Place, sw1, now occupies the site.

> On the northern side of St James's Park, fronting Pall Mall, is Carlton House . . . [which] contains several magnificent apartments in a fine modern taste. . . . The principal front is divided from Pall Mall by a low screen, surmounted with a beautiful colonnade. . . . Here have been held, since the

Prince became Regent, some of the most splendid and magnificent Banquets, known to the courts of modern Princes, which have cost immense sums. In short, the Prince lives in a style of magnificence, equalled by none of his Royal Predecessors, and maintains a court which would as much astonish even the Oriental Auringzebe, as it did his late Royal Visitors, the Emperor of Russia, and the King of Prussia.

Charing Cross [WC2]. A traditionally busy crossroads, the meeting-point of Whitehall, the Strand, St Martin's Lane, and The Mall.

Charles Street, Covent Garden. Now renamed Wellington Street [WC2].

Cleveland Court. A small street off St James's Place [SW1]; HTA's bank was there 1801–4.

Cleveland Row [SW1]. Close to Cleveland Court; HTA's friend Mr Gordon had his home and/or business premises there.

Cork Street [W1]. Mr Benjamin Langlois had a house there.

Coventry Street [W1]. A shopping area; in JA's time close to Leicester Square, and in later years rebuilt to lead into the Square.

Cranbourn Alley. A tiny street between Cranbourn Street and Bear Street, off Leicester Square [WC2].

Drury Lane Theatre, Covent Garden [WC2].

This externally substantial and internally superb and well contrived theatre, was rebuilt in 1811, on the ruins of the former building, which had been burnt down in 1809. . . . This house is built to afford sitting room for 2,810 persons, 1,200 in the boxes, 850 in the pit, 480 in the lower gallery, and 280 in the upper gallery. . . . The colour of the interior is gold upon green, and the relief of the boxes is by a rich crimson upon the face of the wall, forming the back of the boxes. There are three circles of boxes, each containing twenty-six boxes. This theatre is altogether a master-piece of art, and an ornament of the metropolis. . . . The Drury Lane Company commence their performance in September, and close in July.

Golden Square [W1]. Created in the late seventeenth century, but none of the original houses survives; Revd Dr J. S. Clarke's No. 37 was on the N side.

Grafton House (Wilding & Kent), on the corner of Grafton Street and 164 New Bond Street [W1].

Grosvenor Place [SW1]. The street was created c.1805–10, part of the ever-continuing expansion of London.

Hans Place [SW1]. HTA was at No. 23, and the James Tilson family at No. 26. HTA's house was refronted later in the nineteenth century and is now unrecognizable, but bears a plaque commemorating JA's visits there.

The gardens to the s of Hans Place, behind Nos. 23 and 26, were all swept away during the last century, and Pont Street runs across the site.

Henrietta Street, Covent Garden [WC2]. The street was originally laid out in the early seventeenth century; HTA's house, No. 10, was first built in 1726 and has undergone many changes of occupier and usage, but the upper part of the façade is still more or less as JA would have seen it.

Hertford Street [W1]. HTA's friends the Spencers were living there in 1814.

Hyde Park [W1].

Hyde Park is a royal demesne immediately contiguous to the metropolis, at the western extremity. It was originally much larger than at present, being reduced in extent chiefly by inclosing Kensington Gardens from it . . . a spot of great natural beauty, heightened by a fine piece of water . . . the Serpentine River, formed into a wide canal in 1730, by enlarging the bed of a stream flowing through the park . . . Hyde Park is used for the field-days of the Horse and Foot Guards, and other troops, and for occasional grand reviews. These exercises destroy the verdure of the park, converting a large portion of it into a beaten and dusty parade; yet the reviews afford an agreeable entertainment to the people of London, who crowd in tens of thousands to the Park on such occasions.

Hyde Park Corner [W1/SW1]. Distances on roads westbound from London have traditionally been measured from Hyde Park Corner.

Hyde Park Gate. The turnpike across the main west road out of London, near Hyde Park Corner, in use 1761–1825.

Keppel Street, Bloomsbury [WC1]. CJA's in-laws, the Palmer family, lived at No. 22; most of the street, including this house, was demolished in the 1930s for the development of London University.

Leicester Square [WC2]. By JA's time this square and the adjacent streets contained shops that were good, but not so expensive as those in the fashionable West End of London.

Liverpool Museum. Also known as Bullock's Museum of Natural & Artificial Curiosities. 'The collection is one of the most complete of its kind, and contains upwards of thirty thousand different articles, including quadrupeds, birds, reptiles, insects, ancient arms, works of art, &c.' In JA's time the collection was on display at the Egyptian Hall, [22] Piccadilly [W1]; the building was demolished in 1906.

Lyceum Theatre, Wellington Street [WC2]. A building, used for various kinds of entertainment, was in existence in 1765, and *c.*1790 became a theatre, only to have its licence withdrawn after pressure from the rival Covent Garden and Drury Lane theatres. It reopened in 1809 as the English Opera House, and was rebuilt in 1816, only to be destroyed by fire in 1830.

The present Lyceum building, erected as a theatre in 1831 on an adjacent site, is now a dance-hall.

Opera House, Bow Street, Covent Garden [wc2]. Originally called the Theatre Royal; the first early eighteenth-century building was burnt down in 1808, and the second one, modelled by Robert Smirke on the Temple of Minerva on the Acropolis, suffered the same fate in 1856; the third and present theatre on the site is in Roman Renaissance style, and specializes in operatic productions. The *Picture of London* was unenthusiastic about the Smirke building:

> The general character of the interior is simple elegance; there is nothing superior in splendour or attraction. The exterior is characterized by massive and masculine dignity; the interior by a tender and well-proportioned delicacy, of a feminine cast. Perhaps in neither is there enough of that luxuriant brilliancy which animates while it pleases, and seems to assimilate with the nature of the drama, the dresses and vivacity of the inmates of the boxes, and indeed with the general idea of pleasure which should reign in a playhouse.

Palace, the. In JA's time this meant St James's Palace, the low sprawling Tudor building lying between St James's Street and The Mall [sw1].

> The external appearance of this palace is inconsiderable, yet venerable from its age. It is a brick building; that part in which the rooms of state are, being only one storey, gives it a regular appearance on the outside. Although there is nothing very superb or grand in the decorations or furniture of the state apartments, they are commodious and handsome.

Buckingham House, then also known as the Queen's House, did not achieve its present size and status as Buckingham Palace until later in the nineteenth century.

Pall Mall [sw1]. Originally laid out in the seventeenth century and by the end of the eighteenth century was a stately thoroughfare containing private mansions and a few smart shops and clubs, leading up to Carlton House.

Park Street Chapel, Green Street [w1]. One of the smart proprietary chapels which sprang up during the late eighteenth and early nineteenth centuries; on the SE corner of the crossing of these two Mayfair streets.

Russell Square, Bloomsbury [wc1]. By the early nineteenth century this was the area where the wealthy mercantile members of society lived — see Thackeray's *Vanity Fair*.

St James's Church, Piccadilly [w1]. Designed by Sir Christopher Wren, 1674.

St James's Square [sw1]. Wedgwood's showrooms for his luxury ceramics were in 8 St James's Square, on the corner with [Duke of] York Street.

St Paul's Church, Covent Garden [WC2]. Built by Inigo Jones in the mid-seventeenth century, burnt down 1795 and rebuilt 1798 in the same style; a long, low, plain building with a deep portico on the east end towards the Piazza, that in later years became the setting for the opening scene of Shaw's *Pygmalion*, alias *My Fair Lady*.

Sloane Street, Chelsea [SW1]. Laid out in the late eighteenth century. The HTAs lived at No. 64 1809–13; the house was refronted and a further storey added in 1897, but some of the internal layout seems to have survived.

Somerset House, also known as Somerset Place, off the Strand [WC2].

The *Royal Academy* at Somerset House . . . was established by royal charter in 1768. . . . The *Annual Exhibition* . . . generally opens on the first of May, and every person who visits it, pays one shilling for admission, and one shilling for a catalogue, if he chuses to have one. The number of works of art exhibited, consisting of paintings, sculptures, models, proof engravings, and drawings, are generally upwards of one thousand.

Spring Gardens [SW1]. Home of the Society of Painters in Water Colours, '. . . formed in 1804, for the purpose of giving due emphasis to an interesting branch of art that was lost in the blaze of Somerset House, where water-colours, however beautiful, harmonized so badly with paintings in oil . . .'

Tavistock Street, Covent Garden [WC2]. Shopping and commercial area.

Temple, the [EC4]. A district extending S from Fleet Street down to the Thames, which since medieval times had been occupied by lawyers, law students, and legal offices.

Upper Berkeley Street [W1]. The HTAs lived at No. 24 1801–4; the house survives as a small hotel.

White's Club. At [37–8] St James's Street [SW1].

Ludgershall, Wilts. (Not now spelt 'Luggershall'.) Country town 7 miles W of Andover on the A 342.

Lyme Regis, Dorset. Seaside resort, 152 miles SW of London and 30 miles E of Exeter on the A 35; the coaching inns were the Three Cups and the Golden Lion. The geological foundations of Lyme are notoriously unstable, and storms often cause coastal changes; the sea-front that JA knew, including the Cobb, has been repaired and remodelled many times in the ensuing years. As early as 1827, according to Constance Hill, publicity-conscious landladies were claiming their cottages as being either where JA had stayed or else where she had placed the characters in *Persuasion*, and ever since then various houses have been similarly identified, and some have likewise disappeared due to coastal erosion. It seems most likely that the Austens stayed first in the cottage now known as Pyne House, 10 Broad Street, and then moved into Hiscott's boarding-house higher up the street, on the site of the present Three Cups hotel. The Assembly Rooms were built at the bottom of Broad Street, overlooking the sea, in the 1770s, and were demolished in 1927 to make way for car-parking.

Lyncombe. Southern suburb of Bath, across the river Avon.

Maidstone, Kent. County town, 37 miles SE of London, 19 miles from Ashford, and 8 miles from Rochester.

Manydown, Wootton St Lawrence, Hants. A fourteenth- to eighteenth-century house, home of the Bigg-Wither family from 1789 until its demolition in 1965; 1 mile from Worting on the B 3400 and 6 miles from Steventon.

Marcou (St Marcouf). Two small islands off the coast of Normandy, at that time occupied by a British garrison.

Margate, Kent. Seaside resort; 76 miles SE of London, and 16 miles from Canterbury on the A 28.

Matlock, Derbyshire. Inland spa town, 148 miles N of London on the A 6.

Mersham le Hatch, Mersham, Kent. House designed by Robert Adam 1762–6, and home of the Knatchbull family; 3 miles from Ashford on the A 20.

Midgham House, Berks. Home of the Boyle family; just north of the A 4, between Reading and Newbury, so that a traveller to Midgham from Portsmouth would go by Winchester, Popham Lane, and Basingstoke.

Milgate, Bearsted, Kent. The sixteenth-century Milgate House, home of the Cage family, still survives; 3 miles from Maidstone on the A 20.

Mounter's Lane: see Chawton.

Mystole, Chartham, Kent. Eighteenth-century house, home of the Fagg family; 4 miles from Godmersham on the A 28; modernized at the turn of this century and now divided into flats.

Nackington, Kent. Home of the Milles family; 2 miles S of Canterbury on the B 2068. Nackington House itself was demolished in 1921, but the domestic quarters and stabling survive.

Nash Court, Boughton-under-Blean, Kent. Home of Gen. Sir Henry Montresor; rebuilt in the mid-nineteenth century, and privately owned.

Neatham, Hants. Hamlet in the parish of Holybourne, just off the A 31, and part of the Chawton estate.

Netherton, Hants. Hamlet off the A 343, 3 miles N of Hurstbourne Tarrant, and 1 mile W of the hamlet of Faccombe; Revd David Lance was rector of Faccombe 1792–1848, but actually lived at Netherton. The former rectory survives, in private ownership.

Netley, Hants. Originally a hamlet on the E side of Southampton Water, containing little more than the ruins of Netley Abbey, and two country villas, shown on a 1791 map as Netley Castle and Netley Lodge. The village developed suddenly during the last century as a result of the creation in 1856 of an enormous military hospital; the hospital in turn has been demolished and the Royal Victoria Country Park covers its site.

Netley Abbey was a thirteenth-century Cistercian house, dissolved in 1536 and converted for domestic use, but in picturesque ruins by the mid-eighteenth century. It became a popular excursion from Southampton—'most frequently made by water . . . but those who prefer crossing the ferry and walking thither, will find the road extremely pleasant, and the distance about three miles'.

Netley Castle had originally been one of the Solent forts built in 1542 close to the water's edge; it was converted to residential use 1627, enlarged and remodelled later in the nineteenth century. Netley Lodge was near the village of Hound, overlooking Southampton Water.

Newbury, Berks. Country town 60 miles W of London on the A 4, 17 miles from Basingstoke, 13 miles from Whitchurch, and approximately 20 miles from Steventon.

Northam, Hants. Originally a shipbuilding hamlet 1 mile N of Southampton, on the river Itchen; a bridge was built across the river in 1796 and a new road made to link Southampton with Portsmouth, and Northam has now become a suburb of Southampton.

Norton Court, Kent. Home of the Lushington family; between Faversham and Sittingbourne, S of the A 2.

Oakley, Hants. Village, 4 miles W of Basingstoke, just off the B 3400, and between Worting and Ashe. Oakley Hall was the home of the Bramston family; the house is now called Hilsea College and for some years has been used as a boarding-school.

Ospringe, Kent. Village, now almost part of Faversham, 9 miles from Canterbury on the A 2, and 9 miles from Godmersham by Chilham; the coaching inn was the Red Lion.

Overton, Hants. Country town 58 miles SW of London, 9 miles from Basingstoke on the B 3400, and 3 miles from Steventon, for which it was the post-town; in 1791 the post-office was at the New Inn, and John Beazley was the postmaster.

Oxford, Oxon. County town and ancient university, 56 miles NW of London; the coaching inns were the Angel, King's Arms, Roebuck, and Star. Most of JA's male relatives completed their education at Oxford.

Painshill Park, near Cobham, Surrey. A remarkable landscape garden was created 1738–73 by the Hon. Charles Hamilton, but fell into dereliction in recent years. The Painshill Park Trust has been formed to re-create the gardens, and they are again open to the public.

Penzance, Cornwall. Seaside town and fishing port, 292 miles sw of London.

Petersfield, Hants. Market town 56 miles sw of London on the A 3, and 12 miles s of Chawton; the coaching inns were the Dolphin, Red Lion, and White Hart. HTA's branch bank, Austen Vincent & Clement, was in The Square 1810–14.

Pett Place, Charing, Kent. A fifteenth- to eighteenth-century house, which still survives; Edward Hussey was the tenant in 1813.

Popham, Hants. Hamlet 5 miles from Basingstoke just off the A 30/A 33, and 2 miles from Steventon via North Waltham. The Wheatsheaf Inn lies at the junction of Popham Lane with the main road.

Portsmouth, Hants. Seaport and great naval dockyard on the Hampshire coast, 74 miles sw of London on the A 3, and 19 miles from Southampton; the coaching inns were the Crown, Fountain, George, and Navy Tavern. The landward fortifications of moats and drawbridges were gradually removed during the nineteenth century, and much of the old town itself was destroyed in the Second World War, so one can no longer approach Portsmouth by the route William and Fanny Price took nor guess at finding the small house in the 'narrow street, leading from the high street', where the Price family were located by JA. The Garrison Chapel is a roofless ruin, preserved as a war memorial, but one can still walk on the nearby ramparts as Mrs Price did; the sea walls are mostly intact and are still used by the inhabitants to view the traffic of the harbour. The dockyards have become an outdoor museum complex, with HMSS *Victory* and *Warrior* on view; the great brick and stone storehouses are now display areas, including the wreck of the *Mary Rose* salvaged in recent years from the Solent waters. The buildings of the Royal Naval Academy, where both FWA and CJA studied, also remain in the dockyard, though naval training there ceased in 1837.

Provender (earlier spelt Provendar), Norton, Kent. A Jacobean house, owned by the Knatchbull family; in her widowhood FCK lived there for many years till her death in 1882.

Ramsgate, Kent. Seaside resort and port, 78 miles SE of London on the A 253, 20 miles from Dover, 17 miles from Canterbury, and 4 miles from Margate. FWA's wife Mary Gibson was living in the town when he met her; JA was a visitor in 1803; and in August 1804 EAK had to rent both 7 and 8 Sion Hill to accommodate his large family party.

Reading, Berks. County town 40 miles w of London on the M 4/A 4, and 17 miles from Basingstoke on the A 33; the coaching inns were the Bear and the Crown. JA and CEA were there from spring 1785 until autumn 1786 at

Mrs Latournelle's school; this was accommodated in the old Reading Abbey gateway and a large house adjoining it which overlooked the ruins of the Abbey itself. The gateway survives, though much restored, but the house site is now a car-park for local municipal offices; ruins of the Abbey still exist.

Ripley, Surrey. Village 25 miles SW of London on the A 3; the coaching inn was the Talbot.

Rochester, Kent. Town 31 miles SE of London on the A 2, 9 miles from Gravesend and 10 miles from Sittingbourne; the coaching inns were the Bull, Crown, and Old King's Head.

Romsey, Hants. Market town 75 miles SW of London on the A 27/A 31, and 11 miles from Winchester.

Rowling, Kent. Small country-house owned by the Bridges family, 1 mile E of Goodnestone; the home of EAK and Elizabeth Bridges following their marriage, and birthplace of their first four children; in private ownership.

Rugby, War. Market town, and now industrial and railway centre, 83 miles NW of London; a boys' grammar school had been founded in 1567, and Edward Cooper's eldest son Edward-Philip was sent there in 1809. Later in the nineteenth century the school was much improved and enlarged by Dr Thomas Arnold, Headmaster 1828–42, and became famous as the setting for Thomas Hughes's *Tom Brown's Schooldays.*

St Alban's Court, near Wingham, Kent. Home of the Hammond family.

St Boniface Cottage, Isle of Wight. Country villa between Bonchurch and Ventnor, belonging to a family named Hill, and possibly therefore some connection of Revd Herbert Hill of Streatham; in 1824 it was described as

> most agreeably seated at the foot of a steep mountainous down, from which its name is derived. Its design is elegant and appropriate, built with free-stone and thatched; the situation possesses every beautiful feature of this romantic country, and unites in an uncommon degree the comfort of sheltered retirement, with the advantage of a sea-prospect.

St Helen's Bay, Isle of Wight. On the NE side of the island, looking towards Portsmouth.

St Mary's, Southampton. Home of the Butler-Harrison family; on the site of the original Saxon settlement of Hamwic, outside the walls of the medieval town of Southampton.

Salisbury, Wilts. Cathedral city, 83 miles W of London, 37 miles from Basingstoke, and 23 miles from Southampton.

Sandling Park, Hythe, Kent. Home of the Deedes family, 10 miles from Ashford on the A 20/A 26; the house was remodelled by Bonomi in 1799, and destroyed by bombs 1940.

Scarlets, Kiln Green, Wargrave, Berks. Home of the Leigh-Perrots from 1765 until Mrs LP's death in 1836; between Maidenhead and Reading, just off the A 4, and 2 miles SE of Wargrave. Mrs LP bequeathed the property to JEAL, who enlarged and then sold it in 1863; the gardens have been built over, but the house still survives, now divided into three private properties.

Seal, Kent. Village 2 miles NE of Sevenoaks, on the A 25. The Walter family lived there 1785–1811.

Seaton Wood: see **Godmersham.**

Selborne, Hants. Village 3½ miles S of Chawton, on the B 3006. Home of Revd Gilbert White, the naturalist and author; and after his death, of his nephew John White and family.

Shalden, Hants. Village 2 miles N of Alton, and part of the Chawton estate.

Sheerness, Isle of Sheppey, Kent. Naval dockyard for the defence of the rivers Medway and Thames, 46 miles E of London and 10 miles N of Sittingbourne; hence CJA's command of HMS *Namur*, the guard ship at the Nore, outside the harbour.

Sherborne St John, Hants. Village 3 miles N of Basingstoke. The Vyne lies in this parish, and James Austen became the vicar in 1791.

Monk Sherborne is a hamlet 1 mile NW of Sherborne St John. The Revd Dr Henry Hall was vicar here 1793–1829.

Shrewsbury, Shropshire. County town, 161 miles NW of London.

Sidmouth, Devon. Seaside resort, 15 miles E of Exeter, 17 miles from Lyme Regis, and 10 miles S of Honiton, on the B 3175/B 3176.

Sittingbourne, Kent. Country town 46 miles SE of London on the A 2, 15 miles from Canterbury, and 16 miles from Godmersham; the coaching inns were the George and the Rose.

Southampton, Hants. Ancient town and seaport, 77 miles SW of London on the A 33, 19 miles from Portsmouth, and 13 miles from Winchester; the coaching inns were the Coach & Horses, Dolphin, George, Star, and Vine. In the late eighteenth century there were some local attempts to turn it into a spa resort, but the district did not possess enough natural resources to be successful in this respect, and the town remained merely a pleasant residential area with commercial interests. A number of gentry built country villas in the neighbourhood—e.g. Bannister's Court, Bellevue, Chessel House— and from 1785 onwards assembly balls were held fortnightly on Tuesdays at the Dolphin Inn, from the beginning of November until the end of April.

The suburb of St Mary's, where the Austens' cousins the Butler-Harrisons lived, was on the site of the Saxon settlement of Hamwic, outside the walls of the later settlement of Southampton.

The ruins of the central keep of the medieval castle were rebuilt into a Gothic fantasy by the Marquis of Lansdowne, but after his death and his widow's departure from Southampton the new house was sold in 1816, and since then various other buildings have occupied the site; the present one is a tower-block of council flats. Castle Square, the area round the keep, where the Austens lived 1806–9 in a house that had a large garden running up to the old town walls, was likewise redeveloped in the later nineteenth century, and furthermore in recent years has been excavated for archaeological reasons (other buildings of the castle complex lay beneath the post-medieval development), and the latest replacement residential layout is totally different. It is still possible to stand on the top of the town walls at approximately the place where the Austens' garden would have ended, but the view beyond is no longer what JA saw, because modern land reclamation has completely filled in the bay whose tides originally washed the base of the walls.

The High Street ran the whole length of the medieval town, from the water's edge up to the Bar Gate which was the N entrance through the walls; on the other side of this the street was known as 'Above Bar'. The High Street suffered severely in the Second World War, but the Dolphin Inn luckily still survives. The boarding-house JA visited at No. 17 was kept by a William Harland, and most of the other tradesmen whom she mentions can be traced in local directories.

The Theatre was in French Street, but no longer survives.

The Polygon was planned to be a smart architectural feature of twelve large houses with gardens and a central hotel for visitors and social events, to the north of the old town (part of the attempt to upgrade Southampton into a fashionable resort); but the developer failed and the estate was never completed.

Southend, Essex. Seaside resort 45 miles E of London on the A 13.

Speen Hill, Berks. Village 1 mile W of Newbury on the A 4. The old Misses Hulbert lived there, and also the widowed Mrs Craven.

Spithead. An area of the Solent, off Portsmouth, where ships could safely lie at anchor.

Staines, Middx. Country town 17 miles SW of London on the A 30; the coaching inn was the Bush.

Starcross, Devon. Village 4 miles N of Dawlish on the A 379, and 9 miles S of Exeter.

Start Point. Headland on the Devon seacoast, and one of the main landmarks for ships coming up the Channel from the Atlantic, as described in the sea-shanty 'Spanish Ladies':

The first land we made it is known as the Deadman,
   Next Ram Head near Plymouth, Start, Portland, and Wight;
We sailed past Beachy, past Fairley and Dungeness,
   And then bore away for the South Foreland Light.

Steventon, Hants. Village 55 miles sw of London, just s of the B 3400, and NW of Popham Lane on the A 30. There is not now very much left that JA would have known except the church of St Nicholas, and even that has been restored and had a spire added since her time. The rectory in which she was born was demolished by EAK in 1824, when he built a new rectory on the hill opposite for the occupation of his son Revd William Knight; this has now become a private residence, and the site of the old rectory and its gardens has reverted to pasture. The Elizabethan manor-house of Steventon, which the Digweeds rented from EAK, went through many vicissitudes later in the nineteenth and twentieth centuries, and was eventually totally demolished a few years ago. A new house has been built recently close to the earlier site.

Stoneleigh Abbey, War. Home of the senior branch of the Leigh family, and inherited by Mrs GA's cousins in 1806; on the A 444 between Leamington Spa and Coventry. Most of the estate has been acquired by the Royal Agricultural Society as the venue for its Agricultural Show, and the house itself was recently sold by the present Lord Leigh.

Streatham, Surrey. Originally a separate village 5 miles sw of London on the Croydon road; now London sw16. The Revd Herbert Hill was rector 1810–28; the rectory JA knew was demolished early this century.

Sunninghill, Berks. Village approximately 6 miles s of Windsor and 25 miles sw of London, on the A 30. Mr Jeremiah Crutchley purchased Sunninghill Park in 1769.

Tangier Park, Hants. A seventeenth-century house in the parish of Wootton St Lawrence, near Manydown; the Limbrey-Sclater family lived there 1710–1833, when it was purchased by the Bigg-Wither family; in private ownership.

Tenby, Pembrokeshire. South Wales seaside resort overlooking Carmarthen Bay; 246 miles w of London.

Tewkesbury, Glos. Country town 105 miles NW of London; Mrs Lloyd had lived there for a time before her marriage, and her companion Mrs Stent was a friend from that period and place.

Tollard Royal, Wilts. Village sw of Salisbury on the B 3081, between Ringwood, Hants, and Shaftesbury, Dorset. The Henry Rice family lived there for a time.

Tonbridge, Kent. Country town 35 miles SE of London on the A 21; its later spa development, Tunbridge Wells, is 38 miles from London on the A 26. Many earlier branches of the Austen family lived in the Tonbridge/Sevenoaks area of Kent.

Twerton, Somerset. Originally a village 2 miles W of Bath, now overtaken by the development of the city.

Uxbridge, Middx. Country town 16 miles NW of London on the A 40; now part of Greater London.

Ventnor, Isle of Wight. '. . . a very clean, pleasant hamlet, half a mile from Bonchurch, situated under St Boniface Down . . . the favourite resort of fishermen . . .'

Waltham, North, Hants. Village 2 miles SE of Steventon and just W of the A 30; Revd Clement Cottrell was rector 1800–14.

Wantage Down, Berks. Wantage is a small town on the Berkshire Downs at the crossroads of the A 417/A 338, 75 miles W of London, and equidistant between Newbury and Oxford.

Weston, Somerset. Originally a village 2 miles NW of Bath, but now nearly overtaken by the development of the city.

Westwell, Kent. Village between Charing and Ashford, E of the A 20. Revd Joseph Sherer held the living 1806–24 in plurality with that of Godmersham.

Weyhill, Hants. Village 3 miles W of Andover on the A 303; an ancient and famous agricultural fair was held there for a week at Michaelmas, but its prosperity gradually diminished during the nineteenth century and the last cattle sale took place in 1957.

Weymouth, Dorset. Seaside resort, 131 miles SW of London and 8 miles S of Dorchester on the A 354. Gloucester House was the villa where the Duke of Gloucester had stayed in earlier years, and where George III and his Queen stayed in 1789.

Wheatfield, Oxon. Village just over 40 miles NW of London, on the A 40, near Stokenchurch.

Whitchurch, Hants. Village 12 miles W of Basingstoke and 8 miles E of Andover on the B 3400; the coaching inn was the White Hart.

White Friars: see Canterbury.

Widcombe. A southern suburb of Bath, across the river Avon.

Wight, Isle of ('the Island'). Off the Hampshire coast, 5 miles across the Solent from Portsmouth, and linked by ferries with Portsmouth, Southampton, and Lymington. The three main towns are Newport, Ryde, and Cowes, and the Island is famous for its small but beautiful hills, villages, and bays.

Winchester, Hants. (Sometimes abbreviated to 'Winton'.) Ancient city, county town of Hampshire, bishop's diocese, and once the capital of Wessex and of Saxon England; 64 miles from London on the A 30/A 33, 16 miles SW of Chawton and 14 miles from Steventon; the coaching inns were the George and the White Hart.

JA died in 8 College Street (privately owned, not open to the public), and is buried in the north aisle of Winchester Cathedral, with a ledger stone in the floor and a brass memorial inscription on the wall above. JEAL was at Winchester College, as also were EAK's sons and some of their Bridges and Deedes cousins.

Windsor, Berks. The ancient royal Castle is on the hill commanding the river Thames, and the town grew up below it; 23 miles W of London on the A 4.

Mrs GA's old friend Mrs Birch lived at Barton Lodge, just outside the town.

Winnigates: see **Godmersham.**

Wood Barn. 1 mile SW of Chawton.

Woolwich, Kent. Originally a little river port on the Thames, 9 miles E of London; then grew into a sprawling garrison town, with the creation of the Royal Dockyard in the sixteenth century, the Royal Arsenal in the seventeenth century, and the Royal Military Academy in the mid-eighteenth century; now London SE18.

Wootton St Lawrence, Hants. Village 2 miles W of Basingstoke. The Bigg-Wither family lived there in Manydown House, and also at one time owned Tangier Park in the same parish.

Worldham, Great or **East,** Hants. Village on the B 3004, 2½ miles E of Chawton.

Worthing, West Sussex. Seaside resort; 58 miles S of London and 14 miles W of Brighton. Mrs GA and her daughters stayed there during the autumn of 1805.

Worting, Hants. Village 2 miles W of Basingstoke on the B 3400. The Clarke family lived there.

Wrotham, Kent. Village 27 miles SE of London, and 11 miles W of Maidstone, at the crossroads of the A 20/A 227. Revd George Moore was rector 1800–45; it was said to be the best living in Kent, and as such usually reserved for close relatives of the Archbishop of Canterbury. Mr Moore's rectory still survives, now known as Court Lodge.

Wyards. In JA's time a farmhouse, 1 mile N of Chawton; now in private ownership. Anna and Ben Lefroy went to live there in 1815, then sharing it with a local farm bailiff.

Wye, Kent. Country town off the A 28, 9 miles SW of Canterbury and 2 miles S of Godmersham. Wye College was originally founded by Archbishop Kemp in 1432, as a secular establishment for priests together with a school; the buildings were converted 1894 into the South Eastern Agricultural College, and this has been part of London University since 1900.

Yarmouth, Isle of Wight. Originally the most important town on the Island, but by 1800 it had dwindled to a mere village; linked by ferry to Lymington on the Hampshire coast opposite.

Yarmouth, Great, Norfolk. Fishing town and port on the East Anglian coast, 135 miles NE of London on the A 12; HTA's militia regiment was stationed there in 1796.

York, York. The capital of the North Country, situated at the junction of the three Ridings of Yorkshire, and 209 miles N of London.

GENERAL INDEX

Notes: (1) In accordance with modern biographical conventions, Edward Knight and his children are indexed under 'Knight', although their change of name did not take place officially until 1812; similarly, James Austen's son James-Edward is indexed as 'Austen-Leigh'; and James's elder daughter Anna appears under her married name of 'Lefroy'.

(2) JA frequently used place-names as a short reference to the family or families living in that village or district; cross-references from places to persons are given where appropriate.

(3) For information on the life of JA and her family, not mentioned in her correspondence, see the chronology in *Family Record*, xv–xxiv.

General Index

Bigeon, Mme 210, 218, 220, 230, 246, 255, 257, 321, 339
Bigg, Alethea 2, 4, 8, 45–6, 129, 133, 148, 154, 205–6, 219, 229, 234, 254, 289, 311, 326–8, 341
Bigg, Catherine, see Hill, Mrs Herbert
Bigg, Elizabeth, see Heathcote, Mrs William
Bigg-Wither, Harris 34, 37, 50, 57
Bigg-Wither, Lovelace 34, 37, 59
Binns, John 154, 164, 170
Birch, Mrs 21–2, 163, 233, 271, 273
Birchall, Robert 224
Birmingham 193
Bishopstoke 50
Bissett, Revd John 191
Blachford, Jane 73
Blachford, Winifred 29, 34, 37, 104, 289
Blackall, Revd Samuel 19, 216
Blackheath 125
Blackstone, Mrs 289
Blackstone, Mrs H. and daughters 35
Blairs, the 226
Blake, Captain 298
Blandford 92
Blount, Mr and wife 61
Bolton, Lord, and family 25, 35, 37, 53
Bond, Miss 87
Bond, John 18, 24, 42, 66, 70, 73, 160, 201, 205
Bond, Lizzie 24
Bonham, Miss 92
Bonham, Mr F. 104
Bookham, Great 33, 44, 128, 135, 138, 146, 162–6, 191, 248, 254, 265; see also Cooke
Booth, Mr and Misses 140
Bourne, Robert 162, 163
Bowen, William 96–7, 100, 123
Boyle, Capt. Courtenay 79–80
Boys, Daniel 14, 109, 125
Bradshaws, the 90
Bramston, Augusta 50, 62
Bramston, Wither 49, 62, 81, 199, 221
Bramston, Mrs Wither 35, 49, 53, 62, 73, 88, 200, 221
Branfill, Jemima 252, 332
Brecknell, Joseph 186
Brecknell & Twining 261
Brentford 141

Breton, Revd Dr Moyle and wife 234, 251
Brett family 62, 107, 238, 250
Bridges, Dowager Lady (née Fanny Fowler) 8, 10, 110, 130, 136, 138, 141, 145, 146, 150, 188, 193, 221, 237–9, 248, 252, 254, 258, 260
Bridges, Revd Brook-Edward 8, 30, 107–10, 112, 136, 145, 153, 230, 234–5, 237–8, 246, 253
Bridges, Mrs Brook-Edward (née Harriet Foote) 68, 153, 155, 231, 246, 253
Bridges, Brook-George 8
Bridges, Brook-George, jun. 139
Bridges, Revd Brook-Henry 6, 8, 109, 110, 111, 221, 252, 254, 258
Bridges, Mrs Brook-Henry 6, 8, 252, 254, 258
Bridges, Brook-Henry, jun. 205, 207
Bridges, Revd Brook-John 108–10, 126, 130, 134, 136, 138, 148, 153, 163, 188
Bridges, Mrs Brook-John 345
Bridges, Sir Brook-William 8, 124, 159, 244, 249, 251, 253, 273
Bridges, Lady (née Eleanor Foote) 68, 83, 124, 153
Bridges, Lady (née Dorothy Hawley) 249, 251–3, 273
Bridges, Brook-William, jun. 68, 139
Bridges, Eleanor 139, 300
Bridges, Harriot-Mary, see Moore, Mrs George
Bridges, Louisa 6, 8, 126–8, 130, 134, 221, 238, 245, 252, 254, 258, 260, 281
Bridges, Marianne 8, 10, 109–12, 119
Bridlington 321
Briggs, Mr 38
Brighton 227, 237, 307, 311
Bristol 62, 68
Broadstairs 127, 316, 319
Bromley, Mrs 40
Brompton 96, 132, 139; see also Austen, Henry-Thomas
Brooklands 115
Broome Park 112
Brown, Bob 23
Browns or Brownes, the 99
Brown(e), Captain and wife 121
Browning, Mrs 264

Remnant, T. (shop) 211
Reynolds, Sir Joshua, PRA, 212–13
Rhodes 80
Rice, Mrs Henry (née Sarah Sampson) 74, 78
Rice, Revd Henry 29, 62, 71, 74, 78, 91
Rice, Mrs Henry (née Jemima-Lucy Lefroy) 9, 28, 62, 79, 91, 99, 104
Richard, manservant 260, 271, 298, 300
Richis, maidservant 8
Richmond, Duchess of 333
Rider/Ryder, Mrs 16, 76
Rider/Ryder, Mr 50
Ripley 210, 244
Ripley, Revd Thomas and wife 246
Ripley, a young 99
Rivers, Lady, and family 1, 4, 236 (?fictional)
Robert, manservant 101, 164
Robinson, Dr 92
Robinson, Mary 7, 12
Robinson, Revd Matthew 62
Rochester 14
Roden, Earl and Countess 105
Rogers, Mrs 76
Roland, Mr 51
Rolle, the Misses 179
Romsey 263
Roope, Mr 34
Rosalie, maidservant 61
Rowe, Miss, *see* Wroe
Rowling 5–13, 36, 108–9, 112
Roworth, C. 297–8, 300
Roxburghshire 230
Rugby 172
Russell, Mrs 19, 28, 37
Russell, manservant 131
Russia, Emperor of 263–4

S., Miss 332–3
Sa(y)ce, maidservant 108, 218, 228
Sackree, Susanna 48, 108, 128, 171, 205, 225–7, 233, 264
Sackville, Viscount 131
St Albans Court 112
St Boniface 274
St Helen's Bay 23
St Helens, Lord 311
St John family 1, 20, 60
St Lawrence, Lady Frances 151

St Mary's or St Maries, *see* Southampton
St Vincent, Earl of 23, 29
Salisbury 64–5, 151
Salkeld, Mrs 108, 238
Sally, maidservant (probably more than one of this name) 78, 170, 196, 324, 325
Salusbury, Mr 333
Sandling Park 50–1, 111, 126, 135, 137, 225–6, 244, 300, 318; *see also* Deedes
Sanford, Caroline 212
Sanford, Henry 287
Sankey, Mr 110
Saunders, Mr 105
Sawbridge, Miss 153
Saye and Sele, Lady 63
Scarlets 71, 94, 200, 206, 294, 314, 336; *see also* Leigh Perrot
Scarman, Mr 271, 273
Schuylers, the 94
Sclater, Mrs Penelope Lutley 206, 316
Scotland 215, 230–1
Scott, Sir Walter 203, 277, 297, 313
Scott, Mr 9
Scrane, Mrs 318
Scudamore, Mr and wife 131, 148, 217, 222, 245–6, 329, 336
Seagraves, the (?fictional) 236
Seal 14, 135
Selborne 190–1, 193, 321
Serle, Mr 50
Sevenoaks 14, 297, 306
Seward, Bridger, and wife 10, 22, 150, 173
Seymer, Maria-Bridget 99
Seymour, Viscount 131
Seymour, William 174, 175, 183, 291, 302, 311, 318
Shalden 140, 234
Sharp, Miss 104
Sharp(e), Anne 107, 112, 120, 127, 130, 141, 149, 173, 188, 190, 192–3, 219, 250, 265, 321, 340–1, 346
Shaw, Anna-Maria 333
Sheerness 39, 240
Sherborne, Monk or West 17
Sherer, Revd Joseph and family 226, 231, 233, 243, 249, 251, 253
Shipley, Mr 53, 61
ships: *Ambuscade* 99; *Caledonia* 181;

General Index

Camilla 101; *Cleopatra* 184; *Elephant* 217; *Endymion* 39, 53, 58, 75, 80, 89, 91; *Excellent* 23; *Expedition* 102; *Haarlem* 75; *London* 23, 28; *Mercury* 63; *Namur* 206, 241, 244; *Neptune* 172; *Petterel* 32, 52, 57, 75, 80; (?)*Ponsborne* 2; *Pyramus* 207; *St Albans* 131, 137–8, 150, 163; *Scorpion* 28–9; *Tamar* 32, 36, 39; *Triton* 12–13; *Urania* 101
Shrewsbury 64
Shropshire 105
Sibley, the Misses 199
Siddons, Mrs 184, 287
Sidmouth 71
Simpson, Capt., and brother 183–4
Sittingbourne 14–15, 125, 239–40, 244
Skeete, Mrs 35
Sloane, Mr 63
Sloper, Mr 157
Small, Miss 24
Smallbone, Jenny 138
Smallbone, Mary 138
Smith, Lady (Drummond) 212
Smith, Captain 168, 170
Smith, Col. 'Cantelo' and wife 180–1
Smith, Mr and Mrs 180–1, 184
Smith, Miss 257
Smith, James and Horace 198
Smith, Robert 292
Smithson, Mr 71, 79
Somerset 135, 216
Somerville, Mrs Maria 87
Sondes, Lady 9, 159, 161, 173
South, Mr 35
Southampton: general references 61, 114, 117, 123, 126, 129, 132, 135, 137, 142–4, 150, 154–5, 160, 162–3, 167–8, 172, 194, 204, 313, 331; Argyle's Inner House 140; Bellevue 155; Chessell/Chiswell 156, 158; Polygon 156; St Maries/St Mary's 141
Southend 216
Southey, Herbert 328
Southey, Robert 141, 235, 327–8
Spain 171
Speen 71, 99, 154, 315
Spence, Mr 219–20, 223
Spencer, Lord 23, 28–9, 31
Spencer, Mr and Miss 218, 256, 260–1

Spicer, Mr 210
Spithead 102
Stacey, Mary 226
Staffordshire 37
Staines 5, 15, 16–17
Stamford Bridge 113
Standert, Revd George 191
Stanhope, Adm. and wife 86, 105
Staples, Dame 18, 31, 323
Staples, Hannah 31
Starcross 268
Start Point 79
Steele & Meyer (shop) 72
Steevens, John and wife 18
Steevens, Mary 31
Stent, Mrs 59, 64, 103, 197
Stephens, Catherine 260–1
Steventon: general references: Revd George Austen's family in residence 1, 5–6, 8, 10, 12, 15–17, 26, 38, 40, 42, 44, 45, 47, 50, 53, 65, 73, 77, 79, 80; Revd James Austen's family in residence 88, 98, 107, 129, 132, 135, 138, 146, 148, 150–1, 154–5, 157, 161, 166, 173, 184, 188, 196–7, 199–204, 206, 214, 228, 246, 248, 272, 300, 314, 316–18, 323, 327, 331, 337, 340
Stirling 270
Stockwell, Mrs 234
Stoneleigh 116, 126, 154, 216
Storer, Dr and wife 321
Streatfeild, Henry 297
Streatham 181, 199, 249, 254, 259, 266, 274, 289, 326–8; *see also* Hill, Revd Herbert
Street, (?)Revd George 38
Street, Mr 242
Suffolk 27
Summers, Miss 61
Sunninghill 273
Sussex 135
Sussex, Duke of 80
Sweden 214–15, 229
Sweny, Mr 318–20
Switzerland 341

Tangier Park 316
Taylor, Edward 10, 26, 57
Temple, Frank and family 29
Tenby 127